Automotive Electrical and Electronic Systems

Fourth Edition

By Chek-Chart

William J. Turney CMAT, *Editor*
Richard K. DuPuy, *Contributing Editor*

Copyright 2000 by Chek-Chart Publications

Automotive Electrical and Electronic Systems, Fourth Edition

Classroom Manual and Shop Manual

Copyright 2000 by Chek-Chart Publications

Automotive Electrical and Electronic Systems (Chek-Chart Automotive Series) v.1 Classroom Manual, v.2 Shop Manual. All rights reserved. Printed in the United States of America. No part of this publication may be reproduced, stored in a retrieval system, or duplicated in any manner without prior written consent of the publisher.

International Standard Book Number: 1-57932-246-8
Library of Congress Catalog Card Number: 99-067757

Chek-Chart Publications
320 Soquel Way
Sunnyvale CA 94086
408-739-2435
"Chek" us out on the web at www.chekchart.com.

General Manager
Peter Monte

Executive Editor
Roger Fennema

Technical Publications Editor
Richard K. DuPuy

Editor
William J. Turney

Contributing Editors
William Renke
Dennis L. Shortino

Managing Editor
Steven D. Schaefer

Technical Consultant
Jerry Mullen

Manufacturing Coordinator
Thomas Hedrick

Production Team
Troy Barnes, *Team Supervisor*
Kristy Nash, *Production Coordinator*
Carl Pierce, *Proofreader*

ACKNOWLEDGEMENTS

In producing this series of textbooks for automobile technicians, Chek-Chart has drawn extensively on the technical and editorial knowledge of the vehicle manufacturers and their suppliers. Automotive design is a technical, fast-changing field, and Chek-Chart gratefully acknowledges the help of the following companies and organizations that provided help and information allowing us to present the most up-to-date text and illustrations possible. These companies and organizations are not responsible for any errors or omissions in the instructions or illustrations, or for changes in procedures or specifications made by the manufacturers or suppliers, contained in this book or any other Chek-Chart product:

Allen Testproducts
American Isuzu Motors, Inc.
Automotive Electronic Services
Bear Manufacturing Company
Borg-Warner Corporation
Champion Spark Plug Company
DaimlerChrysler
DeAnza College, Cupertino CA
Fluke Corporation
Ford Motor Company
Fram Corporation
General Motors Corporation
- Delco-Remy Division
- Rochester Products Division
- Saginaw Steering Gear Division
- Buick Motor Division
- Cadillac Motor Car Division
- Chevrolet Motor Division
- Oldsmobile Division
- Pontiac-GMC Division

Honda Motor Company, LTD
Jaguar Cars, Inc.
Marquette Manufacturing Company
Mazda Motor Corporation
Mercedes-Benz USA, Inc.
Mitsubishi Motor Sales of America, Inc.
Nissan North America, Inc.
The Prestolite Company
Robert Bosch Corporation
Saab Cars USA Inc.
Snap-on Tools Corporation
Toyota Motor Sales, U.S.A., Inc.
Vetronix Corporation
Volkswagen of America
Volvo Cars of North America

The comments, suggestions, and assistance of the following reviewers were invaluable:

Rick Escalambre, *Skyline College, San Bruno CA*
Jerry Mullen, *DeAnza College, Cupertino CA*
Eugene Wilson, *Mesa Community College, Mesa AZ*

The authors have made every effort to ensure that the material in this book is as accurate and up-to-date as possible. However, neither Chek-Chart, nor any related companies, are responsible for mistakes or omissions, or for changes in procedures or specifications by the manufacturers or suppliers.

Contents

On the Covers:
Front — Fluke 98 Automotive Scope Meter, Series II

Copyright 2000 by Chek-Chart Publications

Copyright 2000 by Chek-Chart Publications

Introduction to Automotive Electrical and Electronic Systems

Automotive Electrical and Electronic Systems is part of the Chek-Chart Automotive Series. The package for each course has two volumes, a *Classroom Manual* and a *Shop Manual.*
Other titles in this series include:

- *Automatic Transmissions and Transaxles*
- *Automotive Brake Systems*
- *Automotive Heating, Ventilation, and Air Conditioning*
- *Automotive Steering, Suspension, and Wheel Alignment*
- *Automotive Engine Repair and Rebuilding*
- *Engine Performance, Diagnosis, and Tune-Up*
- *Fuel Systems and Emission Controls.*

Each book is written to help the instructor teach students to become competent and knowledgeable professional automotive technicians. The two-manual texts are the core of a learning system that leads a student from basic theories to actual hands-on experience.

The entire series is job-oriented, designed for students who intend to work in the automotive service profession. Knowledge gained from these books and the instructors enables the student to get and keep a job in the automotive repair industry. Learning the material and techniques in these volumes is a giant leap toward a satisfying, rewarding career.

The books are divided into a *Classroom Manual* and *Shop Manual* for an improved presentation of the descriptive information and study lessons, along with representative testing, repair, and overhaul procedures. The manuals are to be used together: The descriptive material in the *Classroom Manual* reinforces the application material in the *Shop Manual.*

Each book is divided into several parts and each of these parts is complete by itself. Within each part are several related chapters. Instructors enjoy the complete, readable, and well-thought-out presentation of the chapters. Students benefit from the many learning aids included, as well as from the thoroughness of the presentation.

The series was researched and written by the editorial staff of Chek-Chart. Chek-Chart has been providing vehicle specification, training, and repair information to the professional automotive service field since 1929. Chek-Chart maintains a complete, up-to-date automotive data bank, which was used extensively to prepare this textbook series.

Because of the comprehensive material, the hundreds of high-quality illustrations, and the inclusion of the latest automotive technology, instructors and students alike find that these books maintain their value over the years. Many master technicians form the core of their professional library with Chek-Chart publications.

Copyright 2000 by Chek-Chart Publications

How To Use This Book

Why Are There Two Manuals?

Unless you are familiar with the other books in this series, *Automotive Electrical and Electronic Systems* is unlike any other textbook you have used before. It is actually two books, the *Classroom Manual* and the *Shop Manual*. They have different purposes and should be used together.

The *Classroom Manual* teaches what a technician needs to know about electrical and electronic theory, systems, and components. The *Classroom Manual* is valuable in class and at home, both for study and for reference. The text and illustrations are used for years to refresh the memory—not only about the basics of automotive electrical and electronic systems but also about related topics in automotive history, physics, and technology.

The *Shop Manual* teaches test procedures, troubleshooting techniques, and how to repair the systems and components introduced in the *Classroom Manual*. The *Shop Manual* provides the practical, hands-on information required for working on automotive electrical and electronic systems. Use the two manuals together to understand fully how the systems work and how to make repairs when something is not working properly.

What Is In These Manuals?

These key features of the *Classroom Manual* make it easier to learn and to remember the material:

- Each chapter is divided into self-contained sections for easier understanding and review. This organization clearly shows which parts make up which systems, and how various parts or systems that perform the same task differ or are the same.
- Most parts and processes are fully illustrated with drawings or photographs. Important topics appear in several different ways, to make sure other aspects of them are seen.
- Important words in the *Classroom Manual* text are printed in **boldface type** and are defined on the same page and in a glossary at the end of the manual. Use these words to build the vocabulary needed to understand the text.
- Review questions are included for each chapter. Use them to test your knowledge.
- Every chapter has a brief summary at the end to help review for exams.
- Every so often, sidebars—short blocks of "nice to know" information—are included in addition to the main text.

Copyright 2000 by Chek-Chart Publications

The *Shop Manual* has detailed instructions on test, service, and overhaul procedures for modern electrical and electronic systems and their components. These are easy to understand and often include step-by-step explanations of the procedure. The *Shop Manual* contains:

- Helpful information on the use and maintenance of shop tools and test equipment.
- Safety precautions.
- Clear illustrations and diagrams that help in locating trouble spots while learning to read service literature.
- Test procedures and troubleshooting hints that help you work better and faster.
- Repair tips used by professionals, presented clearly and accurately.
- A sample test at the back of the manual that is similar to those given for Automotive Service Excellence (ASE) certification; use this test to help study and prepare when ready to be certified as an electrical and electronics expert.

Where Should I Begin?

If you already know something about automotive electrical and electronic systems and know how to repair them, this book is a helpful review. If you are just starting in automotive repair, then the book provides a solid foundation on which to develop professional-level skills.

Your instructor has designed a course to take advantage of what you already know and what facilities and equipment are available. You may be asked to read certain chapters of these manuals out of order. That is fine. The important thing is to really understand each subject before moving on to the next.

Study the vocabulary words in boldface type and use the review questions to help understand the material. When reading the *Classroom Manual*, be sure to refer to the *Shop Manual* to relate the descriptive text to the service procedures. When working on actual vehicle systems and components, look to the *Classroom Manual* to keep the basic information fresh in your mind. Working on such a complicated piece of equipment as a modern automobile is not easy. Use the information in the *Classroom Manual*, the procedures in the *Shop Manual*, and the knowledge of your instructor to guide you.

The *Shop Manual* is a good book for work, not just a good workbook. Keep it on hand while actually working on a vehicle. It folds flat on the workbench and under the chassis, and is designed to withstand quite a bit of rough handling.

When performing actual test and repair procedures, a complete and accurate source of manufacturer specifications and procedures is needed for the specific vehicle. Most automotive repair shops have either the annual service manuals from the vehicle manufacturer, which lists these specifications, or an independent guide, such as the Chek-Chart *Car Care Guide*. This unique book, with ten-year coverage, is updated each year to provide service instructions, capacities, and troubleshooting tips needed to work on specific vehicles.

Copyright 2000 by Chek-Chart Publications

PART ONE

Basic Electrical Test Procedures

Chapter One
Circuit Tracing, Troubleshooting, and Wiring Repair

Chapter Two
Electrical Faults and Basic Test Equipment

Chapter Three
Battery Service

Copyright 2000 by Chek-Chart Publications

Chapter 3

1 Circuit Tracing, Troubleshooting, and Wiring Repair

Finding and repairing the cause of an electrical problem requires a logical and organized troubleshooting technique. Although it may be possible to repair some electrical failures simply by replacing parts in a haphazard manner, this hit-or-miss approach to electrical service is inefficient, inaccurate, and unacceptable. An unorganized technician wastes time and effort, which leads to unnecessary expense for the customer and often does not solve the root cause of the problem. An organized approach to electrical service is a tried and proven method that consists of a step-by-step examination of the symptoms, isolation of the cause, and repair of the problem.

Part One of this *Shop Manual,* which consists of the first three chapters, details basic electrical test procedures, electrical service tools and equipment, and battery service procedures. The information contained in these chapters is fundamental for all automotive electrical system repairs.

Chapter One begins with a review of basic shop and vehicle system safety precautions to be observed during any automotive service situation. A review of automotive wiring diagrams, schematics, circuit diagrams, and component locators follows. These items are valuable troubleshooting aids and indispensable tools for servicing vehicle electrical systems. Next, the chapter provides a number of sources for obtaining service specifications and procedures that are essential for successful troubleshooting. A 10-step troubleshooting checklist, which is designed to guide the technician through any problem to guarantee an accurate diagnosis and successful repair, is included. The chapter concludes with some common wiring and connector repair techniques and procedures.

Chapter Two examines the use of common troubleshooting tools and equipment. Electrical troubleshooting always begins with checking the condition of the battery. Battery service is detailed in Chapter Three.

ELECTRICAL SAFETY

Most professional technicians work for years without ever suffering a serious injury simply by following a few commonsense rules of safety. Apply these rules at all times to avoid personal injury to yourself or to others in the vicinity, and to prevent accidental damage to a vehicle or the shop.

Shop Safety

Observe the following precautions during any shop activity.

Copyright 2000 by Chek-Chart Publications

- Know the location of shop first-aid supplies and the number to call for emergency medical assistance.
- Know the location of all fire extinguishers and have one readily available when working with solvents and other flammable materials.
- Never use gasoline as a cleaning solvent unless it is specifically recommended.
- Never smoke in the shop, or in outside areas where there are any flammable liquids and combustible materials.
- Keep flames and sparks away from a charging battery. Highly explosive hydrogen gas forms during the charging process.
- Never arc the terminals of a battery to see if it is charged. A spark ignites the explosive hydrogen gas as easily as an open flame.
- Always wear safety goggles in any area or during any job where an eye hazard could exist.
- Remove all jewelry, such as rings and watches, before starting work. Tuck in loose clothing and tie back long hair.
- Never use a tool, machine, or test equipment without being familiar with its safe operation and proper use.
- Make sure your hands, the floor, and the entire work area are dry before using any electrical equipment or touching any electrical switches and plugs.
- Keep floors, aisles, and the work area clear of all tools, parts, and materials. Mop up any spilled liquids immediately.
- Carry sharp tools such as screwdrivers, awls, or scrapers in your hand with the cutting edge facing downward. Never carry sharp tools in a pocket.
- When using a vise, make sure the component being held is properly secured and the vise is firmly attached to the bench before working on the part.
- Avoid splashing cleaning solvents when putting parts into, or removing them from, a cleaning tank.
- Always wear gloves and eye protection when working with cleaning solvents and other chemicals.
- When using an air nozzle to dry cleaned parts, direct the airflow away from you and anyone else in the immediate area.
- Before starting an engine, set the parking brake, block the drive wheels, and place the transmission in neutral or park.
- Never run an engine in a closed area or room without proper ventilation. Connect the vehicle exhaust pipe to shop exhaust ducts or make sure there is sufficient ventilation to prevent the accumulation of poisonous exhaust gases.
- Keep hands and other body parts away from hot exhaust components. Catalytic converters heat up rapidly and retain their heat for a long time after the engine is shut off. Wear gloves if working around such objects when they are hot.
- Never drive a vehicle faster than five miles per hour in, or when entering or leaving, the shop.

Vehicle Safety

Observe the following precautions during vehicle electrical system testing or service.

- Always disconnect the negative battery cable before disconnecting any electrical wires that are directly linked to it, such as those attached to the alternator or starter.
- Disconnect the negative battery cable when replacing components or making electrical system repairs, unless a test procedure specifies otherwise.
- Observe correct polarity when connecting battery cables. On most batteries, the negative or ground terminal is marked with a minus (-) sign and the positive or insulated terminal with a plus (+) sign.
- When charging a battery, connect the charger to the battery terminals before plugging it into the power outlet. Also, disconnect the vehicle battery cables before charging to prevent accidental damage to the electrical system.
- When jump starting a vehicle with booster cables, always make the final ground connection on the engine or chassis instead of the battery itself. An electrical arc, which occurs when this connection is made, may cause an explosion if it is near the battery.
- When disconnecting electrical wires, carefully separate the connector if one is used. Never pull directly on a wire to separate it from a terminal, as this causes internal damage. Instead, carefully pry the wire from the terminal with a terminal removal tool.
- Remove spark plug cables from the plug by twisting the boot one-half turn in both directions to break the seal, then pull upward on the boot to remove the wire from the plug terminal. Pulling on the cable causes internal damage. Use a spark plug cable tool to pry the boot off of the plug if needed.

Copyright 2000 by Chek-Chart Publications

- Never short, ground, or apply battery voltage directly to any electric or electronic components or circuits, unless specified in a test procedure.
- Always make sure the ignition is switched off before separating or connecting wiring harness connectors to an electronic control module (ECM) or component.
- A nonconductive grease is used on some electronic connections to prevent corrosion. Be sure the connection is protected with the correct type of grease after servicing.
- Never disconnect a spark plug wire to conduct a spark check if the cable runs directly above or alongside a pick-up coil. An arc from the wire may damage the pick-up coil.
- Never use a 12-volt test lamp to check for voltage or continuity on an electronic circuit or component.
- Use a high-impedance digital multimeter (DMM) to check amperage, voltage, or continuity on an electronic circuit or component. Never use an analog test meter.

TRACING SPECIFIC CIRCUITS

Attempting to diagnose an electrical or electronic system problem without an electrical diagram would be like attempting to drive across the United States without a road map. It is critical to understand how to read and use the various types of electrical diagrams.

Electrical Diagrams

Every automotive electrical system is built using an illustration called an electrical schematic, figure 1-1. The schematic is not always drawn to a particular scale like a blueprint, but it illustrates the layout of the electrical system. Schematics are often many pages in length. The parts are laid out for simplicity of illustration and are not necessarily shown with respect to their physical location on the vehicle.

A schematic can be very complicated. Typically, the electrical diagrams produced for servicing a vehicle are available in two basic types:

- Vehicle system schematic diagrams
- Vehicle component layout diagrams.

A system schematic diagram uses symbols to identify wires, connectors, grounds, and power on the vehicle electrical system illustration. Where electrical parts, harnesses, and connectors are located on the vehicle is shown on a component layout diagram. Typically, both types of diagram are used together to locate and identify the source of an electrical failure.

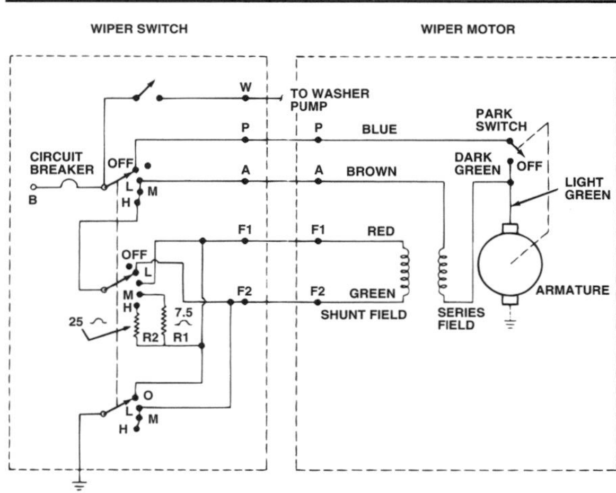

Figure 1-1. A schematic shows the power source, loads, and primary wiring of the electrical system.

The electrical system illustrations vary from manufacturer to manufacturer. Each manufacturer has unique methods of displaying the electrical systems. In general, understanding the principles of electricity, as explained in the *Classroom Manual,* knowing how to read the diagrams, and being able to trace out a circuit on the vehicle schematic make repair of electrical and electronics problems faster and easier. In order to use a schematic, it is important to understand:

- Color code information
- Circuit numbering
- Component symbols used on the diagram.

Color codes

Manufacturers design automotive electrical systems so individual circuits can be identified on the vehicle from other circuits by using color-coded wires. Electrical system diagrams may illustrate the color code on the schematic. Other forms of circuit identification used on system drawings have letters and numbers printed near each wire. A code table accompanying the drawing shows what color wire the letters and numbers stand for, figure 1-2. As you can see, the Chrysler code contains information on wire gauge and circuit numbers, as well as wire color. On a diagram without a color code table, "L" is used to denote blue, while "B" indicates black, and "BR" is used for brown, figure 1-3. Note that this Toyota diagram shows the color of the wires only; wire gauge is not identified in the drawing.

There are hundreds of circuits in a modern vehicle. Identifying a particular circuit or wire in the vehicle requires the ability to understand the color code in the electrical diagram. The abbreviations used to denote the color codes vary between manufacturers, but they

Copyright 2000 by Chek-Chart Publications

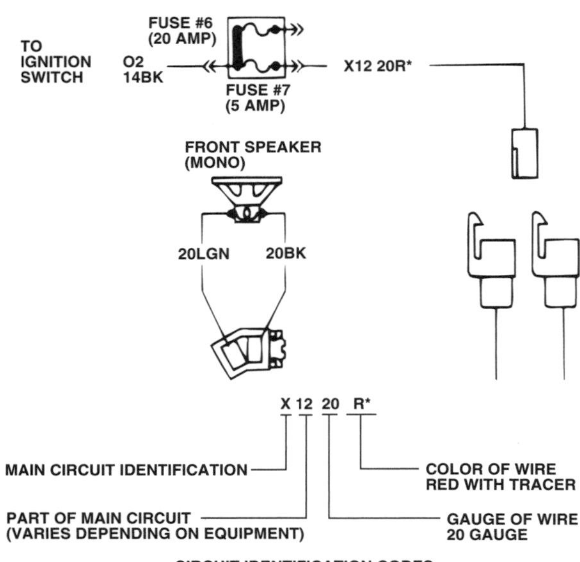

COLOR CODE			
BK	BLACK	P	PINK
BR	BROWN	R	RED
DBL	DARK BLUE	T	TAN
DGN	DARK GREEN	V	VIOLET
GY	GRAY	W	WHITE
LBL	LIGHT BLUE	Y	YELLOW
LGN	LIGHT GREEN	*	WITH TRACER
O	ORANGE		

Figure 1-2. Wire codes on this Chrysler diagram identify the circuit and the gauge and color of the wire.

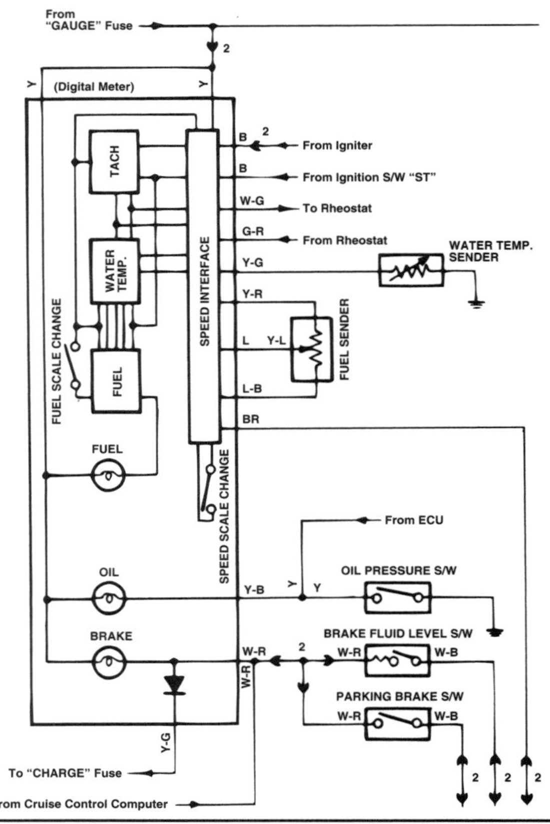

Figure 1-3. On diagrams without a color code table, standard abbreviations are used to show the color of each wire.

are usually self-explanatory. There are three ways colors are used to identify wires:

- Solid colors—black (BK), white (WT), light blue (LB), dark blue (DB), violet (VT), yellow (YL), dark green (DG), light green (LG), orange (OR), brown (BR), tan (TN), pink (PK), gray (GY), red (RD). Any other colors used are similarly abbreviated.
- Solid color with complementary strips or tracers—such as black with white (BK/WT) and white with green (WT/GN). The trace or stripe is a continuous line of color that runs the entire length of the wire.
- Solid color with complementary dash colors—such as black with white (BK/WT) and white with red (WT/RD). The hash appears as a broken line that repeats along the entire length of the wire.

Most original equipment manufacturer (OEM) electrical diagrams are illustrated in black and white. Color codes and circuit numbers will be listed either on the schematic or on an auxiliary legend. Some General Motors shop manuals illustrate the electrical system by using individual electrical circuit diagrams. Commonly called *Valley Forge* diagrams, after the company that originally devised them, these diagrams are sometimes printed in color. The color of the lines used to denote wires on a Valley Forge diagram closely matches the actual color of the wires on the vehicle, figure 1-4. Since not all service manuals are printed in color, an abbreviation of the color name is also printed beside the wire and the abbreviations are spelled out in an accompanying chart, figure 1-5. Some illustrations may also show the wire gauge or the wire size in metric dimensions printed immediately before the color name. Rather than print the size on all the wires in a diagram, General Motors includes a statement indicating all of the wires are of a certain gauge, unless otherwise identified. Therefore, the only wires in the drawing that have a gauge number printed on them are those that are not the specified gauge.

Circuit numbers

Because there are so many circuits in a modern vehicle, it is impossible to use a different color wire for each individual circuit. Therefore, the same color

Copyright 2000 by Chek-Chart Publications

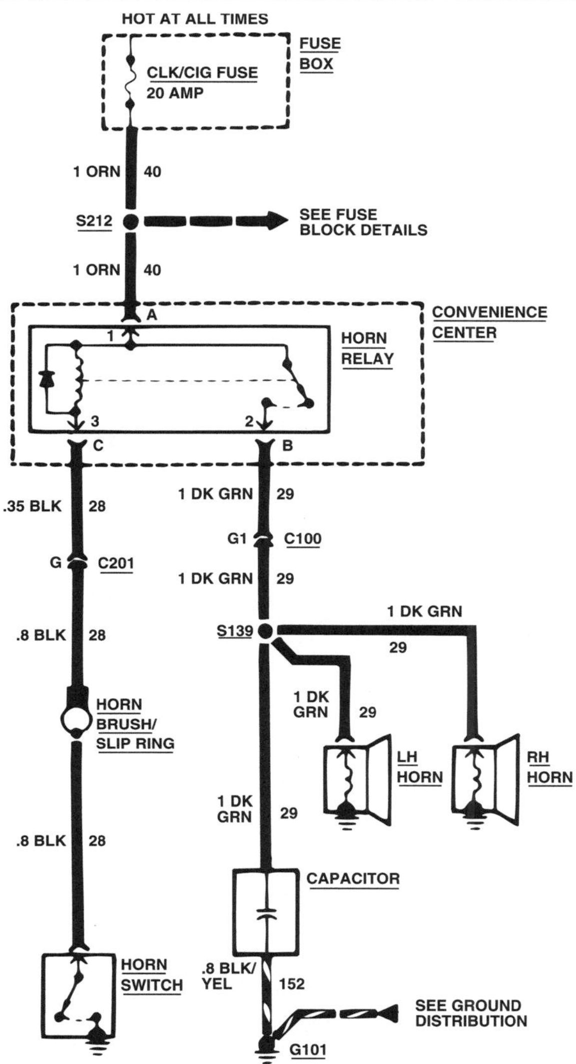

Figure 1-4. This Valley Forge horn circuit schematic may be printed in color, but also has a color abbreviation printed at each wire.

WIRE IDENTIFICATION CHART			
COLOR	**SYMBOL**	**COLOR**	**SYMBOL**
ALUMINUM	AL	NATURAL	NAT
BLACK	BLK	ORANGE	ORN
BLUE-LIGHT	BLU LT	PINK	PINK
BLUE-DARK	BLU DK	PURPLE	PPL
BROWN	BRN	RED	RED
GLAZED	GLZ	TAN	TAN
GREEN-LIGHT	GRN LT	VIOLET	VLT
GREEN-DARK	GRN DK	WHITE	WHT
GRAY	GRA	YELLOW	YEL
MAROON	MAR		

Figure 1-5. A color key is used to define Valley Forge abbreviations.

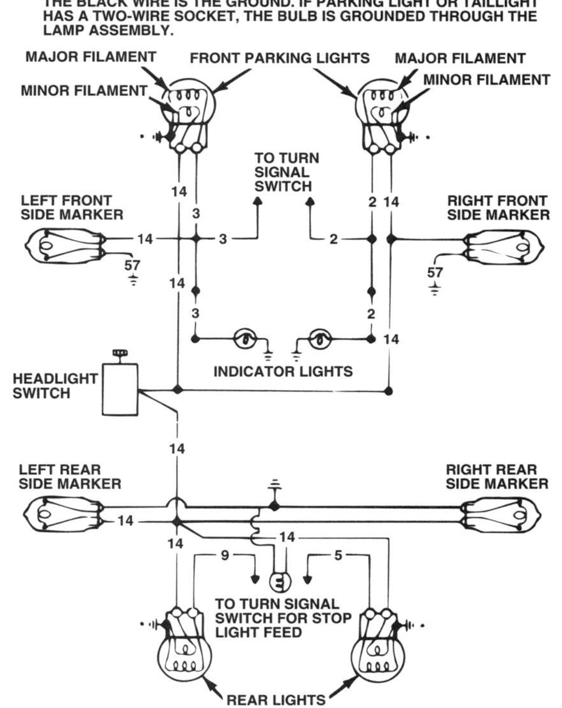

Figure 1-6. Wires are identified by a circuit number only on this Ford exterior lighting wiring diagram.

wires are used on more than one circuit, both on the vehicle and on the schematic. To help identify the circuit and to coordinate diagnostic information in a service manual, most manufacturers identify the circuits with number codes. It is common to see entire vehicle wiring diagrams with only circuit numbers for late-model vehicles, figure 1-6. Some manufacturers, such as Chrysler, use a combination of letters and numbers to identify the circuits, figure 1-7. Any two wires with the same circuit number are connected within the same circuit.

Color coding the wires is not the only method of identifying the circuits in a vehicle. In some systems, each wire is numbered at selected, repetitive intervals along its length for identification. No matter where the wire runs in the vehicle, the number on it stays the same. No two wires have the same number. The vehicle diagrams use the corresponding number and also have a legend of component-to-number and number-to-component listings.

Component symbols

Besides being able to identify the wires and the circuits in a vehicle and on a schematic, it is important to be able to identify the type of components. Symbols are used to show the components and the connectors on a circuit diagram. Generic electrical symbols are used for different types of electrical devices in each diagram, figure 1-8. Although these symbols are similar on different diagrams, they are not identical across

Copyright 2000 by Chek-Chart Publications

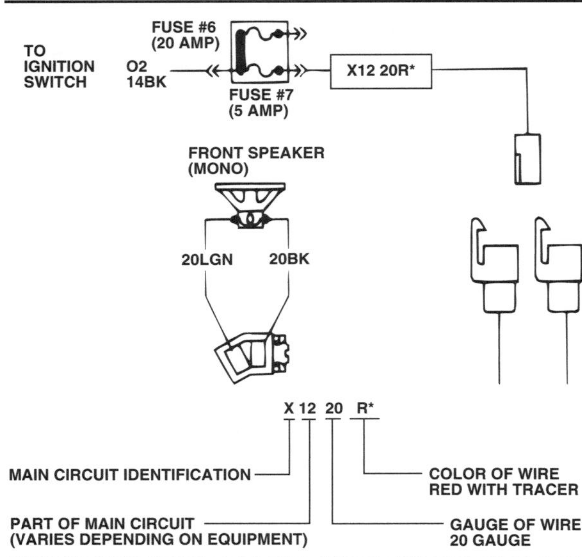

Figure 1-7. This Chrysler radio speaker wiring diagram uses a combination of letters and numbers to identify wires and circuits.

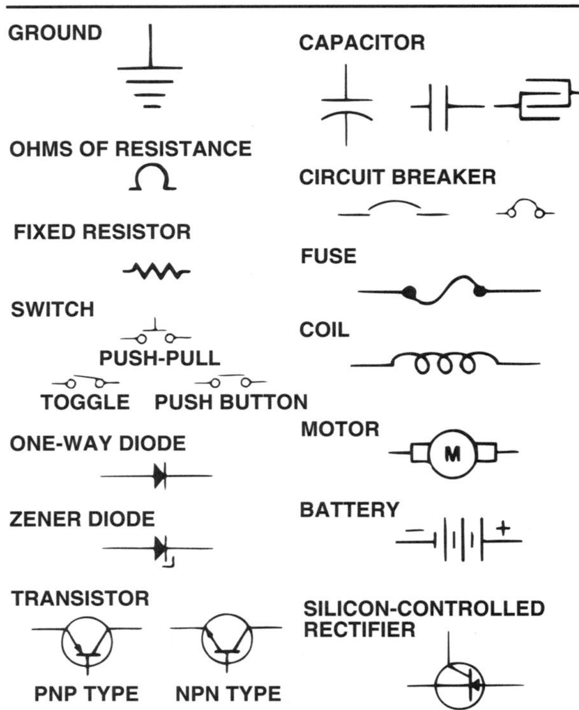

Figure 1-8. Symbols are used to represent the different types of electrical devices on a diagram.

manufacturers, figure 1-9. Manufacturers generally include a chart to identify the symbols used in the diagrams somewhere in the manual. Some manufacturers print the name of key components alongside their symbol on the diagrams, figure 1-10.

The increasing use of sophisticated electronics in automobiles has brought about the appearance of a new type of electrical circuit diagram containing logic symbols. Logic symbols are used to simplify a complex electrical circuit and show how current is directed under operating conditions, figure 1-11.

Types of Electrical Diagrams

The color codes, circuit numbers, and symbols discussed above are combined to create a variety of electrical diagrams. Most technicians tend to refer to any electrical diagram simply as a "wiring diagram," but there are at least three distinct types of diagrams commonly supplied by automotive manufacturers. These electrical diagrams are needed to troubleshoot electrical problems efficiently. It is very important to be familiar with and know how to use each of the three types:

- System diagram
- Circuit diagram
- Installation diagram.

System diagram

A system diagram, also properly called a "wiring diagram," is a drawing of the entire automobile electrical system. The system diagram may cover many pages of a manual or it may be printed on a special, oversized, fold-out page, figures 1-12. System diagrams show the wires, the type of connectors used, connections to loads, and switches. But a system diagram does not show how the loads or switches work.

Most system diagrams are laid out to show current moving horizontally across the page. That is, they read from left to right. Some manufacturers provide reference coordinates along the edges of their system diagrams. An index is included listing system components alphabetically, along with the specific grid coordinates. This method is similar to that found on a road map and is used in the same manner.

Some European manufacturers, such as Volkswagen, show current moving vertically across the page on their diagrams. That is, the diagram is read from top to bottom, figure 1-13. These German diagrams use lines across the top of the page to represent the fuse panel connections. Wires are identified by the metric gauge system and a color-code abbreviation.

Circuit diagram

A circuit diagram is more focused than a system diagram, as it displays only a small portion of the overall system diagram. Commonly referred to as a "schematic", these diagrams are easier to use for troubleshooting a specific circuit because unrelated systems and components are not included in the diagram. For example, one schematic might illustrate only the starting system or the lighting system.

Copyright 2000 by Chek-Chart Publications

LEGEND OF SYMBOLS USED ON WIRING DIAGRAMS			
+	POSITIVE		CONNECTOR
−	NEGATIVE		MALE CONNECTOR
	GROUND		FEMALE CONNECTOR
	FUSE		MULTIPLE CONNECTOR
	CIRCUIT BREAKER		DENOTES WIRE CONTINUES ELSEWHERE
	CAPACITOR		SPLICE
Ω	OHMS	J2 2	SPLICE IDENTIFICATION
	RESISTOR		OPTIONAL WIRING WITH / WIRING WITHOUT
	VARIABLE RESISTOR		THERMAL ELEMENT (BI-METAL STRIP)
	SERIES RESISTOR		"Y" WINDINGS
	COIL	88:88	DIGITAL READOUT

Figure 1-9. Although electrical symbols are somewhat universal, they do vary slightly between manufacturers.

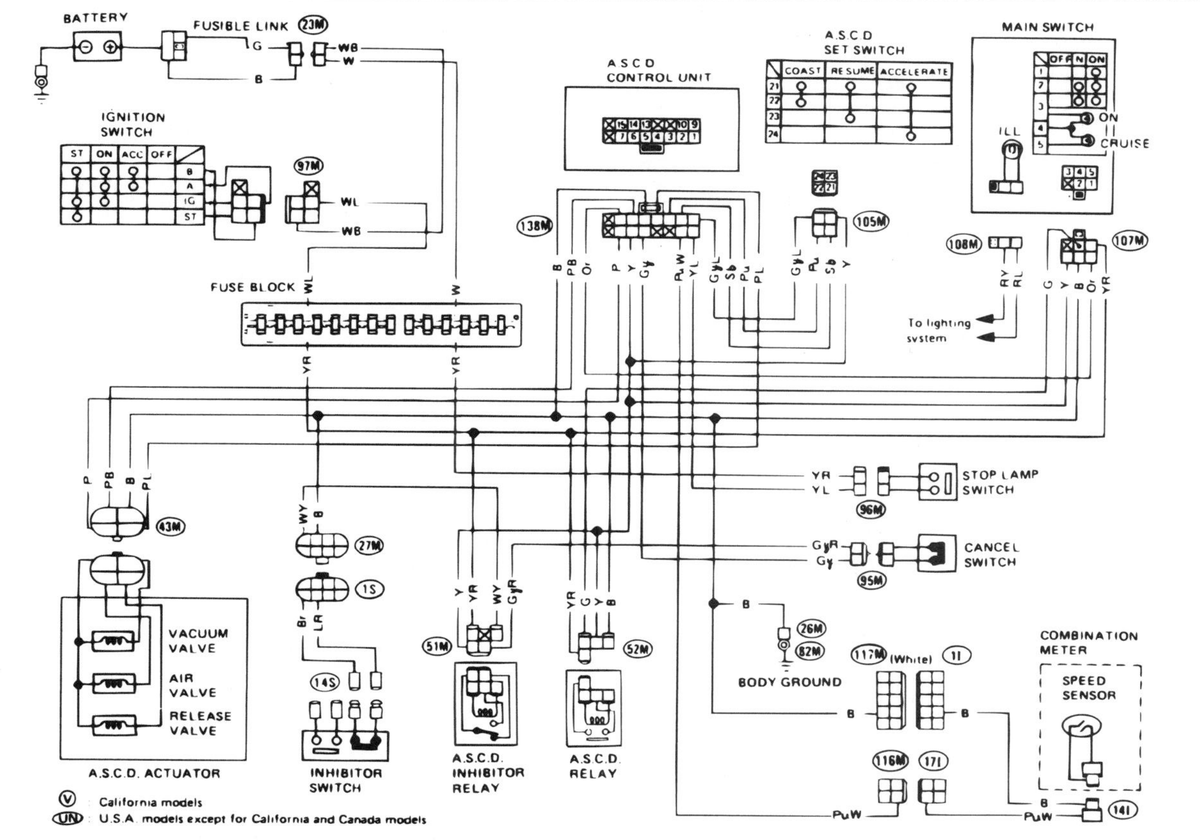

Figure 1-10. On this Nissan cruise-control system diagram, the name of key components appears alongside the symbol.

Copyright 2000 by Chek-Chart Publications

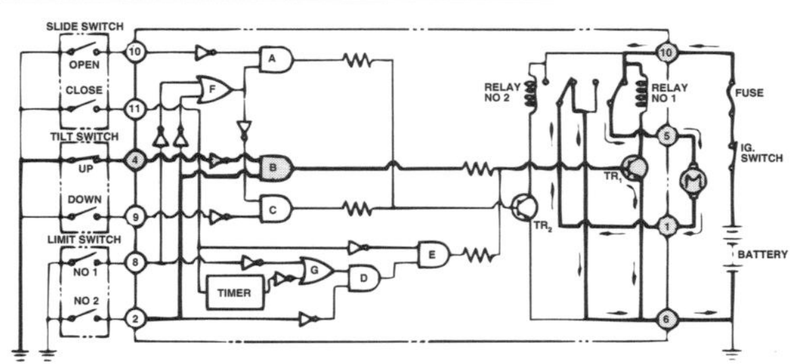

Figure 1-11. An electronic diagram uses logic symbols to show how current is directed through this Toyota sunroof motor circuit.

Circuit diagrams vary somewhat between manufacturers, but always contain electrical information about a complete automotive circuit in a single drawing. The diagram illustrates the power source, circuit protection, switches, connectors, loads, and other devices included in the circuit, figure 1-14.

The radio system circuit diagram shown in figure 1-14 is typical of the format Chrysler extensively uses throughout its shop manuals for individual circuits. Note that some of the wires are fully identified with circuit numbers, wire gauge, and wire color, while other wires, such as those connected to the front speaker, are identified only by wire gauge and color. The "20LGN" indicates a 20-gauge, light green wire.

Ford typically does not specify wire gauge or wire color on its circuit diagrams. When servicing a Ford, determine wire color code by looking them up in a table of circuit numbers to color code or circuit number to wire size. General Motors specifies wire gauge and color on some, but not all, of its circuit diagrams. To determine what the wire size and color codes are on a General Motors vehicle, refer to the system wiring diagram.

One potential problem with using circuit schematics is that frequently there are parallel circuits. These may share fuse power or ground circuits with the particular circuit being worked on. It is very important to keep parallel circuits in mind when using a schematic. Remember, a failure in a parallel circuit may be affecting the circuit being worked on. Since the companion schematic does not appear, it is easy to forget to consider it. Look the circuit diagram over for indications of a connection to a parallel circuit. For example, a note at the upper right corner of the Oldsmobile keyless entry system schematic shown in figure 1-15 states "see I/P fuse block/relay center for details." This shows that another circuit, *S251,* shares the same 15-amp fuse. Do not forget to find out what is on that circuit, especially if the fuse is blowing. Note also that this circuit has another parallel connection on the left side at circuit *S227,* which is accompanied with another note and connects to a common circuit breaker. Additional circuit diagrams are referenced for the ground side of the circuit as well. A broken line outlining a device, such as on the relay center, I/P fuse block, and remote accessory control module, indicates a partial circuit. The remainder of these circuits are detailed on other pages in the manual. Consider the potential of interference from all parallel circuits when troubleshooting with a circuit schematic.

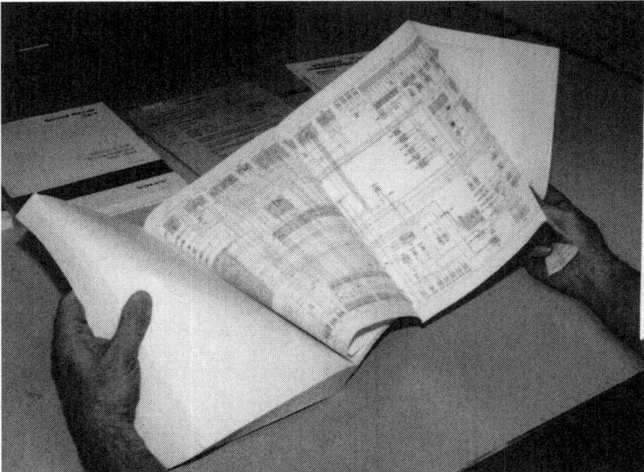

Figure 1-12. Some system diagrams are printed in the service manual on large, fold-out pages.

Installation diagram

None of the diagrams shown so far have indicated where or how the wires and other circuit components are installed in the automobile. If working only with a schematic and color codes, it would be a very difficult task to find out where the parts are on the vehicle. Many are completely hidden from sight behind the dash or under the carpet. Most vehicle manufacturers provide installation diagrams or component locator charts showing the positions of various parts. Component location diagrams are sometimes called pictorial diagrams. These diagrams are helpful for locating a harness, circuit, or component on the vehicle.

The Chrysler installation diagram in figure 1-16 includes the wiring for the radio speakers and shows the major wiring for this area of the vehicle. An installation diagram for a Ford side lamp assembly details wiring along with the placement of the bulbs and lenses, figure 1-17.

This Chrysler illustration clearly shows the left fender, strut tower, brake master cylinder, and the engine harness for easy reference on the vehicle, figure 1-18. The illustration also points out the location of certain relays, the ECM, and the diagnostic connector.

Though each manufacturer offers the same type of information, each one presents it differently. For

Copyright 2000 by Chek-Chart Publications

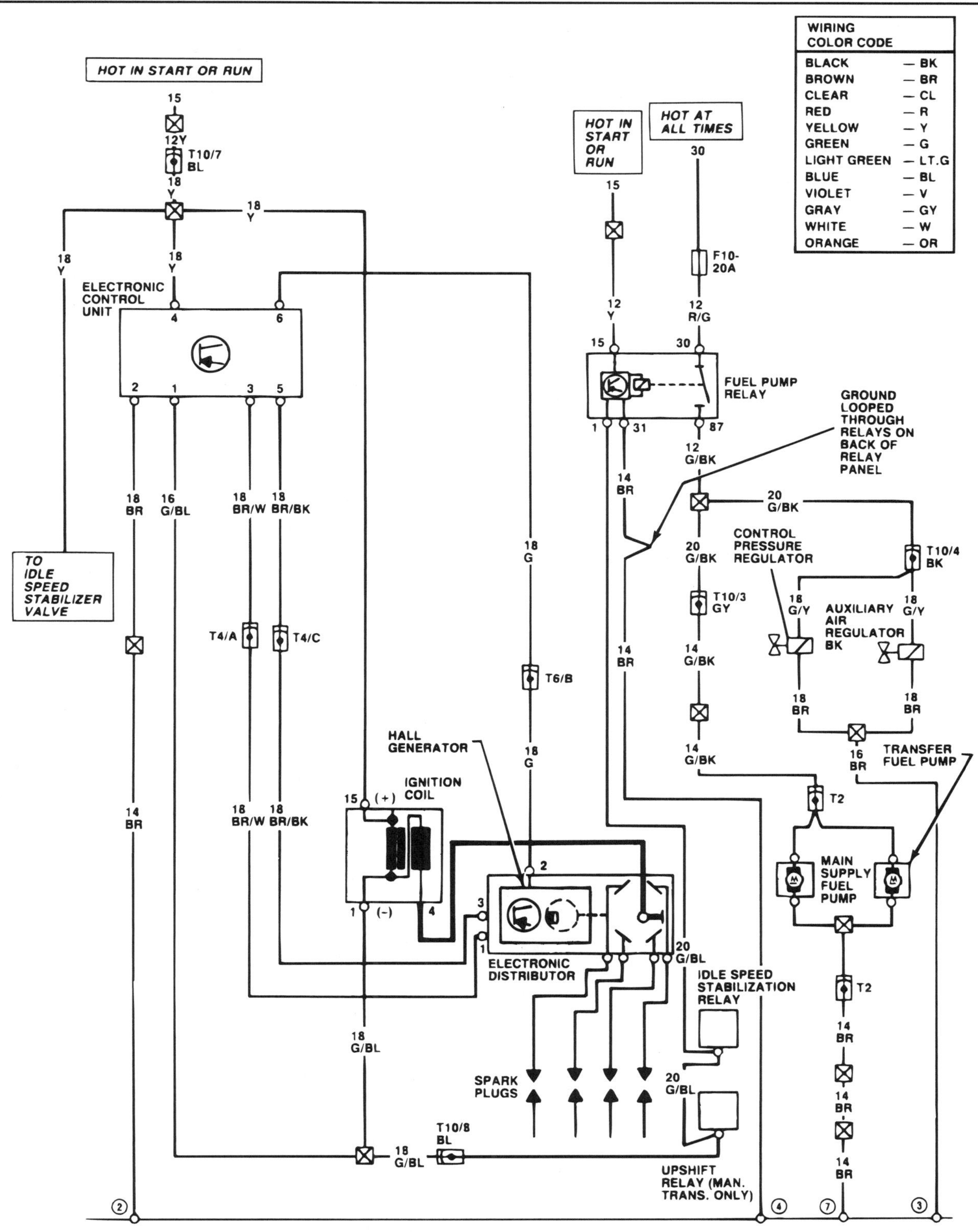

Figure 1-13. A portion of a Volkswagen diagram, which is read from top to bottom.

Copyright 2000 by Chek-Chart Publications

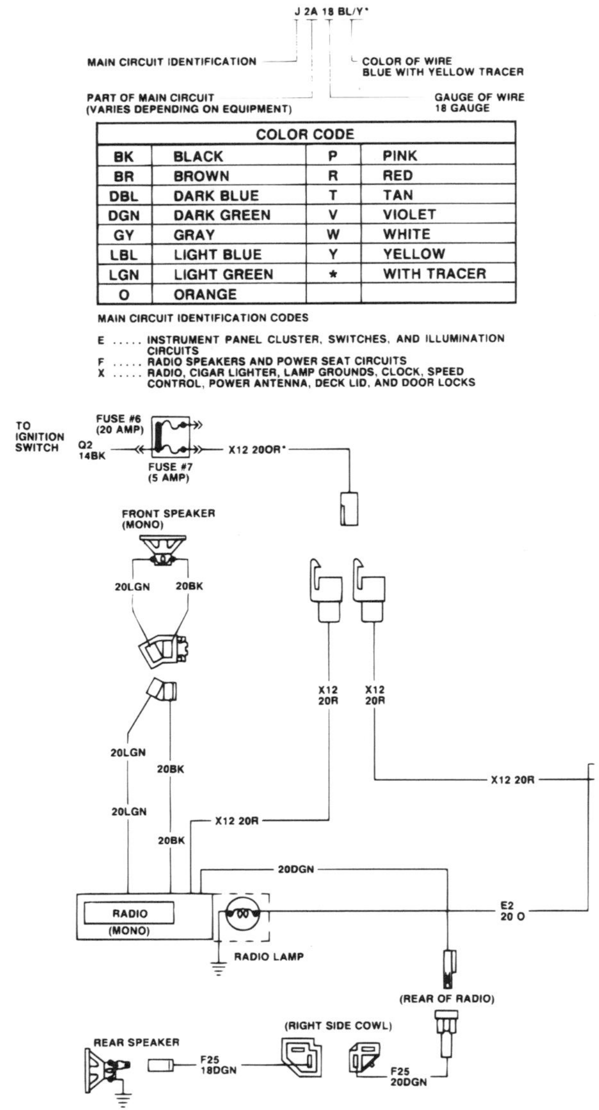

Figure 1-14. This Chrysler radio circuit diagram illustrates only the devices within the radio system.

example, Nissan provides two different system component diagram formats, each with different detail levels, figure 1-19. To further refine the location of the electrical components, Nissan provides a harness connector location diagram, figure 1-20.

To get a complete understanding of how any circuit works and where the components are located, review the circuit schematic. Note the circuit color codes, and study the component locator chart.

SERVICE INFORMATION SOURCES

Successfully troubleshooting an automotive electrical system requires access to accurate specifications and service procedures for the particular vehicle being worked on. Complete and accurate specifications are the only tool that tells you how the system *should* operate. Without specifications, all the sophisticated test equipment in a shop is useless. Test results mean nothing until they are compared to specifications that indicate what the test results should be. Service procedures go hand-in-hand with specifications. It is important to know the procedure peculiar to a particular system in order to obtain the correct test results. The following paragraphs describe what specifications and procedures are commonly available and where to find them.

There are two main sources of electrical specifications and procedures: the vehicle manufacturer and aftermarket sources.

Vehicle Manufacturer Service Manuals

Manufacturers usually publish a new service or factory shop manual for each model year. Often, these shop manuals cover only one model, so a number of manuals are needed to cover the entire model range each year as well, figure 1-21. Service manual information is often divided and scattered throughout the manual, separated by the repair and overhaul information that is also included.

Manufacturer service manuals are available to vehicle owners, schools, and independent service technicians through dealer parts departments or directly from the manufacturer. Import dealers sell factory service manuals through their parts department, or can supply addresses from which they can be ordered. Domestic vehicle service manuals are also available through the dealer parts department, and can also be ordered from the addresses listed below. Upon request, most of these companies will send a catalogue of available publications and an order blank.

Chrysler Corporation
Service Training
26001 Lawrence Avenue
Centerline MI 48015
1-800-626-1523

Ford Motor Company
Helm, Inc.
Ford Department
P.O. Box 07150
Detroit MI 48207
1-800-782-4356

General Motors Corporation
Helm, Inc.
G.M. Department
P.O. Box 07130
Detroit MI 48207
1-800-782-4356

Copyright 2000 by Chek-Chart Publications

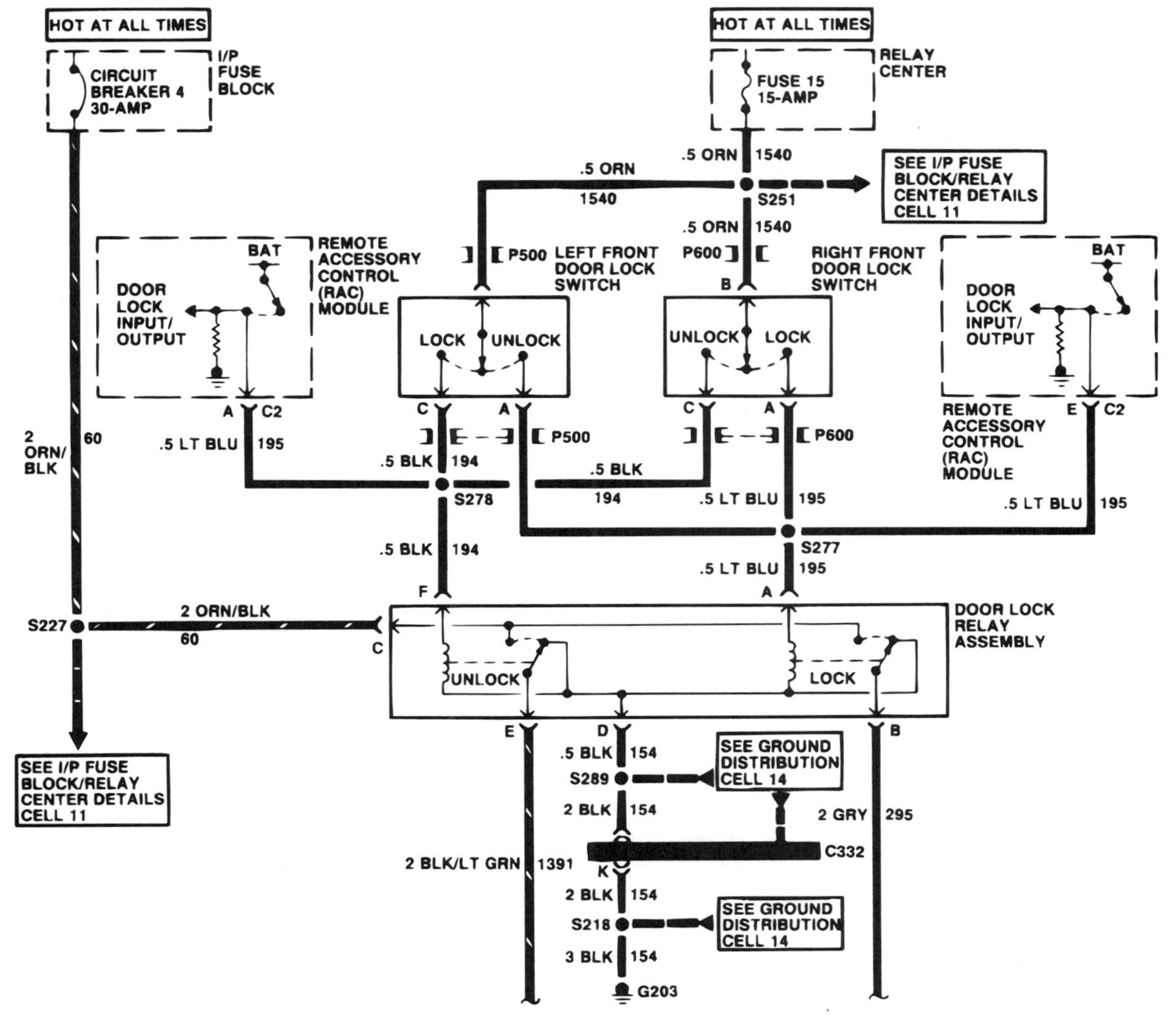

Figure 1-15. Parallel circuit links, both power and ground, are shown as notes on this Oldsmobile keyless entry system diagram.

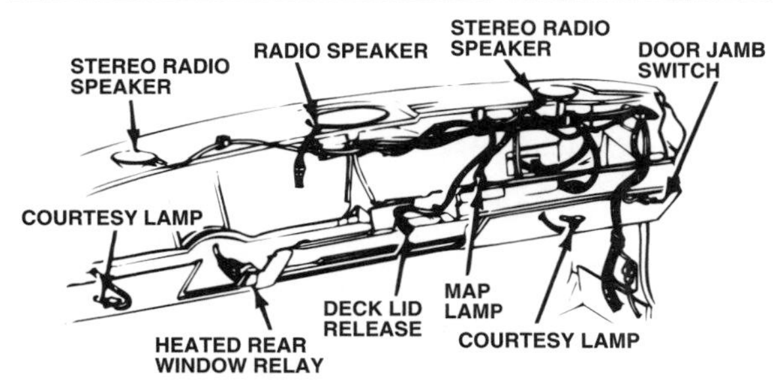

Figure 1-16. This Chrysler installation diagram shows the wiring for the radio speakers.

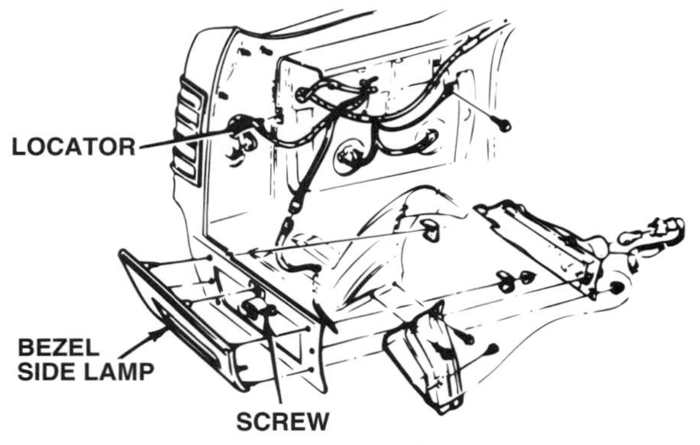

Figure 1-17 This is a Ford installation diagram for a rear side marker lamp assembly.

Copyright 2000 by Chek-Chart Publications

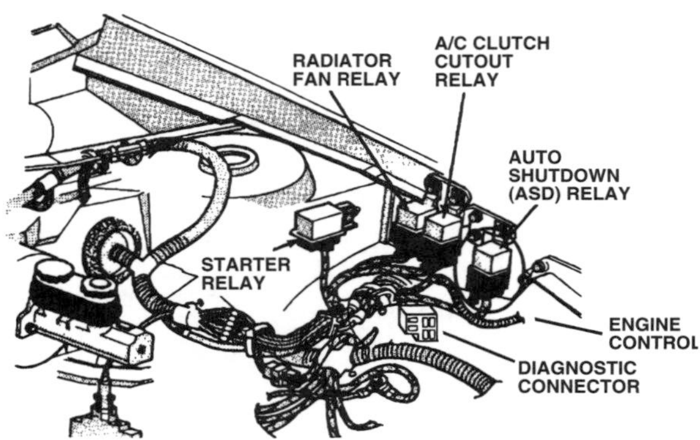

Figure 1-18. This Chrysler installation diagram provides a visual reference for locating components on the left inner fender.

A drawback to factory manuals is that they are produced only once at the beginning of the model year. They do not address any changes made during production. Manufacturers produce technical service bulletins to update the manuals when changes are made during the year. Therefore, it is important to have access to these service bulletins when using the service manual. Service bulletin subscriptions are available through the same sources as manuals.

Aftermarket Repair Manuals

A number of publishing companies, such as Chek-Chart, produce specification and procedure manuals that cover a number of manufacturers and models. Although these manuals are usually published annually, they generally cover a span of model years. These aftermarket manuals typically cover only specific systems, rather than the entire vehicle, figure 1-22. Because the books cover a number of model years, any changes advised by the manufacturer in a service bulletin are incorporated into the next printing of the manual.

Independent manufacturers of replacement components and test equipment often print books of specifications and procedures as well. These manuals are usually highly specialized and apply to installing a particular component or operating a certain piece of equipment only.

Online Services

The Internet is fast becoming one of the most valuable sources of service information to the working technician. A number of vehicle, equipment, and replacement parts manufacturers maintain a web site, as do many aftermarket publishers and training providers. These web sites provide rapid delivery of updated service information to the field. For example, the Chek-Chart web site (chekchart.com) offers free access to selected service bulletin information from the vehicle manufacturers.

Online organizations dedicated to automotive repair, such as the International Automotive Technicians Network (iatn.com), provide valuable service and troubleshooting information. Networking with other technicians across the country and around the world often helps solve those most difficult problems that seem to defy your best diagnostic efforts. These online forums are also a great way to spot pattern failures on a certain model, often before they are addressed by the manufacturer in a service bulletin. In addition, many technicians offer tips and advice for performing certain repairs that can only be learned through experience.

TROUBLESHOOTING ELECTRICAL FAILURES

Many customers bring their vehicle in for service when they have a specific problem. The most common electrical faults are opens, shorts, and grounds that cause electrical components to malfunction. Electrical system diagrams and test meters are used to track down these faults to determine what repairs are required.

Organized Approach

The complexity of a modern automobile electrical system demands that any diagnosis and repair be approached in a logical, systematic, and well organized manner. A thorough electrical problem diagnosis and repair procedure is a 10-step process:

1. Identify the complaint.
2. Verify the complaint.
3. Know the system.
4. Check mechanical operation.
5. List possible causes.
6. Isolate the problem circuit.
7. Systematically test the circuit.
8. Verify test results.
9. Make repairs.
10. Verify a successful repair.

Identify the complaint

If possible, talk to the person who was driving the vehicle when the problem first appeared. Questions to ask include:

- Has this problem occurred before? If so, what repairs were made?
- Were there any sparks, odors, noises, or other unusual signs?

Copyright 2000 by Chek-Chart Publications

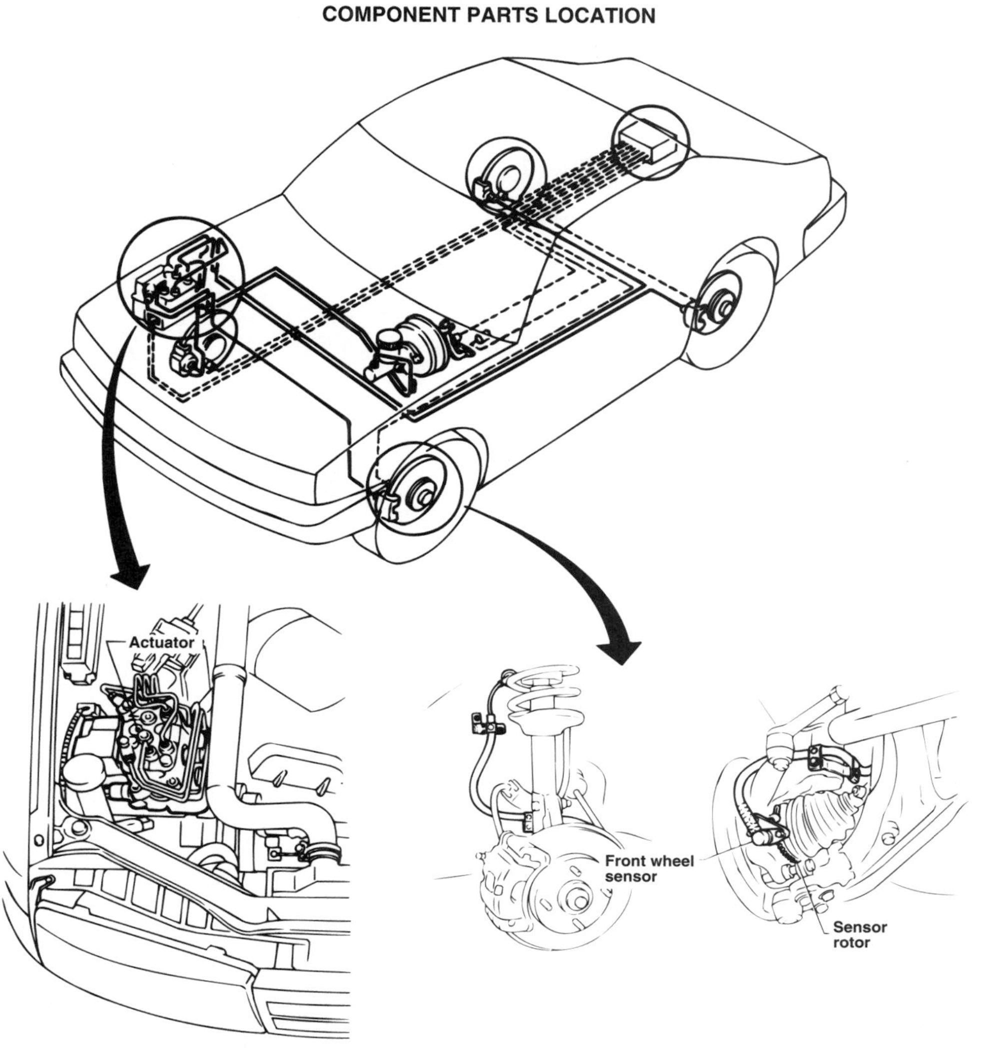

Figure 1-19. Breakout drawings identify and locate antilock brake (ABS) components on this Nissan diagram.

- What other circuits and accessories were being used when the problem occurred?

Many shops have a service writer who talks to the customers and prepares a work order for the technician to follow. If you cannot speak directly to the customer, make sure the service writer includes all this information on the work order.

Verify the complaint

Be aware that the way a customer describes a problem may be very different from the way you would describe it. If possible, ride along while the customer operates the vehicle and pinpoints the symptoms of the problem when it occurs. Otherwise, drive the vehicle yourself to experience the symptoms.

Remember, if there are no symptoms, there is no problem. Never attempt to make a repair unless you actually experience the symptoms of a problem. Verifying the complaint is an important early step in troubleshooting any automotive electrical problem.

Know the system

Now is the time to locate the electrical system diagrams, test specifications, and service procedures for the vehicle being repaired. These are essential items that are used as reference material during diagnosis and repair. Review this material, along with the appropriate chapters in the *Classroom Manual* as needed, to get a general idea of what circuits and loads are involved.

Check mechanical operation

Visually inspect the vehicle for obvious faults and try to eliminate simple problems first. Check for loose or broken wires and connectors, oil, coolant, and other

Copyright 2000 by Chek-Chart Publications

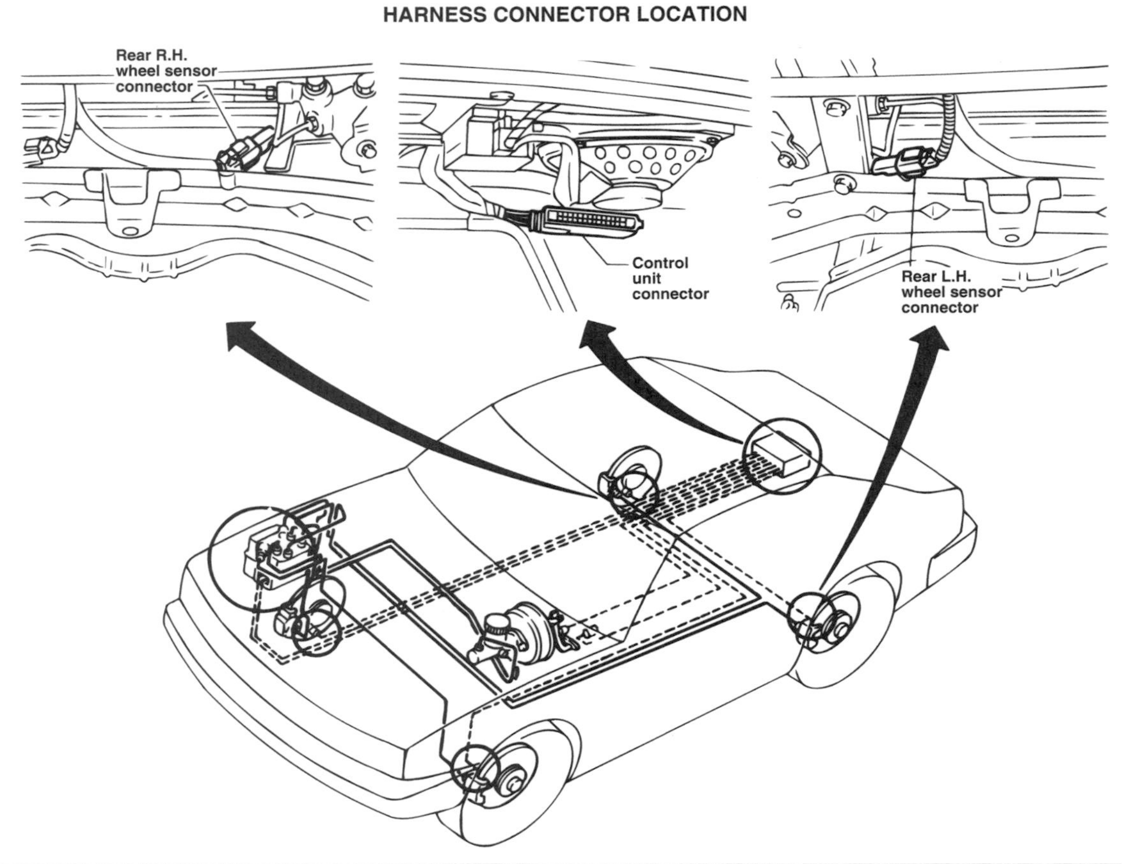

HARNESS CONNECTOR LOCATION

Rear R.H. wheel sensor connector

Control unit connector

Rear L.H. wheel sensor connector

Figure 1-20. Nissan provides another ABS system breakout illustration that shows electrical harness connector locations.

Figure 1-21. All of these manuals are needed to cover the Chrysler, Dodge, and Plymouth model line for one year only.

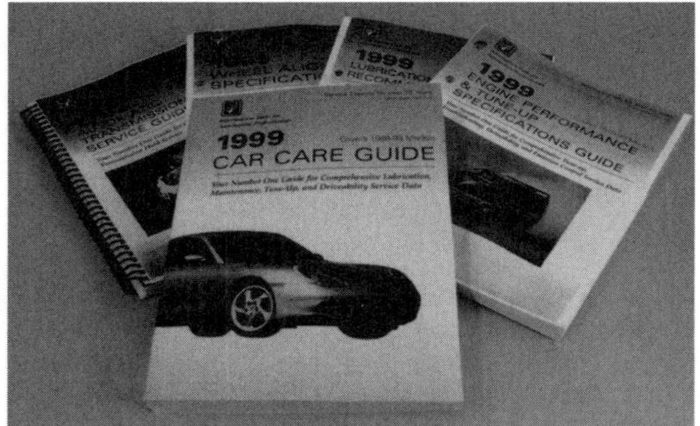

Figure 1-22. Aftermarket manuals generally span a number of years, but only cover specific areas of the vehicle.

fluid leaks, worn or damaged drive belts and hoses. Also, look for any signs of mechanical and electrical tampering and collision damage.

Next, operate the controls for the electrical circuits in question to make sure switches and other mechanical devices function correctly in all settings. Make note of any conditions that may help narrow the focus of your diagnostic investigation. For example, if the service order says, "repair headlamp high beams",

Copyright 2000 by Chek-Chart Publications

turn on the high beams and see if they are totally out, glow dimly, or if only one side is not working. At the same time, look for related problems that may not have been noticed or mentioned by the owner or service writer. For example, is the high-beam indicator also completely out? These related symptoms provide clues to the circuit problem.

List possible causes

Jot down, or make a mental note of, possible causes of the problem based on what has been revealed thus far. Look over the system diagram and the circuit diagrams to see other possible causes. For example, if the complaint is that a certain fuse frequently burns out, see what circuits share that fuse. If the fuse serves the turn signals, the backup lamps, the radio, and the windshield washer pump, then the source of the problem could be in any one of those circuits. A list of possible causes helps to organize your thoughts before actually testing the system. Always begin with the simplest possible cause and avoid overlooking the obvious.

Isolate the problem circuit

If the list of possible causes includes several circuits, narrow the list to locate the problem circuit. For example, the sample list of possible causes in the last step included the turn signals, the backup lamps, the radio, and the windshield washer pump as the source of a blown fuse. To narrow this list, turn off all other accessories and operate the suspected circuits one at a time. If the fuse blows, then the trouble will be within the particular circuit that is switched on.

Systematically test the circuit

Once the offending circuit is isolated, study that circuit diagram in detail to determine:

- Where the circuit receives battery current
- What switches control current
- What circuit protection is involved
- How the loads operate
- Where the circuit is grounded.

Understanding the total circuit is necessary to troubleshoot efficiently and test systematically.

All direct current (dc) automotive circuits are connected to the positive battery terminal at one end and to the negative battery terminal, or ground, at the other end. There may be more than one ground path through parallel circuit branches, but the basic pattern remains. Because of this pattern, the most logical way to troubleshoot an electrical circuit is to start at one end and work toward the other end.

Keep these general guidelines in mind when troubleshooting a problem on a circuit with multiple components:

- If the failure occurs in a single component of a multiple-unit circuit, start the test at that device.
- If the failure affects all the units in a multiple-unit circuit, start the test at the point where the circuit gets its power.

For example, for a lighting circuit problem where only one bulb in the circuit does not operate, start testing at the bulb. If all the lights in a circuit do not operate, start testing at the point where the current first enters the circuit.

With some systems, such as electronic ignitions or engine control systems, the best approach is to perform an area, or general, test of the overall system operation. This helps to narrow down the cause of a problem to a specific subsystem. At that point, detailed tests are performed to isolate the faulty component. Access the onboard diagnostic program to help isolate faulty circuits on an electronic control system.

Verify test results

Once the exact trouble spot of a circuit is located, be sure it is the source of the failure before replacing any parts or attempting repairs. Use test meters to verify that all electrical signals to the component in question are present and at their correct levels. Also make sure that all electrical connections are clean and tight. Never replace an electronic component before verifying the integrity of the signal circuit and system grounds. Remember, loose and corroded connections cause more electrical problems than component failures.

Make repairs

Repairs are made only after narrowing the problem down to a specific component or point in the circuit. Bench test components after removing them from the vehicle as a final confirmation. Defective new parts do exist, so it pays to bench test new parts before installing them as well.

Be meticulous when wiring harness repairs are called for, especially on electronic systems. Electronic circuits that carry low-voltage signals have a very narrow margin of tolerance for resistance. The wrong gauge wire or a sloppy splice may cause worse symptoms than the original problem. Work carefully and pay attention to detail.

Verify a successful repair

This is the final step of the troubleshooting process. Operate the controls or drive the vehicle to test the problem circuit. If the symptoms are gone, then the repair is successful. Sometimes, a circuit has more than one problem and the second one does not become apparent until the first has been repaired. In these

Copyright 2000 by Chek-Chart Publications

cases, resume troubleshooting from the point at which repairs were made.

Once repairs are made, drive or test the vehicle once again to ensure that the symptoms are no longer present.

WIRING REPAIR

The primary circuits used in most automotive applications are made of multi-strand copper wire covered with colored plastic insulation, as explained in Chapter Five of the *Classroom Manual.* Solid-core copper wire generally is used inside starter motors, alternators, and other high-amperage components. Repair of solid-core wire circuits in these parts is generally not a part of normal automotive service but is left to a specialized rebuild shop.

Some General Motors vehicles use aluminum, rather than copper, wiring in their forward body harnesses. Some repairs are possible on these General Motors harnesses, but a special repair kit is required. In addition, engine control and other electronic harnesses may contain shielded cables or circuits made of two twisted leads. These types of wiring, which are designed to protect low-current circuits from signal interference, require special handling techniques.

Whenever wiring is replaced, replacement wire must be the same size as the damaged wire. As explained in Chapter Five of the *Classroom Manual*, wire sizes are specified by American Wire Gauge (AWG) or metric specifications. Be sure to use replacement wire with the same color insulation to preserve the color coding for the next technician who may work on the circuit.

Safety

Several steps of wire and conductor repair involve special procedures that must be fully understood before beginning. Completely read all instructions before attempting any repair job.

To correctly repair some conductors, a soldering tool is used to heat the copper wire and then melt solder onto the hot wire strands. Solder is a soft tin-lead compound that melts at a relatively low temperature. Be aware, soldering tools can reach 500°F (260°C) , so keep them away from your skin, clothing, wiring insulation, and all flammable materials. Avoid breathing the fumes created when soldering, as melting solder gives off dangerous fumes that should not be inhaled.

Tools and Supplies

Most wiring repairs are performed using a few simple tools and supplies, figure 1-23. These include:

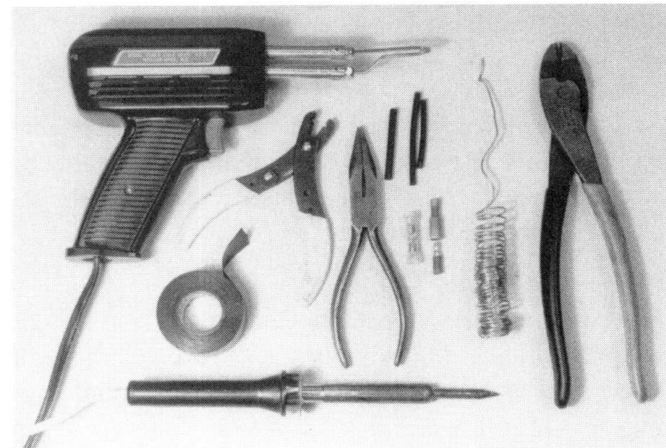

Figure 1-23. A few simple tools and supplies are all that is needed for most wire repairs.

- Wire cutting, stripping, and crimping tools. This can be a combination tool or separate units. A knife and pliers cannot do the job properly, but may be used in an emergency.
- Assorted styles and sizes of terminals.
- Soldering tool. A soldering gun heats faster than an iron and often has a smaller tip for delicate work.
- Pliers for holding heated wiring and metal parts. During electronic circuit repairs, heat sinks, which absorb excess heat from the soldering, are used to hold wires and prevent overheating the circuit.
- Resin-core solder. Never use acid-core solder for electrical soldering because residue from the acid promotes corrosion.
- Electrical tape or heat-shrink tubing, which is used to insulate the repaired area.

Repair Methods

The most common wiring repair methods are:

- Splicing
- Connector attachment
- Insulation repair
- Aluminum wiring repair
- Twisted or shielded cable repair.

Splicing

Connecting two or more wires without using a terminal is called splicing. This repair method is commonly used to insert a fusible link or to replace a section of damaged wire. When using heat-shrink tubing for insulation, remember to slip a piece of tubing slightly larger then the splice area over one of the sections of wire before soldering.

If there are one or more damaged wires in a harness, it is not necessary to replace the entire harness.

Copyright 2000 by Chek-Chart Publications

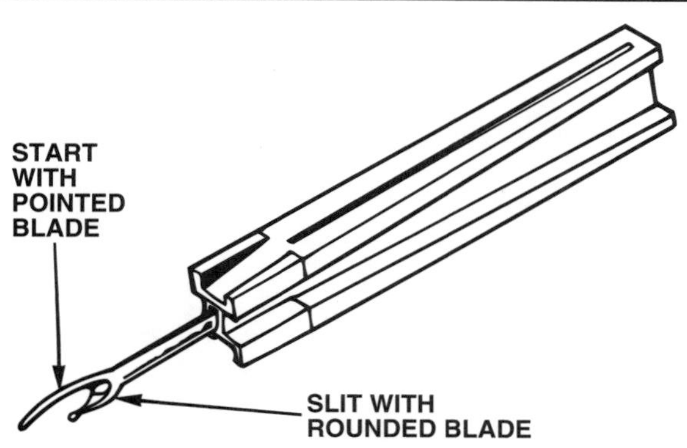

Figure 1-24. A seam splitter cuts open a taped wiring harness without damaging the wire insulation.

If the harness is enclosed in a plastic conduit, just open the conduit and pull out and repair the damaged wires. If the harness is wrapped with tape, use a seam splitter to cut open the tape, figure 1-24. A seam splitter is an inexpensive tool available from sewing supply stores. Take care to avoid damaging the insulation on the wires inside the harness when splitting insulation.

To splice a wire in a taped harness, use the pointed end of a seam splitter to start a small slit in the tape. Make sure the cutting blade of the tool faces away from the wires. Then, work the seam splitter down the harness to cut open the tape. Work carefully to avoid damaging wire insulation. Once the damaged section of wiring is exposed, splice as follows:

1. Cut out the damaged section of wire. Cut a length of replacement wire approximately two inches longer than the removed piece. Use the same color and size of wire. Use the correct opening in the wire stripping tool to remove about one inch (25 mm) of insulation from the ends of the replacement wire and the ends of the original harness wire, figure 1-25. If uncertain of the wire size, start with the largest stripper hole and work down until a clean strip of insulation is removed without nicking or cutting the wire strands.
2. If heat-shrink tubing is to be used for insulation after the repair, cut off a length of tubing about one inch (25 mm) longer than the splice and slip the tubing over one of the sections of wire before soldering.
3. Braid the bare strands of the new piece of wire and the original wire and twist them securely, figure 1-26. Keep in mind, the integrity of the connection is in the contact of the wires, solder is only used to hold them in place.
4. Place the broad side of the soldering tool on the braided bare wires to heat the wires, figure 1-27. For most repairs, the wire strands are heated with an 80 to 120 watt iron or gun.
5. Lightly touch the resin-core solder to the heated bare wire, figure 1-28. Be careful not to touch the solder to the soldering tool. Solder must melt from the heat of the wire splice and flow evenly through all of the strands. If the wire is not heated enough, the solder cannot flow and the result is a *cold* solder joint. The solder is not a conductor; its only purpose is to hold the conductors together. Excess solder creates resistance in the circuit.
6. Use only enough solder to flow into the cracks, not a large amount, figure 1-29. Too much solder makes a weak splice and traps contamination that causes high resistance.
7. Allow the splice to thoroughly cool, then wrap it with tape or use heat shrink tubing to insulate the repair. To use heat-shrink tubing, slide the length of tubing installed on the wire before soldering over the splice. Apply heat to the tubing and it shrinks down to seal and insulate the repaired area, figure 1-30.

Whenever soldering electronic components, use a heat sink to prevent overheating the part. Hold the component with a pair of pliers between the component and solder point. This draws heat away from the component when soldering the leads. An alternate method is to clamp the component in an alligator clip attached to a vise. Always disconnect any computers from the harness before soldering wires.

Another method of splicing wires together is to use a splice clip, crimping tool, and the procedure in the next section, figure 1-31. Once the clip is crimped onto the wires, heat the front side of the clip with the soldering iron or gun and apply solder to the hole on the back of the clip, figure 1-32.

Connector attachment

Connectors may be attached with solder or simply by crimping, depending upon the service conditions in which they are used. Attach connectors as follows:

1. Match the terminals to the wire size. Most terminals fit a small range of wire gauges.
2. Use the correct opening in the wire stripping area of the crimping tool to remove just enough insulation from the wire so that the bare wire will fit into the terminal barrel. Avoid nicking or cutting the wire strands.
3. Insert the bare end of the wire into the terminal barrel, figure 1-33.

Copyright 2000 by Chek-Chart Publications

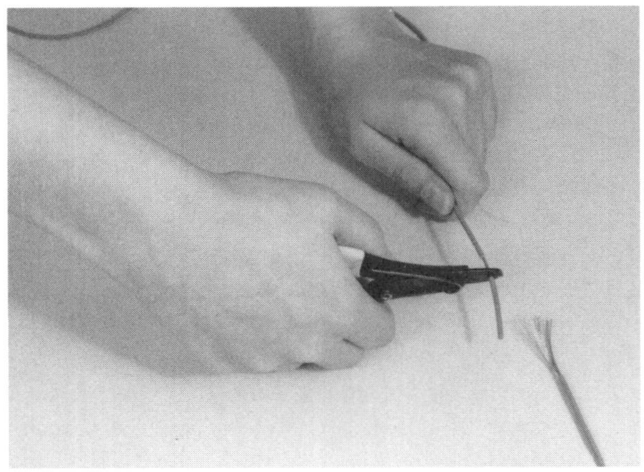

Figure 1-25. Take care not to cut, nick, or scratch the conductor wires when removing insulation with the stripping tool.

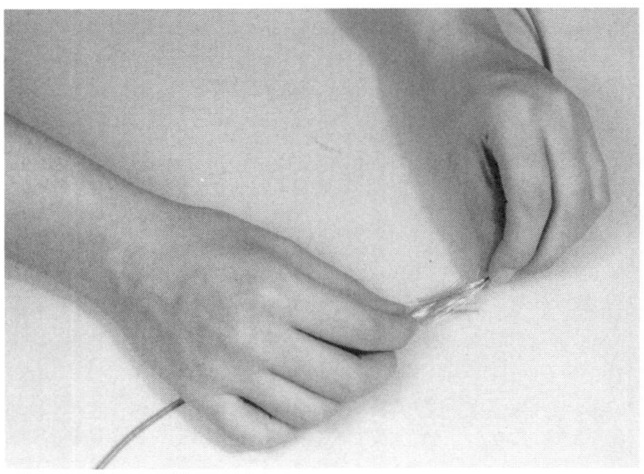

Figure 1-26. Tightly braid the strands of bare wire together to make the splice.

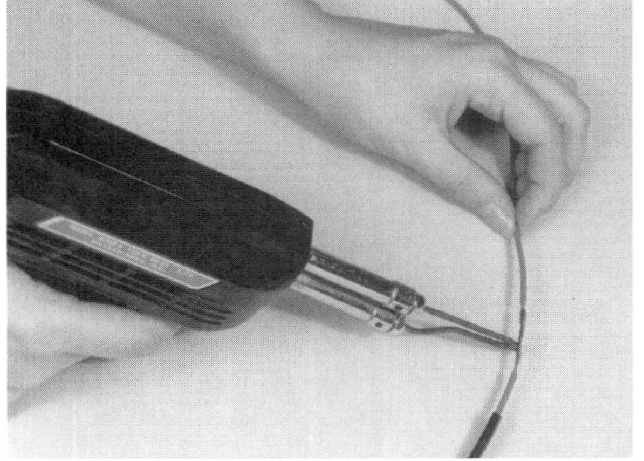

Figure 1-27. Heat the braided wires with the soldering gun or iron.

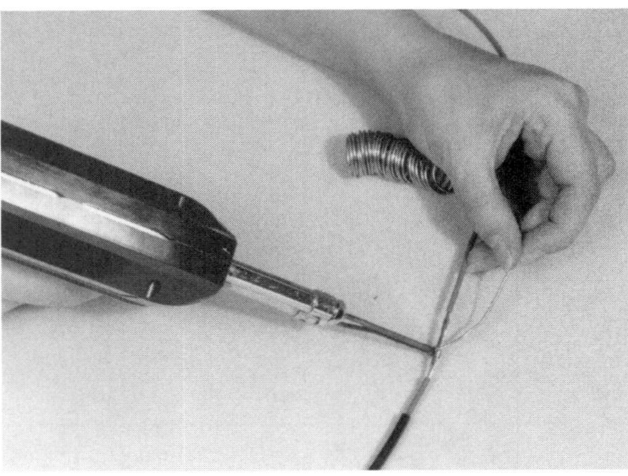

Figure 1-28. Apply resin-core solder to the hot, braided wires. Never melt solder on the tip of the soldering tool.

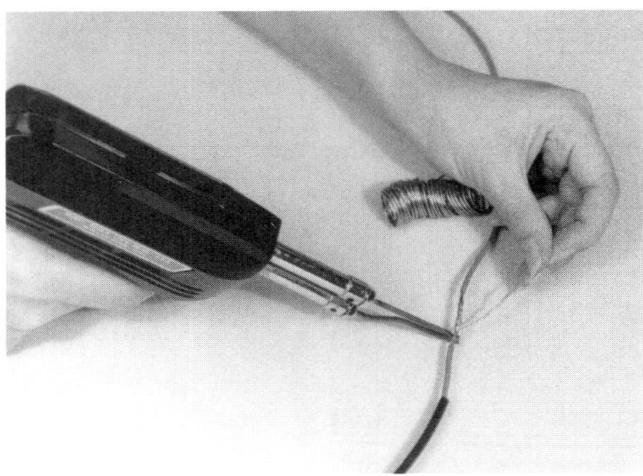

Figure 1-29. Use only enough solder to coat the cracks between the wires. Too much solder creates circuit resistance.

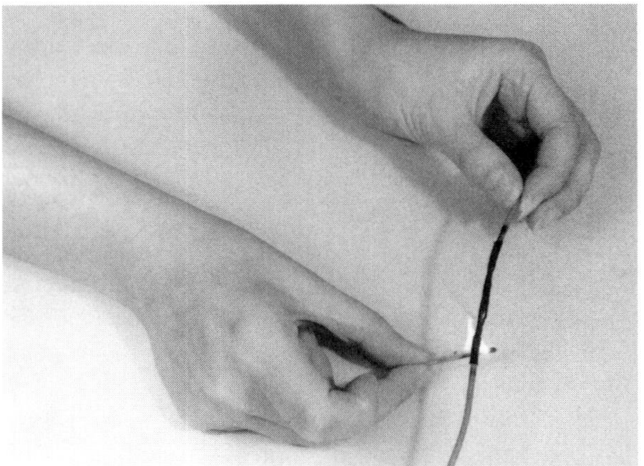

Figure 1-30. A flame or heat gun collapses heat-shrink tubing around the splice to insulate it.

Copyright 2000 by Chek-Chart Publications

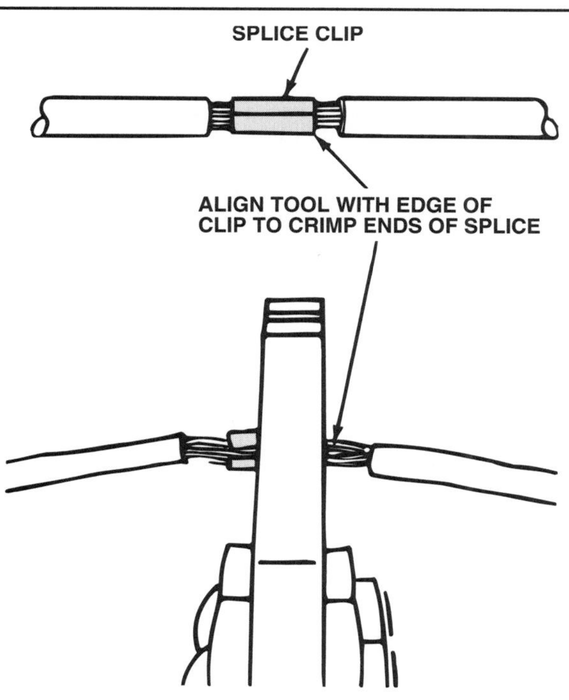

Figure 1-31. A splice clip clamps the two bare wire ends together so they do not need to be braided.

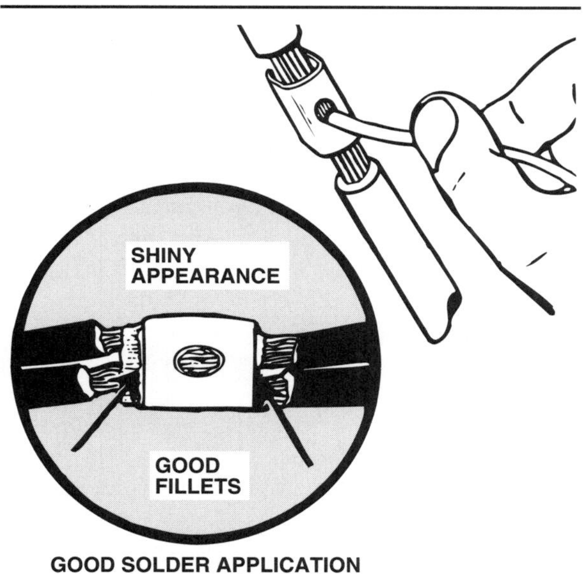

Figure 1-32. Heat the splice clip with a soldering tool and flow solder into the hole on the clip.

4. Place the crimping tool over the terminal barrel. When installing a bare metal terminal, the seam on the barrel must face toward the convex anvil in the jaw of the crimping pliers, figure 1-34. Tools used for crimping insulated terminals do not have an anvil, so the position of the terminal seam is not critical, figure 1-35. With either type, firmly squeeze the pliers to crimp the connector barrel onto the wire, figure 1-36.
5. Use electrical tape or heat-shrink tubing to insulate the splice.

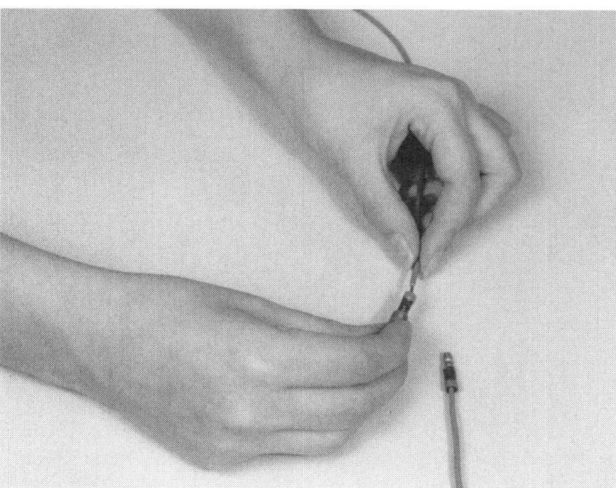

Figure 1-33. Insert the stripped end of the wire into the barrel of the terminal.

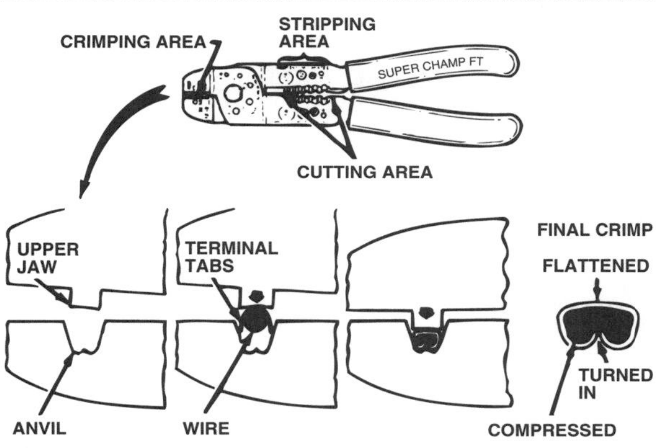

Figure 1-34. With a bare metal terminal, the seam of the barrel must be correctly positioned on the tool to ensure a good crimp.

Insulation repair

Insulation repair is required whenever wiring has been repaired, or when the insulation is damaged but the conductor inside is not affected. There are two ways to repair insulation: with plastic electrical tape or heat-shrink tubing.

If electrical tape is used, wrap three turns of tape over the repair area and overlap the tape about one-half inch (13 mm) onto the undamaged insulation at each end of the repair, figure 1-37. If the repaired section of wire is not protected in a conduit or another harness covering, tape it a second time to entirely overlap the first piece of tape.

Copyright 2000 by Chek-Chart Publications

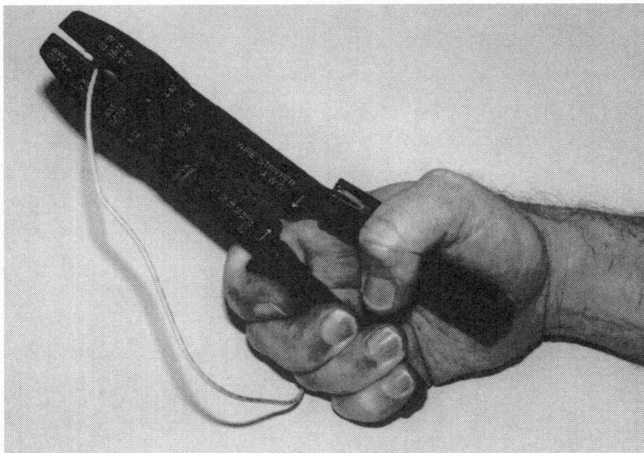

Figure 1-35. With insulated terminals, squeeze the pliers firmly, but not enough to break the plastic insulator, when making a crimp.

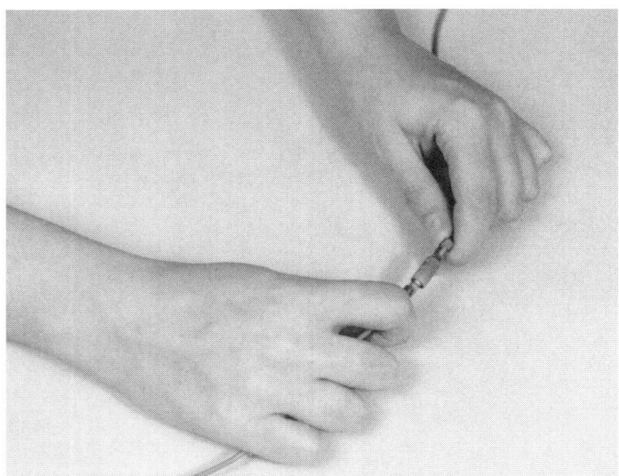

Figure 1-36. Once crimped, the terminal is solidly attached to the wire and ready to use.

Heat-shrink tubing is a plastic tube that shrinks when heated. It is available from electronic and automotive supply stores in various diameters, lengths, and colors to cover specific wire sizes. When heat-shrink tubing is used, it must be cut to size and installed on the wire before the wire is spliced or attached to a connector. After the repair has been made, slide the tubing into place over the splice and heat it with a heat gun, lighter, or match. This shrinks the tubing to the diameter of the wire and insulates the repaired area.

Aluminum wiring repair

Many late-model General Motors vehicles have a front body wiring harness made of solid core aluminum wires enclosed in a plastic conduit. Special procedures and a special repair kit are required to repair these harnesses, which use 14-gauge and 16-gauge wires.

Figure 1-37. When using electrical tape, the splice must be tightly wrapped and completely sealed to the wire insulation.

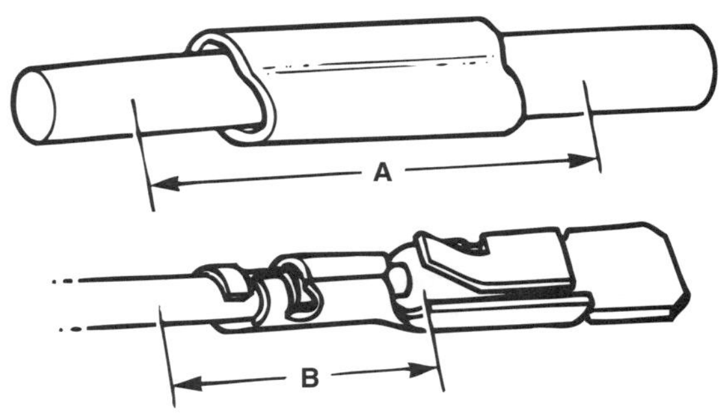

Figure 1-38. Solid aluminum wire terminals are crimped, then coated with petroleum jelly for protection.

The special repair kit includes an assortment of aluminum wires, splice clips, and anticorrosion petroleum jelly. Wires are supplied in six-inch (15-cm) lengths with terminals attached to one end. Any splice made in the harness should be at least an inch and a half (38 mm) away from other splices, connectors, or harness branches.

If a solid aluminum wire has been damaged and a section must be replaced:

1. Pull the damaged wire out of the conduit.
2. Cut out the damaged section of wire.
3. Strip one-quarter inch (6 mm) of insulation from both ends of the wire on both sides of the damage.
4. Fit in a replacement section, install a connector, and firmly crimp.
5. Coat both the crimp area and aluminum-core wire with petroleum jelly, figure 1-38.
6. Wrap the splice area with insulating tape to seal out moisture.

If a terminal in this type of harness fails, replace as follows:

1. Separate the defective terminal from the connector.
2. Remove the defective terminal by cutting it and about six inches (15 cm) off of the harness.
3. Strip about one-quarter inch (6 mm) of insulation from the end of the wire being repaired and from the replacement wire.

Copyright 2000 by Chek-Chart Publications

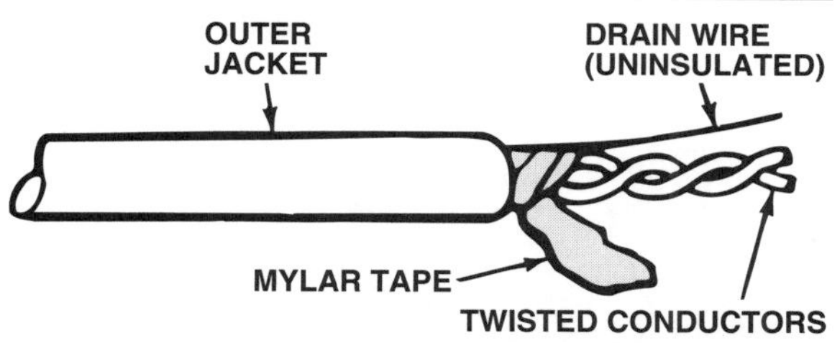

Figure 1-39. Cut the outer jacket and unwrap the Mylar tape to expose the conductors on this General Motors low-current cable.

4. Place wire ends in a splice clip and firmly crimp.
5. Apply petroleum jelly to the terminal crimp area and aluminum wire to prevent galvanic corrosion.
6. Wrap the splice area with insulating tape and insert the terminal into the connector.

Twisted or shielded cable repair

Late-model vehicles with electronic engine control systems may use wire that carries very low current, typically in the 0.1 to 0.2 ampere range. General Motors vehicles use a two-conductor twisted cable between the electronic control module and the distributor. Similar shielded cable designs are used by other vehicle manufacturers. This type of wiring is used to prevent radio frequency interference (RFI) or electromagnetic interference (EMI) from disrupting the circuit signals. To repair this type of wiring:

1. Carefully remove and discard the outer jacket. Do not cut into the drain wire or any metallic Mylar tape shielding, figure 1-39.
2. Unwrap but do not remove the Mylar tape. This tape is used to rewrap the conductors after the splice is made.
3. On two twisted-pair wires, untwist the conductors and strip the insulation as described above in the *Splicing* section. If both conductors are broken, be sure to stagger the splices to prevent the possibility of shorts or interference. Strip the single inner conductor on shielded cables.
4. Splice and tape each wire using splice clips and resin-core solder. Wrap each wire splice with tape to insulate it, then rewrap the conductors, but not the drain wire, with the Mylar tape.
5. Splice the drain wire in similar fashion, then wrap it around the tape-covered, twisted conductors, figure 1-40.
6. Seal the spliced area with electrical tape using a winding motion to replace the section of jacket cut away and discarded earlier.

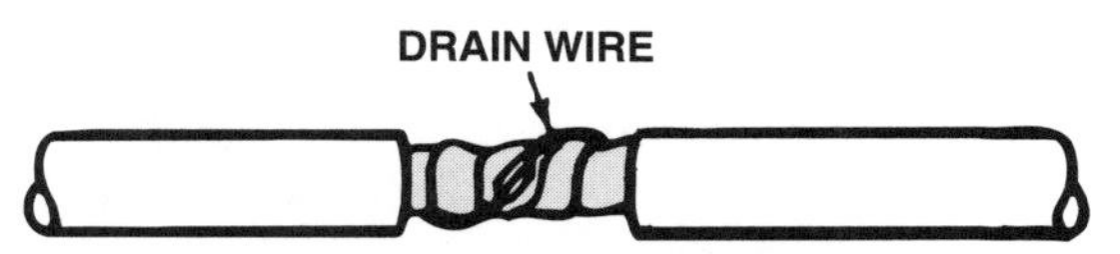

Figure 1-40. After taping the conductors, the bare drain wire wraps around them.

Figure 1-41. This drawing identifies the sockets and pins on the two halves of a multi-plug connector.

CONNECTOR REPAIR

The electrical connectors used on late-model vehicles may join together from one to over fifty pairs of wires. This makes connector and terminal identification essential for efficient troubleshooting and successful repairs. Connectors are shown on wiring diagrams and in schematics. Most manufacturers also provide drawings, commonly called pin charts, for identifying the terminals or cavities of a multi-plug with their circuit numbers, figure 1-41.

Molded or Single-Wire Connectors

Connectors used with 1 to 4 wires are generally molded units in which the individual wires and terminals cannot be separated for repair. Molded single wire connectors are repaired by cutting out the damaged wire or connector from both halves of the connector. Next, splice a new connector with pigtail leads in place. Some aftermarket replacement connectors are available for repairs of alternators, sensors, headlights, and taillights.

Hard-Shell Connectors

Many multiple-wire connectors are a two-piece hard plastic shell that houses the terminals of individual circuits, figure 1-42. One half of the shell holds the male, or pin, terminals, while the other half holds the female, or socket, terminals. Circuit operation is checked without separating the connector shells. Simply use the test meter leads to probe the rear of the individual connections.

Individual terminals also can be replaced in this type of connector. After separating the connector halves or disconnecting the connector from the component, the damaged terminal is released from the shell with a special terminal removal tool, pick, or small screwdriver, figure 1-43.

Copyright 2000 by Chek-Chart Publications

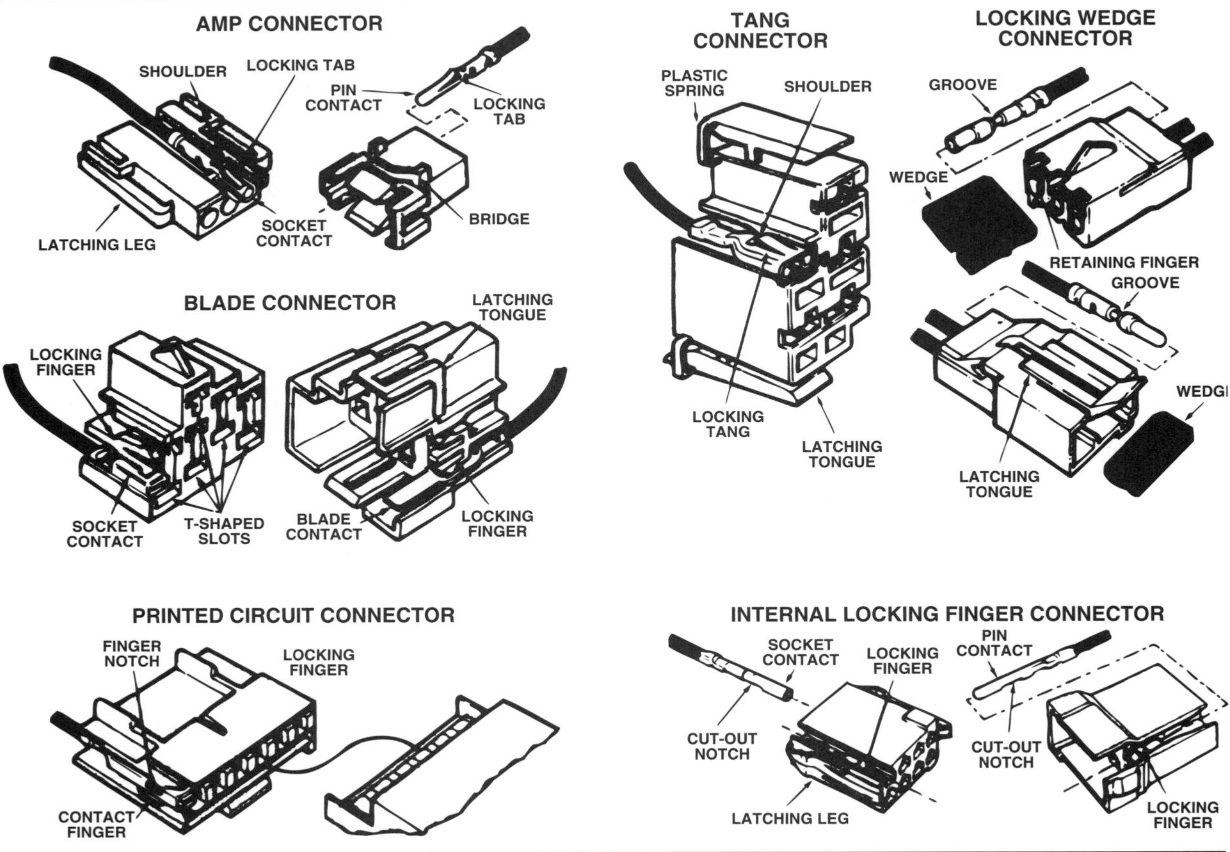

Figure 1-42. There is a wide array of hard-shell connectors; these are some Ford designs.

Replace the damaged terminal by soldering or crimping a new one on as previously described. Then, install the new terminal into the connector shell. Most terminals used in this type of connector have a locking tang of some kind. In cases where the terminal is removed from the shell but is not damaged, the locking tang must be reformed to make sure it latches when reinstalled, figure 1-44.

Weather-Pack® Connectors

Special weatherproof connectors are used in engine and body harnesses of late-model General Motors vehicles. This type of connector uses a rubber seal on the wire ends of the terminals. On small connectors, a secondary sealing cover is used on the rear of each connector half. These Weather-Pack® connectors should never be replaced with a nonweatherproof type. To service a Weather-Pack® connector:

1. Separate small connectors by simply pulling them apart, figure 1-45. To separate large connectors, remove the bolt from the center of the connector body before pulling it apart.
2. Flip the secondary lock hinges downward on small connectors, figure 1-46. On large connectors, push the locking nib up as far as possible with a wide pick, then pull the retainer out.
3. Insert a Weather-Pack® pick in the front of the terminal cavity and push the terminal free of the connector. Pull the pick out and carefully remove the terminal, figure 1-47.
4. If the same lead and terminal are to be reinstalled, reform the locking tang on the terminal, figure 1-48.
5. If the lead or terminal requires replacement, splice a new terminal and cable seal onto the wire, figure 1-49. Crimp the seal carefully to avoid damaging it.

Copyright 2000 by Chek-Chart Publications

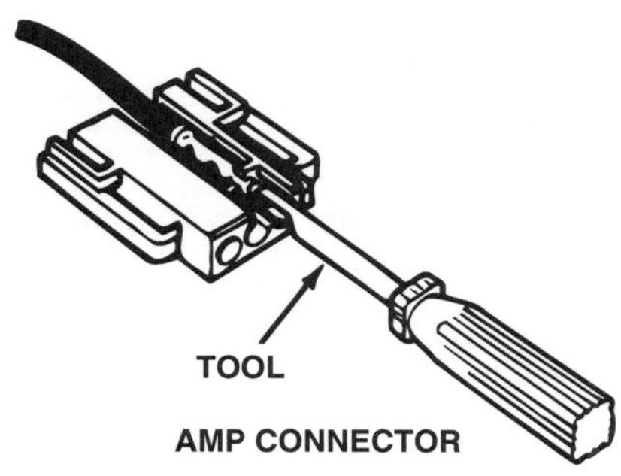

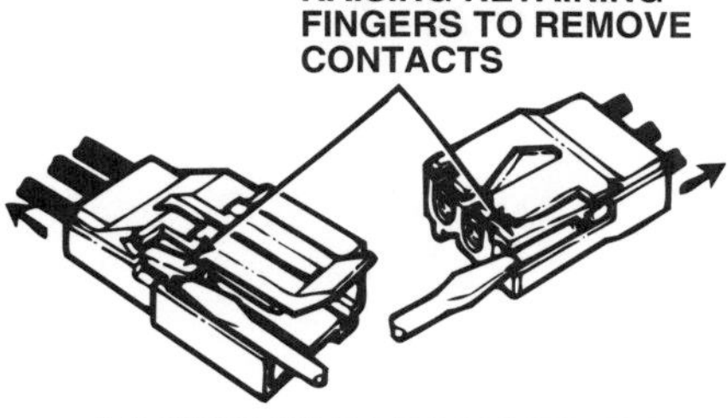

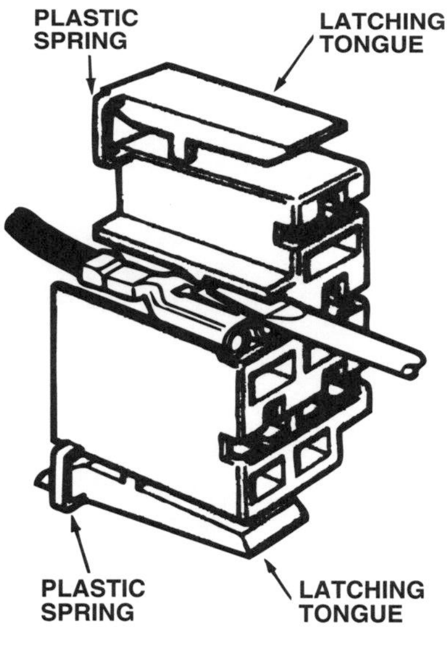

Figure 1-43. Use a removal tool or small screwdriver to release terminals from the connector shell.

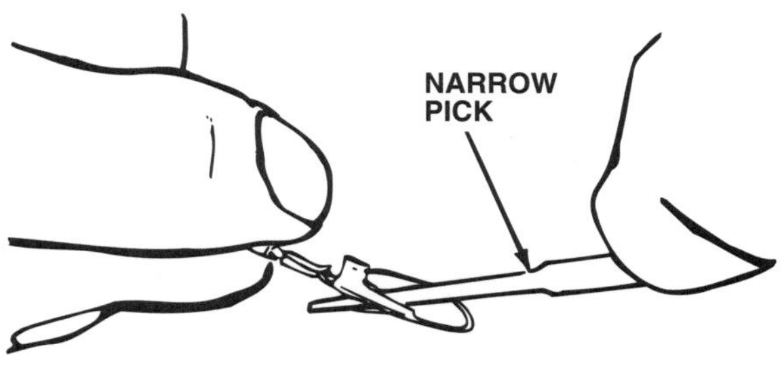

Figure 1-44. Reform the locking tang when reinstalling a terminal in the connector shell.

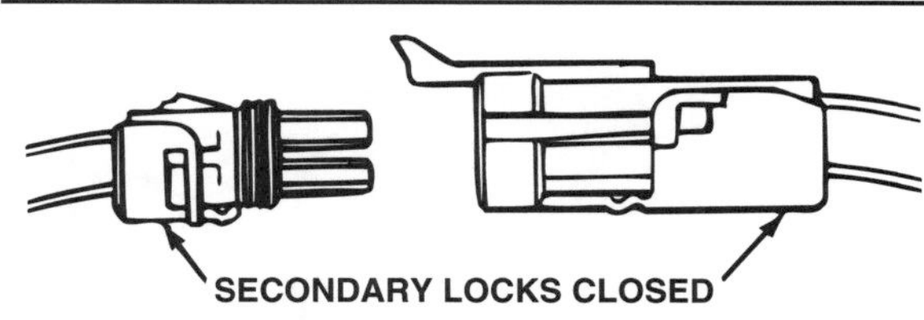

Figure 1-45. Separate a Weather-Pack® connector by opening the lock and pulling it apart.

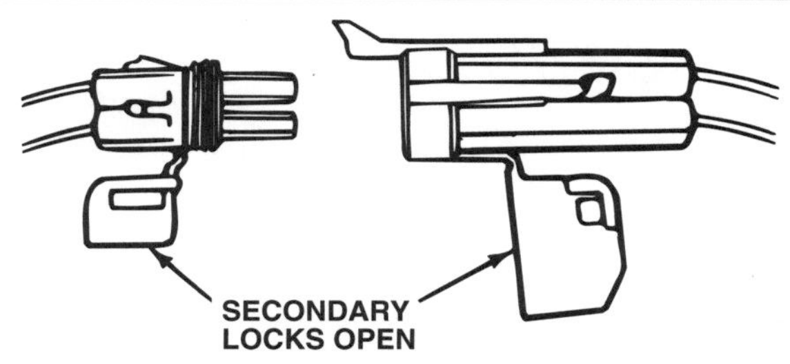

Figure 1-46. The secondary locks help retain the terminals in the connector shell.

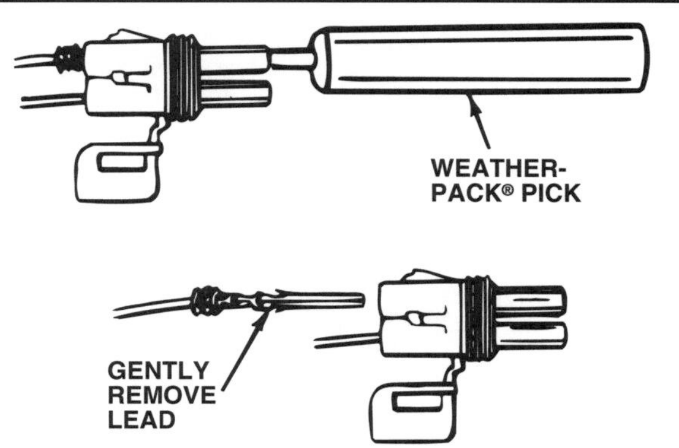

Figure 1-47. Insert the pick tool to collapse the lock tangs and pull the wire and terminal from the connector.

Copyright 2000 by Chek-Chart Publications

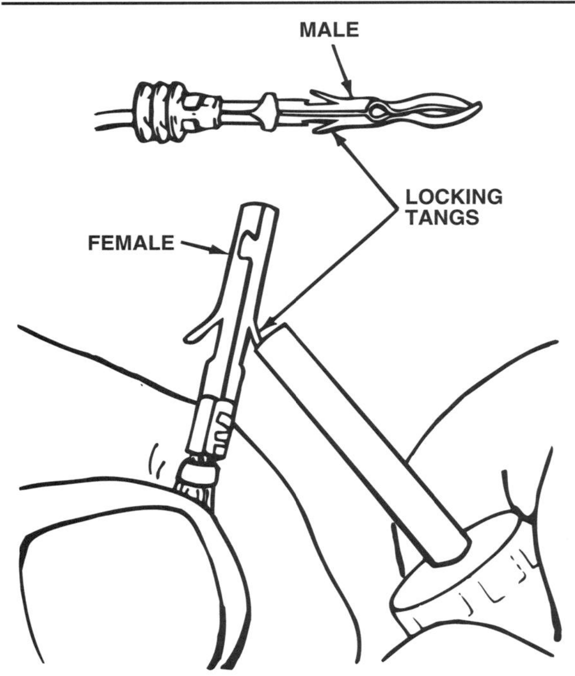

Figure 1-48. Reform the locking tangs before reinstalling a terminal into the connector shell.

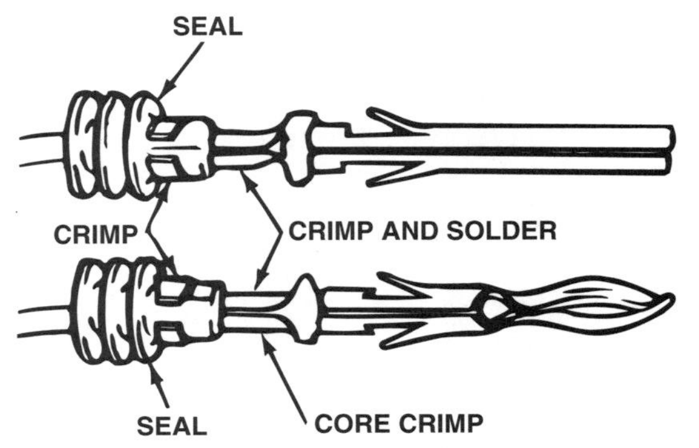

Figure 1-49. Replacement terminals are spliced to the wire and installed along with a new seal.

Copyright 2000 by Chek-Chart Publications

2 Electrical Faults and Basic Test Equipment

ELECTRICAL FAULTS

As explained in the *Classroom Manual,* switches, relays, fuses, and other circuit protection devices regulate current through a circuit. Failure of any of these components usually opens the circuit so that current stops at that point. However, some electrical failures damage components by allowing too much current through the circuit. Electronic components are especially vulnerable to high-amperage failure. Care must be taken during service to prevent accidental damage. Basically, there are two types of failure that stop or affect current in a circuit:

- High-resistance faults
- Low-resistance faults.

This chapter discusses electrical faults and ways to identify and find the source of a problem. Troubleshooting any electrical failure requires the use of test equipment. The design and use of common test equipment is detailed in the text.

High-Resistance Faults

High resistance impedes current in the circuit. An open circuit, which results from a broken wire, no contact between connectors, or a defective part, creates maximum resistance, figure 2-1. The resistance across an open circuit, or simply, an "open," is infinite, therefore, there is no current whatsoever in the circuit. Other high-resistance failures allow some, but not all, of the current through the circuit. Corrosion on connections, damaged wires, defective parts, loose connections, and failed components are typical sources of high-resistance, figure 2-2.

Low-Resistance Faults

Low resistance promotes current in the circuit. A shorted circuit, or "short," is the result of an unwanted connection between two conductors. Shorts allow current to bypass all or part of the normal circuit. Circuit resistance is also altered, figure 2-3. Remember, current always follows the path of least resistance. Low-resistance circuit failures result from a:

- Short to ground
- Short to power.

A short to ground, or simply, a "ground," is the result of an unwanted connection between a conductor and ground. All or part of the normal circuit and normal resistance is bypassed.

From the point where the short, or "ground," occurs, the current bypasses all remaining circuit conductors and loads, traveling directly to ground, figure 2-4. The short circuit path is simply a short to

Copyright 2000 by Chek-Chart Publications

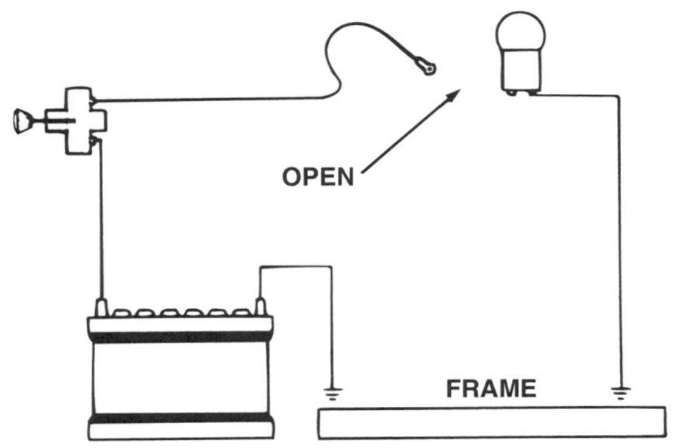

Figure 2-1. An open circuit creates infinite resistance, so there is no current in the circuit.

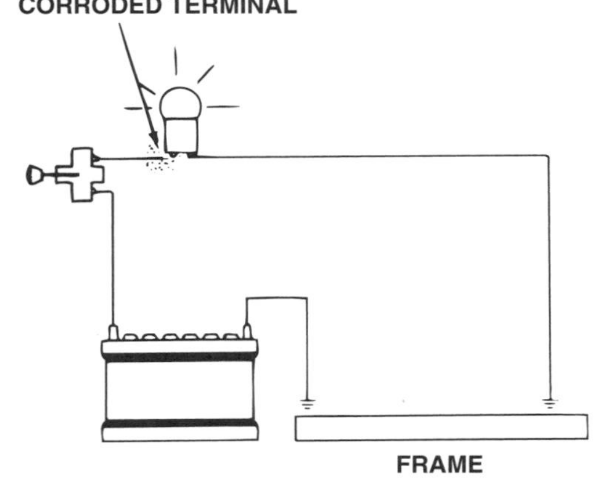

Figure 2-2. Corrosion at this bulb terminal connection creates high-resistance, which reduces current.

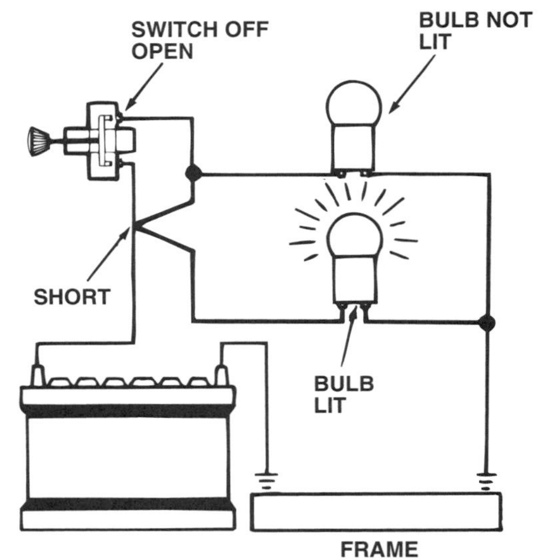

Figure 2-3. A short circuit bypasses current around all or part of a circuit.

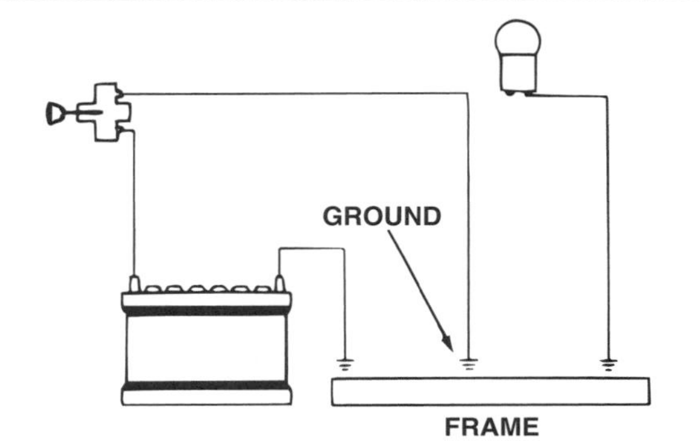

Figure 2-4. A short to ground directs current back to the battery, so there is no current in the circuit past the short.

ground. Because automotive electrical systems are single-wire systems using a common chassis ground, most short circuits occur as shorts to ground. It is possible, however, to find a short circuit within a circuit component, such as a short across part of the windings in an alternator rotor or stator.

A short to power is the result of an unwanted connection between a power source and a circuit conductor, figure 2-3. This type of failure allows current through a portion of the circuit, possibly activating and damaging loads. Remember that all grounds are shorts, but that not all shorts are grounds.

Isolating the cause of a circuit problem requires the ability to measure current, voltage, and resistance in a circuit with some type of test equipment. The test equipment can take on many forms, from simple 12-volt test lights to more sophisticated meters. Each tool has its place and supplies information in different ways. It is not always necessary to use the most expensive or sophisticated piece of test equipment to find the root cause of an electrical problem.

SIMPLE TEST DEVICES

A considerable amount of electrical troubleshooting can be performed using simple test lights and continuity testers. While an ohmmeter is the ideal continuity tester because it shows the degree of continuity, the quick and easy go/no-go feature of jumper wires and test lights makes them ideal to locate problem areas.

Exercise caution when using these tools to test circuits that contain solid-state components. Diodes, transistors, microprocessors, and other solid-state devices typically operate at relatively low voltage and amperage. Using the incorrect test equipment

Copyright 2000 by Chek-Chart Publications

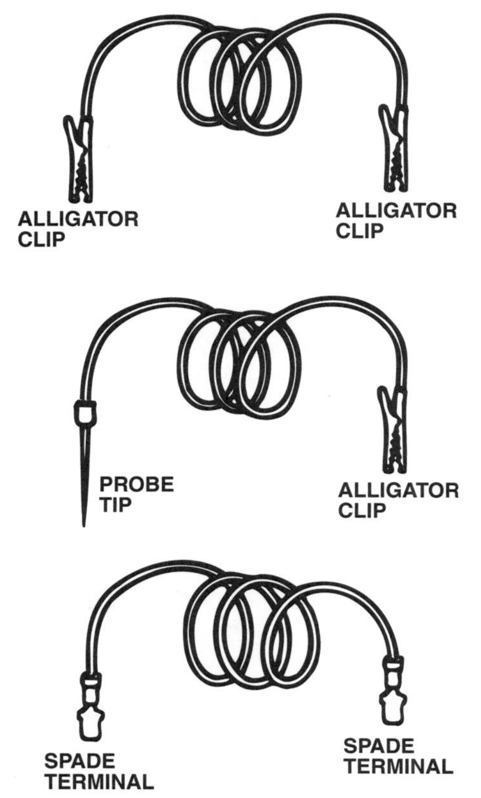

Figure 2-5. A jumper wire is simply a length of wire with terminals at either end and a fuse.

damages solid-state components by allowing them to draw more current than they were designed to handle.

Jumper Wire

A jumper wire is a simple length of wire with alligator clips or some other type of connector on both ends, figure 2-5. The jumper wire is used to temporarily bridge, or "jump," any two points in a circuit, figure 2-6. Jumper wires come in handy for bridging suspected "opens" or "gaps" in a circuit, such as a switch, connector, relay, or any other nonresistive circuit part, to direct current through the rest of the circuit. If everything else in the circuit functions normally, the bypassed part must be defective.

Never use a jumper wire to bypass a load or a circuit component with fairly high resistance, such as a heater or motor. Bypassing a resistive component with a jumper wire has the same effect as a low-resistance short parallel with the device. The jumper reduces circuit resistance and allows excessive current. This may damage other circuit components or even start an electrical fire. For similar reason, to avoid damage due to high amperage, jumper wires should not be used on

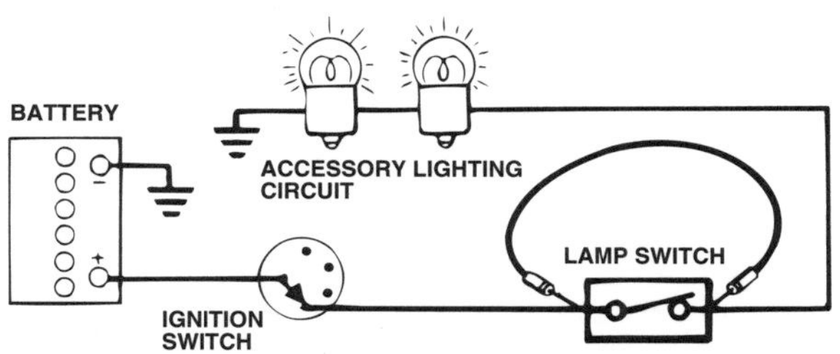

Figure 2-6. A jumper wire installed to bypass a lamp switch and power the circuit.

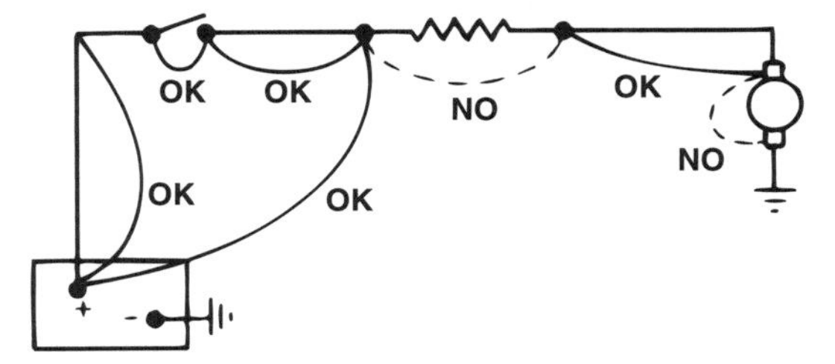

Figure 2-7. Never bridge a resistive load with a jumper wire.

electronic circuits unless specified by the manufacturer for a particular procedure.

Technically, the jumper wire is a continuity tester, but it does not provide any form of output value. Circuit devices either operate or do not operate with the jumper wire installed. To test a circuit with a jumper wire:

1. Turn on all switches to power the circuit to be tested.
2. If the lamps, motors, or other loads do not operate, bypass the switch or relay with a fused jumper wire.
3. If the circuit operates, the switch or relay is defective.

Jumper wires should include an inline fuse or circuit breaker to protect the circuit being tested. Do not use a jumper to bypass a resistive load, figure 2-7.

Test Lamp

A test lamp is a simple continuity tester containing a bulb that glows when there is power in the circuit or to the component being checked. Test lamps are used to quickly check for open circuit conditions. There are two basic types of test lamp: external-powered and self-powered.

External-powered

This device is similar to a jumper wire, but it contains a bulb that illuminates when there is power in the circuit being checked. This type of test light, which is

Copyright 2000 by Chek-Chart Publications

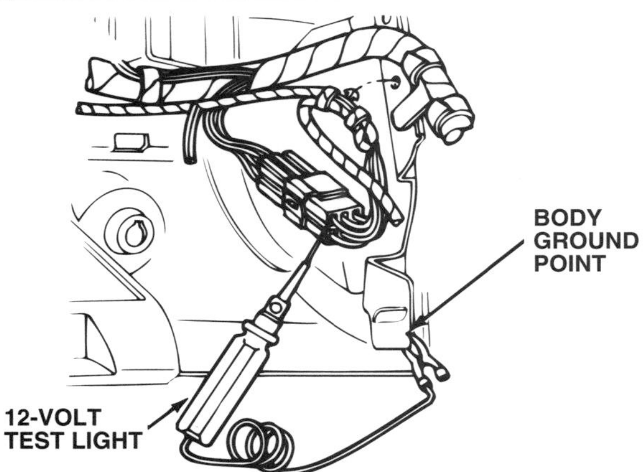

Figure 2-8. A 12-volt test lamp clamped to ground and probing for power.

used to quickly check for open circuits, relies on the vehicle battery to power the circuit or component being tested. It is an effective go/no go test tool to check for the presence of circuit voltage. It can be connected either way in a circuit since it is not polarity-sensitive. However, it is not a recommended practice to use a 12-volt test light on circuits that contain electronic components. Certain electronic devices, such as transistors, may be damaged by the added current draw of the test light.

Once you become familiar with the 12-volt test lamp, it becomes easy to recognize high-resistance circuits by the effect they have on the illumination of the bulb. As current drops in a high-resistance circuit, the usual bright glow of the bulb dims.

A typical 12-volt test lamp has a sharp probe tip and a lead with an alligator clamp. The probe is used for back probing a connector for testing. The clamp attaches to a ground or power source, figure 2-8.

Two checks are made with a 12-volt test lamp: voltage-seeking and ground-seeking tests. The voltage-seeking test indicates whether or not voltage is available to the circuit at a particular point. This is an effective way to troubleshoot a lighting circuit. Always check the operation of the test lamp before testing a circuit. To check the test lamp:

1. Connect the test lamp lead clamp to a known chassis ground.
2. Touch the probe tip of the test lamp to the positive battery terminal.
3. If the lamp lights, it is ready to use.

Leave the test lamp connected to ground, then conduct voltage-seeking tests by touching the probe to various points of the circuit, figure 2-9. If the lamp lights at one test point, but not at the next, the circuit is open between these two points.

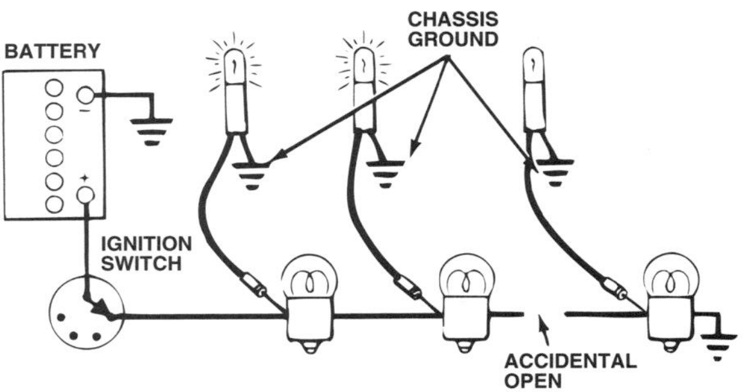

Figure 2-9. A voltage-seeking test with a 12-volt test lamp checks for available voltage along the circuit.

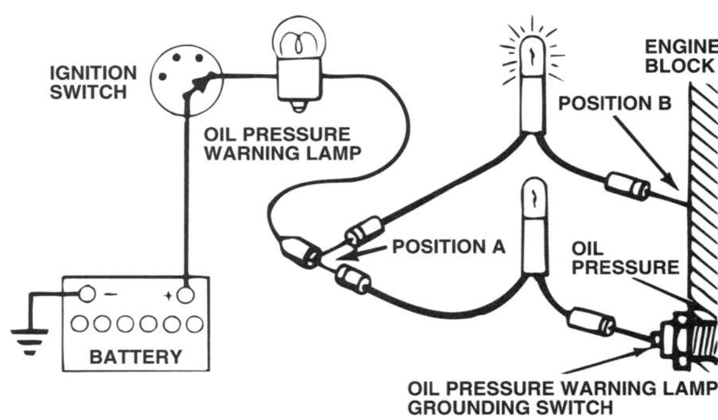

Figure 2-10. Performing a ground-seeking test with a 12-volt test lamp on a oil pressure warning lamp grounding switch.

The ground-seeking test indicates whether or not a conductor, switch, or load is grounded. This test could be used on a warning lamp circuit that has a grounding switch, such as an oil pressure warning lamp, figure 2-10. To test an oil pressure switch circuit:

1. Disconnect the sending unit and connect the test lamp between the disconnected wire and the sending unit.
2. The lamp should light when the ignition switch is on with the engine not running.
3. If the lamp does not light, disconnect it from the grounding switch and connect the test lamp lead to the engine block or another good ground.
4. If both the test lamp and the warning light illuminate, a defective grounding switch, or sending unit, is the likely cause.

Self-powered

Often called a continuity lamp, this tester is similar to the 12-volt test lamp just described. However, rather than using the vehicle battery, the test lamp contains its own battery to power the circuit or component being checked, figure 2-11. Always disconnect the vehicle battery before using a self-powered test lamp to check a circuit. Connecting the test lamp to a circuit

Copyright 2000 by Chek-Chart Publications

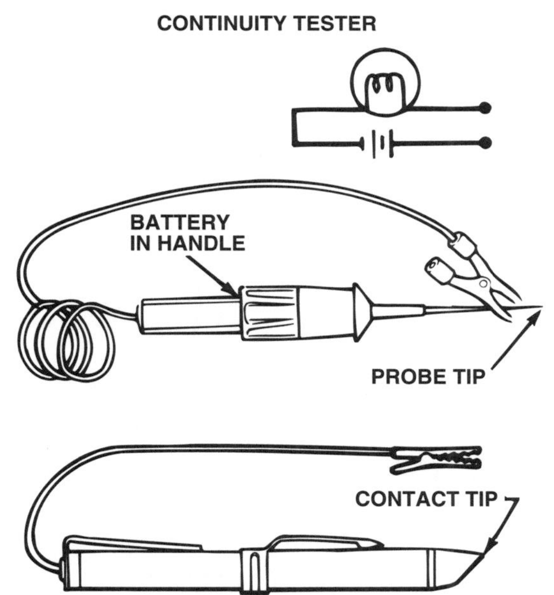

Figure 2-11. Self-powered test lamps contain a battery and usually have a clamp and probe to connect to a circuit.

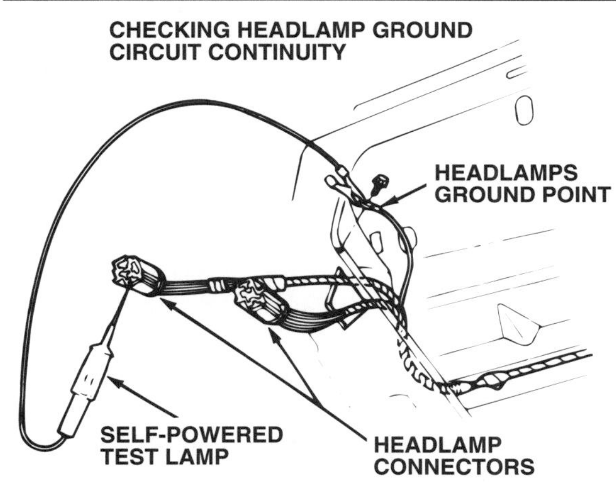

Figure 2-12. Using a self-powered test lamp to check the headlamp circuit.

carrying power may burn out the bulb or otherwise damage the tool.

The self-powered test lamp is used to check for open or short circuits. The test lamp bulb illuminates whenever the tool is connected to a complete circuit, figure 2-12. Check the tool battery before use by connecting the clip lead to the probe tip. If the bulb lights, the battery is good.

As with a 12-volt test lamp, this tester should not be used on electronic circuits, as too much voltage from the tool battery may damage some electronic components. Use jumper wires to bypass loads when

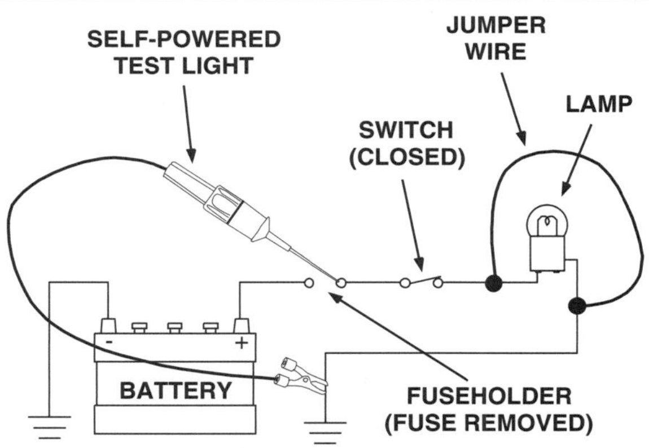

Figure 2-13. Bypass loads with a jumper wire when using a self-powered test lamp to check a circuit.

using a self-powered test lamp to check a circuit, as the normal resistance of the load may be more than the low-voltage lamp battery can overcome, figure 2-13. These test lamps cannot be used to check high-resistance components, such as suppression-type ignition cables, because the lamp battery cannot overcome the normal component resistance.

Logic Probe

A logic probe is a rather simple tool that is the electronic equivalent of a test lamp, figure 2-14. While a test lamp has low impedance and places a high load on the circuit being tested, a logic probe has high impedance and places a minimal load on the circuit. Therefore, a logic probe can be used for checking low-voltage, low-current electronic circuits without interfering with the signal.

The logic probe is an externally powered, solid-state test lamp used extensively by the electronics industry for troubleshooting circuitry. Any 5 to 15 volt direct current (dc) source may be used to power the logic probe. It is important that a higher voltage power source be used, if possible, because the probe can be damaged if the measured voltage exceeds the power source voltage. The device should not be used to test voltages in excess of 15 volts dc.

The easiest power source to use is the vehicle battery. A logic probe has two power leads, black and red. Connect them to the power supply observing the correct polarity, usually red to positive and black to negative, figure 2-15. If the leads on the tool are not long enough, they can be extended with jumper wires. Be sure to use jumper wires that are the same gauge as the original leads. Most logic probes come with small alligator clips on the lead ends. These are easily changed to larger clips for connecting directly to the vehicle battery.

Copyright 2000 by Chek-Chart Publications

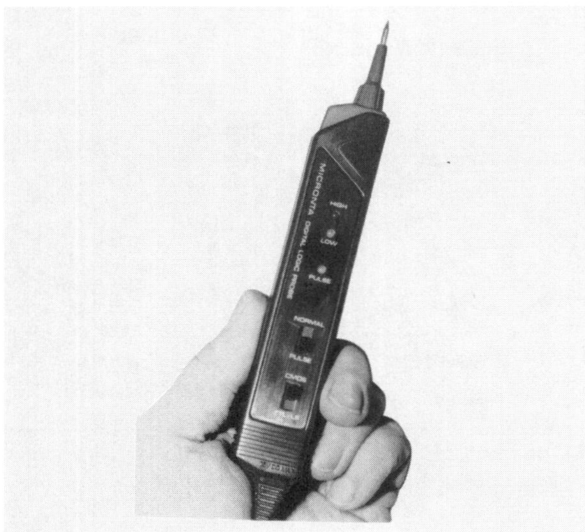

Figure 2-14. A logic probe is an electronic test lamp used to check circuit continuity.

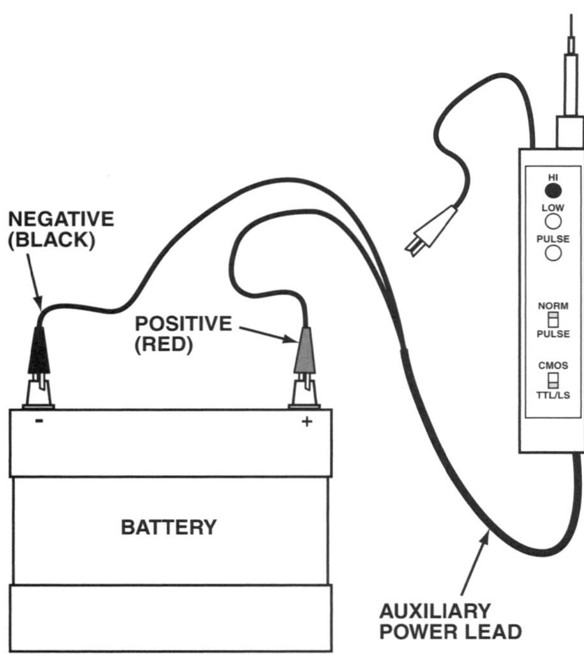

Figure 2-15. A logic probe connected to the vehicle battery and ready to test.

An alternative power source to the vehicle battery is a 9-, 12-, or 15-volt dry cell battery. This method is convenient and much safer for checking electronic circuits. The logic probe has an auxiliary ground lead used for testing when the power source is not the vehicle battery, or when troubleshooting suspected ground circuit problems. Unlike a self-powered test lamp, the logic probe power source does not power the circuit

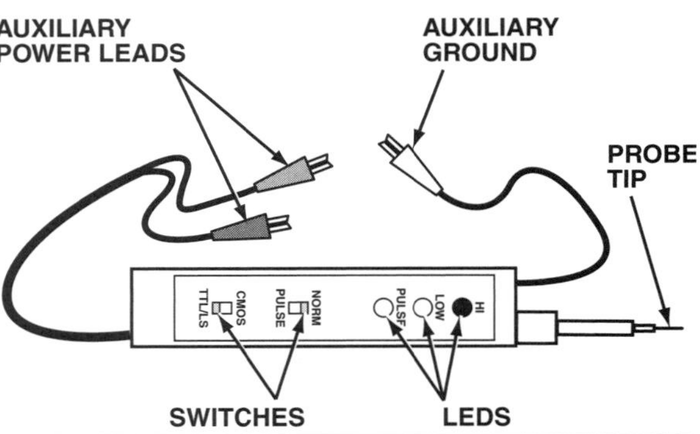

Figure 2-16. Three LEDs on the logic probe indicate circuit conditions.

being tested. The logic probe battery only powers the internal circuitry of the tool.

A logic probe indicates the presence of voltage in a circuit and, to some degree, the amount of voltage. Although it cannot provide specific voltage readings, it does differentiate between a steady or pulsed signal. This makes it a good tool for checking the presence of a frequency-based signal, such as a camshaft position (CMP) sensor, crankshaft position (CKP) sensor, ignition pick-up, and other pulse or frequency-based computer signals.

A typical logic probe has three light-emitting diodes (LEDs): a red one, normally labeled "high;" a green one, labeled "low," and an amber one, labeled "pulse," figure 2-16. It also has two two-position switches. The settings for one switch are *Normal* and *Pulse*. The tool is set to *Pulse* for checking most automotive signals. Be aware, false pulse signals are common when testing with the engine running and the tool set in pulse mode. This is because the ignition signal is inductively picked up by the probe The second switch offers a selection of *TTL/LS* and *CMOS* modes. These stand for transistor-transistor logic/link state and complementary metal-oxide semiconductor, which are the types of tests being performed. Most automotive tests are made with the tool in the *CMOS* position.

With the probe set in the *TTL/LS* mode and connected to a power source, the red, or high, LED illuminates whenever the probe tip is connected to any voltage source that is 2.2 volts or higher. The green, or low, LED illuminates when the voltage source at the probe tip is 0.8 volt or less.

If the probe is set in the CMOS mode, the red LED illuminates only when the probe is connected to a voltage that is 70 percent or more of the power source. For example, voltage at the probe tip must be 8.5 volts or more to light the red LED if the tool is connected to a 12-volt power source. Similarly, the green LED

Copyright 2000 by Chek-Chart Publications

illuminates when the tip touches any voltage source that is 30 percent or less than that of the source power, which is 3.6 volts with a 12-volt battery. Note that the voltage needed to illuminate the red and green LEDs varies as percentages of the power supply when it is set in the CMOS position. It is fixed, at 0.8 volt and 2.2 volts, when the probe is in the TTL position regardless of the power source voltage.

The amber, or pulse, LED illuminates whenever the probe tip contacts a voltage source. Then, the LED flashes each time the test voltage goes above or below zero. The frequency of a pulsed voltage is observed by noting the rate at which the amber lamp flashes. On some probes, an audible tone sounds as it corresponds to the voltage level being measured sounds. A low tone indicates low voltage, and a high tone indicates high voltage.

To prevent tool damage, never expose the probe tip to over 15 volts dc. Logic probes work well for checking electronic circuits, but be very cautious if trying to test the operation of a magnetic generator, such as a magnetic pick-up, wheel speed sensor, or engine speed sensors. Normal signals from these devices often exceed 15 volts.

Logic probe checks of any engine sensor are made while the engine is cranking only, not running. Remember, charging system output is almost 15 volts. Normal charging system output voltage fluctuations often exceed what the logic probe can handle. Conduct wheel speed sensor tests by rotating the wheel by hand. This generates a low-voltage signal to protect the probe and still allow a valid test for output from the magnetic generator. Checking for the presence of an output signal from a Hall-effect type CKP sensor is an example of using a logic probe:

1. Connect the probe power leads to the vehicle battery, observing proper polarity.
2. Use a circuit diagram to identify the power, signal, and ground wires for the circuit being tested. If no schematic is available, testing can still be successful.
3. Disable the fuel system to prevent the engine from starting while testing.
4. A typical single Hall-effect sensor has three leads: dc power, ground, dc pulsed signal output. Probe each of the three wires while cranking the engine and observe the results on the LED display.
5. The results of a test with the logic probe should show one wire that lights the green LED continuously. This lead is the ground. The amber LED also blinks as the probe tip touches the ground.
6. Probe the power wire and both the red LED and the amber LED should light continuously.

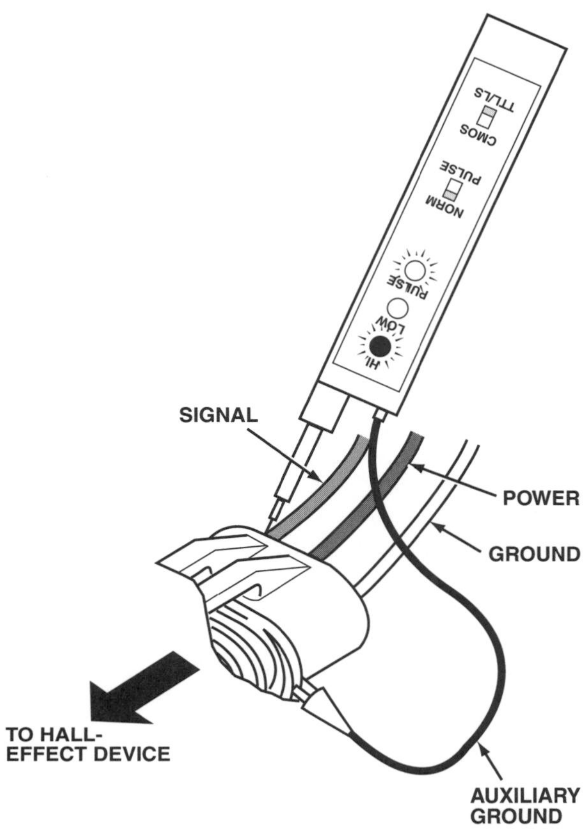

Figure 2-17. Both the red and amber LED should pulse when checking a Hall-effect switch signal circuit.

7. The third, or signal, wire should cause both the red and amber LEDs to pulse as the engine is cranked, figure 2-17.

When testing a Hall-effect device, if no output signal is present while the engine is cranking, measure the signals at the other two leads before determining the device is faulty. If the green LED does not illuminate and there is no blink of the amber LED when probing the ground lead, continue to test for a potential failure of the ground circuit. This could be a broken wire or poor connection. If neither the red nor amber LED illuminates with the probe connected to the power circuit while cranking, the power circuit is open. The Hall-effect device cannot function without power.

TEST METER DESIGN

Repairing an electrical problem involves finding and identifying the underlying cause. Many tools exist to help in this search. These tools range from the simple test devices just described to complex, expensive programmed engine analyzers. Measure voltage, current, and resistance in the circuit in order to determine how

Copyright 2000 by Chek-Chart Publications

well an electrical circuit is functioning. Measurements are taken using three basic test meters:

- Voltmeter
- Ammeter
- Ohmmeter.

All three of these test meters may be either analog or digital devices. However, digital meters are required for testing late-model vehicles with electronic control systems. Today, analog gauges may still be found on equipment designed for testing high-current circuits, such as starting and charging systems. The most common automotive meter design is the multimeter, which is a single unit with the ability to measure voltage, current, and resistance. Many meters are also equipped with a light or a buzzer that indicates continuity in the test circuit.

Test meters have two leads—long pieces of wire with connectors on the end—to make contact with the circuit being tested. The leads may be permanently connected to the meter, or they may plug into various sockets in the meter for different uses.

When measuring voltage or current in a circuit, the polarity of the test meter and the leads must correspond to the polarity of the circuit being tested. One lead is usually colored red, for positive (+), and should be used on the part of the circuit or component being tested that is nearer to the highest positive voltage. This is generally the battery positive post, except for some charging system tests when it is the alternator output terminal. The other meter lead is usually colored black or white, for negative (-), and should be connected to the test point nearer to the highest negative voltage.

Analog Meters

Analog meters use a mechanism called a D'Arsonval movement to move a needle over a printed scale to indicate test values. They are called analog meters because the needle indicates a continuous range of values across the scale, figure 2-18. Analog meters have a low input impedance, which is the combined opposition to current resulting from the inductance, resistance, and capacitance of the meter.

When the meter is in use, current passes through a coil to create a magnetic field. This coil assembly is mounted in bearings and surrounded by a horseshoe-shaped permanent magnet. When energized, the magnetic field of the coil interacts with the permanent-magnet field causing the bearing mounted assembly to rotate, figure 2-19. The coil can move in either direction. The direction of rotation is controlled by the direction of current. The needle coil, which attaches to the coil, indicates the value of voltage, current, or resistance on the printed scale. The meter is designed so that the value it measures is proportionate to current in the meter coil. Some analog meters are calibrated, or adjusted for accuracy, with adjustment screws. If so, it is highly recommended that you calibrate, or "zero," the meter before each use.

The low input impedance of an analog meter lowers the resistance of the circuit under test. This may cause the circuit to draw more current than it is designed to carry. This characteristic somewhat

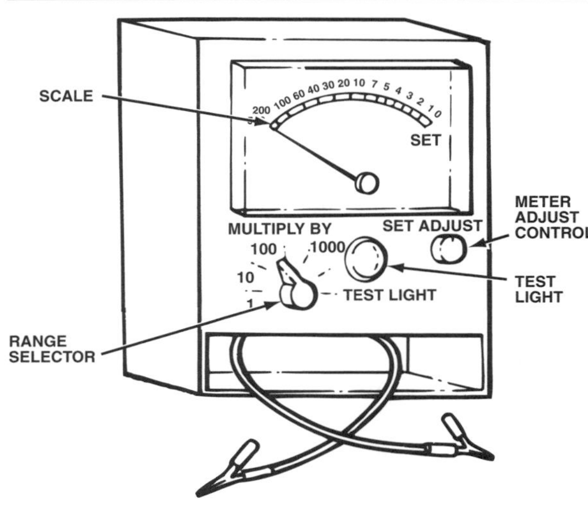

Figure 2-18. The sweep of the needle indicates a continuous range of values across the scale of an analog meter.

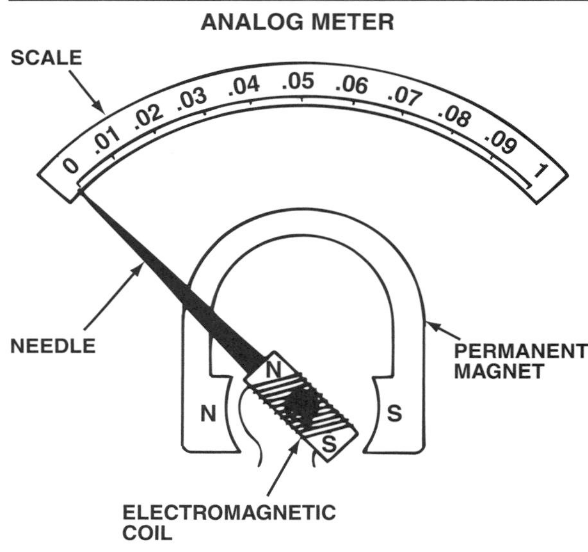

Figure 2-19. Interaction between the electromagnetic coil field and the permanent-magnet field moves the needle of an analog meter.

Copyright 2000 by Chek-Chart Publications

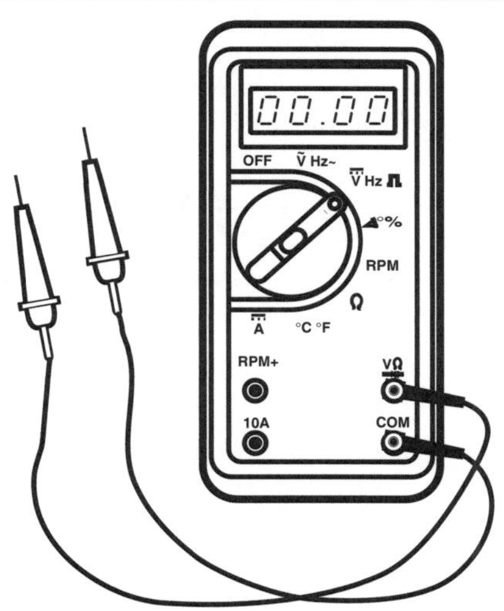

Figure 2-20. A high-impedance digital meter is needed to test electronic circuits.

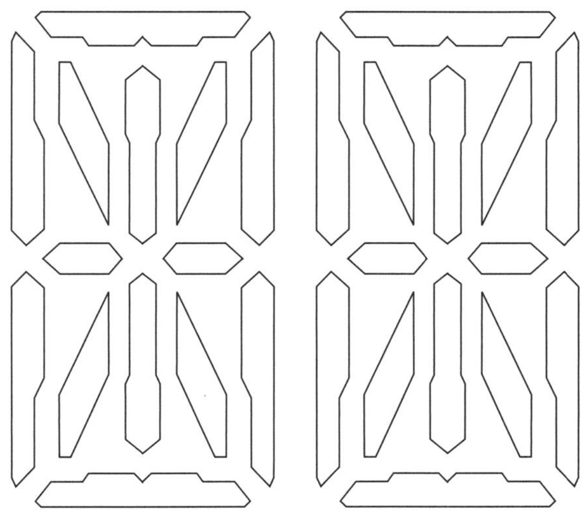

Figure 2-21. A microprocessor energizes different segments of a LCD to display numerals on the screen.

distorts—sometimes considerably—the accuracy of the measurements. If the added current draw of the meter exceeds the circuit design, which is often the case with low-current electronic circuits, component failure results. The input impedance of most analog meters is in the range of 5,000 to 20,000 ohms per volt. Analog meters are *not* recommended for automotive electronic system testing, unless specified by the vehicle manufacturer for a particular procedure.

Digital Meters

Digital test meters have a very high input impedance, usually greater than ten megohm, or ten million ohms, figure 2-20. High input impedance is an important requirement for testing components in computerized control systems because the load the meter places on the circuit does not distort the measurements.

A digital meter converts the analog current, voltage, or resistance signals into a digital format and displays them as digits, or numbers, on a LED or liquid crystal display (LCD) panel. A LCD screen displays numerals by energizing different segments of the screen, figure 2-21. Each segment has its own electrical contact and is activated by a low-voltage signal from a microprocessor, which is part of the meter. An LED display is arranged in a grid, and each LED in the grid has a separate circuit that is switched on or off by the microprocessor to display values, figure 2-22.

A digital display presents data more accurately because it reads to several decimal places, rather than spotting the position of a floating needle on a scale. Digital meters also eliminate the possibility of parallax error, which occurs when the needle of an analog

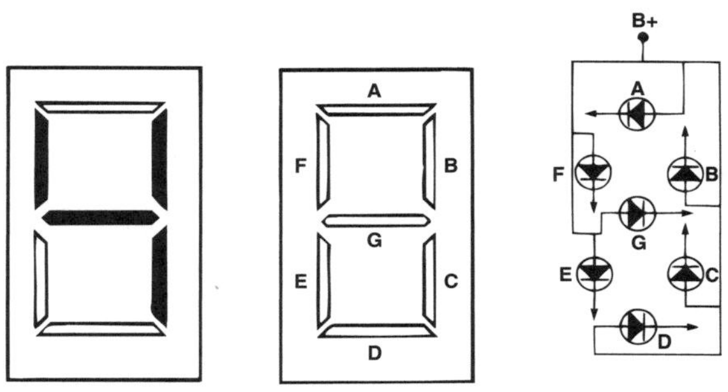

Figure 2-22. Individual LEDs on a grid are energized to display numerals on the screen.

meter is viewed from an angle. In addition, most digital meters also have automatic range selection, a floating decimal point, and automatic polarity indication, which make them much easier to use than analog meters. There is no need to "zero" an electronic, digital meter before use because it is self-calibrating.

AMMETER

An ammeter is a gauge that is used to measure current and to check continuity in a circuit. An ammeter is always connected in series with the circuit or component to be tested. The meter connection can be either intrusive or inductive. On an intrusive connection, the meter bridges the gap in an open circuit so that all the current passes through the meter, figure 2-23. An inductive pickup is a clamp that fits around the circuit being tested. The meter reads the strength of the electromagnetic field created by the current passing through the inductive clamp, figure 2-24.

Copyright 2000 by Chek-Chart Publications

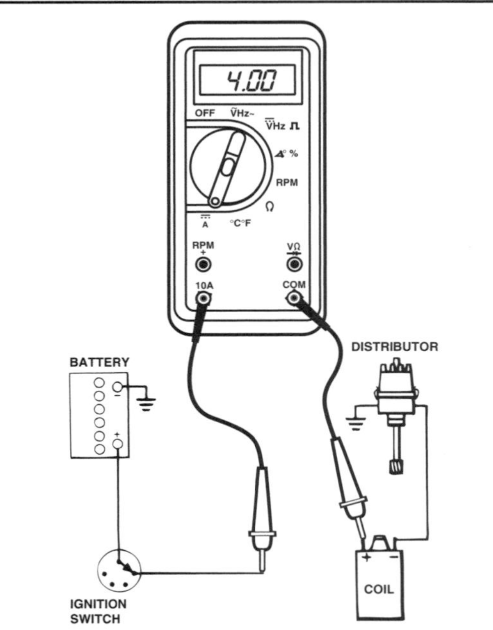

Figure 2-23. An intrusive ammeter connection bridges an open circuit so that all the current passes through the meter.

Figure 2-24. An inductive ammeter pickup clamps around the test circuit and measures the electromagnetic field of the current.

When using an ammeter, if any current is allowed to travel through an alternate path and bypass the meter, the ammeter reading is inaccurate. If the ammeter alters the resistance of the circuit, the accuracy of the meter reading is affected as well. Analog ammeters generally have a shunt resistor parallel to the meter movement to minimize meter impact on the circuit and test results. The high input impedance of a digital ammeter results in an extremely low amount of current being drawn off the circuit when the meter is connected in series. Since all ammeters have low resistance, they act as a jumper wire to create a short circuit if connected in parallel.

Using an Ammeter

According to Ohm's law, current is equal at all points in a series circuit, or within any single branch of a parallel circuit. When the current specifications for a circuit or component are known, ammeter testing determines the presence of either a short circuit or high resistance. A current value greater than specified indicates less resistance in the circuit, possibly a short. An ammeter also detects high circuit resistance, which causes current readings to be below normal. For example, on a simple lamp circuit, resistance that results from corrosion at the bulb terminals causes a low current reading on the ground side of the load, figure 2-25.

Ammeter polarity

Correct polarity is important when connecting either an intrusive or inductive ammeter. Failure to maintain polarity produces inaccurate readings and may damage the meter. Intrusive test leads are usually color-coded and inductive clamps are typically marked with an arrow. The arrow points in the direction of current travel when properly connected.

Ammeter ranges

Most ammeters have either more than one current scale and a range selector switch or an automatic ranging feature, which switches the meter to a higher or lower scale depending on the current being measured. If using a meter without automatic ranging, it is important to set the selector switch to the range above the maximum expected current draw before connecting the meter. Too much current passing through the meter on any given range may overload the internal fuse and possibly damage the test instrument.

Each setting of the range selector switch on a digital ammeter generally increases the maximum amperage capability of the meter by a factor of 10. Typical selections are labeled 200mA, 2A and 20A. Each setting indicates the maximum amperage that particular range will accommodate. Although the higher ranges test currents well below their maximum, they may not display as many digits as a lower range would display. Therefore, the reading is not as accurate as it would be on a lower scale. When using an ammeter, set the selector switch to the highest

Copyright 2000 by Chek-Chart Publications

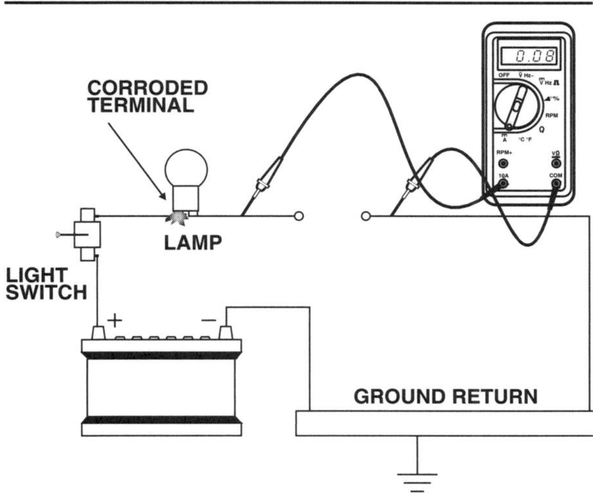

Figure 2-25. High resistance from a corroded bulb terminal shows up as low current with the ammeter connected on the ground side of the load.

current range before testing, then switch ranges downward to provide a greater number of digits for more accuracy.

A digital ammeter may have two separate current scales. If so, one is for direct current (dc) and the other is for alternating current (ac). All automotive systems operate on dc. However, the alternator generates ac then converts it to a dc output signal. Use the correct ammeter scale. Readings taken using the ac scale *are not accurate* for dc circuits.

Ammeter Tests

Always connect an ammeter in series with test components so that current travels through both the part and the meter for measurement. The extremely low resistance of the ammeter compensates for the additional current draw created by the intrusive connection to minimize voltage drop across the meter. If connected parallel across a live circuit, the low resistance of the ammeter creates a short circuit. Excessive current that results could possibly damage both the meter and the circuit.

Once an accurate reading is obtained on the ammeter, compare the reading to the current specifications provided by the vehicle manufacturer. Current specifications are not always available, so it may be necessary to use Ohm's law and calculate the proper amount of current for a particular circuit. In general:

- If the ammeter shows *no current,* the circuit is *open* at some point. This indicates no continuity.
- If the ammeter shows *less current* than normal, the circuit is complete but there is either *too much resistance* in the circuit or *not enough voltage* applied to it. This may be caused by defective components or by loose or corroded connections.
- If the ammeter shows *more current* than normal, some of the normal circuit resistance is being bypassed by a *short circuit.* Short circuits are caused by faulty components or defective wire insulation.

Inductive Ammeters

Inductive ammeters measure current without being physically connected into the circuit. The inductive pickup simply clamps around the conductor. This does not require opening a connection to place the meter in series with the circuit. An inductive pickup is typically used for high-voltage electrical work or for simply checking the presence of current, rather than measuring for an exact amount.

In automotive applications, an inductive ammeter is a convenient way to measure starter draw or charging current. These measurements are in a relatively high range, so the slight inaccuracy of the readings is not enough to affect performance. Most charging-starter-battery analyzers have an inductive pickup for the built-in ammeter.

Inductive ammeters are not as accurate as a standard digital ammeter, especially for testing low-current circuits. However, a current, or amp, probe, which is a self-powered inductive pickup that converts current to a voltage signal, makes testing low-current circuits easy.

Many manufacturers provide current draw specifications for ignition coils. The coil is quickly tested with an amp probe and a scope or a graphing multimeter (GMM). Current draw exceeds 10 amps on some coils, so set the probe on the 100mV per amp scale. To test, simply clamp the amp probe around the negative primary wire of the coil and either start or crank the engine according to service instructions for the vehicle being tested. Current should quickly rise to specifications and abruptly switch to zero as the field collapses, figure 2-26. The powertrain control module (PCM) regulates and limits ignition coil current on some systems. The GMM or scope trace rises quickly, levels off, then drops to zero on these peak and hold systems, figure 2-27.

No current draw indicates an open primary circuit or no continuity. The ignition system would not operate at all in this case. A low current reading indicates a discharged battery, high resistance in the primary wiring or primary coil winding, or loose or corroded connections.

Copyright 2000 by Chek-Chart Publications

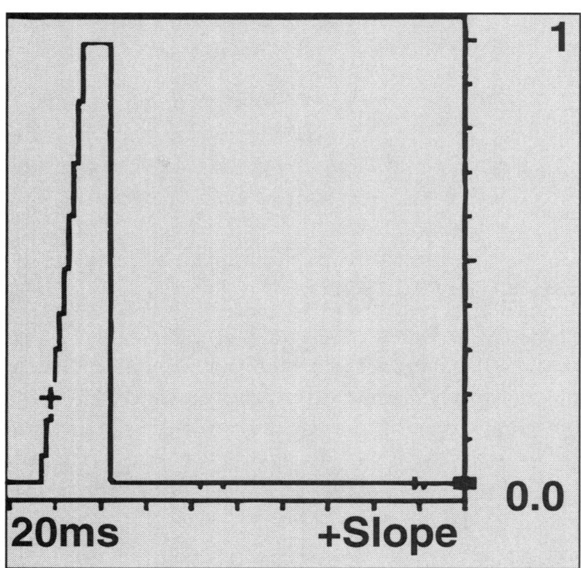

Figure 2-26. Ignition coil current draw captured with an amp probe and GMM.

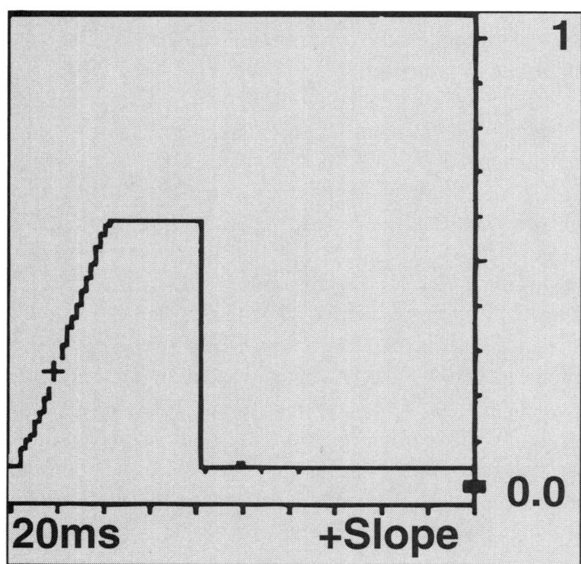

Figure 2-27. The trace momentarily levels off if current is internally limited by the PCM.

VOLTMETER

A voltmeter is a gauge that measures the electrical pressure differential, or potential difference, between two points in a circuit. The meter displays the results in volts. Voltage is a force that is applied to, or impressed on, a circuit and exists even when there is no current in the circuit. In an automotive electrical system, voltage is supplied by the battery and the alternator.

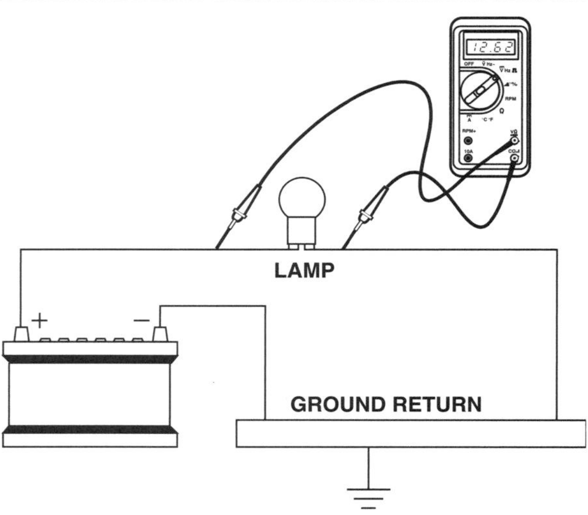

Figure 2-28. Connect a voltmeter in parallel with the load or circuit being tested.

A voltmeter, which can be either a digital or analog instrument, is normally connected parallel with a circuit or across a voltage source. This parallel connection allows a very small amount of current to bypass the normal circuit path and travel through the voltmeter, figure 2-28. The current draw of the meter is so small that enough current travels through the normal circuit path while allowing the test component to function normally. The voltmeter is calibrated to determine the voltage across the component from the small amount of diverted current. Voltmeters may be connected to "live" circuits to measure component voltages under actual operating conditions.

As with a digital ammeter, a digital voltmeter has high input impedance to prevent high current from damaging the meter and limit the additional load placed on the circuit by the meter. Both analog and digital voltmeters also have an internal resistor parallel to the test circuit to protect the meter from too much current. This resistor must be at least one megohm. A good digital meter uses a 10-megohm resistor. Because of this high internal resistance, the meter draws very little current from the test circuit. The effect of the meter on circuit voltage is insignificant.

Using a Voltmeter

A voltmeter is probably the most versatile and frequently used test meter in automotive electrical repair. Voltmeter tests include checking:

- Source voltage of a circuit
- Voltage drop caused by a load
- Continuity of a circuit
- Voltage at any point in a circuit.

Copyright 2000 by Chek-Chart Publications

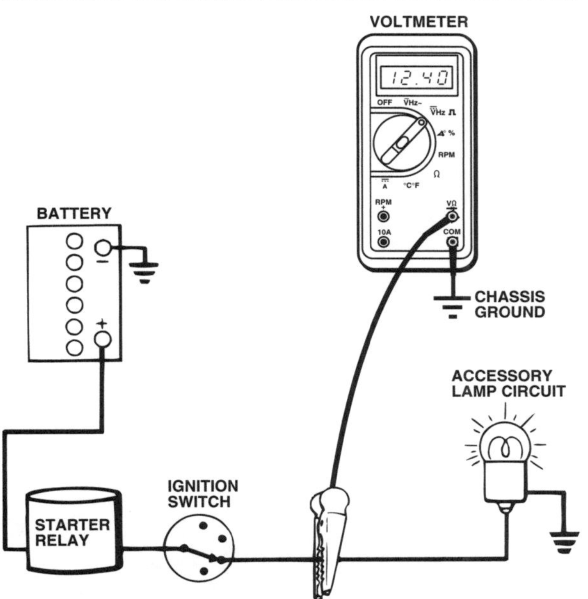

Figure 2-29. A voltmeter connected in parallel measures voltage available at the test point.

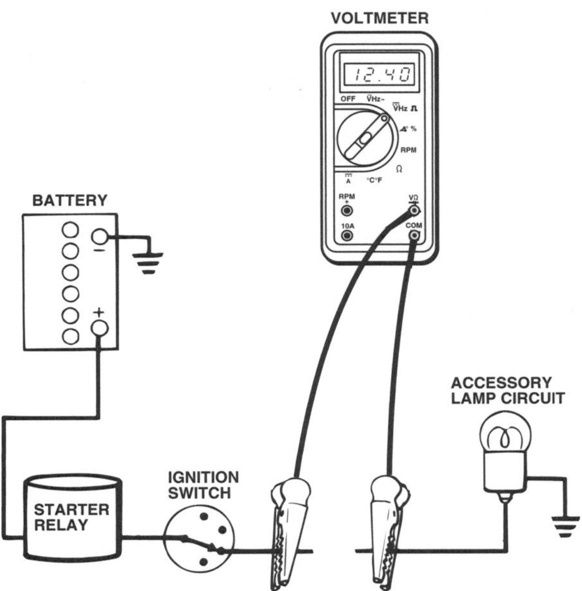

Figure 2-30. A voltmeter connected in series checks continuity from the test point to ground.

Voltage is impressed equally on all branches of a parallel circuit. The sum of the voltage drops across all of the loads in a branch or a series equals the source voltage. For measuring available voltage, source voltage, and voltage drop, the voltmeter is connected parallel with the circuit or part, figure 2-29. When checking for circuit continuity, the voltmeter is connected in series with portions of the circuit, figure 2-30.

Voltmeter polarity

Whether the meter is connected in series or in parallel, the polarity of the test leads must be maintained. This prevents meter damage with an analog unit and avoids confusion in understanding the voltage readings with a digital meter. Reversing the polarity of the leads on an auto-ranging digital voltmeter causes the display to show a minus sign indicating negative voltage. Incorrect polarity on an analog meter may damage the meter movement when the needle travels in the opposite direction against the needle stop.

Voltage ranges

Most voltmeters designed for automotive use feature automatic ranging. However, some digital and most analog voltmeters have a range selector switch for choosing the proper voltage scale. When selectable, range settings are labeled to indicate the *maximum* voltage that particular range will accommodate. Although the higher ranges will test voltages well below their maximum, results are not as accurate as they would be in a lower range. For greatest test accuracy, use the lowest *safe* voltage range. Always set the selector switch to the range above the maximum expected voltage before connecting the meter to the circuit. Then, switch the ranges downward to provide a greater number of digits for more accurate readings.

A digital voltmeter may have two separate voltage scales. If that is the case, one is for dc and the other is for ac. All automotive systems operate on dc voltages, and readings taken using the ac scale *are inaccurate* for dc circuits. The ac setting on the meter is useful for checking alternator voltage ripple, figure 2-31.

Voltmeter Tests

To use a voltmeter efficiently, keep the following points in mind when testing circuits and components:

- Voltage is the same across all branches of a parallel circuit.
- The sum of the voltage drops across the components of a series circuit is equal to the applied source voltage.
- The sum of the voltage drops across the components of any branch of a parallel circuit is equal to the applied source voltage.

With the exception of the ignition secondary circuits, the maximum available source voltage for most automotive circuits is battery voltage, or a nominal 12 volts. Most vehicle electrical systems and devices are designed to operate on this 12-volt source voltage. However, this source voltage is often reduced in electronic control system circuits, which commonly operate on 5 volts.

Copyright 2000 by Chek-Chart Publications

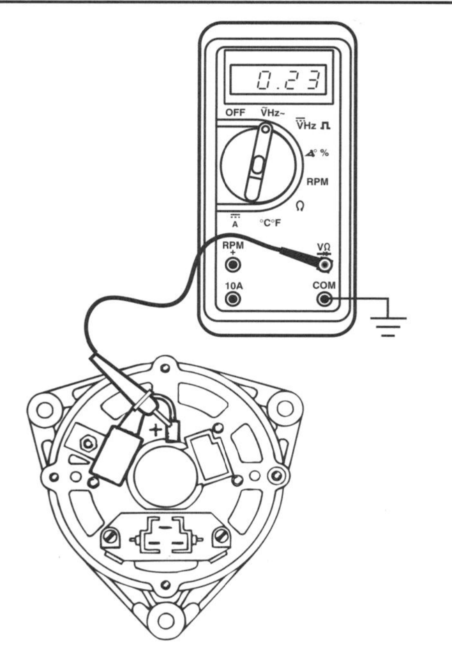

Figure 2-31. Measuring ac voltage ripple from the alternator using the ac scale of the voltmeter.

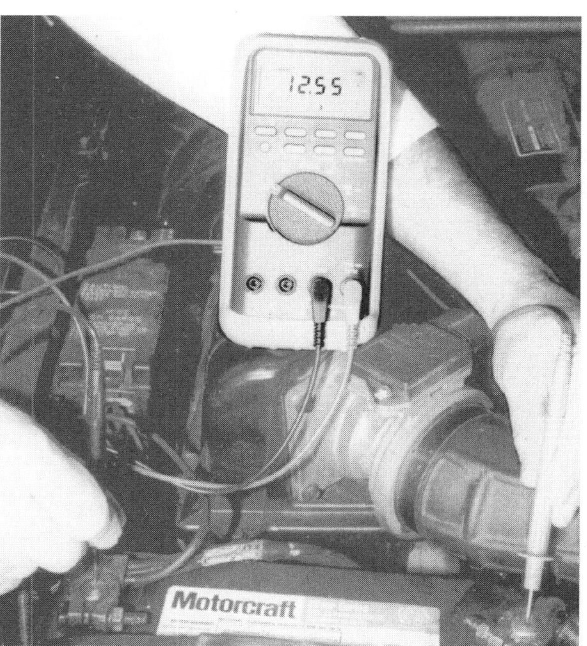

Figure 2-32. Checking no-load battery voltage with a voltmeter.

One reason for using low-voltage electronic circuits is to reduce the current draw on the battery. Because late-model vehicles have many electrical devices and electronic components, the accumulated drain of all these components puts a great strain on battery resources.

Source voltage

The source, or available, voltage within a circuit may be measured with or without current applied. The vehicle battery provides the source voltage for all dc automotive circuits. Check the battery by connecting the positive lead of the voltmeter to the positive battery (B+) terminal and the negative lead to the negative battery (ground) terminal, figure 2-32. This measures no-load, or open-circuit, battery voltage, which should be about 12.2 to 12.5 volts with the engine not running. Next, turn on the headlamps and air conditioning. Note if the voltmeter reading is lower than the no-load voltage. This indicates the condition of the battery and the current draw of the electrical system.

Once source voltage is known, the amount of voltage available at any point along a circuit may be checked in a similar fashion. Simply ground the negative meter lead and probe the supply wire with the positive meter lead. Low source voltage in a circuit is the result of high resistance. Loose or corroded connections are often at fault. A loss of source voltage indicates an open circuit.

Available voltage in a circuit

Sources of low-voltage problems and high resistance faults are isolated by systematically taking available voltage readings along a circuit while it is carrying current. These available voltage tests provide a quick way to determine overall circuit condition. For example, if an accessory motor is not turning fast enough, available voltage testing can pinpoint the problem area of the circuit. Begin testing at the point of highest potential voltage, or closest to the power source. Then, work down the circuit and take readings at each load, figure 2-33. The meter readings in the illustration show that there is not enough available voltage to correctly operate the motor. Therefore, the problem is either in the switch or the circuit between the switch and the motor.

Voltage available to a component may be measured with or without current in the circuit. Checking available voltage when there is no current in the circuit is a quick way to locate an open, figure 2-34. The meter readings in the illustration reveal that the circuit is open at some point between the second and third test points.

Remember, work from the most positive point in the circuit to the most negative, which is usually ground, when checking available voltage. Tests are performed in the direction that voltage is dropped as the loads in the circuit operate. To perform the tests, connect the voltmeter negative lead to ground, and use

Copyright 2000 by Chek-Chart Publications

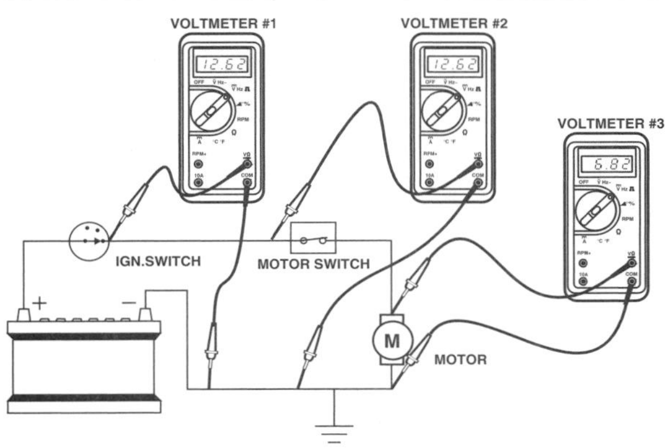

Figure 2-33. Checking available voltage at each load quickly locates source voltage problems.

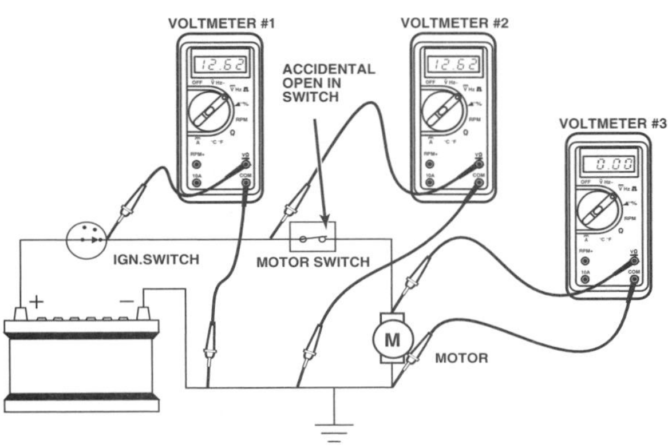

Figure 2-34. With no current in the circuit, available voltage testing isolates the location of an open.

the positive lead to probe each test point until the problem is found. For accurate test results, *all measurements must be made from the same ground reference point.*

Voltage drop

Voltage drop is the amount of voltage that an electrical device normally consumes to perform its task. Voltage drop is a normal part of circuit operation because every load device has resistance. However, excessive voltage drop causes a decrease in current and reduces the voltage available to other devices in the circuit. Too much voltage drop is often the result of undesired, high resistance in a circuit caused by bad connections, malfunctioning components, or wiring problems. Keep in mind, *the sum of the individual component and wiring voltage drops in a circuit equals the source voltage.* Checking voltage drop is one of the most important diagnostic tests for troubleshooting circuit problems.

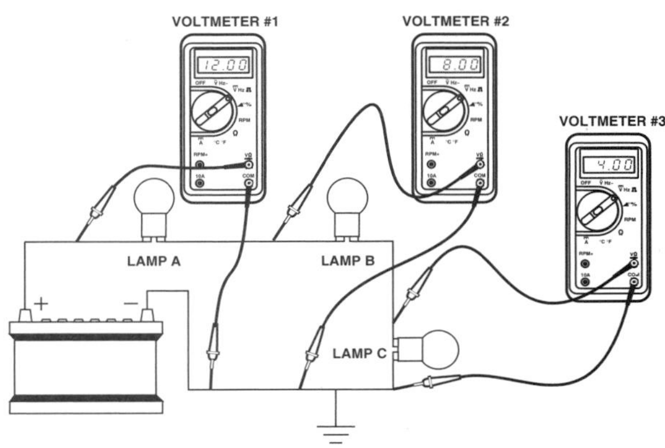

Figure 2-35. A series of available voltage tests are used to calculate voltage drop across each load.

To check voltage drop, the circuit must be carrying the maximum amount of current it was designed to operate with under normal conditions. The amount of voltage drop that is considered acceptable varies by circuit. A low-current circuit that draws milliamps is affected by a very small voltage drop, while the same amount of voltage drop has a negligible effect on a high-current circuit. The two ways to determine voltage drop are by measuring available voltages and calculating the voltage drop, or by measuring it directly.

Calculated voltage drop

By conducting available voltage tests and applying some simple math, the voltage drop across any part of a circuit can be calculated. This method for determining a voltage drop is especially helpful when it is difficult or impossible to physically reach a portion of the circuit to connect the voltmeter directly. Voltage drop is equal to the *difference* between the two readings; therefore, subtract one from the other. For example, consider a series circuit of three lamps. To test, simply take available voltage readings at each lamp, figure 2-35. To calculate voltage drop:

- Voltmeter #1 shows 12 volts available on one side of lamp "A" and 8 volts on the other side. Subtract 8 volts from 12 volts and the difference is 4 volts; therefore, the voltage drop across lamp "A" is 4 volts.
- Similarly, voltmeter #2 shows the voltage drop across lamp "B" to be 4 volts as well because 8 minus 4 equals 4.
- Voltmeter #3 shows the voltage drop across lamp "C" is 4 volts as well, because 4 minus zero is 4.

One important fact to remember about ground is: *Ground is considered to be at a potential of 0 volt.* It

Copyright 2000 by Chek-Chart Publications

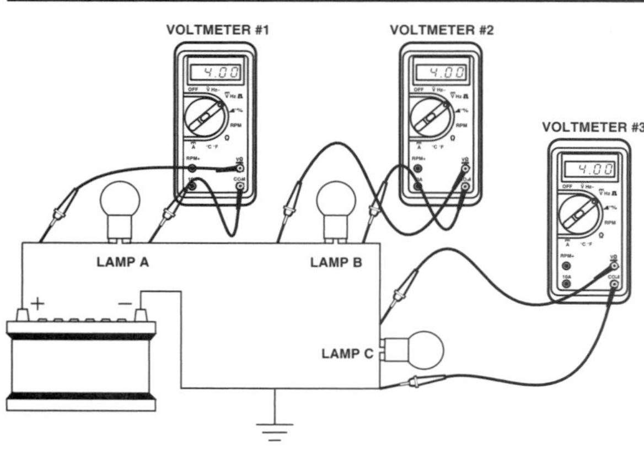

Figure 2-36. The voltmeter is connected across the load to take direct voltage drop readings

is actually defined that way to make calculations easier, and is one reason it is almost always chosen as the reference point from which voltage measurements are made.

A typical test situation where the calculated voltage drop method is used would be when it is impossible to reach lamp *"B"* in the illustrated circuit to take a reading. Using the readings from voltmeters #1 and #2 alone, the voltage drop across lamp *"C"* is easily determined. Measurements indicate a voltage drop of 4 volts each for lamps *"A"* and *"B,"* or a combined drop of 8 volts on the circuit. Because total voltage drop is equal to the battery voltage, or 12 volts, simply subtract the combined 8-volt drop for lamps *"A"* and *"B"* to determine that the voltage drop across lamp *"C"* is also 4 volts.

Direct voltage drop

In some cases, voltage drop is measured directly, rather than being computed from two voltmeter readings. A single, direct voltage drop test is useful only when it is known what a normal drop should be for the load being measured. Direct voltage drop readings are taken by connecting the voltmeter across the load. That is, the positive voltmeter lead attaches to the power side of the load and the negative meter lead attaches to the ground side of the component or circuit, figure 2-36. Remember, the circuit must be carrying current to measure voltage drop. Also, the sum of all the voltage drops in a circuit equals the source voltage.

Circuit continuity

Continuity testing is similar to no-load voltage testing since both procedures reveal if system voltage is being applied to a part of the circuit. However, the voltmeter is connected in series, rather than in parallel, with the circuit for a continuity check.

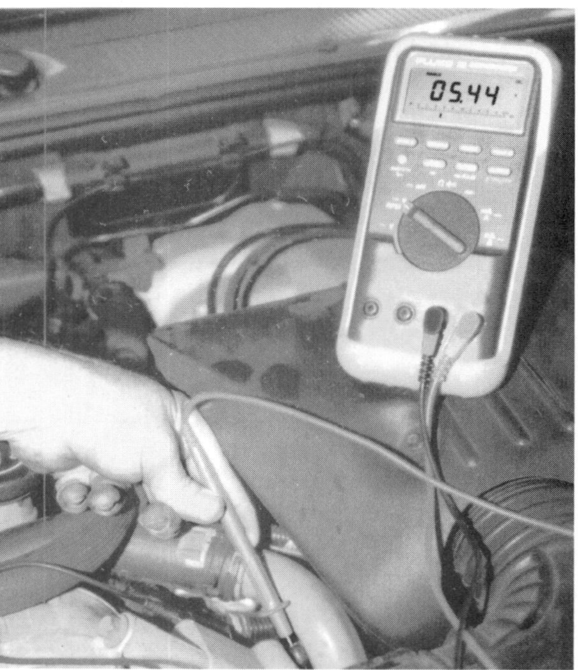

Figure 2-37. A voltmeter connected in series confirms continuity on this low-voltage electronic circuit.

When connecting a voltmeter to check continuity, the circuit must be open so that it is not carrying current. Open the circuit by disconnecting the power wire at the test point. Then, attach the positive voltmeter lead to the battery side of the open circuit and connect the negative voltmeter lead to the ground side of the test point. Next, energize the circuit and note the voltmeter reading. If the voltmeter reads system voltage, or reference voltage on an electronic circuit, the circuit is complete, figure 2-37. If the voltmeter reads near zero voltage, the circuit is open.

OHMMETER

An ohmmeter is a self-powered test instrument that is used only when there is no voltage applied to the circuit device being tested. Any current from an outside source results in inaccurate readings on a digital ohmmeter and could damage an analog meter. Make sure the circuit is not under power before connecting an ohmmeter, or simply remove the component to be tested from the circuit.

An ohmmeter, whether analog or digital, operates on the voltage drop principle. When the leads of an ohmmeter are connected for testing, the meter directs a low-voltage current from its internal power source through the test circuit. Since the source voltage and the internal resistance of the meter are known, the resistance of the test device can be determined by the amount of voltage dropped as current travels through

Copyright 2000 by Chek-Chart Publications

it. The ohmmeter makes this calculation and directly displays the resistance of the test device in ohms.

Be aware, ohmmeter testing may not always be conclusive. Resistance faults in wiring and connections often generate heat, which further increases the resistance of an operating circuit. In these cases, the fault may not be apparent unless the circuit is under power. The device may be able to relay the low-voltage signal of an ohmmeter, but not be able to carry the signal when system voltage is applied. Another consideration is the fact that most ohmmeters read only as low as 0.1 ohm, yet smaller amounts of resistance can cause problems. This is especially true on electronic and high-amperage circuits. Some low-resistance faults are detected only through voltage drop testing. However, an ohmmeter has definite advantages for many test situations and is particularly useful to:

- Measure the resistance of parts that have specific resistance values that fall within the usable range of the meter.
- Measure high-resistance items for which specifications are available, such as secondary ignition cables and electronic pickup coils.
- Test the resistance of internal parts of components that require disassembly to reach the test points.
- Bench test parts such as switches, circuit breakers, and relays before assembly or installation.
- Check circuit continuity of components.

Using an Ohmmeter

To compensate for internal temperature, resistance changes, and battery strength, it is important to calibrate, or "zero," analog ohmmeters before use. To zero the meter, set the range selector switch to the desired resistance scale, hold the test leads contacts together, and adjust the calibration control to set the needle at zero on the scale. A digital ohmmeter is generally self-calibrating, so there is no need to zero it.

Ohmmeter polarity

Since an ohmmeter generates its own signal to measure resistance and test circuit continuity, the polarity of the meter leads is usually not important. However, ohmmeter polarity is a factor when checking some semiconductors such as diodes and transistors. These devices require a small signal voltage of the proper polarity to switch them on for continuity testing.

Ohmmeter ranges

Analog ohmmeters show increasing resistance values as the needle moves from *right* to *left* over a printed scale. Digital ohmmeters are much easier to read and operate because the display screen directly presents measurement values as digits.

As with ammeters and voltmeters, ohmmeters may feature automatic ranging or use a range selector switch for choosing the proper meter setting. A range selector switch is labeled to indicate the maximum resistance value the instrument displays in that range. Resistance values outside the selected range do not display properly. For the greatest accuracy when testing, use the lowest safe resistance range that provides the greatest number of digits.

Typically, values far too small for a given range display on a digital ohmmeter as "0.00," although the *true* resistance value is not zero ohm. Values greater than a given range may display as "1," which does *not* mean the resistance is one ohm. Rather, it means the true value is not displayed properly, which is an indication that the ohmmeter is over-ranging. If the ohmmeter is set for its highest range and the "1" is still displayed, the true resistance value is so high it cannot be displayed on the meter. This is considered an infinite resistance.

Ohmmeter Tests

Connect an ohmmeter across the component to be tested. This is similar to the parallel connection used with a voltmeter, figure 2-38. However, this is not a true parallel connection because there is no current in the circuit under test. Ohmmeter measurements are used to pinpoint high resistance faults, or open circuits, and low resistance faults, or short circuits.

- When a device has an excessively high resistance, the ohmmeter indicates this higher resistance value. In the rare case when the resistance is extremely high, the ohmmeter may indicate "infinity," which may display as "1," or "OL," for out of limits, on a digital ohmmeter, figure 2-39. This indicates an open-circuit condition.
- If a device has an excessively low resistance, the ohmmeter display indicates this low resistance value on the selected scale. In the extreme case, the meter may register zero ohm. This indicates a short-circuit condition.

Digital meters have a "diode test" selection, which is an enhanced ohmmeter function. Remember, an ohmmeter actually measures voltage drop across the device being tested. A diode must be energized by a specific amount of voltage in order to operate, and this voltage is often greater than the bias, or test, voltage applied by the meter. In the "diode test" mode, a higher bias voltage is applied to ensure the diode is energized. The operation of some semiconductor devices, such as diodes, is quickly checked with an ohmmeter. Results are displayed as ohms. To check diodes:

Copyright 2000 by Chek-Chart Publications

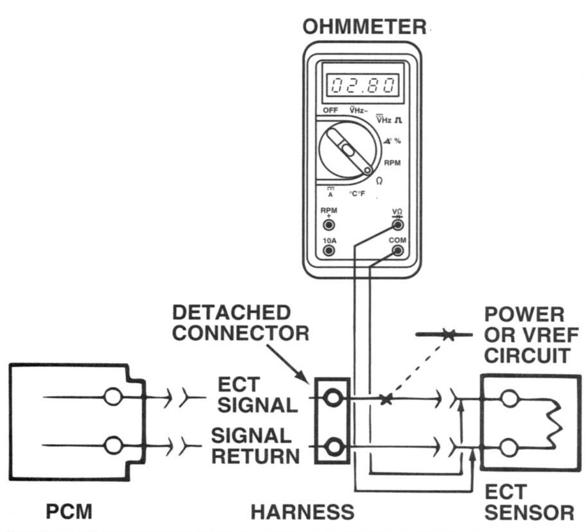

Figure 2-38. Ohmmeter readings are taken with leads connected in parallel to the test circuit.

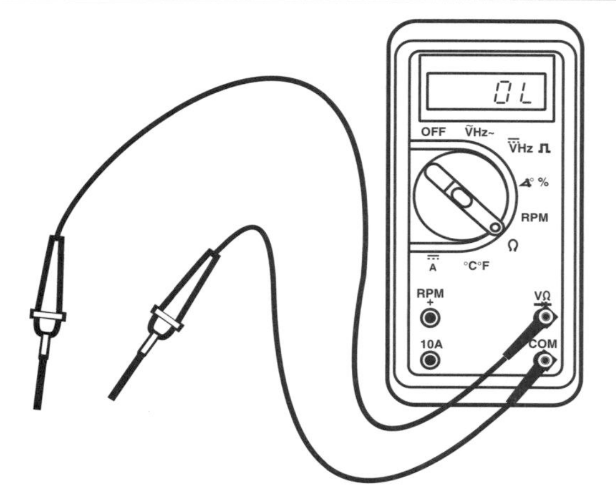

Figure 2-39. An "OL" displayed on the ohmmeter screen indicates that circuit resistance is greater than the meter can measure.

1. Connect one meter test lead to the diode lead and the other test lead to the diode base. Observe the ohmmeter reading.
2. Reverse the test leads, then read the ohmmeter again.
3. Compare the two meter readings, figure 2-40.

A good diode has very high or infinite resistance in one direction and very low resistance in the other direction. Either high resistance or low resistance in both directions indicates a bad diode.

DIGITAL MULTIMETER

A high-impedance digital multimeter (DMM) is a necessary piece of equipment for any automotive

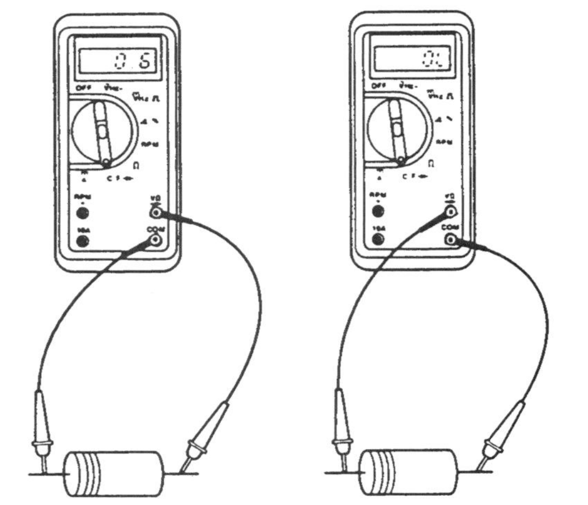

Figure 2-40. A diode should have continuity in only one direction when the ohmmeter leads are reversed.

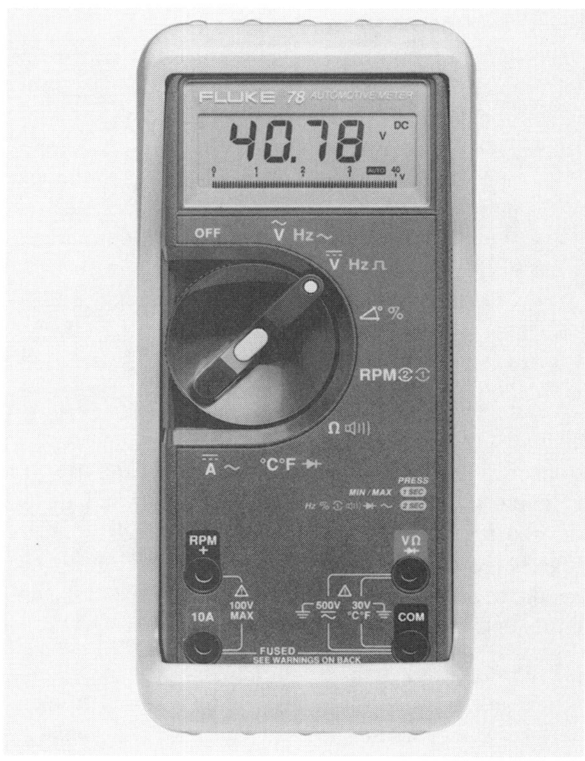

Figure 2-41. A digital multimeter combines ammeter, voltmeter, ohmmeter, and other test functions into a single unit.

technician, figure 2-41. The DMM combines the functions of several test instruments into a single, hand-held unit. For automotive use, a DMM must be able to perform as a voltmeter, ohmmeter, and ammeter. Additional functions, such as the ability to monitor pulse width and frequency, are available on some DMM models.

Copyright 2000 by Chek-Chart Publications

The DMM is the ideal tool for checking circuit conditions. However, a slow instrument screen update rate makes a DMM inaccurate for monitoring circuit activity. If the display responded immediately to the rapidly changing conditions of an operating circuit, values would appear as a blur on the display screen. To make the display legible, the instrument is designed to sample the test circuit, compute an average or representative figure based on the sample, then update the display at predetermined intervals according to the computed figure. Some instruments sample the test circuit at intervals, rather than take a constant reading.

The maximum update rate for displaying readable numbers on a LCD screen is 250 milliseconds, or four times a second. At this rate, it is impossible to see a quick, intermittent electrical glitch. In fact, when using a DMM to read voltage on a circuit that pulses from 0 to 12 volts at a 50-percent duty cycle, the meter most likely displays 6 volts, which is the average reading.

To compensate for this slow screen update, a good-quality DMM has a minimum/maximum, or min/max, feature and some have an analog bar graph on the display screen as well. On this min/max setting, the meter captures the lowest and highest sample signal and makes it available for recall. An analog bar graph makes it easy to spot fluctuations on the circuit, but it is difficult to get an accurate reading from one. On a top-quality DMM, the analog bar graph updates 40 times per second, but some units simply update the graph at the same rate as the readout. Again, these features provide circuit condition information, but do not provide circuit activity data. In spite of these shortcomings, the DMM is an indispensable diagnostic aid because of its versatility, ease of use, quick setup time, and precise results.

Graphing Multimeter

The digital graphing multimeter (GMM) is a fairly new type of test instrument designed for automotive use. These powerful tools perform all the functions of a top-quality DMM and also plot voltage measurements in a graph over a period of time, figure 2-42. At first glance, the GMM display appears similar to an oscilloscope waveform. However, there are important differences between what is seen on a GMM display and a scope screen.

Like a DMM, a GMM measures and displays voltage, frequency, and pulse width. However, the two instruments sample the signal and generate their screen display in different ways. A GMM has a fast sampling rate and is constantly monitoring the minimum and maximum voltage levels occurring on the circuit. A microprocessor in the tool stores these readings in a buffer until there is enough information to generate a screen display. Based on the measured samples, the GMM internally calculates and plots voltage over time to create a display screen trace that represents circuit conditions. As soon as the screen updates, the buffer clears and the meter immediately returns to sampling and storing signal activity.

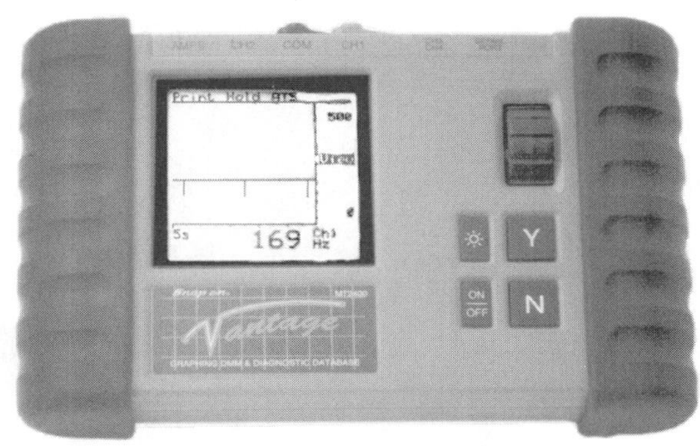

Figure 2-42. A graphing multimeter displays circuit conditions as a graph of voltage over time.

Although the screen update rate of a GMM is fairly slow, it has the capability of capturing fast-occurring glitches because of the way it samples the signal. This feature allows the GMM to display voltage spikes that do not show up on a lab scope trace unless the controls are at ideal settings. A quality GMM also records circuit activity over an extended period of time, a feature that is extremely valuable when troubleshooting intermittent problems or trying to locate the source of a battery draw.

OSCILLOSCOPE

An oscilloscope is a two-dimensional voltmeter that displays measured voltage and time in graph form. For many years, oscilloscopes have been used in the automotive repair industry to test primary and secondary ignition circuits, as well as charging system components. Recently, technicians have begun using small laboratory oscilloscopes, or lab scopes, to troubleshoot delicate electronic circuits. The lab scope is a versatile tool that helps in locating intermittent problems.

Like other test instruments, both analog and digital oscilloscopes are available and both types can be used for automotive applications. The primary difference between an analog and digital scope is the way in which they display a voltage trace. Analog traces display voltage as a continuous sweep, based on the signal at the tip of the probe, figure 2-43. On a digital storage oscilloscope (DSO), a computer generates the

Copyright 2000 by Chek-Chart Publications

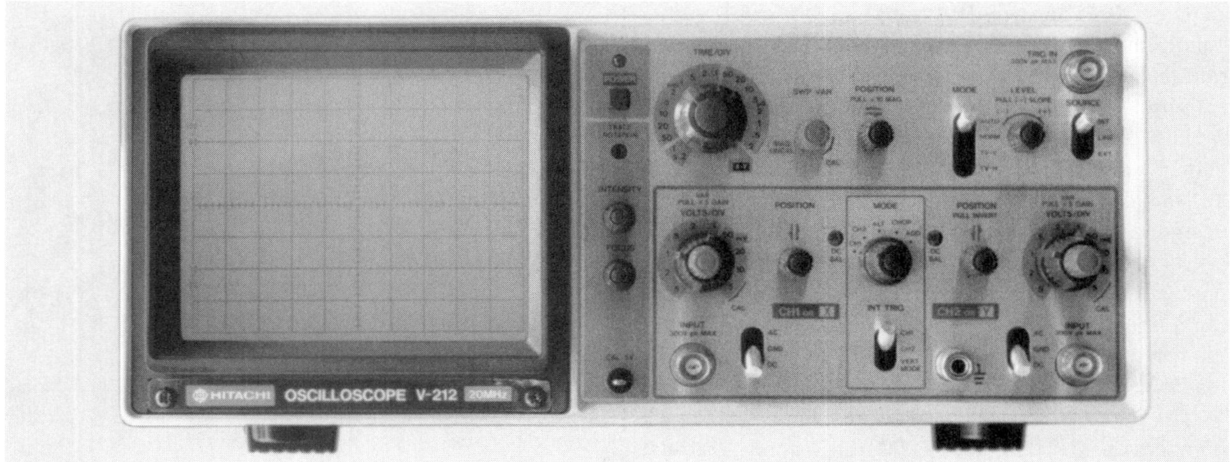

Figure 2-43. Voltage displays as a continuous sweep across the screen of an analog oscilloscope.

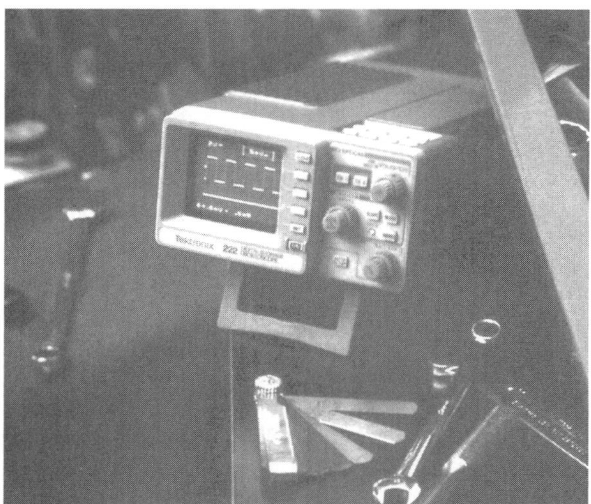

Figure 2-44. The computer of a digital storage oscilloscope generates the screen trace based on circuit sampling.

trace by drawing a line to connect sampling points, figure 2-44. An analog to digital converter within the computer creates the sampling points based on the analog signal input from the probe.

Most test instruments, such as a scan tool, DMM, or GMM, display only the peak, calculated, or average voltage. The update rate of the information being displayed is comparatively slow. A scope displays circuit conditions that result from the operation of a load and update the screen display much faster than any other test instrument. Remember, as a load operates, circuit resistance, or current, or both either increase or decrease. Therefore, voltage must change in response to load operation as well. This changing voltage, commonly referred to as an event, is displayed on the scope screen. However, to capture the event on the screen, the scope must be correctly adjusted for the test circuit signal.

Similar to other digital test instruments, a typical DSO screen updates only about 7 times per second. However, the information a DSO presents provides a very detailed picture of the signal being monitored. Special features, such as min/max capture, data recording, and graphing, are available to overcome the slow screen update rate of a DSO designed for automotive use.

Any lab scope reveals exactly how an electrical charge is moving through a circuit and displays any changes that take place in the measured portion of the circuit. Like other test instruments, a scope has a positive test lead and a negative one. The screen displays the circuit activity occurring between the two test leads. Scope traces are an image of voltage over time and can be used to determine voltage levels, state changes, frequency, and pulse width. The voltage level and the time interval of the display screen are adjustable and must be set correctly to successfully capture an event. Many automotive scopes have automatic presets for common circuit tests.

As with any other automotive test equipment, there is a wide selection of oscilloscopes available. Regardless of who manufactures the scope or how many special features are built into the unit, the basic function of all oscilloscopes remains the same. On all scopes, the screen always displays voltage over time.

AMPERAGE PROBE

The amperage, or amp, probe is an extremely useful tool for diagnosing vehicle electrical problems. An accessory item that is used with a DMM, a GMM, or a lab scope, the amp probe is a self-powered inductive clamp that measures amperage, then converts the

Copyright 2000 by Chek-Chart Publications

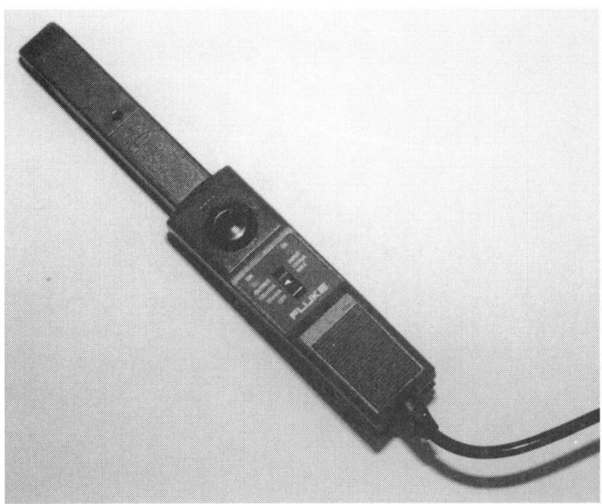

Figure 2-45. An amp probe makes measuring current quick and easy.

measured current into a voltage signal, figure 2-45. Therefore, the voltage displayed on the test instrument represents the amperage, or current, moving through the circuit. Although the probe measures up to 100 amps, its real advantage is that it accurately displays current on a low-amperage circuit.

Most amp probes have two settings. One displays 10 mV per amp of measured current, so a 0.6-volt reading equals 60 amps. The other setting displays 100 mV per amp, so a 0.6-volt reading equals 6 amps. Typically, the tool is powered by a 9-volt, dry-cell battery.

SCAN TOOL

A scan tool is a handheld computer that communicates with the onboard computers of a vehicle. Scan tools are the only diagnostic tool capable of displaying internal electronic control module (ECM) information. Any other electronic test instrument is limited to accessing the external input and output circuits only. A quality scan tool provides:

- Easy diagnostic trouble code (DTC) retrieval
- Access to the ECM data stream
- The ability to record data during a road test
- A means to actuate onboard test procedures.

The information the vehicle communicates to the scan tool is a function of the onboard computer, not the scan tool. Most vehicle manufacturers market scan tools designed specifically for servicing their systems. Aftermarket scan tools are also available from a number of equipment manufacturers, figure 2-46. Interchangeable software cartridges and cable connectors are used to adapt an aftermarket scan tool to different control system designs, figure 2-47.

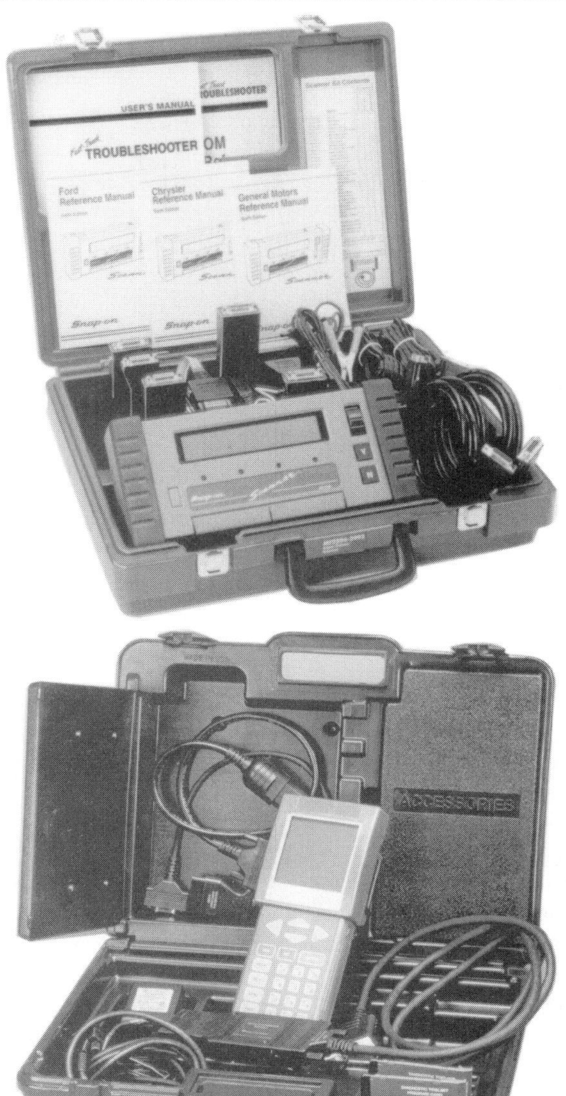

Figure 2-46. A number of scan tools are available from aftermarket manufacturers.

A scan tool is essential for diagnosing problems in the electronic control system. The most recent units provide a great deal of valuable diagnostic information that is difficult, or impossible, to obtain in any other way. Because a scan tool is portable, it can be connected to the vehicle to monitor conditions during a road test. Watching "live" data on the scan tool provides the opportunity to catch an intermittent problem as it happens. One of the most useful features of a scan tool is its ability to record data during a road test and then play it back later for analysis.

Copyright 2000 by Chek-Chart Publications

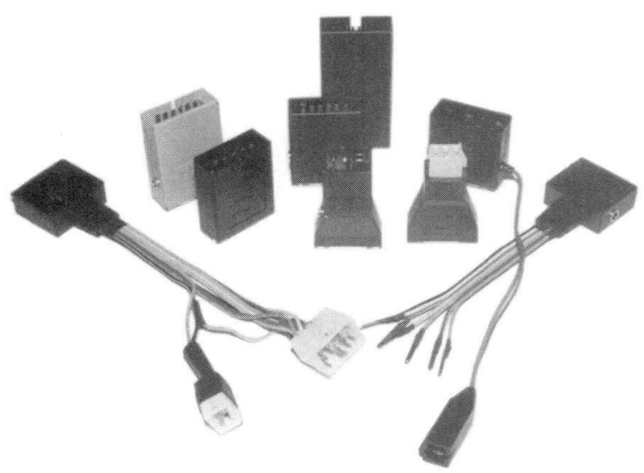

Figure 2-47. An assortment of adapters permit connecting the scan tool to different control systems.

This recording feature allows close scrutiny of sensor and actuator activity at a relaxed pace for a more accurate diagnosis. These data recordings, which are called snapshots, movies, or events, by the various scan tool manufacturers, can either be viewed on the scan tool or downloaded to a personal computer or printer. Scan tool use is detailed in the electronic control system chapter later in this *Shop Manual.*

PROGRAMMED ENGINE ANALYZER

These large, expensive pieces of shop equipment are constructed around a computer that is programmed to identify problems that affect all major engine systems. A number of different analyzers are available from aftermarket equipment manufacturers, such as Snap-on, SPX, and Bear, as well as from the vehicle manufacturers under their own brand name. As with a scan tool, the analyzer must have the correct software for the year, make, and model of the vehicle being serviced. These so-called analytical analyzers vary considerably in what they are capable of doing and how well they do it. While many handle a high percentage of problems quite well, there are still situations that require interpretation of data and additional testing to isolate the source of a problem.

In general, an analyzer "talks" to the technician by asking questions and provides test procedure sequences on a screen. Some models allow the technician to "talk back" using a photocell light pen or keyboard. Once the vehicle identification number (VIN) is entered into the analyzer, the program compares the operational characteristics of the test vehicle to diagnostic logic stored in its memory bank. Then, the analyzer performs a troubleshooting process to identify the system or component that is causing the problem.

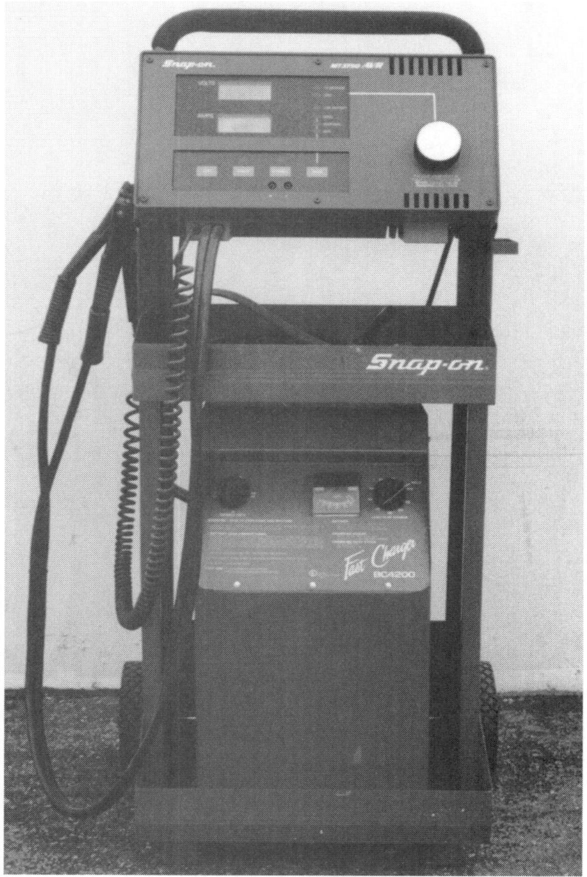

Figure 2-48. A CSB analyzer provides a quick method of checking the high-current circuit devices of a vehicle.

The analyzers are programmed to recognize out-of-specification conditions, pinpoint the malfunctioning component, and determine the necessary adjustment or repair. In addition, most analyzers provide a printout of the test procedures and results.

CHARGING-STARTER-BATTERY ANALYZER

A charging-starter-battery (CSB) analyzer is a common piece of shop equipment designed to quickly check the high-current circuit devices of a vehicle. The instrument contains a resistor, usually a carbon pile, that places the test circuit under load. Test results display on the built-in voltmeter and ammeter, figure 2-48.

Some analyzers feature an adjustable carbon pile, while others use a fixed resistor. Typically, newer units are digital, while older ones have analog gauges. Either type may be used since signal interference is not a concern on the analyzer-tested high-current circuits. Specific test procedures with a CSB analyzer are detailed later in Part Two and Part Three of this *Shop Manual.*

Copyright 2000 by Chek-Chart Publications

3

Battery Service

A weak or dead battery causes problems in all areas of the electrical system. Therefore, a quick check of the battery is always the first step in electrical troubleshooting. The battery must be restored to a full state of charge, then tested prior to diagnosing and testing other electrical system components.

Batteries do not last forever. All batteries eventually wear out through normal use. However, a weak or discharged battery is most often the symptom of a problem elsewhere in the electrical system. The battery must be fully charged in order to locate the source of the system problem. If the battery is not in good condition, service or replace it using the procedures detailed in this chapter. Then, continue testing any other circuits to complete the diagnosis and repair.

Automotive batteries are hazardous and must be handled properly. Batteries contain caustic acid, toxic lead, and are potentially explosive. Always observe safety precautions when handling, servicing, or working near a battery. Used batteries are recycled. Follow the proper disposal procedure and observe all applicable regulations.

BATTERY SAFETY

Treat a battery with respect. If spilled, the sulfuric acid in the battery electrolyte not only quickly damages paint and corrodes metal, it also causes severe skin burns and permanent eye injury. Wear safety glasses and acid-resistant gloves to protect your eyes and hands while handling a battery.

In the event of skin or eye contact with the electrolyte, immediately flush the area with cold water for several minutes. Then apply a neutralizing eyewash or flood the affected area with a solution of baking soda and water. Never rub the eyes or skin because this spreads the acid and the injury. Call for emergency medical assistance immediately.

When a battery is charging or discharging, it releases *highly explosive* hydrogen gas. Hydrogen, which is always present in battery cells, escapes through the battery vents and may form an explosive atmosphere around the battery. An errant spark or flame may ignite this hydrogen gas causing the battery to violently explode. Make sure the work area is well ventilated. Be aware, it is possible for explosive gas formations to remain in or around the battery for several hours after charging.

Charging a battery at too high of a charge rate or attempting to charge a frozen battery may explode the battery. When a battery explodes, the case disintegrates and the adjacent area and any bystanders are showered with acid and case fragments. Often, personal injury and considerable damage to the vehicle

Copyright 2000 by Chek-Chart Publications

and shop equipment result. Follow these instructions to minimize the possibility of explosion:

- Keep sparks, open flame, and smoking materials far away from batteries at all times.
- Operate charging equipment only in a well-ventilated area.
- Never "short" across battery terminals or cable connectors.
- Never connect or disconnect battery charger leads at the battery terminals while the charger is turned on. This always causes a spark.
- Remove wristwatches, rings, and other jewelry before doing any electrical work. This helps to prevent the possibility of arcing and burns.

Batteries are heavy and awkward to handle. If dropped, a battery may smash a foot, spill electrolyte, and/or self-destruct. Always use an insulated lifting strap or battery carrier to make battery handling easier and therefore safer, figure 3-1.

As previously mentioned, passing current through a frozen battery may cause it to rupture or explode. Always check the electrolyte in all cells for signs of freezing before charging or boost-starting a dead battery in cold weather. Battery electrolyte in a fully charged battery freezes between -160° and -90°F (-5° and -68°C). However, if the battery is discharged or partially discharged, the freeze point of the electrolyte is considerably higher. In some instances, the electrolyte may freeze at temperatures as warm as 5°F (-15°C). This means that winter temperatures in many areas are cold enough to freeze a weak battery. If ice or slush is visible, or if the condition and level of the electrolyte cannot be determined, allow the battery to thaw at room temperature before servicing.

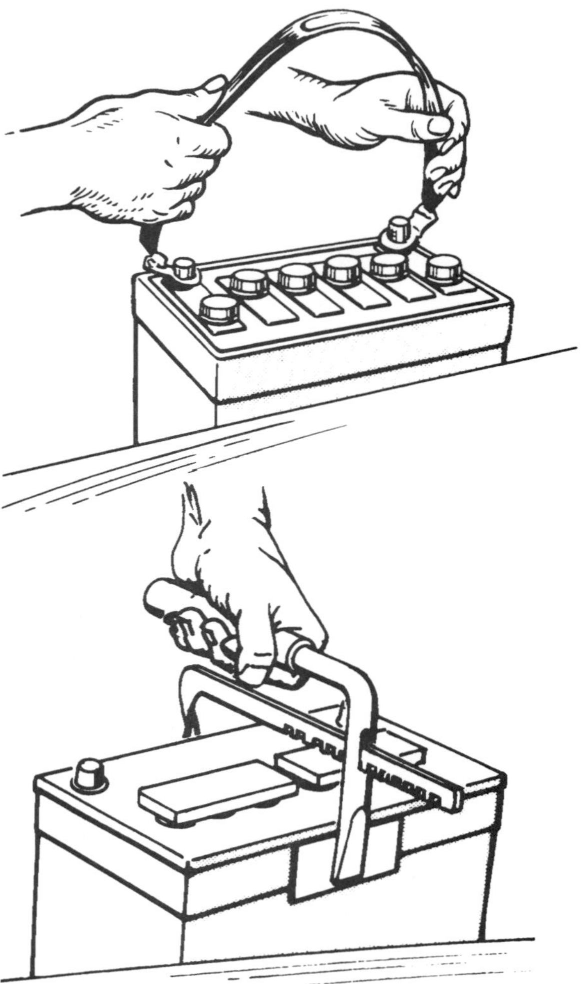

Figure 3-1. Battery carriers provide a convenient, easy, and safe way to handle a battery.

INSPECTION, CLEANING, AND REPLACEMENT

Inspection, cleaning, and replacement are often the only services a battery requires. A few simple tools and supplies are all that are needed to service a typical battery, figure 3-2. Have the following available:

- Baking soda or other neutralizing solution
- Cleaning brushes
- Pliers and wrenches
- Battery terminal puller
- Terminal cleaning tool
- Terminal clamp spreader
- Battery strap or carrier
- Anticorrosion coating or pads.

Battery Inspection

Any electrical service begins with an inspection of the battery. Inspect as follows:

- On a battery with vent caps, check to make sure the electrolyte level is above the tops of the plates or at the indicated level within the cells, figure 3-3. Top off the electrolyte with distilled or mineral-free water as needed.
- Look for accumulated dirt and grease on the battery cover that could draw voltage to ground.
- Check the battery case for cracks, loose terminal posts, a raised top, and other physical damage. Replace the battery if damage is found.
- Check for corrosion around the battery terminal connections and on metal parts of the holddown and battery tray, figure 3-4.

Copyright 2000 by Chek-Chart Publications

Figure 3-2. Simple tools and supplies are all that are needed to service a battery.

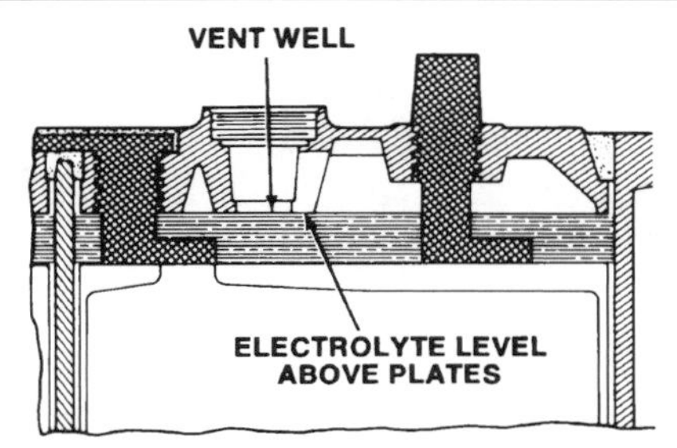

Figure 3-3. The electrolyte level must be above the cover top of the battery plates in each cell.

- Replace missing or damaged cell caps.
- Check the battery cables for broken or corroded wires, worn insulation, and loose or damaged connectors. Replace parts as needed.
- Check the tray and holddown for looseness, damage, and missing parts. Make sure any heat shields are properly installed. Repair or replace as needed.

Battery Cleaning

Always wear gloves and eye protection when servicing batteries. Begin battery cleaning by neutralizing acid corrosion on terminals, connectors, and other metal parts. This is done with a solution of baking soda and water or a commercial neutralizing agent. The solution may be applied with a brush, or stored in a spray bottle and sprayed onto the corroded areas. Once the acid is neutralized, rinse thoroughly with clear water. Be careful to keep corrosion off painted surfaces and rubber parts. Never allow any of the soda

Figure 3-4. Corrosion forms on battery terminals, cable clamps, and metal holddown parts.

solution to enter the battery, as this neutralizes the electrolyte.

If the battery terminals and cable connectors are corroded, remove the cables from the battery for a thorough cleaning. Always disconnect the negative cable first, then the positive cable, from the terminals. This reduces the possibility of creating a spark that results in an explosion. Use a cable puller to remove terminal clamps that are stuck on a post, figure 3-5. Using a screwdriver to pry a terminal off or a hammer to loosen one damages the battery. After disconnecting, neutralize residual corrosion on the cable clamps with a solution of baking soda and water.

If corrosion is heavy, it is a good idea to remove the battery from the engine compartment for a thorough cleaning. This prevents any corrosion from falling into various body and frame crevices where it can react with the metal. Neutralize corrosion formations on terminal clamps and holddown hardware before removing the battery from the vehicle. Disassemble and remove the holddown along with any heat shield components. Then, remove and clean the battery, the battery tray, and the holddown straps with a baking soda and water solution to neutralize the acid, figure 3-6.

Use a stiff-bristled, nonmetallic brush to clean heavy deposits from the terminals, figure 3-7. Use a soft-bristle brush and baking soda solution to neutralize the battery case, then remove dirt and grease with a detergent solution or solvent, figure 3-8. Avoid splashing and do not let the cleaning solution enter the battery vents. Once free of corrosion and dirt, rinse the battery, tray, and holddown parts with fresh water. Dry the clean parts with low-pressure compressed air.

Copyright 2000 by Chek-Chart Publications

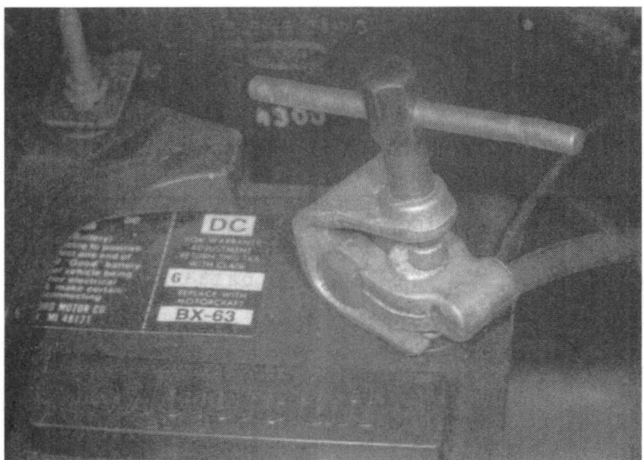

Figure 3-5. A battery connector puller removes the cable without damaging the battery post.

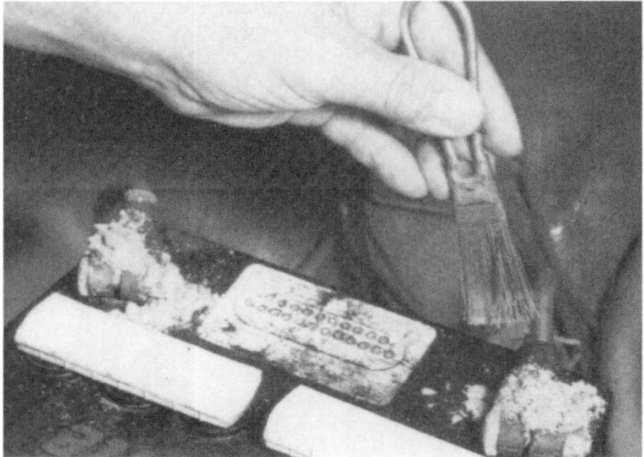

Figure 3-7. Use a stiff-bristled, nonmetallic brush to remove heavy corrosion.

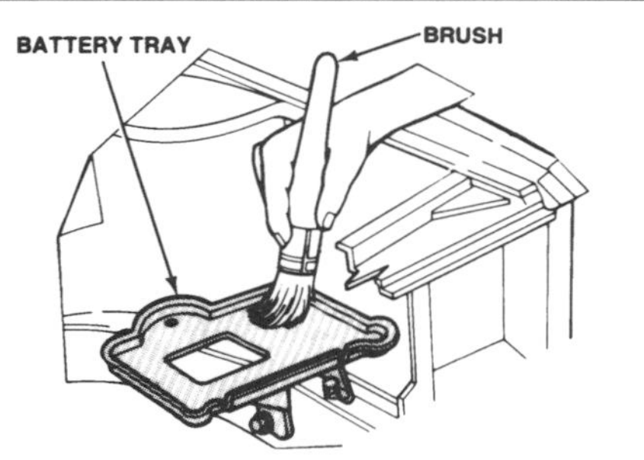

Figure 3-6. Neutralize and clean corrosion and dirt from the battery tray and holddown assembly.

A terminal cleaning tool is used to remove corrosion from the contact surfaces of the battery terminals and the cable clamps. A combination wire brush with internal and external bristles is used for cleaning the battery posts and the inside of the cable clamps on a top-post battery. Similar tools with reamer blades, rather than brushes, are also available. With either type, one end of the tool cleans the inner surface of the cable clamp, figure 3-9. The other end of the tool fits over the battery post and turning it cleans the contact surface, figure 3-10. Use a small, round brush to clean the contact surfaces of the cable end and the bolt on a side-terminal battery, figure 3-11. The same brush is used to clean both the battery terminals and the cable connectors, figure 3-12. With either type of terminal, make sure the contact surfaces are completely clean for a good, low-resistance connection.

Use a battery strap or carrier to lift the battery into the vehicle. Then, secure the battery by assembling the holddown along with any heat shield components. Avoid overtightening the holddown because this damages the battery case. If necessary, open clamp-type cable connectors with a spreading tool so they fit easily onto the battery posts, figure 3-13. Connect the

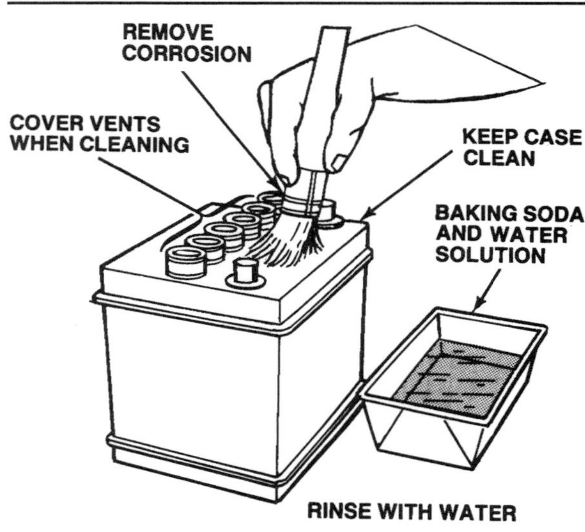

Figure 3-8. Use a solution of baking soda and water to neutralize and clean the battery case.

positive cable to the battery first; then connect the negative cable. To help prevent corrosion, apply a light coat of anticorrosion compound to exposed metal surfaces on the terminals and connectors after installation.

Battery Replacement

Vehicle manufacturers provide battery cold-cranking amperage (CCA) requirements for each model. A replacement battery must meet or exceed these requirements. The replacement battery must properly fit into the vehicle. A group number that appears on the battery label defines its size and other physical characteristics. The Battery Council International (BCI), an association of battery manufacturers, assigns these group numbers. Each BCI group reflects

Copyright 2000 by Chek-Chart Publications

Figure 3-9. Using a battery brush to clean a cable clamp.

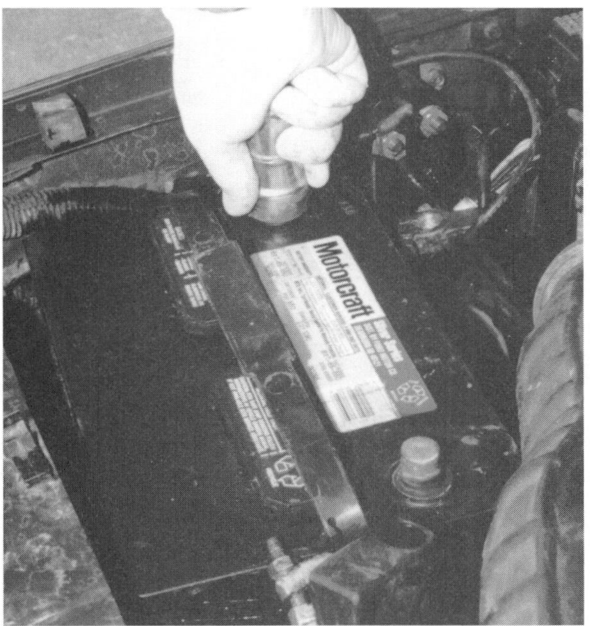

Figure 3-10. Cleaning a post terminal with a battery brush.

maximum dimensions, terminal type and location, cell layout, and case construction of the battery. Make sure the replacement battery is the same group and meets or exceeds the CCA rating of the original. Battery group and CCA specifications are provided in the BCI Replacement Battery Data Book, which is produced by Chek-Chart, figure 3-14.

Once the correct replacement battery is selected, review the safety precautions given earlier in this chapter before installing it. Remember, handle batteries

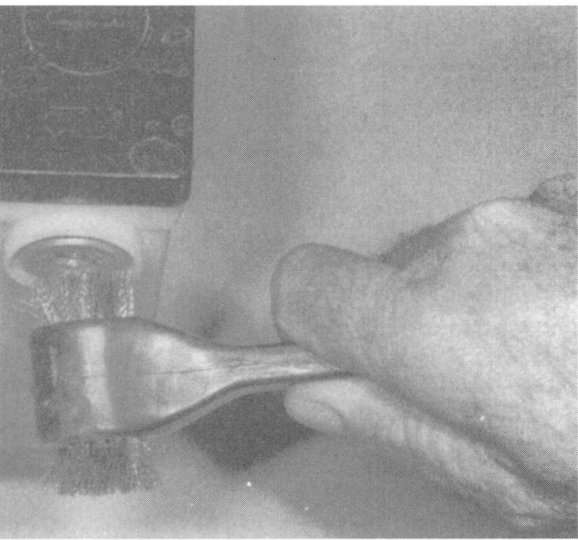

Figure 3-11. A small, round brush works well for cleaning side terminals.

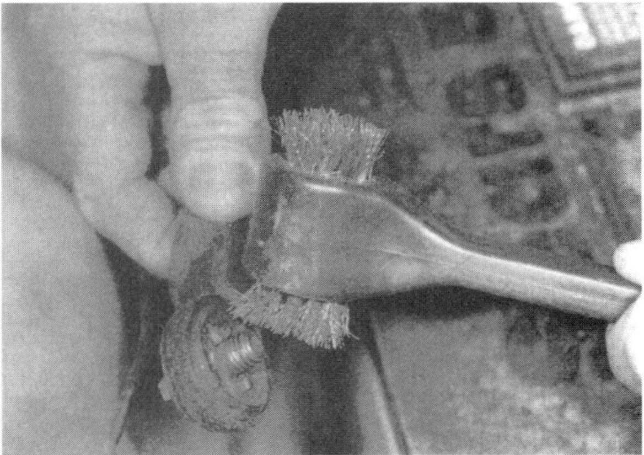

Figure 3-12. Using a brush to clean a side-terminal cable connector.

only with a lifting strap or battery carrier. Be aware that disconnecting the battery erases the operator-programmed and adaptive memory of most onboard computers. Many late-model vehicles have theft-resistant audio systems that become inoperative anytime battery power to the radio is disconnected. A special code must be entered into the radio to reactivate it once the battery is connected. Make sure the customer is aware of this and has the code to activate the system before disconnecting the battery. If the customer does not have the code, he or she must go through a dealer to get the code from the manufacturer. This may involve removing the radio to get the serial number.

Maintaining correct polarity is critical when replacing a battery. Some battery cables are color-coded red for positive and black for negative, but many are not. Simply follow the cable from the

Copyright 2000 by Chek-Chart Publications

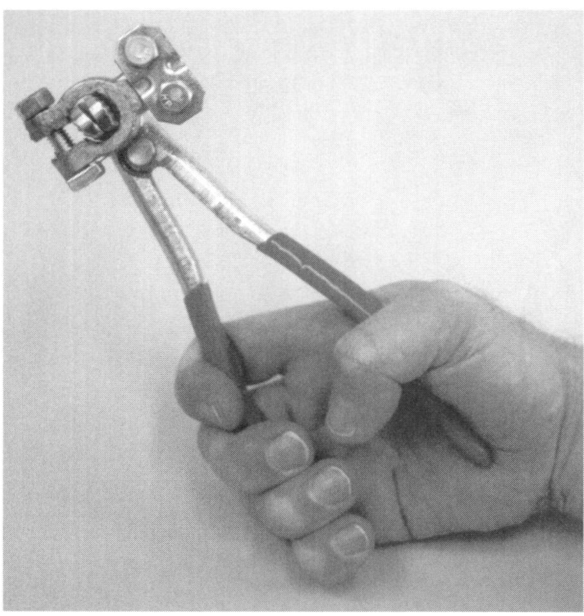

Figure 3-13. A spreading tool opens the cable clamp so it fits easily onto the battery post.

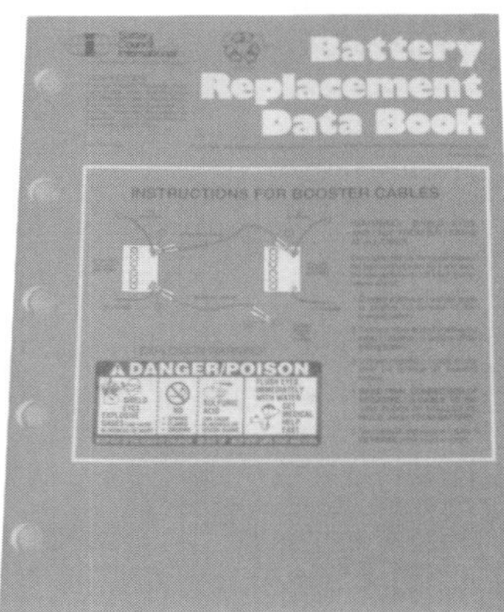

Figure 3-14. Replacement batteries must meet CCA and BCI group specifications for the vehicle.

Figure 3-15. Use the correct-size wrench to loosen the cable clamp.

battery to the first connection to determine polarity. Terminal identification is usually provided by a stamped or raised "POS" or "+" in the battery case beside or on top of the positive terminal post, and "NEG" or "-" beside or on top of the negative terminal post. On a top-post battery, the positive post is always larger in diameter than the negative post. Side-terminal batteries generally use bolts with different thread pitch for the positive and negative terminals. These features help ensure that the correct cable is connected to its corresponding terminal and thus prevent reversed battery polarity from incorrect installation. Reversing polarity causes severe damage to the vehicle electrical system. If there is any question, mark the cables before removing them from the old battery.

To eliminate the chance of creating an arc should a wrench accidentally touch a ground, always disconnect the negative, or ground, cable from the battery first; then remove the positive, or insulated, cable. Loosen the nut on clamp-type connectors using the correct-size wrench, figure 3-15. Locking pliers or battery pliers are used if corrosion has damaged the nut to the point where a wrench no longer fits. Some cables use a spring-type clamp that is loosened with conventional pliers, figure 3-16. Once the fastener is loose, use a puller to remove clamp-type connectors from battery posts. To disconnect a side-terminal battery cable, use the correct size wrench to back the bolt out, figure 3-17.

Loosen and remove the battery holddown and any heat shields that require removal. Many newer batteries have a handle built into the case making it easier to remove and install them, figure 3-18. If the battery does not have a handle, attach a lifting strap or carrier to remove the battery from the vehicle. Inspect and clean the tray, cables, terminals, holddown, and other parts as previously described. If new cables or other parts are needed, install them at this time.

Attach the strap or carrier to the new battery and fit the battery into the tray. Assemble the holddown to secure the battery and install any other parts removed. Clean the terminals of the new battery. If necessary, use a clamp-spreading tool so the cable clamps fit easily onto the posts.

Copyright 2000 by Chek-Chart Publications

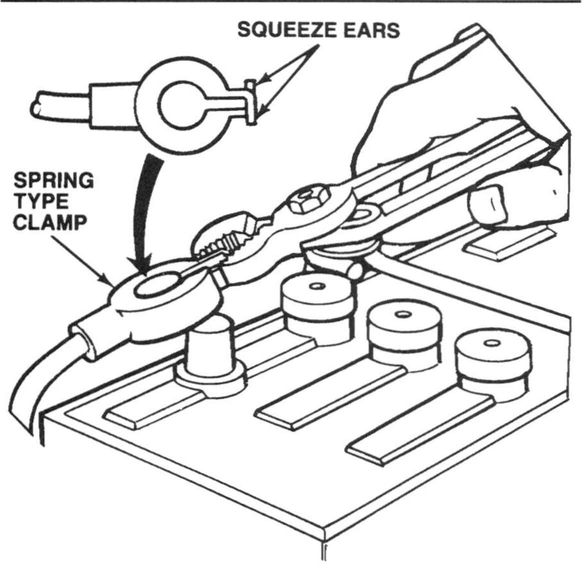

Figure 3-16. A pair of pliers spreads a spring-type clamp to loosen it.

Figure 3-17. Back the bolt out to disconnect a side-terminal battery cable.

Connect the positive cable to the battery first; then connect the negative cable. Install clamp-type connectors flush with or slightly below the tops of the posts, figure 3-19. Avoid overtightening the bolts of side terminal clamps, as this strips the threads on the battery. To help prevent corrosion on top terminal batteries, apply a light coat of nonconductive anticorrosion compound to the terminals and connectors after installation. As an alternative, install anticorrosion pads over the posts before connecting the cables, figure 3-20.

Figure 3-18. Many newer batteries have a lifting handle built into the case.

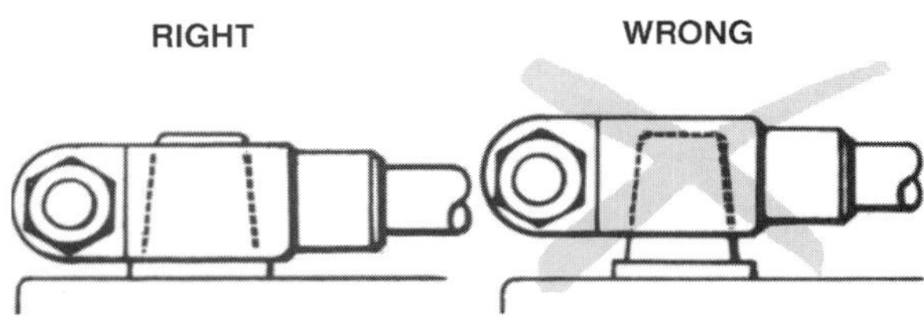

Figure 3-19. The cable clamp must be correctly seated on the battery post.

BATTERY TESTING

State-of-charge and capacity tests are performed to determine the condition of the battery. In addition, a preliminary evaluation on a low-maintenance or maintenance-free battery is required to determine if the battery is capable of accepting a recharge.

State-of-Charge Test

A hydrometer is used to measure the specific gravity of the electrolyte in a vent-cap battery. If the battery is a fully closed, maintenance-free design, use the capacity test or the open-circuit voltage test described later in this chapter to determine its state of charge.

Specific gravity check

Testing the specific gravity of the electrolyte with a hydrometer was a universal method of determining battery condition before the introduction of sealed, maintenance-free batteries. However, the procedure can be used today only on the minority of batteries that are unsealed and have removable filler caps.

Copyright 2000 by Chek-Chart Publications

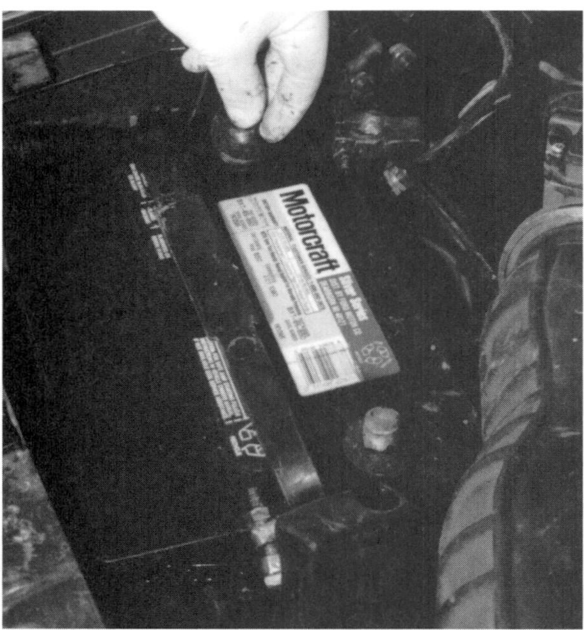

Figure 3-20. Anticorrosion pads help prevent acid deposits from forming on the battery terminals.

When performing a hydrometer test, do not add water to the cells before testing unless the electrolyte level is too low to obtain a sample. If the electrolyte level is low, add distilled water to the correct level in each cell and charge the battery for 5 to 10 minutes before proceeding with the test. When testing in very cold weather or when using a hydrometer with a built-in thermometer, draw electrolyte into the tool several times to normalize the temperature of the hydrometer tube before taking a reading.

To perform a specific gravity test, remove the cell caps and insert the tube of the hydrometer into one of the end cells. Gently draw electrolyte into the hydrometer until the indicator is floating freely without touching the sides or top of the tube, figure 3-21. A false reading results if the float indicator touches the top or sides of the chamber. Hold the hydrometer at eye level and read the specific gravity on the tool scale. After reading, return the electrolyte to the cell from which it was withdrawn. Repeat to sample the electrolyte in each of the cells and note the readings.

The specific gravity of the electrolyte determines the battery state-of-charge, figure 3-22. With an electrolyte temperature of 80°F (27°C), the specific gravity of a fully charged battery is approximately 1.260. A battery should always be recharged when the specific gravity drops below 1.225. Replace the battery if there is a specific gravity variation of more than 50 points (0.050) between cells.

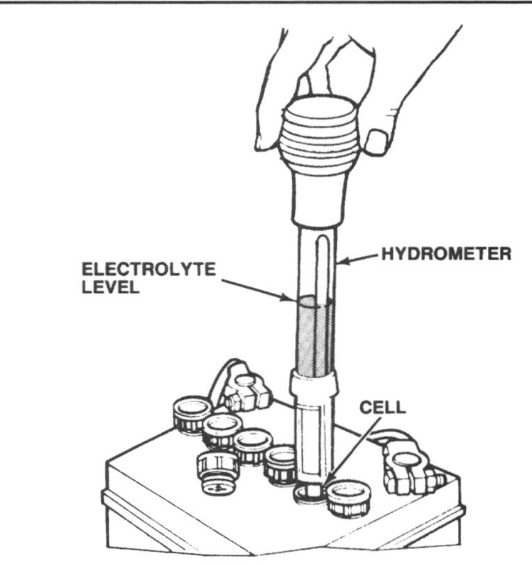

Figure 3-21. Using a hydrometer to measure electrolyte specific gravity.

If the electrolyte temperature is above or below 80°F (27°C), the specific gravity reading must be corrected. Corrections to the measured specific gravity are made by adding or subtracting 4 points (0.004) for each 10°F (5.6°C) that the electrolyte temperature is above or below 80°F (27°C). For example:

- If the electrolyte temperature is 10°F (-12°C) and the hydrometer reading is 1.230, the specific gravity must be corrected for a 70°F (39.2°C) temperature variation. Therefore, subtract 28 points (0.004 x 7 = 0.028) from the indicated reading of 1.230 to get a corrected reading of 1.202, which is the true specific gravity.
- If the electrolyte temperature is 120°F (49°C) and the hydrometer reading is 1.235, the specific gravity must be corrected for a 40°F (22°C) temperature variation. Therefore, add 16 points (0.004 x 4 = 0.016) from the indicated reading of 1.235 to get a corrected reading of 1.251, which is the true specific gravity.

Battery hydrometers often contain a thermometer to make temperature correction quick and easy. The thermometer has a scale that shows the relationship between that temperature and the correction necessary for an accurate specific gravity reading, figure 3-23.

State-of-charge indicators

Sealed maintenance-free batteries are often equipped with a built-in state-of-charge indicator in one cell. This indicator has two functions: It shows whether electrolyte has fallen below a minimum level and also serves as a go/no-go hydrometer. The indicator is a plastic rod inserted in the top of the battery and

Copyright 2000 by Chek-Chart Publications

Hydrometer Specific Gravity Readings	
Specific Gravity	**State of Charge**
1.260-1.280	100 percent
1.230-1.250	75 percent
1.200-1.220	50 percent
1.170-1.190	25 percent
1.140-1.160	Very little useful capacity
1.110-1.130	Discharged

Figure 3-22. Electrolyte specific gravity is a direct indicator of battery state-of-charge.

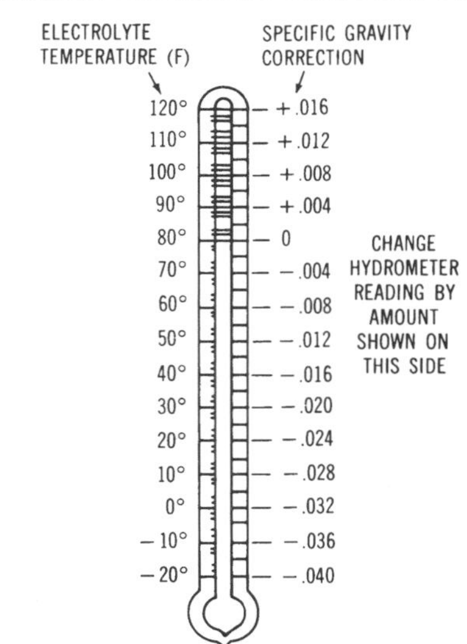

Figure 3-23. Many battery hydrometers have a thermometer with a temperature correction scale.

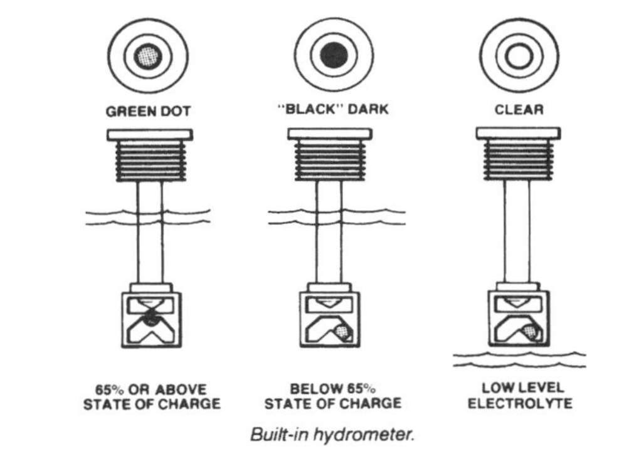

Figure 3-24. The color of a single-ball indicator of a maintenance-free battery reflects electrolyte level and state-of-charge.

extends into the electrolyte. One indicator design uses a single plastic ball, usually colored green, red, or blue, suspended in a cage from the bottom of the rod, figure 3-24. Depending on the specific gravity of the electrolyte, the ball floats or sinks in its cage, changing the appearance of the indicator "eye."

Generally, a green dot in the indicator means the battery has a sufficient charge for testing. If this dot is not visible, the battery must be charged before it is tested. An indicator eye that is black or has no visible color indicates the battery is below a 65-percent state of charge. If the indicator is clear or light yellow, the electrolyte level has fallen below the bottom of the indicator assembly. When the eye is clear or light yellow, lightly tap the top of the indicator to dislodge any gas bubbles that might be giving a false indication of a low electrolyte level. If the color does not change, replace the battery. Never attempt to recharge a battery if the electrolyte level is too low.

Some battery indicators contain both a red and a green ball, which gives the indicator a green, black, red, or yellow appearance, figure 3-25. A red dot means the battery is approaching complete discharge and must be charged before being tested. Complete indicator information is printed on a label attached to the battery. Refer to this label for an accurate interpretation of the built-in indicator readings.

If the built-in indicator shows a sufficient charge, perform a capacity test to determine the condition of the battery.

Open-Circuit Voltage Check

A fully sealed, maintenance-free battery that does not have a state-of-charge indicator may be checked with an open-circuit voltage test instead of using a hydrometer specific gravity test. As a battery charges and discharges, the same internal chemical changes that affect the electrolyte specific gravity also result in minor voltage variations. Because of this, an accurate no-load voltage reading is an indicator of battery state-of-charge.

Open-circuit voltage readings are taken with the battery temperature between 60° and 100°F (16° and 38°C). For accurate results, allow battery voltage to stabilize with no load applied for at least ten minutes before taking readings. It may be necessary to disconnect the negative battery cable to stabilize voltage on vehicles with high parasitic drains. If the battery has just been charged, apply a load for about 15 seconds to remove the surface charge. Then allow voltage to stabilize before measuring.

Once voltage has stabilized, use a digital voltmeter to measure the open-circuit battery voltage. Make sure

Copyright 2000 by Chek-Chart Publications

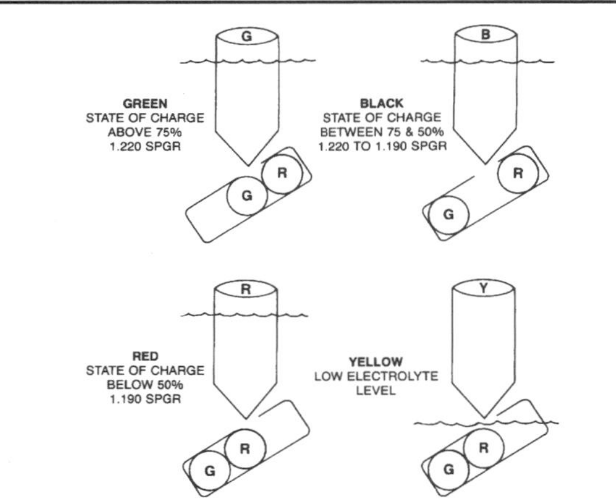

Figure 3-25. Some indicators use two different color balls to display state-of-charge.

all of the vehicle electrical circuits are switched off. Connect the voltmeter to the battery terminals and read voltage to the nearest tenth of a volt, figure 3-26. Open-circuit voltage determines the state-of-charge of the battery, figure 3-27. As a general rule, a battery is ready for capacity testing if readings are 12.4 volts or higher.

Capacity Test

State-of-charge and open-circuit voltage tests cannot determine if a battery has enough current capacity to supply all the needs of a vehicle. All of the previous procedures simply determine if the battery is ready for a capacity test. Never perform a capacity test if any preliminary tests indicate that the battery has less than a 75-percent state-of-charge. Charge the battery as needed, then perform a capacity test to determine the condition of the battery.

A battery capacity, or load, test determines how well a battery can perform when under load. Test results indicate the capacity to supply adequate starting current while maintaining sufficient voltage to effectively operate the ignition system. Tests are performed using either a charging-starter-battery (CSB) analyzer or a battery tester. As explained in Chapter Two of this *Shop Manual*, a CSB analyzer consists of a voltmeter, ammeter, resistance pile, and the cables for connecting it to the vehicle. Some equipment uses a fixed resistor, while others have a variable resistance pile that permits adjusting the load applied to the battery. A battery tester also applies a resistive load to the battery, but results are usually displayed on a scale rather than as ammeter and voltmeter readings, figure 3-28.

A battery may be tested either in or out of the vehicle if it is at or near a full state of charge. The electrolyte temperature should be approximately 80°F

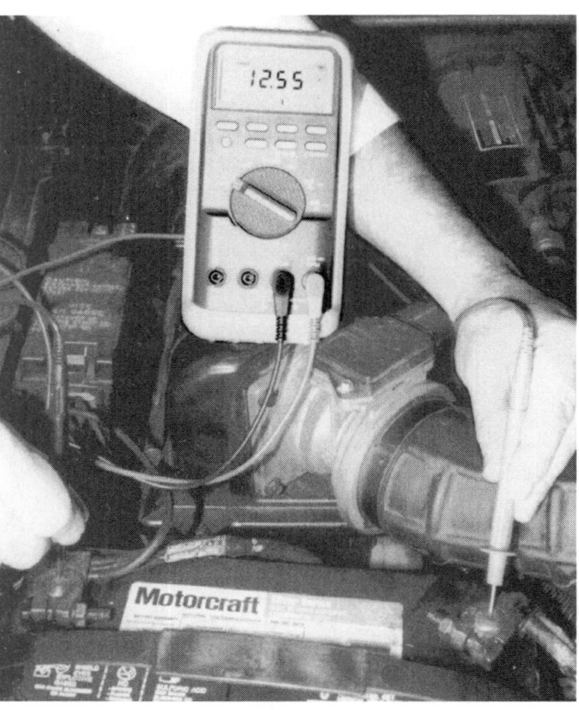

Figure 3-26. Connect a digital voltmeter to read open-circuit battery voltage.

OPEN CIRCUIT VOLTS	STATE OF CHARGE
12.6 or greater	100%
12.4 - 12.6	75 - 100%
12.2 - 12.4	50 - 75%
12.0 - 12.2	25 - 50%
11.7 - 12.0	0 - 25%
11.7 or less	0%

Figure 3-27. Minor changes in the open-circuit battery voltage reflect changes in the state-of-charge.

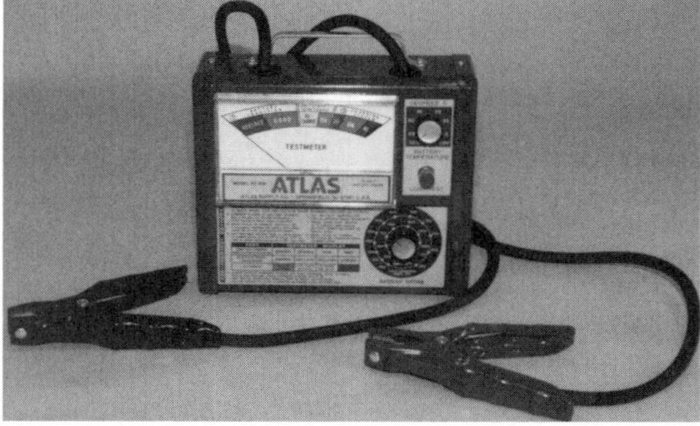

Figure 3-28. A battery tester applies resistance and displays results on a scale.

(27°C) for best results. A cold battery has a considerably lower capacity. Battery testers come in a variety of designs, and exact test procedures vary, so refer to

Copyright 2000 by Chek-Chart Publications

Figure 3-29. Observe correct polarity when connecting the test leads.

the equipment instructions for proper procedures. In general, to load test a battery:

1. Switch the machine off and connect the test leads to the battery. Be sure to observe correct polarity and make certain the test lead clamps make good contact on the battery terminals, figure 3-29. Special adapters are used to connect the test leads to a battery with side terminals, figure 3-30.
2. If the analyzer has a temperature adjustment, select the setting that matches electrolyte temperature. If possible, place a thermometer in one cell to determine the electrolyte temperature. Estimate the temperature on sealed batteries. Be aware, minimum capacity test voltages vary significantly with battery temperature, figure 3-31.
3. Determine the CCA rating of the battery, which should be included on a label attached to the battery.
4. On a tester with a variable resistor, turn the load control knob to draw battery current at a rate equal to one-half the CCA rating of the battery. On a fixed-resistance tester, set the battery size indicator to the appropriate position.
5. Apply and maintain this load for 15 seconds while monitoring the voltmeter or the scale on the tester. Turn off the load control knob immediately after 15 seconds of current draw and note the meter readings. Discontinue loading if voltage drops too low before 15 seconds are up.
6. On a 12-volt battery, voltage should not fall below 9.6 volts after 15 seconds. If voltage is lower, replace the battery.

If load test results are marginal, a 3-minute charge test may help confirm a faulty battery. This procedure is not recommended for some batteries, such as the Delco Freedom. To test, connect a battery charger, set the charge rate to 40 amps, and charge for three minutes. Connect a voltmeter across the battery terminals

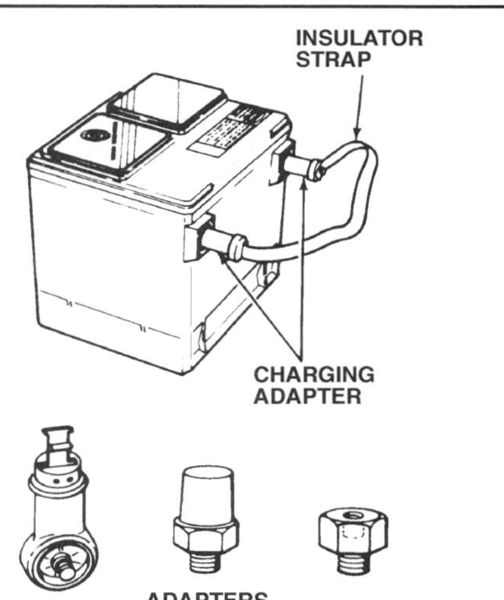

Figure 3-30. Adapters are used for connecting cables to side-terminal batteries.

BATTERY TEMPERATURE °F (°C)	MINIMUM TEST VOLTAGE
70° (21°) or above	9.6 volts
60° (16°)	9.5 volts
50° (10°)	9.4 volts
40° (4°)	9.3 volts
30° (−1°)	9.1 volts
20° (−7°)	8.9 volts
10° (−12°)	8.7 volts
0° (−18°)	8.5 volts

Figure 3-31. Minimum capacity test voltage varies significantly with battery temperature.

to check the charging voltage. If charging voltage exceeds 15.5 volts after three minutes, the battery has failed the test. A battery that passes the 3-minute charge test is able to accept a charge. One that fails is sulfated or severely discharged and must be replaced.

Alternative capacity test

If a battery tester is not available, use the starter motor to load the battery and conduct a capacity test. This test is valid only if the battery is at or near a full state of charge and the starting circuit and starter are known to be in good operating condition. To test:

1. Disable the ignition system to prevent engine startup. Be aware, prolonged engine cranking damages some electronic system components. Refer to instructions from the vehicle manufacturer to properly disable the ignition.
2. Connect a digital voltmeter to read open-circuit battery voltage.

Copyright 2000 by Chek-Chart Publications

OPEN CIRCUIT VOLTAGE	BATTERY SPECIFIC GRAVITY*	STATE OF CHARGE	CHARGING TIME TO FULL CHARGE AT 80° F**					
			at 60 amps	at 50 amps	at 40 amps	at 30 amps	at 20 amps	at 10 amps
12.6	1.265	100%	FULL CHARGE					
12.4	1.225	75%	15 min.	20 min.	27 min.	35 min.	48 min.	90 min.
12.2	1.190	50%	35 min.	45 min.	55 min.	75 min.	95 min.	180 min.
12.0	1.155	25%	50 min.	65 min.	85 min.	115 min.	145 min.	280 min.
11.8	1.120	0%	65 min.	85 min.	110 min.	150 min.	195 min.	370 min.

*Correct for temperature **If colder, it'll take longer

Figure 3-32. Battery charging times vary according to state-of-charge, temperature, and charging rate.

3. Engage the starter and crank the engine continuously for 15 seconds, then take a voltmeter reading.

For accurate results, voltmeter readings must be corrected for battery temperature, figure 3-31. As with a conventional capacity test, voltage on a 12-volt battery should not fall below 9.6 volts after 15 seconds of cranking. However, these alternative test results are not conclusive because a starting system that is drawing too much current has the same effect on voltage as a battery in poor condition.

BATTERY CHARGING

Charging a battery replaces energy that was drained during service restoring the battery to its full capacity. The more discharged the battery has become, the greater the charge required to revive it. There are no shortcuts when charging a battery. A battery is charged by applying a charging current rate in amperes for a period of time in hours. For example, a 20-ampere charging rate for three hours would be a 60-ampere-hour charging input to the battery.

Typically, a battery is either slow charged at a rate of about 3 to 15 amperes, or fast charged at up to 50 amperes. The method used depends on the condition of the battery and the charging equipment available. Fast chargers are the most widely used charging equipment in repair shops. Most fast chargers can be set to charge at a slow rate as well. Slow chargers, or trickle chargers, charge a battery only at a slow rate and are a consumer item designed for home use. A trickle charger is typically left on overnight while the vehicle is not in use since slow charging takes several hours.

Generally, a battery may be charged at any current rate as long as electrolyte gassing and spewing do not occur. Charging current raises the electrolyte temperature in the battery. The higher the charging rate, the greater the increase in electrolyte temperature. Electrolyte temperature must remain below 125°F (52°C) while charging to prevent internal damage. Monitor temperature and reduce the charge rate as needed to keep temperature within range. The length of time a battery must charge at a given rate depends upon the state-of-charge of the battery, figure 3-32. When possible, charge at a slow rate of 5 to 15 amperes for best results.

Whether charging at a slow or a fast rate, begin by checking the electrolyte level. Electrolyte should be about 0.25 inch (6 mm) above the tops of the separator plates in each cell. Charging with the electrolyte level too low damages the battery plates. If the electrolyte level is too high, the electrolyte tends to overflow through the vents as it expands due to the heat generated by charging. The proper electrolyte level is especially important for fast charging. Leave the cell caps in place during charging, but be sure the vent holes are clear. Placing a damp cloth over a battery while it is charging helps prevent hydrogen from escaping. Do not allow the damp cloth to create a short across the battery terminals.

When charging a battery, observe these precautions:

- Charge in a well-ventilated area away from sparks and open flames.
- Be sure the charger is switched off or unplugged before connecting or disconnecting cables at the battery.
- Never attempt to charge a frozen battery because it may explode.
- Always wear suitable eye protection.
- Never fast charge a battery that has failed a 3-minute charge test.
- Never fast charge a battery that is sulfated or has plate or separator damage.
- Monitor electrolyte temperature closely and stop charging or reduce the charge rate if it rises above 125°F (52°C).

Charging Guidelines

Always make sure that the alternating current (ac) power line connected to the charger is delivering full

Copyright 2000 by Chek-Chart Publications

power. Never connect the charger to a heavily loaded circuit. Be aware, an ac voltage drop of 20 percent reduces charger output by up to 40 percent. If an extension cord is necessary, it should be less than 25 feet (8 meters) long and made of at least 14-gauge wire. The charger cord, extension cord, and outlet should all be of the 3-wire grounded type.

A completely discharged battery may not accept a high charging current because the electrolyte is almost pure water and thus a poor conductor of electricity. Since the weak electrolyte solution is highly resistant to the charger current, the amount of current accepted is very low at first. As the battery continues to charge, more sulfuric acid forms and the electrolyte eventually accepts the full charging current. If a load test indicates that the battery is fully discharged, monitor the initial charging rate and terminal voltage carefully. If terminal voltage exceeds 15.5 volts, reduce the charge rate to a setting low enough to keep terminal voltage below 15.5.

Although slow charging at a rate of 5 to 15 amperes produces the best results, it may require 12 to 24 hours to restore the battery to a full charge. Fast charging takes considerably less time, but does not always restore a battery to its full potential. However, a fast charge is adequate for most service situations.

Before connecting the charger, clean any corrosion from the battery terminals to ensure good electrical contact. Charge at the recommended rate. If possible, occasionally check electrolyte specific gravity with a hydrometer during the first stage of charging and every hour as the battery approaches full charge. Unless otherwise specified by the battery manufacturer, a battery is fully charged when all cells are gassing, the specific gravity reading is between 1.260 and 1.280 when corrected for an electrolyte temperature of 80°F (27°C), and hydrometer readings show no increase during three consecutive hourly readings. After charging, wash, neutralize, and dry the top of the battery to remove any acid condensation due to gassing.

Be aware, if the battery terminals are disconnected for cleaning, charging, or for any other reason, power is lost to all of the onboard computer modules of the vehicle. This erases diagnostic trouble code records, as well as the radio and clock settings. Other accessory settings, such as memory for power seats, steering wheels, and mirrors may also be lost. On some systems, the vehicle must be driven to restore the adaptive memory for idle speed and transmission shifting. It is possible to keep these memories alive on some vehicles by providing power into the cigarette lighter or other circuits; follow procedures from the manufacturer.

Specific Gravity Reading	Length of Fast Charge
1.150 or less	Up to 1 hour
1.150 to 1.175	Up to 3/4 hour
1.175 to 1.200	Up to 1/2 hour
1.200 to 1.225	Up to 1/4 hour
Above 1.225	Slow charge only

Figure 3-33. Estimated fast charging time based on specific gravity readings.

Fast-Charging Precautions

Fast charging a battery delivers a much higher charging rate for a shorter period of time. Normally, fast charging a battery takes less than an hour. The equipment operating instructions for charging rate and length of charge should always be followed. However, charge time can generally be estimated based on a preliminary specific gravity reading taken at an electrolyte temperature of 80°F (27°C), figure 3-33.

While charging, check electrolyte temperature frequently and reduce the charging rate if temperature rises above 125°F (52°C). Also monitor voltage across the battery terminals while charging. Lower the charging rate if readings exceed 15.5 volts for a 12-volt battery or 7.75 volts for a 6-volt battery. Maintain the charge rate low enough to keep electrolyte temperature and voltage below the specified maximums. Whenever possible, follow a fast charge with a slow charge to completely restore the battery. Continue charging at a slow rate until a specific gravity reading of 1.260 at an electrolyte temperature of 80°F (27°C) is achieved.

Maintenance-Free Battery Precautions

Maintenance-free batteries require special precautions during charging. A battery with a state-of-charge indicator should not be recharged if the "eye" indicates the electrolyte is below the level of the built-in hydrometer. A high initial charging current heats the electrolyte of a maintenance-free battery and causes it to gas. Since the battery is sealed, venting is minimal and a high charging current can cause internal battery damage or an explosion.

Follow specifications from the manufacturer for charging rate and time when servicing a maintenance-free battery. Monitor battery temperature by touch and check the state-of-charge indicator hourly for the

Copyright 2000 by Chek-Chart Publications

green dot while charging. If the dot is not visible, gently shake the battery and continue charging. Once the green dot appears and remains visible, the battery is charged. Switch the charger off and disconnect it.

BATTERY CABLE SERVICE

Two heavy-gauge cables connect the positive battery terminal to the starter motor and the negative battery terminal to a chassis ground. These cables must be in good condition and securely connected to ensure sufficient current in the circuit. Most battery cable failures occur as a result of corrosion at the battery terminal connection.

The terminal clamps that connect most cables to the battery can be replaced individually, so battery cables seldom require replacement unless physical damage or corrosion has started to deteriorate the cable. Corrosion or other cable damage causes an increase in resistance, which reduces the current-carrying capability of the cable. Too much cable resistance reduces the amount of battery voltage available to the electrical system. Poor starter performance is a common symptom of high cable resistance.

Inspect the battery cables whenever battery services are performed. Look the entire length of the cable over for corrosion, damage, and correct mounting. If the battery terminals are heavily corroded, check the cables carefully. Corrosion attacks the cable strands and works its way down the cable, which causes the insulation to appear swollen, blistered, or cracked. Corrosion on the outside of the cable damages the insulation; neutralize and clean all deposits, figure 3-34.

Sometimes the corroded end of a battery cable can be trimmed off and a new terminal clamp installed. Replacement clamps either bolt or crimp onto the end of the cable and are readily available, figure 3-35. However, there is little slack on the battery cables of many newer vehicles. Typically, if corrosion has traveled more than an inch or so down the cable, the entire cable must be replaced.

In addition to the heavy-gauge wire lead connecting the battery to the starter motor, most positive battery cables have at least one smaller-gauge wire lead coming off the terminal. Commonly called pigtails, these wires provide current to the various vehicle circuits that require battery power with the ignition switched off. These leads generally connect to a fuse block or junction box and may also include a fusible link. Most replacement battery cables have crimp-type connectors on the pigtails for attaching them to the vehicle wiring. Use techniques discussed previously in this *Shop Manual* to trim the original wire to the correct length, strip the insulation, and connect it to the new cable.

Figure 3-34. Corrosion deposits on a cable cause insulation damage.

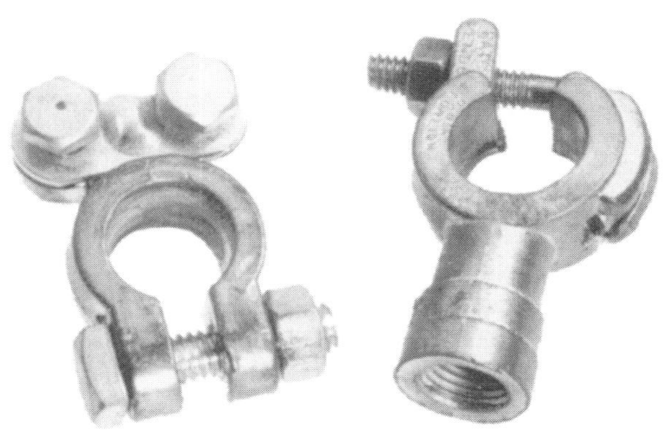

Figure 3-35. Replacement battery cable terminals are readily available.

Some negative battery cables also have a pigtail lead to provide an additional ground path to the vehicle body or frame. Other negative cable designs have a terminal connector somewhere along their length that attaches to the vehicle body, while the end of the cable attaches to the engine. Be sure to inspect all of these leads and connections carefully when servicing the battery cables or terminals.

Copyright 2000 by Chek-Chart Publications

Cable Replacement

To replace the negative, or ground, cable, first disconnect the terminal end from the battery, then disconnect the other end of the cable to remove it. To replace the positive cable, first disconnect the negative cable at the battery. Then, remove the positive cable terminal at the battery and disconnect the opposite end of the cable from the starter solenoid or relay. Disconnect any smaller-gauge leads that supply accessory circuits, then remove the cable from the vehicle. Be sure the replacement cable includes all of the necessary leads, is the same length and gauge as the original, and has the correct terminal ends. Route the new cable along the same path as the old one, making connections in reverse order of removal. Cable connections must be clean, dry, and tight for good continuity. Be sure to install any brackets, clamps, or tie wraps used to secure the original cable in the chassis.

JUMP STARTING

A booster battery and jumper cables are used for jump starting a vehicle with a dead battery. Although jump starting is a simple procedure, many vehicles are damaged each year as a result of incorrect execution. Improper jumper cable connections damage electronic control and charging system components on the disabled vehicle. In addition, connecting jumper cables produces sparks that have the potential of causing a battery explosion. Always wear eye protection when jump starting a vehicle.

Jump starting is performed either with a second vehicle that has a fully charged battery and operating charging system, or with a separate booster battery that is fully charged. With either method, it is extremely important to properly route the jumper cables and make the cable connections in the correct order, figure 3-36. To jump start a disabled vehicle:

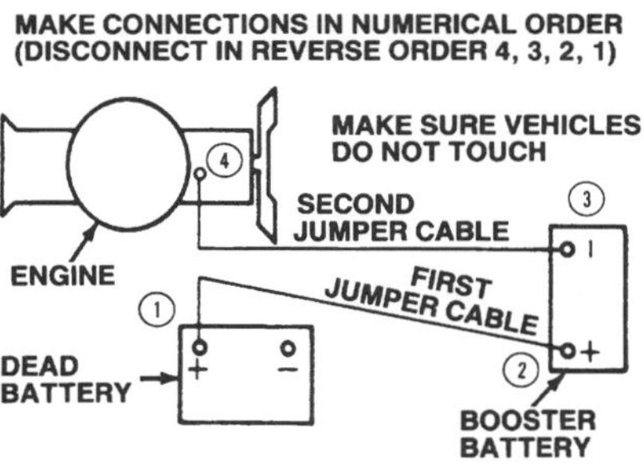

Figure 3-36. Proper cable routing and connection sequence for jump-starting a disabled vehicle.

1. On the disabled vehicle: Switch off the ignition and all electrical accessories, set the parking brake, and place the transmission in either neutral or park.
2. Attach one end of a jumper cable to the positive terminal of the discharged battery, then connect the other end of the same cable to the positive terminal of the booster battery.
3. Connect one end of the other jumper cable to the negative terminal of the booster battery and attach the remaining jumper cable end to a good ground on the engine block of the disabled vehicle. This final cable connection must be at least 12 inches (30 cm) from the discharged battery. Some vehicles have a remote jump start terminal specifically for this purpose.
4. If jump starting from another vehicle, make sure that the two vehicles are not touching each other. Also make sure that the clamps of one cable cannot accidentally contact the clamps of the other cable.
5. Switch on the ignition and attempt to start the disabled vehicle.
6. Once the disabled vehicle starts, remove the cables by disconnecting them in reverse order. First, the engine block connection, then the negative battery terminal connection. Once the negative cable is removed, disconnect and remove the cable linking the two positive battery terminals.

Using a 24-volt booster to quickly spin the starter motor and jump start a vehicle with a dead battery used to be a common practice. Most commercial battery chargers had a setting to provide this boost voltage for jump starting disabled vehicles. However, this 24-volt boost causes immediate, severe, and costly damage to vehicles with electronic control systems. Never use a 24-volt booster charger to jump start a late-model vehicle.

Dual-Battery Vehicles

Heavy-duty trucks and other Diesel engine vehicles require a high cranking current that exceeds what is available from a standard 12-volt automotive battery. Two 12-volt batteries connected in parallel usually provide this additional cranking current. Large trucks may use up to six batteries. It is possible to jump start

Copyright 2000 by Chek-Chart Publications

these dual-battery vehicles by modifying the previous procedure. However, the booster battery must be able to provide the cranking current capacity required by the engine. A low-capacity battery cannot to supply enough current to crank the engine, especially in cold weather.

In a typical dual-battery installation, the positive terminal of the "main" battery connects to the starter motor solenoid or starter relay. The other "auxiliary" battery connects in parallel to the main battery. Always connect the booster battery positive cable to the positive terminal of the "main" battery. This minimizes starting circuit resistance. The negative jumper cable connects the negative terminal of the booster battery to a ground point on the engine of the disabled vehicle, figure 3-37. Make sure the engine ground connection is at least 18 inches (45 cm) from both batteries.

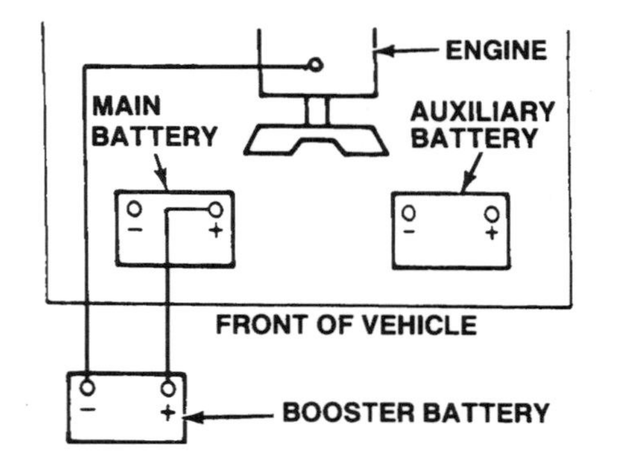

Figure 3-37. Typical dual-battery jump-start cable connection pattern.

Copyright 2000 by Chek-Chart Publications

PART TWO

Charging System Service

Chapter Four
Charging System

Chapter Five
Alternator Overhaul

Copyright 2000 by Chek-Chart Publications

4 Charging System

All modern vehicles use an alternating current (ac) generator to charge the battery and supply the electrical system while the engine is running. Commonly called an alternator, this generator is the heart of the charging system. Wiring circuits connect the alternator to the battery through the ignition switch. These circuits, the alternator, and all the components used to regulate alternator output are included in the charging system.

Part Two of this *Shop Manual* consists of two chapters that detail charging system service. This chapter explains inspection, diagnostic, and test procedures used to isolate the source of a charging system problem. If tests indicate a faulty alternator, the alternator must be removed from the vehicle for repair or replacement. Alternator removal, repair, and installation procedures are discussed in Chapter Five.

INSPECTION, DIAGNOSIS, AND TESTING

Like all electrical circuits, the charging system is subject to four basic electrical failures:

- Short circuits
- Open circuits
- Grounded circuits
- High-resistance circuits.

Short circuits are unwanted connections that allow current to bypass part or all of the circuit. An open circuit occurs when a break in the circuit causes extremely high or infinite resistance. There is no current in a completely open circuit. Grounding a circuit creates an unwanted connection between the insulated, or power, circuit and the ground circuit. This allows current to bypass part or all of the insulated circuit. High circuit resistance is usually the result of either poor or corroded connections or frayed and damaged wires that impede the current.

Always keep safety in mind when working with the charging system. Remember:

- Remove any jewelry and keep hands, hair, and clothing away from moving parts.
- Keep the ignition switched off at all times except when specified during actual test procedures.
- Disconnect the negative battery cable before removing any leads from the alternator.
- The alternator output terminal has battery voltage present all the time while system connections are in place.
- Observe correct polarity when connecting battery cables.
- Disconnect the battery ground cable before charging the battery.
- Never operate an alternator without an external load connected to the unit.

Charging system service begins with a visual inspection.

Copyright 2000 by Chek-Chart Publications

Inspection

In order to operate at peak efficiency, the alternator must be securely mounted, the drive belt must be in good condition and correctly tensioned, belt pulleys must be aligned, the battery connections must be clean and tight, and the battery must have a sufficient state of charge. Visually checking these items, as well as the overall condition of the wiring, is the first step in charging system repair. Look for indicators, such as cracked, swollen, or melted wiring insulation, loose or corroded component mounts and ground connections, and signs of tampering that might create short, open, grounded, and high-resistance circuits. To inspect:

1. Check the battery state of charge and electrolyte level as explained in Chapter Three of this *Shop Manual*. A worn battery causes charging system failure symptoms.
2. Inspect the alternator drive belt for wear or damage, proper tension, and correct pulley alignment, figure 4-1. Adjust and replace belts as needed before conducting system tests. Service procedures are detailed later in this chapter.
3. Inspect all system wiring and connections. Be sure to inspect fusible links and other circuit protection devices for signs of overheating or failure. Make sure multiple plug connectors are latched correctly.
4. Check the alternator mountings for loose or missing fasteners. Also check for worn or damaged bushings where applicable. With a remote voltage regulator, check its mounting as well. Replace or tighten as needed.

If any mechanical repairs are needed to restore the integrity of the charging system, make them now. If charging system failure symptoms persist, continue with a basic diagnosis, then test to isolate the faulty component or circuit.

Basic Diagnosis

Diagnosing charging system problems requires a familiarity with basic system operations. Although there are numerous design variations, all charging systems operate in a similar manner. On any charging system:

- The regulator is energized through the ignition switch.
- The voltage regulator controls current through the alternator field windings.
- The regulator is connected to battery voltage to sense charging voltage.

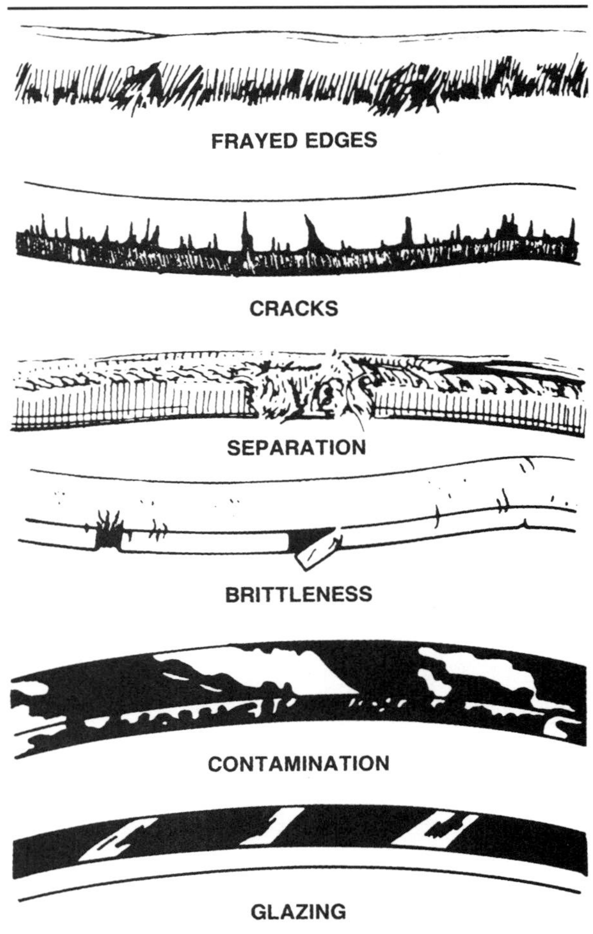

Figure 4-1. Replace any drive belts that are frayed, cracked, separated, brittle, contaminated, glazed, or otherwise damaged.

The regulator may be energized by either system voltage from the ignition switch or a reduced voltage provided by an electronic control module (ECM). Only one volt is needed to initially energize the field circuit. Some systems use the ground circuit of the instrument cluster warning lamp to energize the regulator and field circuit.

With an electronic regulator, the ground side of the alternator field circuit is usually controlled by a pulse-width modulated signal. The regulator varies the pulse width of the signal to adjust the amount of time that the ground circuit is complete. The greater the pulse width, the longer the field circuit is energized. Therefore, alternator output current increases and decreases in direct proportion to the pulse width of the regulator signal.

Electronic voltage regulators may be mounted externally, internally in the alternator, or built into the

Copyright 2000 by Chek-Chart Publications

powertrain control module (PCM). With a PCM controlled regulator, charging system output is adjusted according to the current operating conditions of the vehicle. Typically, these systems vary the alternator load to maintain a smooth idle and good driveability. Some systems do not energize the regulator and field circuit until the engine has started.

A voltage regulator senses charging voltage. When maximum charging voltage is reached, the regulator switches off the field circuit. The regulator switches the field circuit back on whenever the charging voltage level drops below the set point. The regulator must have a good ground for reference.

An original equipment electromechanical regulator uses a set of contact points to vary the voltage on the power side of the field circuit. Spring force and the air gap across the points determines the alternator current output, which is adjustable. Replacement regulators for these older systems are usually a solid state device.

The first tool used in diagnosis is a circuit diagram of the charging system, figure 4-2. The diagram shows how the system operates determines where and how to test the system. Most charging system problems are diagnosed with a charging-starter-battery (CSB) analyzer. Tests may also be conducted using the ammeter, voltmeter, and ohmmeter functions of a digital multimeter (DMM). However, a carbon pile is required to apply a load during some tests. Make an initial diagnosis based on charging system symptoms, figure 4-3.

A good way to quickly evaluate regulator function is to capture the charging voltage trace on a graphing multimeter (GMM) as the engine starts, figure 4-4. The test circuit is fed through the charging system warning lamp on the instrument cluster; therefore, there is no voltage as the trace begins with the ignition switched off. When the ignition is switched on, a 2.8-volt signal energizes the field circuit and turns on the warning lamp. Voltage drops to zero while the starter is cranking, then rises to charging voltage as the engine starts and the warning lamp switches off.

There are three types of charging system problem:

- No charge
- Undercharge
- Overcharge.

No charge or undercharge

If a charging system has a lower than normal charging rate, or is not charging at all, check for:

- Loose or broken drive belts, pulleys, or supporting brackets
- Voltage on the energizing circuit
- Defective diodes or stator windings

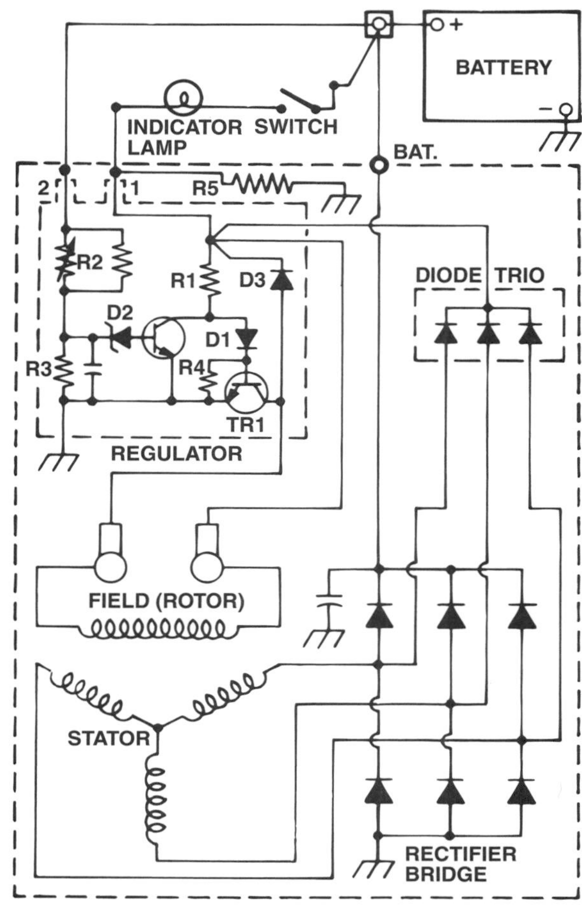

Figure 4-2. Typical solid-state charging system circuit diagram.

- Defective voltage regulator
- High resistance or an open circuit in the wiring connecting the alternator and the battery
- High resistance in the alternator field circuit
- Sulfated battery.

Overcharge

An excessive charging rate can be caused by a:

- Defective voltage regulator—on some systems, the voltage regulator is part of the powertrain control module (PCM); if defective, replace the PCM
- Shorted field wire—shorted to ground in a system with an externally grounded field, or shorted to power in a system with an internally grounded field
- High resistance in the wiring between the battery and main fuse panel—this results in an inaccurate voltage to the field circuit from the ignition switch

Copyright 2000 by Chek-Chart Publications

SYMPTOMS	POSSIBLE CAUSE	REPAIR
• The meter reading flutters • Warning lamp flickers	1. Loose connections in system wiring 2. Loose or worn brushes 3. Defective regulator	1. Repair system wiring 2. Repair or replace alternator 3. Replace regulator
• Ammeter reads discharge • Voltmeter shows low system voltage • Warning lamp stays on • Battery is discharged	1. Faulty alternator drive belt 2. Corroded battery cables 3. Loose system wiring 4. Defective regulator 5. Defective battery 6. Alternator output low	1. Check and adjust belt 2. Replace battery cables 3. Repair system wiring 4. Replace regulator 5. Replace battery 6. Repair or replace alternator
• Ammeter reads charge • Voltmeter shows high system voltage • Battery is overcharged	1. Loose system wiring 2. Poor regulator ground 3. Defective regulator	1. Repair system wiring 2. Tighten regulator ground 3. Replace regulator
• Warning lamp stays on when ignition switch is off	1. Shorted positive diode	1. Repair or replace alternator
• Alternator makes squealing noise	1. Loose or damaged drive belt 2. Worn or defective rotor shaft bearing 3. Defective stator 4. Loose or misaligned pulley	1. Adjust or replace drive belt 2. Repair or replace alternator 3. Repair or replace alternator 4. Adjust pulley
• Alternator makes whining noise	1. Shorted diode	1. Repair or replace alternator

Figure 4-3. Diagnose common charging system problems by symptom.

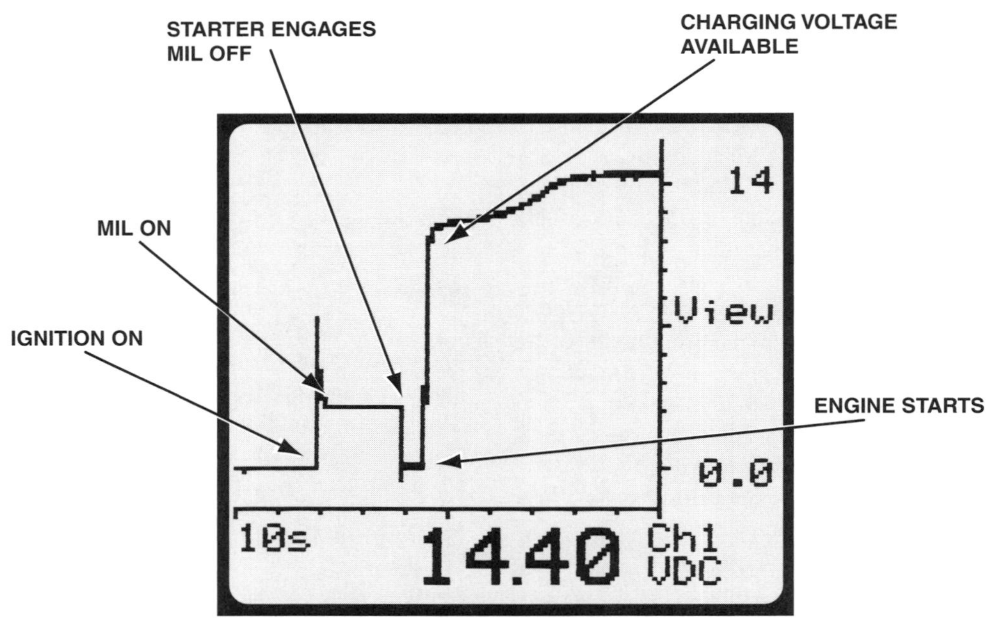

Figure 4-4. The alternator voltage at engine startup, captured on a GMM, shows regulator operation.

- Battery with an internal short that accepts a charge with little resistance
- A faulty component that is drawing excessive current.

Once the type of electrical system failure is determined, the source of the failure is located by conducting systematic tests.

Testing

To check the charging system, several test meter readings are taken to test the alternator. These alternator tests are essentially the same regardless of the vehicle. However, meter test points, specifications, and exact procedures do vary slightly by make and model. This section contains general descriptions of common on-vehicle tests:

Copyright 2000 by Chek-Chart Publications

- System output
- Circuit resistance
- Current output
- Voltage regulator.

Not all manufacturers require all of these tests, and some suggest additional tests. Procedures for testing specific alternators are discussed later in this chapter.

Tests are conducted with the alternator installed in the vehicle and operational. Accurate specifications, whether from the vehicle manufacturer or a reliable aftermarket source, are essential. Comparing test results to specifications is the only way to determine how well the alternator and charging system are performing. If on-vehicle testing determines the alternator must be removed for service, refer to Chapter Five of this *Shop Manual* for procedures.

System output

To measure charging system output, the alternator must be under load. The most efficient way to check system output is with a CSB analyzer. A DMM and an adjustable carbon pile may also be used. As an alternative, load the alternator using vehicle electrical devices, such as the headlights and heater blower fan. Be aware, these alternative test results are not very accurate because the amount of load applied is uncertain.

To test the charging system with a CSB analyzer:

1. Follow the equipment instructions and connect the analyzer to the vehicle.
2. Set the CSB test selector switch to the charging test position.
3. Switch the ignition on without starting the engine and note the ammeter reading. This reading, which is the current required by the ignition and accessory circuits, is not included in the maximum output reading.
4. Start the engine and run it at the specified test speed. Run the engine at 2,000 rpm if no speed specification is given.
5. Adjust the load to obtain the maximum ammeter reading while keeping the system voltage above 12 volts. Note the ammeter reading and remove the load immediately when the voltmeter drops below 12 volts. Always keep load time to a minimum. Make sure the load is completely switched off before proceeding.

Compare the ammeter reading to specifications. If the ammeter reading is not within 10 percent of specifications, continue by checking the alternator. Continue by checking the voltage regulator if output is within 10 percent of specifications.

Alternator check

Check the alternator with the engine running at test speed and the CSB test selector switch set to the charging test position. To test:

1. Apply a load with the CSB analyzer to discharge the battery while monitoring the meters.
2. As system voltage drops, the voltage regulator should increase alternator output.
3. When amperage begins to decrease, note the meter reading and immediately reduce the load. Make sure the load is completely off before continuing.
4. To determine alternator output, add the current required by the ignition system and accessory circuits measured earlier to the highest ammeter reading taken here.

Compare the total to alternator output specifications. Measured output should be within 10 percent of specifications. Readings below specifications indicate field circuit and regulator failures. With an internal regulator, test other alternator input voltages.

Voltage regulator check

With the engine running at the specified test speed, check voltage regulator output with a CSB as follows:

1. Set the test selector switch to the regulator test position.
2. Monitor the voltmeter and allow voltage to stabilize. The amount of time required for the voltage to stop rising varies according to battery state of charge.
3. Once voltage stabilizes, take a meter reading.

Compare the voltmeter reading to specifications. If readings are not within specifications, replace the voltage regulator and retest. If readings are within specifications, continue testing.

Circuit resistance

High circuit resistance reduces charging system performance. Resistance checks are made on both the positive, or insulated, circuit and the negative, or ground, circuit. Areas of high circuit resistance are located by conducting voltage drop tests. Replace or repair any loose or corroded connections or damaged wiring before testing the charging system to prevent inaccurate test results.

Voltage drop readings are taken with the charging system under load, the engine running at a fast idle, and the alternator producing a specific current. Typically, tests are made with the engine running at 1,500 to 1,800 rpm and the alternator supplying 20 amps to the battery.

Copyright 2000 by Chek-Chart Publications

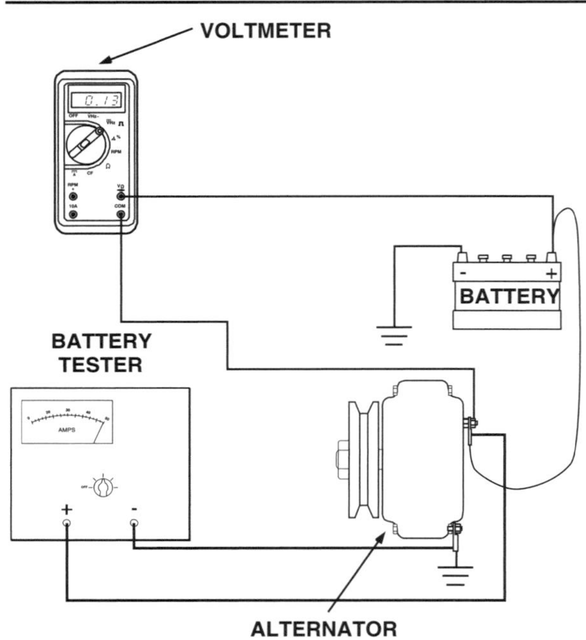

Figure 4-5. Checking voltage drop on the insulated, or positive, alternator circuit.

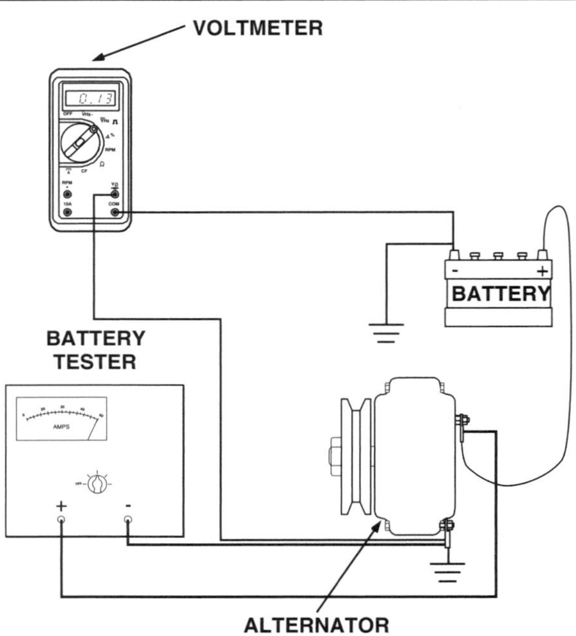

Figure 4-6. Voltage drop should be less than 0.2 volt on the ground, or negative, alternator circuit.

Begin by testing the insulated circuit. To check voltage drop, connect the positive DMM lead to the positive battery terminal and the negative, or common, meter lead to the output, or battery, terminal of the alternator, figure 4-5. Compare readings to specifications. If the voltage drop is higher than specified, move the test connection down the circuit from the alternator to pinpoint the area of high resistance.

Check voltage drop on the ground circuit of the alternator in similar fashion. This ground circuit test is performed only when the alternator has enough output to charge the battery at a 20 amp rate. It is fairly common to see a negative (-) voltage under these conditions. To check, connect the positive DMM lead to the alternator frame and the common meter lead to the negative battery terminal, figure 4-6. If voltage drop is excessively high, install an external ground strap between the alternator housing and the engine. This ground strap is always required when the alternator is mounted in rubber bushings. The normal limit of voltage drop on this circuit is 0.2 volt.

Current output

There are two stages to an alternator current output test. Some manufacturers suggest doing only one stage or the other. Obtain specifications and follow procedures in the service manual for the vehicle being tested. Both test stages are performed using either a CSB analyzer or a voltmeter, ammeter, and adjustable carbon pile. The voltmeter connects between the positive battery terminal and ground. The ammeter installs between the alternator output terminal and the positive battery terminal.

First stage

With the engine running at specified test speed, typically 1,200 rpm, apply a load to the system. Adjust the load to either maintain a steady 14.5-volt charging level or to get the greatest possible ammeter reading. Note the ammeter reading, then immediately reduce the load. Make sure the load is completely removed, then continue testing.

When the load is applied, system voltage drops and causes the regulator to increase the output amperage. Compare the ammeter reading taken to specifications from the manufacturer. This first stage tests the component parts of the charging system for proper operation. If readings are out of specification, perform the second stage test.

Second stage

Perform the second stage test by bypassing the regulator. This test is commonly called full-fielding the alternator because bypassing the voltage regulator supplies maximum output to the field coil. The voltage regulator limits the strength of the magnetic field by changing the current going to the field coil. Therefore, it regulates the alternator voltage output according to the electrical system demand. System

Copyright 2000 by Chek-Chart Publications

voltage can increase to over 16 volts under full-field conditions, which is an unsafe level. Immediately remove the bypass once it is determined if the alternator can produce the required voltage. Never full field the alternator with a dead battery; this causes inaccurate results and may overload and damage the system.

On some systems, the regulator is bypassed to ground to full-field the alternator. On others, power is applied to the regulator to get maximum output. It is important that the right method be used to prevent system damage. Check the service manual for procedures. If the regulator is controlling the ground circuit of the field windings, bypass to ground. If the regulator is controlling the power circuit of the field, apply battery power to full-field the alternator.

With the alternator full-fielded, it is possible for the system voltage to go excessively high. This high voltage can present problems with electronic components. Therefore, full-fielding is often recommended only after it has been determined that the voltage regulator is not properly functioning. This test is used to see if there is an additional problem with the alternator.

To bypass a remotely mounted regulator, use a jumper wire to provide battery voltage or ground the field wire. There are several methods to bypass an internal voltage regulator. Some designs cannot be full-fielded for testing. Follow service manual instructions for the vehicle being serviced.

To test, note the ammeter reading with the engine running at fast idle, usually about 1,200 rpm, the system under load, and the voltage regulator bypassed. Disconnect the bypass and switch off the load immediately after taking readings. Compare the ammeter reading to specifications. If output is within ten percent of specifications, the alternator is working and the voltage regulator may be faulty. If output is below specifications, remove the alternator for further testing.

Voltage regulator

Check the regulated voltage with a voltmeter connected between the alternator output terminal and ground, or between the positive battery terminal and ground. Start and run the engine at a fast idle for several minutes to stabilize the charging system. The amperage charge rate into the battery should be low. If voltage readings are too low, confirm the amperage output at the alternator before condemning the voltage regulator. High alternator amperage output can cause a low voltage reading. If the readings are too high, replace the voltage regulator.

Oscilloscope Testing

An oscilloscope, or scope, offers a quick and effective way to check the voltage output and internal operating condition of the alternator. A digital graphing multimeter (GMM) is used in a similar manner to perform the same tests. On either tool, results display as a graph of voltage over time in what is commonly called a waveform. The waveform illustrates circuit voltage activity between the two leads of the test equipment. It is important to understand how voltage creates, or structures, this waveform in order to use a scope or GMM to diagnose alternator problems.

Waveform structure

The waveform, or trace, that appears on the display screen is a graph of circuit activity with vertical movement indicating voltage and horizontal movement representing time. A flat horizontal line reflects a stable voltage at a constant level. Diagonal lines indicate a linear change as voltage rises or falls at a steady rate. Vertical lines or sharp angles represent sudden voltage changes as a circuit switches off or on, figure 4-7. Some common electronic terminology applies to different aspects of a waveform. All waveforms have rising and falling edges, as well as an amplitude and peak voltage, figure 4-8. In addition, there may be ringing or noise on the waveform.

A waveform is a pulse that occurs whenever work is being done on the circuit. Where this pulse begins depends upon what work the circuit is doing. When a circuit switches to ground to perform work, voltage drops as the load is applied. On a circuit where the power supply switches, work begins as voltage rises. This increasing voltage is called the rising edge of the trace, while decreasing voltage is the falling edge of the waveform.

Rising edge

The rising edge, also known as the positive slope, is the portion of the wave that is making a transition from low to high voltage. A rising edge may vary anywhere from a sudden, vertical rise to a slow, gradual climb. Digital signals instantaneously change state from low to high voltage. This produces a vertical rise in the trace, forming a right angle where it switches on and where it levels off at peak voltage. The span between the low and peak voltage is the rising edge. Analog signal voltage changes are more linear, so the trace angles up as voltage climbs from low to high.

Falling edge

The falling edge, or negative slope, is the section of the waveform that indicates a change of state from high to low voltage. Again, a digital signal switches

Copyright 2000 by Chek-Chart Publications

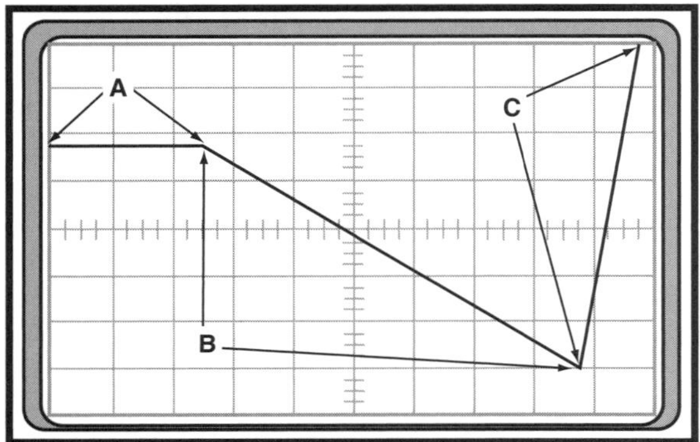

Figure 4-7. A horizontal trace (A) indicates steady voltage, a diagonal line (B) indicates a linear voltage change, and a sharp angle (C) indicates a sudden voltage change.

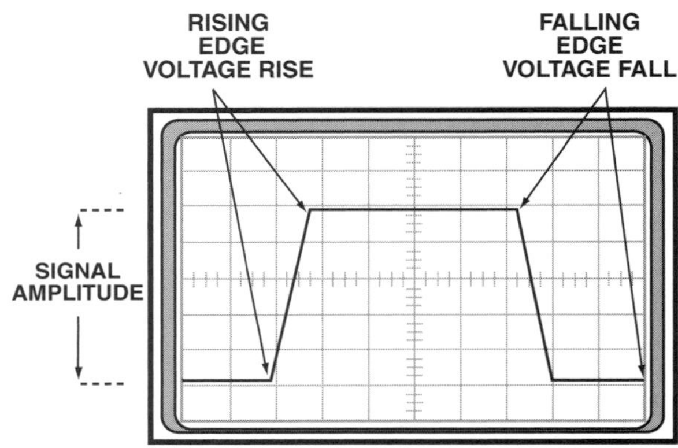

Figure 4-8. The rising edge is increasing voltage, the falling edge is decreasing voltage, and amplitude is the total difference between the highest and lowest voltage.

off immediately, so the falling edge trace plummets straight down. An analog signal drops progressively from high to low voltage, so the trace angles to form the falling edge.

Amplitude

The amplitude of the signal is the difference between the lowest voltage and the highest voltage achieved. Amplitude is the total amount of voltage change on the circuit and does not refer to positive or negative voltage. Therefore, the signal of a device that switches from a low state of negative 2 volts and a high state of positive 2 volts has an amplitude of 4 volts. The amplitude of a signal that switches from zero to 4 volts would also be 4 volts, as would that of a circuit switching from 6 to 10 volts. Always investigate the cause of any deviation that exceeds ten percent of the amplitude.

Peak voltage

Peak voltage is the highest point of a waveform, or the maximum voltage that a signal develops, figure 4-9. Peak voltage is a concern on circuits such as fuel injectors and ignition coils that produce a voltage spike. Before connecting a scope, make sure the controls are set to accommodate the highest expected peak voltage. These spikes, also known as inductive kicks, damage the scope if peak voltage exceeds the setting.

Ringing

Ringing is a term that applies to a series of small oscillations in an analog waveform. These oscillations generally result from excess energy being dissipated by an induction coil in the circuit. Some ringing is considered normal if the test circuit contains a coil. The ringing pattern from a good coil produces oscillations that diminish in amplitude as energy dissipates. Ringing is actually a type of noise or interference.

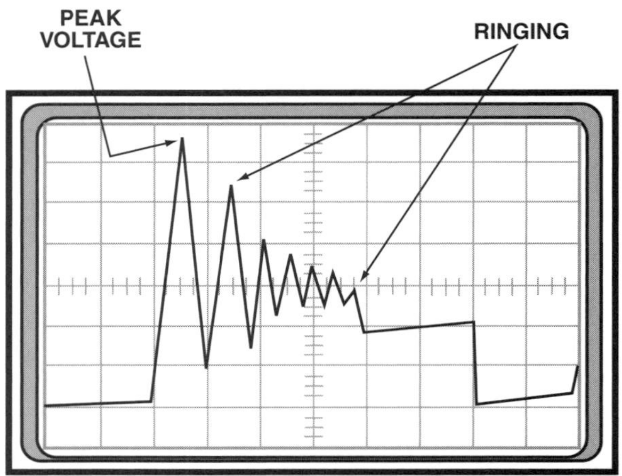

Figure 4-9. Peak voltage is the maximum voltage of a signal, and ringing is a series of oscillations that result from a release of energy.

Noise

Electrical noise is a loosely defined term used to describe abnormal voltage levels on one circuit, resulting from electrical activity on a second circuit or some other external source. The two circuits share no common connection. The interference, or noise, is induced through the insulation of the wiring.

An electromagnetic field is created whenever there is current in a conductor. The strength of the field changes when current stops and starts. Each change in field strength creates an electromagnetic signal that increases in frequency in proportion to the speed of the current changes. When strong enough, this electromagnetic signal may be induced into an adjacent circuit where it disrupts or distorts the signal.

Copyright 2000 by Chek-Chart Publications

A scope is a sensitive instrument. Even low levels of electrical noise interfere with a trace. Shielded test leads eliminate a considerable amount of distortion, but not all of it. In addition, a probe that is not properly shielded acts as an antenna to attract any random signals. The ignition system and charging system, as well as all motors, switches, and relays, naturally produce electrical noise. In fact, it is common to find some noise on almost any wire in the engine compartment. Minor interference can be disregarded, but high noise levels can disrupt input signals and erratically trigger output devices. In general, any noise that produces spikes peaking at 0.5 volt or higher could be a problem on an electronic circuit.

Pattern diagnosis

Alternating current transmits a two-directional signal with voltage constantly shifting from positive to negative. An ac signal forms a sine wave trace on a scope screen when the directional changes are repetitive, figure 4-10. Alternating current is rated in cycles per second. One cycle begins at the baseline, or zero voltage, climbs to a positive peak, drops to a negative peak, then returns to baseline voltage. Specification may be listed in hertz or simply in cycles.

Although the alternator is an ac generator, a sine wave pattern is not displayed on a scope connected to the alternator output circuit. This is because the alternator has a built-in circuit that converts, or rectifies, the ac signal to the dc signal required to charge the battery. Rectifying the signal filters out most of the sine wave pattern and converts negative portions of the signal to a positive voltage. However, portions of the sine wave are displayed if the scope controls are set properly. The automatic ranging function of many GMMs and digital storage oscilloscopes (DSOs) makes capturing the waveform easy. With a conventional lab scope, select a low VOLT/DIV setting and coupling to ac to capture the alternator signal. At these settings, the peak of each pulse, or wave, appears on the scope screen in what is known as a "ripple" pattern, figure 4-11. This ripple, which is voltage above the constant dc output of the alternator, is an ac signal coupled to a dc voltage.

Remember, the alternator voltage trace shown on the scope is the result of wave rectification, so only the peak portion of the signal is visible. Look for equal spacing between pulses and even peak voltages on the waveform, figure 4-12. Any defective alternator diodes or stator windings affect the trace. By studying the trace, which is current moving through the circuit, it is possible to determine what is wrong with the alternator.

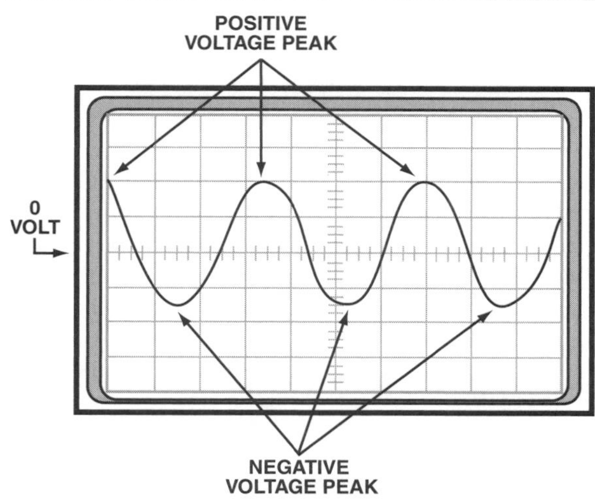

Figure 4-10. Alternating current forms a sine wave as its polarity changes from positive to negative in a regular cycle.

In general, a shorted diode tends to break up the trace and disrupt the pattern, figure 4-13. A shorted diode has a greater effect on the trace than an open diode because it not only reduces the output of its own phase, it also allows current back through the stator to oppose the current of the next phase. When two diodes of the same polarity are shorted, only one phase produces output voltage. In this case, two waves are missing from the trace, figure 4-14.

An open diode disrupts current, so the scope pattern drops out, or spikes down. The trace of an open diode appears to have one pulse missing and the adjacent pulses are compressed, figure 4-15. If two diodes in the same phase are open, two full pulses are missing from the trace, figure 4-16. When two diodes of the same polarity are open, two output phases are affected, figure 4-17. The scope pattern spikes down in a regular pattern when there is one open positive diode and one open negative diode in different phases, figure 4-18.

DRIVE BELT SERVICE

The alternator is driven by a belt which is powered by the engine crankshaft pulley. For the alternator to operate properly, this belt must be in good condition, properly tensioned, and aligned. Drive belt condition must be checked periodically, as belts wear and stretch with age. Most manufacturers recommend checking and adjusting drive belts about every six to twelve months. Replace the belt if needed.

Copyright 2000 by Chek-Chart Publications

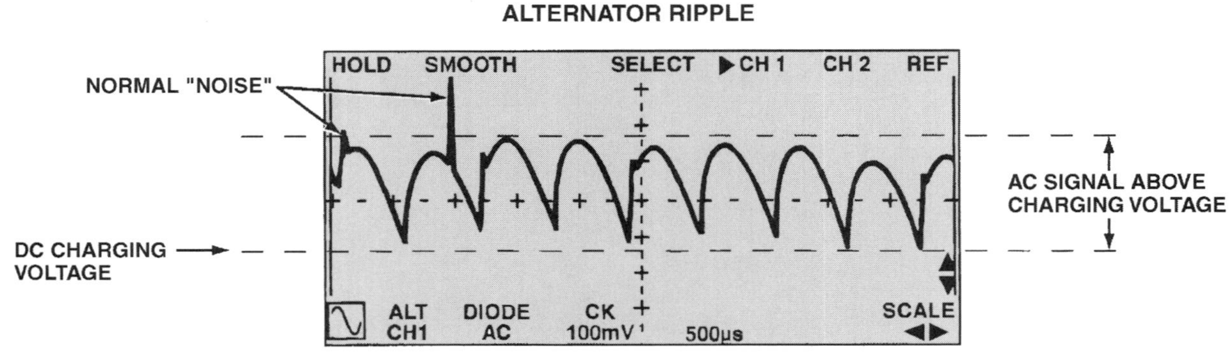

Figure 4-11. An ac ripple pattern shows only the portion of the waveform that is higher than the dc output voltage.

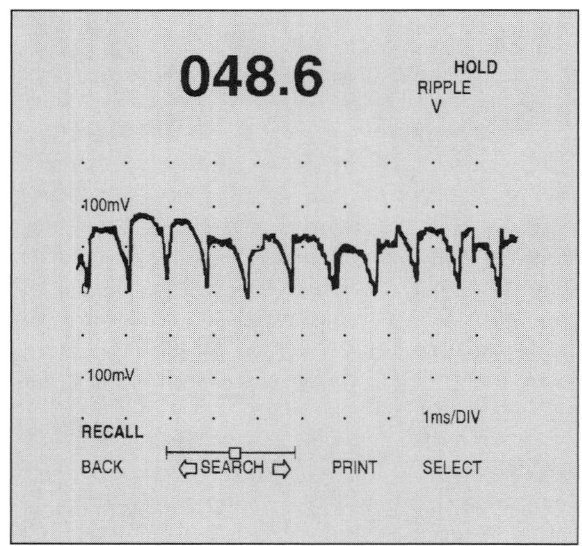

Figure 4-12. Look for a repetitive pattern of evenly spaced, equal height waves on a rectified alternator scope trace.

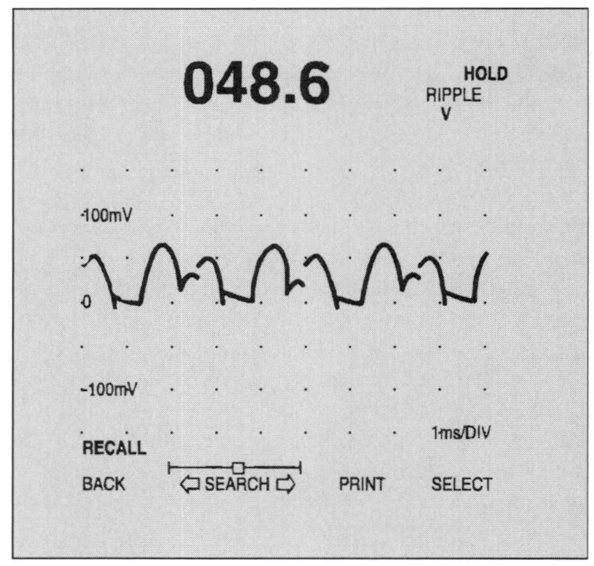

Figure 4-13. A shorted alternator diode breaks up the trace and disrupts the pattern.

Inspection

A damaged drive belt prevents the alternator from operating at full capacity. A low or fluctuating alternator output and noises under the hood are indicators of belt damage. Common types of belt damage include:

- Frayed edges
- Cracks
- Separation
- Brittleness
- Oil contamination
- Glazing.

Inspect the drive belt for these conditions and any other signs of age, wear, and damage. As a precaution, disconnect the negative battery cable before inspecting drive belts. If the vehicle being serviced has an electric cooling fan, disconnect the electrical connector for the fan before checking the belts.

The alternator is driven by one of two types of belt: V-belt or serpentine belt. A V-belt is thick with a V-shaped cross section, while a serpentine belt is flat with a number of small, V-shaped ribs on the underside. Most late-model vehicles use a serpentine belt to drive the alternator, figure 4-19.

The top of a V-belt does not exhibit wear, so twist the belt to inspect the underside and sides. Turn the engine over a few times to examine the full length of the belt. If the sides are shiny and hard, the belt is glazed, which causes the belt to slip on the pulley and eventually crack and fail. Replace the belt.

Copyright 2000 by Chek-Chart Publications

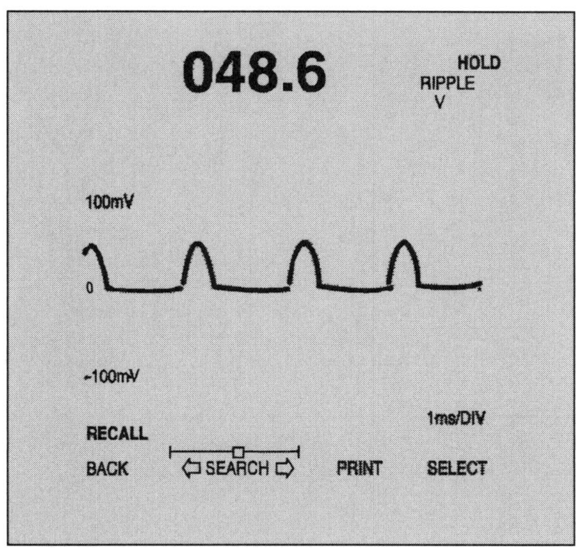

Figure 4-14. Two shorted diodes of the same polarity produce a trace with two missing waves.

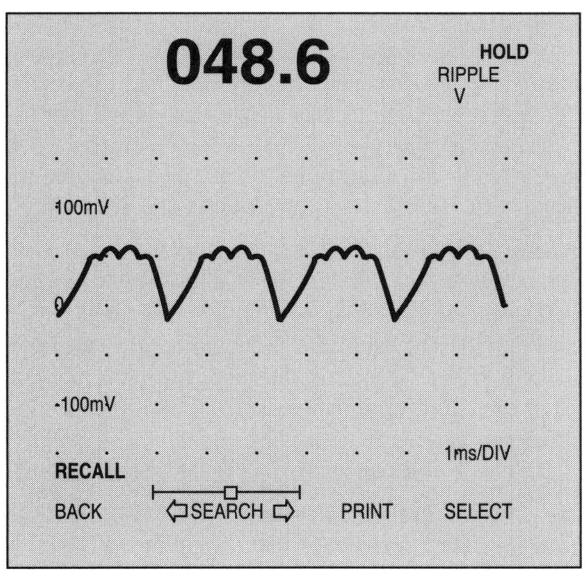

Figure 4-15. With an open diode, the scope pattern drops out, or spikes down.

Check both V-belts and serpentine belts for oil contamination, which breaks down rubber, causing it to crumble. Replace oily belts and repair the source of the oil leak.

Never twist a serpentine belt more than 90 degrees when checking for wear, as this can damage the belt. Inspect a serpentine belt as you would a V-belt, plus check the ribs for cracking. A few random cracks across the belt are normal, but a series of cracks is not.

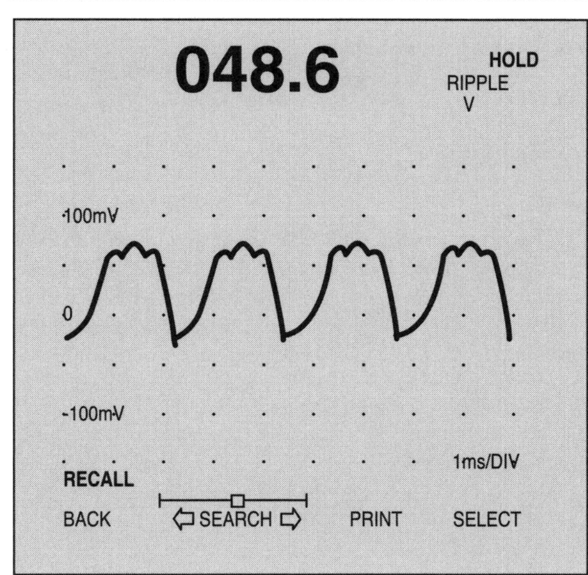

Figure 4-16. Two pulses are missing from the trace if two diodes in the same phase are open.

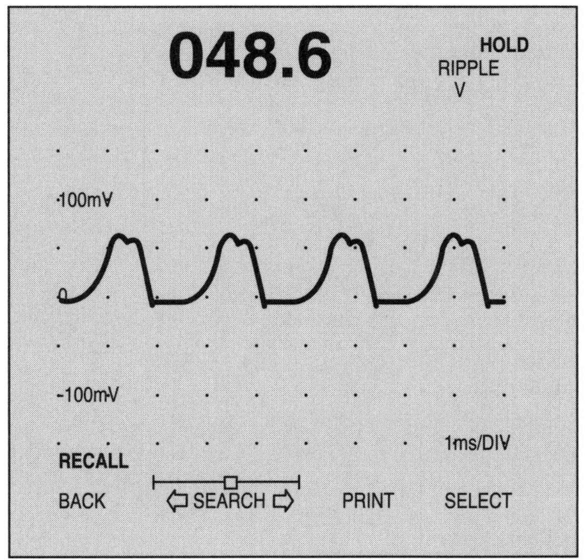

Figure 4-17. The trace drops for two pulses if two diodes of the same polarity are open.

Replace a serpentine belt if there is a series of cracks within an inch (25 mm) of each other.

Inspect the alternator and crankshaft pulleys for signs of wear and damage. A worn pulley allows a V-belt to ride too low in the pulley groove, which causes overheating and premature wear. The top edge of a V-belt should be even with or ride about 1/16 of an inch (2 mm) above the top of the pulley, figure

Copyright 2000 by Chek-Chart Publications

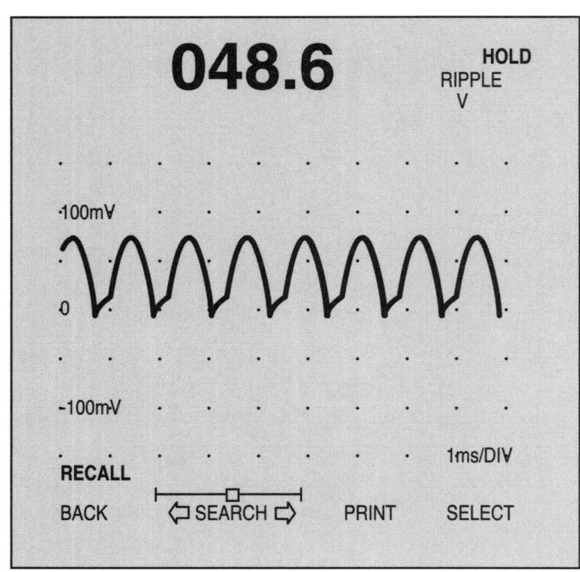

Figure 4-18. With one positive diode and one negative diode open in different phases, the trace spikes down in a regular pattern.

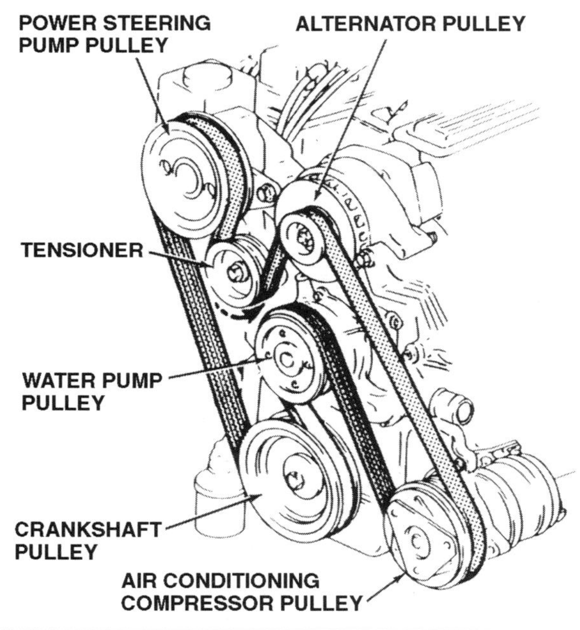

Figure 4-19. A flat, ribbed serpentine belt drives the alternator and other accessories on most late-model vehicles.

4-20. Also, check pulleys for nicks, burrs, and cracks that may accelerate belt wear. Replace the belt if any damage is found.

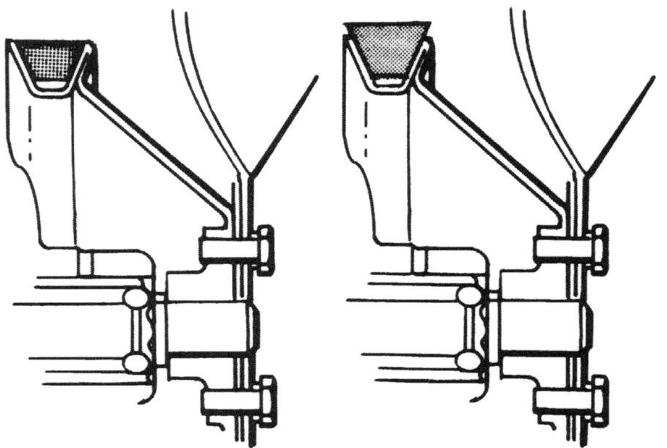

Figure 4-20. A properly fitted V-belt rides flush with or slightly above the top of the pulley grooves.

Tension

A loose drive belt slips under load, and a tight belt wears out quickly and damages bearings. Decreased alternator output and a high-pitched squeal from the engine compartment, especially while under heavy loads, are signs of a slipping alternator drive belt.

Check and adjust belt tension as part of a general inspection and whenever replacing drive belts. Tension specifications vary depending on whether the belts are new or used. Vehicle manufacturers often give two specifications, one for new belts and one for used belts. Be sure to use the correct specification.

Checking

There are two methods of checking belt tension: deflection and tension gauge. Manufacturers often provide specifications for both methods. However, using a tension gauge is the more accurate method. After checking tension, adjust the belt if needed, as described later in this chapter.

To check belt tension using the deflection method:

1. Locate the longest length of drive belt between two pulleys, then find the midpoint of this length.
2. Hold a ruler alongside the belt and use moderate hand pressure to either push or pull on the belt, figure 4-21.
3. Measure the amount of deflection from the normal belt position and compare it to specifications. Typical drive belt deflection falls into the 0.50 to 0.75 inch (13 to 19 mm) range.
4. Adjust belt tension, if needed, using one of the methods described later in this chapter.

Copyright 2000 by Chek-Chart Publications

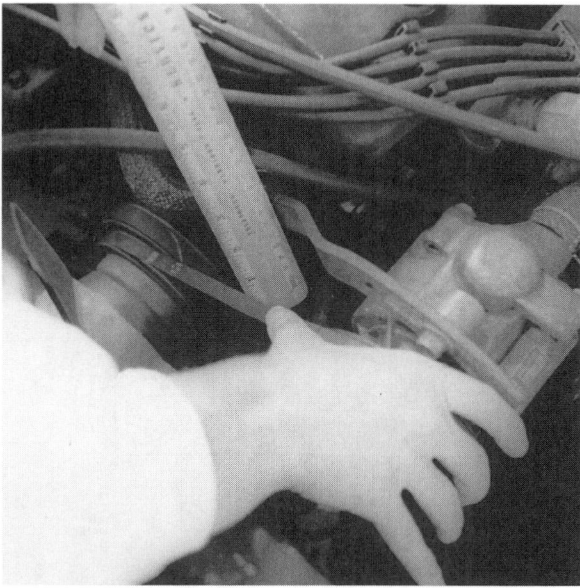

Figure 4-21. Measuring drive belt tension by deflection.

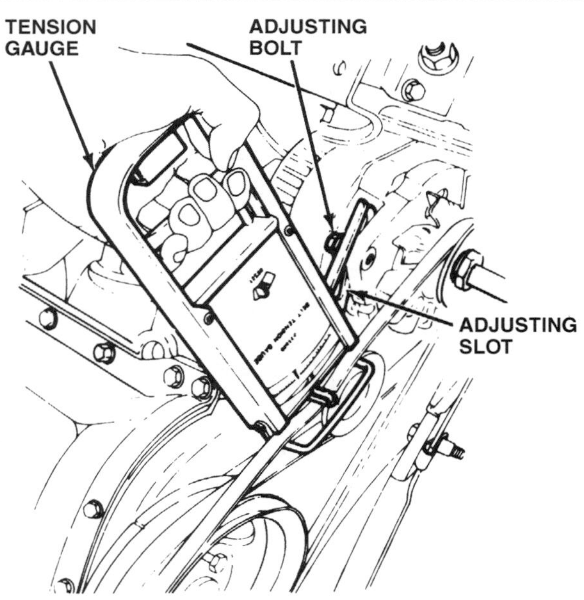

Figure 4-22. Using a gauge is the most accurate way to check belt tension.

To check belt tension using a tension gauge:

1. Locate the longest length of drive belt between two pulleys, and find the midpoint of this length.
2. Place the tension gauge on the drive belt at this point and press the gauge handle, figure 4-22.
3. The gauge measures the pounds of force needed to deflect the belt. Compare the gauge reading to the specifications. New V-belts typically deflect at about 120 to 150 pounds (530 to 670 N) of force, while used belts deflect at about 90 to 120 pounds (400 to 530 N) of force. Serpentine belts normally require more force to deflect. Be aware, a belt is considered used after only a few minutes of operation.
4. Adjust belt tension, if needed, using one of the methods described in the next section.

Serpentine belts usually have a self-adjusting tensioner pulley that maintains proper tension as the belt wears and stretches. However, belt tension should be periodically checked to verify proper operation of the tensioner pulley.

Adjusting

Most alternator V-belts are adjusted by loosening one or more retaining bolts and moving the alternator in an elongated slot in an adjusting bracket, figure 4-23. Some systems that use a pivoting bracket to tension the belt have an adjustment, or draw, bolt, while others do not. Generally, the alternator pivots to adjust

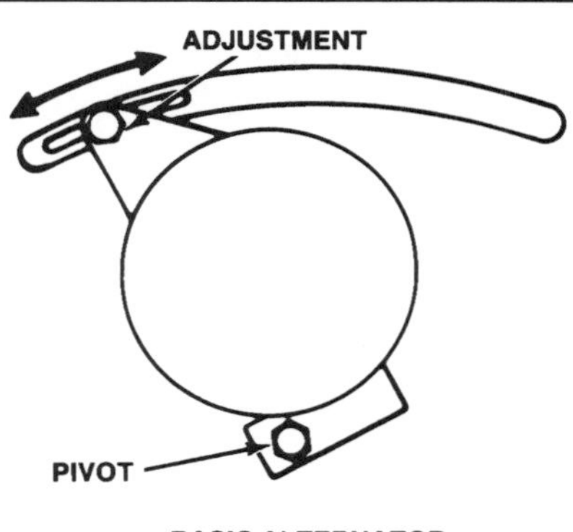

Figure 4-23. Accessories generally have a pivot bolt and an adjusting bolt that are loosened to reposition the assembly.

Copyright 2000 by Chek-Chart Publications

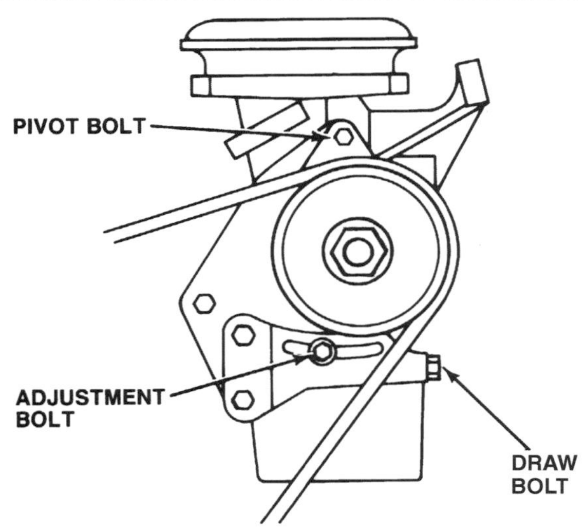

Figure 4-24. Some belt tensioning designs use a draw bolt to reposition the assembly once the pivot and adjustment bolts are loosened.

belt tension, but some other accessory, such as the power steering pump, moves to adjust the belt on some models. Also, one or several bolts hold the alternator in position to maintain correct belt tension, and the assembly usually pivots on a long through bolt. To adjust, locate the pivoting component, then loosen the adjustment bolt, or bolts, and the pivot bolt. If a draw bolt is used, turn it in or out to move the bracket, figure 4-24. If the bracket does not have a draw bolt, use a prybar, screwdriver, or piece of wood to lever the bracket into its new position. Never pry against the alternator itself, as the housing may bend or crack. Tighten the bolts holding the bracket in place and the pivot bolt, then recheck belt tension.

For a serpentine belt with an automatic belt tensioner, belt tension is released by levering the tensioner up or down, figure 4-25. An automatic tensioner generally has either a half-inch square bore to accept a breaker bar for applying leverage or a reinforced area for using a prybar. Simply apply pressure on the breaker bar or prybar to release tension so the belt can be slipped off or on the pulley. Once the belt is in place, release the automatic tensioner and check with a tension gauge.

After adjusting belt tension, regardless of belt or tensioner design, run the engine for fifteen to twenty minutes. Then, recheck tension to make sure it is within the range specified by the manufacturer for a used drive belt.

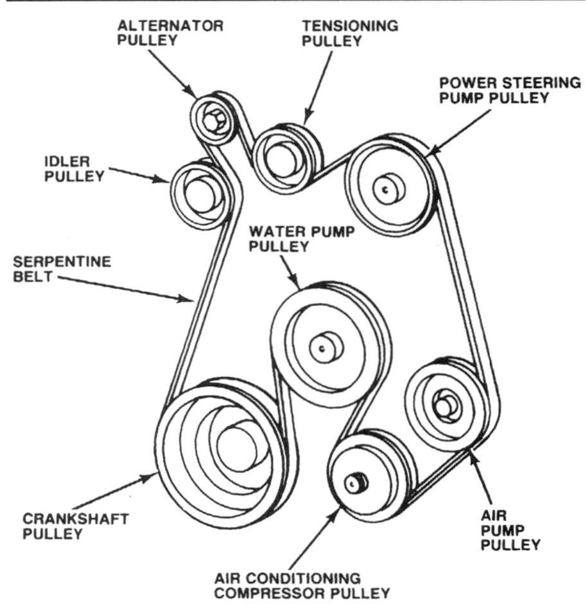

Figure 4-25. Serpentine belt tension is released by levering the tensioning pulley away from the belt.

Replacement

Drive belts are fairly inexpensive and generally easy to replace. However, space in the engine compartment is limited on some vehicles, which makes removing and replacing belts a little more difficult. Use the following procedures to remove a V-belt or serpentine belt, inspect the pulley system for damage, and replace the belt.

V-belt removal

If damage is found when inspecting the belts, the belt or belts must be replaced. Remove a V-belt as follows:

1. Disconnect the negative battery cable. Although this is not absolutely necessary, it is a safety precaution, especially if the vehicle has an electric cooling fan. Also disconnect the electrical connector for the fan.
2. Loosen the pivot and adjustment bolts on the pivoting accessory bracket, figure 4-26.
3. Ease the tension on the belt by pivoting the accessory, loosening the draw bolt, or repositioning the idler pulley. When using leverage, apply pressure against the bracket, not the accessory housing.
4. Once the tension is relieved, slip the belt off of the pulleys.

Copyright 2000 by Chek-Chart Publications

Figure 4-26. Loosen the alternator or pivot and adjustment bolts.

Serpentine belt removal

Before removing a serpentine drive belt, locate a diagram of how it is routed around the accessory pulleys. Belt routing is often illustrated on an underhood decal and is also shown in the service manual. If a belt layout diagram cannot be located, sketch one before removing the belt. Routing a serpentine belt can be confusing if the belt path is not known. Installing a serpentine belt incorrectly may drive accessories in the wrong direction and cause extensive damage. To remove a serpentine belt:

1. Disconnect the negative battery cable. Although this is not absolutely necessary, it is a safety precaution to prevent an electric fan from switching on during the procedure.
2. Most vehicles with serpentine belts use a self-tensioning pulley. Loosen belt tension by levering the pulley away from the belt, figure 4-27.
3. Slip the belt off of the tensioner, then off of the other pulleys.

Checking for causes of belt wear

After removing a drive belt, inspect the pulleys for defects that may contribute to belt wear before installing the new belt. Also look the old belt over for signs of damage that were not noticeable with the belt installed. To inspect:

- Turn each pulley by hand while listening for noise and feeling for roughness. Either condition is an indication of worn bearings. Replace bearings as needed.

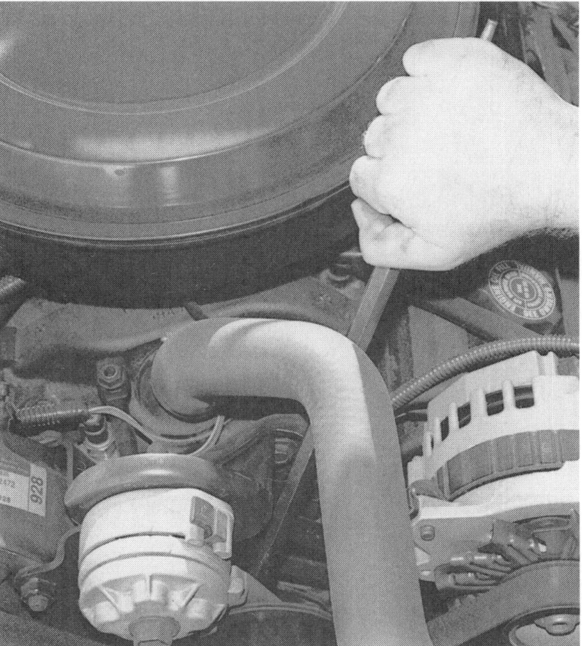

Figure 4-27. Loosen a serpentine belt by levering the tensioner pulley away from the belt.

- Look the belt over for signs of oil, power steering fluid, or other liquids. Locate and repair the source of any fluid leaks that may be contaminating belts.
- Check for dirt and grease embedded in the groves of the pulleys. This is especially important for serpentine belt systems where belt ribs ride in shallow grooves, figure 4-28. Use a wire brush to clean the pulleys if needed.
- Check the belt contact areas of the pulleys for chips, nicks, or cracks that may damage the belt. Replace pulleys if needed.
- Check pulley alignment to make sure they mount squarely on the driveshafts. Also, spin each pulley to make sure it turns true and does not wobble or appear out-of-round.
- Make sure the pulleys line up with each other, figure 4-29. The belt must lie flat as it runs along the pulleys. This is especially true for a serpentine, where even a slight deviation in pulley alignment greatly accelerates belt wear.

Drive belt installation

Use the correct size and type of belt, as recommended by the vehicle manufacturer, when replacing a damaged drive belt. To install a new drive belt:

1. Route the belt over the accessory pulleys. With a serpentine belt, refer to the routing diagram to make sure it is correctly installed.

Copyright 2000 by Chek-Chart Publications

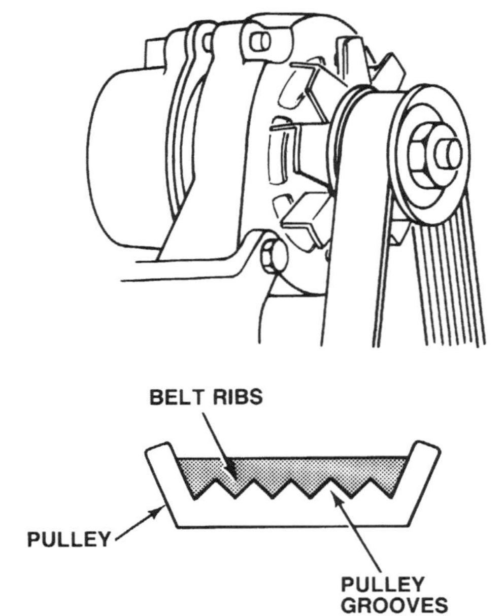

Figure 4-28. Serpentine belt pulleys must be free of dirt and grease, which can become embedded in the pulley grooves.

2. If the belt uses a self-tensioning pulley, route the belt around all of the pulleys except the tensioner first. Then lever the tensioning pulley forward, slip the belt onto the pulley, and slowly release the self-tensioning pulley.
3. If the belt system uses an idler pulley or pivoting accessory bracket, move the idler pulley or accessory bracket in as far as possible so the belt can slip over the pulleys. Once the belt is in place, use leverage or the draw bolt to reposition the bracket and tension the belt. Apply leverage to the bracket, not the accessory housing, to avoid damage. Tighten the securing bolts and verify that belt tension is within specifications for a new belt.
4. Reconnect the negative battery cable.
5. Start and run the engine for about ten to fifteen minutes. Then, shut the engine off and check belt tension once again. Adjust the drive belt tension if it is not within the specified range for a used belt.

VOLTAGE REGULATOR SERVICE

Electromechanical and most solid-state regulators can be tested as described above. Different procedures are used to test electronic regulators. On most electronic regulators, the field current switches on and off at a fixed frequency, typically about 400 Hz. Alternator output voltage is determined by the duty cycle, or proportion of on-time to off-time, of the field current signal. Direct testing of the voltage regulating circuitry on a computerized system is unnecessary unless the onboard diagnostics system detects a charging system problem and stores a diagnostic trouble code (DTC) in memory.

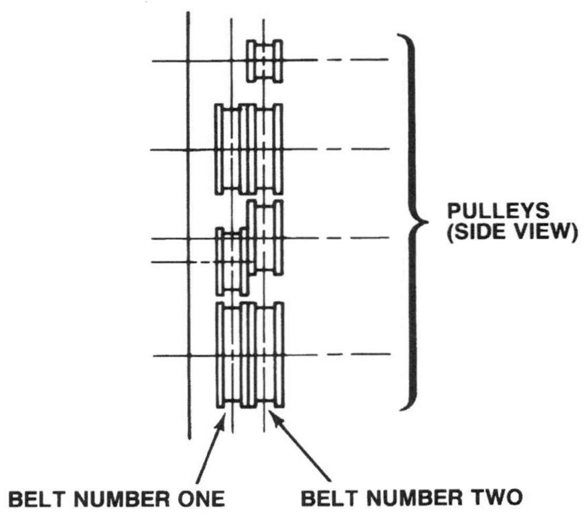

Figure 4-29. Pulleys must be installed correctly on their driveshafts so that they line up with each other.

Size, shape, and mounting position vary among regulators. Some regulators mount inside the alternator housing and include the brush holder. Others attach on the outside of the alternator end frame, while still others are remotely mounted away from the alternator, figure 4-30.

Replacing an external voltage regulator consists of unplugging the electrical connector and removing one or more fasteners. Integral regulator replacement may require partial disassembly of the alternator. Computerized regulator replacement involves installing a new powertrain control module (PCM).

TESTING SPECIFIC ALTERNATORS

This section contains detailed testing procedures as recommended by the manufacturer for a number of commonly used alternators. If needed, refer to the *Classroom Manual* to determine what type of alternator is used on the vehicle being serviced.

Delco-Remy SI Series

A circuit resistance test and a current output test are recommended for Delco-Remy 10-SI, 12-SI, 15-SI, and 27-SI alternators.

Copyright 2000 by Chek-Chart Publications

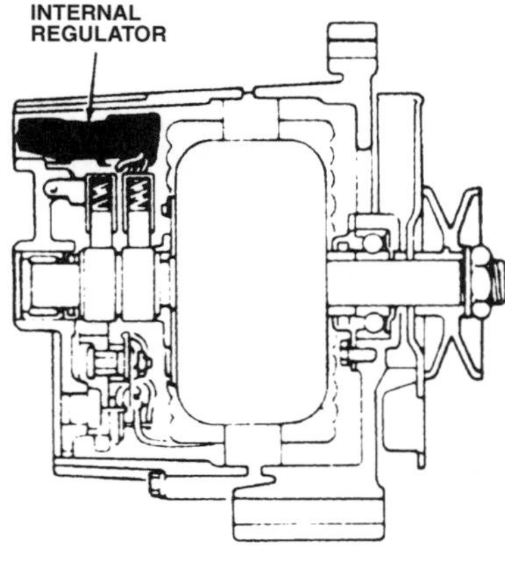

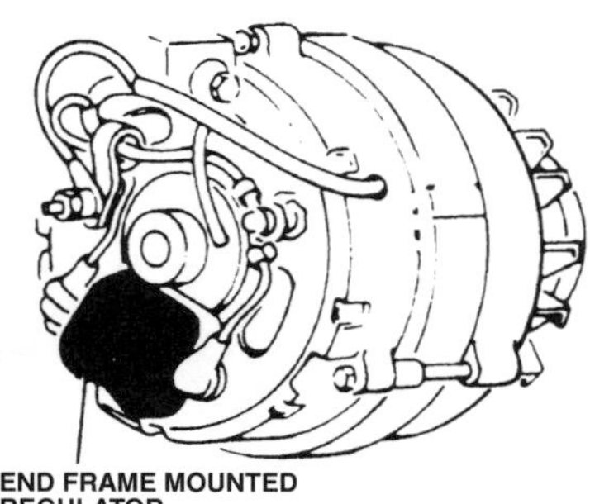

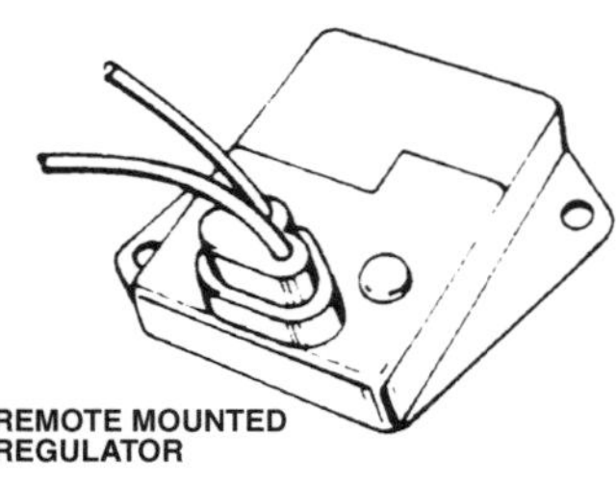

Figure 4-30. The voltage regulator may be inside the alternator, attached to the alternator end frame, or remotely mounted.

Circuit resistance test

Check circuit resistance by taking available voltage readings with the ignition switched on and the engine not running. Connect the negative, or common, voltmeter lead to the negative battery cable or a good chassis ground. Connect the positive meter lead to check for available voltage at:

- The battery terminal at the alternator
- Terminal "1" at the alternator
- Terminal "2" at the alternator.

Battery voltage should be available at all three points with the key on and engine off, figure 4-31. A zero voltage reading at any of these test points indicates an open circuit between the test point and the battery. Locate and repair any open circuits, then retest. Voltage at terminal "2" should be low with the ignition on and the engine off, and should be at charging voltage with the engine running. Suspect a faulty diode trio if engine running readings are below 9 volts, and an open positive diode if readings are 16 volts or higher. Remove the alternator for further testing.

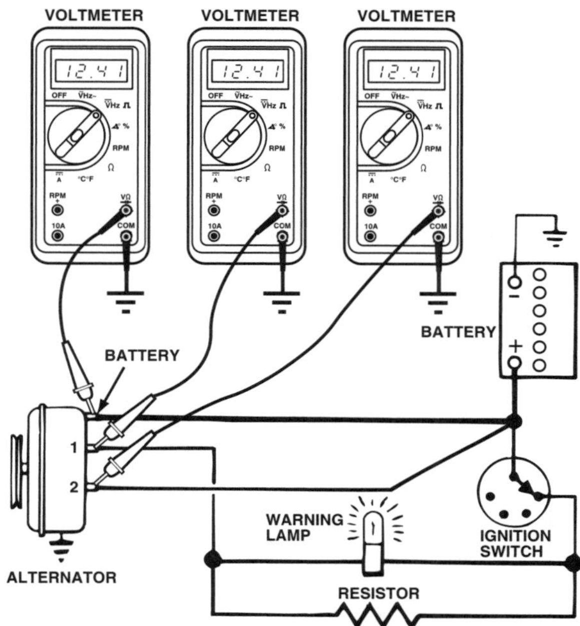

Figure 4-31. Take three available voltage readings on a Delco SI-series alternator to check circuit resistance.

Current output test

The current output test is performed with a CSB analyzer or an ammeter and carbon pile. Connect the equipment and test as follows:

1. Start and run the engine at moderate speed.
2. Switch on the headlights, heater fan, and other accessories.
3. Apply a load to the battery to obtain the maximum possible ammeter reading, figure 4-32. Note the amperage and remove the load.
4. Compare the meter reading to specifications. If the reading is within ten percent of specifications, both the alternator and the regulator are operating properly. Continue testing if the reading is below specification.
5. Insert a small screwdriver blade into the test hole on the back of the alternator to a depth of one inch, figure 4-33. This bypasses the regulator and grounds the field winding to full-field the alternator.

Copyright 2000 by Chek-Chart Publications

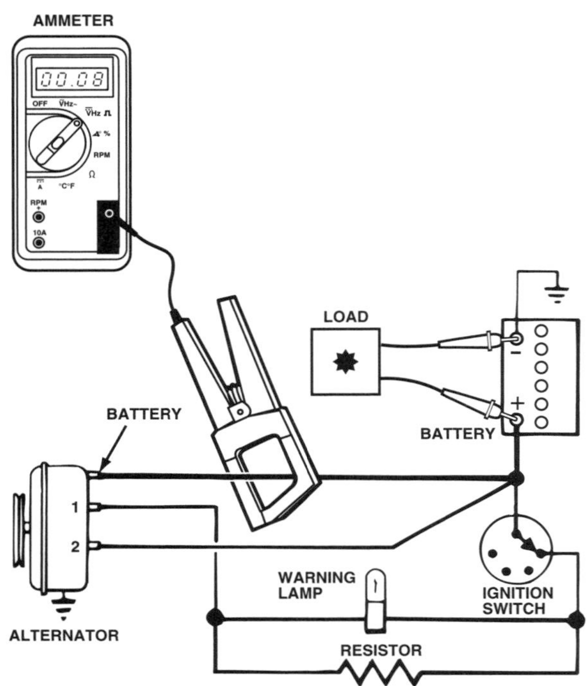

Figure 4-32. Load the battery to get maximum amperage when checking current output of a Delco SI-series alternator.

6. Note the ammeter reading, then remove the screwdriver. Compare the ammeter reading to specifications.

Readings should be within ten percent of specifications. If not, remove the alternator for further testing of the rectifier, the diode trio, and the stator. If current is within specifications, the charging system problem may be caused by a defective voltage regulator or alternator field winding. Remove the alternator to check the regulator and windings

Delco-Remy CS Series

Perform a preliminary system check using the instrument cluster warning lamp before conducting circuit resistance and current output test on systems with a Delco-Remy CS Series alternator. To perform the check, simply switch the ignition on without starting the engine while watching the indicator lamp. The indicator lamp should come on.

If the indicator lamp fails to light, disconnect the harness connector from the voltage regulator. With the ignition on and engine off, check available voltage at terminal "L" of the harness connector, figure 4-34. Readings of 12 volts indicate a bad connection or alternator failure, and zero-volt readings indicate an open circuit between the connector and the ignition switch. If the lamp illuminates with the connector disconnected, start and run the engine. Check voltage at terminal "L". High readings, 14-volts or more, are caused by a grounded circuit and low readings indicate an alternator failure.

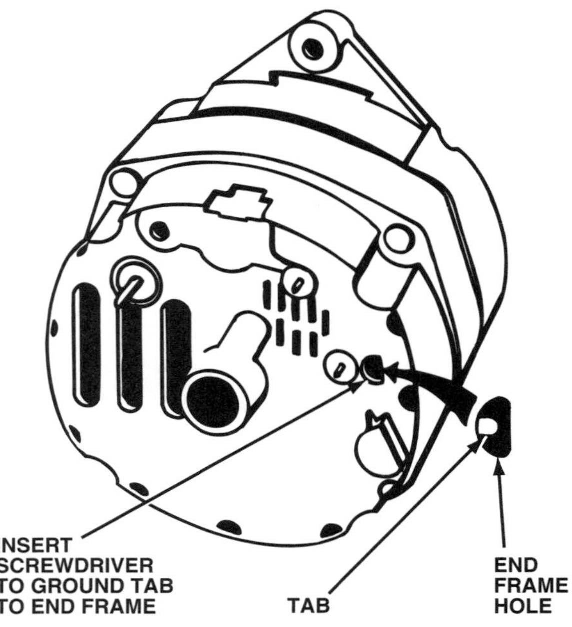

Figure 4-33. Insert a screwdriver into the test hole on the end frame to full-field a Delco SI-series alternator.

Reconnect the regulator harness, then start and run the engine at moderate speed. If the lamp remains on, disconnect the alternator harness connector. If the lamp switches off, remove the alternator for further testing. A lamp that remains on indicates a circuit ground between terminal "L" of the alternator and the ignition switch.

Circuit resistance test

Test circuit resistance with a voltmeter as follows:

1. Connect the negative lead of the voltmeter to the negative battery terminal or a good ground.
2. Disconnect the wiring harness from the alternator.
3. On models with a terminal "I" on the alternator, install a jumper wire between it and the positive voltmeter lead.
4. Connect the positive voltmeter lead to terminal "L" in the harness connector.
5. Switch the ignition on without starting the engine and take a meter reading. No voltage indicates an open "L" circuit in the wiring harness. If voltage is present, continue testing.

Copyright 2000 by Chek-Chart Publications

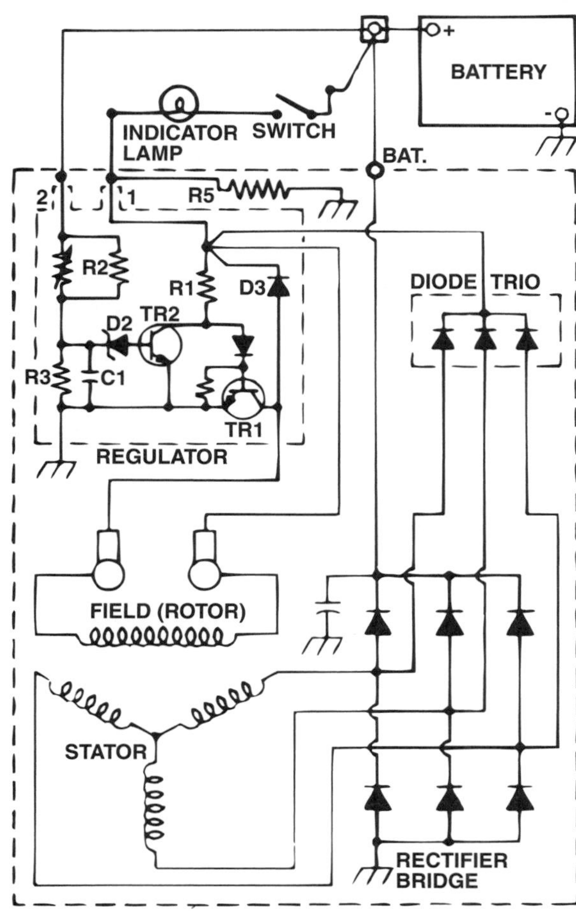

Figure 4-34. Typical Delco-Remy CS alternator wiring schematic.

6. Reconnect the alternator harness. Then, start and run the engine at moderate speed, about 2,000 rpm, with all accessories off.
7. Connect the voltmeter across the battery and take a system voltage reading. If above 16 volts, replace the regulator. If below 16 volts, perform a current output test.

Current output test

Connect a CSB analyzer or an ammeter, voltmeter, and carbon pile to test current output. With the engine running at moderate speed, apply a load to the battery so that maximum charging current is at approximately 13 volts. Note the ammeter reading and remove the load. If the reading is not within 15 amperes of rated output, repair or replace the alternator.

Motorcraft External Voltage Regulator

Test procedures are the same for any Ford charging system with a Motorcraft alternator and external voltage

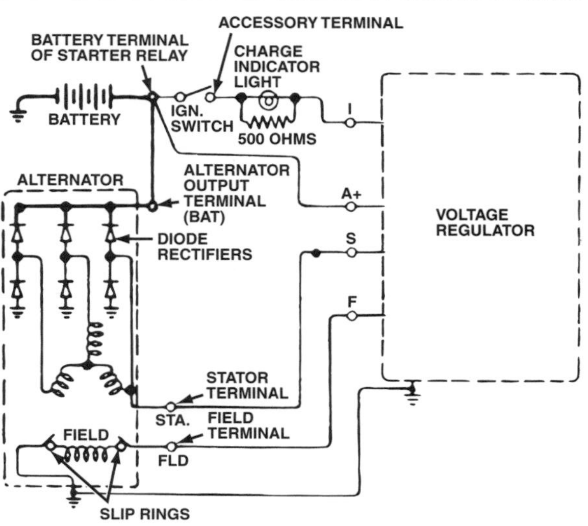

Figure 4-35. Typical Motorcraft EVR charging system diagram with a warning lamp.

regulator. Perform a regulator circuit test, voltage regulator test, and voltage output test to check the alternator.

Regulator circuit test

On the Motorcraft external voltage regulator (EVR) system, a voltmeter is used to check the regulator circuits. The regulator circuitry varies depending upon whether the vehicle has an ammeter or a warning lamp on the instrument cluster, figure 4-35. With the ignition switched off, disconnect the voltage regulator wiring harness connector. Switch the ignition on without starting the engine and take a voltage reading at each of the four harness connector terminals. Interpret results as follows:

- There should be one to two volts at terminal "I", which energizes the regulator.
- There should be at least 12 volts at terminal "A", which senses battery voltage.
- There should be zero volts at terminal "S", which is the stator neutral circuit.
- There should be twelve volts at terminal "F", which is the field circuit.

Next, connect the harness, start the engine, and take a second set of readings at each of the harness connector terminals. If the charging system is functioning properly, expect to see:

- Battery voltage at Terminal "I"
- Charging voltage, about 14 volts, at terminal "A"
- One-half of charging voltage, about 7 volts, at terminal "S"
- Twelve volts at terminal "F" if alternator output is high, and 6 volts at terminal "F" if output is low.

Copyright 2000 by Chek-Chart Publications

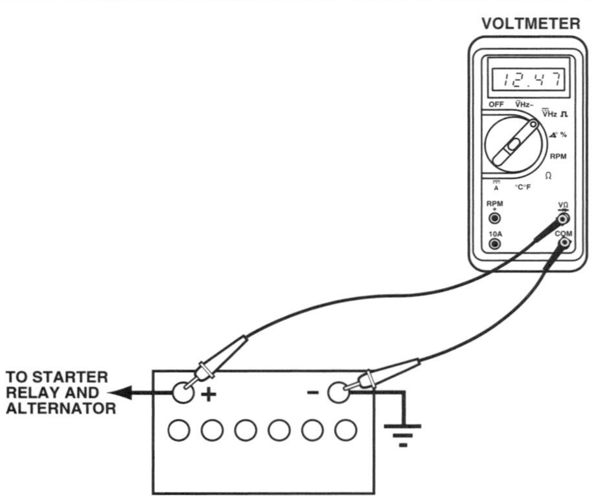

Figure 4-36. Measure open-circuit battery voltage to test the regulator on a Motorcraft EVR system.

Voltage regulator test

To check voltage regulator operation, connect a voltmeter to read open-circuit battery (B+) voltage, figure 4-36. Charge the battery if voltage is low. Next, connect the voltmeter to the field, or "F," terminal of the regulator. Monitor the voltage while starting the engine. Voltage should be high, about 12 volts, as the engine is first started. As the engine continues to run and the battery charges, field voltage should gradually drop, then level off at the regulated voltage.

If both the charging voltage and the field voltage are high, check that the "A" circuit is supplying the correct charging voltage signal. If "A" circuit voltage is correct, suspect a faulty regulator ground.

If both the charging voltage and the field voltage are low, check voltage at the stator "S" terminal. Readings should be one-half of charging voltage. If there is no stator voltage, the regulator may be unable to provide enough voltage to the field. Typically, anything over 4 volts is enough to power the regulator and field. If stator voltage is available, suspect a faulty regulator. Full-field the alternator to verify.

If the charging voltage is too low and the field voltage is high, check the alternator output amperage. A high output amperage keeps charging voltage low. If output amperage is low, remove the alternator for further testing.

Voltage output test

Before performing a voltage output test, check for battery voltage available at the battery terminal of the alternator and terminal "A" of the regulator connector, figure 4-37. If either reading is zero, repair the wiring between the test point and the positive battery terminal. To perform a voltage output test:

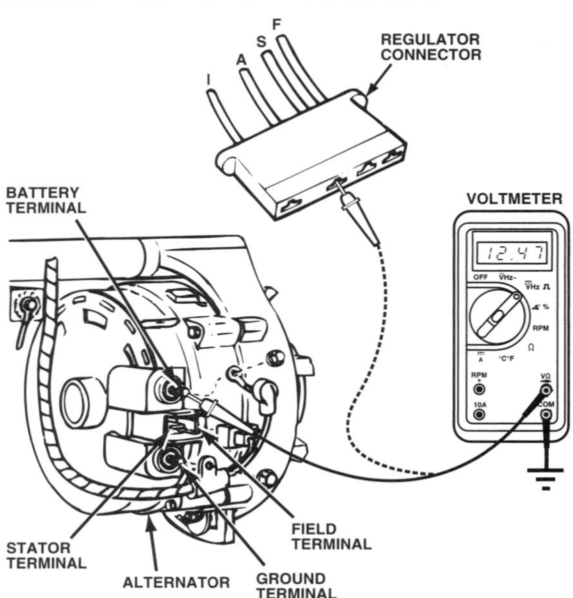

Figure 4-37. Battery voltage must be available at the battery and "A" terminals of the alternator.

1. Switch the ignition off and disconnect the regulator wiring harness.
2. With an electromechanical voltage regulator, install a jumper wire between terminals "A" and "F" of the connector. With a solid-state voltage regulator, install a jumper wire between battery voltage and terminal "F" of the connector, figure 4-38.
3. Check no-load and loaded charging voltage. If loaded voltage remains below specifications, continue testing.
4. Remove the jumper wire but leave the regulator harness disconnected. Check regulator continuity with an ohmmeter, figure 4-39. Typically, there should be 2.4 to 250 ohms between the "F" and battery terminals, and zero ohms between terminals "I" and "F." Replace the regulator and retest if either reading is out of specifications.
5. Install a jumper wire between the field terminal and the battery terminal of the alternator, figure 4-40.
6. Check no-load and loaded charging voltage.

Repair the wiring between the alternator and the regulator if readings are now within specifications. Then retest. If readings are not within specifications, remove the alternator for further testing.

Copyright 2000 by Chek-Chart Publications

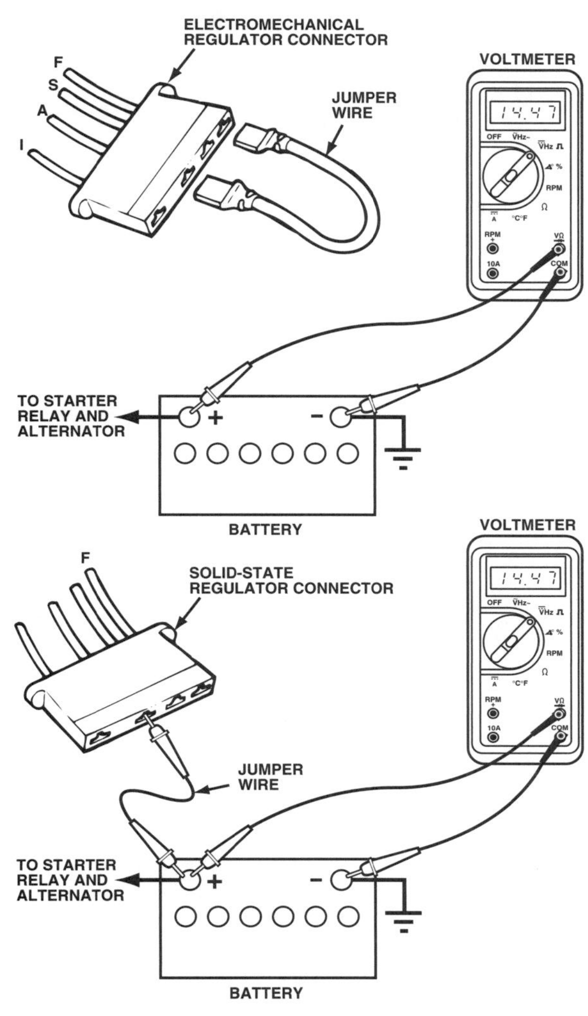

Figure 4-38. Install a jumper wire to full-field a Motorcraft EVR alternator for output testing.

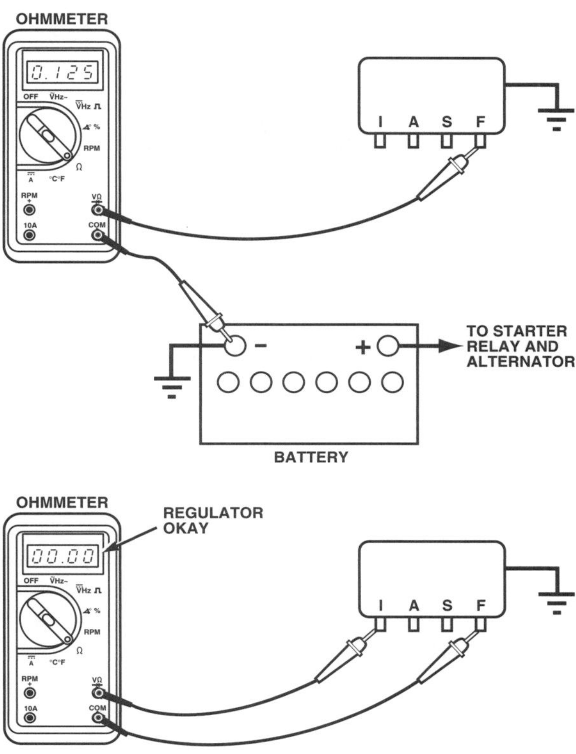

Figure 4-39. Check internal circuitry of Motorcraft EVR regulator with an ohmmeter.

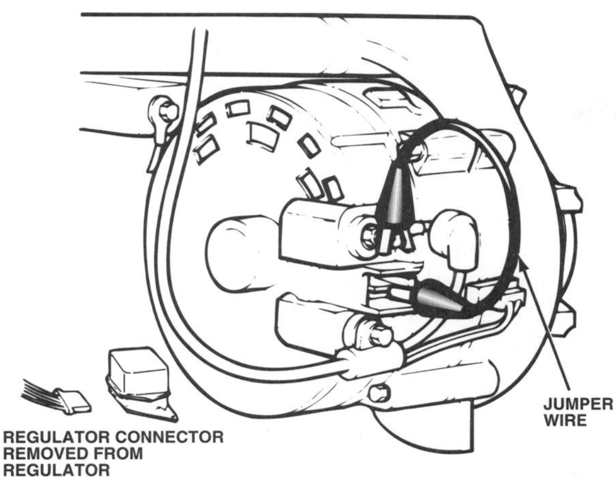

Figure 4-40. Connect the field of a Motorcraft EVR alternator to battery voltage for output testing.

Motorcraft Integral Alternator Regulator

Ford specifies a circuit test procedure for checking a Motorcraft integral alternator regulator (IAR) charging system. A voltmeter, ohmmeter, and jumper wires are used to conduct the charging circuit test. A second test procedure, the field circuit drain check, is used to locate the cause of current drain through the alternator field circuit when the ignition is off.

Charging circuit test

Make sure the battery is at a full state of charge and the drive belt is in good condition, then test the charging circuit as follows:

1. Connect the voltmeter to read open-circuit battery voltage. Note the voltmeter reading with the ignition switched off.
2. Start and run the engine at 1,500 rpm with all accessories off. Take a voltmeter reading; it should be 2 volts more than open-circuit battery voltage. If the reading does not increase, skip the next step and continue testing. If voltage increases by more than 2 volts, skip ahead to the final step of this procedure.

Copyright 2000 by Chek-Chart Publications

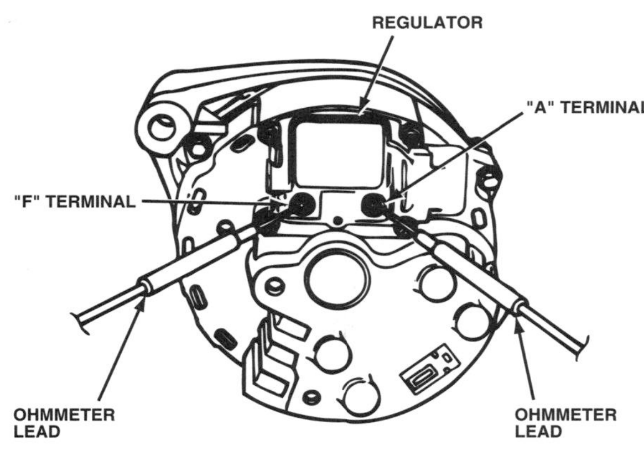

Figure 4-41. Check resistance with an ohmmeter connected between the "A" and "F" terminals of a Motorcraft IAR regulator.

3. If voltage increases by less than 2 volts, check output under load. Increase engine speed to 2,000 rpm, switch all electrical accessories to high, and note the voltmeter reading. If the reading increases by 0.5 volt or more, check for a battery current drain. Locate and repair any current drains, then retest. If voltage does not increase by 0.5 volt, continue testing.
4. Switch the ignition off and disconnect the regulator wiring harness at the rear of the alternator.
5. Use an ohmmeter to measure resistance between terminals "A" and "F" on the regulator, figure 4-41. If resistance is 2.4 ohms or less, remove the alternator, replace the regulator, and check the alternator for a shorted rotor or field circuit. Continue testing if resistance is greater than 2.4 ohms.
6. Reconnect the regulator harness to the alternator, switch the ignition on, and connect a voltmeter to read available voltage at terminal "A" of the regulator. If readings are less than open-circuit battery voltage, repair the wiring in the "A" circuit and retest. Continue testing if battery voltage is available.
7. Switch the ignition off and connect the voltmeter to measure available voltage at terminal "F" of the regulator. No available voltage is likely caused by an open or grounded field circuit in the alternator. Remove the alternator for further testing. If battery voltage is available, continue testing.
8. Leave the voltmeter connected to terminal "F," then turn the ignition switch on without starting the engine. Note the voltmeter. Terminal "F" voltage of 1.5 volts or less indicates a wiring problem on the alternator-to-starter relay circuit. Continue testing if voltage exceeds 1.5 volts.

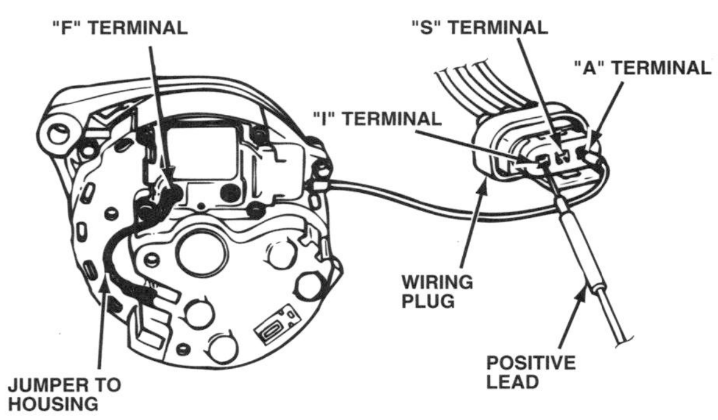

Figure 4-42. Install jumper wires to connect the "A" circuit and to ground terminal "F" of a Motorcraft IAR alternator for output testing.

9. Switch the ignition off and disconnect the regulator harness at the rear of the alternator.
10. Install a jumper wire to complete the circuit between terminal "A" of the regulator and pin "A" of the harness connector. Install a second jumper wire between terminal "F" of the regulator and the alternator housing, figure 4-42.
11. Start and run the engine at idle. Then, measure available voltage at the "S" and "I" pins of the harness connector. If voltage at terminal "S" is approximately one-half of that available at terminal "I," replace the regulator and retest. If the voltage at terminal "S" is out of specifications, remove the alternator for further testing.
12. Remove the jumper wires and reconnect the regulator harness. Switch the ignition on without starting the engine. Take available voltage readings at the starter relay and at terminal "A" of the regulator. Compare the readings. If the difference exceeds 0.5 volt, repair the "A" circuit wiring. If the difference in readings is 0.5 volt or less, check for loose regulator mounting screws and tighten as required.

Field circuit drain check

Use a voltmeter to check for a current drain on the field circuit. To check:

1. Connect the negative voltmeter lead to ground at the alternator housing.
2. With the ignition switched off, check for voltage at terminal "F" of the regulator, figure 4-43. Battery voltage should be available. If less than battery voltage is available, continue testing.
3. Disconnect the wiring harness from the regulator.
4. Take a voltage reading at pin "I" of the harness connector, figure 4-44. Voltage available here indicates a current drain on the "I" circuit

Copyright 2000 by Chek-Chart Publications

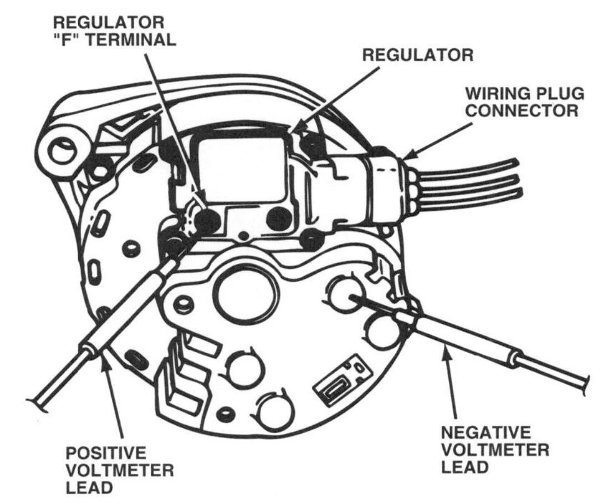

Figure 4-43. Battery voltage should be available at terminal "F" of the regulator with the ignition off.

between the connector and the ignition switch. Locate and repair the cause of the drain. If no voltage is available, continue testing.

5. Take a voltage reading at pin "S" of the harness connector. Voltage available here indicates a current drain on the "S" circuit; locate and repair the cause of the drain. If there is no voltage available, replace the regulator and retest.

Chrysler Transistorized Regulator

Perform circuit resistance, current output test, field current draw, and voltage regulator tests on a Chrysler alternator with a transistorized voltage regulator.

Circuit resistance test

Connect a CSB analyzer, or a carbon pile, ammeter, and voltmeter to check circuit resistance, figure 4-45. To test:

1. Disconnect the voltage regulator field circuit at the alternator. Wrap the disconnected wire terminal in electrical tape to insulate it and prevent accidental arcing.
2. Install a jumper wire between the field terminal of the alternator and ground.
3. Start and run the engine at idle.
4. Load the battery to maintain 20 amperes of charging current.
5. Measure voltage drop across the battery terminal of the alternator and the positive battery terminal, then remove the load.

Voltage drop on the battery circuit must be less than 0.7 volt for the charging system to operate correctly. If the reading exceeds 0.7 volt, perform voltage drop checks along the circuit to isolate the area of high resistance. Repair the wiring and retest.

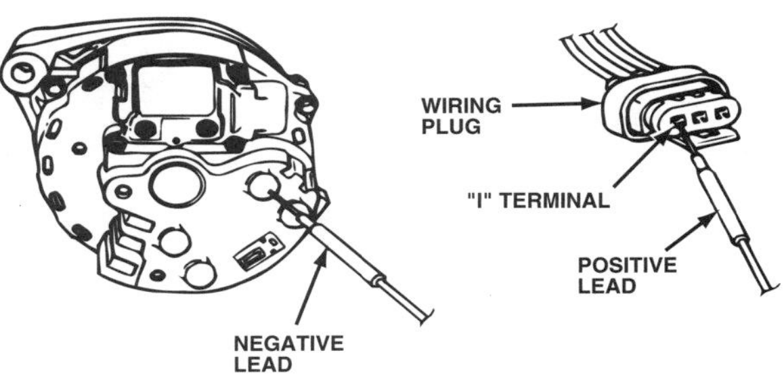

Figure 4-44. Voltage available on the "I" circuit with the ignition off indicates a current drain.

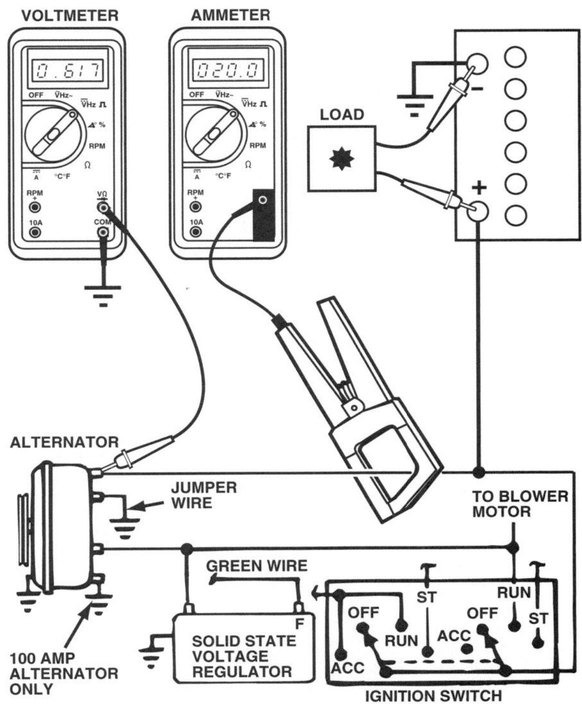

Figure 4-45. Circuit resistance test meter connections for a Chrysler solid-state voltage regulator system.

Current output test

Use a CSB analyzer, or a carbon pile, ammeter, and voltmeter to perform a current output test, figure 4-46. To test:

1. Install a jumper wire between the field terminal at the alternator and ground.
2. Start and run the engine at specified test speed; 900 rpm for a 100-ampere alternator and 1,250 rpm for all others.

Copyright 2000 by Chek-Chart Publications

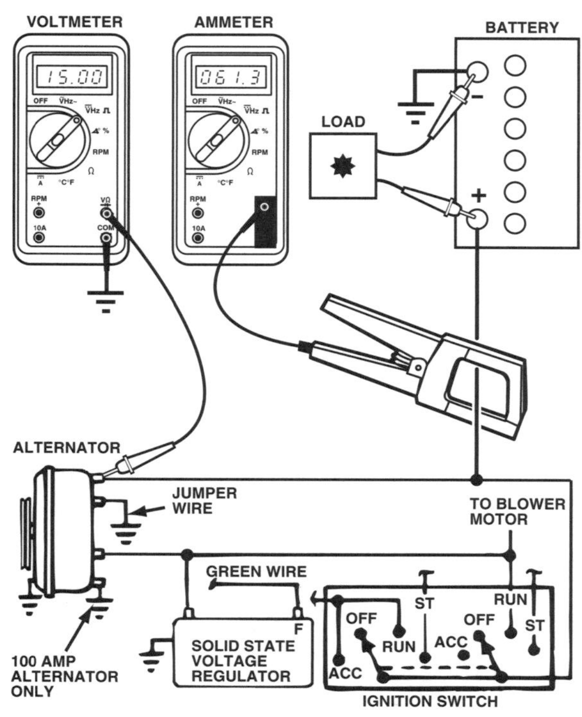

Figure 4-46. Meter connections for current output testing a Chrysler solid-state regulator system.

3. Load the battery to obtain the specified charging voltage; 13 volts for a 100-ampere alternator and 15 volts for all others.
4. Take an ammeter reading, then remove the load.

Compare the ammeter reading to specifications. If current output is within specifications, the alternator and the regulator are operating properly. Remove the alternator for further testing if readings are out of specification.

Field current draw test

Use an ammeter and a jumper wire to check field current draw. To test:

1. Disconnect the wires from both field terminals at the alternator.
2. Install a jumper wire between one field terminal at the alternator and the positive battery terminal.
3. Connect the ammeter between the other field terminal at the alternator and the negative battery terminal, figure 4-47.
4. Slowly rotate the alternator pulley by hand and note the highest amperage.

Compare the ammeter reading to specifications. The alternator field circuit is operational if the reading is within specifications. If field current draw is out of specifications, remove the alternator for further testing.

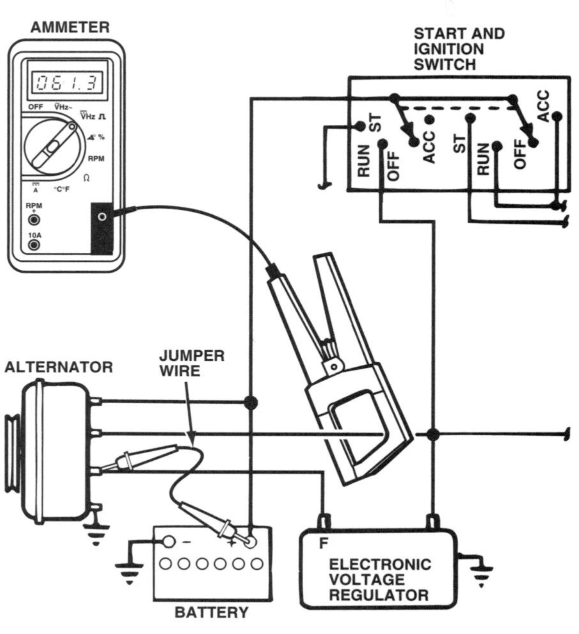

Figure 4-47. Field current draw test on a Chrysler alternator with a solid-state regulator.

Voltage regulator test

Use a voltmeter to check voltage regulator operation. To test:

1. Connect the voltmeter to read open circuit battery voltage.
2. Start and run the engine at 1,250 rpm with all accessories switched off.
3. Take a voltmeter reading and compare it to specifications. If voltage is out of specifications, or if the reading fluctuates, check and repair the voltage regulator ground connections and retest. Continue testing if the voltage reading is within specifications.
4. Switch the ignition off and disconnect the voltage regulator wiring harness. Check the connector for bent or distorted terminals and repair if necessary.
5. Switch the ignition on without starting the engine.
6. Take available voltage readings at both of the regulator connector terminals.

If either reading is zero voltage, check the charging circuit wiring and the alternator field circuit for faults and repair as necessary. Replace the regulator and retest if battery voltage is present at both terminals.

Copyright 2000 by Chek-Chart Publications

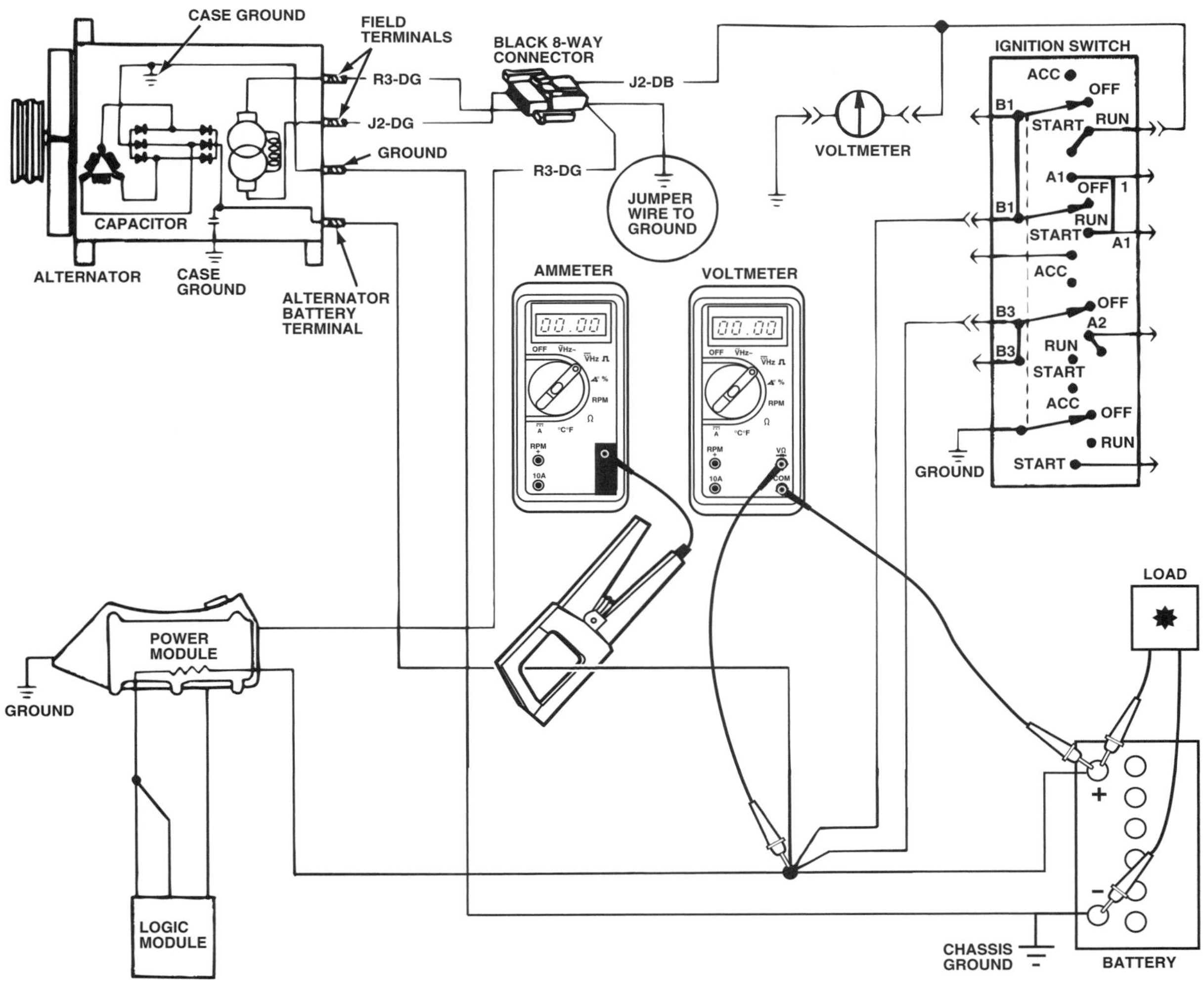

Figure 4-48. Early Chrysler computer-controlled systems are grounded at terminal "R3" of the black 8-pin connector when testing.

Chrysler Computer-Regulated Charging System

Circuit resistance and current output tests for the Chrysler computer-regulated charging system are essentially the same as for systems using an external solid-state regulator. Test circuit resistance and current output using procedures previously described. Note the following differences:

- On 1985-1989 models with a dual-output alternator, ground the field circuit at terminal "R3" on the dash side of the 8-pin black connector to check circuit resistance, figure 4-48. *Do not ground the blue wire at field terminal J2 of the alternator.*
- On 1989 and later models with a single-output alternator, install a jumper wire from alternator terminal "K20" to check circuit resistance, figure 4-49. *Do not ground the "A142" terminal, this overloads and blows the fusible link.*
- On any computer-controlled charging system, maximum allowable voltage drop across the output circuit is 0.05 volt, rather than the 0.7 volt allowed for a circuit with a separate regulator.

Direct testing of the voltage regulating circuitry is generally unnecessary unless the onboard diagnostic (OBD) program of the control system detects a charging system failure and records a diagnostic trouble

Copyright 2000 by Chek-Chart Publications

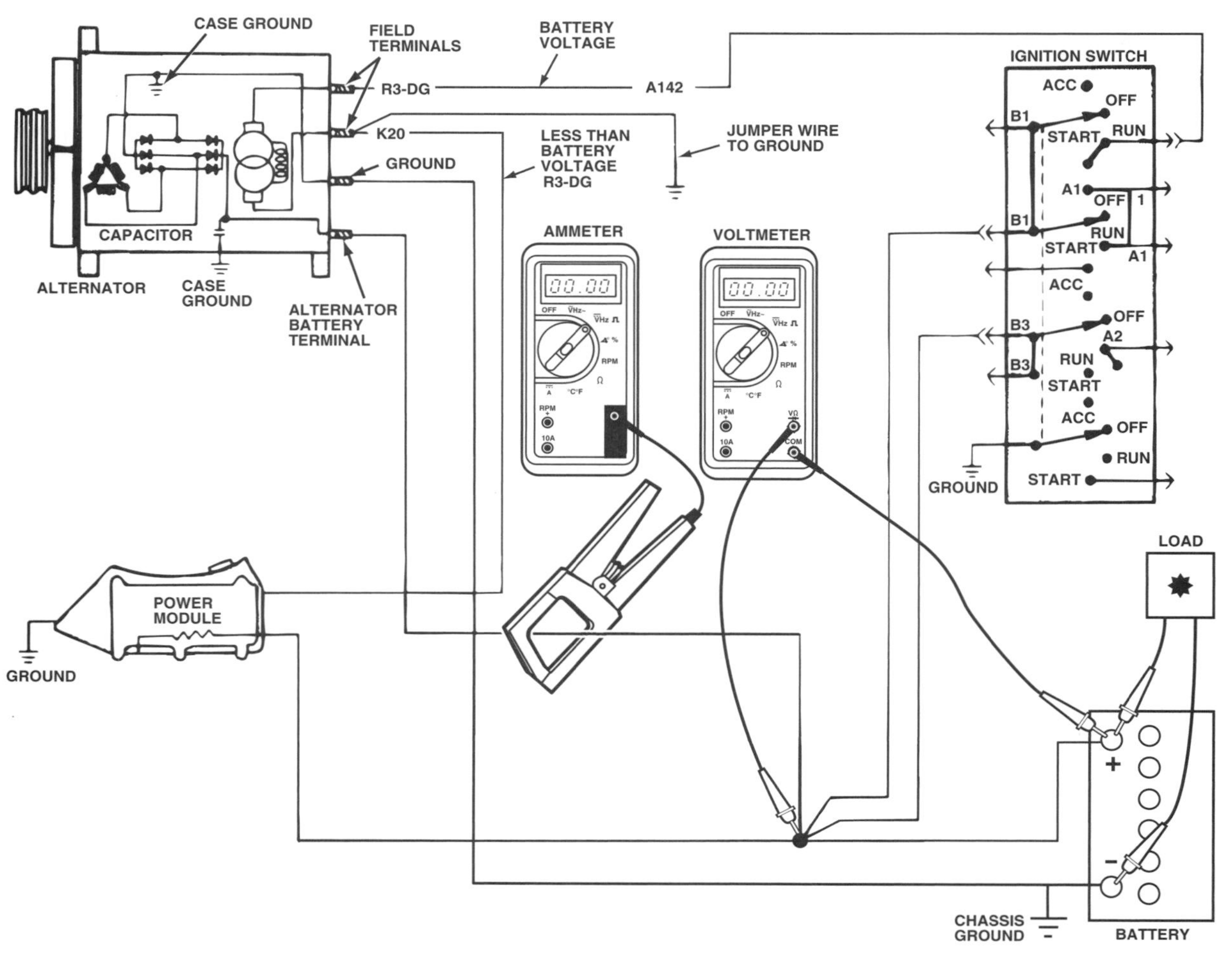

Figure 4-49. Ground the "K20" circuit, not the "142" circuit, when testing a Chrysler computer-controlled single-output alternator.

code (DTC). Some DTC failures illuminate the malfunction indicator lamp (MIL) on the instrument cluster, but others do not.

On Chrysler electronic systems, voltage regulator operation is a powertrain control module (PCM) function. Therefore, DTC information and data parameters for the charging system are available to a scan tool. Use scan tool data to isolate faulty circuits and components, and to verify repairs. The scan tool connects to the diagnostic connector in the engine compartment on older vehicles, and to the OBD II data link connector (DLC) in the passenger compartment of newer models. Refer to Chapter Twelve of this *Shop Manual* for additional information on electronic control system service.

Remember, a DTC is set when the voltage level on the monitored circuit goes outside the normal range of operation, figure 4-50. A number of circuit problems may cause voltage to change and set a code. A DTC does not indicate that a particular component has failed. The DTC simply isolates the defective circuit. The source of the circuit failure is located by voltage drop testing. If more than one DTC is recorded, troubleshoot the codes in the order they display on the scan tool, which is usually ascending numerically. Clear PCM memory and retest after each repair.

Circuit tests and connector terminal numbers vary slightly from one model to another. Consult Chrysler service publications for detailed test instructions.

Copyright 2000 by Chek-Chart Publications

Single-Output Alternator			Dual-Output Alternator		
DTC	**MIL**	**Fault**	**DTC**	**MIL**	**Fault**
12	On	Battery disconnected within last 50 to 100 engine starts.	16	On	Battery voltage below 4 volts, or between 7.5 and 8.5 volts for more than 20 seconds.
41	On	Field circuit problem, improper field control.	41	Off	Field circuit problem, improper field control.
46	On	Charging voltage high. More than 1 volt *above* desired regulating voltage for more than 20 seconds.	44	Off	Battery temperature signal out of range, below 0.04 volt or above 4.9 volts.
47	Off	Charging voltage low. More than 1 volt *below* desired regulating voltage for more than 20 seconds.	46	On	Charging voltage high. More than 1 volt *above* desired regulating voltage for more than 20 seconds.
55	Off	End of diagnostic mode.	47	Off	Charging voltage low. More than 1 volt *below* desired regulating voltage for more than 20 seconds.

Figure 4-50. Chrysler charging system DTC setting conditions.

Chrysler Mitsubishi

Circuit resistance, current output, and voltage regulator tests are performed to check Chrysler charging systems with a Mitsubishi alternator.

Circuit resistance test

Connect a CSB analyzer, or a carbon pile, ammeter, and voltmeter to check circuit resistance. To test:

1. Start and run the engine at idle.
2. Apply a load to the battery to maintain 20 amperes of charging current.
3. Measure voltage drop on the power circuit between the battery terminal at the alternator and the positive battery terminal.
4. Note the reading and remove the load. There should be less than a 0.5-volt drop. If voltage drop is more than 0.5 volt, locate and repair the source of high circuit resistance.

Load the battery and conduct voltage drop tests along the circuit between the alternator and the battery to pinpoint the high resistance. Repair as needed and retest. Then, check current output.

Current output test

To check current output, connect a CSB analyzer, or a carbon pile, ammeter, and voltmeter to the vehicle. Test as follows:

1. Start and run the engine at idle.
2. Adjust the load and engine speed to obtain a 13.5-volt charging rate at 2,000 rpm.
3. Note the ammeter reading, then remove the load.

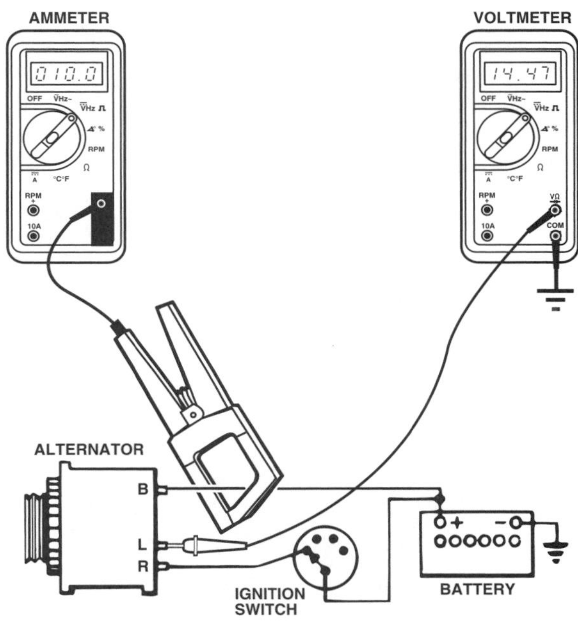

Figure 4-51. Meter connections for testing the voltage regulator on a Chrysler Mitsubishi system.

Compare the ammeter reading to specifications. If the current output is not within specifications, remove the alternator for further testing.

Copyright 2000 by Chek-Chart Publications

Voltage regulator test

A voltmeter and ammeter are used to test the Mitsubishi voltage regulator, figure 4-51. To test:

1. Connect the voltmeter to read available voltage at terminal "L" of the alternator.
2. Switch the ignition on without starting the engine.
3. Take a voltmeter reading. If the reading is above 1 volt, remove the alternator for further testing. If 1 volt or less is available, continue testing.
4. Start the engine and immediately increase the engine speed to between 2,000 and 3,000 rpm.
5. Note output current on the ammeter. To continue testing, the output must be 10 amps or less. If output current is over 10 amps, continue to charge the battery until the reading falls below 10 amps, then continue testing.
6. Note the voltmeter reading. This is the regulated charging voltage; compare it to specifications. If the reading is outside specifications, remove the alternator for repairs.

Copyright 2000 by Chek-Chart Publications

5 Alternator Overhaul

When diagnosis and testing indicate an alternator problem, the alternator must be removed from the chassis for replacement or repair. Although most alternator failures are repairable, many shops simply replace the defective alternator with a rebuilt unit as a convenience to the customer. Overhauling an alternator is a time-consuming procedure, and rebuilt units are often less expensive than an overhaul at shop labor rates. However, some alternator repairs are made quickly and inexpensively without using any special tools or equipment.

This chapter provides general instructions that apply to removing, bench testing, and installing most alternators. Detailed instructions for overhauling common Delco-Remy, Motorcraft, and Chrysler alternators are provided as photographic sequences.

UNIT REMOVAL

Although all alternators mount in the same way, on a bracket attached to the engine, removal procedures vary between models. The main differences are which parts and assemblies need to be moved or removed in order to get to the alternator mounts. Removing the alternator often involves removing, or loosening and relocating, other engine-driven accessories, such as the power steering pump or air-conditioning compressor. On some models, additional parts, such as fan shrouds, splash shields, and intake air ducts, must be removed to access the alternator. Most alternators are accessible from above, but some are removed from underneath the chassis; therefore, the vehicle must be on a hoist or jack stands to remove the alternator.

While working, keep all nuts, bolts, washers, and other hardware organized to avoid confusion during assembly. If necessary, tag parts for reference during assembly. If drive belts are in good condition and are to be reused, mark their direction of rotation and position on the pulleys before removing them. Once belts are removed, carefully inspect their entire length for signs of wear or damage. Never take a chance on a questionable belt; replace it.

Observe all electrical safety precautions and shop safety regulations during alternator service. Remove a typical alternator as follows:

1. Disconnect the negative battery cable.
2. Identify and carefully disconnect all leads from the alternator. Some are held by nuts on terminal studs. Others are plug-in or plug-on connections. Be sure to release any clips or springs holding the plugs in the alternator. Tag the leads for identification at assembly as needed.

Copyright 2000 by Chek-Chart Publications

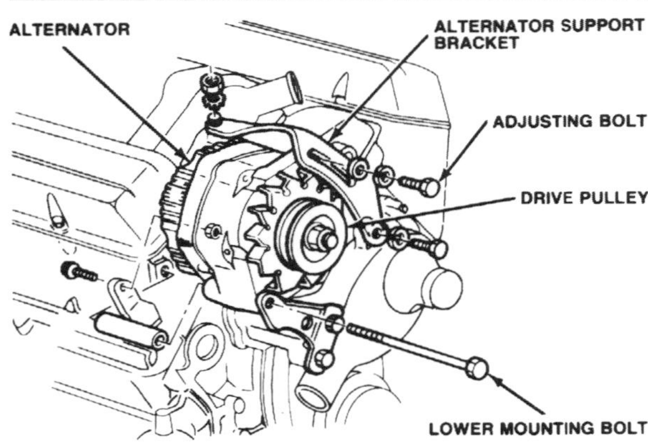

Figure 5-1. Several bolts attach the alternator to the mounting brackets.

3. Loosen bolts holding the power steering pump, air pump, or any other unit that interferes with alternator removal.
4. Move other accessories away from the alternator. Loosen or disconnect hoses, harnesses, and other parts as needed.
5. Loosen the adjusting bolt and pivot bolt or bolts holding the alternator to the support brackets.
6. Move the alternator toward the engine until the drive belt, or belts, can be removed from the alternator pulley.
7. Make sure all belts are clear of the alternator.
8. Remove the pivot bolt and the adjusting bolt and lift the alternator from the bracket, figure 5-1.

DISASSEMBLY, CLEANING, AND INSPECTION

All alternators are held together by several through bolts that connect the front and rear end frame housings, figure 5-2. The stator is sandwiched between the two end frames. The end frames also support the rotor bearings and provide a mounting place for the recti-fier assembly, the brushes, and the internal regulator, if one is used. The front shaft of the rotor assembly is machined to accept the drive pulley, which is generally a slight interference fit. On some models, a cooling fan installs on the shaft behind the pulley. A locknut threads onto the end of the rotor shaft to secure the pulley.

Exact disassembly procedures vary by model; therefore, have accurate service information on hand when overhauling an alternator. The following general procedures apply to disassembling, cleaning, and inspecting any alternator.

Brush any dirt or debris off the outside of the alternator housing, then loosen the fasteners adjoining the drive and stator end frames. Mark the position of the end frames before separating them so they align easily during assembly. Also, note the location of the brush assembly when separating the end frames. Brushes are generally located in the drive end frame. Check brushes to make sure they slide freely in their holders and are making full contact on the rotor shaft sliprings. Replace brushes that are worn to half their original length or less.

Remove the stator and rotor assemblies from the end frames. While disassembling the alternator, clean each part and inspect it for excessive wear or damage. Most parts are easily cleaned with a dry brush and compressed air. For removing heavy dirt buildup, use nonconductive solvents exclusively designed for cleaning electrical parts only. Some types of solvent leave a conductive residue that promotes arcing and short circuits. As part of the overall inspection during disassembly:

- Check bearings for proper clearance, roughness, or galling.
- Remove any oil and dirt from insulation.
- Check insulation condition.

After inspecting and cleaning the alternator, bench test components and replace any defective parts, then reassemble the unit.

BENCH TESTS

The following bench checks are performed during a typical alternator overhaul:

- Rotor continuity
- Rotor ground
- Stator continuity
- Stator ground
- Capacitor continuity
- Rectifier continuity.

These tests, which are similar for all models, may be made at several convenient points during the disassembly and assembly sequences. An alternator with delta stator windings cannot be bench tested for shorts or opens in the stator windings. However, a failed delta stator winding usually causes a noticeable discoloration on the assembly. Standard procedures also apply to the removal and installation of single diodes that are press-fit into heat sinks and end frames.

The following general tests should be made on the alternators covered in the overhaul procedures later in this chapter, as well as on models not covered. Read these test instructions before overhauling any

Copyright 2000 by Chek-Chart Publications

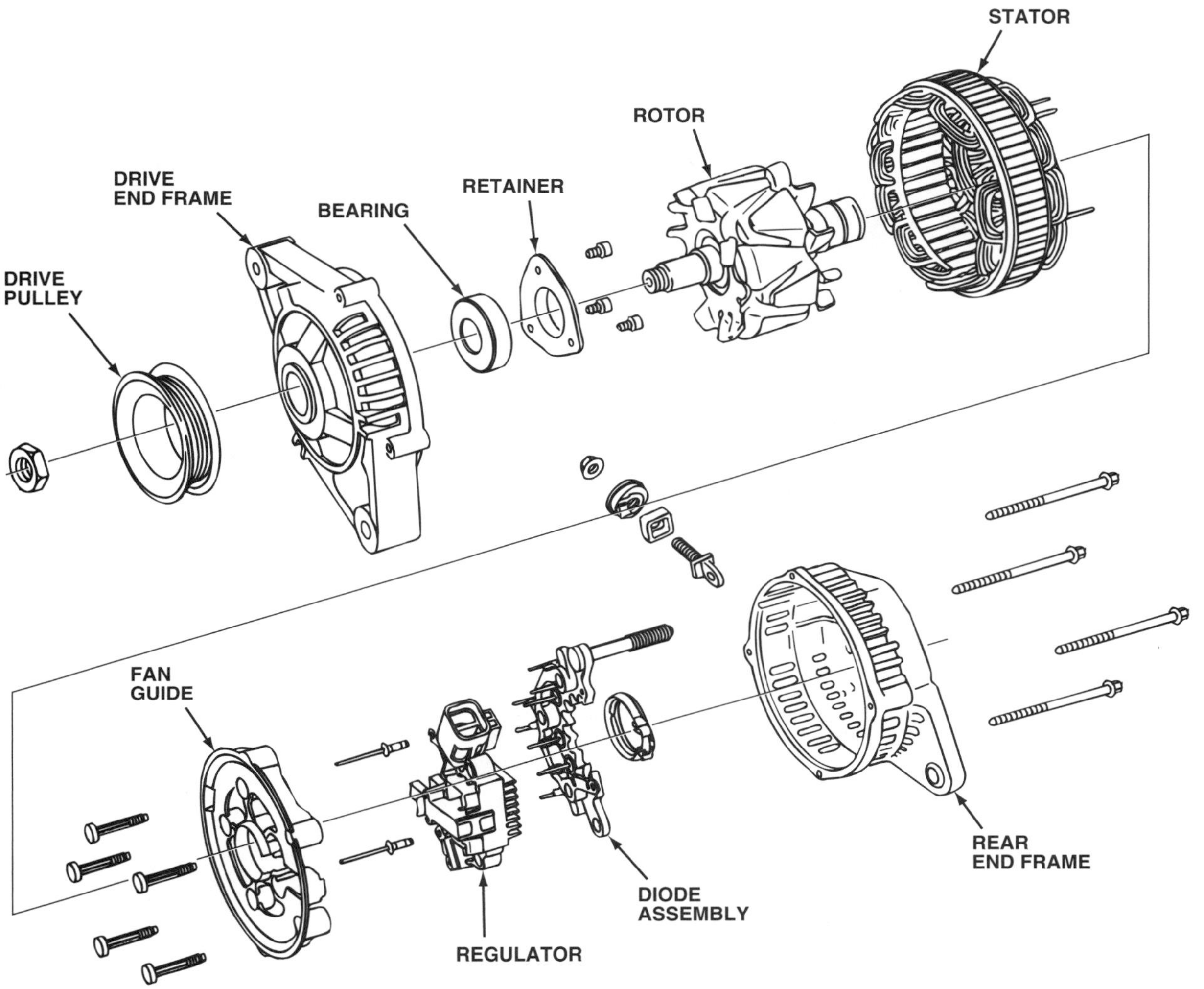

STATOR
ROTOR
DRIVE END FRAME
RETAINER
BEARING
DRIVE PULLEY
FAN GUIDE
REAR END FRAME
DIODE ASSEMBLY
REGULATOR

Figure 5-2. Several through bolts connect the two end frames to hold the alternator assembly together.

alternator and refer to them whenever necessary during an overhaul procedure.

Continuity and ground tests are made with either an ohmmeter or a self-powered test lamp. High resistance or an open circuit is indicated when an ohmmeter gives a very high or infinite reading or when the test lamp does not illuminate. Continuity is indicated when the ohmmeter reads low or zero resistance or the test lamp illuminates.

Rotor Continuity

Check the rotor winding, or field, for open and short circuits by connecting an ohmmeter or self-powered test lamp between the two sliprings, figure 5-3. Look for high or infinite readings on the ohmmeter, figure 5-4. Lower than specified resistance indicates a short and a reading above the specified value indicates an

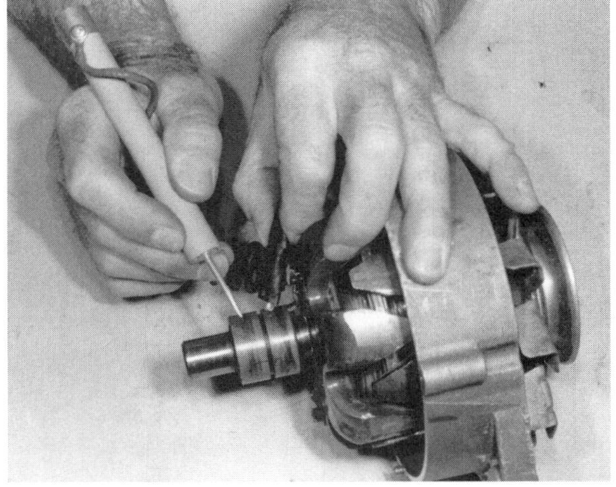

Figure 5-3. Check rotor winding continuity between the two sliprings.

Copyright 2000 by Chek-Chart Publications

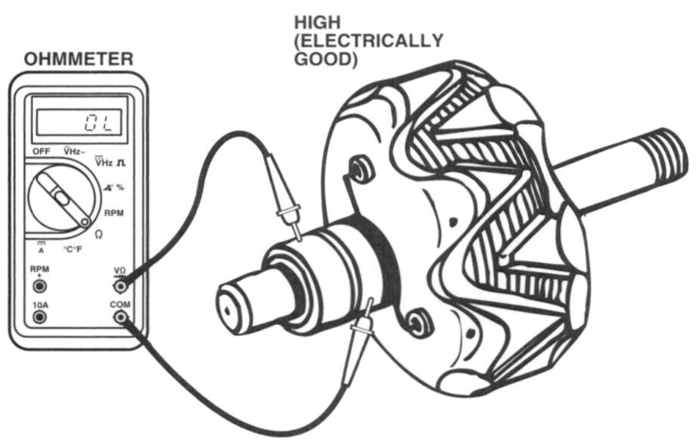

Figure 5-4. There should be high or infinite resistance between the sliprings.

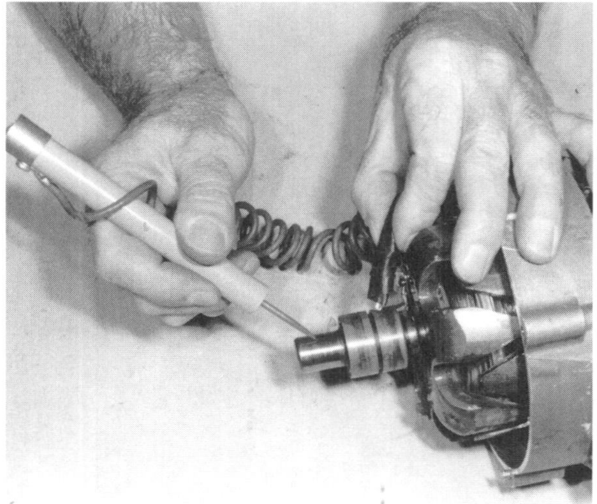

Figure 5-5. Check for grounded rotor windings between each slipring and the shaft.

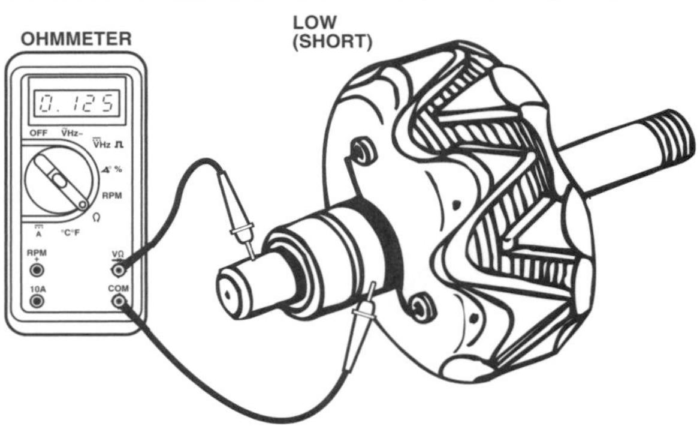

Figure 5-6. Low resistance between a slipring and the shaft indicates a grounded winding.

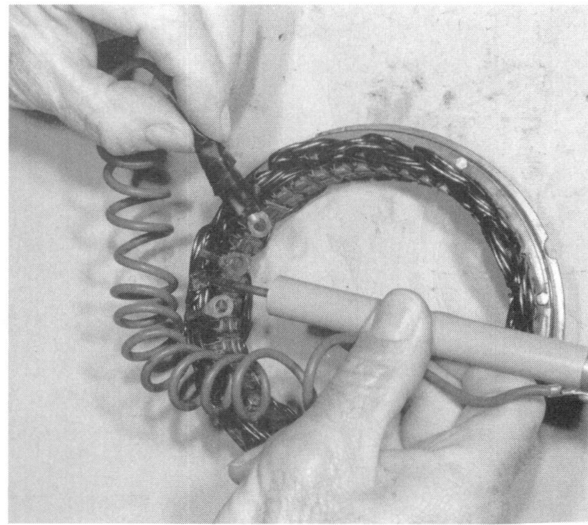

Figure 5-7. Check for stator winding continuity between each of the leads.

open. If a self-powered test lamp does not illuminate when connected to both sliprings, the winding is open.

Rotor Ground

To check for grounded rotor winding circuits, connect an ohmmeter or self-powered test lamp between either slipring and the rotor shaft, figure 5-5. A high ohmmeter reading or the lamp not illuminating means the winding is good. A low ohmmeter reading or a test lamp that lights indicates the winding is shorted to ground, figure 5-6. Test between both sliprings and the shaft for grounded rotor windings.

Stator Continuity

Disconnect stator windings from the end frame and check for open circuits with an ohmmeter or self-powered test lamp. Test stator continuity by connecting one ohmmeter or test lamp lead to one stator lead or to the neutral junction. Systematically touch the other meter or test lamp lead to each remaining stator lead, figure 5-7. A good winding offers little resistance, so look for low ohmmeter readings or an illuminated test lamp when connected between each pair of stator leads, figure 5-8. A high ohmmeter reading or a test lamp that does not light indicates an open circuit.

Stator Ground

Test the stator for grounded windings by connecting one ohmmeter or test lamp lead to the stator frame, figure 5-9. Then, touch the other test lead to each of the stator leads and note the meter reading or lamp condition. The stator windings are grounded if resistance is low or the lamp illuminates at any point, figure 5-10.

Copyright 2000 by Chek-Chart Publications

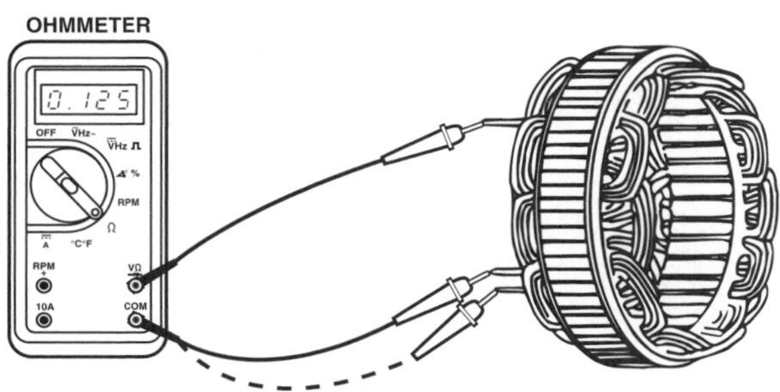

Figure 5-8. There should be low resistance in the stator windings.

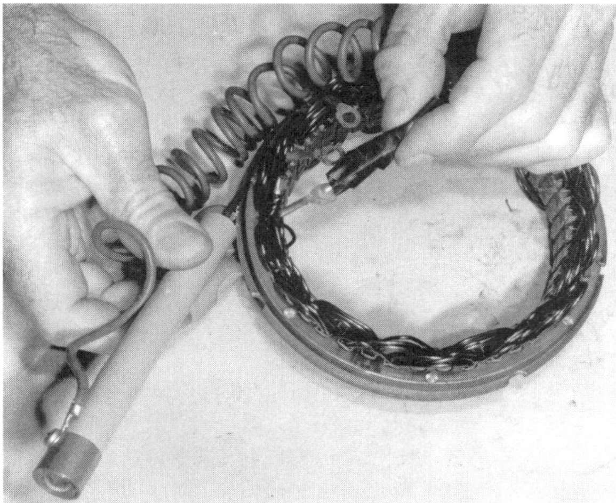

Figure 5-9. Check for grounded stator windings between each lead and the stator frame.

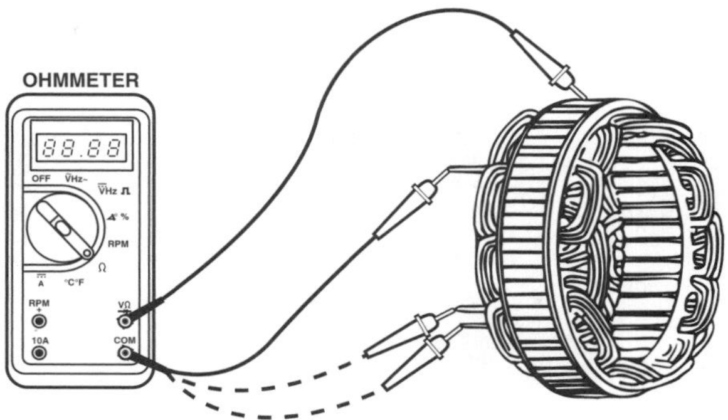

Figure 5-10. There should be high resistance between the leads and the stator frame.

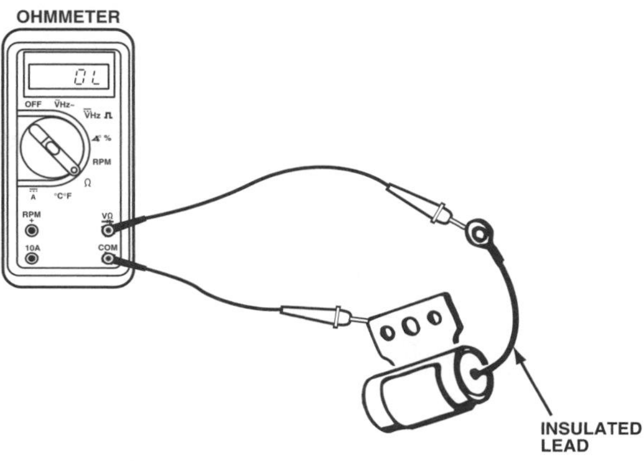

Figure 5-11. There should be infinite resistance between a capacitor lead and case.

Shorted Capacitor

A capacitor, located inside the alternator, is connected between the positive terminal and ground. Although it is seldom the cause of a charging system problem, the capacitor should be visually inspected whenever the alternator is disassembled. The lead must be attached firmly with its insulation intact. Check with an ohmmeter or a self-powered test lamp. On a good capacitor, an ohmmeter displays infinite resistance and a test lamp does not illuminate, figure 5-11. If there is continuity, or the lamp illuminates, the capacitor is shorted and needs to be replaced. A capacitor cannot be tested for an open circuit without the use of a special capacitor tester.

Diode Assembly

The diodes in the rectifier assembly are also checked with either an ohmmeter or a self-powered test lamp. However, the diodes must be disconnected from the circuit. Special diode testers that check diodes connected to the circuit are also available. These testers supply an alternating current that is used to determine diode condition. The tester meter has a pointer at rest in the center of the scale, and a green zone on both sides of the center that indicates a good diode. A red zone at both extremes of the scale indicates a defective diode, positive or negative.

When checking a diode with a test lamp, the lamp should light with the probes connected across the diode in one direction, and not light with the probes switched, which reverses polarity. Test individual alternator diodes with a test lamp as follows:

1. Touch one test lamp lead to the diode lead and the other test lead to the diode base. On some models, the alternator end frame serves as the diode base, figure 5-12.
2. Reverse the test lamp leads, figure 5-13. If the lamp illuminates with the leads connected in both directions or if it does not light at all, the

Copyright 2000 by Chek-Chart Publications

Figure 5-12. Connect test leads between the diode base and the lead to check the continuity of individual diodes.

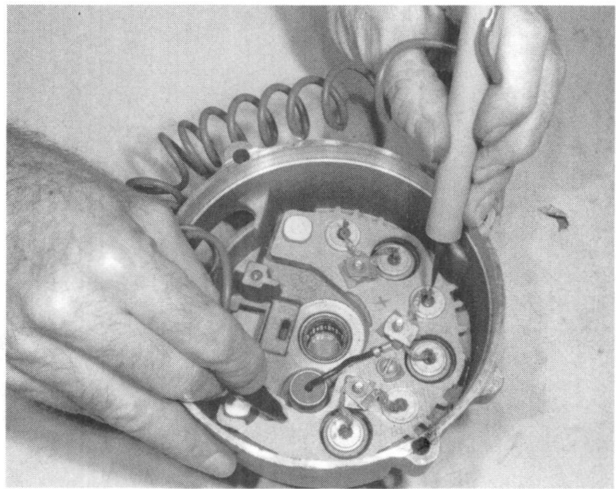

Figure 5-13. Reverse the test leads to check continuity in the opposite direction.

diode is bad. The diode is good if the lamp lights in one direction and not in the other.

A good diode conducts current in only one direction. Therefore, a good diode shows high resistance with ohmmeter leads connected in one way and an infinite reading with the meter leads reversed, figure 5-14. All diodes must be energized, or have voltage applied to them, in order to operate. Often, the minimum voltage required to energize a diode is greater than what is supplied by the ohmmeter. Remember, an ohmmeter applies a low-voltage signal to the test circuit, then determines resistance based on how much voltage is dropped between the two test leads. To compensate,

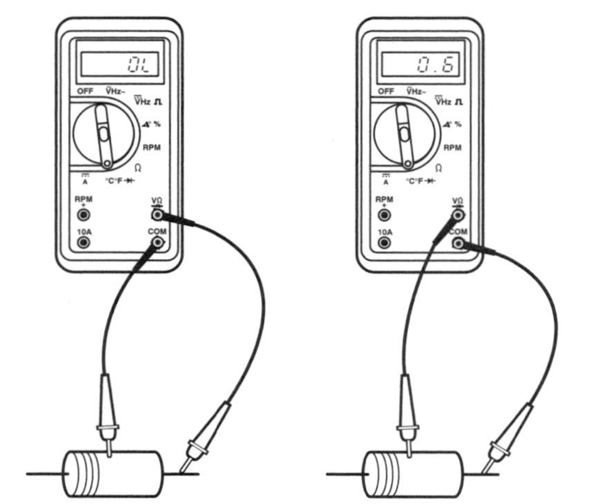

Figure 5-14. A diode should have infinite resistance in one direction and high resistance in the other.

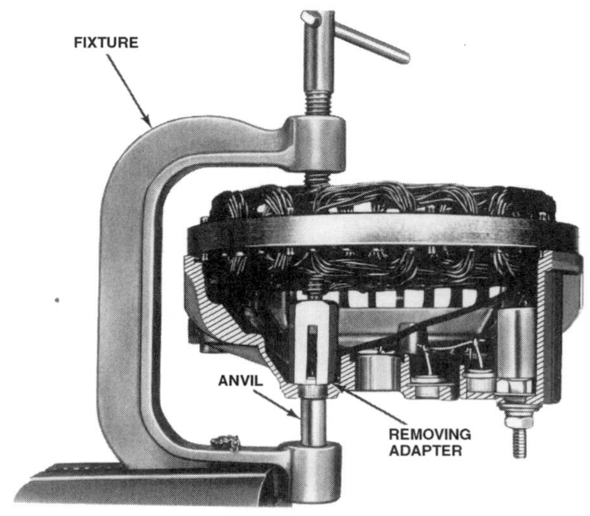

Figure 5-15. Some diodes are press-fit to the heat sink and require special tools to replace.

most meters have a diode test setting in addition to the ohms setting. In this mode, the ohmmeter applies a higher voltage signal in order to energize the diode. Make sure to use the correct meter setting when checking diodes.

On some alternators, a defective single diode is replaced by pressing it out of its heat sink with a special tool. A diode press is a metal sleeve, or removing adapter, with the same inside diameter as the outside diameter of the diode. The sleeve is placed over the large end of the diode, and a press or a C-clamp is used to drive the diode from the heat sink, figure 5-15.

Copyright 2000 by Chek-Chart Publications

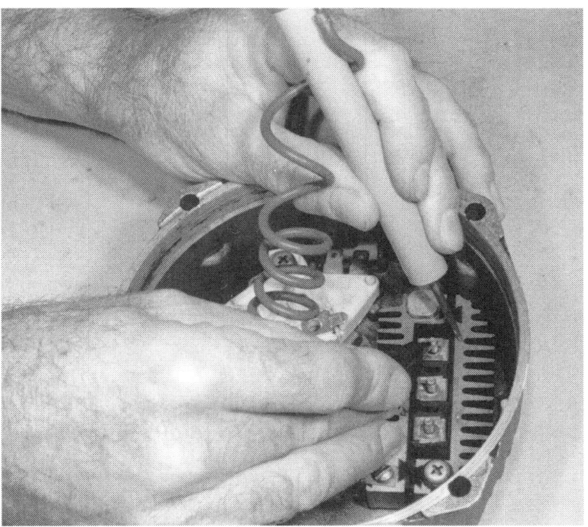

Figure 5-16. Attach one test lead to the base of each diode and touch the other lead to the grounded heat sink to check a Delco-Remy rectifier.

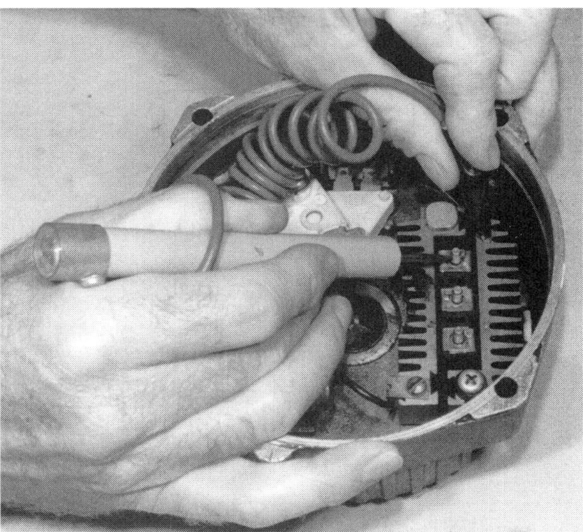

Figure 5-17. Check each diode, then reverse the test leads and check continuity in the opposite direction.

Diodes are not individually serviceable on some alternators, such as the Delco-Remy SI series. On these designs, three diodes are combined in an assembly, which is commonly referred to as a diode trio. Test the diode trio of a Delco-Remy SI series alternator as follows:

1. Touch one ohmmeter or test lamp lead to the base of a diode terminal. Do not touch the lead to the terminal stud. Touch the other test lead to the outer, or grounded, heat sink, figure 5-16.
2. Reverse the test leads for each diode terminal base and the outer heat sink, figure 5-17.
3. A test lamp should light in one direction but not in the other for each diode and an ohmmeter should show high and infinite resistance with the leads switched.
4. Repeat the procedure, but connect the meter or lamp between the inner, or insulated, heat sink and the base of each diode, figure 5-18.

Replace the entire assembly with a new one if any diode has continuity or is open in both directions.

ALTERNATOR INSTALLATION

Before installing the alternator, spin the rotor and pulley by hand to be sure there is no drag or binding. Make sure the rotor and pulley rotate freely, the brushes glide smoothly along the sliprings, and the rotor or the fan blades do not snag the stator windings.

Inspect the drive belts and replace those that are worn, frayed, or damaged. Once the alternator is installed in the vehicle, make sure the pivot bolt is tight before tightening the adjusting bolt for the last time during installation. This prevents binding of the alternator bearings, rotor shaft, mounting bracket, or adjusting bolt.

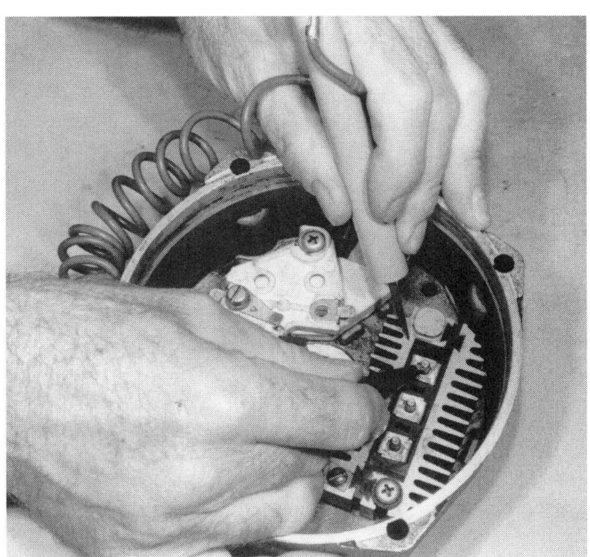

Figure 5-18. Check continuity in both directions between each diode and the insulated heat sink.

Install an alternator that pivots to adjust belt tension as follows:

1. Fit the alternator onto the mounting brackets on the engine. Loosely secure the alternator with the mounting, pivot, and adjusting bolts, figure 5-19.

Copyright 2000 by Chek-Chart Publications

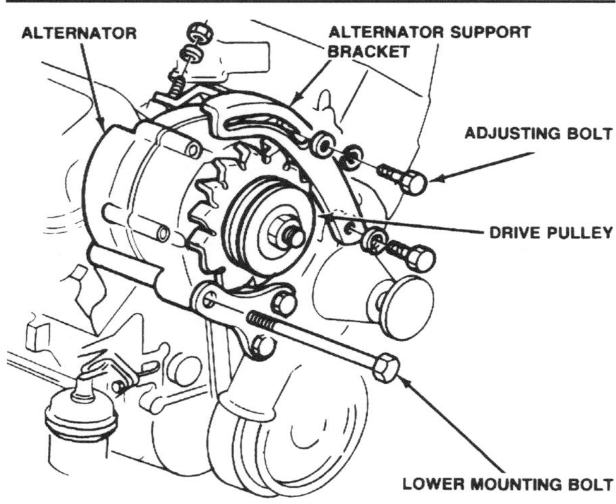

Figure 5-19. Fit the alternator to the engine brackets and loosely install the mounting bolts.

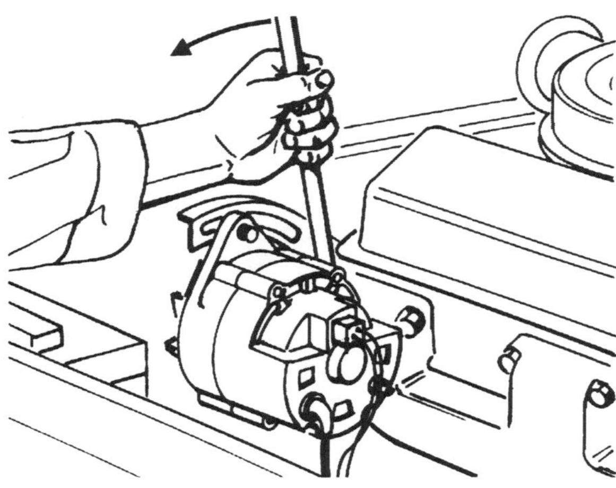

Figure 5-20. Adjust belt tension by carefully prying the alternator away from the engine.

2. Slip the drive belt, or belts, over the alternator pulley and into the grooves. Make sure the belt correctly fits the pulley, all the pulleys are aligned, and the belt is properly routed.
3. Move the alternator along the adjustment slide by hand just enough to keep light tension on the belts. Then, tighten the lower mounting bolt and the adjusting bolt enough to hold the alternator in position.

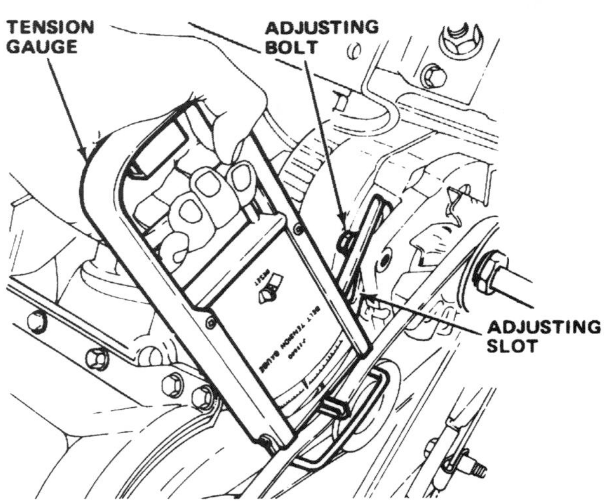

Figure 5-21. Check with a belt tension gauge and adjust to specifications.

4. Using a wooden hammer handle or a pry bar, gently apply leverage to the alternator to adjust the final belt tension, figure 5-20. Do not pry against thin-walled sections of the alternator. Tighten the adjusting and mounting bolts.
5. Use a belt tension gauge to check the tension of the alternator belt, figure 5-21. Loosen the mounting and adjusting bolts and readjust if necessary. Also check and adjust belt tension on all other engine accessories that were loosened to install the alternator.
6. Identify all wiring connections and attach them to their appropriate terminals or sockets.
7. Reposition or install any components that were loosened or removed to access the alternator.
8. Connect the negative battery cable.
9. Start and run the engine and check for noise or vibration from the alternator.
10. Perform output tests as explained in Chapter Four of this *Shop Manual* to verify alternator operation.

Once correct alternator operation is verified, shut the engine off and check drive belt tension again. Remember, if a new belt was installed, now it is adjusted to the used belt tension specifications.

Copyright 2000 by Chek-Chart Publications

ALTERNATOR OVERHAUL PROCEDURES

The following pages contain photographic procedures for the disassembly, overhaul, and assembly of six common domestic alternators:

- Delco-Remy Model 10-SI with integral regulator
- Delco-Remy Model CS-130 with integral regulator
- Motorcraft side-terminal alternator with external regulator
- Motorcraft integral alternator regular (IAR)
- Chrysler standard-duty alternator with external regulator
- Chrysler 40/90-amp alternator with electronic regulator.

Chapter Eight of the *Classroom Manual* contains descriptive information and additional drawings of these alternators. It may be helpful to refer to the *Classroom Manual* for detailed information when overhauling an alternator. Before starting any overhaul, be sure to read and understand the test procedures in the preceding section of this chapter. There is no specific order for conducting these tests. Tests are simply made at convenient points during the overhaul sequence. Read through the entire step-by-step procedure for the specific alternator being serviced before beginning work.

Also, before performing the overhaul, gather all the tools needed. Make sure the work area is clean, well organized, and conveniently arranged. A medium-hot, approximately 100-watt, soldering iron is used when soldering and unsoldering electrical parts. Remember, use only rosin-core solder on electrical connections.

Copyright 2000 by Chek-Chart Publications

DELCO-REMY 10-SI ALTERNATOR OVERHAUL PROCEDURE

1. Draw a reference line across both end frame housings. Remove the four through bolts that secure the housings, then separate end frames.

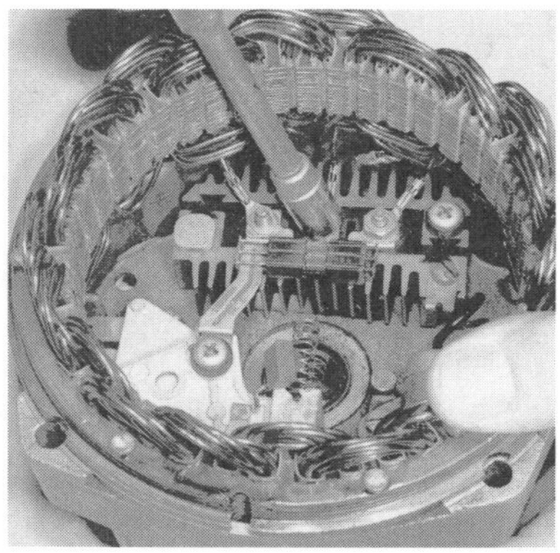

2. Remove the three nuts that attach the stator leads to the rectifier. Lift the stator off of the end frame housing.

3. Test stator windings for opens and grounds with a self-powered test lamp or ohmmeter.

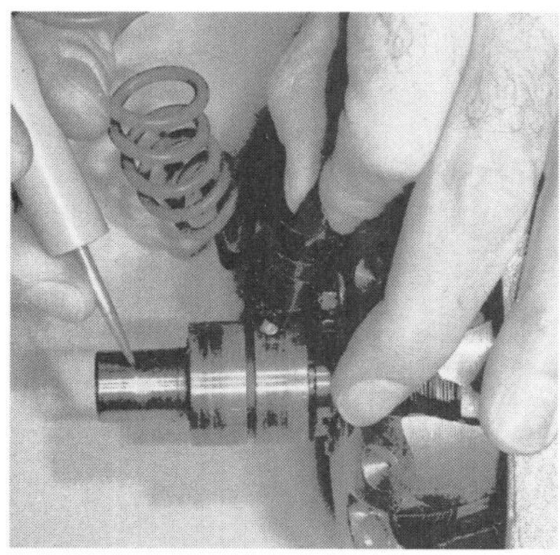

4. This is also a convenient time to test the rotor for opens and grounds. Check with an ohmmeter or a self-powered test lamp.

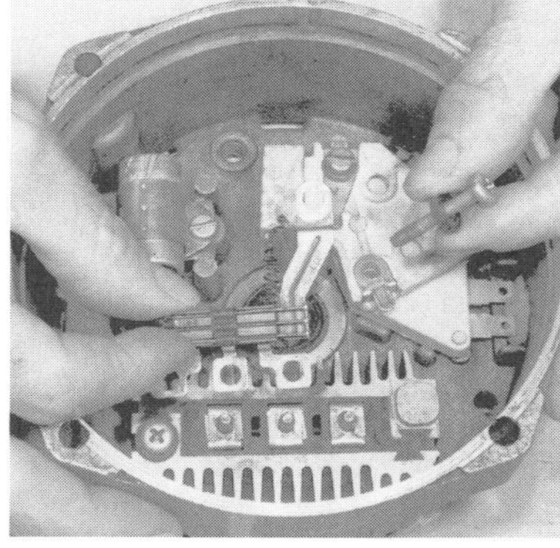

5. Remove the screw that holds the diode trio to the brush holder. Remove the diode trio and test it for opens and shorts.

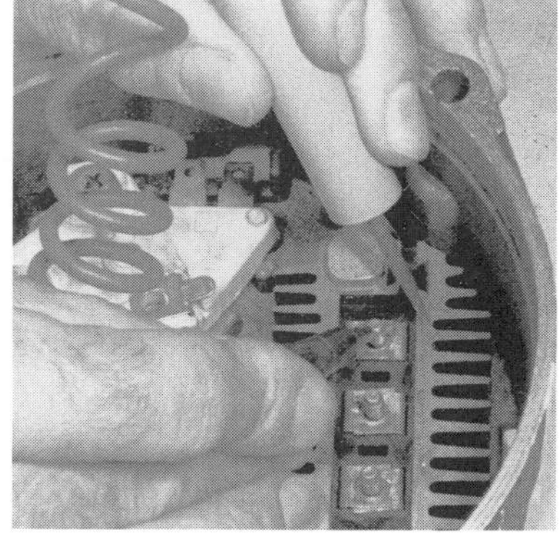

6. Test the rectifier with a self-powered test lamp or ohmmeter while it is still in end frame.

7. Disconnect the capacitor lead from the rectifier. Then, remove the screw, capacitor, and bracket from the end frame.

8. Remove the nut, washer, and insulator from the "BAT" terminal and the terminal assembly. Also remove the ground screw and rectifier.

9. Remove the two screws on the brush holder and regulator. *Be sure* to note the position of insulators and insulating sleeves for later assembly.

Copyright 2000 by Chek-Chart Publications

DELCO-REMY 10-SI ALTERNATOR OVERHAUL PROCEDURE

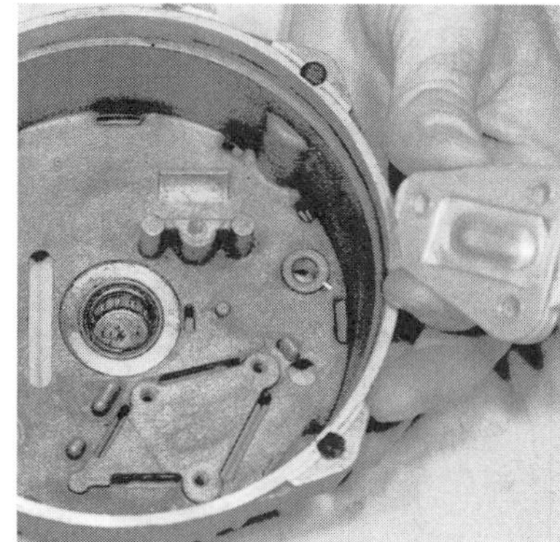

10. Remove the brush holder and regulator. Then, separate the two and inspect the brushes for wear. Replace brushes in matched pairs if necessary.

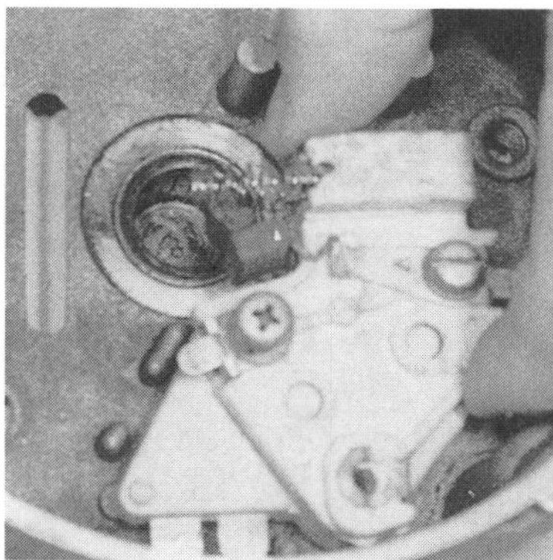

11. Install the regulator and brush holder. Replace insulating sleeves and washers as needed. *Be sure* insulating sleeves and washers are installed as removed.

12. Compress the brushes and springs into the holder, then insert a drill bit or pick through the rear of end frame. This holds the brushes clear of the sliprings as the rotor is installed.

13. Fit the rectifier into the end frame, then insert the "BAT" terminal through the rectifier and end frame. Install the ground screw.

14. Install the nut and insulating washer on the "BAT" terminal to secure it and the rectifier assembly to the end frame.

15. Attach the capacitor lead to the rectifier and secure the capacitor with the mounting screw.

16. Fit the diode trio and secure it with the screw and insulating sleeve. Make sure the three diode leads fit over the rectifier terminals.

17. Fit the stator into the end frame so its three leads fit over the rectifier terminals and the notches in the stator align with the bolt holes in end frame.

18. To service the drive end frame, *carefully* clamp the rotor and loosen the pulley nut. Then, remove the nut, washer, pulley, and fan.

Copyright 2000 by Chek-Chart Publications

DELCO-REMY 10-SI ALTERNATOR OVERHAUL PROCEDURE

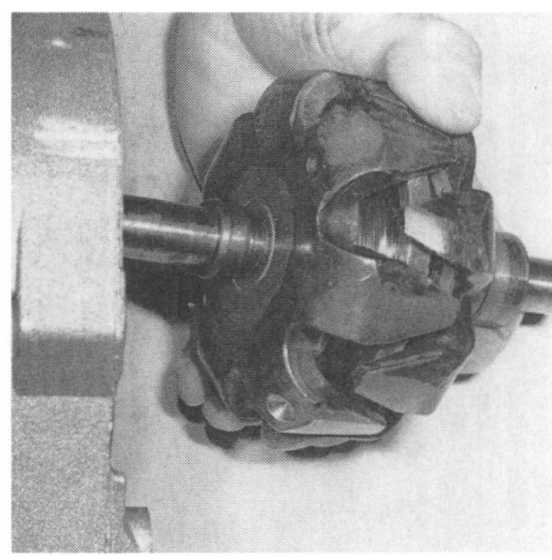

19. Remove the collar from shaft behind fan. Then, separate the rotor and shaft assembly from the end frame.

20. If the bearing is to be replaced, remove three screws holding bearing retainer and remove retainer plate.

21. Support the end frame on a suitable fixture and *carefully* drive or press the bearing from the end frame.

22. Carefully press or drive the new bearing into the end frame. When reusing bearings, lightly pack, but do not overfill, with grease.

23. Replace the bearing retainer if the felt seal is hardened or worn. Fit the retainer and install the retaining screws.

24. Guide the rotor and shaft assembly into the end frame. Install the collar on the shaft.

25. Assemble the fan, pulley, washer, and nut. *Carefully* clamp the rotor to hold it and tighten the nut to 40 to 60 ft-lbs. (54 to 80 Nm) of torque.

26. Align the reference marks on the end frames, assemble the end frames, and loosely install the through bolts.

27. Remove the drill bit or pick holding the brushes. Tighten the four through bolts. The overhaul is complete.

Copyright 2000 by Chek-Chart Publications

DELCO-REMY CS-130 ALTERNATOR OVERHAUL PROCEDURE

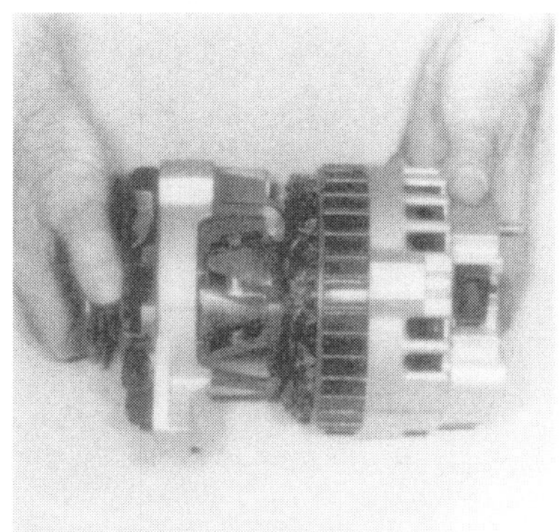

1. Remove the through bolts and carefully separate the drive end frame rotor and shaft assembly from the stator and rear end frame.

2. Inspect the plastic internal fan attached to the rotor shaft for damage or signs of overheating. Replace the entire rotor assembly if damage is found.

3. Remove the pulley nut, spacer, drive pulley, fan, and washer from the drive end housing. Then, separate the rotor and end frame.

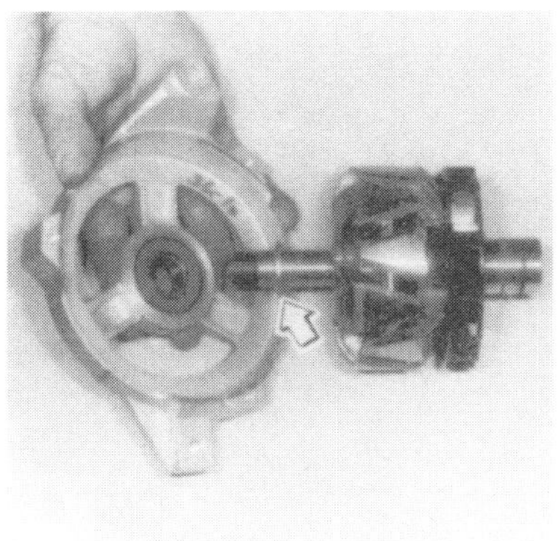

4. Remove the spacer (arrow) from the rotor shaft and check for bearing wear or damage. Replace the end frame and bearing as a unit.

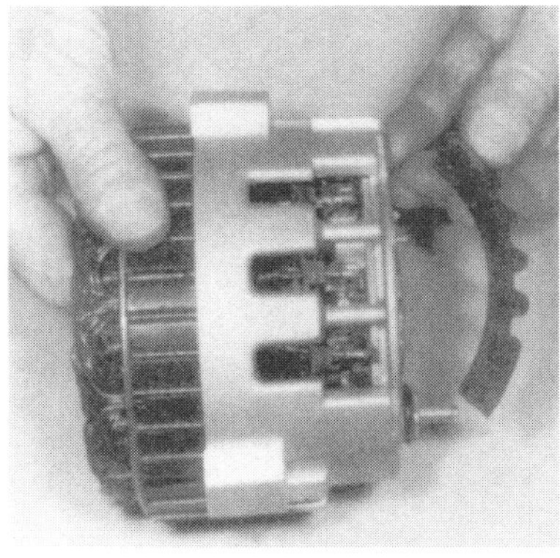

5. Remove the plastic dust cover from the stator lead connections by carefully prying it off the housing.

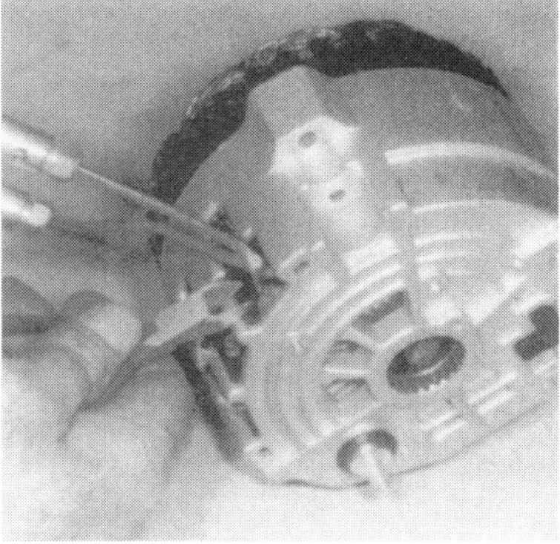

6. Heat one stator lead at a time with a soldering iron, then open the clamp with a pair of diagonal pliers to remove the wires.

7. Use a punch and hammer to carefully drive out the three plastic pins holding the plastic stator cover to the end frame.

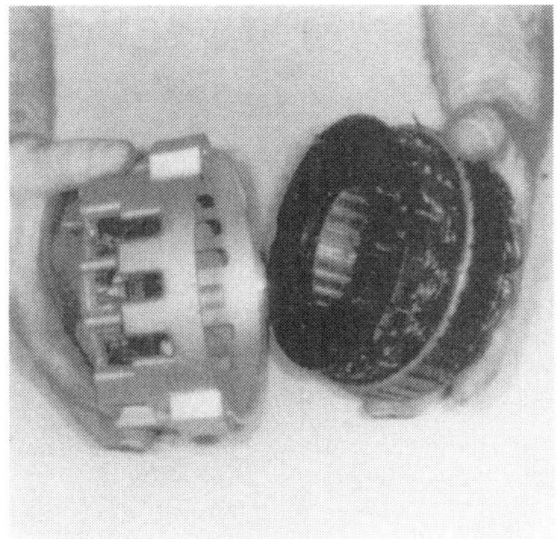

8. Remove the stator along with the cover from the end frame. Remove the cover and test the stator continuity and ground.

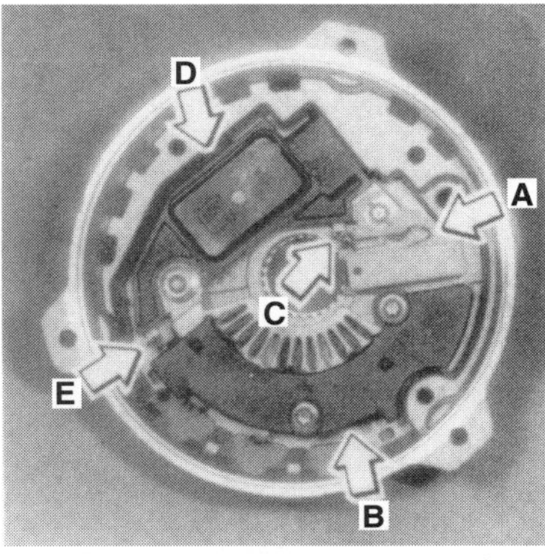

9. Separate the brush holder (A) from the rectifier assembly (B) at the slip-on terminal (C). The regulator (D) to rectifier assembly connection is a soldered terminal (E).

Copyright 2000 by Chek-Chart Publications

DELCO-REMY CS-130 ALTERNATOR OVERHAUL PROCEDURE

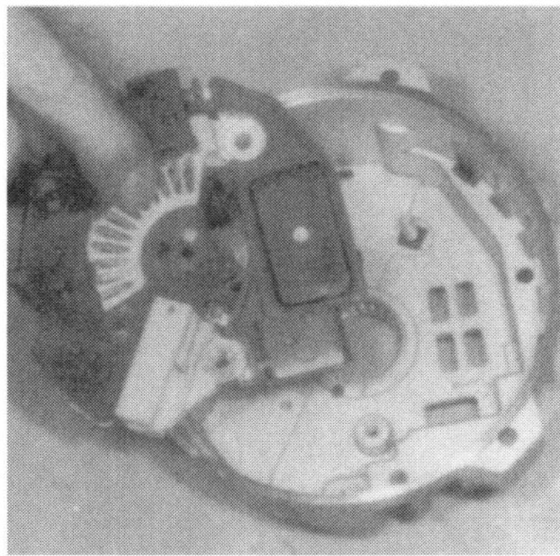

10. Remove the brush holder, rectifier, and regulator from the end frame as a unit. Then, separate the components for testing or replacement.

11. There is no bearing in the stator end frame. This rippled aluminum spacer, or tolerance ring, eliminates play in the machined shaft opening.

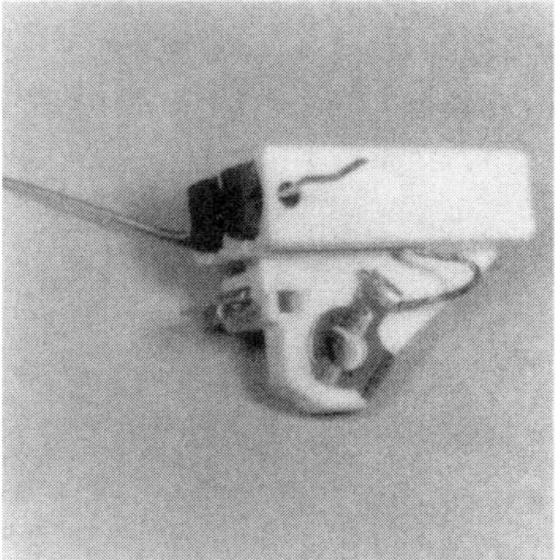

12. Compress the brushes and insert a drill bit or bent paper clip through them and brush holder to hold them during assembly.

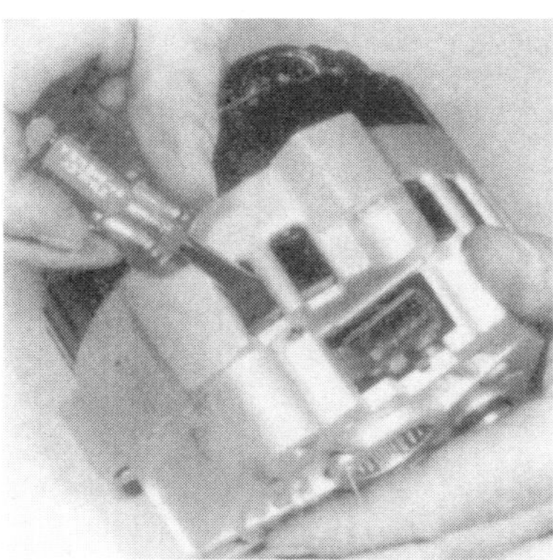

13. Assemble the stator and plastic cover onto the end frame. Press the stator cover pins completely back into the housing.

14. Make sure the stator cover clips snap into place or they may hit the rotor as it turns. Fit the rotor and drive end frame assembly.

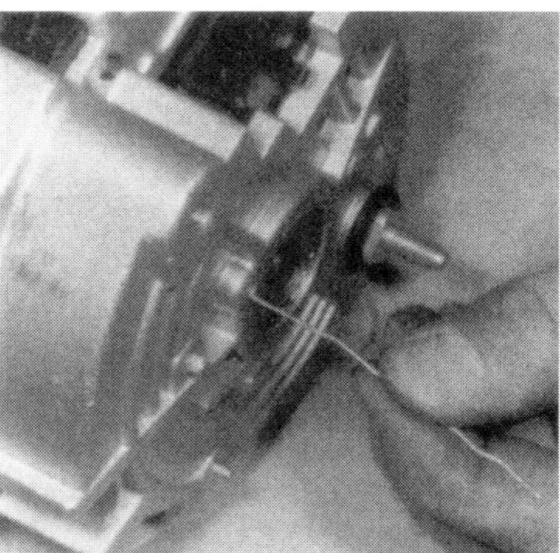

15. Tighten the through bolts, then remove the drill bit or paper clip to allow the brushes to make contact with the rotor sliprings.

Copyright 2000 by Chek-Chart Publications

MOTORCRAFT SIDE-TERMINAL ALTERNATOR OVERHAUL PROCEDURE

1. Draw an alignment mark across both end frames and the stator, then remove the three through bolts securing the assembly.

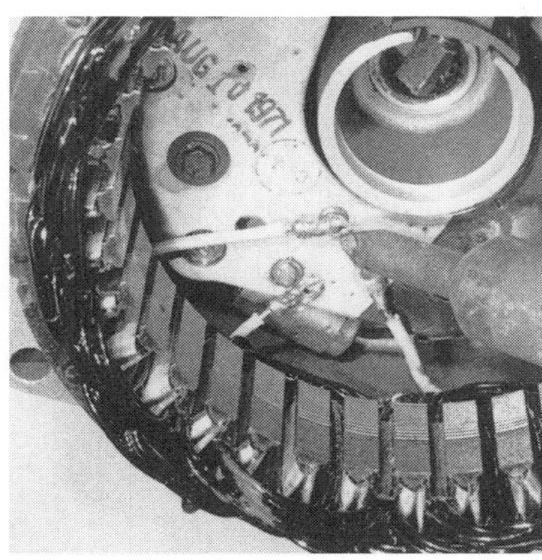

2. Heat and separate the soldered stator lead connections from the rectifier. Then, remove the stator from the end frame.

3. Heat and separate the soldered brush holder lead connection from the rectifier. Remove the retaining screws and brush holder assembly.

4. Remove the "BAT" and "GRD" terminal nuts on the outside of the rear end frame. Remove the insulator from the "BAT" terminal.

5. Disconnect the capacitor lead and remove the rectifier. Note the location of rectifier insulators in the end frame for assembly reference.

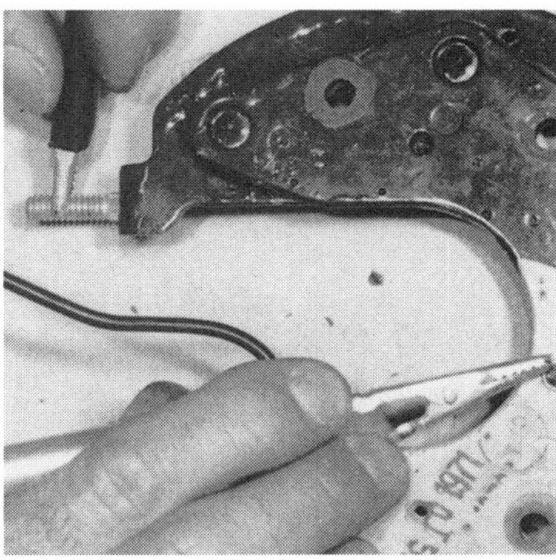

6. Test the rectifier by connecting an ohmmeter or test lamp between the "BAT" terminal and each of the three stator winding terminals.

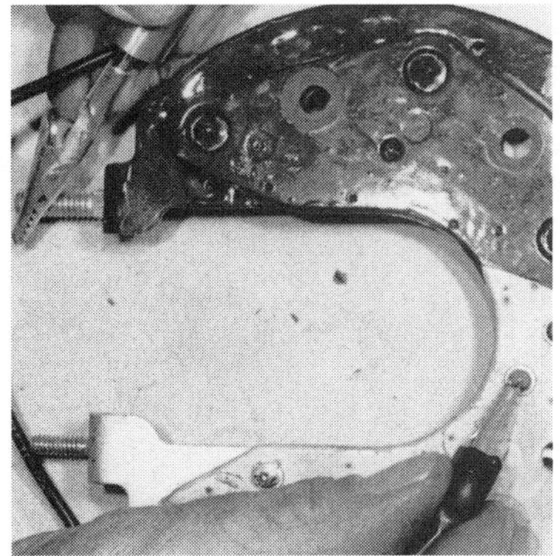

7. Reverse the test leads and repeat. There should be continuity at all three positions in one direction, but not in the other.

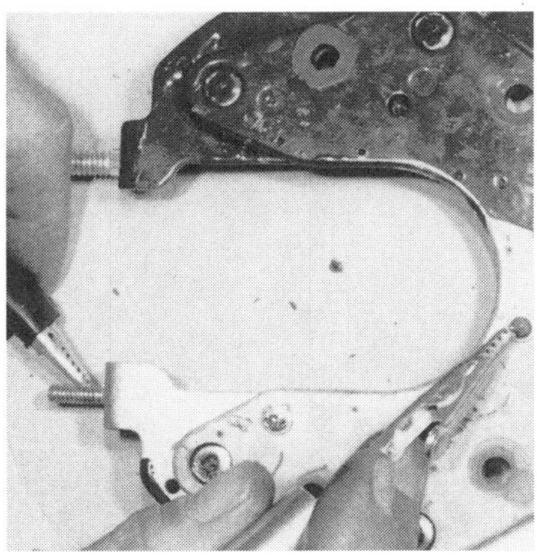

8. Similarly, connect the test leads between "GRD" and the three stator leads to check continuity in both directions. Replace the rectifier if any test fails.

9. Inspect the brushes and replace them if worn. Attach the brush holder and insert a drill bit or wire to hold brushes in place.

Copyright 2000 by Chek-Chart Publications

MOTORCRAFT SIDE-TERMINAL ALTERNATOR OVERHAUL PROCEDURE

10. Install the capacitor. Make sure the two insulators are on the bosses inside the end frame.

11. Fit the rectifier to the end frame and the insulating washer on the "BAT" terminal. Install the four rectifier mounting screws.

12. Fit an insulating washer on the outside of the "BAT" terminal and install the nut. Install the "GRD" terminal nut.

13. Attach the capacitor lead to the rectifier with the screw and solder the brush holder lead to the recti-fier terminal.

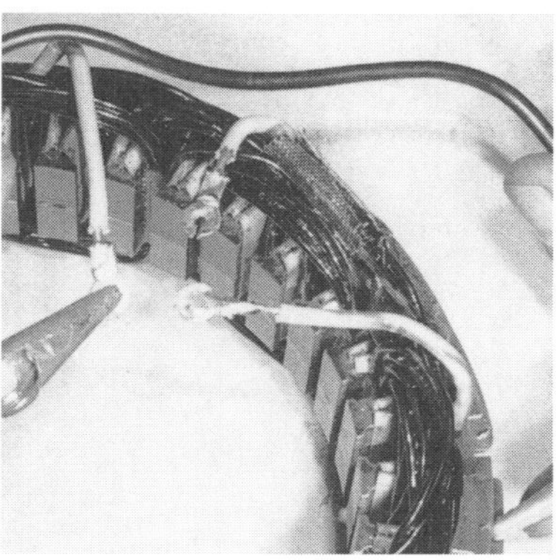

14. Perform stator open and ground, as shown here, tests before assembling the alternator. Replace a defective stator.

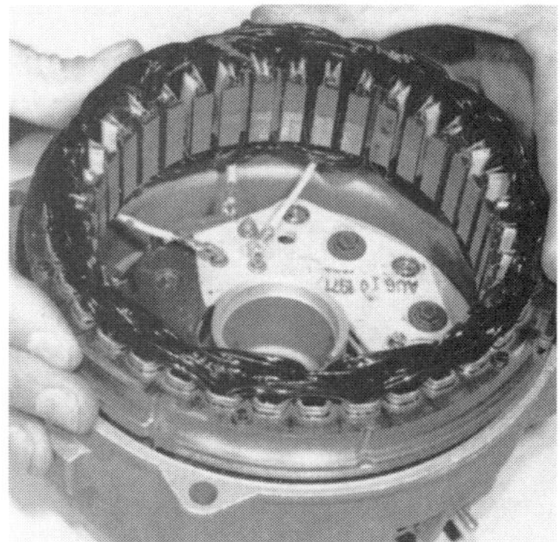

15. Fit the stator to the rear end frame and solder the three stator leads to the rectifier terminal connections.

16. Test the rotor for grounds and opens, as shown here, before assembling the alternator.

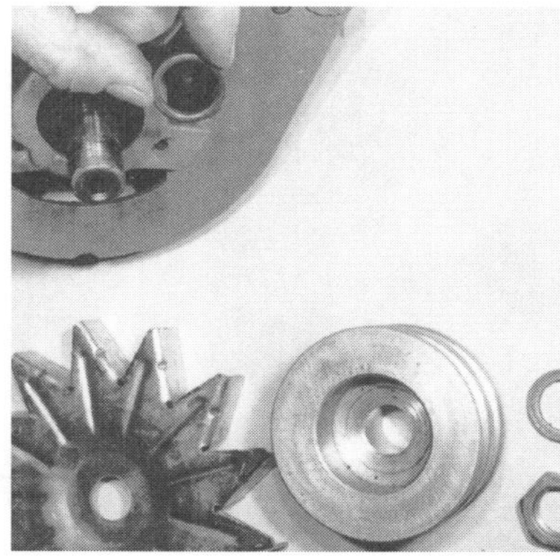

17. If the drive end frame parts are to be removed, *carefully* clamp the rotor in a vise and remove the nut, washer, pulley, fan, and collar.

18. Separate the rotor from the end frame. Note the spacer on the shaft; it must install in the same direction. Leave it on the shaft unless replacing it.

Copyright 2000 by Chek-Chart Publications

MOTORCRAFT SIDE-TERMINAL ALTERNATOR OVERHAUL PROCEDURE

19. Remove the three screws and lift off the retainer plate if the front bearing is to be replaced.

20. Press or drive out the old bearing, then fit the new one into the end frame hub. *Carefully* seat the bearing with a wooden block and a hammer.

21. Fit the bearing retainer plate, install the three screws, and tighten evenly.

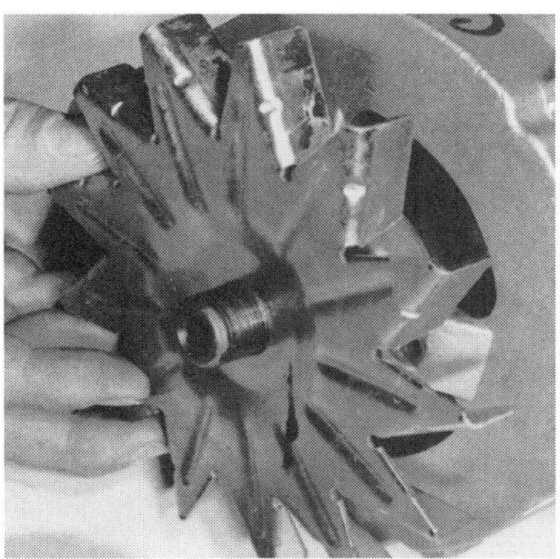

22. Assemble the collar, fan, pulley, and washer. Carefully hold the rotor in a vise while tightening the nut on the rotor shaft.

23. Align reference marks and fit the drive-end frame and rotor assembly into the rear-end frame and stator-rectifier assembly.

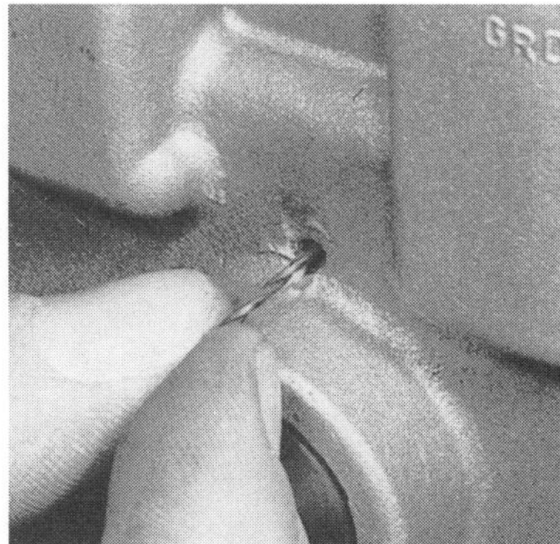

24. Install the through bolts and tighten them evenly. Release the brushes and make sure they contact the sliprings.

Copyright 2000 by Chek-Chart Publications

MOTORCRAFT INTEGRAL ALTERNATOR REGULAR (IAR) OVERHAUL PROCEDURE

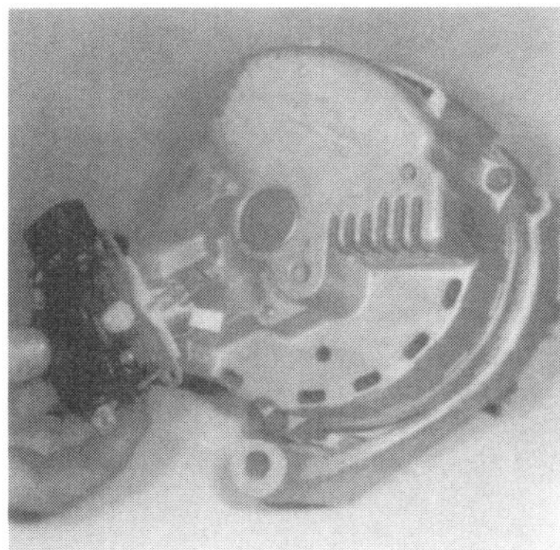

1. Remove the four mounting screws, then lift the regulator and brush assembly from the rear end frame.

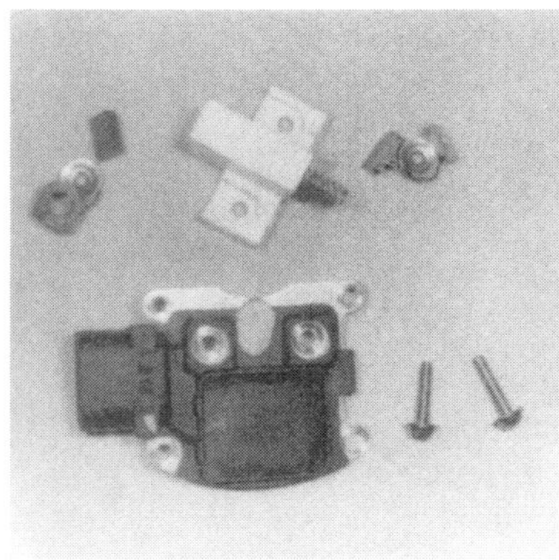

2. To replace brushes, remove the two screws from the regulator and separate the brush holder, brushes with the leads, and retaining nuts.

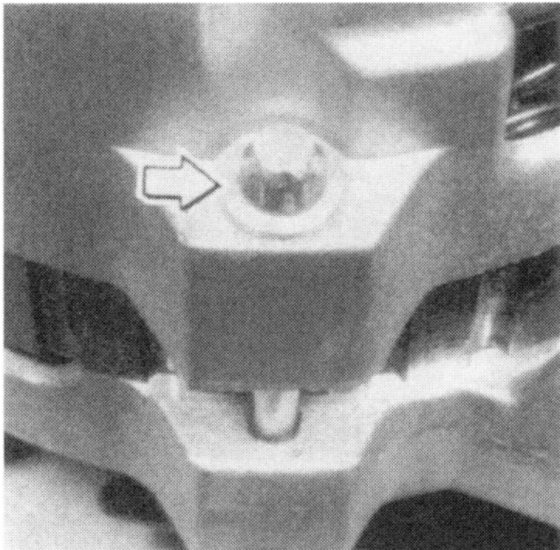

3. Scribe an alignment mark across the end frames with a grease pencil or chalk, then loosen and remove the through bolts.

4. Several through bolt head styles are used; be sure to use the correct socket to remove them.

5. Carefully separate the drive-end frame and rotor assembly from the stator and rear-end frame.

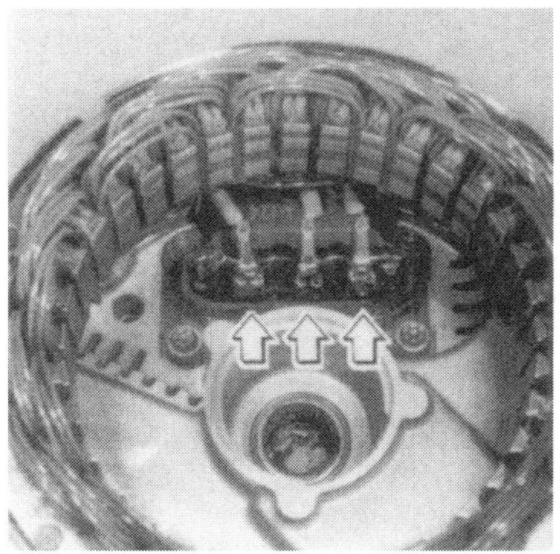

6. To remove the stator from the end frame, heat and separate the three soldered stator lead connections (arrows) at the rectifier assembly.

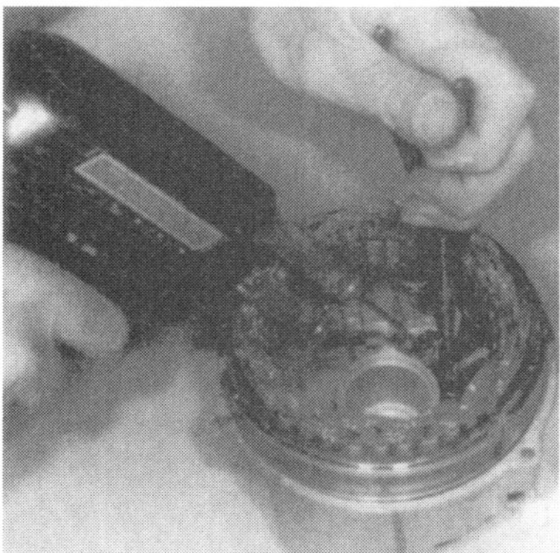

7. Heat one stator lead at a time with a soldering iron and use pliers to pull the leads off the rectifier terminal.

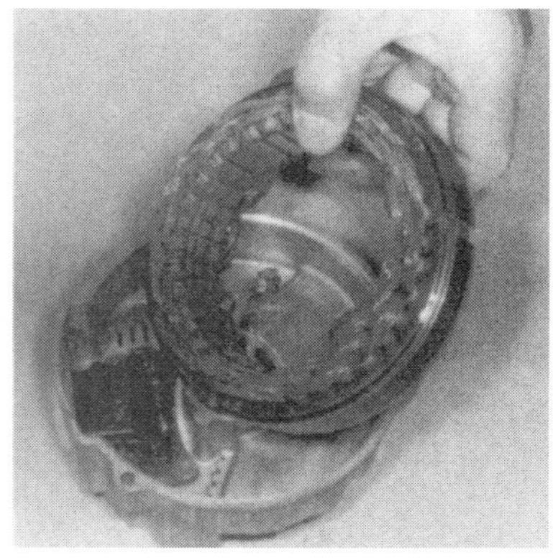

8. Once all three leads are disconnected, lift the stator from the end frame. Test the stator for continuity and ground.

9. Use a Torx T-20 driver to remove the four screws attaching the rectifier assembly to the end frame.

Copyright 2000 by Chek-Chart Publications

MOTORCRAFT INTEGRAL ALTERNATOR REGULAR (IAR) OVERHAUL PROCEDURE

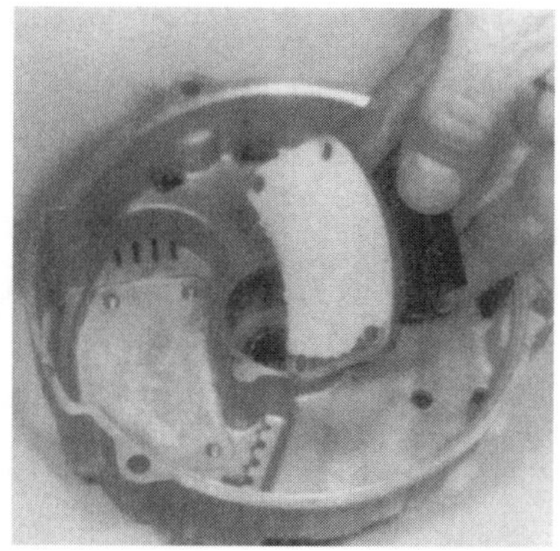

10. Lift the rectifier assembly from the end frame. Note: Silicone grease is applied to the base of the rectifier on assembly.

11. Loosen and remove the pulley nut. Remove the washer, drive pulley, fan, and spacer (arrow), from the rotor shaft.

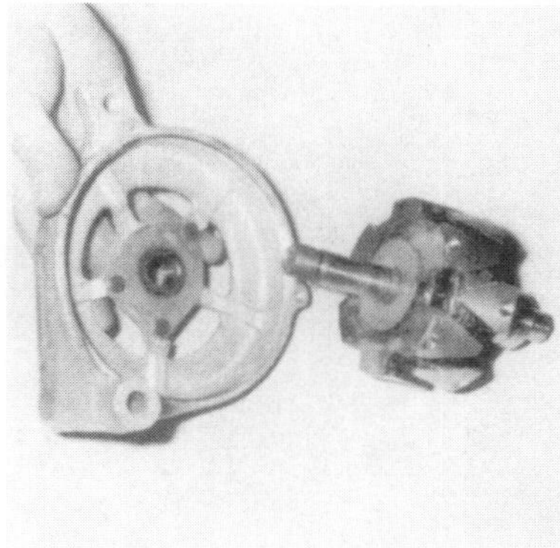

12. Press the rotor from the drive end frame. Test the rotor for continuity and ground and replace as needed.

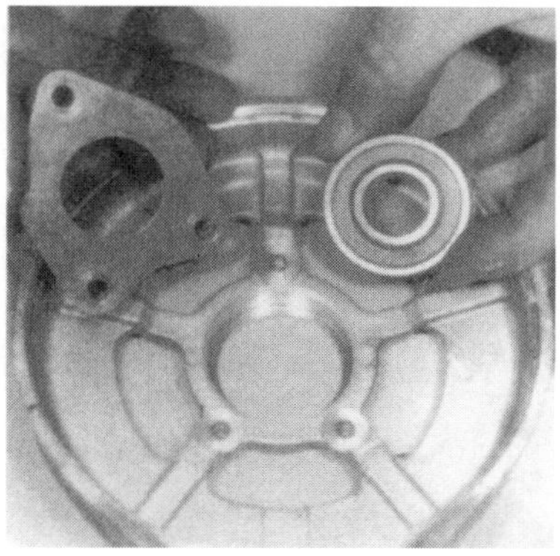

13. Remove the three screws and the retainer plate to replace the drive end bearing. The bearing installs in the frame by hand.

14. Assemble the brush holder to the regulator and insert a drill bit or wire to hold the brushes in place during installation.

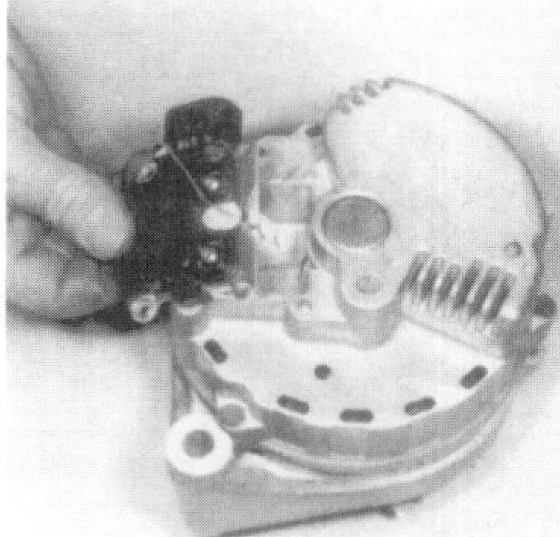

15. Assemble the end frames and tighten the through bolts. Install the regulator and brush holder assembly, then remove the drill bit or wire.

Copyright 2000 by Chek-Chart Publications

CHRYSLER STANDARD-DUTY ALTERNATOR WITH EXTERNAL REGULATOR OVERHAUL PROCEDURE

1. Remove the screws and washers, then lift the two brush holders from the rear-end frame.

2. Draw an alignment mark across both end frames. Then, remove the three through bolts and separate end frames.

3. Remove the three nuts securing the stator leads to the rectifier terminals. Lift the stator off the end frame.

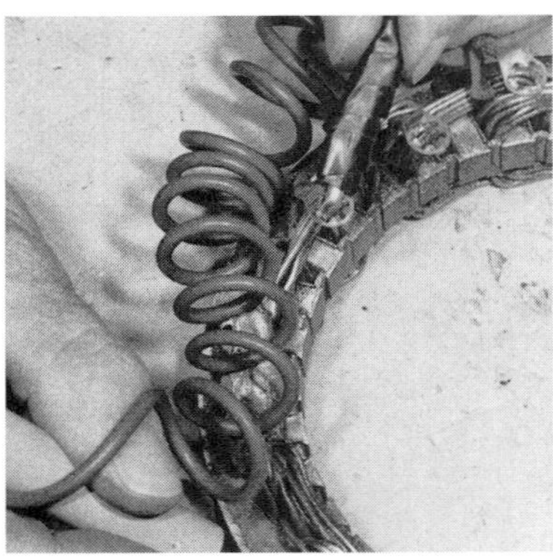

4. Perform stator ground, as shown here, and continuity tests with an ohmmeter or test lamp. Replace the stator as needed.

5. Test the positive rectifier by connecting an ohmmeter or test lamp between the heat sink and the lead for each of the three diodes.

6. Reverse the test leads and repeat. There should be continuity at all three positions in one direction, but not in the other direction.

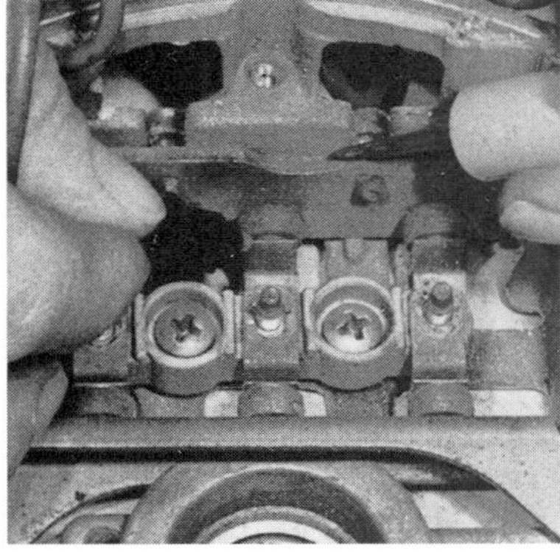

7. Test the negative rectifier in similar fashion by connecting an ohmmeter or test lamp between the heat sink and each diode.

8. Reverse the leads. Again, there should be continuity at all three positions in one direction, but not in the other direction.

9. Remove the nut and mounting screw, then lift the capacitor off the insulated stud. Remove the "BAT" terminal nut and the positive rectifier.

Copyright 2000 by Chek-Chart Publications

CHRYSLER STANDARD-DUTY ALTERNATOR WITH EXTERNAL REGULATOR OVERHAUL PROCEDURE

10. Loosen and remove the four mounting screws, then remove the negative rectifier from the end frame.

11. To replace a rear bearing, carefully press or drive it from end frame. Install the new bearing from outside the end frame.

12. Fit the insulating washer between the rectifier and end frame. Assemble the "BAT" terminal and insulator.

13. Make sure the insulating washer is on the other mounting stud, then install the positive rectifier.

14. Test the capacitor for opens and shorts, then install it. Install the "BAT" terminal and stud nuts to secure the capacitor and the positive rectifier.

15. Fit the negative rectifier and install the four screws through the top of the end frame to secure it.

16. Align the stator with the through bolt holes, fit the stator dowels into the end frame holes, and attach the stator leads to the rectifier terminals.

17. Perform rotor continuity, as shown, and ground tests with a test lamp or ohmmeter.

18. A special pulley puller is used to disassemble the drive end frame. *Carefully* clamp the end frame in a vise and attach the puller to pulley hub.

Copyright 2000 by Chek-Chart Publications

CHRYSLER STANDARD-DUTY ALTERNATOR WITH EXTERNAL REGULATOR OVERHAUL PROCEDURE

19. *Securely* hold the puller with pliers while turning the forcing screw. An impact wrench may be needed to remove some pulleys with the puller.

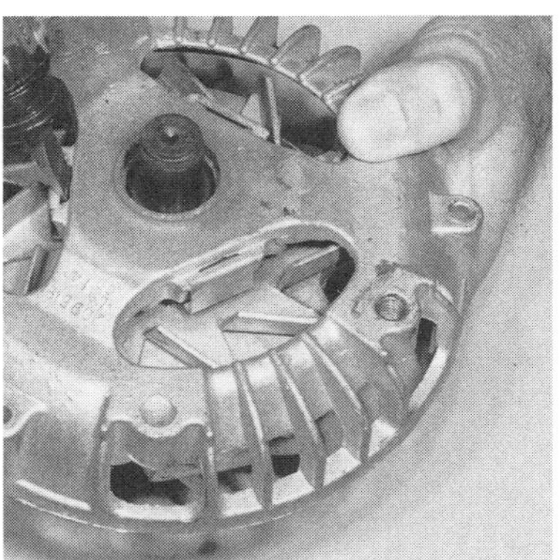

20. Use a screwdriver to release the three tabs for front bearing grease retainer.

21. If the rotor does not separate from the end frame, tap it gently with a soft-faced hammer to loosen it.

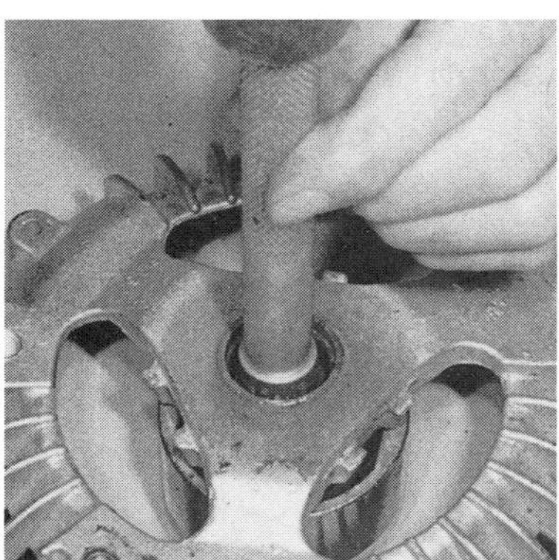

22. To remove the bearing, support the end frame and carefully press or drive the bearing from the end housing.

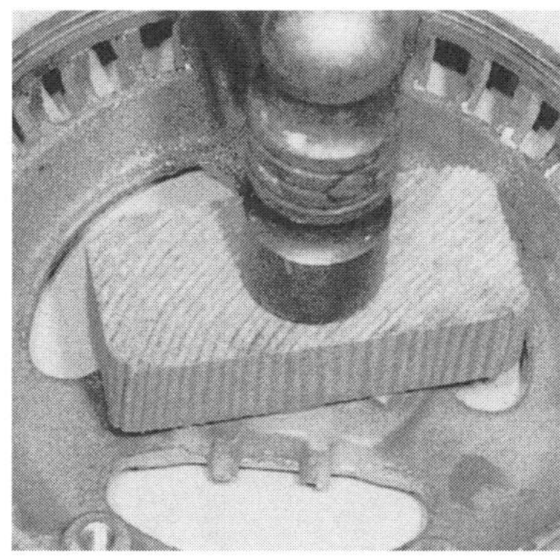

23. Seat the new bearing into the housing using a block of wood and a hammer. Fit the rotor to the end frame and latch the grease retainer tabs.

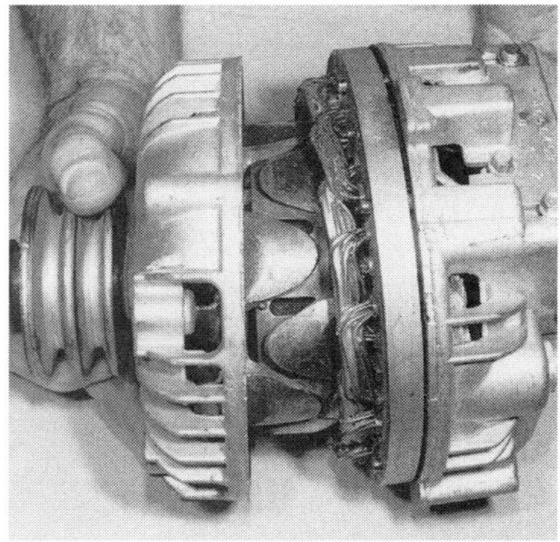

24. The pulley installs on the shaft with press. Align the dowels on the stator with the end frame holes, assemble, and secure with through bolts.

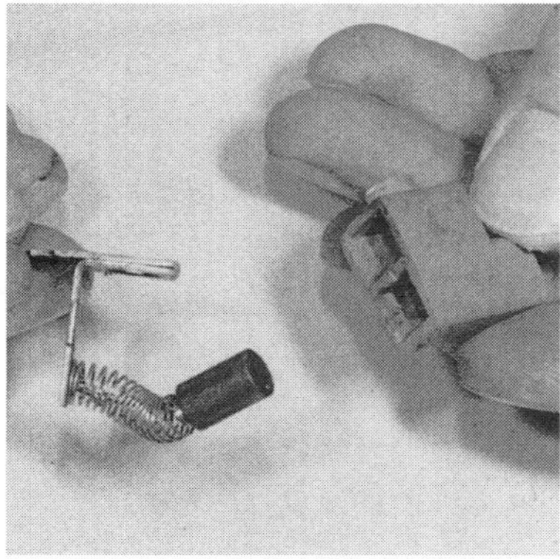

25. Inspect the brushes for wear and replace as a matched pair if necessary. Install the brushes and springs into the brush holders.

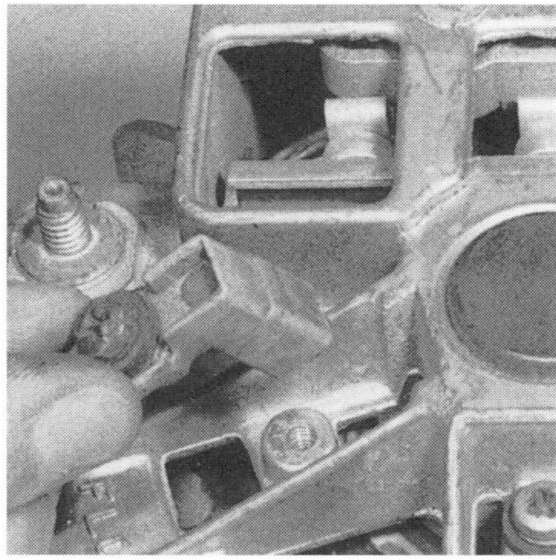

26. Attach the brush holder assemblies to the rear end frame. Make sure the insulators are installed between the brush holders and screw heads.

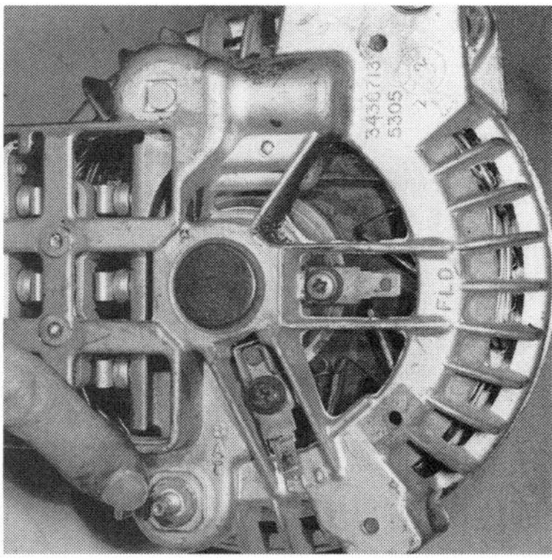

27. Make sure the "BAT" terminal and insulator are secure in the end frame. Install the insulating washer and nut to complete the overhaul.

Copyright 2000 by Chek-Chart Publications

CHRYSLER 40/90-AMPERE ALTERNATOR OVERHAUL PROCEDURE

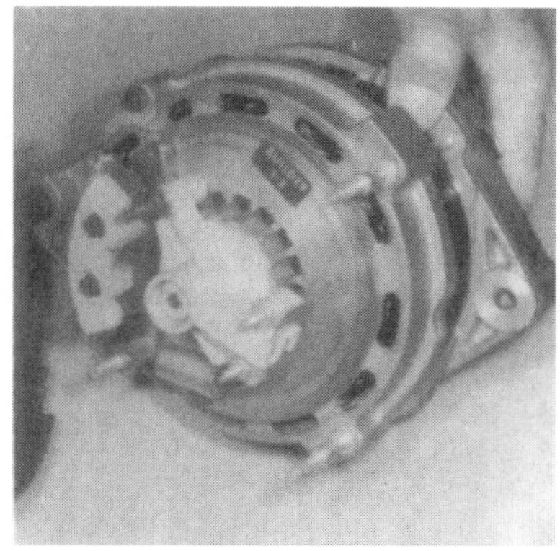

1. Draw an alignment mark across both end frames. Remove the nut from brush holder mounting stud and lift off the dust cover.

2. Use a deep-well socket to remove the two brush holder mounting screws. Lift the brush holder assembly off the shaft carefully.

3. Remove the three screws attaching the stator leads to the rectifier assembly terminals. Separate the leads from the post terminals.

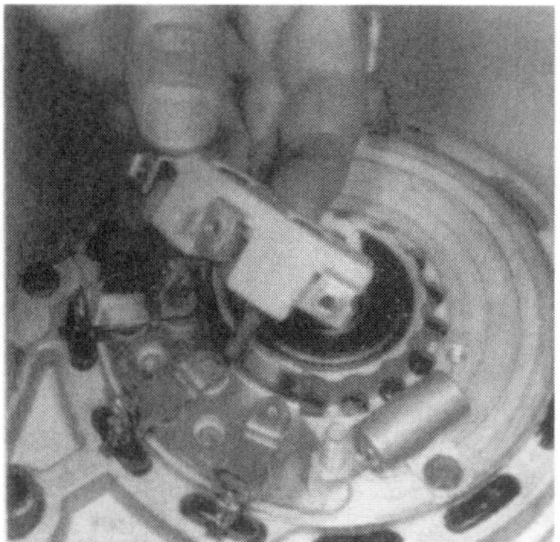

4. Remove the two screws holding the rectifier insulator to the end frame and lift off the rectifier insulator.

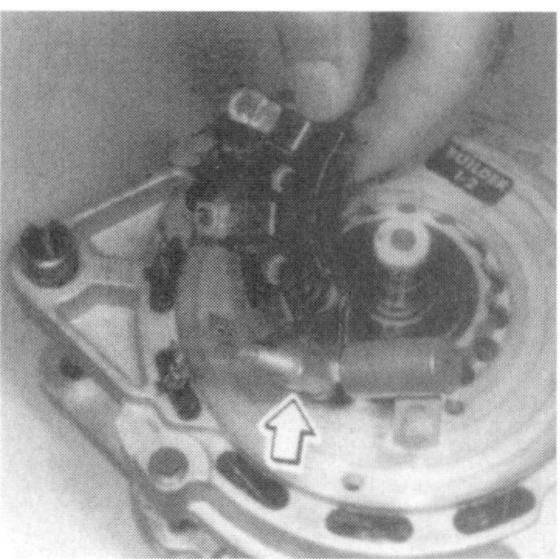

5. Remove the mounting screw from the end frame and lift off the capacitor and rectifier assembly. Remove the large nut (arrow) to separate.

6. Loosen and remove the four through bolts (arrows). Use a deep-well socket for the two bolts with stud ends.

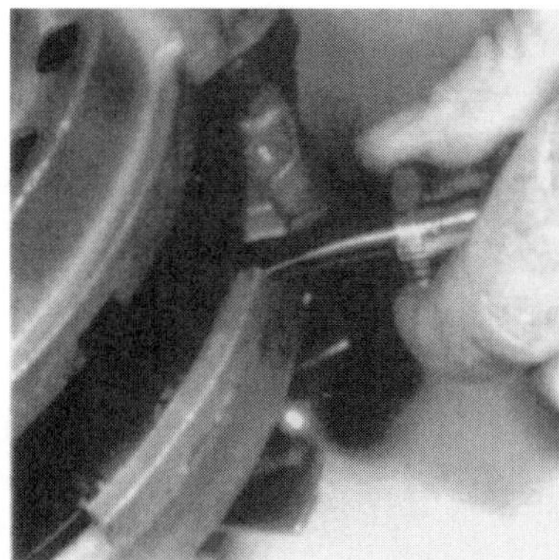

7. Carefully pry apart the rectifier and drive end frames by inserting a screwdriver blade at pry points on each side of the end frame and stator.

8. Guide the stator leads through the insulator openings in the rectifier end frame while separating it from the stator assembly.

9. Check the condition of the plastic stator lead insulator assembly. It is snapped out of the end frame if replacement is required.

Copyright 2000 by Chek-Chart Publications

CHRYSLER 40/90-AMPERE ALTERNATOR OVERHAUL PROCEDURE

10. Separate the stator from the drive end frame. Test the stator for continuity and ground.

11. Remove the pulley nut, washer, pulley, fan, and front bearing spacer from the rotor shaft. The chamfer on the spacer fits toward the rotor on installation.

12. Press, *do not hammer,* the rotor from the end frame, then remove the inner bearing spacer (arrow) from rotor shaft. Test the rotor.

13. To replace a front bearing, remove the four bearing retaining screws. Press the old bearing out and the new one in.

14. This rotor is more delicate than most. The ceramic slipring end of the shaft (A) and the plastic termination plate (B), are easily damaged.

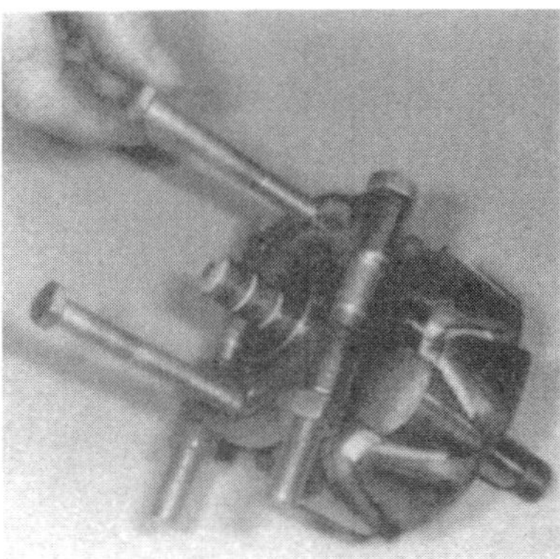

15. Use the Chrysler special tool or a bearing splitter to remove and install bearings. Avoid damaging the shaft end and termination plate.

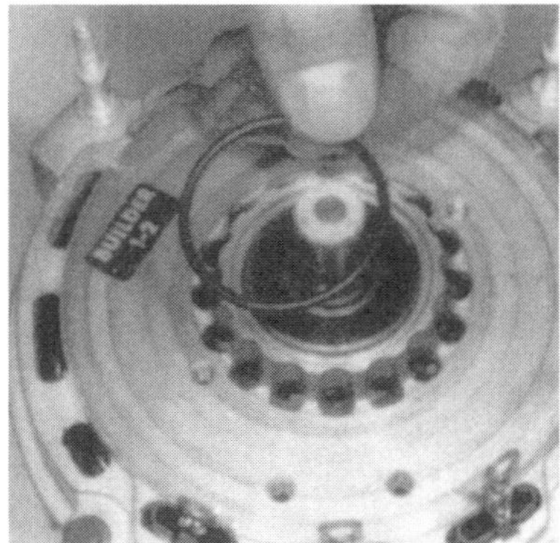

16. Reassemble the end frames and stator, then install the four through bolts. Install a new O-ring on the rectifier end frame.

17. Assemble the rectifier, capacitor, and rectifier insulator to the end frame and tighten in place. Attach the three stator leads to the rectifier terminals.

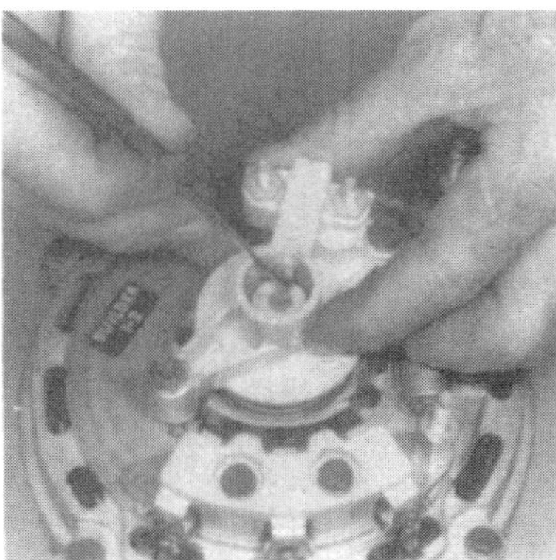

18. Use a pointed tool to push brushes back into the holder while fitting it over the sliprings. Tighten brush holder screws and install the dust cover.

Copyright 2000 by Chek-Chart Publications

PART THREE

Starting System Service

Chapter Six
Starting System

Chapter Seven
Starter Motor Overhaul

Copyright 2000 by Chek-Chart Publications

6 Starting System

The starting system includes the battery, ignition switch, safety switch, solenoid, starter motor, and all the circuitry that links these components. Starting circuits often contain relays, fuses, fusible links, circuit breakers, or similar devices to protect the wiring and deliver the required current to the starter motor. In addition, starter motor operation may be electronically prevented by an anti-theft, clutch interlock, or other accessory systems on many newer models. Wiring and circuit diagrams are needed to troubleshoot and accurately diagnose the starting system. Accurate specifications are needed to test and repair system components.

Part Three of this *Shop Manual* consists of two chapters that detail starting system service. This chapter explains inspection, diagnostic, and test procedures used to isolate the source of a system problem. Typical replacement procedures for components other than the starter motor are included in this chapter as well. If tests indicate a starter motor failure, the starter must be removed from the vehicle for repair or replacement. Starter motor removal, overhaul, and installation procedures are discussed in Chapter Seven.

As with the charging system, the starting system depends on a battery that is at a full state of charge and is supplying sufficient current to drive the motor. Test the battery as explained in Chapter Three of this *Shop Manual* before attempting to diagnose starting problems.

INSPECTION AND DIAGNOSIS

Attempt to start the engine and form a preliminary diagnosis based on what happens when the ignition key is in the START position. A starter motor that cranks slowly or not at all is usually caused by a battery that is discharged or has inadequate reserve capacity. However, internal engine damage that binds the crankshaft produces these same symptoms. If the starter motor does crank, listen carefully to determine which areas of the starting system to focus on during the inspection, figure 6-1.

Inspection

Many problems within the starting system are found with nothing more than a simple visual inspection. Inspect the following areas:

- Battery
- Ignition switch
- Starting safety switch
- Starter solenoid
- Starter motor.

Copyright 2000 by Chek-Chart Publications

SYMPTOMS	POSSIBLE CAUSE	CURE
• Nothing happens when ignition switch is turned to Start	1. Battery discharged 2. Open in control circuit 3. Defective starter relay or solenoid 4. Open in motor internal ground connections	1. Recharge or replace 2. Test control circuit for continuity; repair or replace components as necessary 3. Replace relay or solenoid 4. Replace starter motor
• Solenoid contacts click or chatter but starter does not operate OR movable pole shoe starter chatters or disengages before engine has been started	1. Battery discharged 2. Excessive resistance in system 3. Open in solenoid or movable pole shoe hold-in winding 4. Defective starter motor	1. Recharge or replace 2. Make voltage drop tests; replace components as necessary 3. Replace solenoid or movable pole shoe starter 4. Replace starter motor
• Starter motor operates but does not turn car engine	1. Defective starter drive assembly 2. Defective engine flywheel ring gear	1. Replace starter drive 2. Replace engine flywheel ring gear
• Starter motor turns engine slowly or unevenly	1. Battery discharged 2. Excessive resistance in system 3. Defective starter 4. Defective engine flywheel ring gear 5. Poor flywheel/starter engagement	1. Recharge or replace 2. Move voltage drop tests; replace compo-nents as necessary 3. Replace starter motor 4. Replace engine flywheel ring gear 5. Adjust starter/flywheel engagement
• Engine starts but motor drive assembly does not disengage	1. Defective drive assembly 2. Poor flywheel/starter engagement 3. Shorted solenoid windings 4. Shorted control circuit	1. Replace starter drive 2. Adjust flywheel/starter engagement, if possible, or replace starter motor 3. Replace solenoid 4. Test control circuit; replace components as necessary

Figure 6-1. Attempt to start the engine and form a preliminary diagnosis.

At the battery, check for:

- Loose or corroded terminals
- Loose or corroded ground cable connections
- Frayed or corroded cables
- Damaged insulation.

Check the ignition switch for:

- Loose mounting
- Damaged wiring
- Worn or sticking contacts
- Loose connections.

Check a starting safety switch for:

- Improper adjustment
- Loose mounting
- Loose or damaged wiring.

Check starter solenoids for:

- Loose mounting
- Loose connection
- Damaged wiring.

Inspect the starter motor for:

- Loose mounting
- Improper pinion adjustment
- Loose wiring and connections
- Damaged wiring and connections.

On systems that use a starter relay, check the relay for loose connections and wiring damage. Verify relay operation using a voltmeter and jump wire. If the vehicle has a theft-deterrent system, it is important to have the information necessary to test it.

Copyright 2000 by Chek-Chart Publications

All General Motors and most import vehicles have a solenoid mounted onto, or enclosed within, the starter motor. Ford uses a starter relay to complete the high current circuit and drive the motor. The relay is mounted on the bulkhead or an inner-fender panel. Some older Ford vehicles have a solenoid at the starter in addition to the relay. Chrysler starting systems use both a starter relay, mounted on the bulkhead or a fender panel, and a solenoid at the starter.

Repair any problems found during the inspection. Then, perform tests to isolate the source of any remaining starting system symptoms.

TESTING

Almost all starting system tests are performed while the starter motor is cranking the engine. However, if the engine starts and runs during the test, the readings will be inaccurate. Therefore, bypass the ignition switch with a remote starter switch to prevent the engine from starting, figure 6-2. As an alternative, disable the ignition system and use the key to crank the engine.

In addition to circuit diagrams and accurate test specifications, testing the starting system requires a:

- Voltmeter
- Ammeter
- Variable-resistance load
- Jumper wire
- Remote starter switch.

A charging-starter-battery (CSB) analyzer contains all of these units except the remote starter switch and jumper wires. However, using an amp probe and a graphing multimeter (GMM) or a lab scope is a quick and easy way to get accurate test results, figure 6-3.

When using an amp probe, sample the starter signal before disabling the ignition. To test, clamp the amp probe around the solenoid wire and monitor the signal while turning the key and attempting to start the engine. Remember, a stopped engine creates considerable resistance, which must be overcome by high starter current to get it turning over. Once it is up to speed, the starter requires less current to keep turning the engine. A current trace of a good starter spikes up immediately as the ignition switches on and the pull-in windings energize, oscillates several times as speed builds up, then drops and tapers off to a lower level as the pull-in windings switch off, figure 6-4. Current drops to zero when the ignition switch is moved to the RUN position. Although exact specifications vary by model, current peaks at about 50 to 60 amps and is maintained at about 15 to 20 amps for most starters. Variations in the current trace or the peak and hold amperage indicate internal starter or solenoid problems.

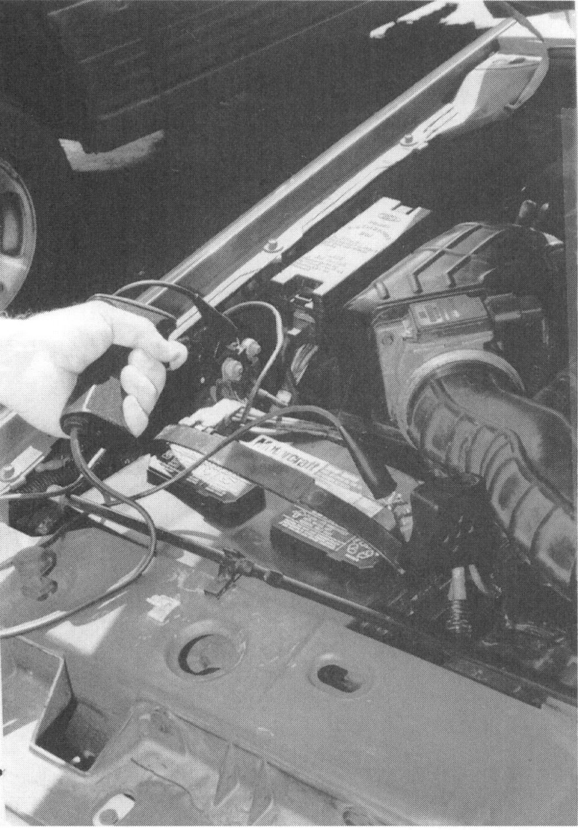

Figure 6-2. A remote starter is a jumper wire with a momentary switch. Depressing the switch applies battery current directly to the starter relay or solenoid.

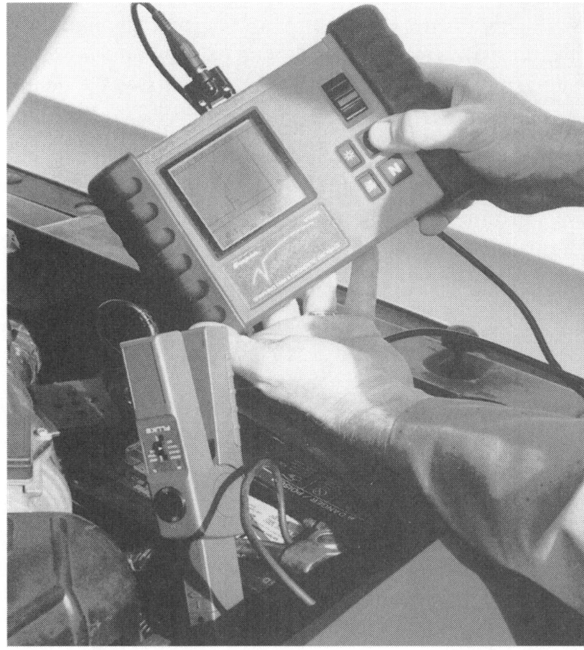

Figure 6-3. Using a GMM and an amp probe to check starter current draw.

Copyright 2000 by Chek-Chart Publications

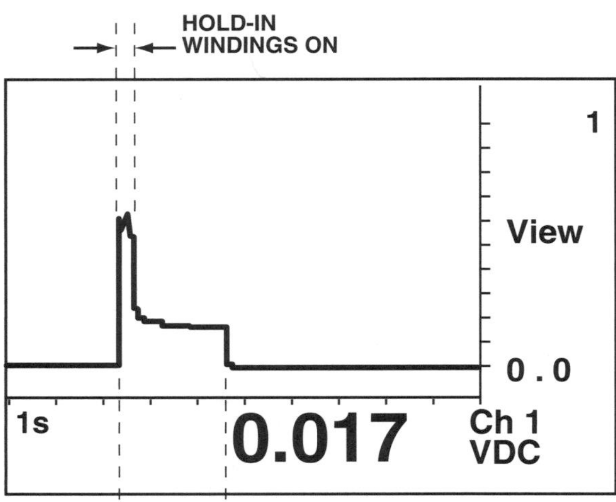

Figure 6-4. A good starter current trace spikes when energized, then drops and levels off as the motor comes up to speed.

Traditionally, the following tests are performed on the starting system:

- Current Draw
- Cranking Voltage
- Circuit Resistance.

Test Precautions

On vehicles that have the ignition starting bypass built into the ignition switch or the starter relay, disable the ignition. Disconnect the wiring harness connector from the distributor or coil pack to disable vehicles with electronic ignition or engine management systems. Be sure any disconnected wires do not contact a ground. When testing, observe the following precautions:

- Make sure the transmission is out of gear and the parking brake set during cranking. Remember, the remote starter switch bypasses the safety switch.
- Do not crank the starter motor for more than fifteen seconds at a time, and allow two minutes between tests for cooling to prevent overheat damage to the motor.
- Disconnect the negative battery cable before making or breaking any connections at the starter motor, solenoid, or relay.

Although disconnecting the negative battery cable is a generally accepted safety procedure to prevent arcing from wrenches and other tools, it is often ignored. This results in burnt hands as well as circuit and component damage. On models with an anti-theft radio, make sure the customer has the programming code before disconnecting the battery. Otherwise, an

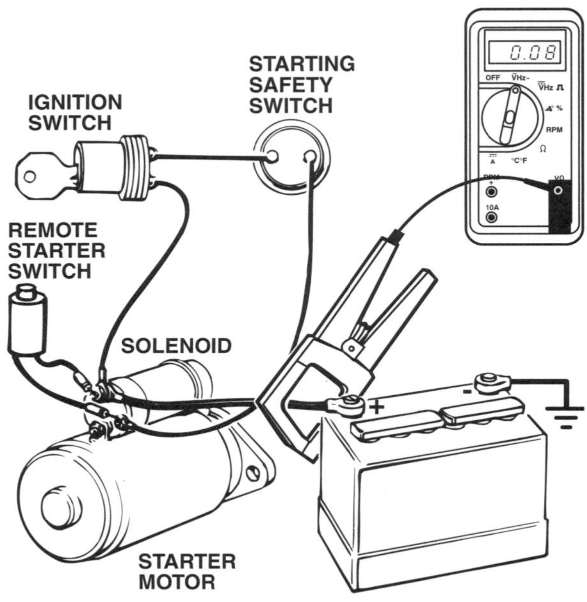

Figure 6-5. Meter connections for testing starter motor current draw.

expensive trip to the dealer to reprogram the radio may result.

Current Draw

The current draw test measures the amount of current, in amperes, that the starter circuit requires to crank the engine. This test, which helps isolate the source of a starting problem, is performed with either a CSB analyzer or a voltmeter and an amp probe or inductive ammeter. To test:

1. Bypass the ignition with a remote starter switch.
2. Connect the voltmeter to read voltage across the battery terminals. Observe correct polarity.
3. Clamp the amp probe or ammeter pickup around the starter motor power cable.
4. Crank the engine for several seconds and note the voltmeter and ammeter readings, figure 6-5.
5. Compare ammeter readings to specifications.

With a CSB analyzer, connect the leads and test according to the equipment instructions. Regardless of the method used, high current draw is caused by either a short in the starter circuit or a binding starter motor or engine. Low current draw is the result of high resistance in the starting system circuitry or an undercharged or defective battery.

High resistance in the cranking circuit causes both high and low current draws. To understand how, it is necessary to know that the starter motor requires high current to get up to speed. Once the starter motor is up to speed, it acts like a generator and produces a

Copyright 2000 by Chek-Chart Publications

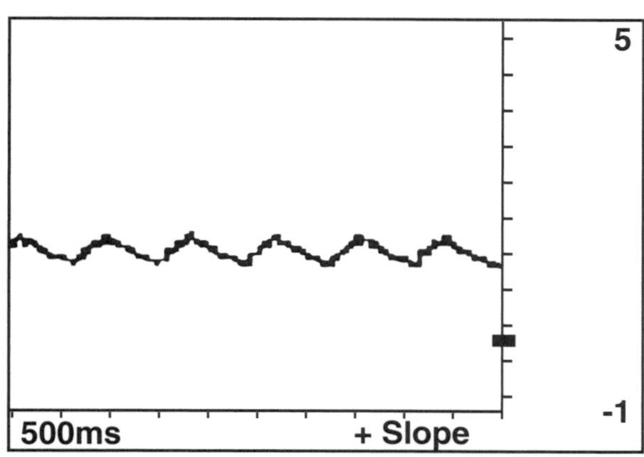

Figure 6-6. An amp probe trace of starter current while cranking shows the resistance created by engine compression.

counter voltage that limits the current. A motor requires high current to begin turning and to turn slowly. High resistance prevents the starter from getting enough current to get up to speed. As a result, the motor turns slowly and does not limit the current.

If resistance is high enough, it limits current to the starter. This low current causes the starter motor to turn slowly or not at all. Suspect high resistance if amperage momentarily spikes high, then immediately drops to a lower amount.

When high resistance is indicated, perform starter circuit resistance tests as described later in the chapter. If testing indicates a starter motor problem, remove the unit for service as described in Chapter Seven of this *Shop Manual.*

High starter circuit resistance is not always caused by an electrical problem. An engine that does not turn freely due to mechanical failure, such as seized bearings, collapsed pistons, or bent connecting rods, creates high resistance that must be overcome for the starter to crank. Other engine problems, such as a slipped timing belt or chain, burnt valves or leaking head gaskets, lower starter circuit resistance because they allow the engine to turn more easily. In this case, the starter cranks faster than normal, but the engine may not start. To quickly check internal engine condition, clamp an amp probe on the battery-to-starter cable, disable the ignition, and crank the starter while monitoring a GMM or scope screen. The signal should go high as the motor first engages, then level off in an even ripple pattern, figure 6-6. Resistance and current rise to a peak as each cylinder approaches top dead center. Look for even peaks on the trace. If compression is low on one cylinder, the current peak of that cylinder is lower than the peaks of the other cylinders.

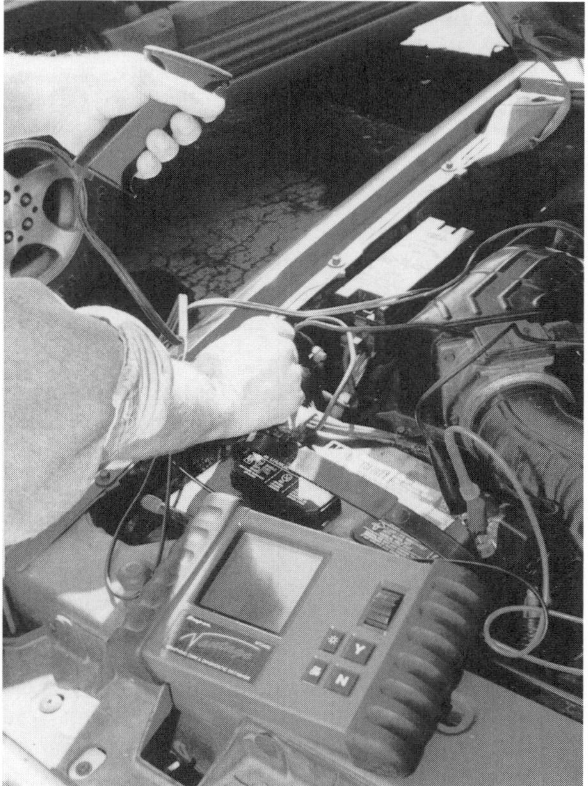

Figure 6-7. Checking starter cranking voltage at the relay.

Cranking Voltage

This test, which must be performed with a fully charged battery in good condition, measures available voltage at the starter during cranking. Test results are read on a voltmeter. To test:

1. Bypass the ignition switch with a remote starter switch.
2. Connect the negative voltmeter lead to a good ground and connect the positive voltmeter lead to high-current starter circuit, figure 6-7. Some manufacturers recommend connecting the voltmeter directly to the starter, while others specify testing at the relay or solenoid. Check the service manual for exact procedures and specifications.
3. Crank the engine while monitoring the voltmeter reading.

If the starter motor cranks poorly, interpret current draw and cranking voltage test results as follows:

- If voltage is 9.6 or more and the amperage is high, the battery is good and the starter motor is getting enough current to operate. The problem is in the motor, the engine is tight and binding, or there is high circuit resistance.

Copyright 2000 by Chek-Chart Publications

- If voltage is 9.6 or more and the amperage is low, the battery is good but there is not enough current to drive the starter motor. The problem is high resistance.
- If voltage is 9.6 or less and the amperage is high, the high amperage draw pulls down the battery voltage and the battery may be faulty. A defective starter motor, overadvanced ignition timing, a tight and binding engine, or high circuit resistance may also be at fault.
- If voltage is 9.6 or less and the amperage is low, the battery should be tested.

Perform a cranking test to check for high resistance in the starter circuit. Starter overloading may be the result of engine seizing, dragging, or preignition.

Circuit Resistance

If the current draw and cranking voltage tests indicate that the problem lies in one of the starting system electrical circuits, use the following tests to pinpoint the problem.

These tests locate the point of high resistance in the circuit that is causing excessive voltage drop. The resistance usually occurs at one of the connections in the circuits, but internally defective wires and cables may also be at fault. As a general rule, acceptable voltage drop in a starting system is less than 0.1 volt across each connection. A greater voltage drop causes starter motor performance problems.

The starting system has three circuits:

- Insulated
- Ground
- Control.

The insulated circuit carries the high current needed to operate the starter motor, the ground circuit provides a return path to the battery for power supplied by the insulated circuit, and the control circuit includes all the low-current wiring and devices used to open and close the insulated circuit. Perform resistance tests on each of the three circuits.

Insulated circuit test

Together, the insulated circuit and ground circuit make up the complete starter motor circuit. The insulated circuit includes all of the high-current cables and connections from the battery to the starter motor. Locate high resistance in the insulated circuit by voltage drop testing:

1. Bypass the ignition switch with a remote starter switch.
2. Connect the positive voltmeter lead to the positive battery terminal. Make sure to connect the meter lead to the post or terminal nut, not to the cable. Otherwise, high resistance in the cable-to-post connection may go undetected. Connect the negative voltmeter lead to the terminal at the starter, figure 6-8.

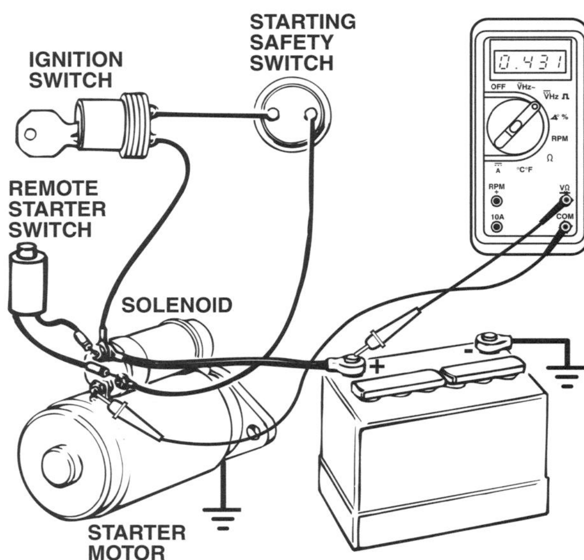

Figure 6-8. Measure insulated circuit voltage drop between the positive battery terminal and the starter power terminal.

3. Crank the engine and take a voltmeter reading. This is voltage drop on the insulated circuit; compare it to specifications. If the reading is within the specifications, usually 0.2 to 0.6 volt, perform a ground resistance test. Continue testing if readings are high.
4. Move the positive voltmeter lead down the circuit toward the battery, taking readings at each connection to isolate the high resistance, figure 6-9. The point of high resistance is between the original test point and the connection where voltage drop falls to within acceptable limits. Work down the circuit and take voltmeter readings while cranking the engine.

A load may be applied with a carbon pile or CSB analyzer as an alternative to cranking the starter, figure 6-10. Momentarily load the circuit to approximately 150 to 200 amps and note the voltage drop. Then, quickly switch the load off to prevent draining the battery.

When high resistance is found, repair or replace any damaged wiring or faulty connections to restore the circuit to operating condition. Retest to confirm the repair.

Ground circuit test

The ground circuit provides the return path to the battery for the power supplied to the starter through the

Copyright 2000 by Chek-Chart Publications

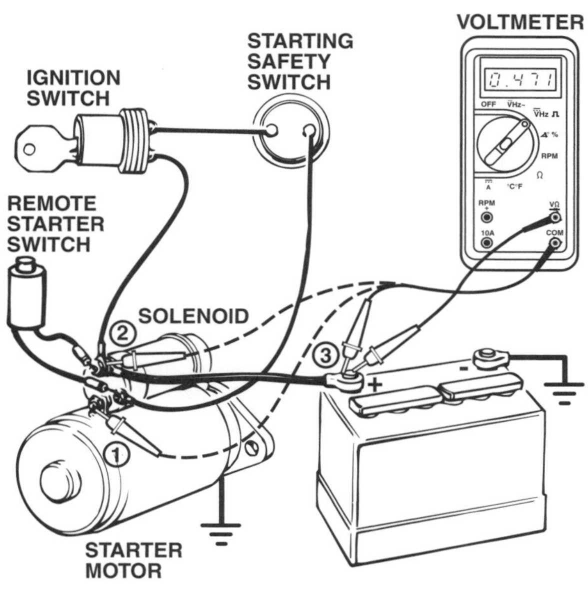

Figure 6-9. Work down the insulated circuit taking voltage drop readings to isolate high resistance.

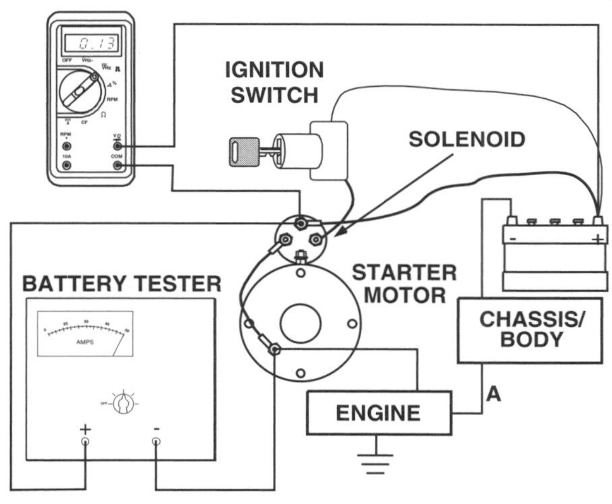

Figure 6-10. Using a CSB analyzer, rather than the starter motor, to load the insulated circuit for voltage drop testing.

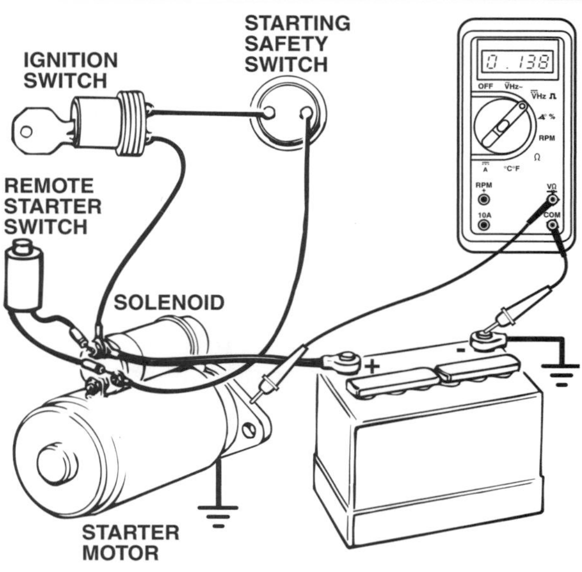

Figure 6-11. Measuring voltage drop across the starter ground circuit.

insulated circuit. It includes the starter-to-engine, engine-to-chassis, and chassis-to-ground terminal connections and cables. Perform voltage drop tests at these locations to check the ground circuit for high resistance. Take readings while cranking the starter, or applying a load with a CSB analyzer, and the ignition bypassed or disabled.

The negative voltmeter lead attaches directly to the negative battery post or terminal nut, not the battery cable. Remember, connecting the meter to the cable overlooks the cable-to-post connection. Take an initial voltage drop reading at the starter housing, figure 6-11. Acceptable ground circuit voltage drop is usually about 0.1 to 0.3 volt for most systems. To isolate high resistance in the ground circuit, take additional readings at the engine-to-chassis ground strap and negative battery cable connections. Work down the circuit from the starter to the battery. If voltage drop is within the specifications, perform a control circuit resistance test.

High ground circuit resistance is often caused by poor connections. Tighten the system ground connections, inspect the negative battery cable, and repeat the test. Replace the negative battery cable or engine-to-chassis ground strap, if necessary.

Control circuit test

The control circuit test checks all the wiring and components used to activate the magnetic switch. Control circuit components and design vary by make and model, so test points and specifications vary as well. In addition, auxiliary circuits for anti-theft and other systems are linked to the starter control circuit on many vehicles. Remember, any parallel circuits must be considered part of the starter control circuit when testing. Modern starter control circuitry is fairly complex and a circuit diagram is required for accurate testing and diagnosis, figure 6-12. Voltage drop tests are performed to check control circuit resistance.

To check voltage drop across the entire control circuit, connect the positive voltmeter lead to the positive battery terminal and connect the negative voltmeter lead to the switch terminal at the starter relay or solenoid. Disable the ignition system and crank the starter

Copyright 2000 by Chek-Chart Publications

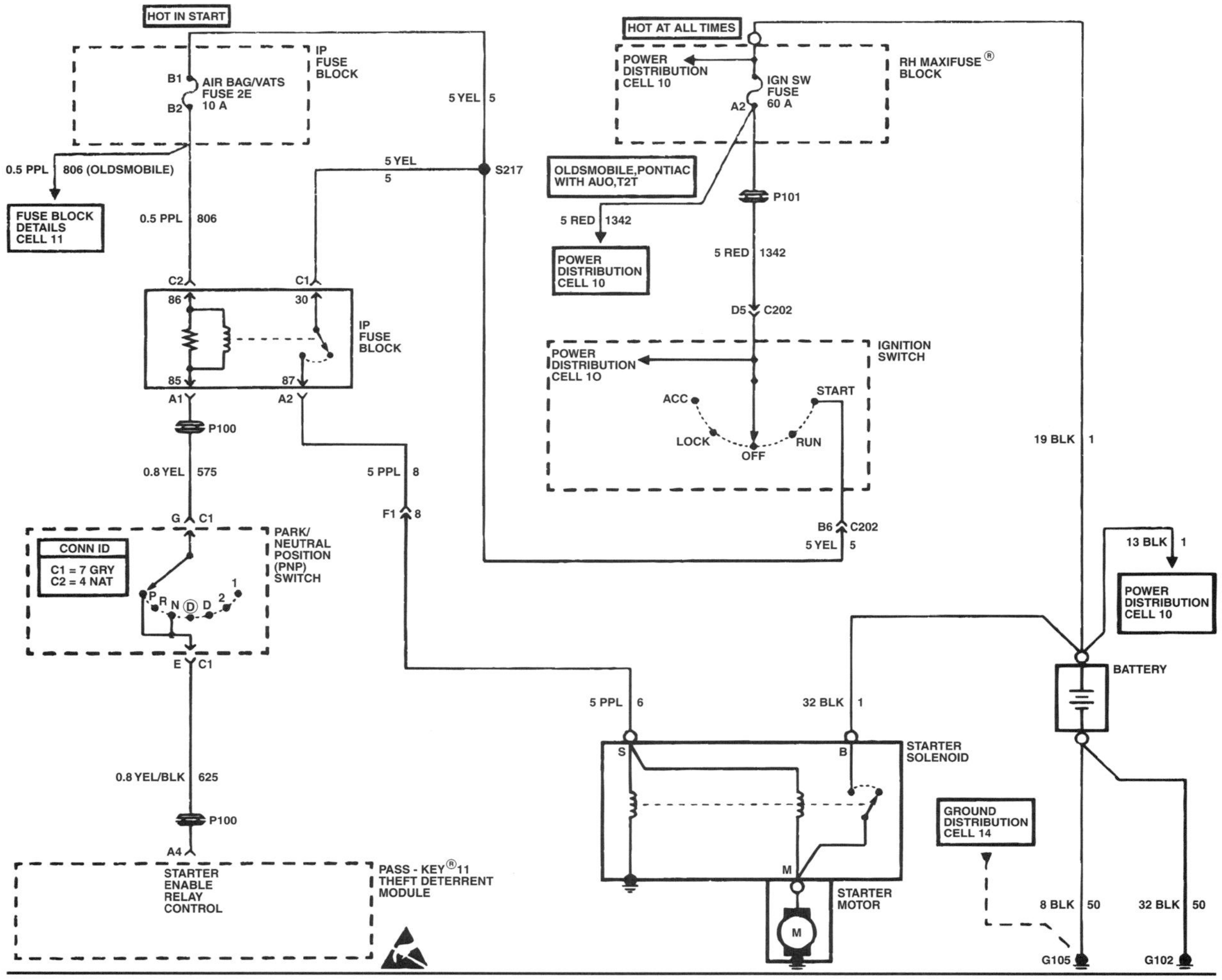

Figure 6-12. Use a starter control circuit diagram to determine current routing and test points.

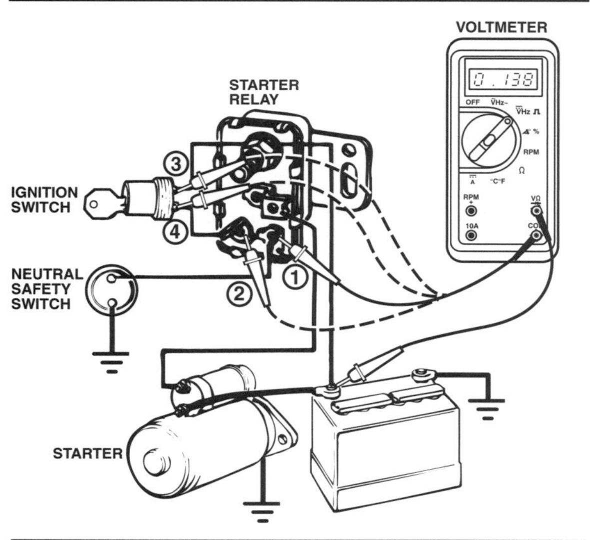

Figure 6-13. Check voltage drop at each control circuit connection to locate high resistance.

to get a reading. Compare the voltmeter reading to the specifications. Typically, up to about a one-volt drop is acceptable on the control circuit. If readings indicate high resistance, refer to a circuit diagram. Work down the circuit toward the battery and measure voltage drop at each connection to locate the source of resistance, figure 6-13. Repair or replace any damaged wiring or faulty connections, then retest.

STARTER CONTROL CIRCUIT DEVICES

A number of different control system devices are used to direct current to, or prevent current from reaching, the starter motor. The control circuit is routed through the ignition switch. The only way to complete the control circuit is to hold the ignition key in the start position. This delivers current to either a starter relay or directly to the starter solenoid.

Copyright 2000 by Chek-Chart Publications

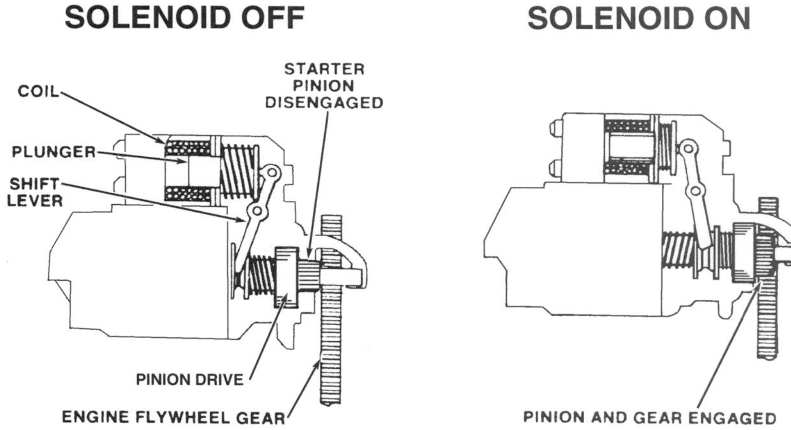

SOLENOID OFF

SOLENOID ON

STARTER PINION DISENGAGED
COIL
PLUNGER
SHIFT LEVER
PINION DRIVE
ENGINE FLYWHEEL GEAR
PINION AND GEAR ENGAGED

Figure 6-14. The starter solenoid is an electromagnetic coil that activates a mechanical linkage to engage the starter drive gear with the ringgear.

The starter relay is an electromechanical switch that connects the starter solenoid to battery current when the switch contacts are closed. The switch contacts of the relay are part of the starter control circuit. Relay contacts close when the ignition key is in the START position, and open when the key is in any other position. The starter solenoid is a coil with a moveable core that completes the high-amperage circuit and may also engage the starter drive with the flywheel.

A starter solenoid is an electromagnetic device that engages the starter drive with the engine ringgear to crank the engine. The heavy solenoid coil is mounted around a plunger. The plunger connects to a shift lever, which is mechanically attached to the starter drive pinion. Closing the starter control circuit activates the solenoid by energizing the coil. This pulls the plunger in and forces the shift lever out to mesh the gears of the drive pinion with those of the ringgear, figure 6-14. As the plunger continues to move, it closes the starter motor switch to energize the starter.

A starting safety, or neutral safety, switch, which prevents the starter from cranking when the transmission is engaged, is used on all vehicles with automatic transmissions and on some vehicles with manual transmissions, figure 6-15. A number of different designs are used. The safety switch may be mounted on the steering column under the dash panel or on the transmission or transaxle. Vehicles with a manual transmission often have a safety switch that is activated by the clutch pedal, so the starter operates only when the clutch pedal is depressed. A clutch switch generally installs between the ignition switch and the starter motor relay coil to maintain an open circuit when the clutch pedal is released.

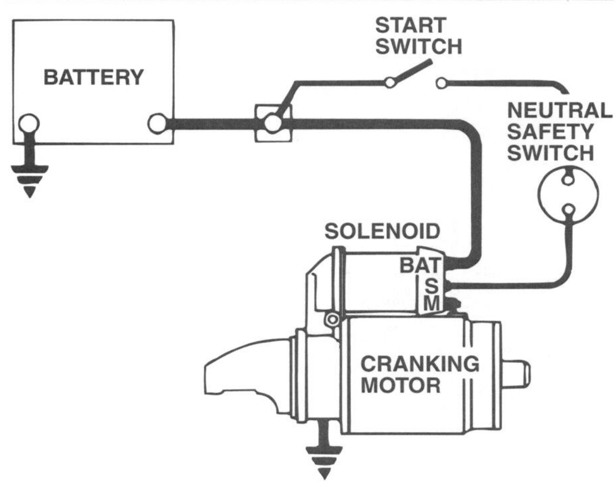

Figure 6-15. A safety switch prevents starter engagement if the vehicle is in gear.

In addition to the safety switch, many newer vehicles have a brake interlock device that prevents starter operation unless the brake pedal is depressed. These may be a mechanical device that holds the ignition lock so that it cannot be turned, or an electric device that opens the control circuit unless certain conditions are met.

A failure in any of these control devices or circuits prevents starter motor engagement.

Ignition Switch

The ignition switch assembles to the ignition lock tumbler and mounts on the steering column. On some models, the switch is an integral part of the lock assembly, while on others the electrical switch is a separate component, figure 6-16. With either design, the switch is easily tested without removing it from the

Copyright 2000 by Chek-Chart Publications

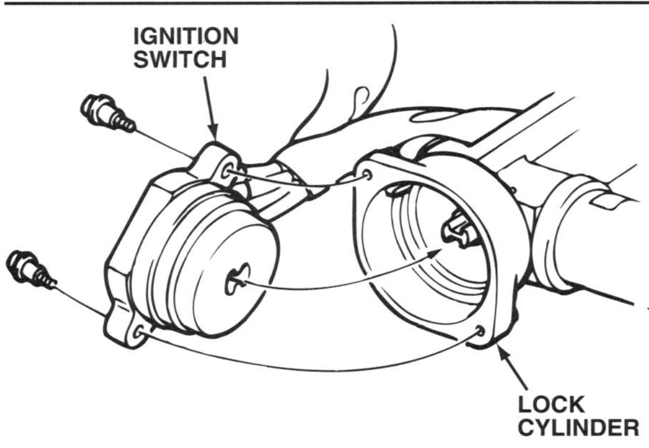

Figure 6-16. This Acura ignition switch bolts onto the ignition lock cylinder.

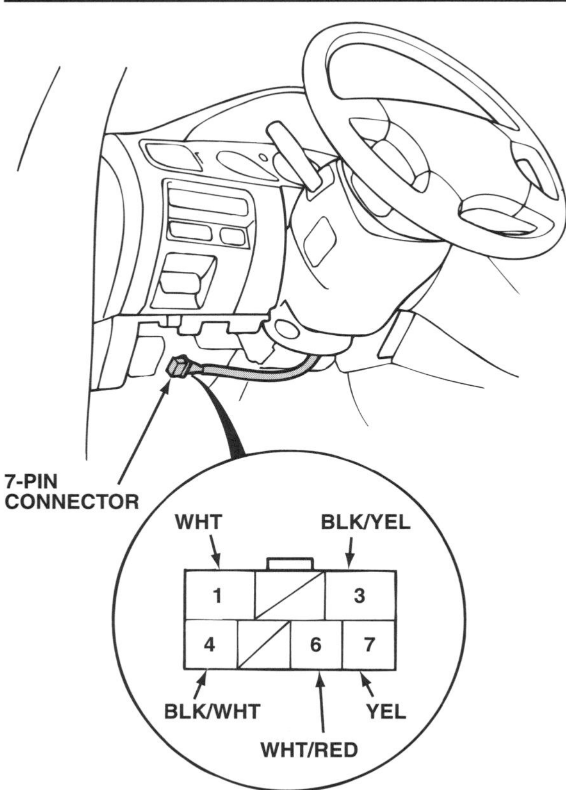

TERMINAL / POSITION	1 (BAT)	3 (IG1)	4 (ST)	6 (ACC)	7 (IG2)
O (LOCK)					
I (ACC)	O			O	
II (ON)	O	O		O	O
III (START)	O	O	O		

Figure 6-17. Use a pin chart to check continuity through the ignition switch.

vehicle. Disconnect the wiring harness multi-plug and check continuity through the switch in all positions. Manufacturers generally include a pin chart for testing the ignition switch in the service manual, figure 6-17.

Ignition switch failures are rare, but do happen on occasion. Most are a result of wear and usually occur on high-mileage vehicles and those used for frequent short trips. A worn ignition switch may work when cold, but not when hot because expansion of the contacts creates high control-circuit resistance. Ignition switches are not repairable and must be replaced when defective.

Refer to the factory service manual when replacing an ignition switch. On models with a supplemental restraint system, disable it to prevent accidental deployment of the air bag. Steering column cover panels must be removed to access the ignition switch for replacement. Tilt mechanisms, interlock linkages, column brackets, and other accessories must be loosened and moved or removed on some models as well. The lock assembly is often secured to the steering column with tamperproof bolts.

Starter Relay

Many vehicles use a starting circuit relay to direct current to the starter motor. A voltage drop test is performed to check relay operation. Measure voltage drop across the battery and switch terminals of the relay while cranking the starter. A voltmeter reading that exceeds one volt indicates excessive resistance in the control circuit, figure 6-18. Continue voltage drop testing to isolate the high resistance. Repair the control circuit as needed and retest.

If voltage drop across the relay is within specifications, below 2.5 volts, but the relay does not close, check for available voltage at the relay. Connect a voltmeter between the switch terminal of the relay and a good ground, then switch the ignition key to the start position and take a voltmeter reading. On a typical 12-volt system, the relay closes whenever voltage reaches approximately 7.7 volts. Next, confirm the relay ground by voltage drop testing. With a metal relay that grounds through the case, connect the voltmeter between the relay case and a chassis ground. If the relay grounds through a circuit, connect the voltmeter between the ground terminal and a chassis ground. The voltmeter reading should be less than 0.1 volt when the starter motor is engaged, figure 6-19. A relay that does not operate with a 7.7 or higher voltage and a good ground is faulty and must be replaced.

Copyright 2000 by Chek-Chart Publications

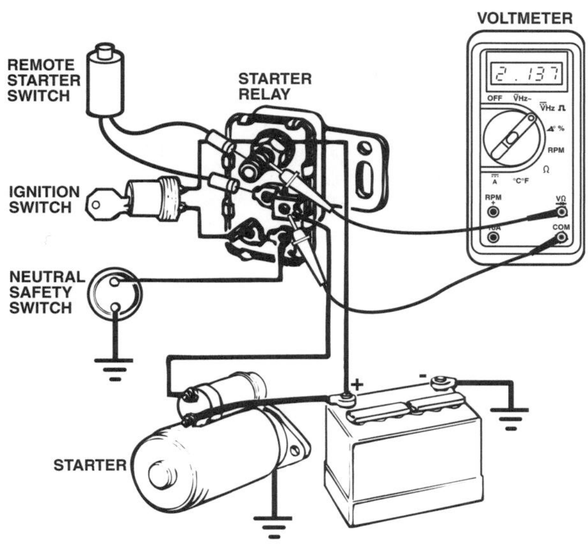

Figure 6-18. Voltage drop across a starter relay should be less than one volt.

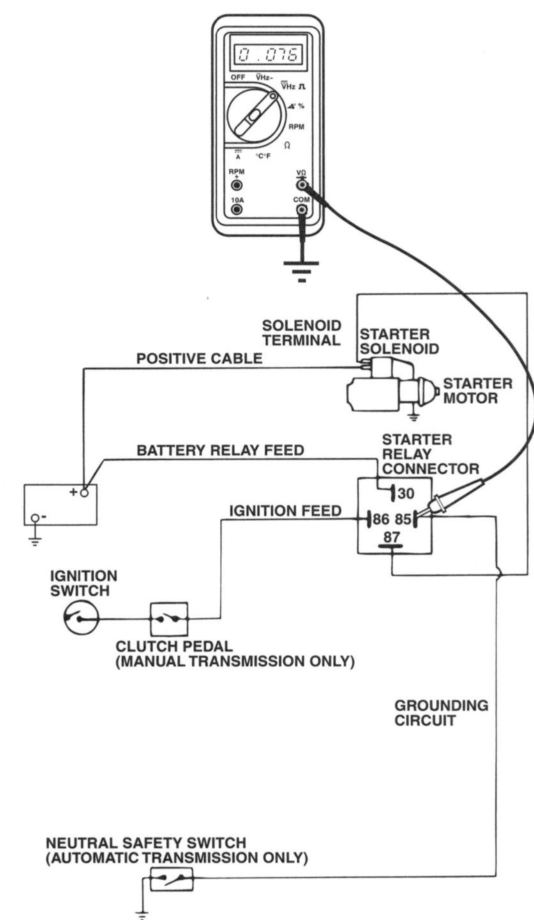

Figure 6-19. Voltage drop across a starter relay ground should be less than 0.1 volt.

Figure 6-20. This Ford starter relay bolts to the inner fender.

Replacing most starter relays is simply a matter of locating the relay, labeling and disconnecting the wires, and removing the relay. On older vehicles, the starter relay is often mounted on the bulkhead or an inner-fender panel, figure 6-20. Newer vehicles generally use a relay that simply plugs into a power distribution center in the engine compartment, figure 6-21.

Starter Solenoid

Starter motor solenoids are a pull-and-hold type of switch with two sets of windings. When the solenoid is first energized, current is applied to both pull-in and hold-in windings to draw in the core. As motor speed builds up and resistance drops, the pull-in windings switch off and the hold-in windings remain energized until the engine starts or the key is released. Solenoid operation is checked with a voltmeter using the same method as described for relays. To test starters and solenoids:

1. Confirm there are at least 8 volts available at the solenoid when cranking.
2. If voltage is present, check for battery voltage to the solenoid, then battery voltage to the starter.
3. Measure voltage drop on the ground circuit. It must be 0.1 volt or less.

Copyright 2000 by Chek-Chart Publications

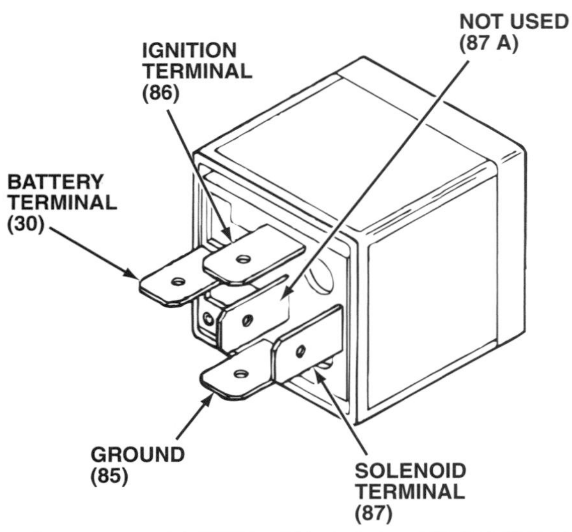

Figure 6-21. Some starter relays simply plug into a socket in the power distribution center.

A starter motor that fails to crank when battery voltage is available and the ground circuit is sound indicates either a seized engine or an internal starter motor failure. A seized engine, caused by liquid filling the cylinders due to a blown head gasket or leaking fuel injection system, is becoming more common. To eliminate this possibility, simply turn the engine by hand using a wrench on the crankshaft pulley nut. A seized engine or starter motor results in low voltage and high amperage readings. An open or high resistance in the ground circuit results in high voltage and low amperage readings.

In most cases, replacing a starter solenoid involves removing the starter motor and partially disassembling it to disengage the plunger from the starter shift lever. The exception would be Ford vehicles that use a remote solenoid that is generally mounted on an inner-fender panel. These Ford solenoids simply bolt on and are serviced the same as a starter relay. Starter motor removal and repair procedures are detailed in Chapter Seven of this *Shop Manual.*

Starter Safety Switch

All vehicles have some type of switch to prevent the vehicle from moving while the starter motor is engaged and cranking the engine. Commonly called a neutral-start, neutral-safety, or park-neutral switch, designs vary by make, model and year. Manufacturers

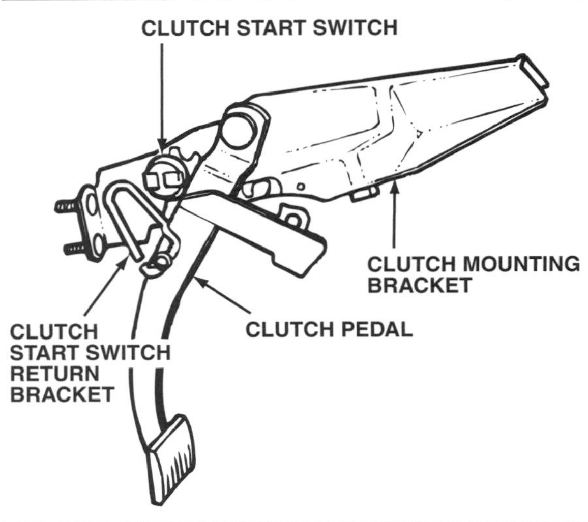

Figure 6-22. Fully depressing the clutch pedal closes a clutch start switch.

may refer to these devices as a park, reverse, neutral, drive, low (PRNDL) switch, manual lever position sensor (MLPS), or park-neutral position (PNP) switch.

Vehicles with manual transmissions or transaxles usually use a mechanical switch activated by the clutch pedal to prevent starting in gear, figure 6-22. The control circuit remains open unless the clutch pedal is fully depressed to activate the switch. A clutch-operated switch is not adjustable. To replace this type of switch, simply remove the defective unit and bolt a new one into the mounting holes of the original switch.

Starter safety switch operation is managed by the powertrain control module (PCM) on late-model vehicles with electronic control systems. Therefore, a diagnostic trouble code (DTC) generally records in the event of a switch or circuit failure. Circuit diagrams, specifications, and procedures from the manufacturer are required to troubleshoot electronic starter safety switch circuits. Electronic safety switches are generally mounted to the transmission or transaxle housing and are easy to replace. Refer to Chapter Twelve of this *Shop Manual* for additional information on electronic control systems.

On Chrysler, and some Ford, automatic transmissions and transaxles, the starter safety switch threads into the transmission housing, figure 6-23. To replace, simply disconnect the wiring and use a wrench to remove the old switch and install a new one. If a sealing washer or O-ring is used, replace it with a new one

Copyright 2000 by Chek-Chart Publications

Figure 6-23. This safety switch threads into the transmission housing and seals with a gasket.

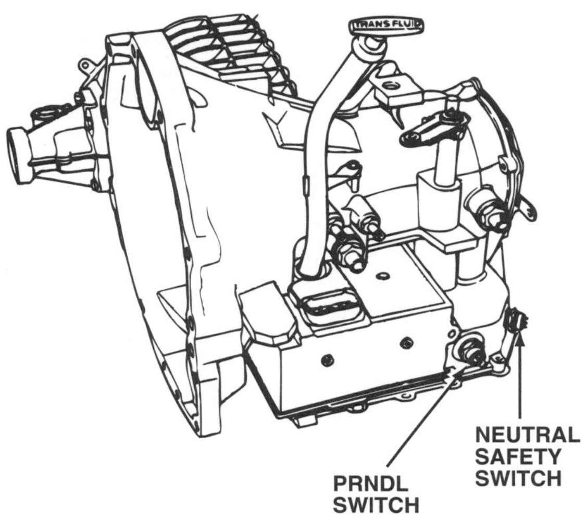

Figure 6-24. Chrysler uses both a neutral safety and a PRNDL switch on some automatic transmissions.

whenever the switch is removed from the housing. Be aware, Chrysler uses both a neutral safety switch and a PRNDL switch on some models, figure 6-24.

Starter control circuit current is routed through the transmission range selector switch on some General Motors, Ford, and import vehicles with automatic transmissions or transaxles. These switches, called PNP by General Motors and MLPS by Ford, bolt onto the transmission housing and connect to the manual valve of the transmission in some way, figure 6-25. Most switches have elongated mounting-bolt holes to allow for adjustment.

Older vehicles with automatic transmissions have a mechanical starter safety switch that is activated by the gear selector lever linkage. Location of the switch

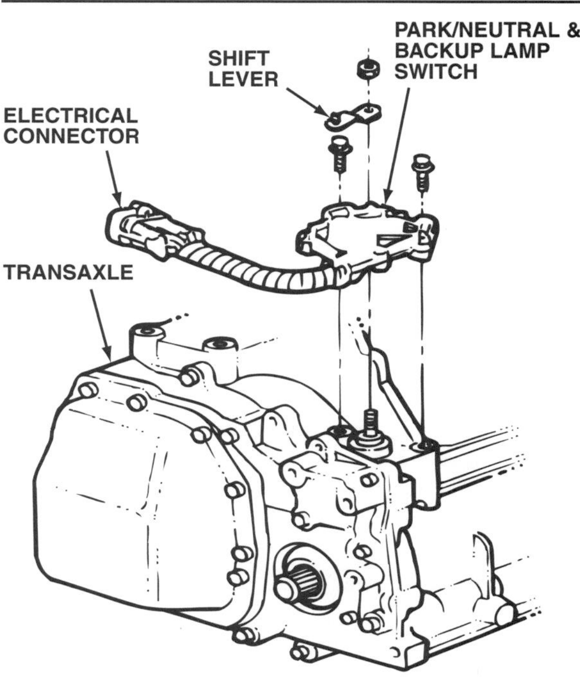

Figure 6-25. This safety switch bolts to the transmission housing and is activated by the manual valve lever.

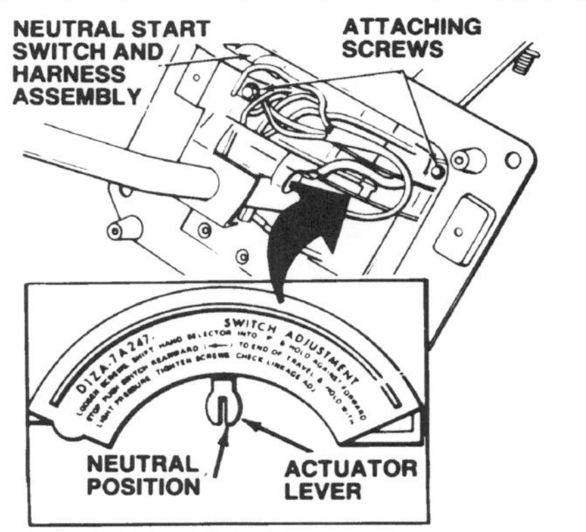

Figure 6-26. Floor-mounted safety switches are adjusted to ensure a complete circuit with the gear selector lever in park and neutral.

varies by make and model. The switch may be on the steering column, floorboard, console, or transmission. Floor-mounted switches are generally adjustable, figure 6-26. To adjust a Ford floor-mounted switch:

1. Remove the gear selector lever handle.
2. Remove the dial housing.
3. Remove the pointer backup shield.

Copyright 2000 by Chek-Chart Publications

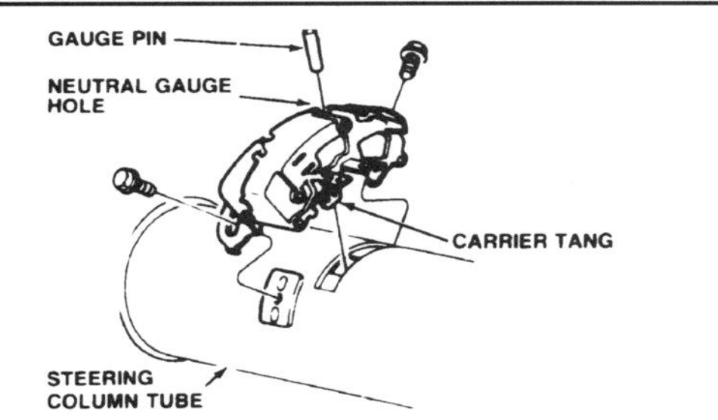

Figure 6-27. A calibrated pin is used to ensure correct adjustment of this General Motors safety switch.

4. Loosen the screws that hold the switch to the gear selector lever housing.
5. Hold the gear selector lever against the forward stop of the Park position.
6. Move the switch rearward to the end of its travel.
7. Tighten the attaching screws.
8. Check that the engine starts when the gear selector lever is in Park or Neutral range only; readjust the switch if necessary.
9. Reinstall the pointer backup shield, dial housing, and gear selector lever handle.

Some column-mount switches have alignment holes and are adjusted using a calibrated gauge pin, figure 6-27. To adjust a General Motors column-mount switch:

1. Disconnect the negative battery cable.
2. Loosen the switch attaching screws.
3. Move the switch until the two alignment holes match.
4. Check hole alignment with a gauge pin of the size specified in the service manual.
5. Tighten the switch attaching screw.
6. Reconnect the battery cable.
7. Check that the engine starts when the gear selector lever is in Park or Neutral range only; readjust the switch if necessary.

Copyright 2000 by Chek-Chart Publications

Starter Motor Overhaul

This chapter contains removal, disassembly, testing, repair, and installation instructions for starter motors. Starter motor removal, bench testing, and installation procedures are presented as general instructions that apply to performing these repairs on most domestic and import vehicles. Be aware, exact procedures and specifications vary by make and model, so additional service information is needed for a successful repair. Overhaul procedures are presented as photographic sequences for five specific Delco-Remy, Motorcraft, and Chrysler starter motor models.

UNIT REMOVAL

When tests indicate a starting system problem is isolated in the starter motor itself, the motor must be removed from the vehicle for further testing and repair or replacement. Starter motor removal procedures vary considerably by make, model, and year. A typical removal involves, figure 7-1:

- Loosening, relocating, or removing exhaust heat shields, support brackets, or pipes
- Loosening, relocating, or removing suspension components
- Loosening, relocating, or removing intake air hoses, ducts, pipes, or manifolds
- Loosening or removing engine mounts or loosening and relocating the engine cradle.

To help avoid confusion on installation, label nuts, bolts, and washers as they are removed from the starter motor and other parts. Also, tag all disconnected wires to prevent incorrect connections and circuit failures on assembly.

Observe all electrical safety precautions and shop safety regulations during removal of the starter motor. Remove a typical starter motor as follows:

1. Disconnect the negative battery cable.
2. Raise the vehicle high enough to gain easy access to the starter motor. Support the vehicle on jack stands or a hoist.
3. If necessary, turn the front wheels and disconnect the tie rods for easy access to the starter motor. On some models, the front wheel nearest the starter motor must be removed as well.
4. Loosen and relocate or remove exhaust pipes and other components that limit access to the starter motor. Also remove any components that may interfere with removing the motor from the engine compartment.
5. Remove any protective covering from the solenoid or motor terminal connections. Disconnect all wires from the solenoid or starter motor. Label the wires and fasteners removed from the solenoid or motor to ensure correct assembly.

Copyright 2000 by Chek-Chart Publications

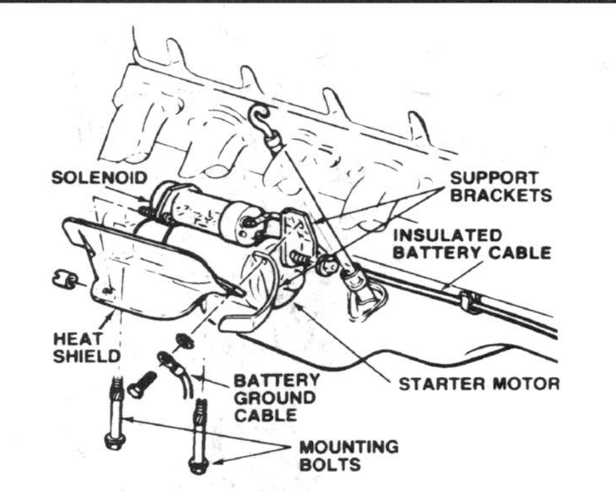

Figure 7-1. A number of brackets, heat shields, and other components must be removed to access the starter motor.

6. Remove the fasteners that secure any heat shields and support brackets to the starter motor. Remove the heat shields and brackets.
7. Remove all mounting fasteners that attach the starter motor to the engine. Separate the motor from the engine and remove any shims that are installed between the two. Save the shims for installation. Carefully guide the starter motor out of the engine compartment.

Once the motor is removed, place it on a clean workbench or clamp it into a vise for bench testing. Always store a starter motor in a safe place where it cannot fall onto the floor. This is especially important with permanent magnet starter motors because the magnets are quite brittle. A fall or any sharp blow damages the magnets and destroys the fields.

As with alternators, faulty starter motors are simply replaced with a new or rebuilt unit at many repair shops. Although overhauling a starter motor is a fairly simple and straightforward procedure, it is time consuming. Replacing the unit offers a quick turnaround time on the job as a convenience to the customer.

BENCH TESTS

Several bench tests are performed to determine the nature of the failure before a starter motor is disassembled for repair. A no-load test is used to locate open or shorted windings, worn bushings, a bent armature shaft, and other problems with the armature and fields. Solenoid tests check the continuity and operation of the pull-in and hold-in windings. Drive pinion clearance is also checked with the starter motor assembled. Incorrect pinion clearance causes pinion damage, stripped flywheel gear teeth, and motor failure. All of these tests are performed twice; once before teardown to isolate the source of a failure, and again after assembly to ensure a successful repair. Current draw and motor speed specifications from the manufacturer for the particular motor being serviced are required for testing.

No-Load Test

The no-load, or free-running, test is made with the starter motor firmly clamped in a vise or bench test fixture. Shops that overhaul starters on a regular basis generally have a special fixture for bench testing that includes all the necessary meters and equipment. Follow the equipment operating instructions to install and test the starter motor. If a test bench is unavailable, a fully charged battery, jumper cables, a remote starter switch, and either a voltmeter, ammeter, and carbon pile, or a CSB analyzer is used to perform a no-load test.

To test a solenoid-actuated starter, connect one jumper cable between the positive battery terminal and the solenoid battery terminal and the other cable between the negative battery terminal and the motor housing. Install the carbon pile across the battery, clamp the inductive ammeter pickup around the positive jumper cable, and connect the voltmeter to read available voltage at the starter motor terminal, figure 7-2. To test, simply close the remote starter switch and note the current draw. Load the battery to maintain a specific voltage if recommended by the manufacturer. Compare test results to specifications.

With a movable pole shoe starter, high amperage is applied directly to the starter motor to drive it. Making this connection causes severe arcing. The connection cannot be made with a remote starter because the amperage exceeds the current-carrying capacity of the remote starter switch. To prevent arcing, use a good starter relay or remote solenoid to connect the battery to the motor, figure 7-3. Then, use the remote starter switch to complete the control circuit and perform the test.

Interpret no-load test results as follows:

- Low no-load speed and high current draw—tight, dirty, or worn bearings, bent armature shaft, or loose field pole screws.
- Low no-load speed and low current draw—open field winding, high resistance due to poor connections, broken or weak brush springs, worn brushes, high mica on the commutator, shorted or grounded armature, or grounded field.
- High no-load speed and high current draw—shorted field windings or, on some models, an open shunt field circuit.
- Starter motor fails to operate under high current draw—grounded insulated terminal or field, or seized shaft bearings.

Copyright 2000 by Chek-Chart Publications

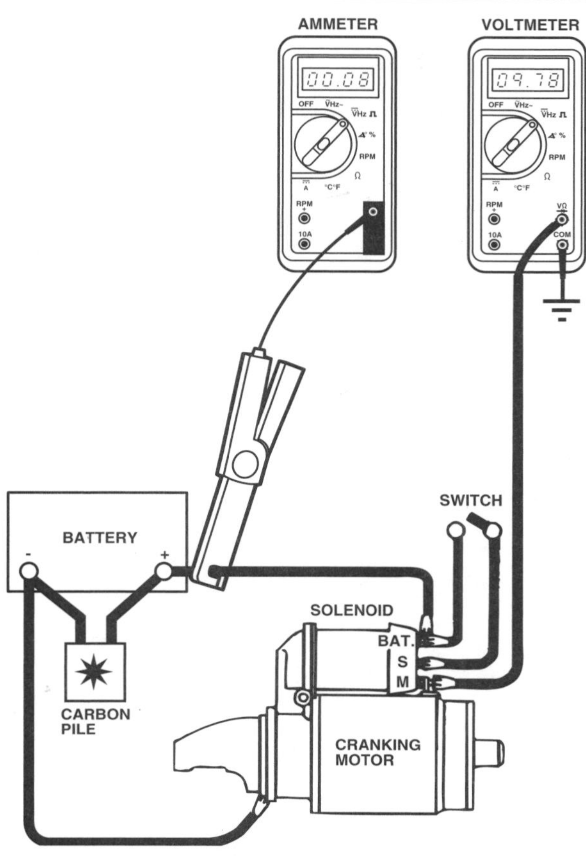

Figure 7-2. Equipment set up for performing a no-load test on a solenoid-actuated starter motor.

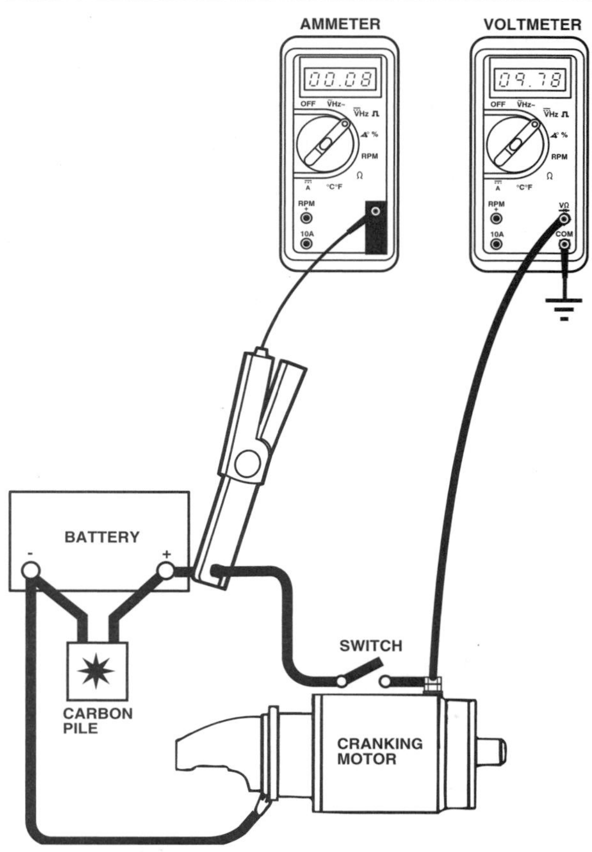

Figure 7-3. Equipment set up for performing a no-load test on a movable-pole-shoe starter motor.

- Starter motor fails to operate with no current draw—open field circuit, open armature coil, broken or weak brush springs, worn brushes, or high mica on the commutator.

Solenoid Tests

The solenoid is tested for current draw and continuity to determine the condition of the pull-in and hold-in windings, figure 7-4. Test procedures vary between manufacturers and models, so accurate service instructions and specifications are needed to test the solenoid. The following are general procedures that apply to checking current draw and continuity on most solenoids.

Current draw check

Solenoid current draw is checked with the starter motor installed in a bench test fixture, or using a battery, test meters, and jumper cables. Two checks are made, one for the hold-in windings and one for the pull-in windings.

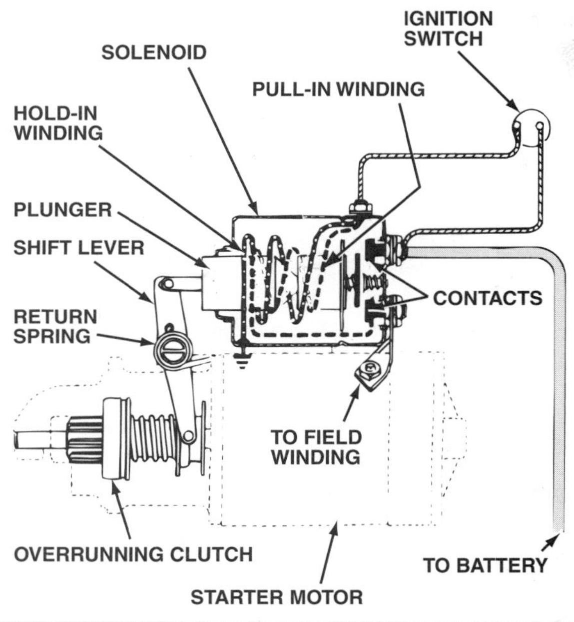

Figure 7-4. Solenoid pull-in and hold-in windings are checked for continuity and current draw.

Copyright 2000 by Chek-Chart Publications

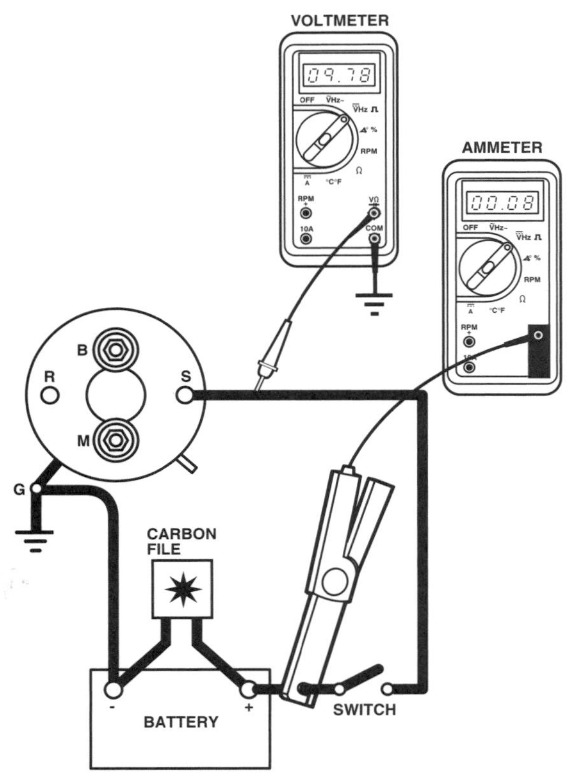

Figure 7-5. Equipment set up to test the solenoid hold-in windings.

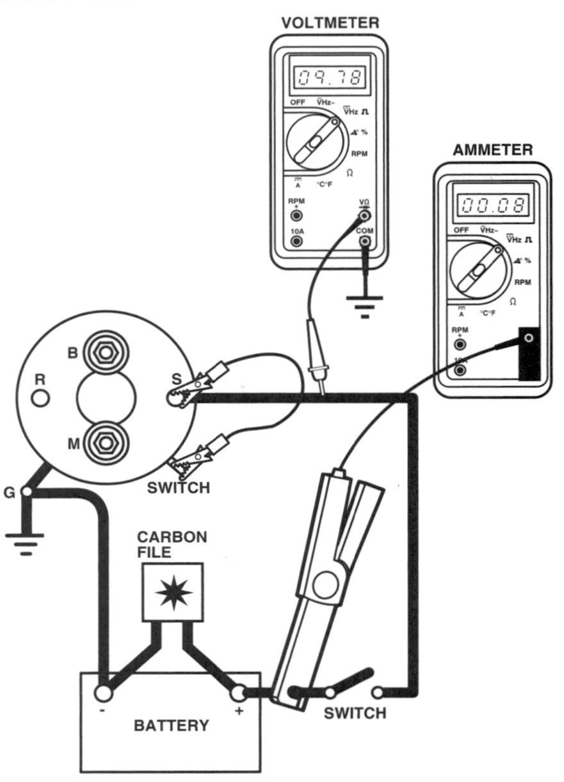

Figure 7-6. A jumper wire is used to energize the solenoid pull-in windings for testing.

To check the hold-in windings, battery current is applied directly to the solenoid switch terminal. Connect a voltmeter to read available voltage and an ammeter to read current at the switch terminal, figure 7-5. Apply a load to reduce battery voltage to between 8 and 10 volts. Note the ammeter reading and compare to specifications.

A jumper wire is installed between the solenoid switch and motor terminals to check the pull-in windings, figure 7-6. Remember, the current draw decreases as the temperature of the pull-in winding increases. Apply a load to maintain battery voltage between 8 and 10 volts, then note the ammeter reading. To prevent damage to the pull-in winding from overheating, do not keep it energized for more than 15 seconds. Compare the ammeter reading to specifications.

If the ammeter reading is higher than specified on either winding, the winding is shorted or grounded. A lower reading indicates high resistance. If either winding does not meet specifications, replace the solenoid.

Continuity check

Solenoid winding continuity is checked with an ohmmeter or a self-powered test lamp. All solenoid electrical connections, including the one to the starter motor, must be disconnected for testing. Connect the ohmmeter or test lamp between the solenoid switch and motor terminals. The meter should show continuity or the lamp should light. Next, connect the test leads between the switch terminal and the solenoid case. Again, there should be continuity. The solenoid has an open circuit if there is no continuity in either test. Replace the solenoid.

Pinion Clearance Test

Although drive pinion clearance cannot be adjusted on all starter motors, it must be correct to avoid a damaged pinion, a stripped flywheel, or a motor failure. Specifications and test and procedures vary somewhat by make and model, so check the service manual. A typical drive pinion clearance check is made as follows:

Check drive pinion clearance with the starter motor assembled:

1. Disconnect the field coil connector from the solenoid motor terminal, and insulate the connector to prevent accidental arcing.
2. Use jumper cables to connect the positive terminal of a battery to the switch terminal on the

Copyright 2000 by Chek-Chart Publications

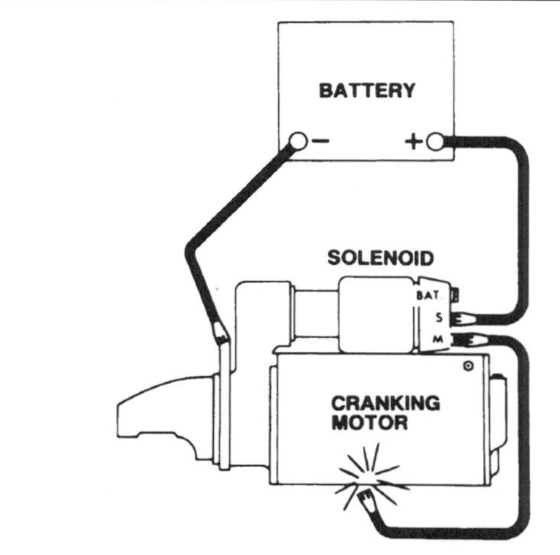

Figure 7-7. Momentarily jumper the solenoid motor terminal to ground to extend the pinion for checking clearance.

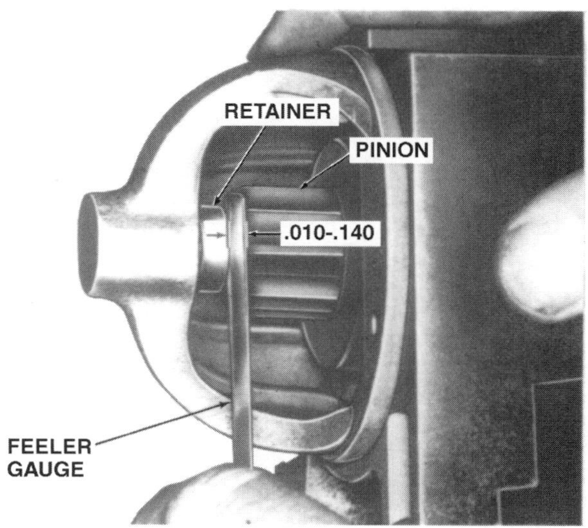

Figure 7-8. Use a feeler gauge to measure clearance between the pinion and gear and retainer.

solenoid and the negative battery terminal to the starter housing.

3. Connect a jumper wire to the solenoid switch terminal and momentarily touch the open end of the jumper wire to the starter motor frame. The pinion should snap into position and stay there as long as the starter remains connected to the battery, figure 7-7.
4. Push the pinion back toward the commutator to eliminate slack or end play on the pinion.
5. Use a feeler gauge to check the pinion-to-pinion stop clearance, figure 7-8. Acceptable clearance typically falls into the 0.010 to 0.140 inch (0.25 to 3.6 mm) range.

If pinion clearance is not within specifications, check the shift fork, pivot pin, and drive mechanism for correct assembly, installation, and wear. Replace worn parts, assemble, and retest. When clearance is adjustable, adjustments are usually made by changing the thickness of a dust cover, shim, or gasket that installs between the solenoid and the starter housing, figure 7-9. Pinion clearance cannot be adjusted on motors with an enclosed shift fork.

DISASSEMBLY, CLEANING, AND INSPECTION

Clean the starter with fresh solvent and dry with low-pressure compressed air before disassembly. During disassembly, clean each part and inspect it for excessive wear or damage. As part of the overall inspection during disassembly:

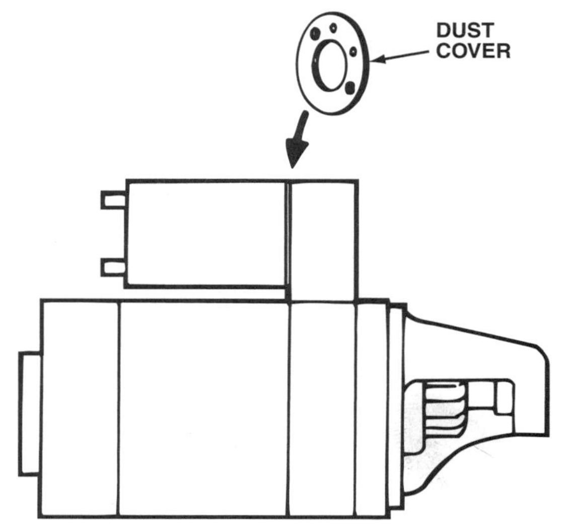

Figure 7-9. Selectively sized dust covers, gaskets, or shims are available for adjusting pinion clearance on some starters.

- Check bearings for proper clearance, roughness, or galling.
- Remove any oil and dirt from insulation.
- Check insulation condition.

Although starter motor designs differ between manufacturers and models, all assemble in a similar fashion. The starter motor assembly is held together by several through bolts that attach the commutator end frame to the drive end frame, figure 7-10. A third housing, the field frame, which contains the field windings, is held between the two end frames. Each of

Copyright 2000 by Chek-Chart Publications

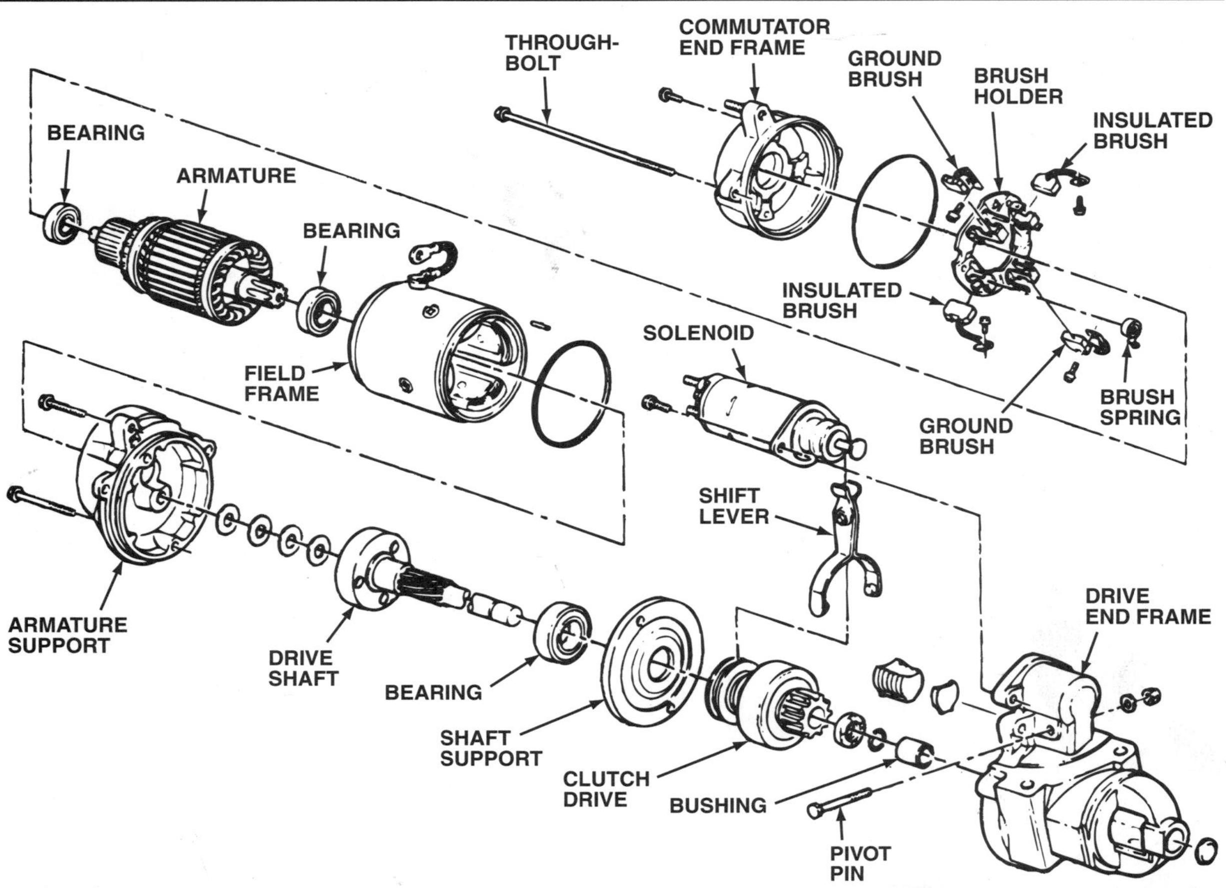

Figure 7-10. An exploded view of the General Motors 28-MT starter illustrates common motor design and assembly.

the end frames contains a bearing or bushing that supports the armature assembly. On some models, the through bolts locate and support the brush holder assembly at the commutator end of the motor. The drive end frame supports the pinion gear and drive, and also provides a mounting for the solenoid where applicable.

Before disassembling the starter motor, mark the position of the end frame and the main frame with chalk or a marker to aid in aligning the parts during assembly. While disassembling the starter, clean each part and inspect it for excessive wear or damage. Most parts are easily cleaned with a dry brush and compressed air. For removing greasy buildup, use only nonconductive solvents exclusively designed for cleaning electrical parts. Some types of solvent leave a conductive residue that promotes arcing and short circuits. Make sure all components are dry before assembly.

To disassemble the motor, loosen the through bolts and remove the commutator end frame. Note the location and position of the brush assembly while removing the end frame. Brushes may be mounted to the end frame or in the field frame. Be careful when removing an end frame that holds the brushes to avoid damaging them. Remember, the spring force holding the brushes on the commutator is suddenly released during removal. Brushes are fragile and brittle and the spring force easily damages them if released too quickly. Check brush movement. Brushes should slide freely in their holders and be making full contact on the commutator. As a rule, brushes that are worn to half their original length or less are replaced. Service brushes as described later in this chapter.

If the starter has an externally mounted solenoid, remove the fasteners securing it to the drive end frame and the field coil lead. Then, remove the solenoid. Slip the field frame and armature off of drive end frame and remove the armature from the field frame.

Clean, inspect, and test the starter motor components. Replace any defective parts, then assemble the unit. After assembly, check and adjust pinion clearance, check current draw, and perform a no-load test to verify repairs.

Copyright 2000 by Chek-Chart Publications

Armature Service

An armature is checked for shaft runout and circuit continuity. Measure armature shaft runout using a set of V-blocks and a dial indicator, figure 7-11. Remember, a bent armature shaft may be the cause of low no-load speed and high current draw test results. Replace the armature assembly if shaft runout exceeds specifications from the manufacturer. A test instrument known as a growler is used to test for shorted armature windings. Either an ohmmeter or a self-powered test lamp is used to check for grounded windings.

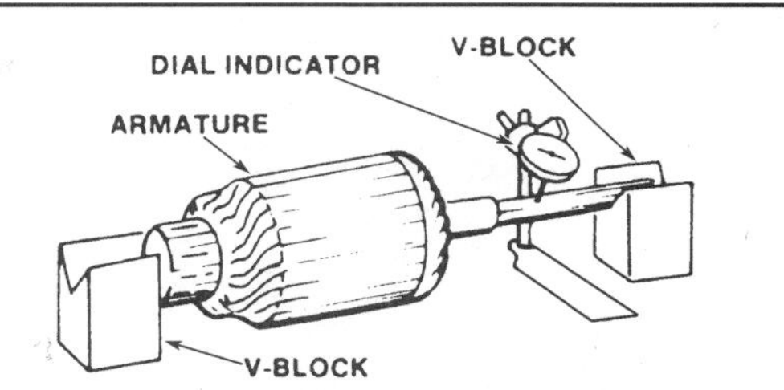

Figure 7-11. Measuring armature shaft runout with a dial indicator and V-blocks.

Growler tests

The growler is an electromagnet operating on a 60-cycle alternating current (ac). At 60 cycles, the magnetic field current reverses direction 120 times each second. This rapid magnetic field shifting causes the test instrument to emit the growling noise for which it is named whenever power is applied to it. To test armature on a growler:

1. Place the armature on the growler and hold a thin strip of steel, such as a hacksaw blade or feeler gauge, against the length of the armature core, figure 7-12.
2. Switch the growler on, then slowly rotate the armature while holding the steel blade against each section of the armature core.
3. If the blade jumps or vibrates over any section of the core, the armature windings are shorted.

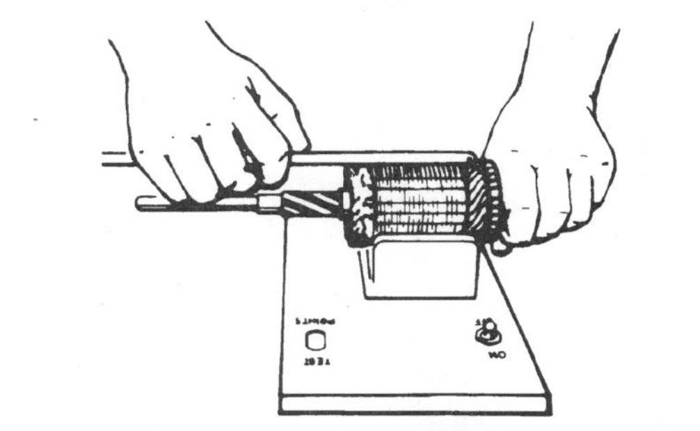

Figure 7-12. Using a growler to check for shorted armature windings.

Shorted windings result from defective insulation that allows adjacent winding coils to touch. This decreases cranking power. Replace the armature if any of the windings are shorted. If no shorted windings are found with the growler, continue by testing for grounded windings.

Grounded winding test

Testing an armature for grounded windings with a self-powered test lamp is quick and easy. Connect one test-lamp lead to the armature shaft and the other to the commutator, figure 7-13. If the lamp lights, the armature is grounded. When testing with an ohmmeter, there should be infinite resistance between the commutator and the shaft. If the ohmmeter indicates continuity or low resistance, the armature windings are grounded to the shaft. Replace the armature if the windings are grounded.

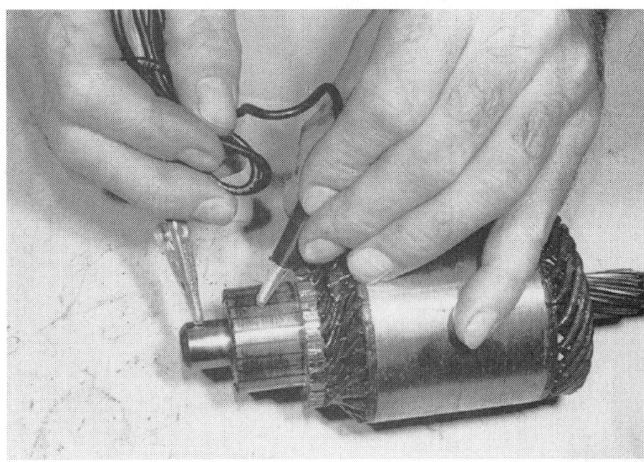

Figure 7-13. Checking for grounded armature windings with a self-powered test lamp.

Commutator service

The commutator contact surface has a tendency to burn and pit due to the high current that passes between it and the brushes, figure 7-14. Emery cloth is used to polish minor blemishes and restore the contact surface. When the commutator is badly damaged, the contact surface is restored using an armature lathe.

Armature lathes are often simple hand-operated devices. Turning the hand crank rotates the armature and draws the commutator along a cutting tool. Adjust the tool bit to take a light cut and keep the amount of metal removed from the commutator to a minimum. After turning, the mica insulation separating the contact segments must be reduced to below the level of the contact surface. Undercut the mica using a hacksaw blade, sharp knife, or other suitable tool. Take care not to scratch the commutator contacts and make sure no metal chips are left lodged between the segments.

Copyright 2000 by Chek-Chart Publications

Figure 7-14. Inspect the brush contact surface of the commutator for burning and pitting.

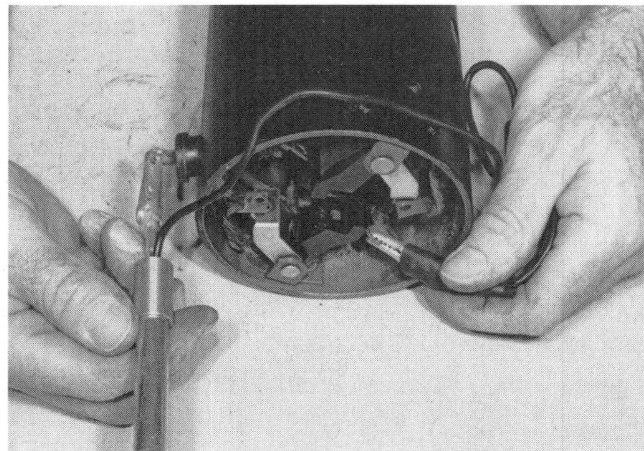

Figure 7-15. Using a self-powered test lamp to check for open field coils.

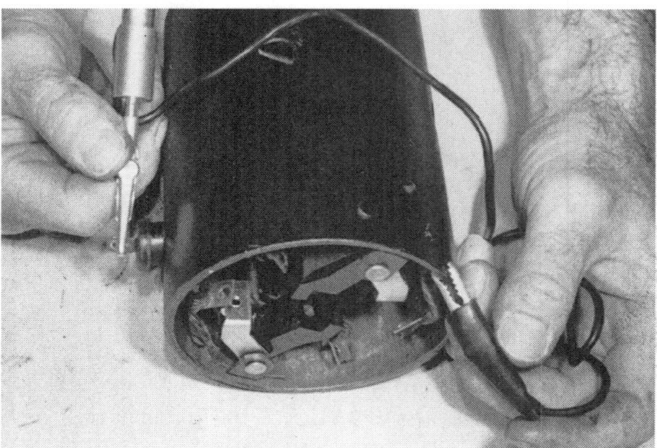

Figure 7-16. Using a self-powered test lamp to check for grounded field coils.

Field Coil Tests

Field coils are tested for open circuits and grounded windings using a self-powered test lamp or an ohmmeter. Most starter motors have four field coils. The field coil circuit runs from the starter power terminal through the coils to the insulated brushes. On a typical starter motor, there are two insulated brushes and two ground brushes. The ground brushes attach to the motor housing. Check the field coils with the brushes installed.

Open-circuit check

Check for open circuits by connecting the test lamp or ohmmeter between one of the insulated brushes and the starter power terminal, figure 7-15. The lamp should light and the ohmmeter should show little or no resistance. The coils are open if the lamp does not light or resistance is high. Move the test lead to the other insulated brush and repeat the test.

Grounded winding check

Check for grounded windings by connecting the test lamp or ohmmeter between the starter power terminal and the motor housing or one of the grounded brushes, figure 7-16. The test lamp should not light and the ohmmeter should show infinite resistance. The field coils are grounded if the lamp lights or the ohmmeter should show little or no resistance.

Brush Service

Before assembling the starter motor, inspect and test the brushes and brush holders. Brushes wear and are the most frequently replaced item in any electric motor. A general rule is to replace the complete brush set if any brush is worn to one-half its original length.

Some brushes are embossed with a logo that is used as a wear indicator, figure 7-17. When any brush is worn to the bottom of the logo, replace the brush set. New starter motor brushes usually range from one-half to three-quarters of an inch (13 to 19 mm) in length. Spring force pushes the brush into contact with the commutator to maintain continuity. As a brush wears, the spring expands to take up play, which reduces force. Insufficient spring force causes the brush to bounce as it moves across the commutator. When a brush bounces, it creates an arc, which reduces motor efficiency and causes burning. Replace brushes that are cracked, chipped, pitted, otherwise damaged, or worn. Also, replace springs as needed if they are broken, distorted, discolored, or otherwise damaged.

Test the insulated, or positive, brush holders by connecting a self-powered test lamp or ohmmeter between the holder and ground at either the field frame or the base of the brush holder assembly, figure 7-18. The test lamp should not light and the ohmmeter should show infinite resistance. If all of the brush

Copyright 2000 by Chek-Chart Publications

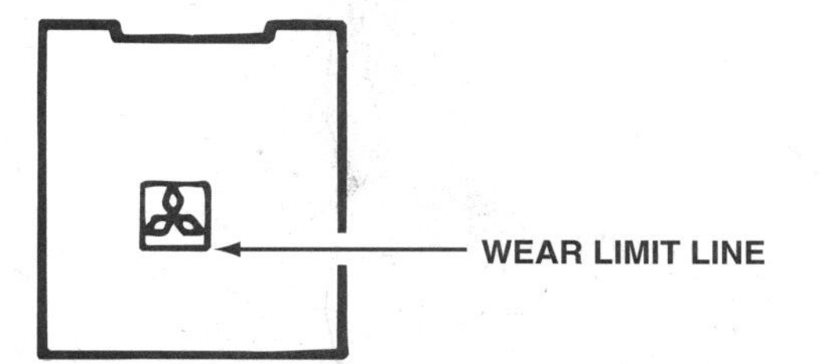

Figure 7-17. The edge of the logo on this Mitsubishi brush serves as a wear indicator.

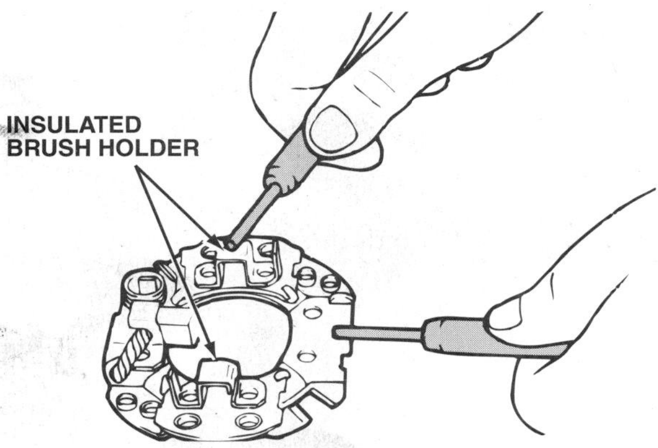

Figure 7-18. Checking for grounded holders on an insulated brush holder assembly.

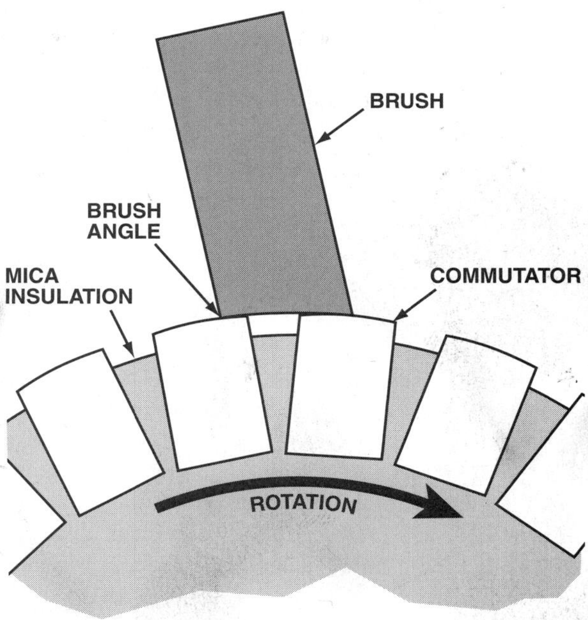

Figure 7-19. Install starter motor brushes so the beveled edge matches the rotation of the commutator.

holders on an assembly are insulated, the lamp should light and the ohmmeter show little or no resistance when connected either to adjacent brush holders or from any brush holder to the base of the assembly. Repair or replace the brush holder assembly if tests indicate it is faulty.

New brushes usually have a beveled edge on the commutator contact surface. It is important to match the contour of the brush face with the curve of the commutator when installing new brushes, figure 7-19. Reversing the brush angle reduces surface contact with the commutator. This causes arcing between the commutator segments, premature brush and commutator wear, and reduced motor efficiency.

Brush replacement

Brush replacement requires partial disassembly of a starter motor and procedures vary by make and model. For example, the entire brush holder assembly can be removed without removing the armature from the frame on a Chrysler permanent-magnet starter. However, on a Delco-Remy permanent-magnet starter, the brush holder assembly is secured on the armature shaft by the commutator end bearing, which is press fit. The armature assembly must be removed from the frame and the bearing pressed off the shaft to remove the brush holder assembly for servicing the Delco brushes.

Ground brushes are generally attached to the field frame with machine screws and are easily removed with a screwdriver. With some late-model starters, the ground brushes are an integral part of the brush holder plate and the entire assembly must be replaced to service the brushes. The assembly mounts to the field frame or the end frame to complete the ground circuit. If machine screws are used to ground and hold the brush holder assembly to the field frame, peen the screws with a punch and hammer after tightening. This helps prevent the screw from vibrating loose during operation.

Original-equipment insulated brushes are usually attached directly to the end of a field coil lead. To replace this type of brush, the lead is cut off as close as possible to the field coil. Then, the pigtail of the new brush is spliced to the field coil and soldered. When soldering brush leads, make the connection on the back of the coil lead to eliminate the possibility of the splice rubbing the armature after assembly. Clean the ends of the coils thoroughly by grinding or filing off the insulating varnish. Remove varnish only as far back as necessary to make the solder connection. Make sure the replacement brush is in the same position as the original, then solder the brush lead to the field coil using rosin core solder. Avoid overheating the lead; this allows solder to run down the cable and reduces flexibility.

Copyright 2000 by Chek-Chart Publications

Small metal clips, used to attach the new brushes to the field coil leads, are supplied in some replacement brush kits. The clips fit around the brush pigtail to coil lead splice and are lightly crimped with pliers. Then, the clip is heated with a soldering iron and rosin-core solder is applied to the connection to ensure a permanent joint with good electrical conductivity. Refer to Chapter One of this *Shop Manual* for additional information and procedures on splicing and soldering connections.

Replacement brushes for many Japanese starter motors do not have a pigtail lead. To replace these brushes, the old brush is crushed with pliers to remove it from the field coil lead. After crushing the brush, remove all trace of brush material from the lead. Clean the end of the lead with sandpaper to ensure good contact with the new brush. Once clean, insert the lead end into the hole in the new brush. Heat the lead with a soldering iron and apply a drop or two of solder into the recessed hole to secure the brush to lead connection, figure 7-20.

After installing the new brushes, assemble the field coil and brush assembly into the field frame. Then, use a test lamp or ohmmeter to make sure soldered connections are not touching the frame and grounding the fields.

UNIT INSTALLATION

To install a starter motor:

1. Transfer support brackets or other hardware from the old motor to the replacement motor as needed.
2. Fit the starter motor into position on the engine and install the mounting fasteners, figure 7-21. Be sure to install any ground cables or brackets that are attached with the starter mounting hardware.
3. Check flywheel-to-starter engagement. Some vehicles require shims to provide correct starter pinion-to-flywheel engagement. These shims are placed between the starter drive housing and the engine block. Remove the flywheel cover and check the starter pinion to flywheel engagement. Add or remove shims to correct.

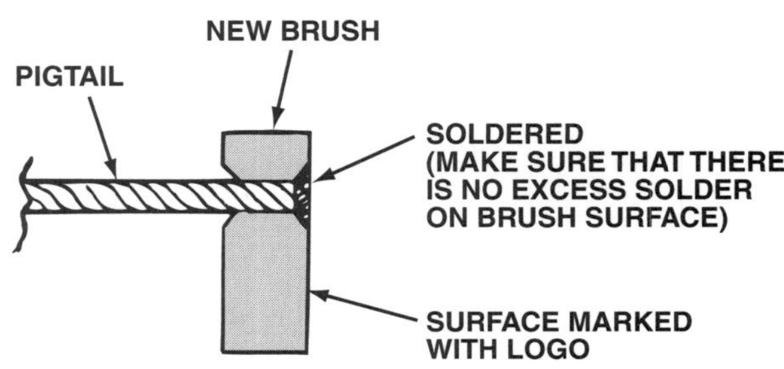

Figure 7-20. Use a minimal amount of solder when connecting a brush directly to a lead.

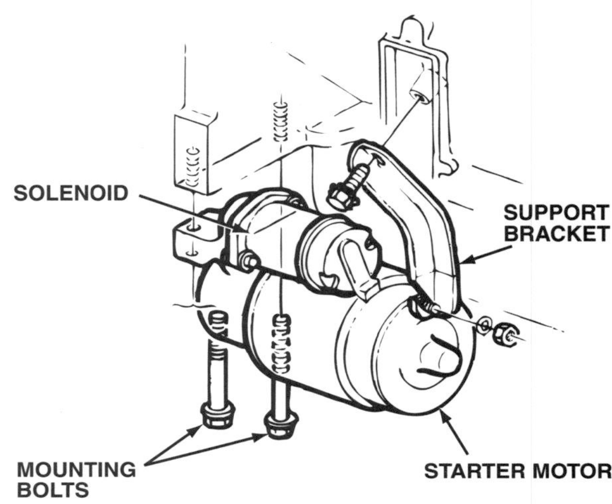

Figure 7-21. Install a starter motor by securing the motor and any support brackets to the engine with bolts.

4. Connect all wires to the solenoid or starter motor terminals.
5. Connect any suspension, exhaust system, or other parts that were loosened or removed.
6. Connect the negative battery cable.

Test starter motor operation by starting the vehicle. Listen for any unusual sounds and check for correct operation of the starting safety switch.

Copyright 2000 by Chek-Chart Publications

STARTER MOTOR OVERHAUL PROCEDURES

The following pages contain photographic procedures for disassembly, overhaul, and assembly of five common domestic starter motors:

- Delco-Remy solenoid-actuated starter
- Motorcraft movable-pole shoe starter
- Motorcraft permanent-magnet, gear-reduction starter
- Chrysler reduction drive starter
- Chrysler permanent-magnet, gear-reduction starter.

Except for the Motorcraft movable-pole shoe, or positive engagement, starter, all of these starters use a solenoid to complete the circuit. The Motorcraft unit uses the moveable pole shoe in place of a solenoid.

Chapter Eleven of the *Classroom Manual* contains descriptions and illustrations of these starter motors. Refer to the *Classroom Manual* for additional information when overhauling a starter motor. It is important to read and understand the test procedures in the preceding section of this chapter before beginning any overhaul. Make the tests previously detailed at convenient points during the overhaul sequence. Read through the entire step-by-step procedure for the specific starter motor being overhauled before starting work.

All soldering and unsoldering of starter motor components are done with a medium-to-high-heat soldering iron, approximately 100 to 300 watts, with a fairly large tip. *Use only rosin-core solder.* Procedures on splicing and soldering connections are detailed in Chapter One of this *Shop Manual.*

Copyright 2000 by Chek-Chart Publications

DELCO-REMY SOLENOID-ACTUATED STARTER OVERHAUL PROCEDURE

1. Draw a reference mark across the commutator end frame and the field end frame. Disconnect the field coil lead from solenoid motor terminal.

2. Remove the two through-bolts and lift off the commutator end frame. Remove the thrust washer.

3. Separate the field frame from the drive end frame; it may be necessary to twist slightly to break it loose. Then slide the field frame off of the armature.

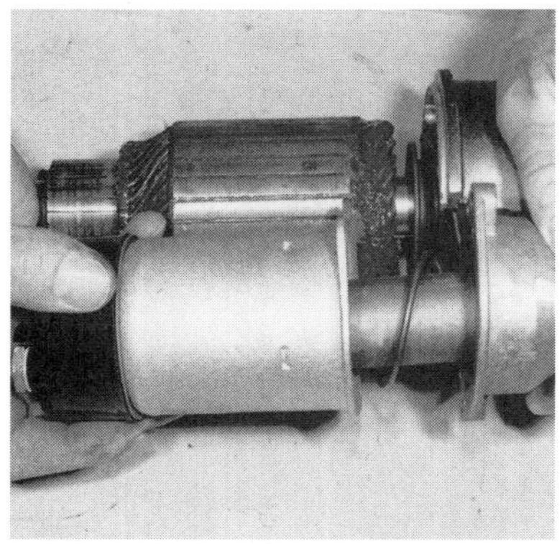

4. Remove the two screws and separate the solenoid from the drive end frame. Remove the solenoid slowly to avoid losing the spring.

5. Lever the shift fork and solenoid plunger assembly back and carefully guide the armature and drive assembly out of the end frame.

6. The shift fork and solenoid plunger pivot on a pin secured to the end frame by a snapring. Remove the snapring, pivot pin, and shift fork and plunger assembly.

7. The commutator end frame bushing and the drive end frame bearing are removed with a puller. New bushings and bearings are pressed or driven into the frames.

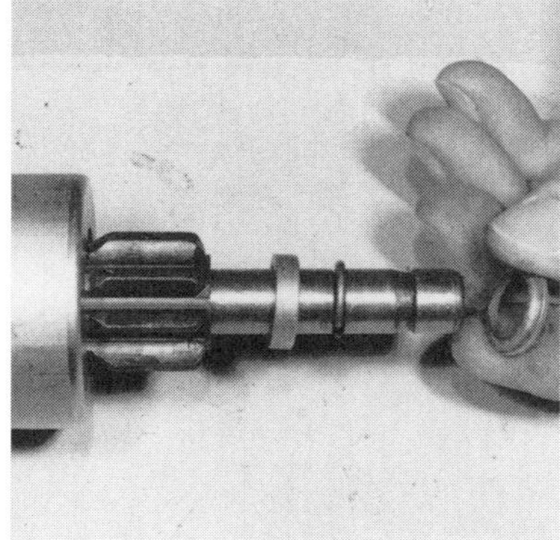

8. Slip the thrust collar from the end of the shaft, then use a deep socket and hammer to drive the pinion stop collar toward the pinion to expose the snapring.

9. Use snapring pliers to remove the snapring. Then, slide the pinion stop collar and the starter drive off of the shaft.

Copyright 2000 by Chek-Chart Publications

DELCO-REMY SOLENOID-ACTUATED STARTER OVERHAUL PROCEDURE

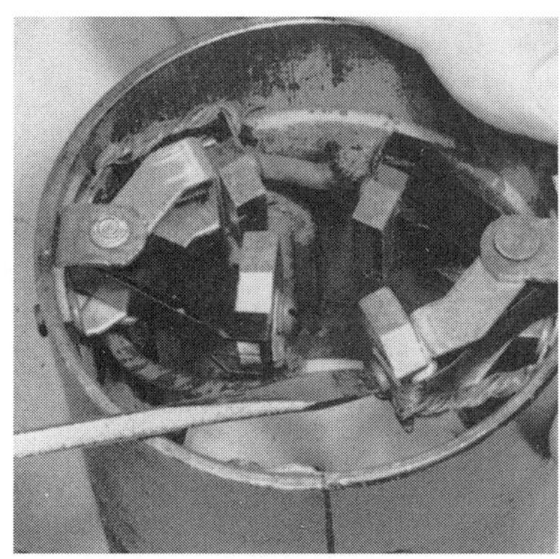

10. Inspect the brushes and replace them if any are worn to one-half original length. Screws attach the brushes and leads to the brush holders.

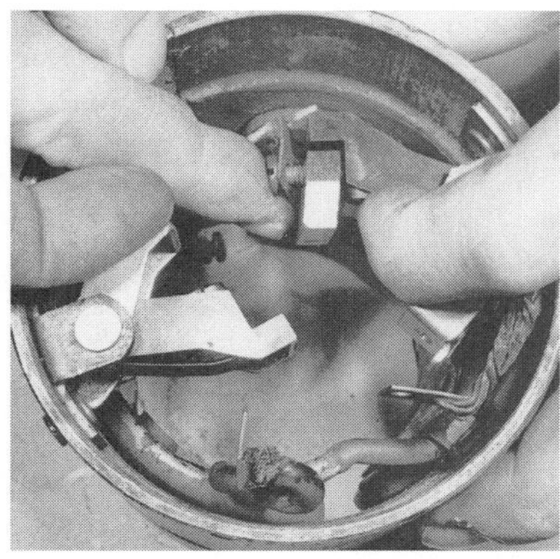

11. Attach new brushes to the brush holders with screws. Damaged brush holders and springs are replaced by removing the pins at the base of the holders.

12. Apply a light coat of silicone lubricant to the drive end of the shaft, then install the drive assembly. Fit the pinion stop collar onto shaft so the cupped side faces the end of the shaft.

13. Install the snapring onto the shaft groove. Fit the thrust collar so the flange is toward the shaft end. Close and clamp the two collars over the snapring using two pliers.

14. Fit the shift fork and plunger into the drive end frame, insert the pivot pin, and secure with the snapring. Some pivot pins are driven in and do not use a snapring.

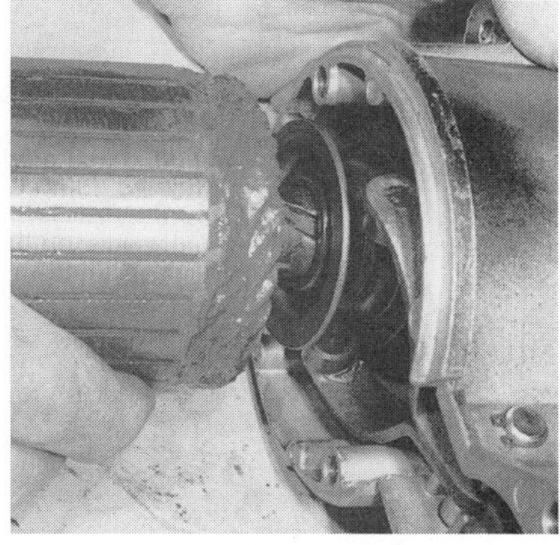

15. Pivot the shift fork and plunger on the pin and install the armature and drive assembly into the drive end frame. Make sure the shift fork engages the drive correctly.

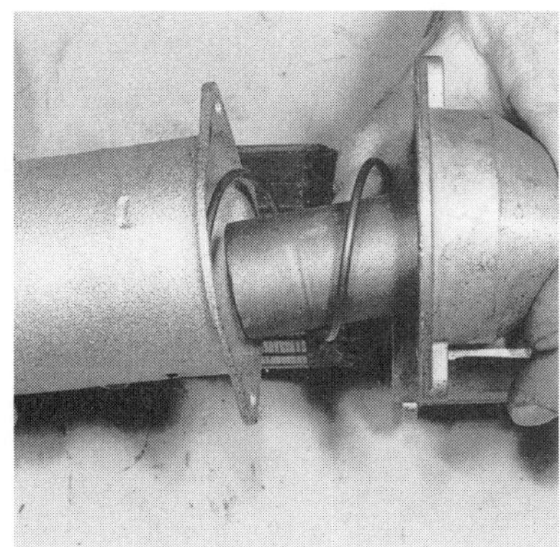

16. Place the solenoid spring over the plunger, fit the solenoid onto the drive end frame, and install the two screws to secure it.

17. Carefully fit the field frame over armature and onto the end frame. Hold all four brushes away from the commutator. Work slowly to avoid bending holders or nicking brushes.

18. Fit the thrust washer on the shaft, align and install the end frame, and secure with the through-bolts. Attach the field coil lead to the solenoid motor terminal.

Copyright 2000 by Chek-Chart Publications

MOTORCRAFT MOVABLE POLE SHOE STARTER OVERHAUL PROCEDURE

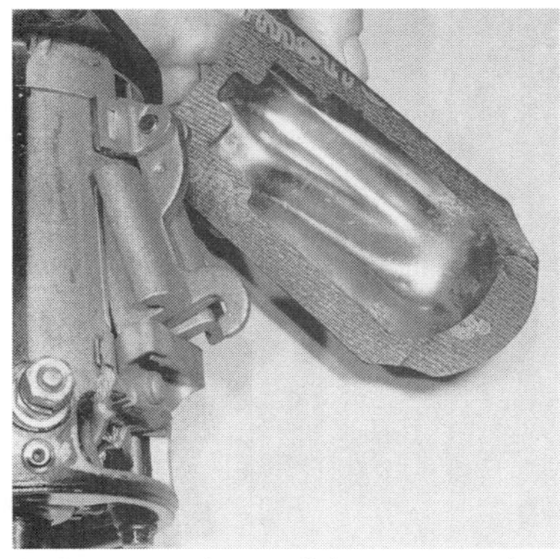

1. Remove the retaining screw, then remove the brush cover band along with the pole shoe cover and gasket from the motor assembly.

2. Use a hooked tool to hold back the brush springs while sliding the brushes out of their holders. Leave the brush leads attached for now.

3. Mark the frame position, then remove the two through-bolts and the end frame. Service bushings as needed using pullers and drivers.

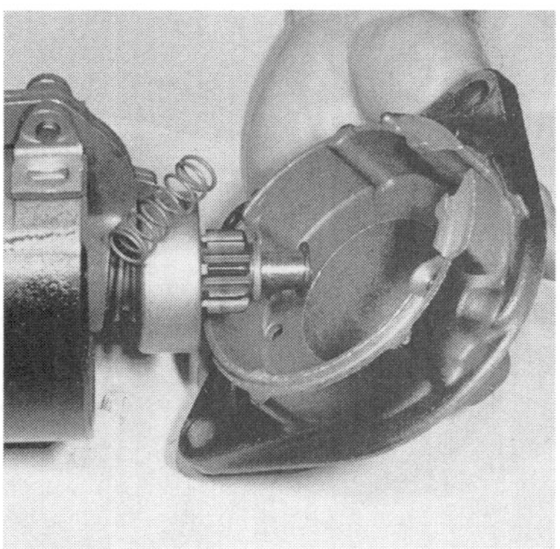

4. Slowly separate the drive end frame from the field frame and armature, taking care not to lose the return spring.

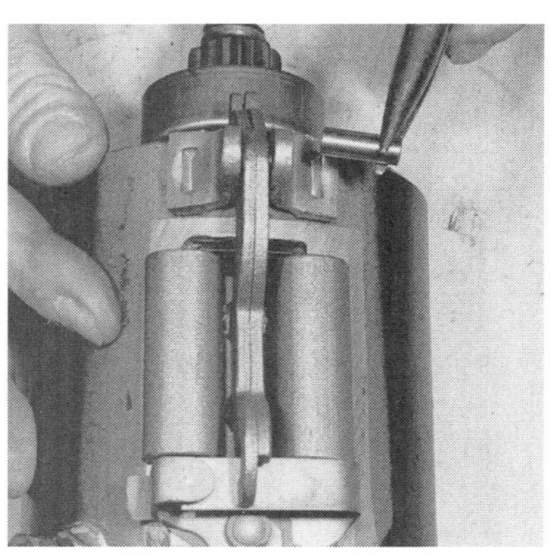

5. Remove the pivot pin attaching the pole shoe plunger to the field frame, then lift off the pole shoe plunger and shift fork assembly.

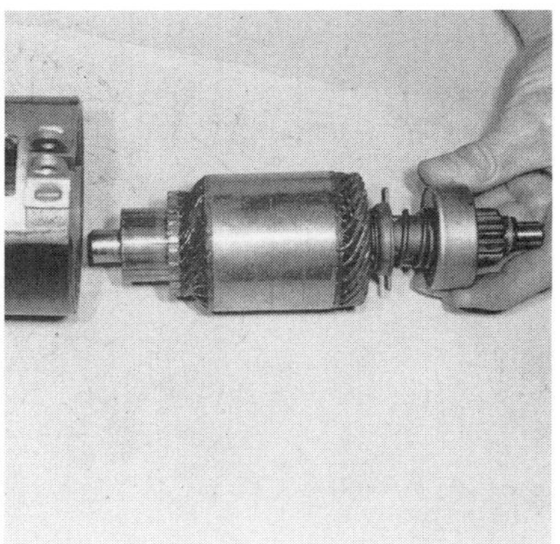

6. Slip the armature and drive assembly out of the field frame. Clean and test the armature and field coils for open and grounded windings.

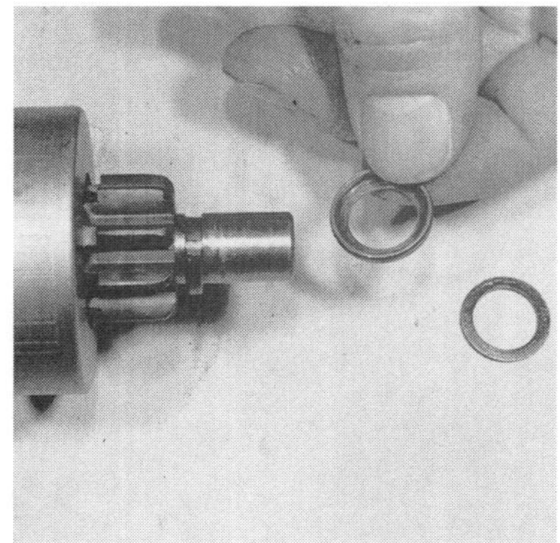

7. To separate the drive assembly from the shaft, first slip the thrust washer and stopring retainer off the end of the armature shaft.

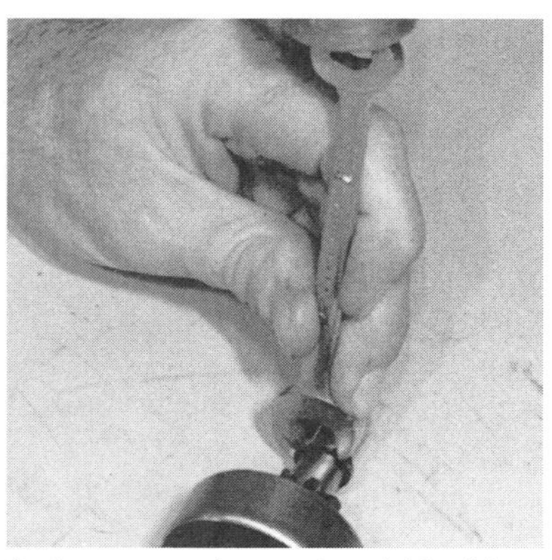

8. An open-end wrench quickly drives the stopring out of the shaft groove. Discard the ring and install a new one on assembly. Slide the starter drive off of the shaft.

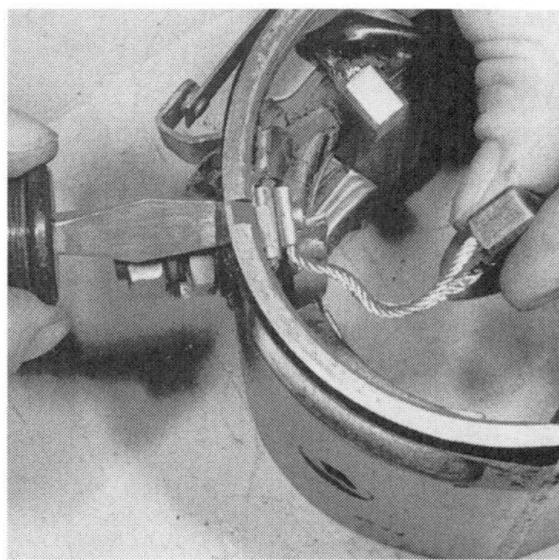

9. Inspect brushes and replace if any are worn to one-half their original length. Ground brushes attach to the field frame with a screw; insulated brush connections are soldered.

Copyright 2000 by Chek-Chart Publications

MOTORCRAFT MOVABLE POLE SHOE STARTER OVERHAUL PROCEDURE

10. When removing insulated brushes, cut the leads as close to the field coil as possible, or apply heat to break a solder connection.

11. On assembly, lightly lubricate the end of the shaft and install the drive assembly onto the armature. Install a new stopring to secure the drive.

12. Fit the stopring retainer and thrust washer onto the end of the shaft, then install the armature and drive assembly into the field frame.

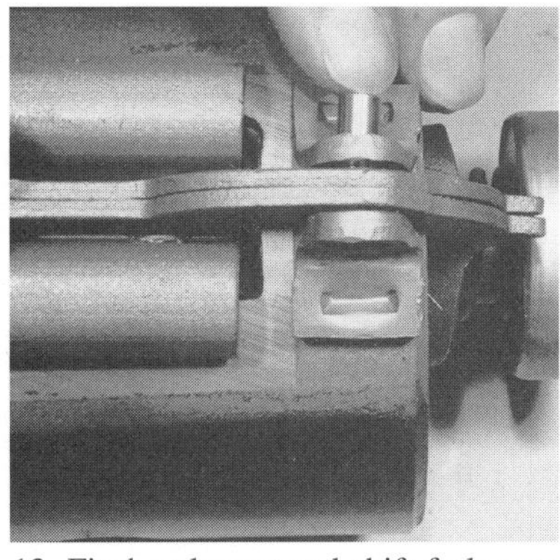

13. Fit the plunger and shift fork onto the starter frame and install the pivot pin to secure the assembly. Make sure the shift fork correctly engages the starter drive.

14. Place the plunger return spring onto position on the plunger arm. The outer end of the spring seats in a machined bore on the drive end frame.

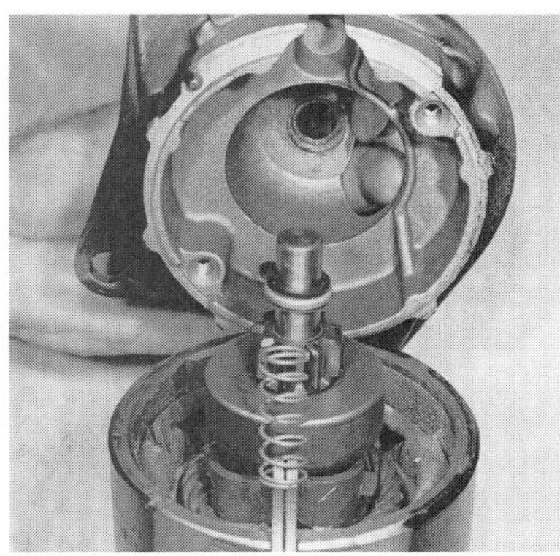

15. Lightly pack the drive end bearing with grease, then fit the drive end frame onto the field frame making sure the plunger spring seats.

16. If a thrust washer is used on the commutator end of the shaft, install it. A thrust washer is not used with a molded commutator. Install the end frame and through-bolts.

17. Pull the brush springs away from the holders and fit the brushes into the holders. Release the springs and make sure the insulated leads do not touch the frame.

18. Fit the pole shoe cover and gasket and the brush cover band. Install the screw to secure the cover and band.

Copyright 2000 by Chek-Chart Publications

MOTORCRAFT PERMANENT-MAGNET, GEAR-REDUCTION STARTER OVERHAUL PROCEDURE

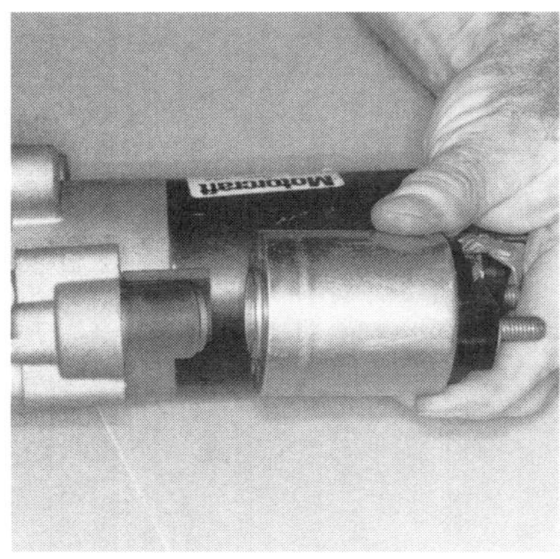

1. Disconnect the field coil lead from the solenoid terminal and remove the solenoid retaining screws. Work the plunger off the drive lever while removing the solenoid housing.

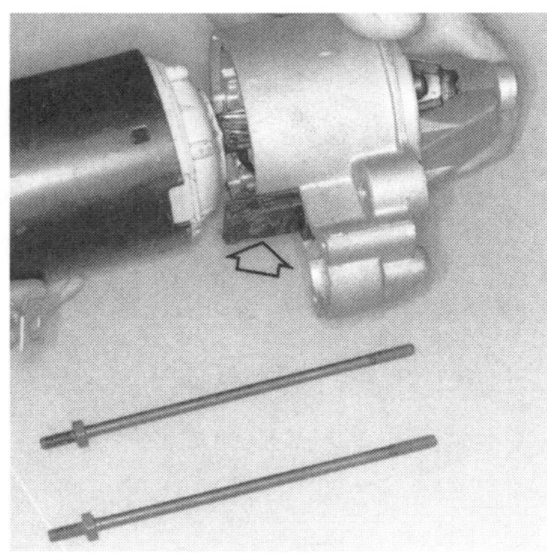

2. Remove the through bolts, separate the drive end frame from the field frame, and remove the drive end seal (arrow).

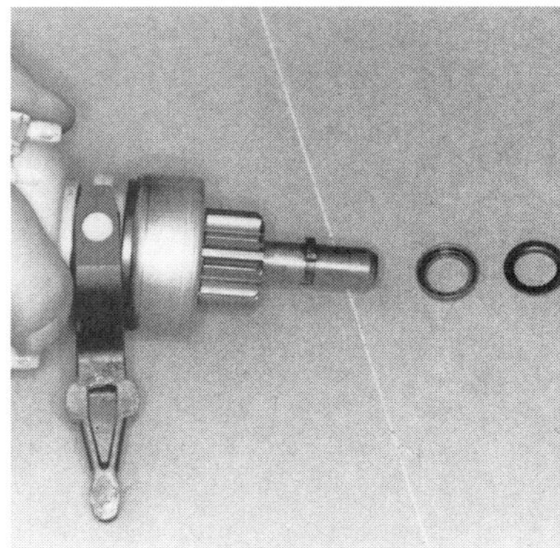

3. Remove the O-ring seal, then slip the stopring retainer off the end of the output shaft and stationary gear assembly.

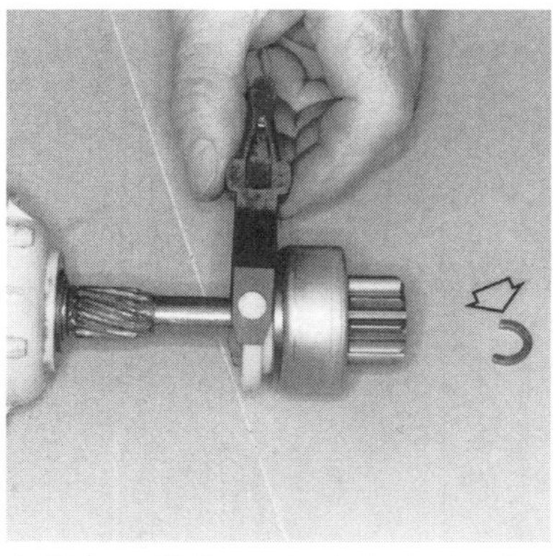

4. Drive off the output shaft stopring (arrow), then slide the drive mechanism from the output shaft.

5. Separate the output shaft and stationary gear assembly from the armature and remove the gear retainer plate.

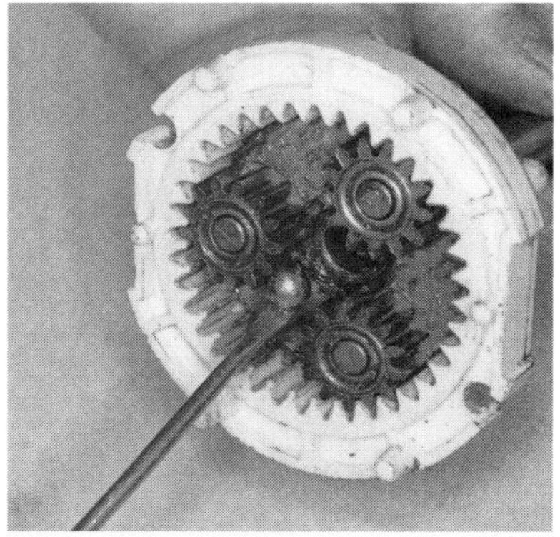

6. A thrust ball is located between the armature shaft end and a seat in the output shaft. Remove the thrust ball from the gear assembly and set it aside.

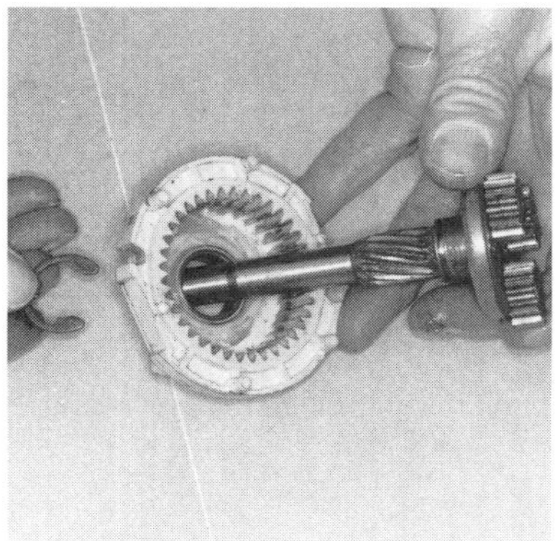

7. Pry the lock ring from the output shaft, remove and set aside the thrust washer, then separate the output shaft from the stationary gear.

8. Remove the three planetary gears from the output shaft. Clean and inspect the planetary gears and stationary gear for wear or damage.

9. The commutator end plate attaches to the brush plate with screws. Remove the screws and lift off the end plate.

Copyright 2000 by Chek-Chart Publications

MOTORCRAFT PERMANENT-MAGNET, GEAR-REDUCTION STARTER OVERHAUL PROCEDURE

10. Slide the armature and brush assembly from the field frame, then separate the brush assembly from the armature.

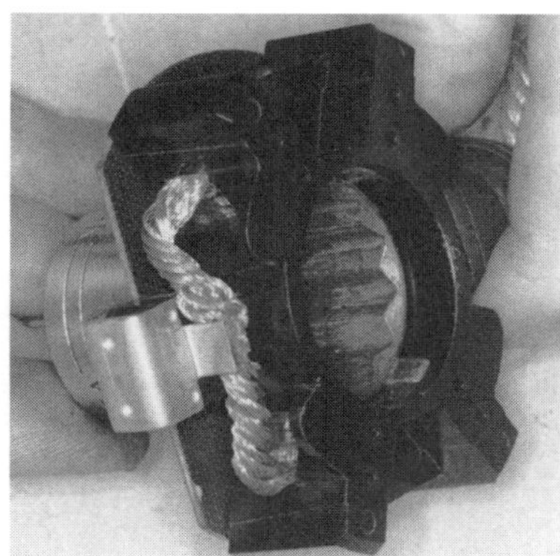

11. To assemble, insert a large socket, about the same diameter as the commutator, into the brush assembly to hold the brushes compressed during installation.

12. Carefully slide the brush assembly onto the armature while pushing the socket free. Install the armature into the field frame.

13. Ensure that the insulated brush lead seal fits correctly into the slot on the field frame. Fit the end plate and install the screws.

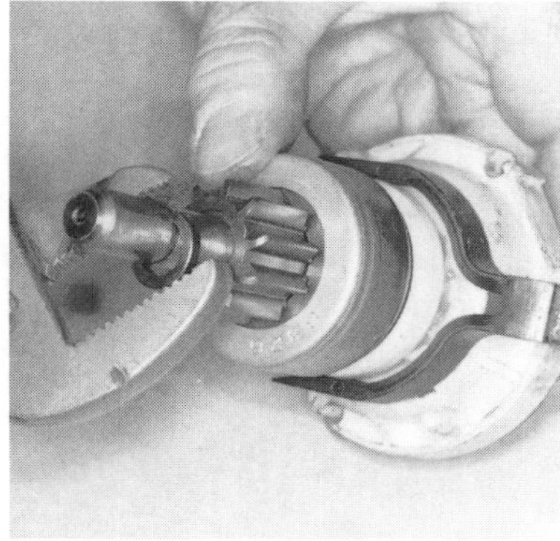

14. Slip the drive mechanism onto the output shaft, fit the thrust washer, and install the lock ring. Use pliers to install a new stopring. Fit the retainer and a new O-ring on the output shaft.

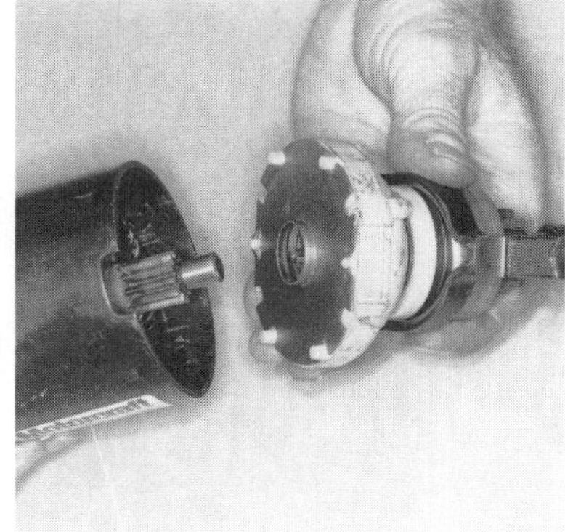

15. Assemble and lubricate the planetary gears, place the thrust ball in its seat, and fit the gear retainer plate. Install the assembly onto the armature shaft.

16. Fit the drive end housing over the drive lever and gear assembly so the shaft engages the bearing, but do not completely seat the assembly.

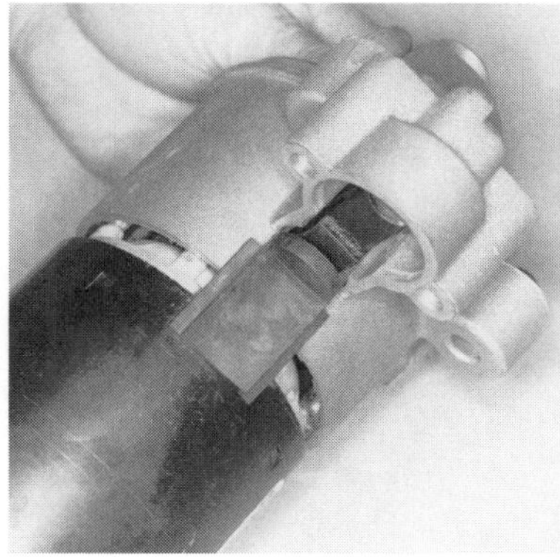

17. Fit the drive lever seal into the slots on the drive end and field frames, then seat the drive frame to the field frame and install the through-bolts.

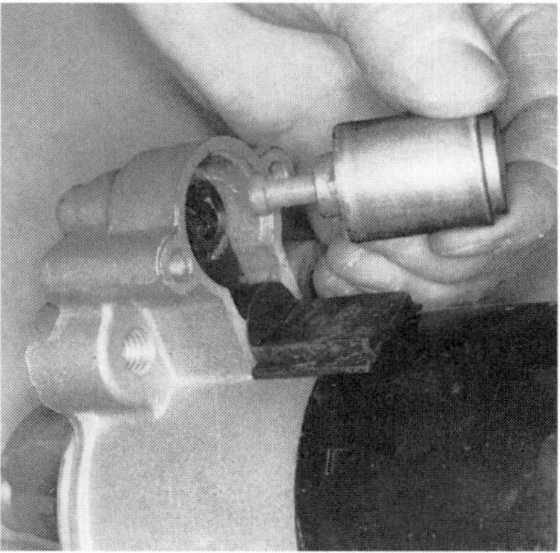

18. Attach the solenoid plunger to the drive lever, fit the solenoid housing, and install the retaining screws. Connect the field lead to the solenoid terminal.

Copyright 2000 by Chek-Chart Publications

CHRYSLER REDUCTION GEAR STARTER OVERHAUL PROCEDURE

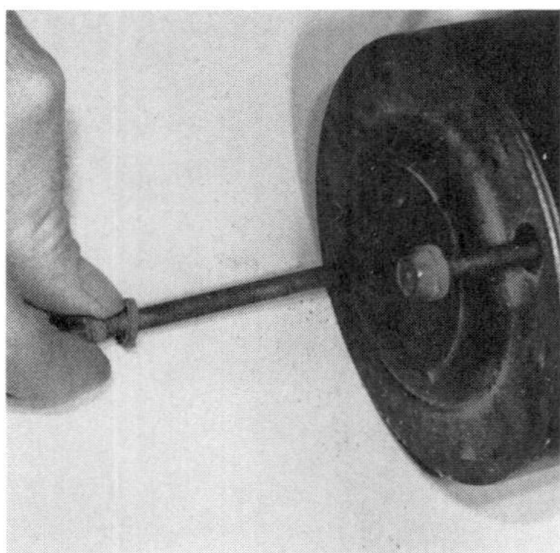

1. Mark frame positions, then remove the two through-bolts and commutator end frame. Remove the armature and the thrust washers from each end of the shaft.

2. Inspect the commutator end frame bushing. Remove old bushings with a puller, and install new bushing with a driver or a wooden block.

3. Separate the field frame and the drive end frame just enough to expose the field terminal screw. Remove screw, then separate the field and end frames.

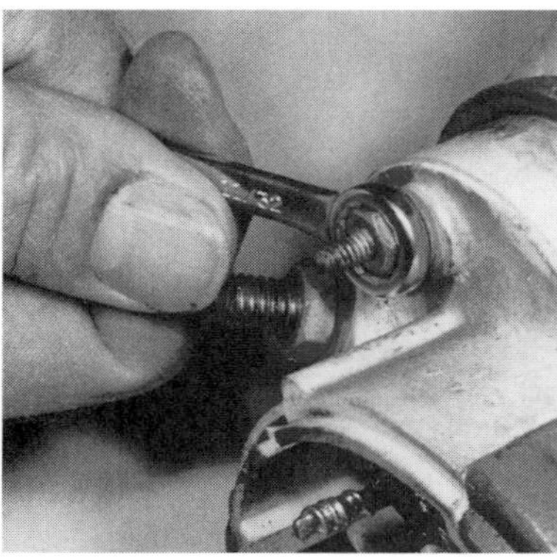

4. Remove the nut, washer, and insulating washer from the solenoid terminal. Heat to unsolder the solenoid pull-in coil lead to brush terminal connection.

5. Unwind the solenoid pull-in coil lead from the brush terminal and remove brush holder from the end frame. Additional screws are used on some brush holders.

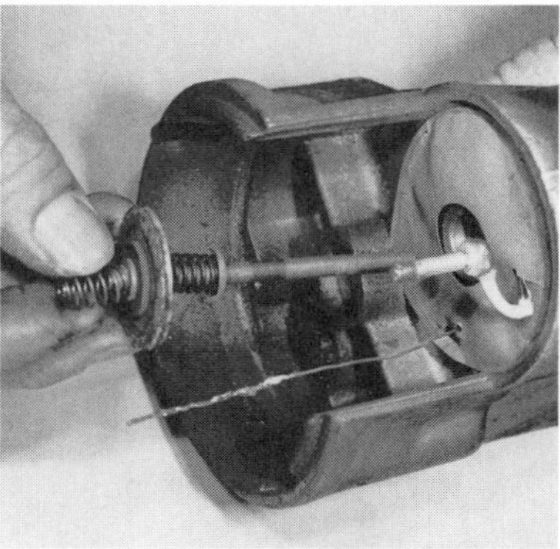

6. Remove the contact and plunger shaft assembly from the solenoid. Also remove the tabbed washer that fits over shaft bore below the solenoid.

7. Separate the solenoid winding from the drive end frame and remove the return spring. Note, the plunger core stays in the end frame with shift fork.

8. Remove the battery terminal nut, washer, and bolt to separate the brush holder from the frame.

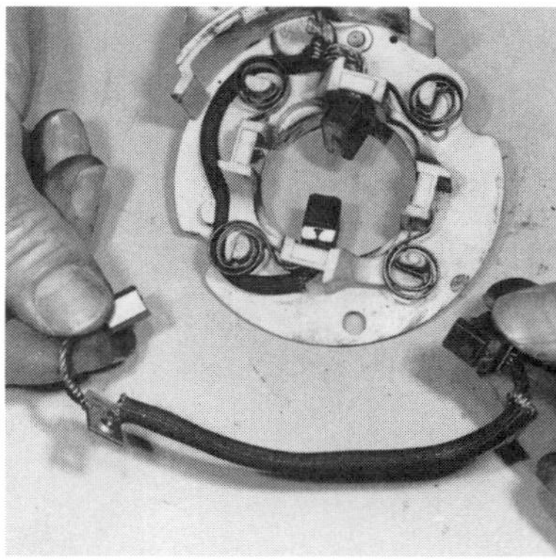

9. Inspect brushes for wear and damaged leads. Replace the complete brush set if any brush is damaged or worn to one-half its original length.

Copyright 2000 by Chek-Chart Publications

CHRYSLER REDUCTION GEAR STARTER OVERHAUL PROCEDURE

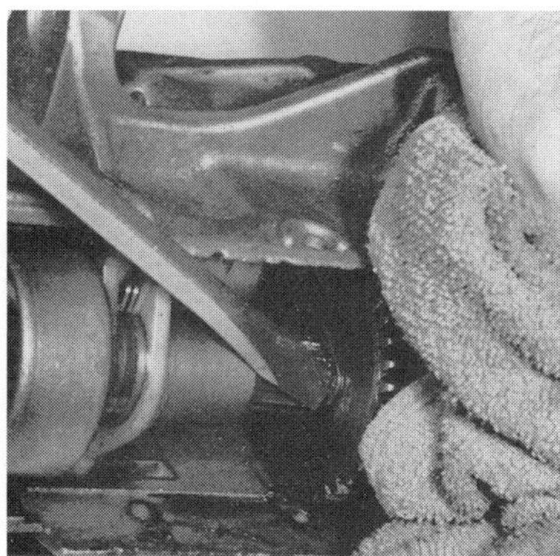

10. Pry off the dust cover and remove the snapring holding the driven gear to the pinion shaft. Lay a rag over the opening to prevent losing the snapring as it comes off.

11. Either a C-clip or snapring is used to retain the assembly on the gear end of the pinion shaft. Carefully remove it.

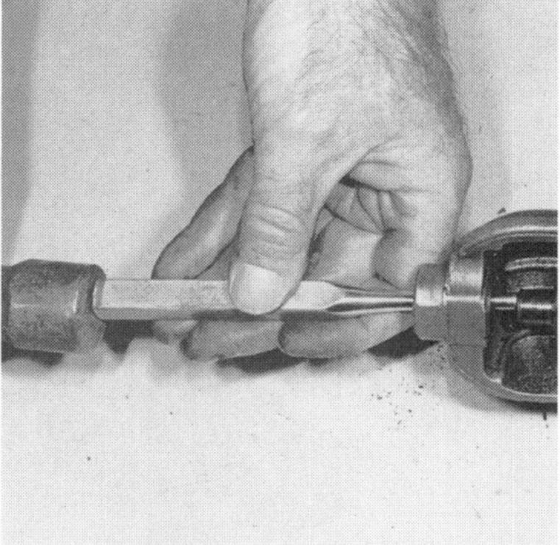

12. Use a punch and hammer to drive the pinion shaft toward the driven gear and out of the end frame.

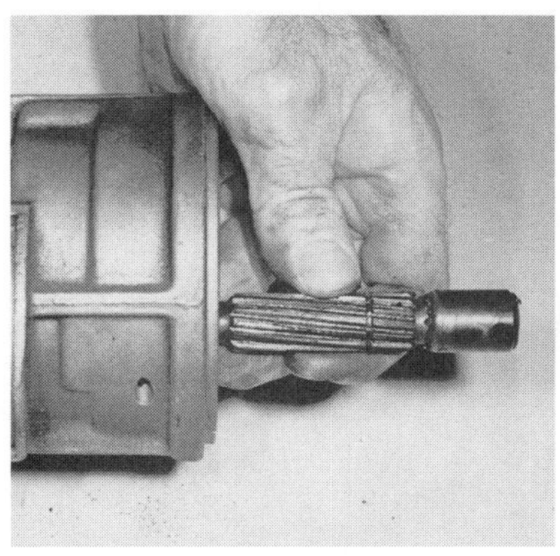

13. Remove the shaft from the gear end of the frame and the pinion, clutch, retainer, washers, and shift fork actuators from the other end. Remove the gear and friction washer.

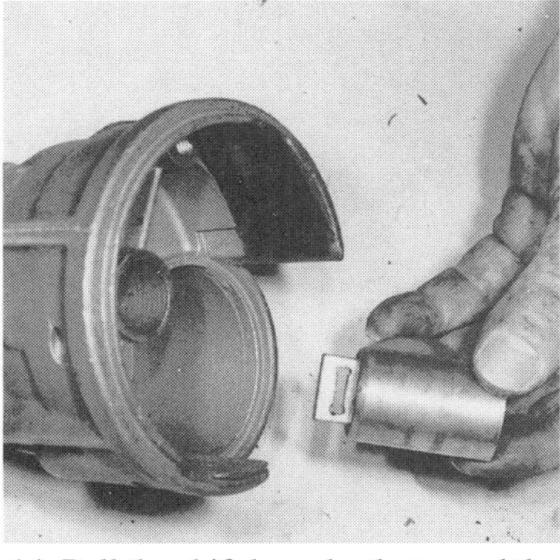

14. Pull the shift lever back, toward the rear of the end frame, to free the solenoid plunger, then remove the plunger core.

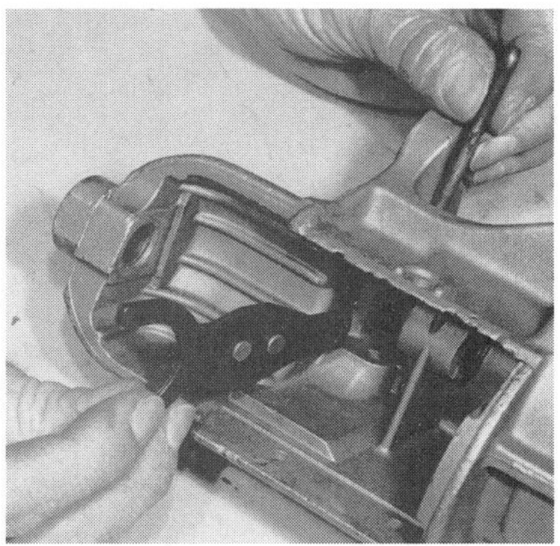

15. Remove the pivot pin using pliers or a punch and hammer, then lift off the shift fork.

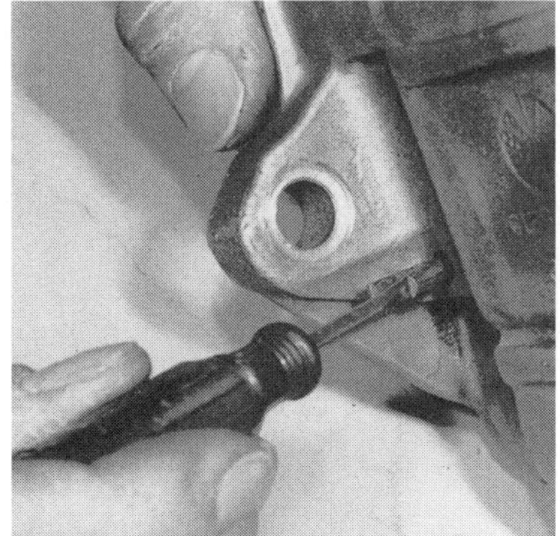

16. Begin assembly by installing the shift fork and pivot pin. Bend one side of the pin after installation to secure it. Attach the solenoid plunger core to the shift fork.

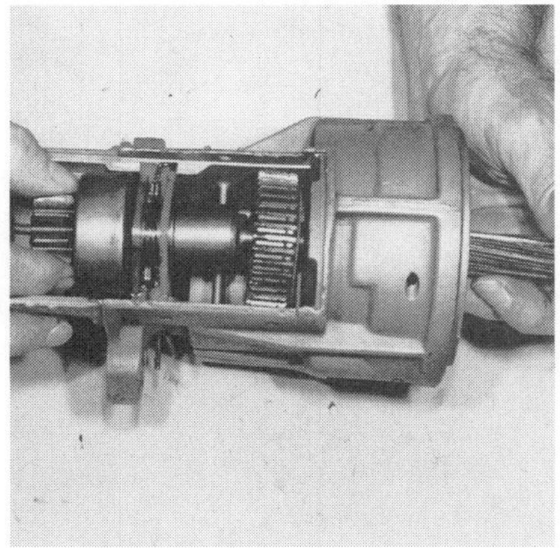

17. Position the driven gear and friction washer and install the shaft through the front of the frame. Fit the pinion assembly from other end so the actuators engage the shift fork.

18. Make sure the friction washer is on the shoulder of the shaft splines before securing the driven gear to the shaft. Install the driven gear snapring.

Copyright 2000 by Chek-Chart Publications

CHRYSLER REDUCTION GEAR STARTER OVERHAUL PROCEDURE

19. Install the pinion shaft C-clip or snapring and fit the assembly to the end frame. Use a soft-faced hammer to drive the pinion shaft into the end frame bushing.

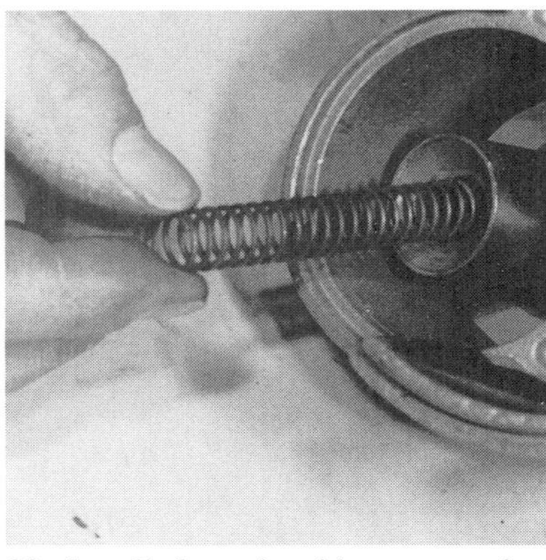

20. Install the solenoid return spring into the bore on the solenoid plunger core.

21. Assemble the brush holder battery terminal, fit the contact plunger to the solenoid, and install the solenoid on the brush holder. Some solenoids attach with screws.

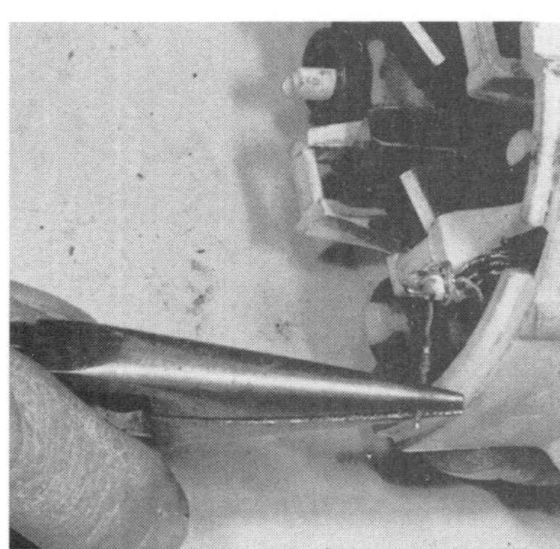

22. Secure the solenoid terminal with the insulating washer and nut. Wrap the pull-in coil lead around the ground brush terminal and solder the connection.

23. Attach the solenoid and brush holder assembly to the drive end frame. Some solenoids attach with screws, others simply snap into place.

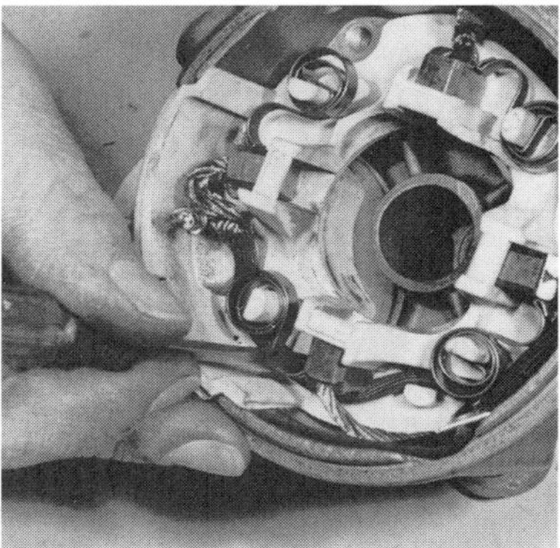

24. Carefully pry the brush springs away from the brushes with a screwdriver, then push the brushes into their holders.

25. Install the thrust washer with the tabs against the brush faces, then place the springs on the brushes. The washer holds the brushes off the commutator during assembly.

26. Test the field coils before assembling the field frame. Align the field frame with the end frame and install the screw to connect the field lead to the brush.

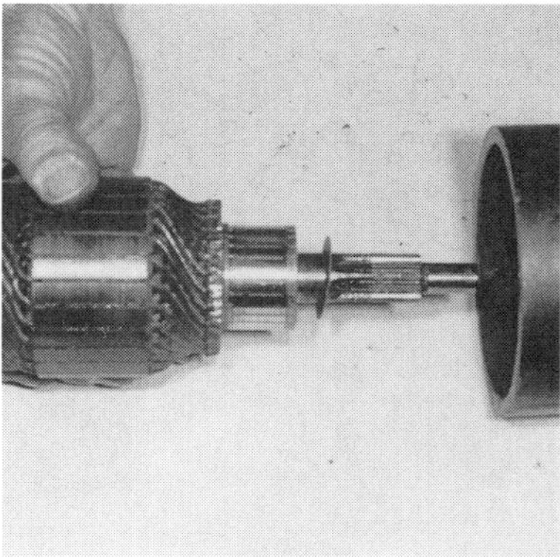

27. Test the armature before assembly. Make sure the thrust washers are on both ends of the shaft, then install the armature. Attach the end frame with the through-bolts.

Copyright 2000 by Chek-Chart Publications

CHRYSLER PERMANENT-MAGNET, GEAR-REDUCTION STARTER OVERHAUL PROCEDURE

1. Remove the nut from the solenoid field terminal, then disconnect the field lead and remove the washer.

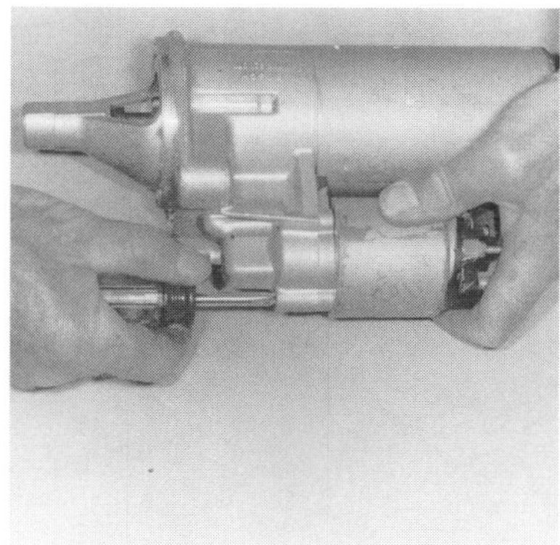

2. Hold the solenoid tightly to the end frame to counteract spring force while removing the three solenoid mounting screws.

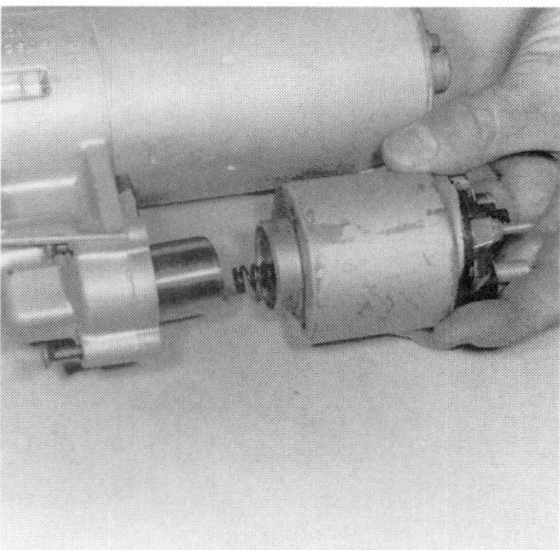

3. Lift off the solenoid housing, then work the solenoid plunger off the shift fork to remove it.

4. Remove the screws and the bushing cap from the commutator end frame. Remove the C-clip and thrust washer from the armature shaft.

5. Remove the through-bolts to separate the commutator end frame from the field frame. If a bushing seal is used on the inside of the end shield (arrow), remove it.

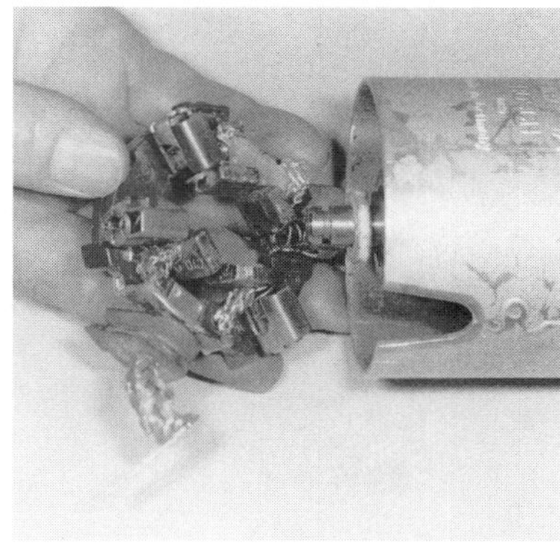

6. Disengage the field terminal insulator from the slot in the field frame and remove the brush plate assembly.

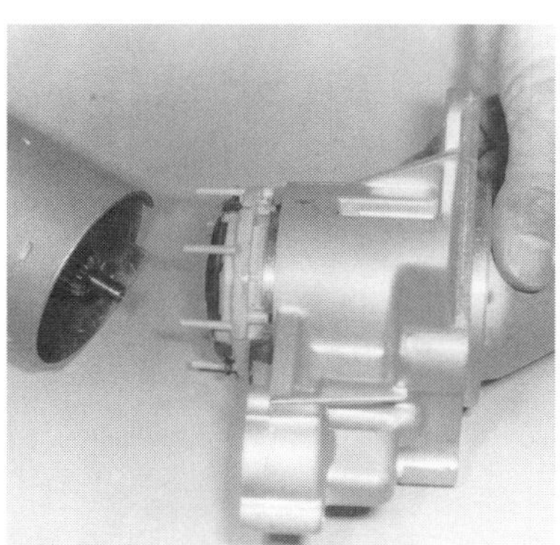

7. Grasp the drive end firmly and carefully separate it from the field frame and armature. The permanent magnets hold the armature in the frame.

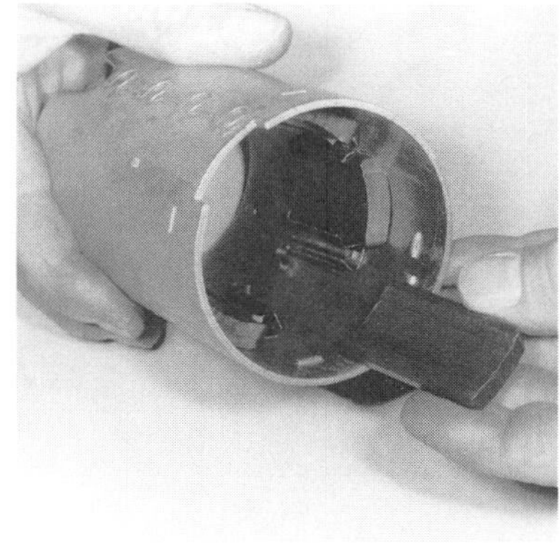

8. The six permanent magnets are held in the frame by clips and are removed by simply sliding them out of the clips.

9. Remove the rubber seal (arrow) from the drive end frame, then lift the starter drive gear assembly free of the frame.

Copyright 2000 by Chek-Chart Publications

CHRYSLER PERMANENT-MAGNET, GEAR-REDUCTION STARTER OVERHAUL PROCEDURE

10. Unsnap the metal dust plate from the plastic ring gear to remove it and expose the planetary gears.

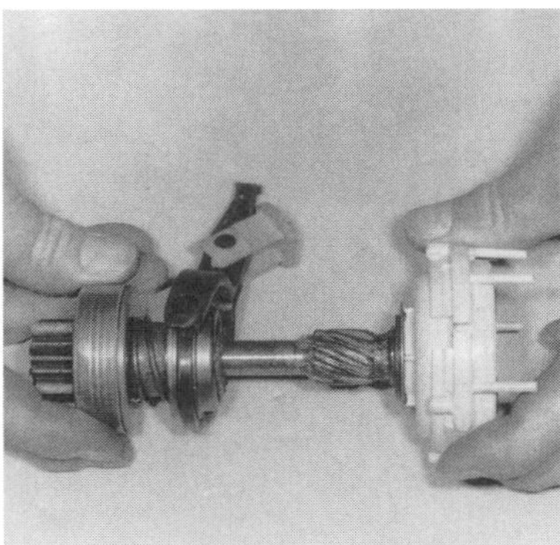

11. Press the stop collar off the snapring with a socket and remove the snapring and collar. Then, slide the clutch assembly off the output shaft.

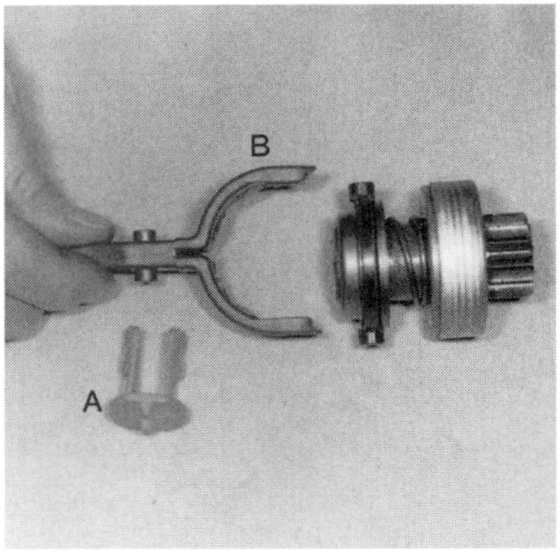

12. Inspect the plastic shift lever bushing (A) and shift lever (B). Separate them from the clutch assembly and replace as needed.

13. Remove the C-clip and thrust washer to separate the ring gear and planetary gears. Clean and inspect the gears for signs of wear and damage.

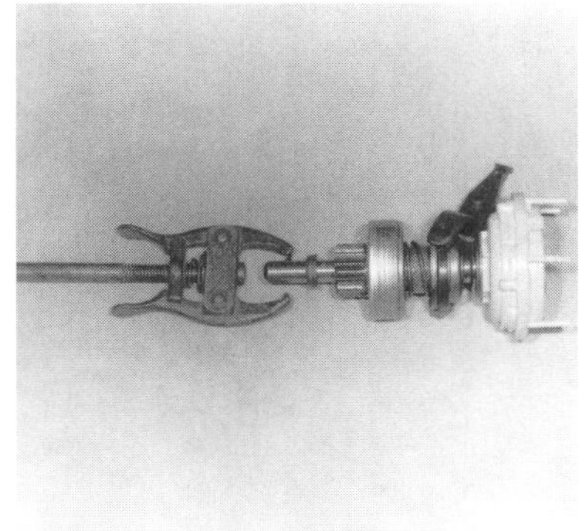

14. Assemble the drive clutch, stop collar, and snapring onto the output shaft. Use a puller to draw the stop collar up around the snapring.

15. Align the shift lever and insert the drive gear assembly into the drive end frame to seat it in the bushing. Then, install the rubber seal.

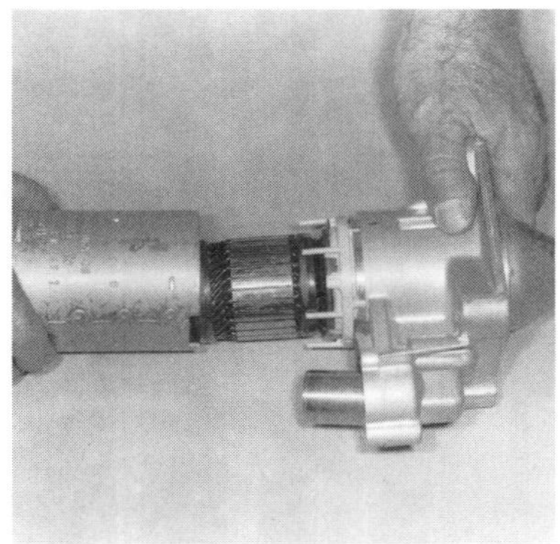

16. Fit the armature to the drive gear. Grasp the frames securely to overcome the magnetic pull while installing the field frame over the armature and onto the end frame.

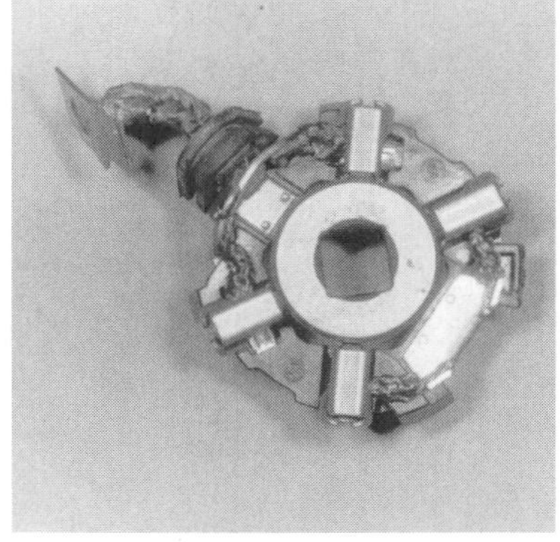

17. Install a large socket, about the same diameter as the commutator, in the center of the brush holder assembly to compress the brushes for assembly.

18. Slip the socket out while installing the brush assembly. Fit the thrust washer, C-clip, and bushing cap. Then, install the solenoid.

Copyright 2000 by Chek-Chart Publications

PART FOUR

Ignition and Electronic Control System Service

Copyright 2000 by Chek-Chart Publications

8

Ignition System Inspection, Diagnosis, and Testing

Part Four of this *Shop Manual,* which includes Chapters Eight through Twelve, details ignition and electronic control system services. This chapter contains general procedures for inspecting, diagnosing, and testing the ignition system circuits and components. Ignition system services, which include testing, removing, and replacing specific ignition system components, are detailed in Chapter Nine. Chapter Ten describes removing, overhauling, and installing a distributor and Chapter Eleven explains checking and adjusting, where applicable, ignition timing. Electronic engine control system service procedures are discussed in Chapter Twelve.

While working, refer, as needed, to Chapter Two of this *Shop Manual* for specific test procedures and to Chapter One for troubleshooting and repair techniques.

IGNITION SERVICE SAFETY

To prevent injury or damage to the ignition system always follow these precautions during ignition system tests:

- Unless the procedure specifically states otherwise, switch the ignition off or disconnect the negative battery cable before separating any ignition system wiring connections. The high-voltage surge that results from making or breaking a connection may damage electronic components.
- Never touch, or short to ground, any exposed connections while the engine is cranking or running.
- Never short the primary circuit to ground without resistance; the high current that results damages circuits and components.
- Never create a secondary voltage arc near the battery or fuel system components. This may cause an explosion.
- Handle high-tension ignition cables carefully. Pulling or pinching cables causes internal damage that is difficult to detect.
- When testing the ignition system, follow the procedure specified by the manufacturer.

Also observe standard safety practices outlined in Chapter One of this *Shop Manual* to prevent accidents.

INSPECTION AND DIAGNOSIS

Ignition service begins with a visual inspection of the system components and circuitry. This is followed by a test drive to experience the symptoms and form a basic diagnosis.

Copyright 2000 by Chek-Chart Publications

Inspection

Check the following items during the inspection:

- Battery
- Secondary ignition components
- Primary ignition components
- Secondary ignition circuitry
- Primary ignition circuitry
- Related components.

Remember, the battery must be at or near a full state of charge and the terminal connections must be clean and tight for *any* electrical system on the vehicle to function properly. The ignition system is no exception. A weak battery or high terminal resistance reduces available voltage and restricts current, which reduces ignition performance.

Check ignition components for secure mounting, correct installation, and good electrical connections. Inspect both the primary and secondary ignition components and their wiring. Check the entire length of wires and harnesses over for signs of damage. Verify the wires are properly routed and all connections are clean and tight.

Inspect any other components related to the ignition system. On a late-model vehicle, this includes all of the electronic engine sensors and actuators and their circuitry. Repair any problems found during the inspection before attempting to diagnose the ignition system.

Basic Diagnosis

If the engine does not start, perform a spark test to check for secondary voltage available from the coil. This is done by disconnecting a spark plug cable from the plug or removing the coil cable at the distributor cap, then attaching the cable to a spark plug simulator. A spark plug simulator is basically a plug without a side electrode and a grounding clamp attached to it, figure 8-1. Connect the secondary coil lead, or plug cable, to the simulator and clamp it firmly on a good ground, figure 8-2. Watch the plug simulator while cranking the engine. The simulator produces a bright blue arc from the center electrode to its side each time the field collapses if secondary voltage is available from the coil.

When secondary voltage is available, the ignition system provides the current required to ignite the combustion charge. Therefore, the cause of the "no start condition" is most likely the mechanical, fuel, or engine control system, rather than an ignition system failure.

No secondary voltage available may be caused by a defective coil or some type of primary circuit failure. As explained later in this chapter, a series of tests is performed using a voltmeter, ohmmeter, and ammeter to isolate the source of the failure.

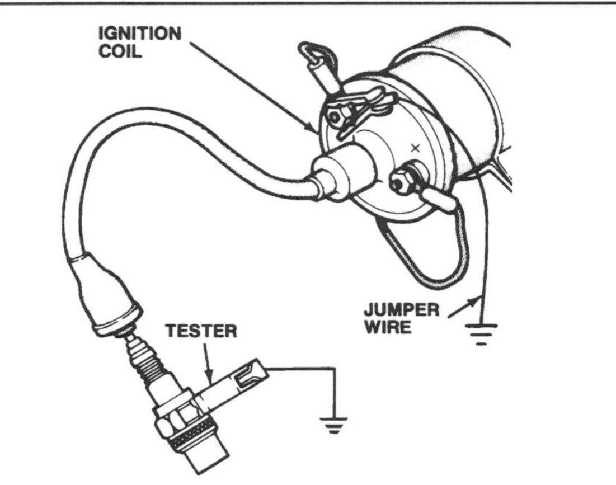

Figure 8-1. A spark plug simulator resembles a plug with a clamp attached to it.

Figure 8-2. Connect the plug simulator, crank the starter, and look for a bright blue arc across electrodes.

If the engine does start, drive the vehicle to experience the symptoms the customer is complaining about. The symptoms experienced during the test drive determine which areas of the ignition system to focus on during diagnosis, figure 8-3. When symptoms indicate a possible ignition failure, use an oscilloscope or engine analyzer to evaluate system performance and condition.

OSCILLOSCOPE DIAGNOSIS

Because an oscilloscope displays voltage changes during a period of time, it is an ideal instrument for examining the variable voltages produced in both the primary and secondary ignition circuits. All oscilloscopes operate on the same principle: A voltage trace, or waveform, is displayed on a viewing screen as a

Copyright 2000 by Chek-Chart Publications

CONDITION	CAUSE	CHECK
• Engine cranks normally but does not start and run	1. Open primary circuit 2. Coil grounded 3. No engine speed signal 4. Incorrect timing 5. Secondary voltage leak 6. Fouled spark plugs 7. No fuel 8. Mechanical failure	1. Circuit connections, coil, pickup coil, module, ignition switch. 2. Test and replace ignition coil. 3. Available voltage to the coil and CKP sensor signal. 4. Check and adjust, where applicable. 5. Coil tower, distributor cap, rotor, and high-tension cables. 6. Clean or replace. 7. Fuel delivery and volume. 8. Engine.
• Engine runs but misfires on one cylinder	9. Defective spark plug 10. Faulty plug wire 11. Defective distributor cap 12. Mechanical failure	9. Replace spark plugs. 10. Inspect and replace. 11. Inspect and replace. 12. Cylinder compression.
• Engine runs but misfires on different cylinders	13. Primary circuit resistance 14. Secondary voltage leak 15. Defective ignition coil 16. Fouled spark plugs 17. Fuel delivery problem 18. Mechanical failure	13. Circuit connections and continuity. 14. Coil tower, distributor cap, rotor, and cables. 15. Inspect, test, and replace as needed. 16. Inspect and replace as needed. 17. Fuel delivery and volume. 18. Engine.
• Engine runs but loses power	19. Incorrect timing 20. No timing advance 21. Fuel quality	19. Check and adjust. 20. Electronic control system. 21. Test and refuel.
• Engine backfires	22. Incorrect timing 23. Ignition crossfire 24. Exhaust leak 25. Fuel quality 26. Mechanical failure	22. Check and adjust. 23. Secondary wiring. 24. Inspect and repair as needed. 25. Test and refuel. 26. Engine.
• Engine knocks or pings	27. Incorrect timing 28. Too much timing advance 29. Lack of EGR 30. Fuel quality 31. Faulty knock sensor	27. Check and adjust. 28. Electronic control system. 29. Inspect and repair as needed. 30. Test and refuel. 31. Inspect and replace as needed.

Figure 8-3. Ignition system troubleshooting chart.

graph of voltage versus time. The vertical scale on the screen represents voltage and the horizontal scale represents time.

The voltage trace of an ignition event, or the firing of one spark plug, is divided into three periods or sections: dwell, firing, and open circuit, figure 8-4. Deviations from a normal pattern indicate a problem, so it is important to know what a good pattern for the system being serviced should look like. Although all ignition waveform patterns appear similar, there are variations between systems. Most scopes designed for automotive use display ignition traces in three different modes. Each mode is best used to isolate and identify particular kinds of malfunctions. The three basic patterns are:

- Superimposed
- Parade
- Raster.

In a superimposed pattern, voltage traces for all cylinders are displayed on top of each other to form a single pattern on the scope screen, figure 8-5. This display provides a quick overall view of ignition system operation and is used to reveal certain major problems.

The parade pattern displays voltage traces for all cylinders one after the other across the screen from

Copyright 2000 by Chek-Chart Publications

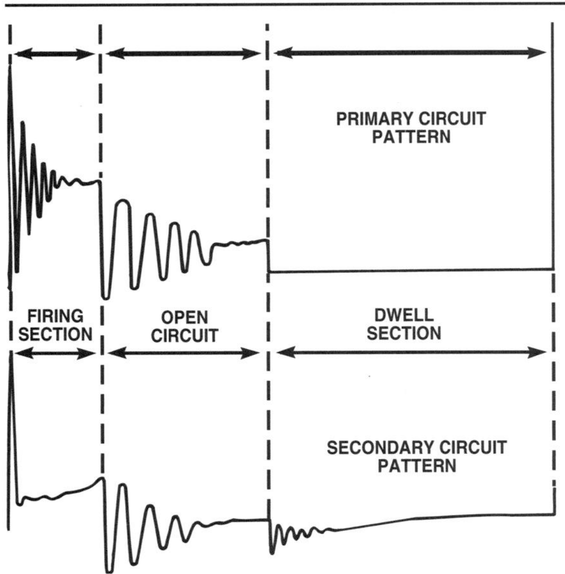

Figure 8-4. Ignition oscilloscope patterns, both primary and secondary, are divided into three distinct periods.

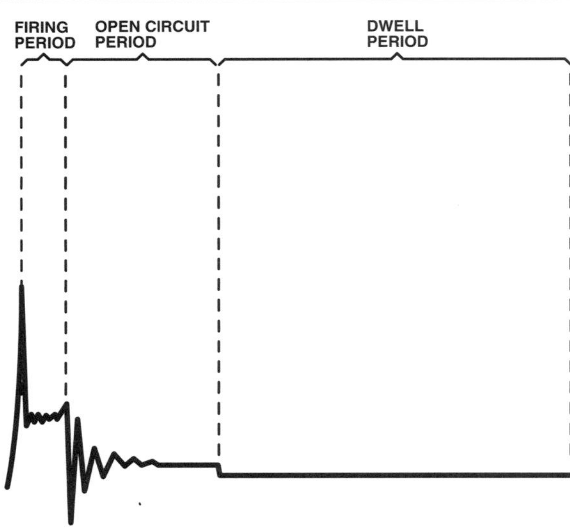

Figure 8-5. A superimposed pattern displays cylinder traces on top of each other.

left to right in firing order sequence, figure 8-6. This allows easy comparison of voltage levels between cylinders. A parade display is useful for diagnosing problems in the secondary circuit.

A raster pattern shows the voltage traces for all cylinders stacked one above the other. The screen displays cylinders from bottom to top in firing order sequence, figure 8-7. This display is used to compare the time periods of the three sections of a voltage trace.

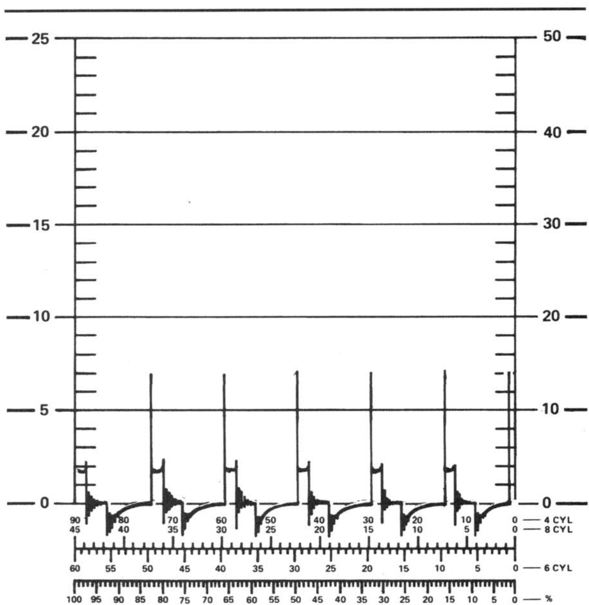

Figure 8-6. Parade pattern displays cylinder traces horizontally across the screen in firing order.

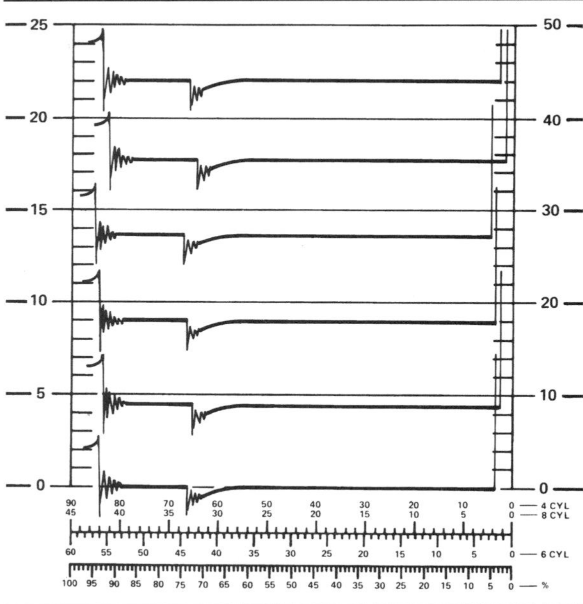

Figure 8-7. Raster pattern stacks cylinder traces vertically up the screen in firing order.

Oscilloscope Settings and Connections

All oscilloscope manufacturers provide instructions for the use of their equipment. Although color codes and connector types vary, there are some basic similarities. Oscilloscopes installed in multifunction engine analyzer units are designed specifically for testing ignition systems and do not require any special considerations. Simply hook up the leads

Copyright 2000 by Chek-Chart Publications

as instructed, then select primary or secondary and the type of display, superimposed, parade, or raster, on the scope control panel. Also select either the high or low voltage scale to be used.

The time base of the scope is automatically set to display one complete cycle of the ignition process. That is, when connected to a six-cylinder engine, the screen displays the firing sequence of the six cylinders, then starts again. As the engine speed changes, the scope maintains the same display, but the time represented changes.

Lab scope settings

It is possible to damage a lab scope if the sampled signal exceeds the capability of the scope. Always be cautious when measuring high secondary voltage to prevent equipment damage. Know the limits of both ac and dc voltage that the scope can safely handle.

To display the signal, both the volts per division (VOLT/DIV) and time per division (TIME/DIV) must be selected on the scope control panel. The VOLT/DIV selection controls the height of the signal trace on the display screen. The lower the VOLT/DIV setting, the higher the displayed image. A higher VOLT/DIV setting results in a lower display. The VOLT/DIV setting determines how many volts are represented in each of the eight vertical grids or blocks on the display screen. As an example, consider a 5-volt square-wave signal. If the VOLT/DIV is set to 1 volt, the signal height changes five grids each time it switches on or off. However, the signal changes only one grid if the VOLT/DIV is set to 5 volts. The type of signal being sampled determines the VOLT/DIV setting to be used.

Ignition system voltage often exceeds the maximum voltage that a lab scope is capable of displaying. If the scope does not have a high-enough VOLT/DIV setting to properly display a higher voltage signal, a 10X probe may be used. These probes have a 10 to 1 attenuation, which reduces the signal by a factor of 10, figure 8-8. When sampling a 400-volt signal with a 10X probe, the signal displays on screen as 40 volts.

Sampling secondary ignition signals requires a special capacitive probe designed specifically for this purpose. These capacitive probes, or inductive clamps, generate a waveform trace based on fluctuations in the strength of the magnetic field and capture a secondary signal without connecting the scope directly to a high-voltage circuit. A capacitive probe for sampling the secondary ignition signals requires about a 1000 to 1 attenuation.

Before attaching the scope leads, adjust the VOLT/DIV switch so the screen displays both the highest and lowest voltage expected on the test circuit. Be aware, some scopes shunt excess voltage to ground

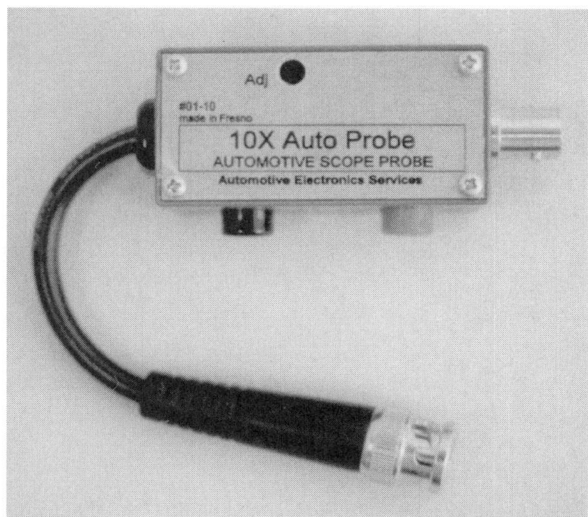

Figure 8-8. A 10X probe increases the display capability of the scope screen by a factor of ten.

to prevent damage to the instrument. If this happens while sampling primary ignition circuits, the collapse of the coil windings is disrupted, which stalls the engine.

Once a trace is visible on the scope screen, adjust the switch to fine tune and maximize the display. Most digital scopes built for automotive use have an automatic range finder that establishes initial settings based on the signal being sampled. Keep in mind, these features are designed simply to make using the scope easier and are not always the ideal settings for diagnosing a problem. Even with the most elaborate automatic ranging features, it is often necessary make adjustments to the settings to maximize the display and get precise readings.

Scope connections

When the scope is part of an engine analyzer, there is an assortment of cables, which are used to conduct a variety of tests, figure 8-9. Be sure to use the right cables, and to connect them correctly. Follow instructions from the equipment manufacturer. Modern engine analyzers often contain onscreen directions for connecting cables and conducting tests.

In general, to sample the primary ignition signal, the positive primary lead on the scope is connected to the primary negative terminal of the coil. The negative primary lead on the scope is connected to a good ground on the engine or battery.

To sample the secondary ignition, the secondary lead on the scope is connected to the coil wire, or clamped to the distributor cap if the coil is internal. This connection is made with an inductive clamp. An additional inductive clamp attaches to the number one spark plug lead to provide a triggering, or synchronization

Copyright 2000 by Chek-Chart Publications

Figure 8-9. Using an engine analyzer to sample ignition waveforms.

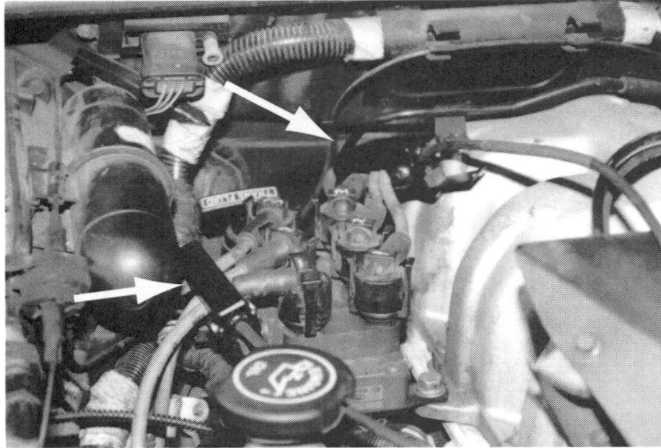

Figure 8-10. Two inductive clamps used to pick up distributorless ignition system voltage signals.

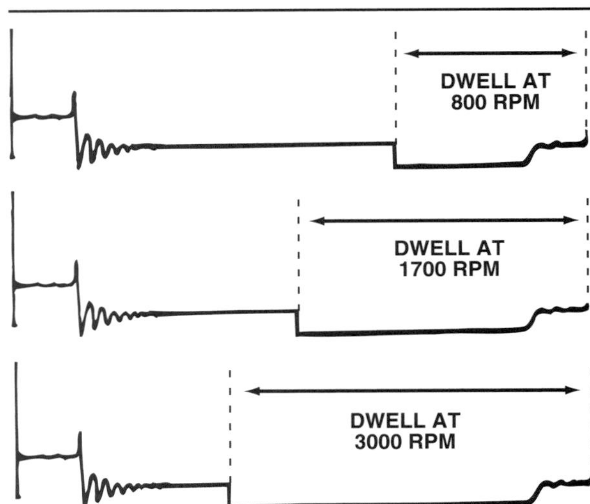

Figure 8-11. A dwell period that increases with engine speed is normal for some ignition systems.

(sync), signal. This ensures that the waveform display begins with the first cylinder in the firing order.

On many late-model vehicles, especially those with distributorless or direct ignition systems, the coil terminals are not readily accessible for attaching the scope leads. Adapters and special test equipment are available for connecting a scope to these systems, figure 8-10. Follow instructions from the equipment manufacturer to connect these devices and test using procedures recommended by the vehicle manufacturer.

Ignition Waveforms

An oscilloscope is the ideal instrument for scrutinizing the variable voltages produced in the ignition circuits. As previously mentioned, all ignition system voltage signals, both primary and secondary, are divided into three periods: dwell, firing, and open circuit. Each period displays specific aspects of the ignition cycle.

Dwell period

The dwell period is when the primary circuit is complete, and low-voltage current is building up the magnetic field of the coil. Dwell begins as the ignition module transistor switches on to complete the primary circuit and continues until the transistor switches off to begin the firing sequence. Dwell time varies for different systems, and some ignition systems also vary the dwell period according to engine speed or other operating conditions, figure 8-11.

A scope trace of the dwell period begins with a sharp drop of the signal as the coil driver completes the primary circuit to ground. This is followed by a relatively flat line which may have a slight ramp as current builds up in the secondary windings of the coil. When viewing a secondary circuit waveform, the signal may ring, or display several diminishing oscillations, as the transistor switches to complete the primary circuit. Some ignition systems offer current limiting. This affects current in the primary circuit and produces a slight hump in the trace toward the end of the dwell period, figure 8-12. The exact shape and other characteristics of this current-limiting hump, appearing on both the primary and secondary trace, vary by system. Therefore, it is important to know the characteristics of the particular system being tested to form an accurate diagnosis. The dwell period ends with the abrupt upward stroke of the firing of the next cylinder.

Firing period

The firing period, also called the spark line on a waveform trace, corresponds to the amount of time an electrical arc is bridging the spark plug gap and igniting the combustion charge. The firing period begins with a high inductive kick as the spark is established across the plug gap. Less voltage is required to maintain the

Copyright 2000 by Chek-Chart Publications

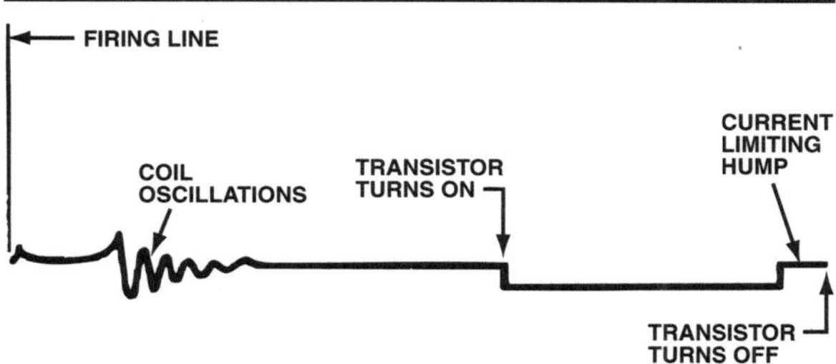

Figure 8-12. A current limiting transistor, when used, causes a small hump to appear on the trace at the end of the dwell section.

arc once it is established, so the trace drops after the initial spike.

When sampling the primary circuit, the trace rings after the inductive kick in a series of diminishing oscillations which continue until the spark extinguishes, figure 8-13. Be aware, some systems suppress the ringing of the firing section, and an inductive kick followed by a relatively flat line is the normal pattern. Again, it is important to know the specific characteristics of the system being tested.

The trace drops following the inductive kick on a secondary pattern, as less voltage is needed to maintain an arc across the spark plug gap once it is established. On a good-running engine, the trace drops to less than one-quarter the height of the inductive kick, then continues as a near-horizontal line. A slight rise in this spark line is normal for some ignition systems, but too much rise indicates a fuel mixture or combustion problem.

The firing period ends when there is no longer enough energy in the secondary windings of the coil to bridge the spark plug gap. This opens the circuit to begin the final period of the ignition cycle.

Open circuit period

The open circuit period begins with a sudden drop of the trace as the spark plug stops firing. The trace continues as a relatively flat line until the transistor switches on to begin the dwell period for the next cylinder in the firing order. When the circuit opens, a considerable amount of energy remains in the secondary coil windings, even though there is not enough to bridge the plug gap. This remaining energy dissipates as heat and appears on both a primary and secondary waveform as ringing, figure 8-14. The primary transistor switches on the moment spark ends on a Chrysler EIS system, so there is no open circuit period. Look for a series of diminishing oscillations that flatten out to a near-horizontal line on an open circuit waveform.

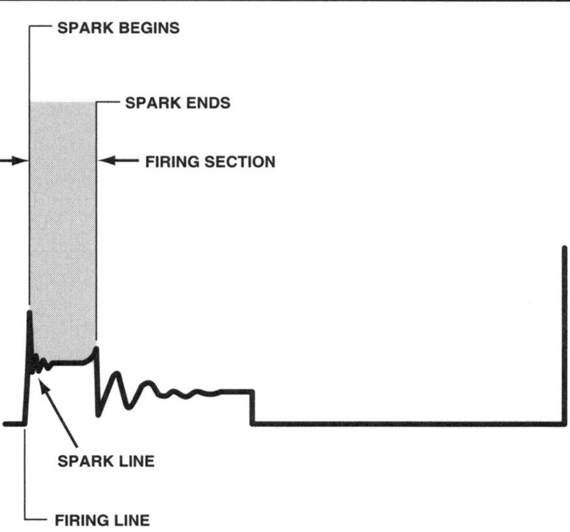

Figure 8-13. A typical primary firing period displays as a high spike followed by a spark line.

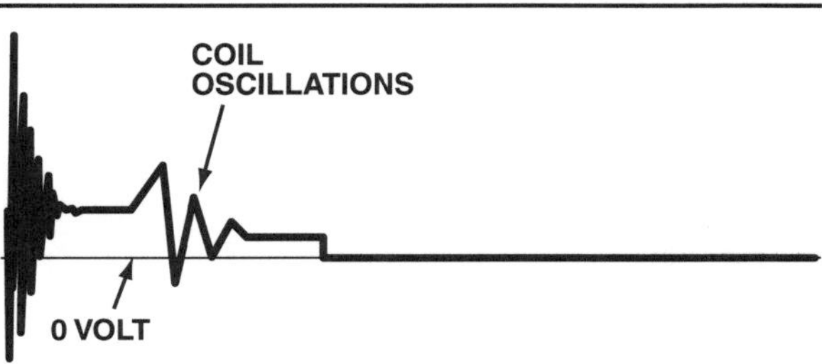

Figure 8-14. Diminishing oscillations appear on the trace as the coil dissipates residual voltage during the open circuit period.

Analyzing Ignition Waveforms

An ignition waveform contains a vast amount of information about circuit activity, mechanical condition, combustion efficiency, and fuel mixture. There are many variables which come into play, and a full explanation of ignition waveforms would fill an entire book. The information included here is simply to show how conditions outside the electronic circuitry can disrupt an ignition waveform. Electronic ignition patterns vary by system, so it is critical to know what is normal for the system being tested. Examples presented here are intended as a general reference only.

A number of ignition, fuel, and internal engine problems interfere with the firing period of a secondary ignition trace. Problems disrupting the firing trace are usually the result of high or low resistance either in the secondary circuit itself, or as the result of combustion problems within the cylinder.

Secondary ignition component failure due to wear is a common problem resulting in high circuit

Copyright 2000 by Chek-Chart Publications

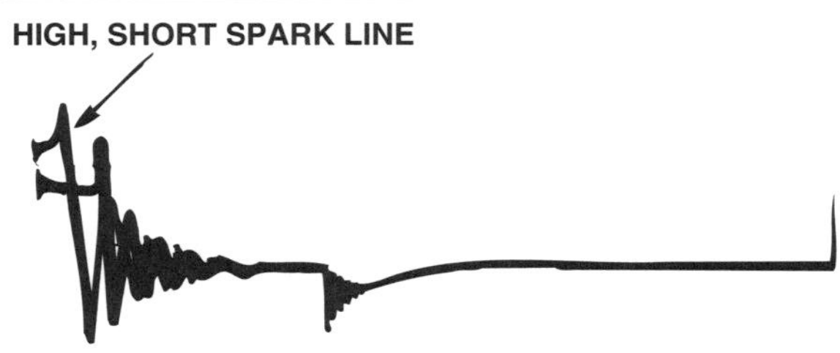

Figure 8-15. High open circuit resistance on one cylinder is quickly spotted on a superimposed display as a high, short spark line on the secondary trace.

resistance. Whether caused by a damaged plug wire, distributor cap wear, or excessive spark plug gap, this additional resistance disrupts current and alters the scope trace. Higher voltage, which is required to overcome this type of resistance, reduces current, and the energy in the coil dissipates more rapidly than normal. As a result, high open-circuit resistance produces a high firing spike followed by a high, short spark line, figure 8-15.

Other problems on the secondary circuit also increase resistance but have a different impact on the waveform. Corrosion on the cable terminals is a common problem that affects the spark line of a trace. Overcoming the resistance created by corrosion requires an increase in voltage to maintain a spark. Secondary terminal corrosion causes the spark line to start high and slope downward sharply as voltage falls off. Poor connections on the primary circuits also add resistance that disrupts the trace. High primary resistance reduces the amount of energy the coil produces, which weakens the spark and results in a trace with a low inductive kick and short burn time.

Current always follows the path of least resistance, and low resistance in the secondary circuit causes current to bypass the spark plug gap. Carbon tracking in the distributor cap, poor secondary cable insulation, and fouled spark plugs are sources of low resistance that disrupt current. Low resistance reduces the voltage requirements and shows up on a trace as a low, long spark line, figure 8-16.

Fuel mixture problems often cause the trace of a spark line to jump erratically, and variations in the fuel mixture show up on the spark line as well. As fuel mixture in the plug gap varies, the voltage requirements to keep the plug firing also vary. Therefore, the spark line always has some variation. Turbulence in the cylinder and fuel mixture changes cause this variation. Diagnosing a fuel mixture problem is best done with an exhaust analyzer, rather than a scope.

Many problems are revealed on a scope only under snap acceleration or engine load. On snap acceleration, a lean mixture produces a scope trace with a high

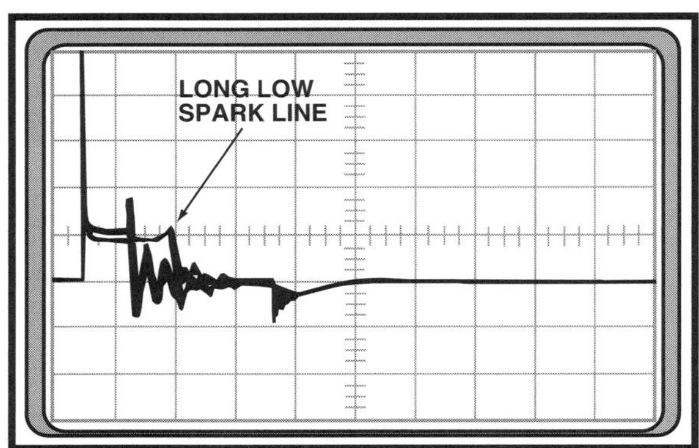

Figure 8-16. Low resistance on a cylinder produces a long, low spark line on the secondary trace.

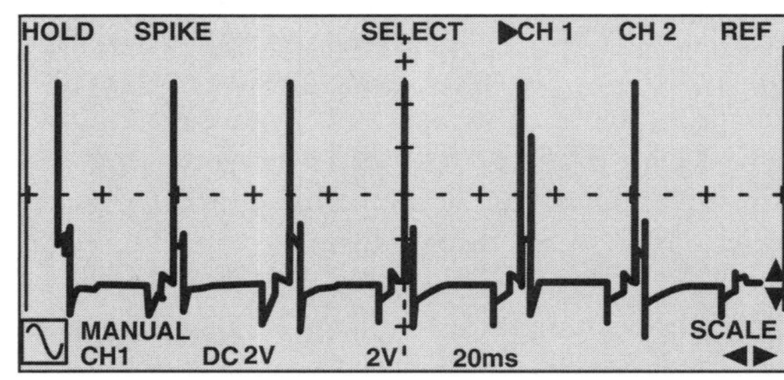

Figure 8-17. A lean mixture produces an inductive kick after the spark line on snap acceleration.

inductive kick after the spark line, figure 8-17. Too wide of a plug gap usually does not show on the scope until snap acceleration, when the firing line goes high.

Primary scope patterns

Although the primary circuit is the low-voltage side of the ignition system, the signal may spike as high as 200 volts on some systems. Be familiar with the system tested and adjust the VOLTS/DIV setting accordingly if using a lab scope.

Firing period

The firing period of the pattern corresponds to the amount of time the spark plug is firing. This is referred to as "burn time." Many engine analyzers record the burn time, which is a good indicator of the firing conditions. A long burn time is the result of low total resistance, such as that caused by low compression. A short burn time is the result of high resistance, such as that caused by high resistance in a plug wire. A normal display of the firing period appears with a high vertical spike, or firing line, as spark begins. This is followed by a relatively flat line until spark ends, figure 8-18.

Copyright 2000 by Chek-Chart Publications

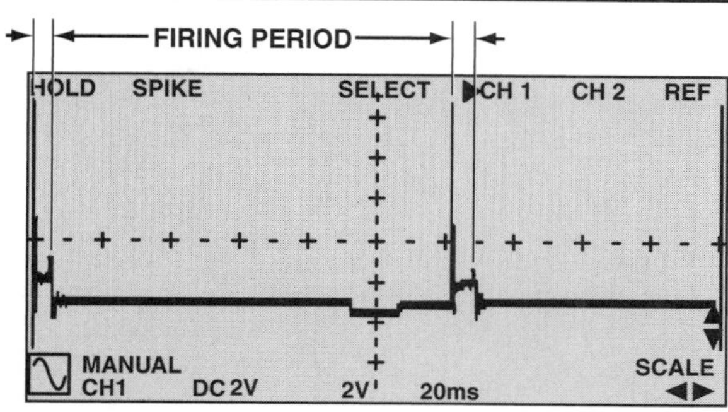

Figure 8-18. Look for an inductive kick and a series of diminishing oscillations in a primary firing period.

Open circuit period

Once spark is extinguished, the open circuit, or intermediate, period begins. This section of the trace continues until an electronic signal from the ignition control module (ICM) or powertrain control module (PCM) switches on the primary circuit transistor. On some systems, such as the Chrysler EIS, there is no open circuit section because the primary transistor switches on the moment spark ends, figure 8-19.

An open circuit voltage trace displays the dissipation of energy remaining in the coil after plug firing is complete. The trace appears as a series of diminishing oscillations similar to those of the firing section, but considerably smaller. There should be at least three distinct coil oscillations on the trace, figure 8-20. Less than five oscillations indicates a defective coil primary winding. The end of the intermediate period is marked by an abrupt drop. This is the point where the primary transistor turns on and dwell begins.

Dwell period

The dwell period is the time the primary circuit is complete. During dwell, a low-voltage current is building up the magnetic field of the coil. Following the sharp drop of the transistor switching on, the trace appears as a relatively flat, horizontal line. The dwell period ends with the abrupt, upward stroke of the first firing oscillation of the next cylinder in the firing order. Small oscillations, or a hump, toward the end of the dwell period should be considered normal on some systems. If the control module contains a current limiting device, the hump indicates that the limiting circuit is activated, figure 8-21.

Use the raster pattern to compare the dwell period for each cylinder. Dwell sections should not vary by more than four to six degrees between cylinders. Dwell variations are generally caused by a worn distributor or timing chain. More important is any variation in the upward spike at the end of each trace. Variation at the end of the trace is variation in timing for each cylinder.

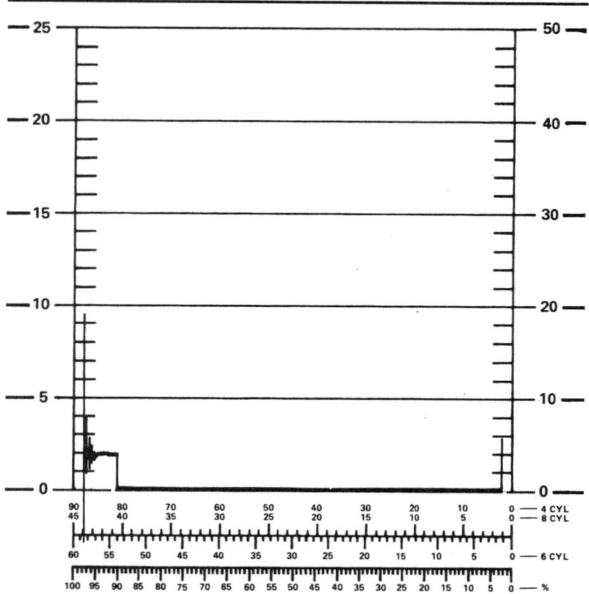

Figure 8-19. There is no open circuit period on some Chrysler systems because the primary transistor switches on as soon as the spark extinguishes.

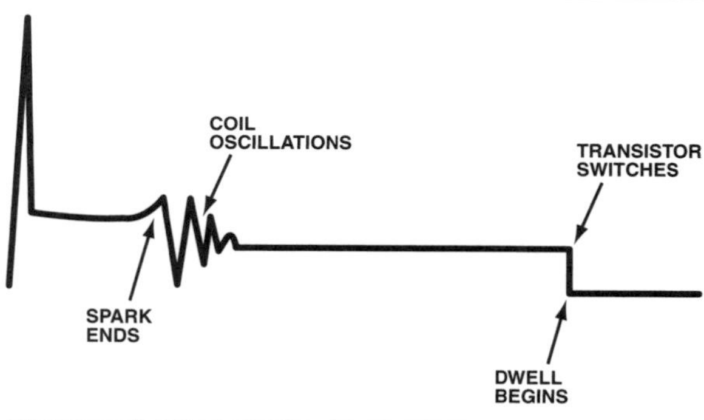

Figure 8-20. Look for at least three distinct coil oscillations in the primary open circuit period.

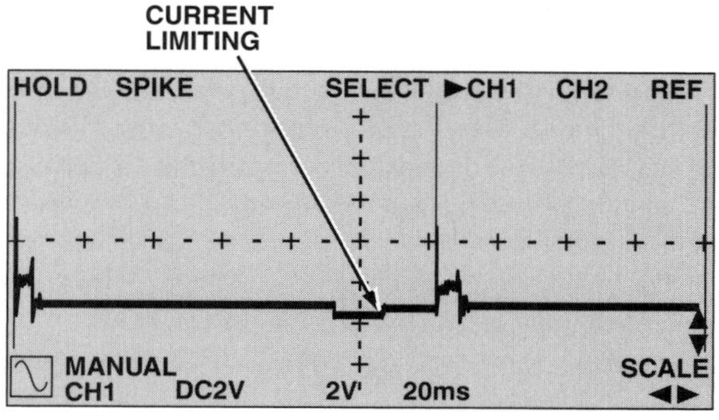

Figure 8-21. Current limiting produces a hump or oscillations toward the end of the dwell period on some systems.

Copyright 2000 by Chek-Chart Publications

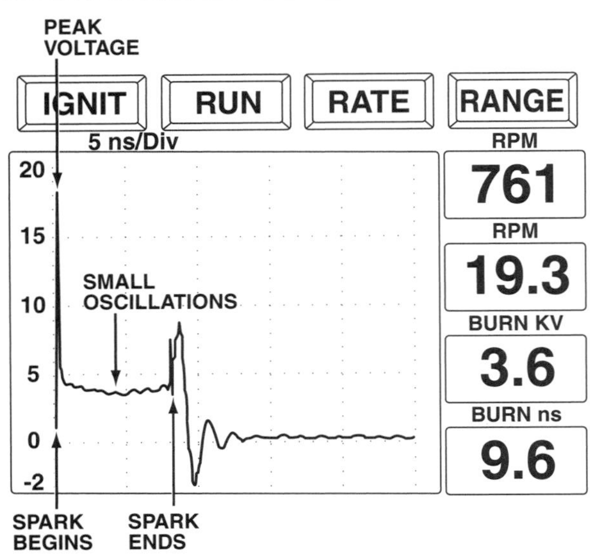

Figure 8-22. Look for small oscillations and a slight rise in the firing period on a secondary trace.

Secondary scope patterns

Secondary voltage traces also move left to right across the screen in firing, open circuit, and dwell sequence. Since normal firing voltage can exceed 40,000 volts, oscillations are displayed on an engine analyzer scope using a high-voltage scale graduated in kilovolt (kV), or thousand-volt increments. With a lab scope, a capacitive pickup with a 10,000 to 1 attenuation is used to capture the entire waveform on the display screen and to protect the scope.

Firing period

The firing period of the secondary pattern starts with a straight, vertical rise called the firing line or voltage spike. The peak of the spike indicates the amount of voltage required to create an arc across the spark plug air gap. Once an arc is established, less voltage is required to maintain it. A normal trace drops to about one-quarter the height of the voltage spike, then continues as a horizontal spark line. A spark line represents continued current across the spark plug gap, and should be relatively flat and stable. However, a series of very small oscillations in the spark line is normal, as is a slight rise toward the end of the firing period, figure 8-22.

Damaged plug wires, worn distributor caps, and excessive plug gaps create high open-circuit resistance. High resistance appears as a high, short spark line. Corrosion on the cable terminals also creates high resistance, but corrosion causes the spark line to start high and slope sharply downward. Carbon tracking in the distributor cap, poor cable insulation, and fouled spark plugs are sources of low resistance. Low resistance shows up as a low, long, spark line. A spark line that jumps erratically or slopes upward or downward generally indicates a fuel mixture problem, figure 8-23. However, an upward sloping pattern may also be the result of a mechanical problem.

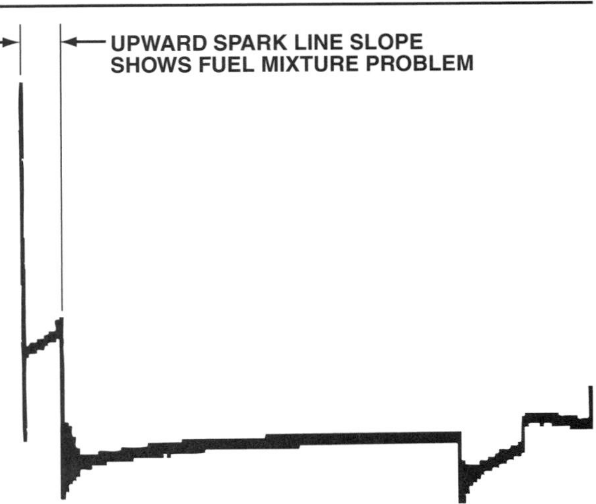

Figure 8-23. A secondary spark line that jumps or slopes upward indicates fuel mixture problems.

The firing period of a secondary trace reveals a number of ignition problems.

- A large firing oscillation with little or no spark line for one cylinder indicates an open circuit between the distributor rotor and the spark plug, figure 8-24. Use the parade display to isolate the faulty cylinder. Check for a disconnected or broken spark plug cable. This pattern can be created deliberately to check coil output on some systems, but causes component damage on others. Perform the check only when recommended by the manufacturer. To check, disconnect the cable from one of the spark plugs and start the engine. The top of the firing line of the open plug is the maximum available voltage from the coil.
- A parade pattern may show a short spark line still exists even when the spark plug cable is deliberately disconnected, figure 8-25. This indicates high voltage is causing a current drain to ground somewhere in the circuit. Current usually drains through the ignition cable insulation, the distributor cap, or the rotor. Carbon tracks tend to accumulate near the leakage over time.
- There should be no more than a twenty-percent difference between the highest and lowest firing spikes when comparing cylinders in a parade pattern, figure 8-26. Peak voltage variations are caused by fuel or electrical system problems. To separate the two, enrich the fuel mixture. If the

Copyright 2000 by Chek-Chart Publications

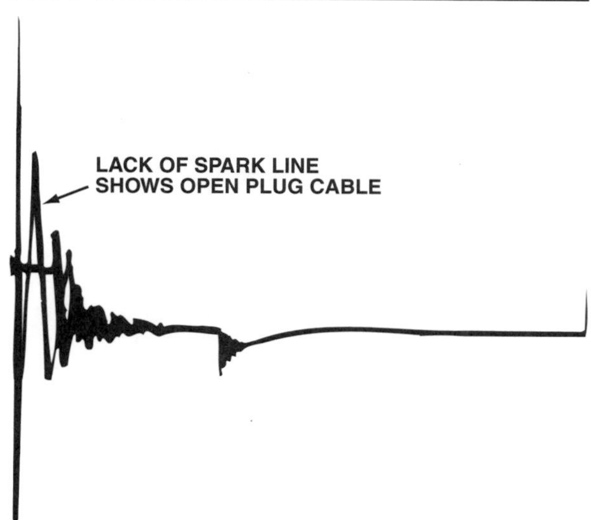

Figure 8-24. A large oscillation without a spark line on a secondary firing period indicates an open spark plug circuit.

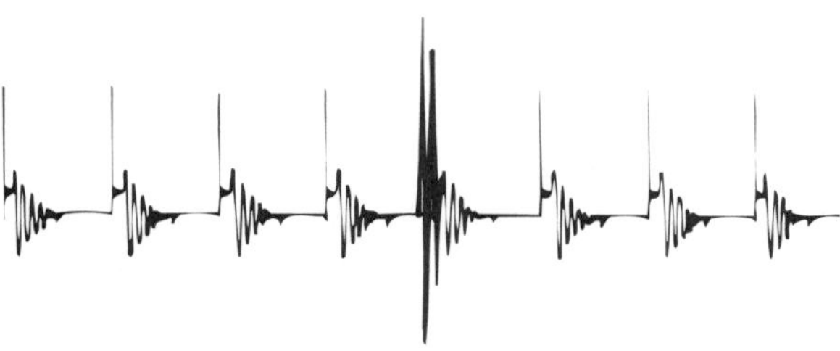

Figure 8-25. An open spark plug circuit displays a high peak and oscillations in a secondary parade pattern as high voltage leaks to ground.

spikes go down and engine speed increases, the problem is fuel related. If the spikes go down and engine speed remains unchanged, the plug gaps may be too great. If a single spike remains the same height, the cable to that plug may be damaged.

- One spark line that is higher and shorter than the rest indicates high resistance from an open circuit between the distributor cap and the spark plug, figure 8-27. A damaged or loose cable or a too-wide plug gap may be at fault. Corrosion on the cable terminals and in the distributor cap causes the spark line for one cylinder to start higher and angle downward more sharply than the others.
- One spark line lower and longer than the rest indicates low resistance in the circuit between the distributor cap and the spark plug, figure 8-28. Check for carbon tracks in the distributor, poor cable insulation, or a fouled spark plug.

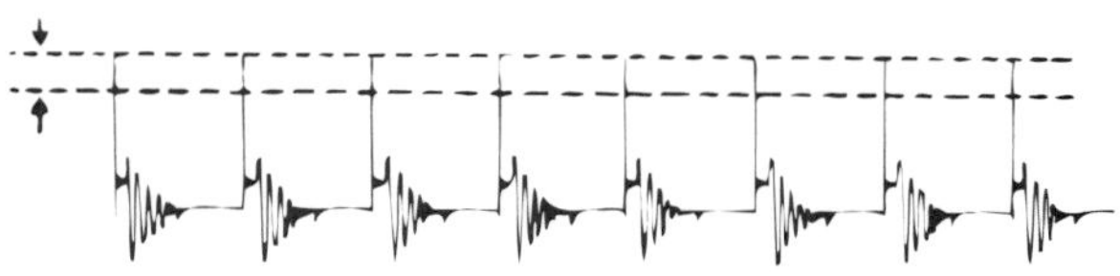

Figure 8-26. Look for fairly even firing line peaks when viewing a secondary parade pattern.

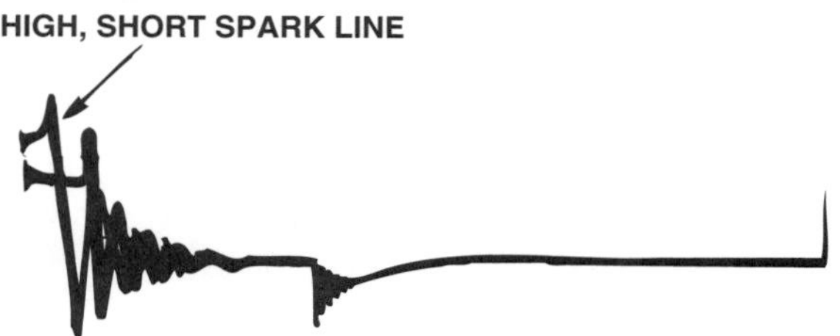

Figure 8-27. A high, short spark line on a secondary superimposed pattern indicates high resistance in one cylinder.

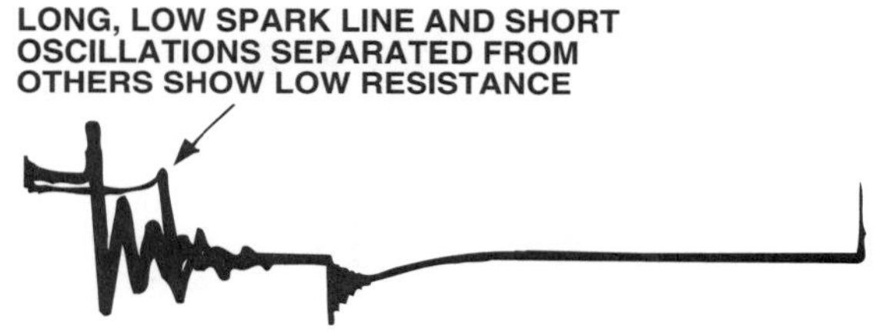

Figure 8-28. A low, long spark line on a secondary superimposed pattern indicates low resistance in one cylinder.

- A spark line that jumps erratically or slopes up rather than down is caused by an incorrect fuel mixture in that cylinder. The problem may be mechanical, such as sticking or worn valves, or caused by intake air leaks, or fuel induction problems.

Open circuit period

A secondary open circuit trace indicates excess coil voltage being dissipated, and appears similar to a primary intermediate pattern. Look for a short vertical rise from the spark line followed by a series of diminishing oscillations, figure 8-29. Oscillations should be of relatively even width and taper down gradually to a near-horizontal line. The open circuit section ends with the module-on signal.

Use the open circuit period of the trace to check coil function. A faulty coil, primary circuit, or high-tension lead between the coil and distributor cap may cause a lack of oscillations. The firing period is used to detect a number of problems:

Copyright 2000 by Chek-Chart Publications

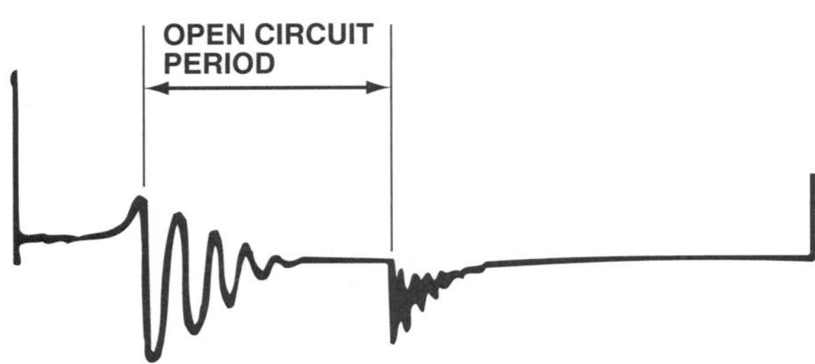

Figure 8-29. A secondary open circuit period displays diminishing oscillations.

- Absent coil oscillations with a normal dwell section are the result of either a faulty coil or a high-resistance short to ground in the primary circuit.
- A pattern displayed upside-down indicates that coil polarity is reversed, usually because of reversed primary connections at the coil.
- The entire pattern jumping on screen results from an intermittent open in the coil secondary winding.
- Reduced coil oscillations along with a missing module-on signal are caused by an open circuit between the coil and the distributor cap.
- A variation in the firing signals on a raster pattern indicates timing differences among cylinders. The cause is generally worn ignition signal parts or a faulty module. Be aware, this is normal for those ignition systems using computer control of timing to regulate idle speed.

Dwell period

The dwell section begins with a sharp vertical drop followed by diminishing oscillations as the trace returns to zero volts. The trace generally remains flat until the module switches off for the next firing sequence.

The length of the dwell section will vary for different systems, and may also be engine speed dependent. As with the primary trace, a slight rise, or hump, towards the end of the dwell period is normal if the control module has a current limiting device.

Dwell variation between cylinders is checked using the raster display, figure 8-30. A dwell variation of more than four to six degrees between cylinders indicates mechanical wear in the distributor, a loose timing chain or belt, or a faulty crankshaft position sensor. An ignition module is also capable of varying dwell. It is possible the dwell variation is normal, as the PCM controls timing to stabilize idle speed on some models.

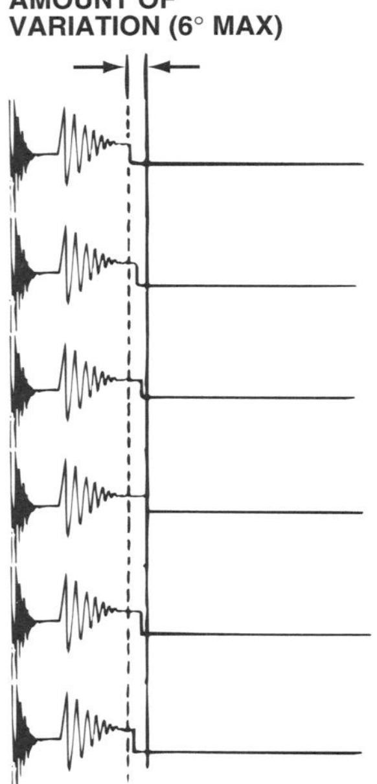

Figure 8-30. Use the raster display to check for too much dwell variation between cylinders.

COMPONENT TESTING

When oscilloscope testing reveals irregularities in the primary or secondary ignition systems, individual components and circuits are checked to isolate the source of the problem. Most ignition failures are the result of either high resistance, which impedes current, or low resistance, which allows too much current through the component or circuit. Component tests are performed using a digital multimeter (DMM), graphing multimeter (GMM), or lab scope.

Test specifications and procedures vary somewhat by manufacturer and model. Therefore, it is important to have accurate service information available for the system being tested. This chapter contains general procedures which apply to most ignition systems. However, it is not to be used as a substitute for the factory service manual. Chapter Nine of this *Shop Manual* contains more detailed procedures for testing specific components. Chapter Twelve of this *Shop Manual* contains information on testing engine management systems incorporating the ignition system on late-model vehicles.

Primary Circuit Testing

Primary circuit voltage has a direct effect on secondary circuit voltage. The loss of a single volt in the primary circuit can reduce secondary circuit voltage by as much as 10 kilovolts (10,000 volts). Common

Copyright 2000 by Chek-Chart Publications

causes of primary circuit voltage loss include: high circuit resistance, insufficient source voltage from the battery, and low charging system output.

Sources of high primary resistance include:

- Loose, corroded, or damaged wiring connections
- An incorrect or defective coil
- A poor ground at the ignition module.

Low source voltage can be caused by the following:

- Excessive starter motor current draw
- Low charging voltage
- A discharged battery.

Resistance problems in the primary circuit are located by voltmeter testing. Begin with a check of available voltage at the battery and ignition coil, then perform voltage drop tests to locate the source of the problem.

Available voltage

Two available voltage checks are performed to determine if the system is receiving enough voltage to operate. Because the ignition system depends on battery voltage, it is important to verify that the battery is at a sufficient state of charge. This is done by checking the voltage available from the battery while cranking the starter. To test, connect the positive voltmeter lead to the positive battery terminal, not to the cable connector, and connect the negative voltmeter lead to ground. Switch the ignition key and take a voltmeter reading while cranking the starter motor.

In general, a reading of ten volts or more indicates that the battery is in good condition. Sources of low voltmeter readings include a voltage drop across the battery ground cable, excessive starter motor current draw, or incorrect charging system output. Refer to previous chapters in this *Shop Manual* as needed to repair the cause of low battery voltage while cranking before proceeding. After repairs are made, retest. If the battery is supplying sufficient voltage, continue by checking the available voltage at the coil.

Turn the ignition switch on without engaging the starter and note the voltmeter readings. Battery voltage should be available on all late-model systems, figure 8-31. Early electronic and breaker point ignition systems that use a ballast resistor normally have about 7 volts available to the coil. Next, crank the engine while monitoring the voltage. A scope or GMM is needed to properly evaluate the voltage drop to the coil. As the engine cranks or runs, the voltage drops because of the amperage when the coil primary is turned on. Any drop in voltage when the primary circuit is turned on is caused by resistance. A ballast resistor creates a large voltage drop because of the resistance of the resistor.

If voltmeter readings are not within specifications, check the primary circuit. Repair or replace any loose or damaged connections and repeat the test. If available voltage readings are still out of range, locate the source of the high resistance by conducting voltage drop tests along the primary circuit.

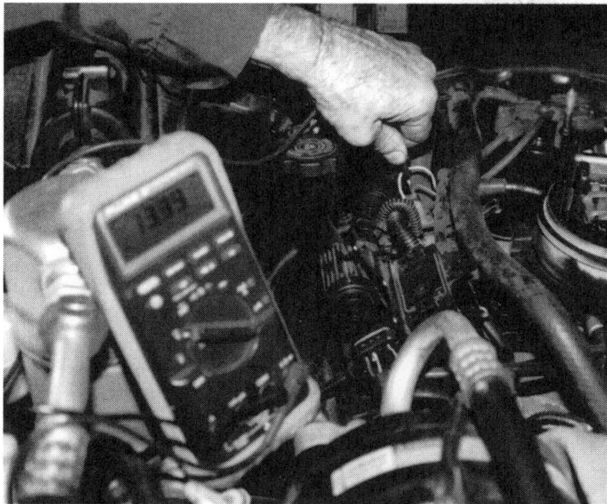

Figure 8-31. Checking for battery voltage available at the ignition coil.

Voltage drop

Voltage drop is the amount of voltage an electrical device normally consumes to perform its task. A small amount of voltage is always lost due to normal circuit resistance. However, excessive voltage drop is an indication of a high-resistance connection or failed component.

To check voltage drop, the circuit must be powered and under load. The circuit must also carry the maximum amount of current it is designed to handle under normal operating conditions. The amount of voltage drop considered acceptable varies by circuit. Low-current circuits that draw milliamps are effected by very small voltage drops, while the same amount of voltage drop has a negligible effect on a high-current circuit.

As explained in Chapter Two of this *Shop Manual,* voltage drop along a circuit is measured by connecting the negative voltmeter lead to ground and probing at various points in the circuit with the positive meter lead. There are two methods of determining voltage drop: computed and direct measurements. Compute voltage drop by checking available voltage on both sides of a load. Then, subtract the voltage reading taken on the ground side of the load from the reading taken on the positive side. Direct voltage drop readings are taken by connecting the positive meter lead to the power side of a load and connecting the negative meter lead to the ground side of the component.

Manufacturers provide voltage drop specifications for various ignition components. High resistance on

Copyright 2000 by Chek-Chart Publications

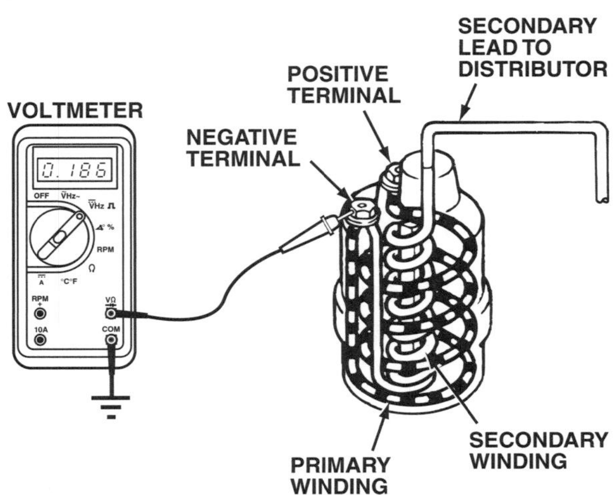

Figure 8-32. Checking voltage drop across the ignition module ground circuit.

the control module ground circuit, often as a result of poor or corroded connections, is a common problem with electronic control systems. Measure the voltage drop across the ignition module ground as follows:

1. Connect the voltmeter positive lead to the negative, or distributor, coil terminal and connect the voltmeter negative lead to a good engine ground. Switch the ignition on and observe the voltmeter. Typically, a reading less than 0.2 volt indicates that the ground is in good condition, figure 8-32.
2. Crank or start the engine. Use a scope or GMM to measure the voltage during the dwell period; it should drop to about 0.5 volt. Be aware, voltage that does not drop below 1 volt is normal for some systems.

High voltage drop is often caused by a poor connection. Check and repair ground circuit wiring and connections, then repeat the test. If readings remain high, work down the circuit taking readings to isolate the source of the high resistance. Voltage drop tests are performed on other ignition components and circuits in a similar fashion to locate high resistance areas. However, the amount of acceptable voltage drop varies by system and circuit. Accurate service specifications are essential for effective troubleshooting.

Ignition Coil Testing

For many years, the only test criteria vehicle manufacturers provided for checking an ignition coil were resistance specifications for the primary and secondary windings. Although checking winding resistance is quick and easy, it is not the most reliable method of testing a coil. To check winding resistance, simply disconnect the primary and secondary wires, take ohmmeter readings, then compare the results to specifications.

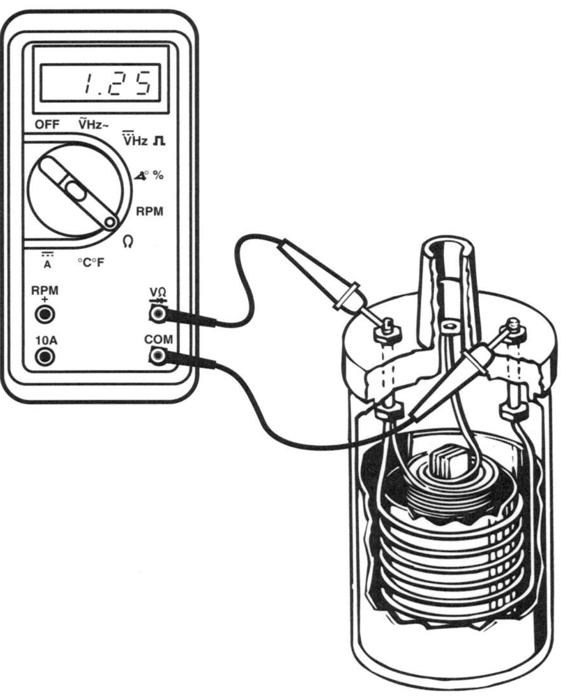

Figure 8-33. Checking primary coil winding resistance with an ohmmeter.

Set the ohmmeter to the lowest scale to check primary winding resistance on an oil-filled coil. Then, connect one ohmmeter lead to the positive, or battery, terminal of the coil, and connect the other meter lead to the negative, or distributor, terminal, figure 8-33. Take an ohmmeter reading and compare it to specifications, which are typically in the 0.50 ohm to 2.00 ohms range.

Secondary winding resistance on an oil-filled coil is measured with the ohmmeter set to the highest scale. To check, connect one ohmmeter lead to the coil tower secondary terminal, then touch the other meter lead to each of the primary terminals and note the meter readings, figure 8-34. Compare the lower of the two ohmmeter readings to specifications, which range anywhere from about 5000 ohms to over 15,000 ohms depending upon the application.

A third ohmmeter check is made to test the coil windings for shorts. With the ohmmeter set on the lowest scale, connect one meter lead to either primary terminal and touch the other lead to the metal case of the coil. The meter should indicate infinite resistance. Any other reading indicates the coil windings are shorted to the case and the coil must be replaced.

Copyright 2000 by Chek-Chart Publications

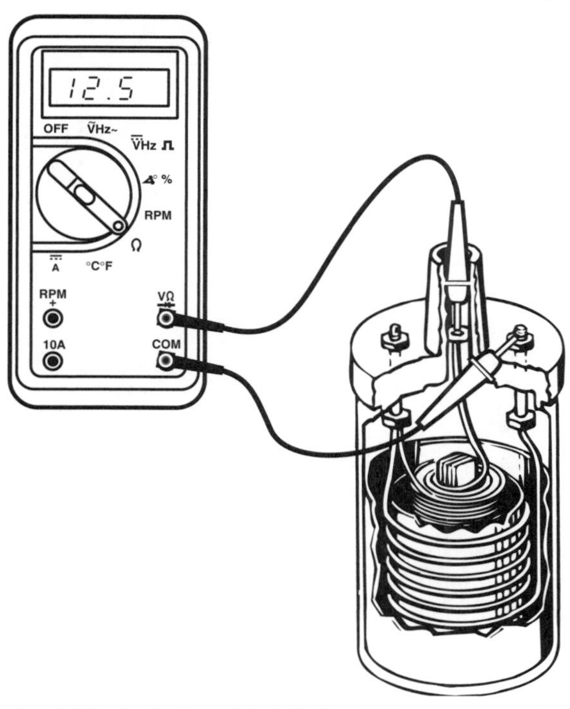

Figure 8-34. Checking secondary coil winding resistance with an ohmmeter.

Although checking winding resistance with an ohmmeter is a quick and easy way to evaluate an oil-filled coil, it is not an accurate method for checking the E-core and direct ignition coils used on modern engines. This is because an ohmmeter determines resistance by transmitting a low-voltage, low-current test signal through the circuit and measures the voltage drop of the test signal. A coil may be perfectly capable of carrying the test signal of the ohmmeter, but not the high-voltage, high-amperage signal produced in the windings during operation. Remember, current generates heat, and heat expands metal. It is fairly common for the windings of a coil to expand enough to create open or short circuits during operation, which often results in a misfire under load. This type of coil failure is impossible to detect with an ohmmeter.

Any leakage in the secondary circuit may cause a carbon track to form. Carbon tracking, the result of the circuit being bypassed, often appears on a rotor, cap, or the spark plug porcelain as a small black track. It is also possible for the ignition coil to carbon track inside between the primary and secondary windings. This type of coil damage does not show up in an ohmmeter test, but allows current to cross between the two windings. The only accurate way of determining the condition of a modern ignition coil is to measure coil current draw.

Coil current draw

Most manufacturers provide current draw specifications and test procedures for checking their ignition coils with an ammeter. However, the most accurate method of evaluating coil operation is to sample the signal on a lab scope or GMM using a current probe. This not only reveals the current draw, it also displays the build-up and release of energy in the windings. Both test methods, ammeter and current probe, are explained below.

Ammeter testing

To test current draw with an intrusive ammeter, disconnect the positive, or battery, primary wire from the coil and connect it to the positive lead of the ammeter. Connect the negative lead of the ammeter to the positive terminal of the coil, figure 8-35. When using an inductive ammeter, fit the inductive pickup over the primary wire to the coil positive terminal leaving the wire connected.

Some manufacturers recommend taking readings with the engine running, while others specify checking current draw while cranking the starter without starting the engine. Follow the recommended procedure for the vehicle being serviced. Observe the ammeter reading and compare it to specifications. When using a DMM for measuring amperage, it must have a min/max feature. A DMM averages the reading and a meter without min/max does not accurately display current because the current in the primary circuit is turned on for such a short time.

If there is no reading, the primary circuit is open. Repair the primary wiring and retest.

Higher-than-specified current draw is usually caused by an internal short circuit in the coil. However, installation of a coil not meeting the original equipment specifications of the vehicle being tested may also result in high current draw readings. In either case, the coil needs to be replaced. Make sure the replacement coil meets specifications. Retest to confirm the repair.

Lower-than-specified current draw indicates a discharged battery, excessive resistance in the coil primary winding, loose or corroded primary connections, or high resistance in the primary wiring to the coil. Service the battery and primary connections as needed and perform voltage drop tests to locate high resistance in the primary wiring. Repair any problems found and retest. If no battery or circuit problems are found, replace the coil.

Current probe testing

Using a current probe and a lab scope or GMM is a quick, easy, and accurate way to measure current draw on any ignition coil. Set the current probe to the

Copyright 2000 by Chek-Chart Publications

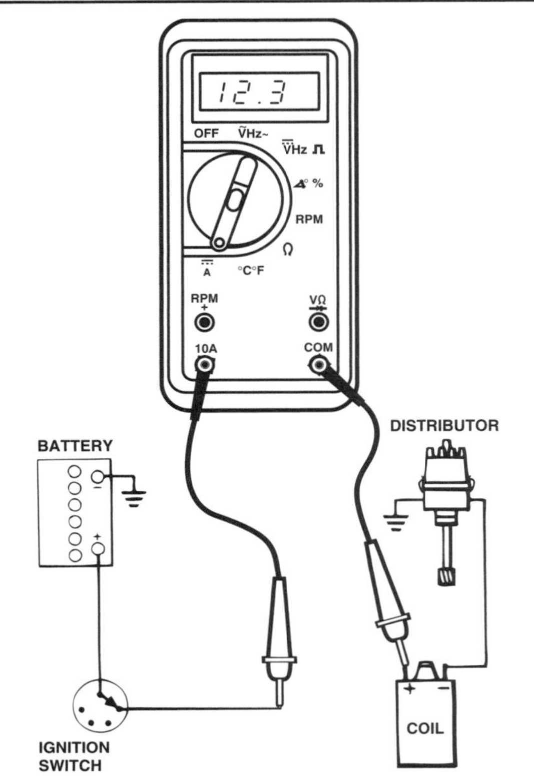

Figure 8-35. Intrusive ammeter connection for checking ignition coil current draw.

100mV per amp scale and adjust the VOLT/DIV setting of the scope or GMM so it is capable of displaying the maximum expected current. Adjust the TIME/DIV setting to capture the firing event. A typical firing event at idle occurs in about 20 milliseconds and delivers up to about 10 amps. Once the equipment is adjusted, simply clamp the current probe around either of the coil primary leads to capture the trace, figure 8-36.

Although the scope or GMM displays a current trace on both the positive and negative primary circuits, sampling from the negative circuit is the preferred method. Both circuits reveal peak current draw, but the negative, or ground side, provides a clearer picture of current build-up and release in the coil windings. However, on some models, especially those with direct ignition, it is difficult to access the negative circuit on each of the coils. Generally, these coils share a common power circuit accessible at a multiplug connection of the harness.

There are basically two types of coil used on electronically controlled systems: those with current limiting and those without current limiting. Before attempting to analyze the current trace of an ignition coil, it is important to know which type is used.

Figure 8-36. Checking coil current draw with a GMM and a current probe.

With current limiting, also known as peak and hold, current build-up in the coil windings stops once it reaches a predetermined level. Current is maintained at this level until the primary circuit opens to release the stored energy and fire the spark plug. A trace for this type of system quickly rises to peak control current, then continues as a horizontal line until the circuit opens and current drops immediately to zero, figure 8-37. Current remains at zero during the dwell period—that is, until it begins building up for the next cycle. Current limiting is an internal PCM or ICM, not an ignition coil, function. When current limiting is used, the PCM varies the dwell time in proportion to engine speed.

On systems without current limiting, the scope trace rises quickly to peak current, then drops immediately to zero as the circuit closes to fire the plug and begins the dwell section, figure 8-38. These systems control peak current with time. The dwell period in time remains constant regardless of engine speed, but changes when measured in dwell.

With either type of current control, look for a trace smoothly rising to the specified peak current and immediately dropping to zero as the primary circuit completes. Irregularities in the slope as current builds indicates resistance in the coil windings. A trace which does not reach the specified peak current indicates either high resistance in the coil or a power supply problem on the positive primary circuit. Ground circuit resistance is indicated by a voltage reading that does not drop close to zero volts. The trace continues as a horizontal line while the primary circuit is completed.

As previously mentioned, it is difficult or impossible to connect the current probe to the negative primary circuit on some models with direct ignition. These systems generally use a single positive circuit to supply all of the coils. Each coil has its own

Copyright 2000 by Chek-Chart Publications

VOLTAGE

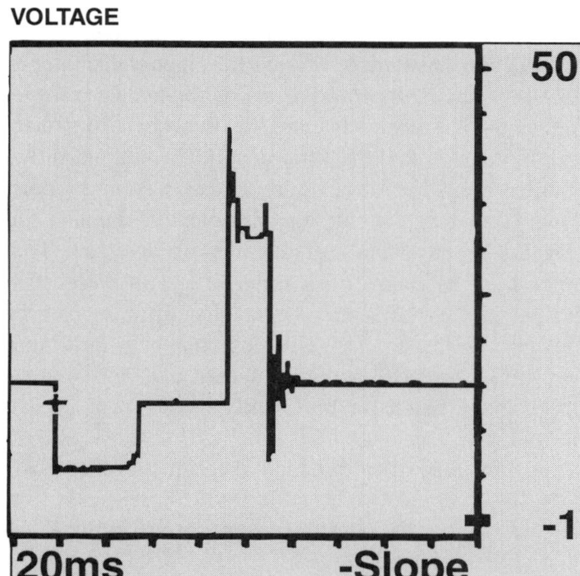

CURRENT

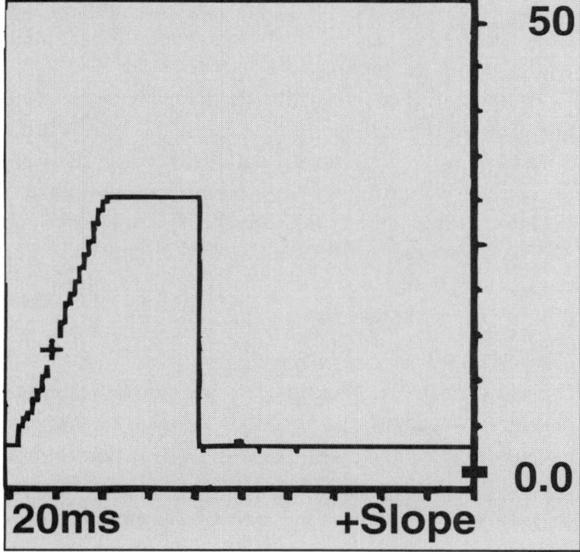

Figure 8-37. Typical primary ignition coil voltage and current trace with peak and hold control.

VOLTAGE

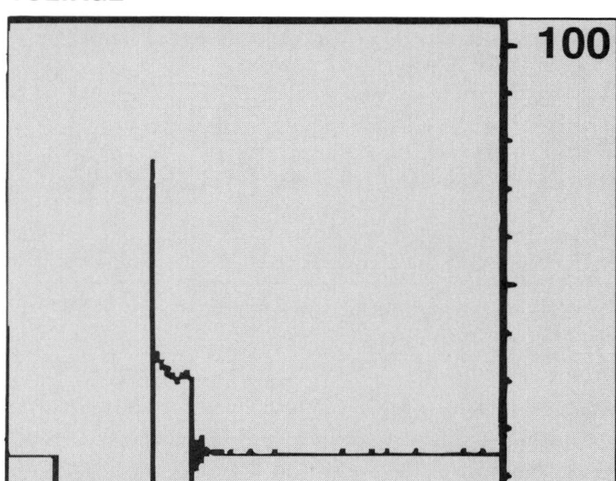

CURRENT

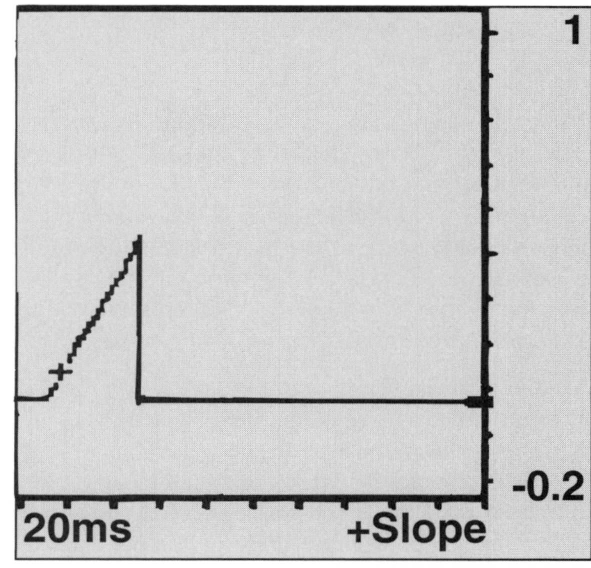

Figure 8-38. Typical primary ignition coil voltage and current trace without peak and hold control.

negative circuit. By connecting the current probe to the common positive circuit and adjusting the TIME/DIV setting of the scope or GMM, a current trace of all the coils is displayed in a parade pattern, figure 8-39. Current peaks should be even for all cylinders and at the level specified by the manufacturer.

Primary Ignition Triggering Devices

Electronic ignition systems rely on the signal of an engine speed sensor to determine when to open and close the primary circuit and fire the spark plugs. A number of different sensor designs are used to perform this task. The sensor, also referred to as a triggering device, may be located in the distributor or mounted on the engine block.

The primary circuit does not energize until the module receives a verifiable engine speed (rpm) signal from the crankshaft position (CKP) sensor. The CKP sensor provides the ignition module or powertrain control module (PCM) information on

Copyright 2000 by Chek-Chart Publications

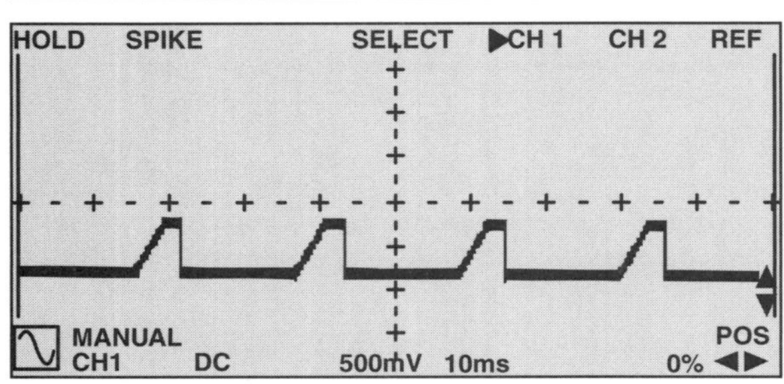

Figure 8-39. Parade display of direct ignition coil current taken on the positive circuit.

crankshaft speed and location. Some systems use an additional camshaft position (CMP) sensor for more precise timing of the ignition firing sequence, figure 8-40. A CMP sensor is used to provide the synchronization signal on distributorless ignition and sequential fuel injection systems, and for misfire detection on OBD II vehicles. There are four basic designs for automotive speed sensors:

- Magnetic pickup
- Hall-effect switch
- Optical sensor
- Magneto resistive sensor.

The most accurate way to diagnose an engine speed sensor problems is to monitor the signal on a lab scope or GMM. A magnetic pickup is a sine wave–producing analog device, while Hall-effect switches and optical sensors are digital and produce a digital or square waveform. For all types, the ignition module or PCM uses the frequency of the signal, or how fast it repeats, to determine the speed of the sensed component.

Magnetic pickup

Whether called a magnetic pickup coil, variable reluctance sensor, or permanent magnet generator, this type of sensor generates an analog alternating current (ac) voltage signal. These sensors are self contained and do not require an applied voltage to produce a signal. Since these sensors produce their own signal, it is possible to get a waveform with correct amplitude and frequency, even though there are problems on the chassis ground circuits.

The pickup coil is wound around a permanent magnet, whose field expands and collapses as the teeth of a rotating trigger wheel pass by it, figure 8-41. The magnetic field generates an ac voltage signal. As the speed of the engine increases, so does the frequency and amplitude of the signal. The PCM uses the frequency of the signal to determine rotational speed.

Pickup coils have a two-wire circuit, a positive lead and a negative lead, connecting them to the PCM. For best results, connect both scope probes directly to the sensor leads as close to the sensor as possible. Backprobe a connector to connect the scope. Avoid piercing the wire insulation. A good trace generally sweeps up the positive slope and drops on the negative slope, figure 8-42. Check for inverted probe or wiring harness connections if the vertical spike is on the positive slope of the waveform, figure 8-43. On some models, the PCM cannot accurately monitor the signal if the harness connections are inverted, or reversed. This may be the source of a driveability problem. The shape of the trace peak varies for different sensor designs, but most signals must reach a minimum amplitude, or peak voltage, before the PCM recognizes them. Look for uniformity in the trace cycles. Remember too, the PCM watches for the signal to switch from positive to negative and negative to positive. This should occur at the 0-volt baseline. If not, check for poor, or resistive, connections on the PCM and chassis grounds.

The resistance of a pickup coil can be checked with an ohmmeter because all pickup coils operate at a specific resistance. However, specifications and test points vary between manufacturers and models. On some vacuum advance distributors, vacuum is applied while testing the pickup coil.

In general, measurements are taken by connecting the ohmmeter leads to opposite sides of the coil. If the reading is not within specifications, replace the coil. To check for a grounded coil, connect one ohmmeter lead to ground and touch the other ohmmeter lead alternately to each of the pickup coil connectors. The ohmmeter should show infinite resistance at all test points. If not, replace the pickup coil.

Air gap check and adjustment

On some magnetic pickups, the air gap between the pickup coil and trigger wheel is adjustable. Air gap has no effect on the dwell period; dwell is determined by the control module. However, the air gap must be set to a specific clearance when a new pickup unit is installed. Although the air gap should not change during service, it should be checked before performing troubleshooting tests. Always use a brass, or other nonmagnetic, feeler gauge to check and adjust air gap. The pickup coil magnet attracts a steel feeler gauge and causes an inaccurate adjustment. Air gap differs between manufacturers, as well as between models. Therefore, the correct specifications are necessary when making adjustments.

Hall-effect switch

A Hall-effect switch uses a microchip to switch a transistor on and off and generate a digital signal transmitted to the PCM. As a shutter wheel passes between the Hall-effect element and a permanent magnet, the

Copyright 2000 by Chek-Chart Publications

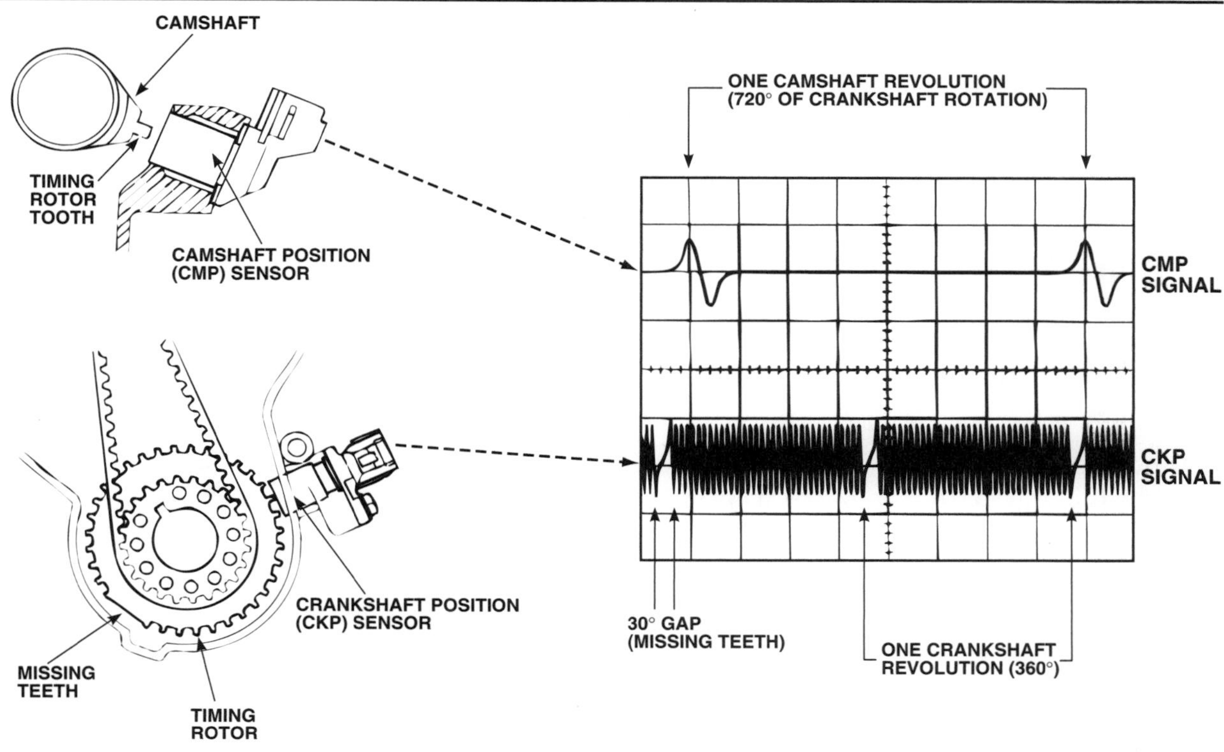

Figure 8-40. Some systems use both a crankshaft position (CKP) sensor and camshaft position (CMP) sensor to control ignition coil firing.

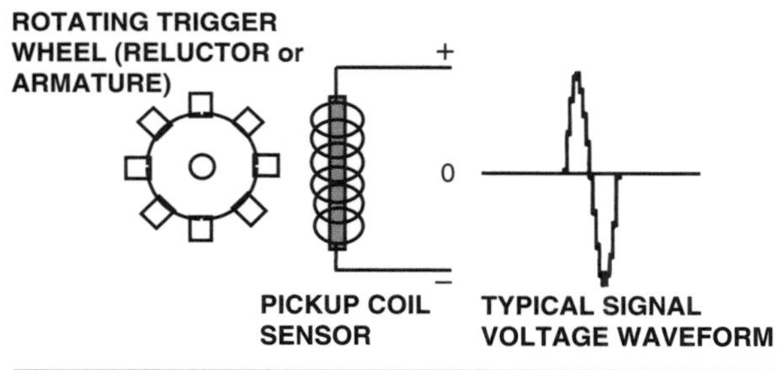

Figure 8-41. A pickup coil is self-powered and generates an analog ac signal as the magnetic field expands and collapses.

magnetic field expands and collapses to produce an analog voltage signal. The Hall element contains an electronic logic gate that converts the analog signal into a digital one. This digital signal is used to trigger transistor switching, figure 8-44. The transistor transmits a digital square waveform at a variable frequency to the PCM.

Hall-effect switches produce a square waveform, whose frequency varies in proportion to the rotational speed of the shutter wheel. A Hall-effect switch does not generate its own voltage, and power must be provided for the device to work.

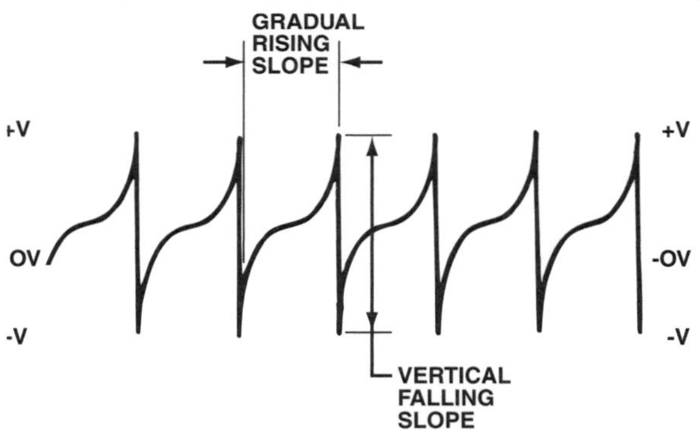

Figure 8-42. A pickup coil generates an ac pattern that ramps up and drops sharply.

Hall-effect operation requires a three-wire circuit—power input, signal output, and ground. The Hall element receives an input voltage from either the ignition switch or the PCM to power it. Activity from the magnetic field and shutter blade opens and closes a switch to ground on the input signal. Be aware, output signal voltage is not always the same as input signal voltage. Therefore, accurate specifications are needed for testing.

A Hall-effect switch creates a square waveform as the transistor switches on and off. To get a good scope

Copyright 2000 by Chek-Chart Publications

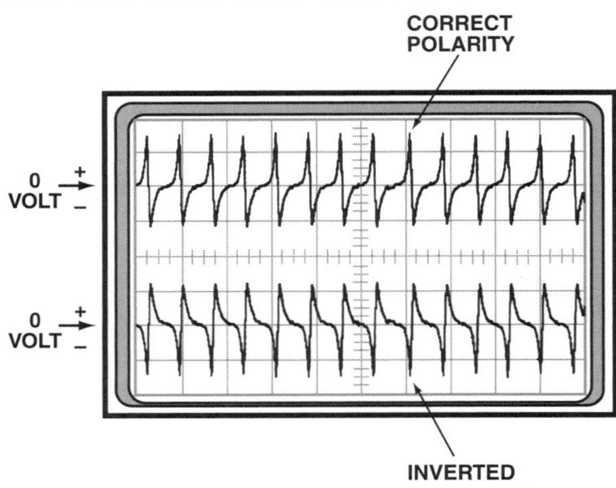

Figure 8-43. Reversed pickup coil polarity, which causes driveability problems, produces an inverted trace.

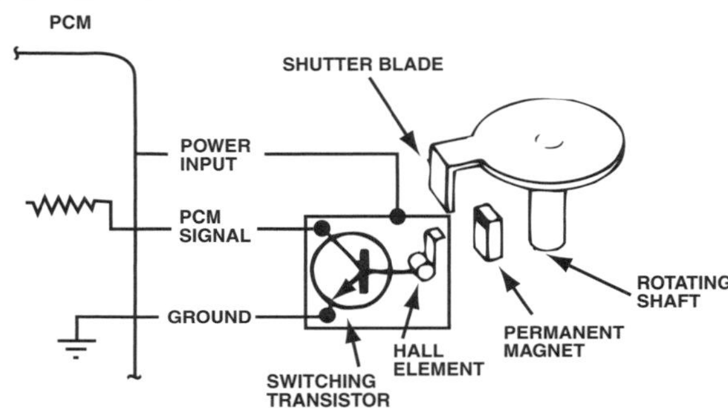

Figure 8-44. A Hall-effect switch uses the analog signal of a magnetic field expanding and collapsing to switch a transistor and generate a digital signal to the PCM.

trace, attach the positive scope probe to the transistor output signal and connect the negative probe to the sensor ground. For optimum results, connect both probe leads as close as possible to the sensor. When a shutter vane is between the sensing element and the permanent magnet, the magnetic field is weak because the shutter blade disrupts it. When there is an open shutter blade window between the element and magnet, the magnetic field is strong. Each time a shutter window opens or closes, the signal generated by the Hall element changes state. That is, it switches on or off, figure 8-45. Depending upon the application, this signal may be amplified or inverted before it is transmitted to the PCM. Therefore, there is no established rule as to whether the signal is high or low with respect to the strength of the magnetic field. Refer to the service manual for procedures and specifications.

When examining a scope trace, look for sharp, clean state change transitions and a signal that pulls

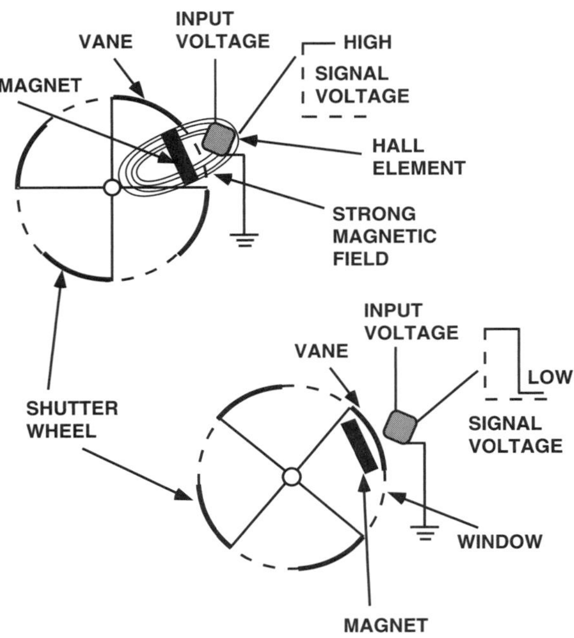

Figure 8-45. The signal of a Hall-effect switches high as the shutter wheel changes the magnetic field from strong to weak.

completely to ground. Amplitude should be even for all waveforms, the pattern should be consistent, and peaks should be at the specified voltage level, figure 8-46. The shape and position of the slots on the shutter wheel determine the shape and duty cycle of the waveform. Some Hall-effect switch patterns have a slight rounding at the top corners of the trace. This is normal for these units and does not indicate a problem on the circuit. Keep in mind, the PCM looks for switching at the midpoint of the voltage range, not at the top or bottom, figure 8-47. However, rounding at the bottom corners of the trace is not normal and does indicate a problem, even though the PCM does not process this portion of the signal. Rounded corners at the bottom of the trace, or a signal not completely dropping to zero, indicates high resistance on the ground circuit. High ground circuit resistance is often the result of a poor connection, making it difficult for the signal to completely ground. Hall-effect sensors produce an output signal by grounding the signal voltage supplied. This voltage must be applied to the sensor by the PCM or other component. Disconnect the sensor to check for the correct bias voltage on the signal wire. Also, check for the correct voltage on the power circuit to the Hall element. A problem here causes problems on the signal circuit.

As a quick check, a logic probe may be used to verify the voltage signal is switching from high to low.

Copyright 2000 by Chek-Chart Publications

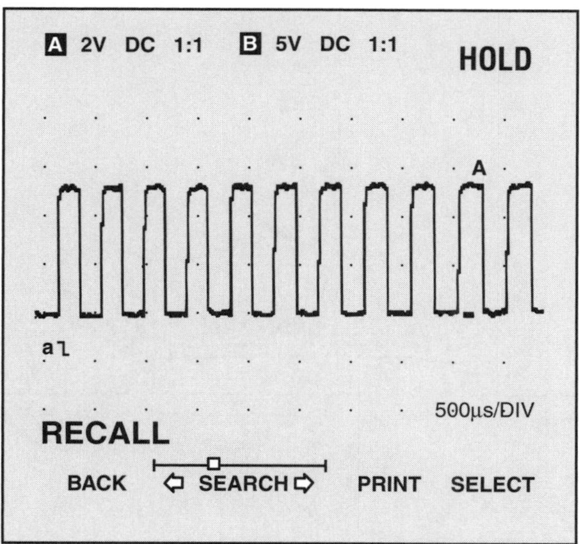

Figure 8-46. Look for sharp transitions, a signal that pulls completely to ground, and consistent amplitude on a Hall-effect switch waveform.

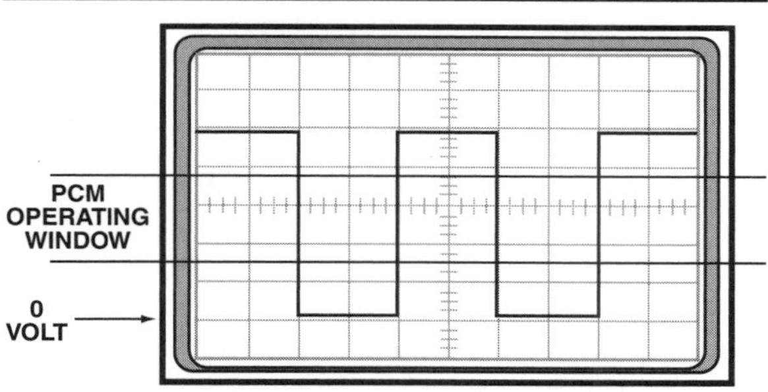

Figure 8-47. The PCM monitors the midpoint of the voltage range to determine the frequency of a Hall-effect switch signal.

Optical sensor

An optical sensor uses a light-emitting diode (LED), a shutter wheel, and a phototransistor to produce a digital signal that changes frequency in proportion to rotational speed, figure 8-48. As with a Hall-effect switch, an optical sensor requires an external power source and uses a three-wire circuit. One wire carries power to operate the LED, one is the signal generated by the transistor, and the third provides a common ground path.

Signal voltage, which is usually 5 volts, switches on and off as the rotating shutter passes between the phototransistor and LED to open and close the ground circuit. When the shutter allows light to shine on the phototransistor, the base of the transistor switches and the signal voltage changes state. When the reflector plate blocks the light to the phototransistor, the base

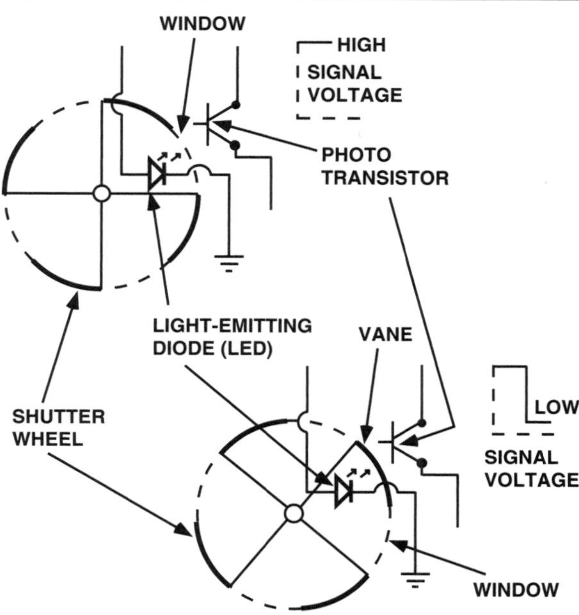

Figure 8-48. Optical sensors use an LED and a light-sensitive transistor to transmit a variable-frequency digital square waveform to the PCM.

of the transistor switches again and signal voltage changes as well.

Optical sensors are more expensive to manufacture and more delicate than a magnetic pickup or Hall-effect switch. Therefore, they are the least common of the three types. However, Chrysler, General Motors, and a few import manufacturers use optical sensors on some of their distributor-type ignition systems. Optical sensors are typically used as vehicle speed sensors and engine speed sensors because their high-speed data rate is more accurate for high rpm applications than other sensor designs.

When viewed on a scope, an optical sensor produces a square waveform similar to that produced by a Hall-effect switch. Optical sensors ground the applied signal voltage to produce an output signal. This applied, or bias, voltage is generally provided to the sensor by the PCM. Disconnect the sensor to check for the correct bias voltage on the signal wire.

Magneto resistive sensor

Many of the late-model systems use a magneto resistive sensor, which is a magnetic pickup with a square wave output. This sensor has the same signal as a Hall-effect switch or optical sensor. A magneto resistive sensor uses a magnetic pickup to produce an analog signal, which is converted to a digital signal inside the sensor.

As with the Hall-effect sensor, three wires are required—power input, signal output, and ground. However, a bias voltage is not required on the signal

Copyright 2000 by Chek-Chart Publications

wire, which provides the full on/off signal. Many magneto resistive sensors are referred to as Hall-effect sensors because of the three wires and square wave signal. A visual inspection of the sensor confirms the type of sensor.

Secondary Circuit Testing

Problems in the secondary ignition circuitry are usually easily detected on the oscilloscope trace. Typical failures are the result of high or low resistance in the high-tension cables, distributor cap and rotor wear or damage, and worn or damaged spark plugs. Caps, rotors, and plugs are inspected and replaced as needed when irregularities appear on the secondary scope trace. High-tension cables are checked with an ohmmeter to confirm their continuity.

Excessive resistance in the secondary circuit causes a number of driveability problems, such as engine misfires, higher burn voltages, and shorter burn times. Damaged high-tension cables are often the cause of excess secondary resistance. High cable resistance often results from:

- Loose or corroded connections at the distributor cap terminal or spark plug
- Damage to the cable conductor from heat, vibration, or mishandling
- A broken terminal at either end of the cable.

Inspect the cables for obvious signs of damage and replace as needed. If damage is not visibly apparent, check the resistance of the cables with an ohmmeter. A typical television-radio suppression (TVRS) cable should measure about 4,000 ohms per foot. Test resistance by removing the high-tension cable from the engine and attaching the ohmmeter leads to each end of the cable, figure 8-49. If meter readings are out of specification, replace the cable.

Replace damaged secondary parts as needed, then check operation on the oscilloscope to confirm the repair.

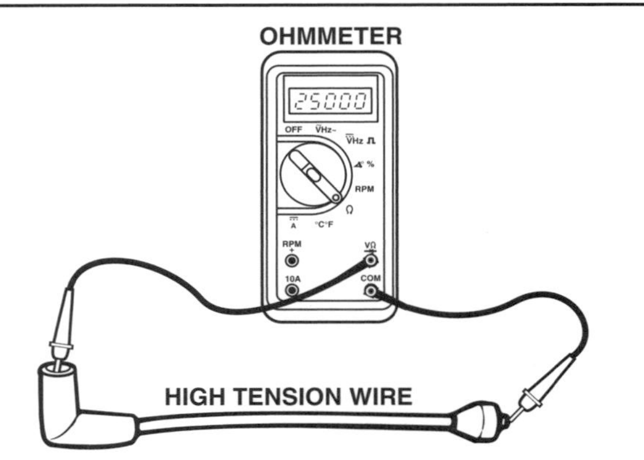

Figure 8-49. A spark plug cable should register about 4,000 ohms per foot of resistance on an ohmmeter.

ELECTRICAL NOISE

Electrical noise is a loosely defined term used to describe abnormal voltage levels on one circuit resulting from electrical activity on a second circuit. The two circuits share no common connection. The interference, or noise, is induced through the insulation of the wiring.

An electromagnetic field is created whenever current travels through a conductor, and the strength of the field changes when the current stops and starts. Each change in field strength creates an electromagnetic signal wave. The frequency of the wave increases in proportion to the speed of the current changes. When the signal wave is strong enough, it may be induced into an adjacent circuit.

In this phenomenon, known as electromagnetic interference (EMI), the signal wave is generated by the source and transferred into the receiver. EMI can be transmitted in four ways:

- Conductive coupling
- Capacitive coupling
- Inductive coupling
- Electromagnetic radiation.

A conductive couple occurs when interference is directly transmitted from the source to the receiver, figure 8-50. Capacitive coupling takes place when applied voltage creates an electrostatic field between the source and receiver, figure 8-51. An inductive couple forms when applied voltage creates an electromagnetic field between the source and receiver, figure 8-52. Electromagnetic radiation occurs when the receiver acts as an antenna and picks up signal waves generated by the source, figure 8-53.

In automotive applications, electrical noise may be classified into two categories: radio frequency interference (RFI) and electromagnetic interference (EMI). Although RFI is a form of EMI, radio frequency signals are much stronger and should be considered separately.

Radio Frequency Interference

Radio frequency interference produces a signal wave strong enough to interfere with radio and television broadcast transmissions. Secondary ignition circuits are capable of producing waves at the rate of thousands of cycles per second, or kilohertz (kHz). Signals of this magnitude fall into the range of commercial broadcast signals. In addition to disrupting broadcast signals, RFI transmissions also create serious

Copyright 2000 by Chek-Chart Publications

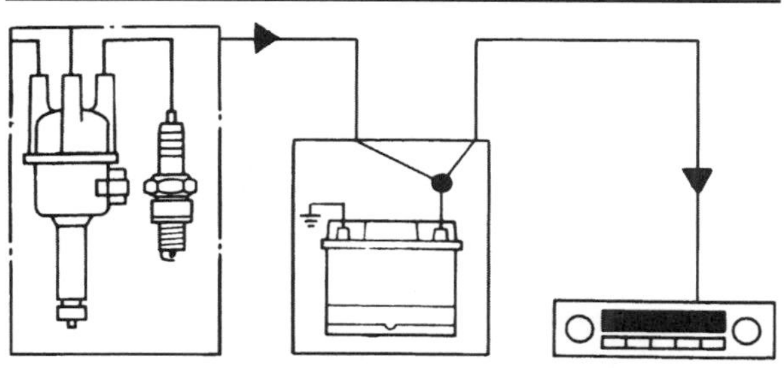

Figure 8-50. A conductive couple forms when a signal from the source is transmitted directly to the receiver.

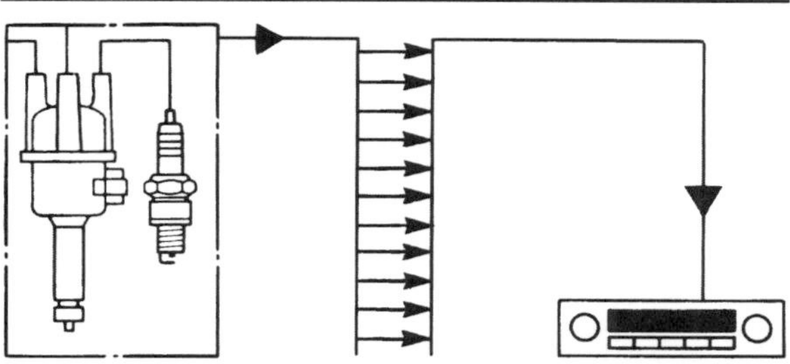

Figure 8-51. A capacitive couple forms when an electrostatic field forms between the source and receiver.

problems on the low-power circuits of an automotive computer control system.

To prevent RFI from affecting commercial broadcasts, vehicle manufacturers are required to use television-radio-suppression (TVRS) cables on the secondary ignition system. These cables have a high-resistance, nonmetallic conductor core, such as carbon, linen, or graphite impregnated fiberglass wrapped into several layers of insulating material, figure 8-54. Due to their high resistance, TVRS cables raise the voltage applied to the spark plugs. This offers the additional benefits of improved ignition characteristics and prevents the formation of some plug deposits. Higher voltage at the spark plug permits the combustion of leaner air-fuel mixtures, and also reduces the amount of current present after ignition is complete. This reduction of current extends the life of the spark plugs and the distributor cap terminals.

In general, RFI transmission is of little concern because vehicle manufacturers have taken steps to eliminate the problem. However, replacement ignition cables that do not meet original equipment specifications, or are incorrectly installed, may cause unwanted signals to be induced into other circuits.

A common RFI problem is cross firing. Cross fire occurs when voltage from one cable is induced into an adjacent cable, causing a spark plug to fire out of sequence. To prevent cross fire, route cables so they do not touch, and avoid running them parallel. This

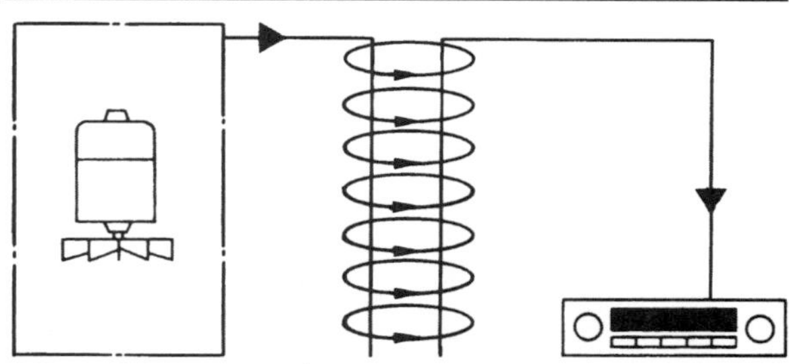

Figure 8-52. Inductive coupling occurs as a magnetic field forms and collapses between the source and receiver.

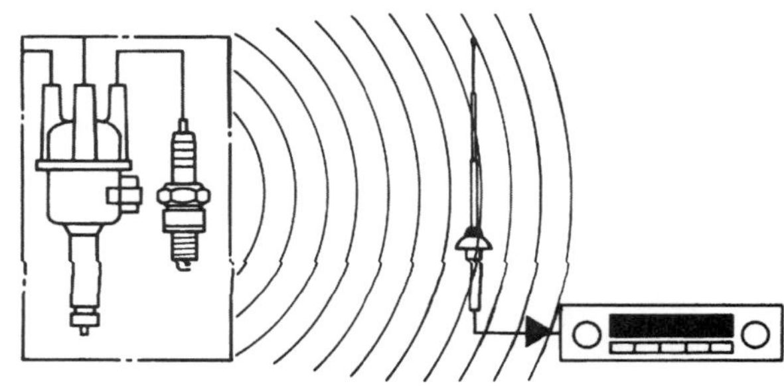

Figure 8-53. Electromagnetic radiation is when the receiver acts as an antenna to pick up signals generated by the source.

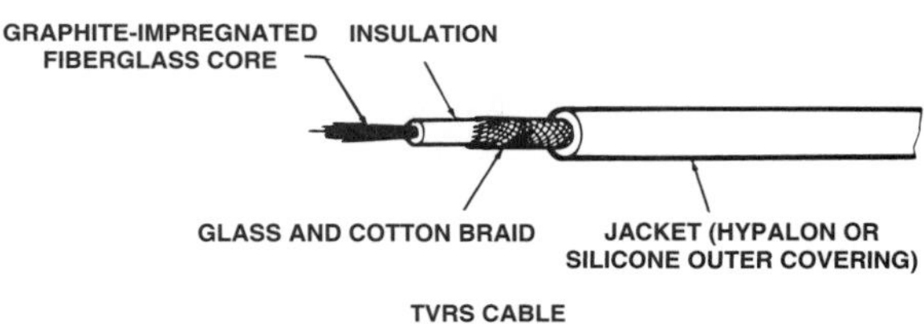

Figure 8-54. A TVRS cable has a non-metallic, high-resistance core surrounded by several layers of insulation.

parallel rule also applies to any primary wiring and harness in close proximity to the ignition cables. When conductors cross each other at an angle, the magnetic field is disrupted and induced voltage is prevented.

Electromagnetic Interference

The revolving commutator in motors, the natural fluctuations in the alternator output circuit, electromechanical voltage regulators, and vibrating horn contacts all produce EMI transmissions. In addition, a wave is created whenever a relay or switch opens or closes a circuit, and when a solenoid is activated. Static electric charges developed from the friction of tires contacting the road, drive belts turning pulleys,

Copyright 2000 by Chek-Chart Publications

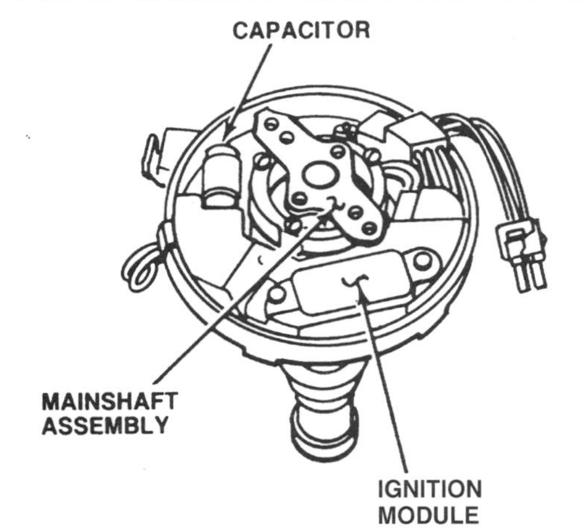

Figure 8-55. A capacitor at the ICM absorbs EMI produced by the primary circuit switching on and off.

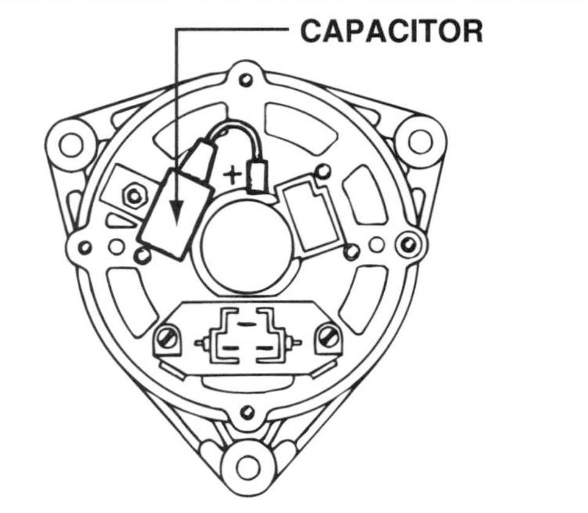

Figure 8-56. A capacitor on the output terminal suppresses the natural ac voltage fluctuations of an alternator to prevent EMI transmissions.

axles and driveshafts rotating, and clutch and brake applications can also produce EMI transmissions.

Manufacturers are aware of this problem and take steps to suppress EMI on suspect circuits. Common suppression methods include the use of capacitors, suppression filters, ground straps, and shields.

A capacitor is a device which absorbs and stores voltage. When installed at the switching point of a circuit, a capacitor absorbs changing voltage and prevents EMI transmission. Manufacturers often install capacitors on the primary circuit at the ICM, figure 8-55, and on the output terminal of the alternator, figure 8-56. Suppression filters, which also absorb unwanted voltage signals, are often used to suppress the natural voltage fluctuations produced by the commutator of an electric motor, figure 8-57. Most replacement parts do not include the capacitor or suppression filter. When replacing parts, it is important to transfer any capacitive suppression device from the old part to the new one to prevent EMI.

Ground straps provide an unrestricted, low-resistance circuit ground path to help suppress EMI conduction and radiation. In a ground path, resistance creates an unwanted voltage drop. The voltage difference across the resistance is a potential EMI source. Ground straps are typically installed between body parts and bushing-mounted components to ensure good conductivity. Some late-model vehicles have a ground strap connecting the hood to the fender or bulkhead. These straps prevent an electrostatic field forming between body panels. If a field does form, it has the potential to couple with electrical harnesses mounted to the sheet metal.

A simple metal shield surrounding a component capable of generating EMI signals effectively blocks any wave transmission. Several manufacturers use a metal shield on their distributors to control RFI radiation. In addition, the metal housing of an onboard computer acts as a shield to prevent EMI waves from entering the unit and causing internal damage.

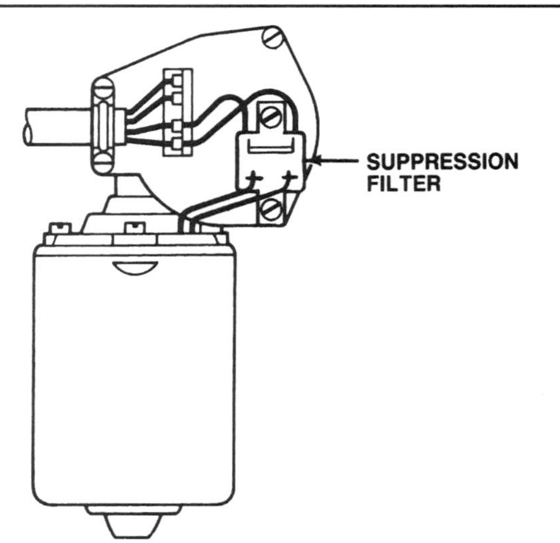

Figure 8-57. Suppression filters absorb interference generated by electric motors.

Any time a suppression device is removed when servicing a vehicle, it is important to reinstall it on assembly. Problems related to EMI transmissions are difficult to diagnose because they are often random and unpredictable. Use a DMM, scan tool, or lab scope to monitor suspect circuits. Then, watch for abnormal circuit activity while activating switches, relays, solenoids, and motors. Also, use a ground strap to make sure your body is grounded when handling components containing a microprocessor. Be aware, simply sliding across a velour seat can generate enough static electricity to damage delicate computer circuits.

Copyright 2000 by Chek-Chart Publications

Ignition System Service

With the exception of the distributor, this chapter addresses testing, repairing, and replacing individual components of the ignition system. Servicing a distributor is detailed in Chapter Ten of this *Shop Manual.* Refer to the appropriate sections of these two chapters to repair ignition failures revealed by the diagnostic and test procedures in Chapter Eight.

Keep in mind, most modern ignition systems contain delicate and expensive electronic components that are easily destroyed by a voltage surge. The high-voltage surge that results from simply making or breaking a connection may cause damage. Always observe the safety precautions outlined in Chapter Eight of this *Shop Manual* to avoid damage and personal injury while working on the ignition system.

The ignition, fuel injection, and emission control operations are electronically linked together by the engine management system on modern vehicles. Every ignition system service includes accessing the onboard diagnostic program to check for and clear diagnostic trouble code (DTC) records. Ignition circuit and component problems commonly set a misfire DTC on OBD II vehicles, which must be cleared before emissions testing. When a DTC is found, follow the troubleshooting procedure recommended by the manufacturer exactly, without skipping steps, to locate the source. Refer to Chapter Twelve of this *Shop Manual* for onboard diagnostic system service information and procedures.

PRIMARY SUPPLY CIRCUIT SERVICE

Failures in the primary supply circuit, which includes all the wiring and devices that connect the positive battery terminal to the positive ignition coil terminal, result in no or low available voltage readings at the coil. Although exactly how the power is delivered to the coil varies significantly by make and model, all ignition systems receive power through the ignition switch. Therefore, the ignition is linked directly to the starting and charging systems. Be aware, low available voltage to the coil may be a symptom of a starting or charging circuit failure.

Locate an accurate circuit diagram before attempting to troubleshoot the circuit. Low available voltage is a result of high circuit resistance and no voltage indicates an open circuit. Check for high resistance and open circuits by voltage drop testing. Almost any nonresistive electrical component can be voltage drop tested with a voltmeter, even if no specifications are available. Nonresistive electrical components of the ignition primary circuit include connectors, relays, and switches. With the engine running, work down the circuit from the coil to the ignition switch taking readings at each circuit connection and component,

Copyright 2000 by Chek-Chart Publications

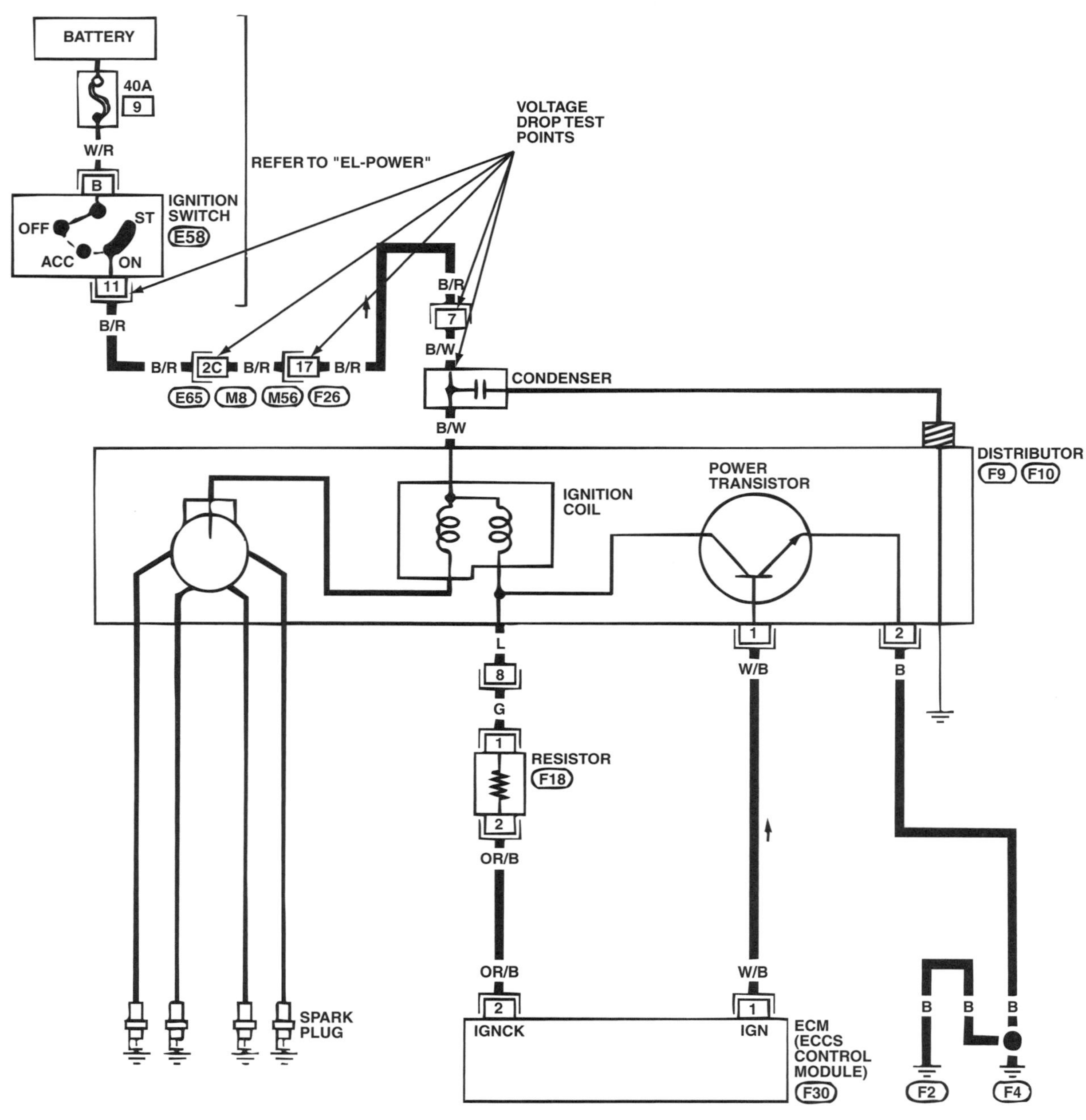

Figure 9-1. Check voltage drop across the condenser, then at connectors "7," "17," "2C," and the ignition switch "11" on this Nissan Altima.

figure 9-1. Make repairs as needed if any high resistance is found.

Testing a Connector

The procedure for voltage drop testing an individual, single-wire connector is the same as for a multi-pin connector. Measure voltage drop across each circuit of a multi-pin connector. A fairly common problem is moisture collecting inside the connector shell, which shorts the individual conductors together. Some short circuits have high resistance, which results in some, but not all, of the current following the short. The remaining current travels the normal circuit path. Use a voltmeter to measure the voltage drop through the connector with the circuit powered and operating. To compute voltage drop across a connector:

Copyright 2000 by Chek-Chart Publications

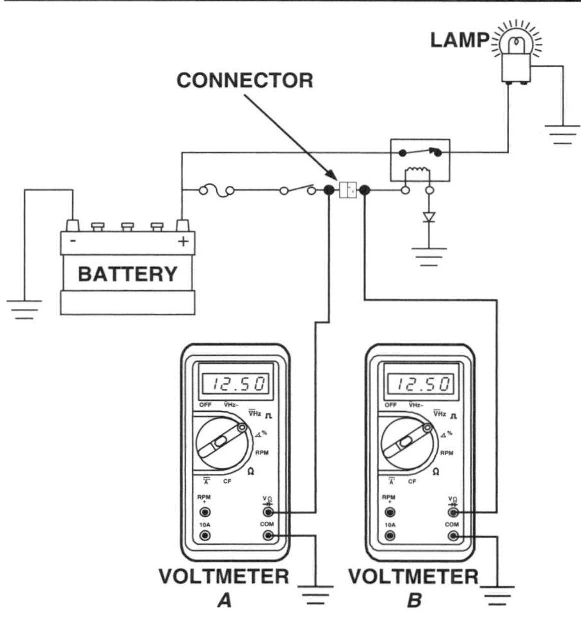

Figure 9-2. There should be negligible voltage drop across a connector, so readings are the same on both sides.

1. Attach the positive voltmeter lead to the power-side circuit wire going into the connector and the negative meter lead to ground. Note the reading.
2. Next, hook the positive voltmeter lead to the load side or ground side circuit wire coming out of the connector, and the negative meter lead to ground. While taking a reading, wiggle or shake the connector and watch for any voltage change. Loose connector contacts cause the voltage to vary when the wire is moved.
3. The voltage readings on both sides of the connector should be the same, figure 9-2. Any difference represents the voltage loss of the connector.

Voltage drop across a connector is directly measured by connecting the positive voltmeter lead to the power side of the connector and the common meter lead to the load side of the connector, figure 9-3. A direct reading across the connector should be zero volt. Any voltage measured indicates resistance in the connection.

Unless the contacts are loose, corroded, burned, or shorted to other contacts in a multi-pin connector, there should not be any voltage drop across a connector. If there is, the connector may need replacement, especially if the contacts are corroded or burned. Clean, tighten, and retest loose connections.

Testing a Relay

A relay, which is a mechanical device that uses a low-current circuit to open and close a switch and control

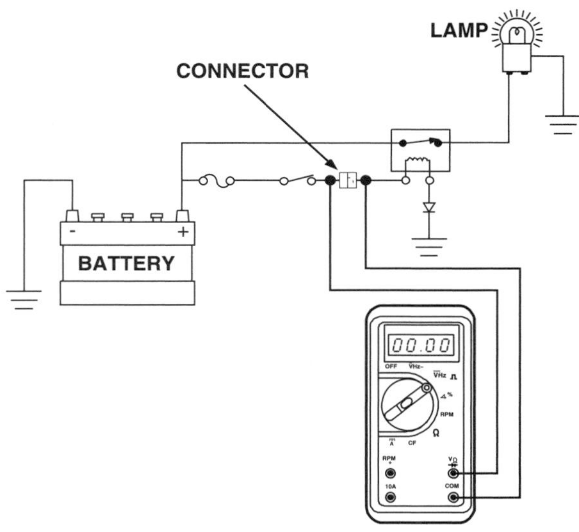

Figure 9-3. A direct voltage drop reading across a connector should be zero.

higher current on another circuit, installs somewhere in the primary ignition circuit on a number of systems. The PCM switches the relay control circuit to energize and deenergize the relay coil. An electromagnet in the coil closes the power circuit contacts to allow a high-current signal through the power circuit. Relays may be switched on either the power or ground side of the circuit. Both types may be used at different locations on the same vehicle. Two common relay failures are defective coil windings and insufficient contact between the points, both of which increase resistance and create a voltage drop across the circuit.

To test the power side of a relay for circuit resistance, use a voltmeter to measure voltage drop. Voltage drop across a relay should be measured with the load drawing current. To compute voltage drop across a relay:

1. Inspect the relay to determine which wires are the primary, or control, leads and which are the secondary, or load, leads. Some relays have one primary and multiple secondary circuits, figure 9-4. Refer to a pin chart or specifications in the service manual to accurately identify the power side of the relay.
2. Connect the positive voltmeter lead to the circuit wire entering the relay on the power side and the common meter lead to a good chassis or engine ground. Activate the relay by powering the primary, or control, circuit and note the voltmeter reading.
3. Leave the common meter lead grounded and connect the positive voltmeter lead to the circuit wire leaving the relay on the load or ground side. With the relay activated, note the voltmeter reading.

Copyright 2000 by Chek-Chart Publications

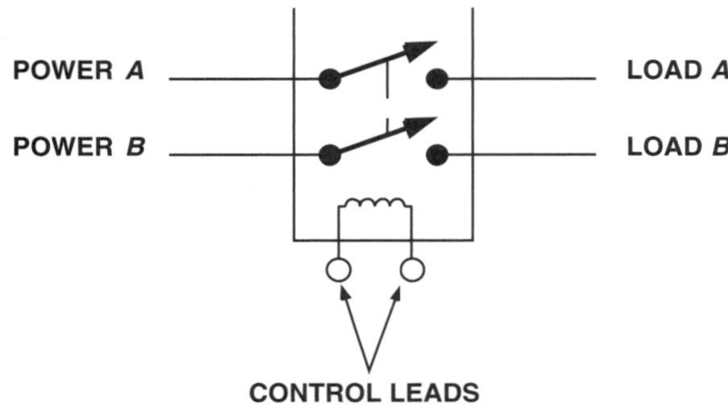

Figure 9-4. A single control circuit operates more than one load circuit on some relays.

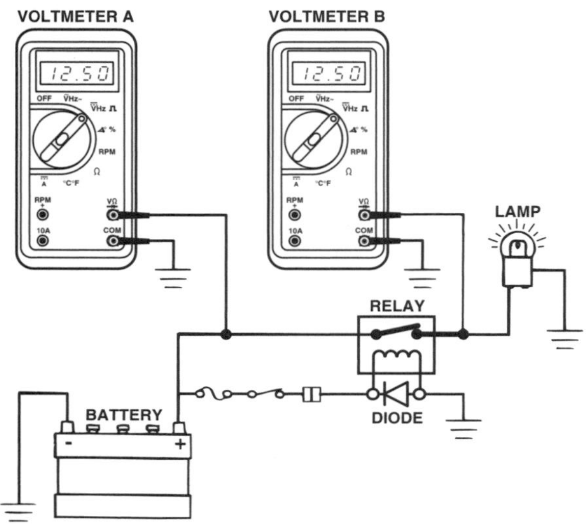

Figure 9-5. Voltage readings should be the same on both sides of a relay load circuit.

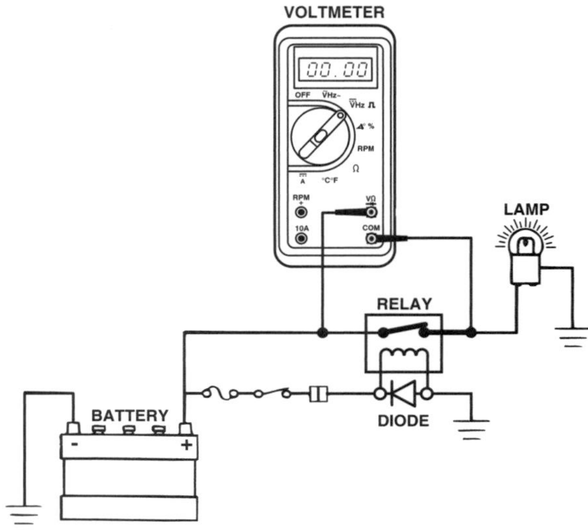

Figure 9-6. Look for a zero meter reading when measuring voltage drop directly across a relay load circuit.

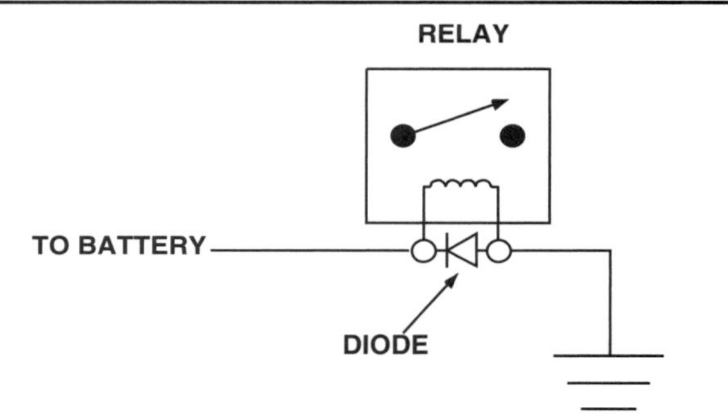

Figure 9-7. A diode in parallel with a relay control circuit protects electronic circuits from voltage spikes.

4. The voltage readings on both sides of the relay should be the same, figure 9-5. The voltage drop is the difference.

Voltage drop across a relay is directly measured by connecting the positive voltmeter lead to the power-side secondary lead and the negative voltmeter lead to the load-side secondary lead. The voltage measured with the relay activated is the voltage drop of the relay, figure 9-6.

On most relays, there should be virtually no voltage loss across the relay contacts, unless they are corroded or burned. Although a voltage drop of 0.1 to 0.2 volt is acceptable on relays that are used to carry starter motor current, it is too much for all other relays. Any excessive voltage loss in a relay means it needs replacement.

Testing a diode

When a relay is used to regulate current through electronic control circuits, a diode is often wired in parallel with the coil, figure 9-7. A diode makes a good one way electrical *check* valve because it offers little or no resistance to current in one direction and is an open circuit to current in the other direction. The diode prevents voltage spikes generated by the coil from entering the electronic circuits.

A diode in parallel with a coil cannot be checked with a DMM. Instead, either an analog ohmmeter or a test lamp is used to check a parallel diode. A good diode has a higher ohms reading in one direction when the leads are reversed. With a test lamp, power the circuit through the test lamp and reverse the leads. The lamp should be brighter in one direction.

A diode in series with a coil is checked by voltage drop testing. Take two voltmeter readings to compute voltage drop: one between the input, or power, side of the diode and ground, and one between the output, or ground, side of the diode and ground. Take readings with the circuit powered. Direct voltage drop readings are taken by connecting the voltmeter across the diode

Copyright 2000 by Chek-Chart Publications

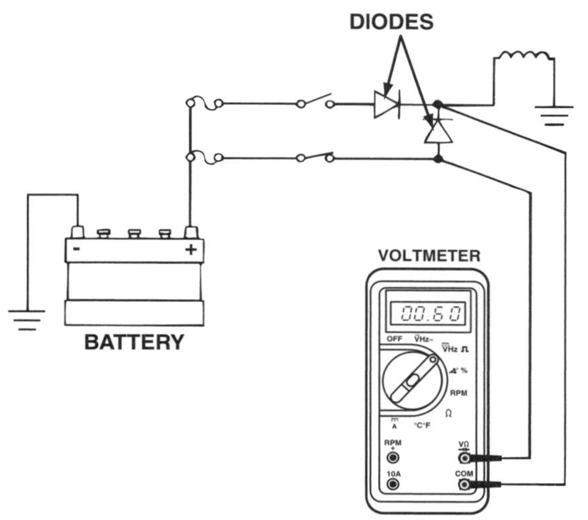

Figure 9-8. Taking a direct voltage drop reading across a diode.

and powering the relay, figure 9-8. With either method, voltage drop across the diode should be about 0.6 volt.

Testing a Switch

To test any switch for circuit resistance, use a voltmeter to measure voltage drop through poles of the switch. Refer to the service manual of the vehicle being repaired to determine how current is routed through the switch in the different positions when testing an ignition switch. Voltage drop readings are taken with the circuit under power and operating. To compute voltage drop across a switch:

1. Connect the positive voltmeter lead to the power-side wire and the common meter lead to a good ground. Activate the switch and note the reading.
2. Leave the common meter lead grounded and connect the positive voltmeter lead to the wire leaving the switch on the load-side. Activate the switch and note the voltmeter reading, figure 9-9.
3. The voltage readings on both sides of the switch should be the same. Any difference is the voltage drop of the switch.

Measure voltage drop directly by connecting the voltmeter across the switch poles and activating the switch, figure 9-10. With either method, there should not be any voltage dropped in the switch. Voltage drop on a switch is usually caused by switch contacts that are corroded, pitted, or burned. If a switch has a voltage drop, replace it.

Ignition Switch

As explained in Chapter Six of this *Shop Manual,* the ignition switch is typically tested without removing it

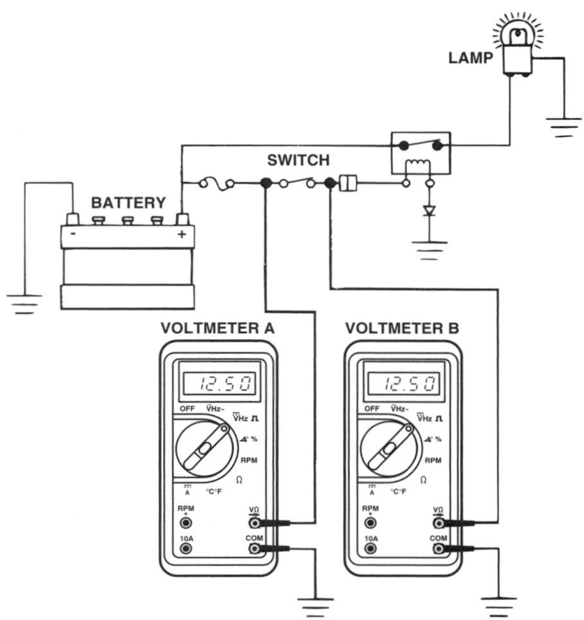

Figure 9-9. Voltmeter readings taken on either side of a switch should be equal.

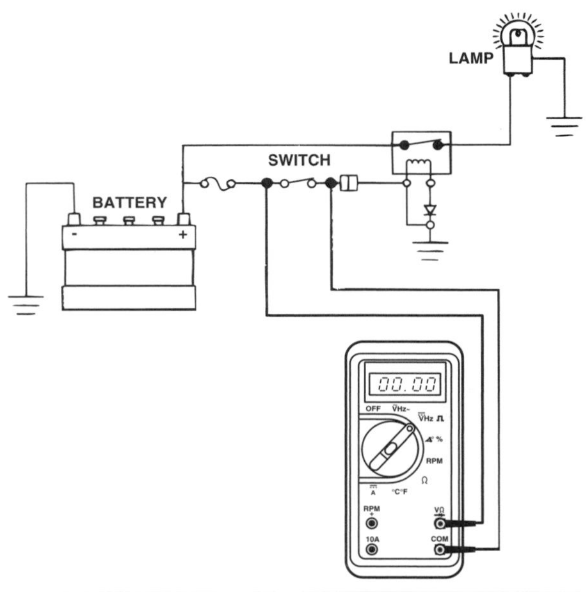

Figure 9-10. Expect a zero reading when measuring voltage drop directly across a switch.

from the vehicle by disconnecting the wiring harness multi-plug and checking continuity through the switch in all positions. Readings are generally taken with an ohmmeter. Locate the pin chart in the service manual for testing the ignition switch, figure 9-11. Replace the switch if continuity is other than specified.

An ignition switch assembles to the ignition lock tumbler, which mounts onto the steering column. On

Copyright 2000 by Chek-Chart Publications

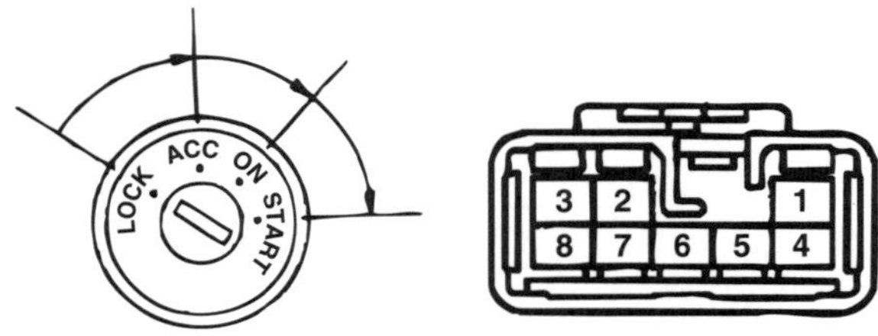

SWITCH POSITION	TESTER CONNECTION	SPECIFIED CONDITION
LOCK	-	NO CONTINUITY
ACC	5 - 7	CONTINUITY
ON	4 - 5 - 7 2 - 3	CONTINUITY
START	4 - 7 - 8 1 - 2 - 3	CONTINUITY

Figure 9-11. Pin chart for testing a 1998 Toyota Celica ignition switch.

some models, the switch is an integral part of the lock assembly, while on others the electrical switch is a separate component. With either type, ignition switches are not repairable and must be replaced when defective.

Ignition switch replacement

Ignition switch replacement procedures vary by make and model. Refer to the factory service manual when replacing an ignition switch. In general, to replace an ignition switch:

1. Disconnect the negative battery cable.
2. On models with a supplemental restraint system, disable the system following the service manual procedure to prevent accidental deployment of the air bag.
3. Remove all steering column cover panels necessary to gain access to the ignition switch for replacement.
4. If the switch is a separate part attached to the lock cylinder, remove the fasteners and lift the switch off the lock.
5. If the switch is an integral part of the lock cylinder, loosen and move, or remove, any tilt mechanisms, interlock linkages, column brackets, and other accessories that connect to the switch and lock assembly.
6. Remove the lock assembly from the steering column. The lock assembly is often secured to the steering column with tamperproof bolts, which are removed with a small chisel and hammer.
7. Install the replacement switch.
8. Connect and secure any linkages and components removed or loosened to access the switch.
9. Fit the steering column cover panels and connect the negative battery cable.

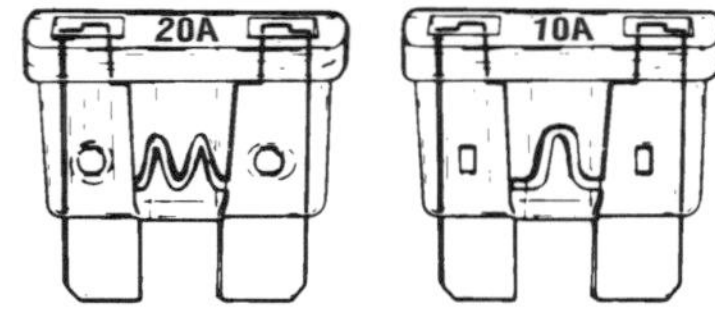

Figure 9-12. Most late-model vehicles use blade-type fuses of various current ratings to protect circuits.

Fuses and Fusible Links

The ignition switch power circuit is protected by a fuse, a fusible link, or both. Check these circuit protection devices if there is no voltage to the ignition switch with the key off. Fuses and fusible links carry a specified current without damage, but if this predetermined rating is exceeded, they open, or blow, to prevent circuit damage. Installing a new part does not solve the problem, as whatever caused the first fuse or link to blow quickly does the same to the replacement. Always determine and correct the cause of the blown device before installing a replacement.

Available voltage at the ignition switch that is lower than battery voltage with the key on indicates high circuit resistance between these two points. Locate the source by voltage drop testing. Repair as needed. If system voltage is available to, but not through, the ignition switch, the problem lies in the switch itself or one of the parallel circuits.

Fuses

Although fuses are available in a range of standard sizes and types, most domestic and import manufacturers use only blade-type fuses in late-model applications, figure 9-12. A miniature version, as well as a larger "maxi" version, of the standard blade-type fuse have gained in popularity in recent years. All fuses are rated by current capacity and the internal filament burns through to open the circuit when current rating is exceeded.

A fuse generally is checked while still in place, using a test lamp. If the lamp does not light on either side of the fuse, turn the ignition switch on and recheck. A voltmeter is used in a similar manner. A burned, or blown, fuse has a hot side and a dead side. Because a fuse is meant to burn out when current is too high, it should never be replaced with one whose rating is higher than the original equipment. A fuse with too high a rating causes circuit or component damage if an overload occurs.

Fusible links

A fusible link is generally used as a backup to fused circuits to prevent harness damage in the event of a fire or major electrical malfunction. Fusible links are made of a special smaller wire and are part of the

Copyright 2000 by Chek-Chart Publications

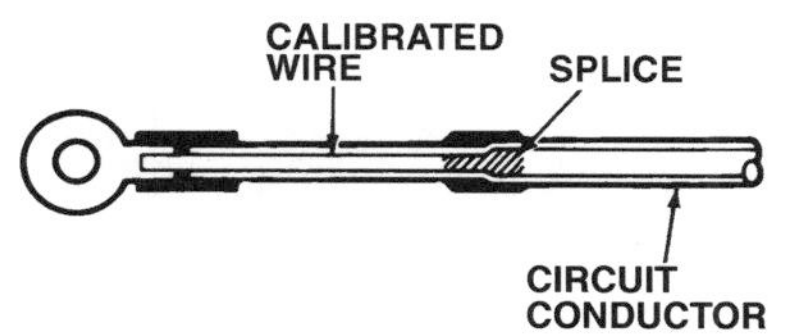

Figure 9-13. The calibrated wire of a fusible link opens to prevent circuit damage if current exceeds its amperage rating.

main wiring harness, figure 9-13. They react the same as a fuse, but have higher current ratings. Each fusible link protects several circuits that have their own fuses with a lower rating. A fusible link usually is connected in series with another accessory fuse. Some late-model vehicles have replaced this type of fusible link with a blade-type maxifuse that plugs into a relay or fuse box in the engine compartment.

When replacing a blown wire-type fusible link, be sure the replacement part is the correct size and properly rated for the circuit load. There are five different sizes, and each has its own current rating. To make the repair, cut out the fusible link at the nearest connector on each side. Attach each end of the replacement wire, which must be the same length as the section removed, to the standard wire and solder the connection with rosin-core solder. Refer to Chapter One of this *Shop Manual* as needed for wire-splicing procedures. Allow the splice to cool, then wrap the connection with tape to insulate it. Never use acid-core solder on an electrical connection, as acid reacts to the electrical current, causing electrolysis that destroys the wire.

IGNITION CONTROL MODULE SERVICE

In general, an electronic ignition system functions as follows: The ignition control module (ICM) processes an input voltage from the distributor signal generator to complete the primary coil circuit and fire the spark plugs. Some signals are generated by a pickup coil or Hall-effect switch mounted in the distributor housing. On these systems, the ICM, which is also referred to as the igniter, generally mounts on or near the distributor. Direct, or distributorless ignition systems (DIS) use a crankshaft position (CKP) sensor, as well as a camshaft position (CMP) sensor on some models, to generate an input signal to the ICM. The ICM generates the output signal to complete the primary circuit and initiate firing, figure 9-14. The ICM is incorporated into the powertrain control module (PCM) on some systems. On other DIS systems, the ICM is a separate component that mounts in the engine compartment. The ICM may bolt to a bracket on the engine, fasten to a fender panel or the bulkhead, or form the base of a coil pack.

Regardless of the ICM design or location, voltage drop tests are performed to locate open or grounded distributor signal generator circuits. Signals available at the ICM provide information on engine speed, timing advance, and cylinder firing. Monitoring these signals on a multi-trace lab scope provides a glimpse of how well the electronic control system is working. The ICM input signals must be correctly synchronized in order to fire the correct spark plug at the right time in the compression cycle. Ignition timing electronically adjusts to compensate for changes in engine speed and load.

Testing

Methods to determine whether an ICM is good or defective vary between manufacturers and systems. Procedures outlined by the vehicle manufacturer must be followed. In general, eliminate all other possibilities before condemning the module. Verify that power is available to the module, and check for voltage drop across connections on the power and ground circuits. Since modules provide the primary circuit ground connection, simply cleaning and tightening the ground circuit connections often solves the problem. Many modules ground through the fasteners that attach the unit to the engine or distributor. Voltage drop on an electronic ground circuit should never exceed 0.01 volt. Always check the ground circuit before replacing a component.

Chrysler systems

Early Chrysler electronic ignition systems have a separate ICM that generally bolts to the engine compartment bulkhead, but the ignition control functions are incorporated into the PCM on all late-model applications.

Several voltmeter checks are made to test the older, standalone units. These systems use an electromagnetic pickup coil in the distributor to open and close the primary circuit. Be aware, there are several wiring harness connector configurations, so check the service manual as needed to identify the correct test points. In general, with the ICM disconnected and the key on, battery voltage should be available to the unit from the ignition switch, and the negative primary coil terminal should read within one volt of battery voltage, figure 9-15. If not, repair the circuits as needed and retest. If voltage readings for power, ground, and magnetic pickup are within specification and the ICM is not triggering the coil to induce secondary voltage, replace the ICM.

The ICM became part of the spark control computer in the late 1970s. In addition to regulating the primary circuit, the spark control computer adjusts ignition timing advance based on input sensor readings. A vacuum transducer, which is part of the spark

Copyright 2000 by Chek-Chart Publications

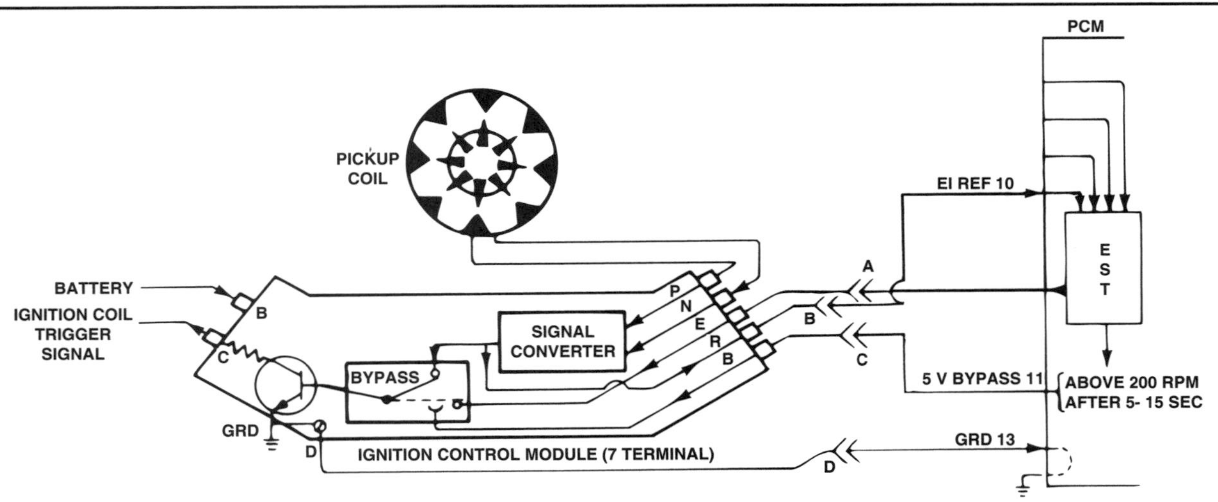

Figure 9-14. The ignition control module on this General Motors system electronically opens and closes the coil primary circuit.

control computer, delivers a signal to the computer to advance timing with high manifold vacuum, figure 9-16. A magnetic pickup or a Hall-effect switch mounts on the breaker plate and provides the primary circuit signal. Access the onboard diagnostic program to check and test the spark control computer; refer to Chapter Twelve of this *Shop Manual.*

Beginning in 1984, all ignition functions were incorporated into the powertrain control module (PCM). Ignition timing advance is electronically regulated by the PCM. Access the onboard diagnostic program to check and test the system; refer to Chapter Twelve of this *Shop Manual.*

Ford systems

Late-model Ford vehicles, those with electronic engine control IV (EEC-IV) and EEC-V systems, use one of two basic ignition systems: the distributor ignition (DI) and the integrated electronic ignition (EI). On EEC-IV applications, the EI system is referred to as the electronic distributorless ignition system (EDIS) and DI is referred to as the distributor ignition system (DIS) in Ford service literature. All EEC-IV systems, as well as EEC-V models with a DI system, have a separate ICM unit. All ignition control functions are incorporated into the PCM on EEC-V models with a EI system.

Ford has very specific self-test programs built into the PCM on all models with electronic control systems. Accessing the self-test program, as explained in Chapter Twelve of this *Shop Manual,* is part of the diagnostic procedure. Results of a self-test determine which pinpoint tests in the Powertrain Control/ Emissions Diagnostic Manual are conducted to isolate the source of the failure. Individual components, such as the ICM, should be tested only as and where instructed by the pinpoint tests.

Regardless of the type of engine management and ignition system, any Ford ICM functions in a similar fashion and provides valuable information for diagnosing ignition and driveability problems. Ford provides specifications and instructions for performing voltmeter checks of the ICM in the pinpoint test procedures. Monitoring the ICM signals on a multi-trace lab scope reveals how well the ignition and control system are operating. Refer to the appropriate service manual to identify the correct circuits for testing.

A typical Ford ICM is a small rectangular unit with either two six-pin connectors, one at either end, or a single twelve-pin connector, figure 9-17. In addition to battery power from the ignition switch, the harness connectors carry input signals from engine sensors and the PCM, feedback signals to the PCM, and output signals to the ignition coil or coils. The ICM size, location, configuration, and number of circuits used vary by model and year. The assembly attaches to a bracket or other mounting surface on the engine with screws. The ICM mounting screws provide the ground circuit connection for both the ICM and PCM, so make sure they are clean and tight. The ICM receives battery voltage from the ignition switch and a parallel circuit delivers voltage to the positive primary coil terminals. A ground circuit connects the ICM to the PCM.

The ICM receives a profile ignition pickup (PIP) signal, generated by either a CKP sensor or a CMP sensor depending upon application, which provides base timing information. On EI models, a magnetic pickup coil type CKP sensor provides input to the ICM through a two-wire, one positive and one negative, circuit. The output of the CKP sensor provides the PIP signal, which is transmitted to the PCM on another circuit. A missing tooth on the CKP sensor tone ring provides a crankshaft position reference that

Copyright 2000 by Chek-Chart Publications

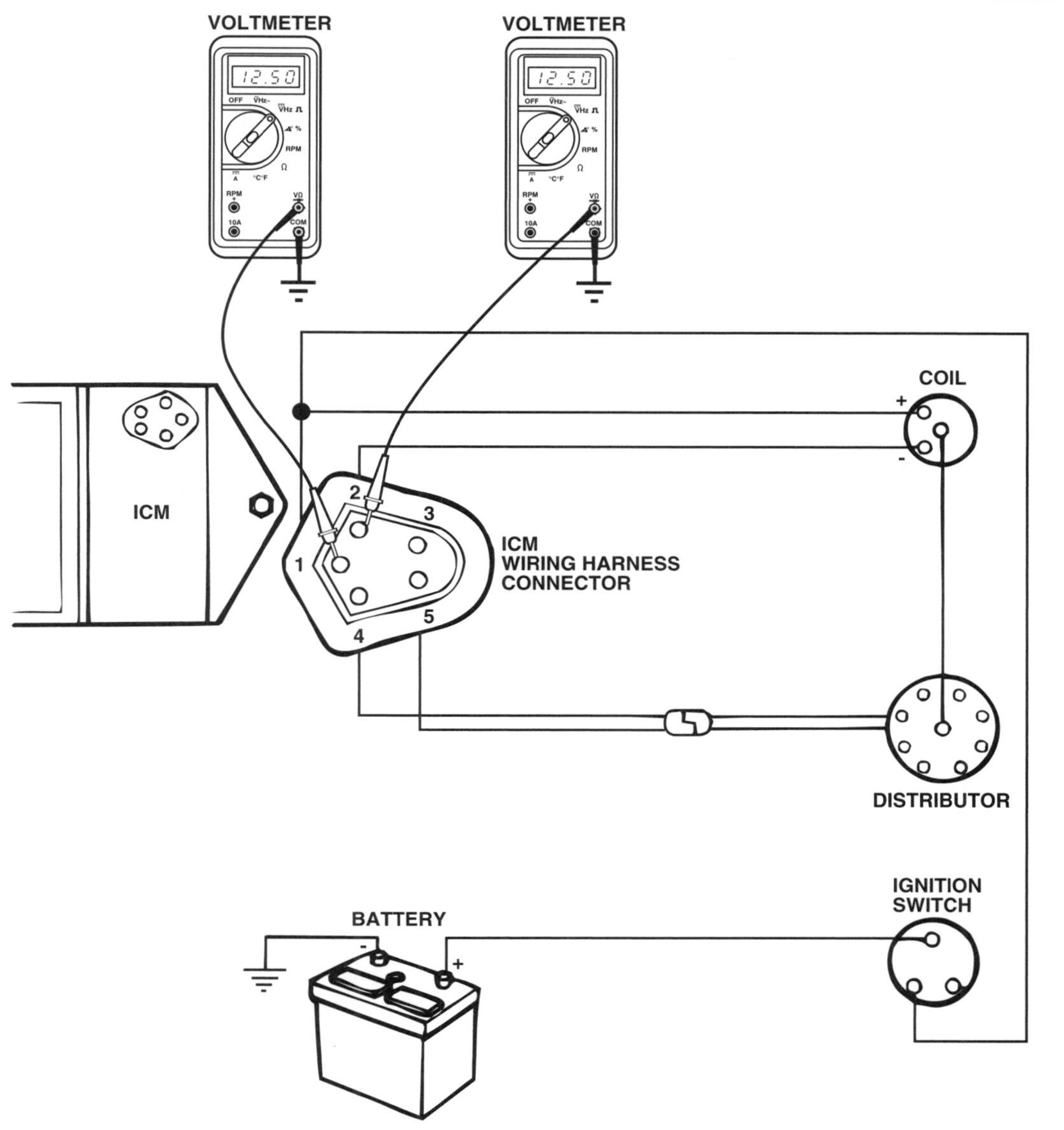

Figure 9-15. Voltmeter connections for testing a typical Chrysler stand alone ICM.

is clearly visible on the scope screen, figure 9-18. The frequency and amplitude of the analog signal increase in proportion to engine speed. Some, but not all, distributorless systems use an additional CMP sensor signal to synchronize ignition timing and sequential fuel injection (SFI). The CMP signal is also used for misfire detection on OBD II systems. The CMP sensor is a Hall-effect switch that provides what Ford calls the cylinder identification (CID) signal to the ICM. Look for a digital square wave that increases in frequency with engine speed and pulls completely to ground.

On late-model DI systems, the distributor houses a Hall-effect CMP sensor that provides a PIP signal to the ICM on a single-wire circuit, figure 9-19. A parallel circuit carries the CMP sensor signal to the PCM. One of the shutter wheel windows is smaller than the other openings, so for each camshaft revolution the pulse width of one cycle in the waveform is different from the rest. This signature waveform provides the timing synchronization reference and the engine will not start if it is absent. Be aware, the same distributor may be used with two different shutter wheels: one with a signature and one without. The signature is used to time SFI, and if installed on a non-SFI engine causes incorrect ignition timing. The frequency of the digital signal increases in proportion to engine speed.

On all systems, the ICM receives an additional input signal from the PCM that actually triggers the opening and closing of the negative primary coil circuit. This is referred to as the spark output

Copyright 2000 by Chek-Chart Publications

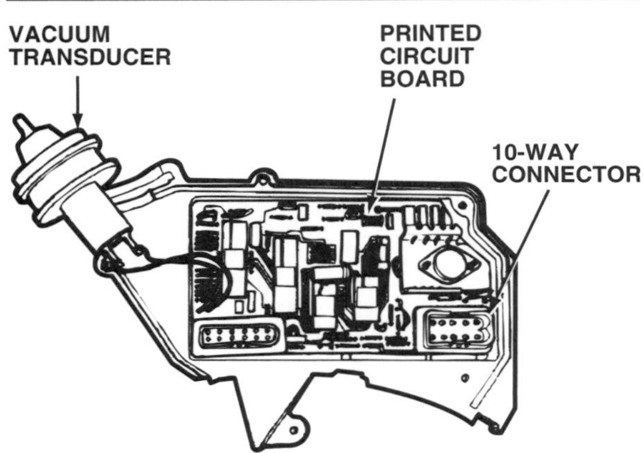

Figure 9-16. The Chrysler spark control computer used a vacuum transducer to advance ignition timing.

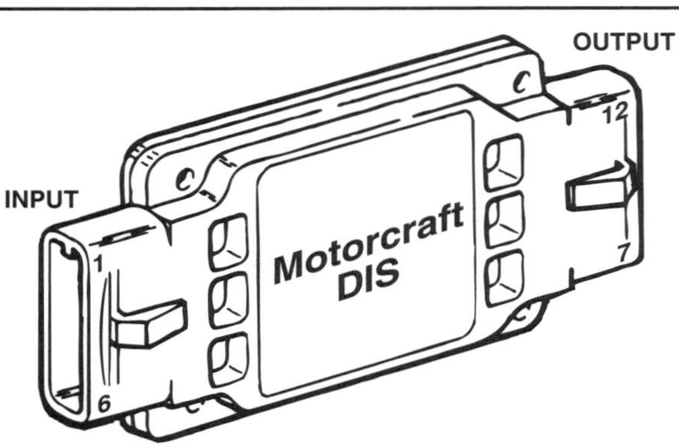

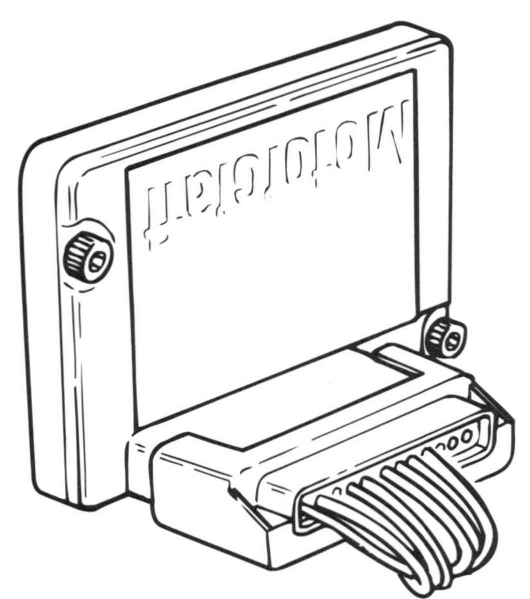

Figure 9-17. There are several versions of the Ford stand alone ICM.

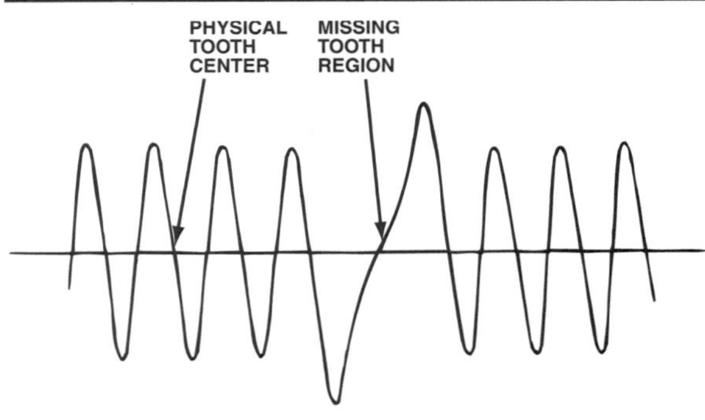

Figure 9-18. A missing tooth provides a crankshaft position signature on this Ford pickup coil signal.

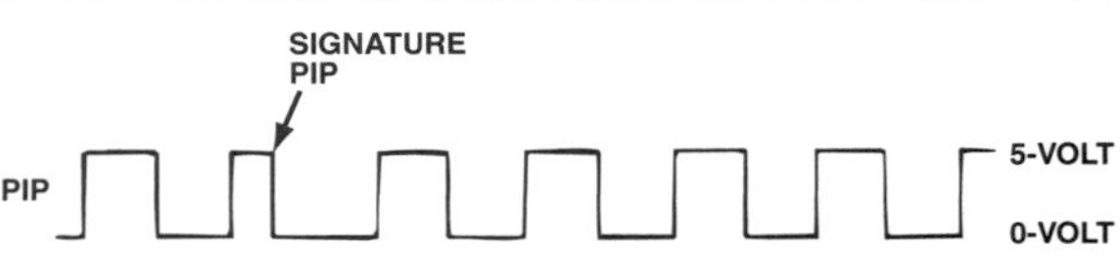

Figure 9-19. Position signature on the PIP signal from a Ford Hall-effect CMP sensor.

(SPOUT) signal on older systems and the spark angle word (SAW) signal on newer models. The difference between the two is in how the computer processes the information; both are a digital square wave signal.

The ICM output circuits connect to the negative primary coil terminals and to the PCM. The number of primary coil circuits varies by system, but, as explained in Chapter Eight of this *Shop Manual,* all are quickly checked using a current probe. The ICM outputs diagnostic feedback information for the self-test program to the PCM on what Ford calls the ignition diagnostic monitor (IDM) circuit. A tachometer signal may be taken off the IDM circuit on some models, and is provided by a separate circuit on others.

General Motors systems

Control of dwell and timing of the primary circuit to generate secondary current is a PCM function on all current General Motors domestic vehicles. Although some models may have a separate ICM, it is used only to switch the primary current off and on. For models with PCM control, refer to Chapter Twelve of this *Shop Manual* for service instructions. The following applies to older ignition systems, both distributor and direct, that use a separate ICM to complete the primary ignition circuit.

On systems with the ICM assembly in the distributor, the module is a separate component that is replaceable, figure 9-20. General Motors distributorless ignition systems have a separate ICM unit that assembles onto the base plate below the coil pack, figure 9-21. Early systems have the CKP signal to the ICM, with the PCM controlling only the timing, while

Copyright 2000 by Chek-Chart Publications

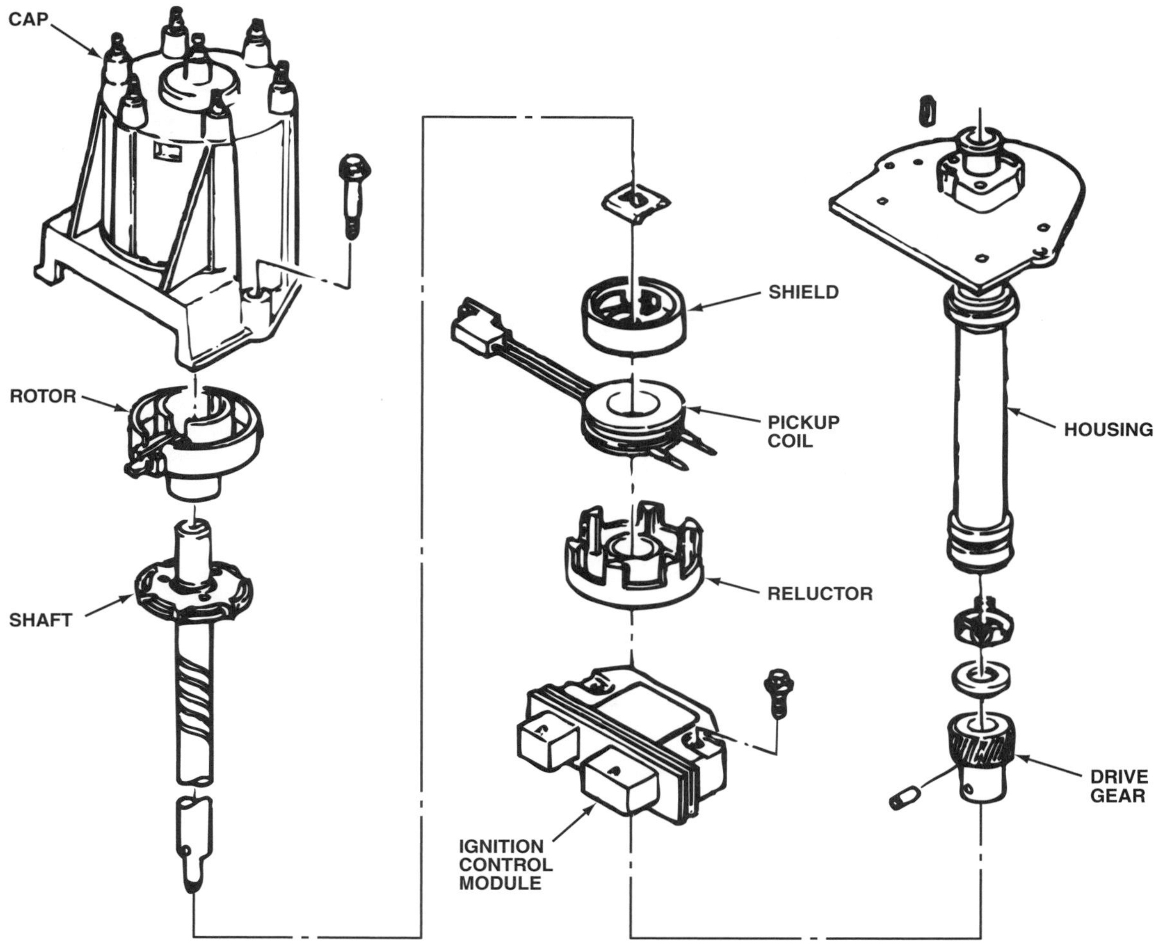

Figure 9-20. Some General motors systems have a separate ICM installed inside the distributor.

later systems have the CKP signal to the PCM, with the PCM controlling both timing and dwell. Test procedures are the same for both types. The integrated direct ignition system used on the Quad Four engine also uses a separate ICM that bolts to the cover shield and connects to the coils with a short harness, figure 9-22.

Although there are several variations of each module design, testing is similar for all of them. Certain signals should be available at select pins of the ICM, but the correct pin must be identified. Check the manual for the vehicle being serviced to identify ICM pin assignments. Most General Motors systems have the following signals at the ICM:

- Battery
- Coil primary
- Crankshaft position
- Reference
- Bypass
- Electronic spark timing
- Ground.

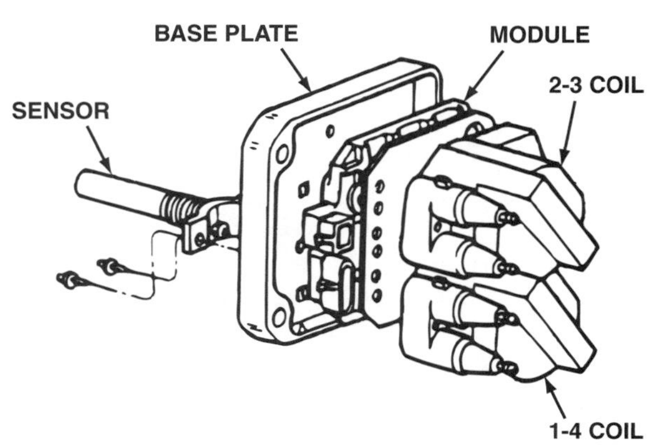

Figure 9-21. The ICM bolts to the coil pack base plate on early direct ignition systems.

Copyright 2000 by Chek-Chart Publications

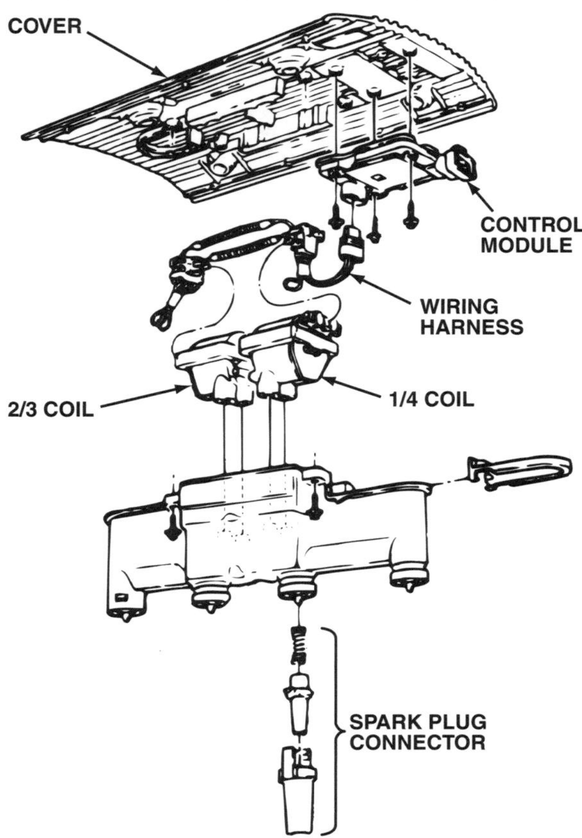

Figure 9-22. A Quad Four ICM bolts to the coil assembly cover.

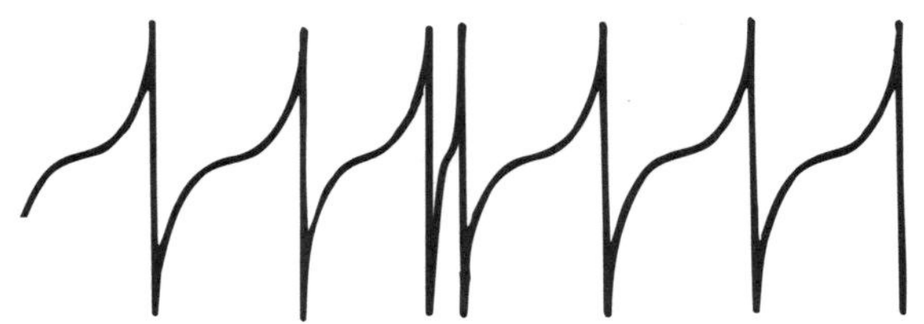

Figure 9-23. A CKP sensor often generates a signature wave to identify the number one cylinder.

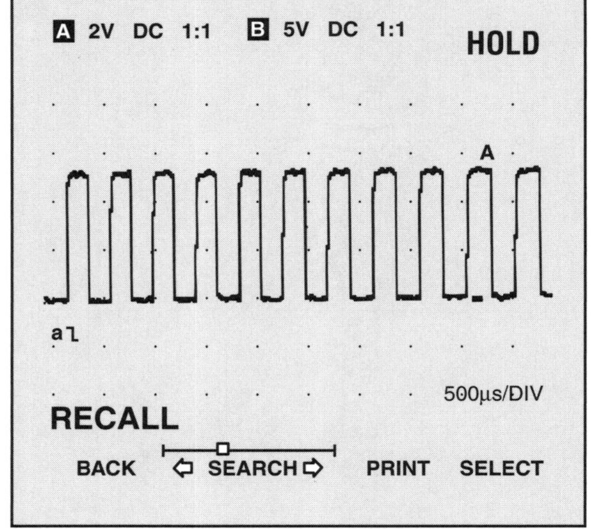

Figure 9-24. The reference circuit of the General Motors ICM cycles on and off with the base timing for each cylinder.

The module receives battery voltage through the ignition switch. This power terminal, which is generally marked either "+" or "B+," should have at least 12 volts available with the key on. The ground circuit connects the ICM to the PCM, but does not provide the ground path for the ignition module. The ICM grounds through the mounting screws that attach it to the distributor base plate, coil-pack base, or cover shield. Make sure these connections are clean, tight, and offer no resistance.

The ICM connects to the negative primary coil on what is commonly referred to as the TACH terminal on earlier models. This terminal is marked "C" or "TACH" on some applications, and is identified only by a number on others. This circuit is sampled with a current probe, as explained in Chapter Eight of this *Shop Manual*, to check coil operation.

Two circuits, often labeled "P" and "N," are the positive and negative circuits from the magnetic pickup coil used as a CKP sensor. Check these circuits on a scope and look for an alternating current (ac) pattern that varies in frequency and amplitude in proportion to engine speed. Some systems have a signature wave that is used to identify the number one cylinder, figure 9-23. The CKP sensor either assembles into the distributor, bolts to the engine, or attaches to the base of the coil pack assembly.

The reference circuit, labeled "R" on some models, carries a 5-volt reference voltage transmitted by the PCM. The ICM internally switches the reference signal on and off to ground as the transistor in the module switches. On a scope, the reference circuit produces a variable frequency square waveform, figure 9-24. Each cycle, or pulse, of the waveform coincides with the crankshaft position of one cylinder for ignition firing.

The bypass and electronic spark timing (EST) terminals, often labeled "B" and "E," are the circuits the PCM uses to control timing advance. Once the engine starts, or exceeds a minimum rpm, the PCM applies a five-volt signal to the ICM on the bypass circuit. The PCM, rather than the ICM, is controlling the opening and closing of the primary circuit when this bypass voltage signal is present. The EST circuit carries a variable frequency digital signal from the PCM to the

Copyright 2000 by Chek-Chart Publications

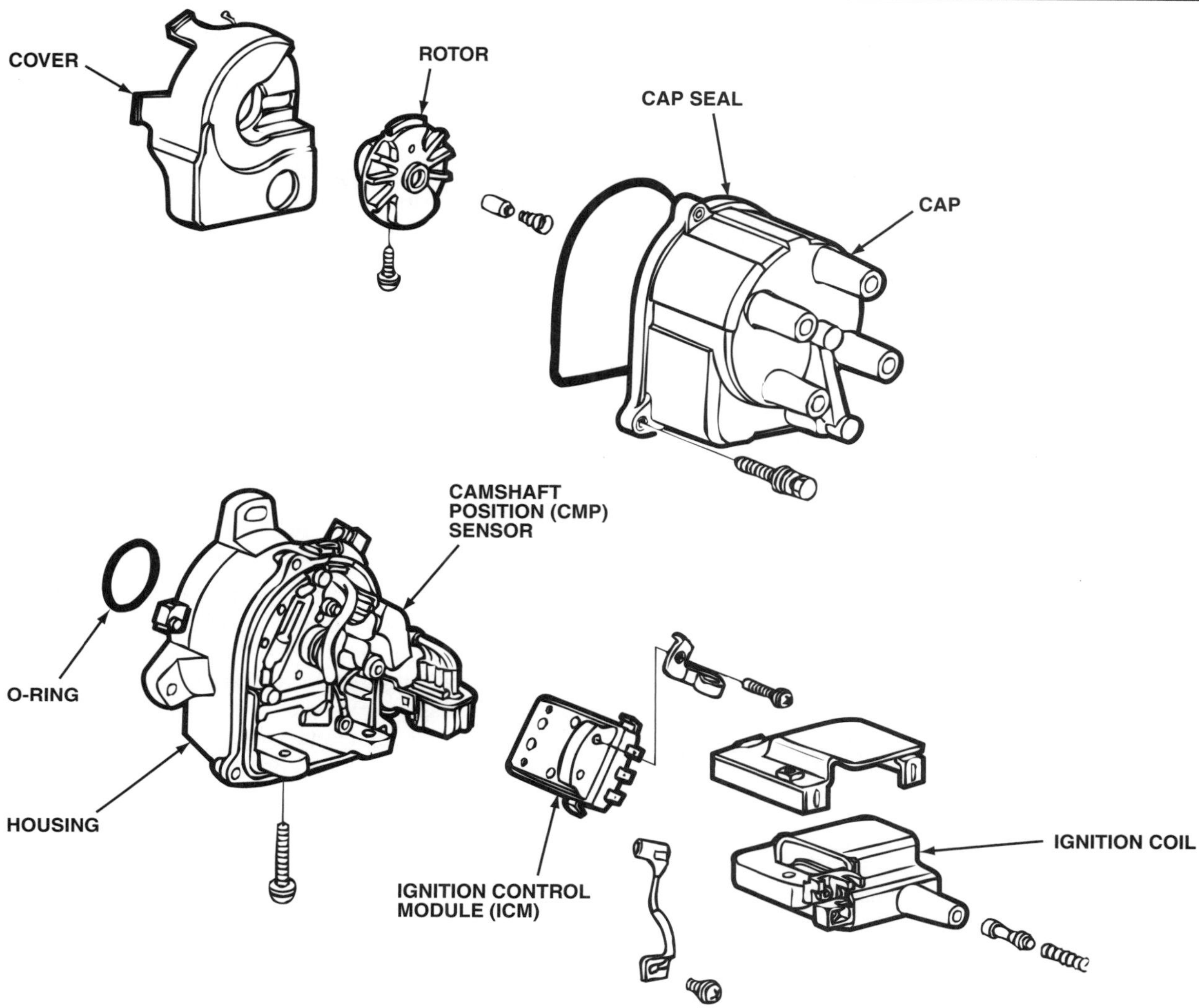

Figure 9-25. The ICM, along with the coil, assembles into this Honda Accord distributor.

ICM that switches the transistor on and off when the system is under PCM control.

The ground circuit provides a ground path between the PCM and ICM, but is not the ground source for the ICM. As previously mentioned, the ICM is grounded through the mounting fasteners.

Import systems

Like their domestic counterparts, the PCM regulates the opening and closing of the primary coil circuit directly on most late-model import ignition systems. When the PCM does all of the control, a simplified ICM is used only as a switch for the primary circuit. This type of ICM is often called a power transistor, or minimum function. An ICM that controls dwell, but the PCM controls timing, typically has more than three wires. Commonly called an ignitor, this type of ICM may be located in the engine compartment or inside the distributor, figure 9-25.

The latest style is the individual direct ignition (IDI) system, which uses an individual coil for each spark plug. These "coil-over-plug" systems may be controlled by either a remote minimum-function ICM or an ICM built into each coil. The PCM transmits a control signal for timing and dwell to each spark plug. Some systems have a positive-switching ICM control signal, while others go negative, or ground, to turn on the primary circuit. The signal, which may include a signature wave, is easily viewed on a scope or graphing multimeter (GMM), figure 9-26.

A number of igniter designs are used and the number of circuits, location and mounting, test procedures, and specifications vary considerably by year, make, and model. Have accurate service information

Copyright 2000 by Chek-Chart Publications

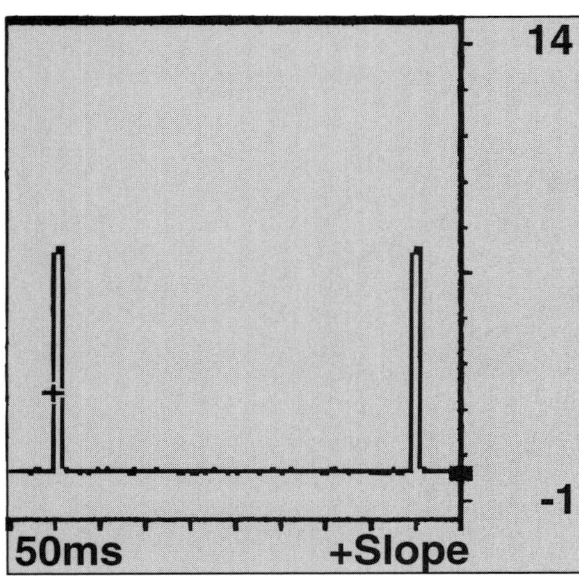

Figure 9-26. A positive switching ICM control signal and signature wave captured on a GMM.

available for the system being repaired. In general, any ICM must have voltage applied, usually battery voltage from the ignition switch, and a nonresistive ground connection. The ICM mounting fasteners often complete the ground circuit. Since the ICM opens and closes the negative primary coil circuit, one of the terminals should carry a signal that switches on and off ground while the engine is running or cranking. If not, replace the ICM.

Replacement

Replacing an ICM that mounts in the distributor requires partial disassembly of the distributor. Often, it is easier to simply remove the distributor from the engine, disassemble it, and replace the ICM on the bench. Distributor removal, disassembly, and assembly techniques are detailed in Chapter Ten of this *Shop Manual*. Refer to procedures in Chapter Ten to service a distributor-mounted ICM.

To replace a Ford ICM, carefully disconnect the harness multi-plugs and remove the mounting screws. A thin coat of silicone grease or heat sink compound is applied to the base of the ICM to increase heat transfer from the unit to the mounting bracket. Avoid getting grease in the mounting bolt holes or on the screws. Remember, both the ICM and PCM ground through the ICM fasteners. Any grease on the threads acts as an insulator and creates resistance in the ground circuit.

On General Motors systems with the ICM at the base of the coil pack, remove the coil assembly from the engine to replace the module. The coils bolt onto the module. With a direct ignition system, the coil housing assembly is removed from the engine as a unit and disassembled on the bench.

SPEED AND REFERENCE SENSOR SERVICE

The PCM or ICM uses the signals of the speed and reference sensors to determine the rotational speed and position of the crankshaft, camshaft, or both. The signal may be an analog ac voltage generated by a magnetic pickup coil, or the digital square wave produced by a Hall-effect switch or optical sensor. Regardless of design, the PCM uses the frequency of the sensor signal to determine the speed of the rotating component. Speed and reference sensors are tested with a digital multimeter (DMM). Operation of the sensor is observed by monitoring the signal on a lab scope or GMM.

Pickup Coil

Whether called a magnetic pickup coil, variable reluctance sensor, or permanent magnet generator, this type of sensor generates voltage as an analog signal. These sensors are self-contained and do not require an applied voltage to produce a signal. However, a slight bias voltage is applied to one coil lead on most systems. Since these sensors produce their own voltage, it is possible to get a waveform with correct amplitude and frequency, even though there are problems on the chassis ground circuits.

The pickup coil is wound around a permanent magnet, whose field expands and collapses as the teeth of a rotating trigger wheel, or tone ring, pass by it, figure 9-27. The magnetic field generates an ac voltage signal and, as the speed of the engine increases, so does the frequency and amplitude of the signal. Two wires, a positive lead and a negative lead, connect the sensor to the PCM. With the addition of a circuit built into this type of sensor, it becomes a magneto-resistive sensor. The analog signal is rectified to a variable-frequency digital square wave signal on these sensors.

For best results, attach scope probes and DMM leads directly to the sensor leads as close to the sensor as possible. Back-probe the harness connector to take readings.

A scope trace of the sensor generally sweeps up the positive slope and drops on the negative slope. Check for inverted probe or wiring harness connections if the vertical spike is on the positive slope of the waveform of most engines, figure 9-28. Be aware, this inverted pattern is normal for some manufacturers, such as Honda and Isuzu. The shape of the trace peak varies for different sensor designs, but most signals must reach a minimum amplitude before the PCM recognizes them. Look for uniformity in the trace cycles broken only by the signature of a missing tooth where

Copyright 2000 by Chek-Chart Publications

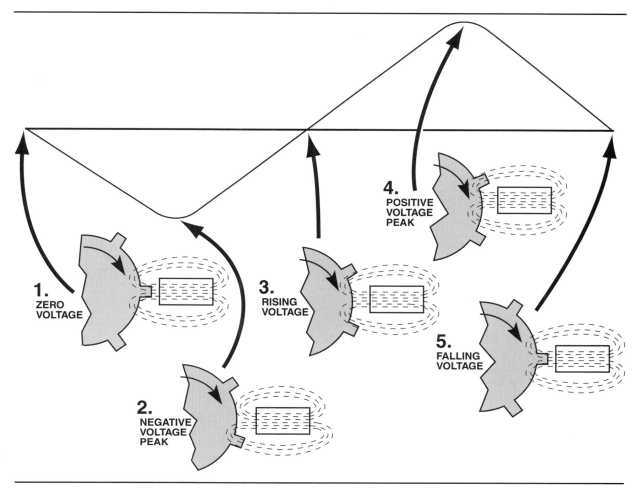

Figure 9-27. The teeth of the trigger wheel disrupt the magnetic field of a pickup coil to produce an ac signal.

applicable. The PCM monitors for the signal to switch from positive to negative and negative to positive, which should occur at the 0-volt baseline. If not, check PCM and chassis grounds.

Manufacturers generally provide resistance specifications for checking internal pickup coil circuits with a DMM. Sensor output voltage can also be checked using a DMM. Magnetic sensor output voltage is related to engine speed. Typically, it ranges between about 500 millivolts at cranking speed to approximately 100 volts at high rpm. When diagnosing an engine that cranks but does not run, the sensor output should exceed the minimum specified output while cranking. A signal that switches slowly typically cannot register on a DMM. An example would be a CMP sensor, which cycles once, or produces one sine wave, for each two revolutions of the crankshaft.

Pickup coil sensors may be mounted in the distributor or on the engine. Refer to Chapter Ten of this *Shop Manual* for servicing sensors mounted in the distributor. Both CKP and CMP sensors mount at various locations on the engine. The tone ring for a CKP

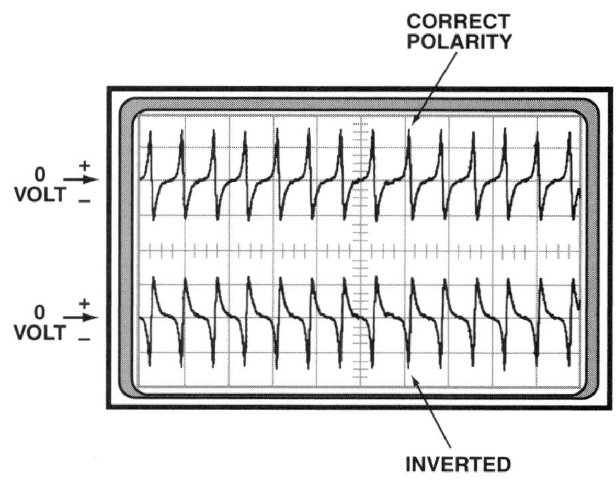

Figure 9-28. Reversed, or inverted polarity on a pickup coil may cause driveability problems.

sensor may be on the crankshaft pulley, flywheel, or the crankshaft. Typically, a sensor has a short harness with a two-pin connector and the assembly attaches to

Copyright 2000 by Chek-Chart Publications

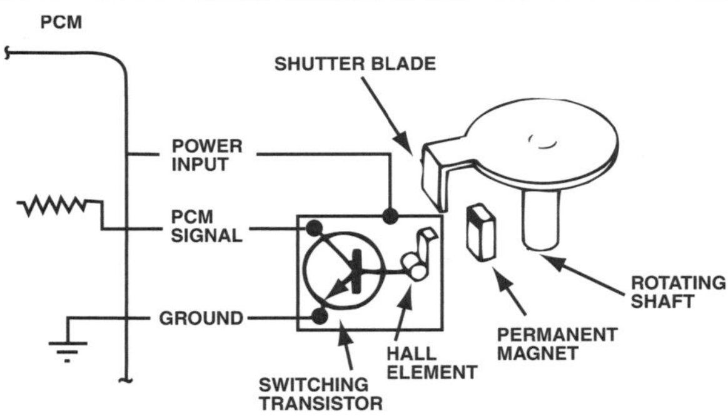

Figure 9-29. A Hall-effect switch consists of the Hall element, a permanent magnet, and the shutter wheel.

the engine with one or two bolts. Note the harness routing before removing the sensor and install the replacement in the same manner.

Pickup sensors are not adjustable. However, they must be properly aligned and installed with a precise gap between the teeth and sensor to function properly. Misalignment, incorrect gap, damage to the tone rings, or accumulated debris may be the cause of an engine that sags, stumbles, hesitates, or diesels. Sensor failure often prevents the engine from starting, or causes it to die immediately after startup. Sensor damage due to road debris or vibration may cause engine misfire, stumble, or intermittent no-start conditions.

Hall-effect switch

A Hall-effect switch uses a microchip to switch a transistor on and off and generate a digital signal that is transmitted to the PCM. As a shutter wheel or the magnet passes between the Hall element and a permanent magnet, the magnetic field expands and collapses to produce an analog signal. The Hall element contains a logic gate that converts the signal into a digital signal, which triggers transistor switching, figure 9-29. Hall-effect switches produce a square waveform, whose frequency varies in proportion to the rotational speed of the shutter wheel.

Applications for Hall-effect switches are similar to those for magnetic pickup sensors. However, since a Hall-effect switch does not generate its own voltage, power must be provided for the device to work. Therefore, Hall-effect operation requires a three-wire circuit—power input, signal output, and ground.

The Hall element receives an input voltage from either the ignition switch or the PCM to power it. Activity of the magnetic field and shutter blade opens and closes a switch to ground on the input signal. Be aware, output signal voltage is not always the same as input signal voltage. Therefore, accurate specifications for the unit being tested are required.

Hall-effect switches seem to function better on a higher voltage signal than other electronic components, and are often an exception to the 5-volt

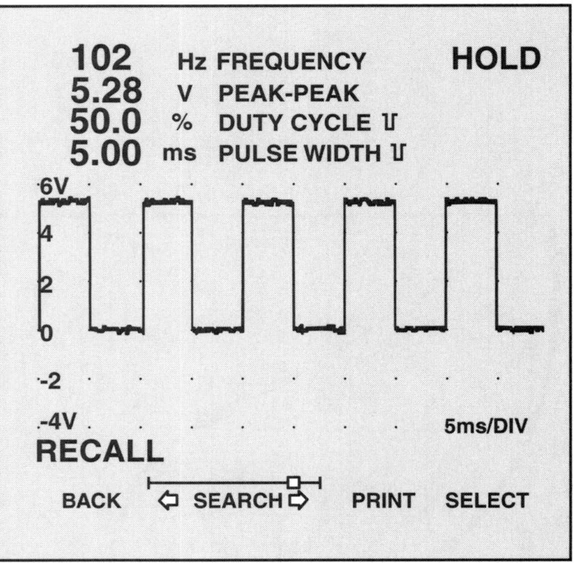

Figure 9-30. Look for clean, sharp transitions and a zero-volt baseline on a Hall-effect switch trace.

reference rule. Keep this in mind when checking supply voltage, the unit may require 7, 9, or even 12 volts to operate properly. On engines that use more than one Hall-effect switch, such as crankshaft and camshaft sensors, a common circuit generally supplies the power.

The most effective way to check a Hall-effect switch is to monitor the signal on a scope. Look for sharp, clean state-change transitions and a signal that pulls completely to ground. Amplitude should be even for all waveforms, the pattern should be consistent, and peaks should be at the specified voltage level, figure 9-30. The shape and position of the slots on the shutter wheel determine the shape and duty cycle of the waveform. Some Hall-effect switch patterns have a slight rounding at the top corners of the trace that can generally be overlooked. Remember, the PCM looks for switching at the midpoint of the voltage range, not at the top or bottom. However, rounding at the bottom corners of the trace is often caused by high resistance on the ground circuit. Also, check for the correct voltage on the power circuit to the Hall element. A problem here causes problems on the signal circuit.

When used as a CKP or CMP sensor, Hall-effect switches generally install in the distributor. Refer to the distributor removal, disassembly, and assembly procedures in Chapter Ten of this *Shop Manual* to service these units. Some Hall-effect sensors mount to the engine at the crankshaft or camshaft. These are replaced by removing the mounting fasteners and separating the wiring harness connector, figure 9-31.

Copyright 2000 by Chek-Chart Publications

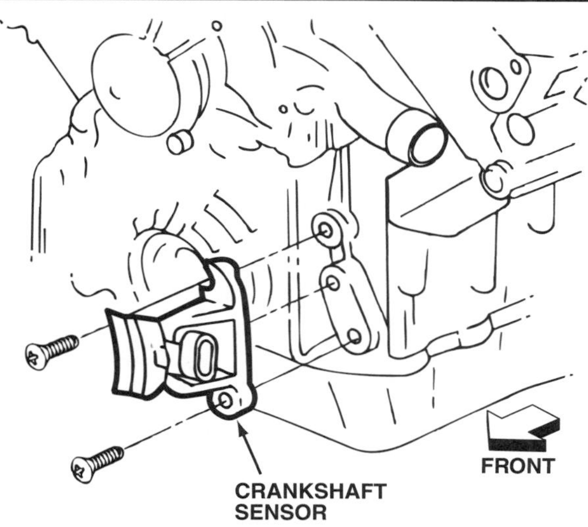

Figure 9-31. This General Motors Hall-effect CKP sensor bolts to the front of the engine.

Optical Sensor

An optical sensor uses a light-emitting diode (LED), a shutter wheel, and a phototransistor to produce a digital signal that changes frequency in proportion to rotational speed. Like a Hall-effect switch, an optical sensor requires an external power source and uses a three-wire circuit. One wire carries power to operate the LED, one is the signal generated by the transistor, and the third provides a common ground path.

Signal voltage, which is usually 5 volts, switches on and off as the rotating shutter passes between the phototransistor and LED. This opens and closes the ground circuit. When the shutter allows light to shine on the phototransistor, the base of the transistor switches, causing the signal voltage to change state. When the reflector plate blocks the light to the phototransistor, the base of the transistor switches again, and signal voltage changes as well.

Optical sensors are more expensive to manufacture and more delicate than a magnetic pickup or Hall-effect switch. Therefore, when used, they generally assemble into the distributor to protect them. Service procedures are detailed in Chapter Ten of this *Shop Manual*. Typically, optical sensors are used as engine speed sensors because their high-speed data rate is more accurate for high rpm applications than any other sensor designs. When viewed on a scope, the waveforms are similar to those produced by a Hall-effect switch.

Magneto Resistive Sensor

The magneto resistive sensor is a later variation of the magnetic inductive sensor. This type of sensor uses a magnetic pickup coil to produce an analog signal, and internal circuitry to convert the signal to a digital signal that is delivered to the PCM. These sensors have three wires, ignition, ground, and the digital signal generated by the sensor. The ac signal cannot be monitored. A magneto resistive sensor produces a signal similar to that of a Hall-effect sensor.

IGNITION COIL SERVICE

Chapter Eight of this *Shop Manual* explains how to check an ignition coil by measuring coil current draw with an ammeter or current probe. An ohmmeter is used to measure the resistance of the primary and secondary windings. If current draw or winding resistance is out of specifications, replace the coil.

Oil-filled and some E-core coils attach to a bracket that bolts onto the engine. Other E-core coils install in the distributor. Refer to Chapter Ten of this *Shop Manual* if the coil is part of the distributor assembly. To replace a remotely mounted coil, disconnect the secondary lead from the coil tower and the primary wires from the terminals. Label the primary leads to ensure proper installation on the replacement coil as needed. Loosen the mounting fasteners and remove the coil. Install the new coil, then connect the primary wires and secondary lead.

A coil pack mounts on a base plate that typically bolts onto the engine block. To remove the unit, label as needed, then disconnect the secondary leads and the primary wiring connectors. Remove the mounting fasteners and lift off the coil pack assembly. Secure the new unit to the engine and connect the primary and secondary leads, figure 9-32.

Direct ignition coils fit onto the spark plug and are often secured by small bolts or screws, figure 9-33. A two-pin connector provides the primary circuit connections. On some designs, each coil is serviced individually. On others, the coils for all of the cylinders remove from the engine as an assembly, figure 9-34. The assembly is torn down on the bench to service the individual coils on some, but not all, designs.

IGNITION CABLE SERVICE

Inspect high-tension ignition leads and measure resistance with an ohmmeter as described in Chapter Eight of this *Shop Manual*. When replacing cables, make sure the new leads meet original equipment specifications. Most ignition systems use 7-mm cables. However, a few use larger 8-mm cables. The larger cables provide additional dielectric resistance in a system where secondary voltage exceeds 40 kV. Use the proper-size replacement cables; they are not interchangeable.

Ignition cables generally push-fit into the distributor cap or DIS coil. Twist and pull up on the boot to remove the cable from the cap. Fit the new cable to the cap so the terminal seats firmly on the tower, figure

Copyright 2000 by Chek-Chart Publications

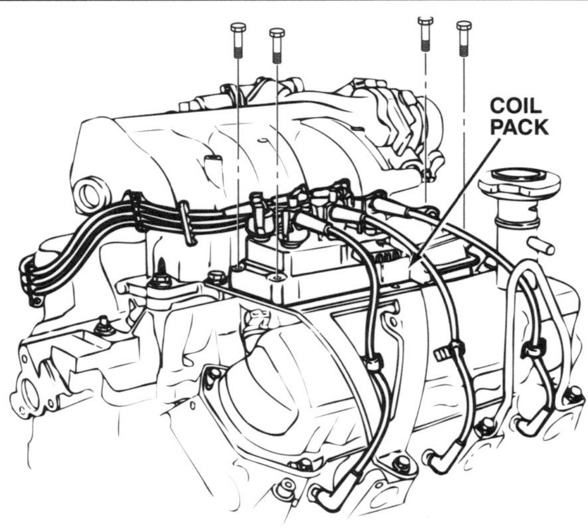

Figure 9-32. A coil pack generally mounts to a base plate on the engine with bolts.

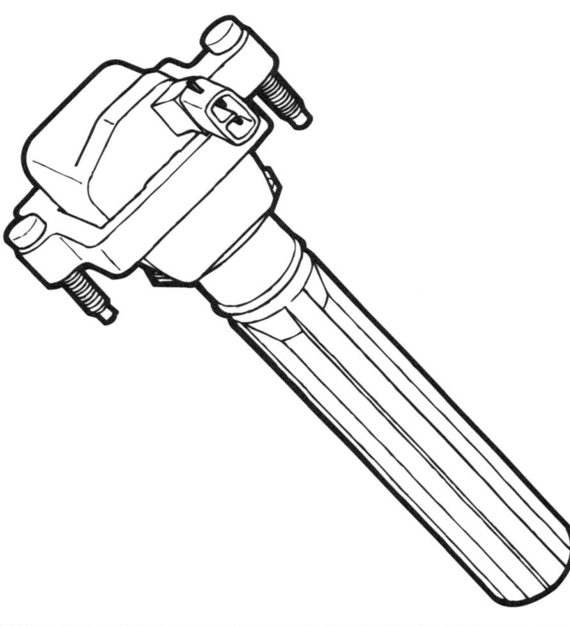

Figure 9-33. Two bolts secure this Chrysler direct ignition coil to the engine.

9-35. Fit the rubber boot seal over the tower, or DIS terminal, and squeeze it to remove any trapped air.

The cables used on some Chrysler engines have locking terminals that form the distributor contact terminal within the cap. To replace this type of cable, remove the distributor cap and compress the terminal ends with pliers, figure 9-36. Some distributor caps use a male ignition cable terminal that looks much like a spark plug. The cable end snaps onto the terminal instead of fitting down inside the cap tower.

Replacing Ignition Cables

To install new ignition cables, follow this procedure to avoid confusion and possible incorrect installation:

1. If the distributor cap uses locking terminals, remove the cap. If it is a traditional cap, leave it on the distributor and begin at cylinder number one and work in firing order sequence.
2. Disconnect only one cable from a spark plug and the distributor cap at a time.
3. Check the cap tower terminal for dirt, corrosion, or damage. Replace the cap if there is a heavy accumulation or damage.
4. Fit the new cable to the cap while squeezing the boot to remove any trapped air when it seats in place. Make sure the terminal is firmly seated and the rubber boot seals over the tower.
5. Connect the other end of the cable to the spark plug. Make sure the terminal and boot fit properly onto the plug terminal and the cable is routed as the original.
6. Repeat this procedure for each remaining cable, including the coil cable. Make sure that the cables are secured in their brackets and cannot contact the exhaust manifold or interfere with other electrical wiring.

DISTRIBUTOR CAP AND ROTOR SERVICE

Inspect the distributor cap and rotor for damage as described in Chapter Eight of this *Shop Manual*. Replace the parts if any sign of wear or damage is found. Never clean cap electrodes or the rotor terminal by filing. If electrodes are burned or damaged, replace the part. Filing changes the rotor air gap and increases secondary circuit resistance.

Replacing a Distributor Cap and Rotor

Most distributor caps are replaced by simply undoing spring-type clips, L-shaped lug hooks, or holddown screws, figure 9-37. Caps generally have a locating lug or slot for proper alignment, figure 9-38. More detailed descriptions are found in Chapter Ten of this *Shop Manual*. Lift the old cap off and install a new one. When replacing the cap, be sure to install the spark plug cables in correct firing sequence.

Rotors may be retained by holddown screws or simply fit onto the end of the distributor shaft. Rotors also use one or more locating lugs to correctly position them on the distributor shaft. Make sure the rotor is fully seated. If not, it can strike the cap and damage both the cap and rotor when the engine cranks and starts.

Copyright 2000 by Chek-Chart Publications

Figure 9-34. The Saab ignition discharge module, or direct ignition coil assembly, is serviced as a unit.

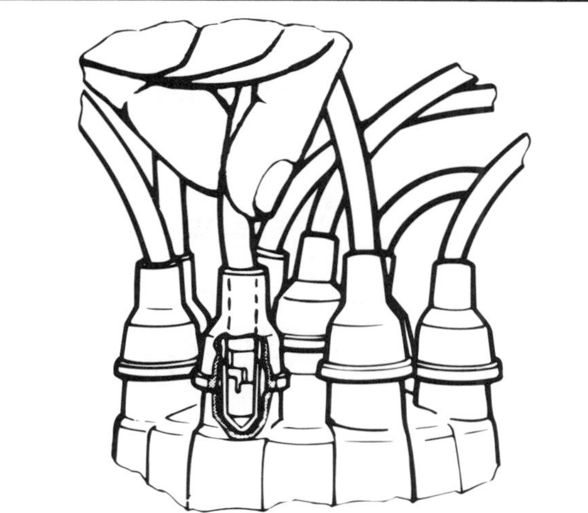

Figure 9-35. Make sure the cable end completely seats in the distributor cap.

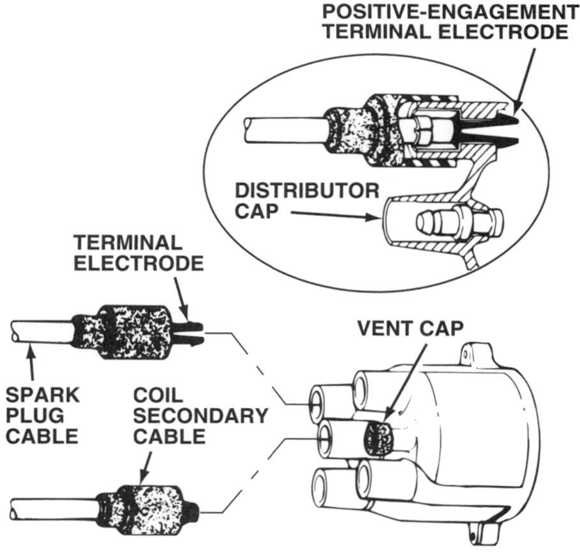

Figure 9-36. Some Chrysler spark plug cable ends lock to the cap and pliers are needed to remove them.

SPARK PLUG SERVICE

Spark plugs are routinely replaced at specific service intervals as recommended by the vehicle manufacturer. However, these intervals are guidelines and actual spark plug service life will vary. Spark plug life depends upon:

- Engine design
- Type of driving done
- Kind of fuel used
- Types of emission control devices used.

Since the spark plugs are the final component in all secondary circuits, the remainder of the circuit cannot perform properly if they are not in good condition.

Copyright 2000 by Chek-Chart Publications

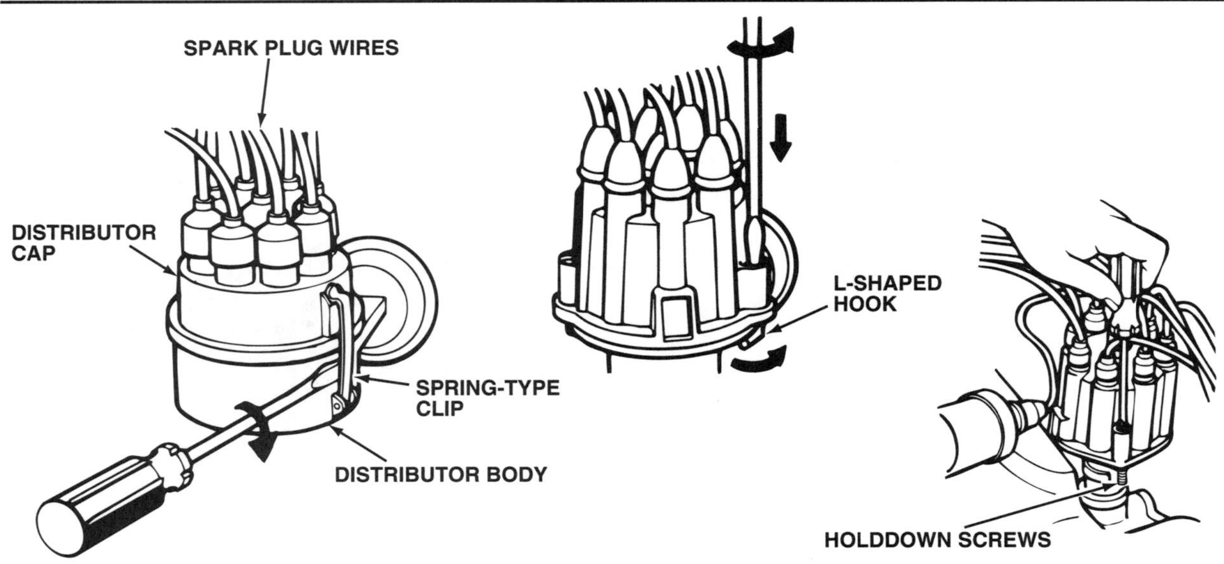

Figure 9-37. A number of methods are used to attach the cap to the distributor housing.

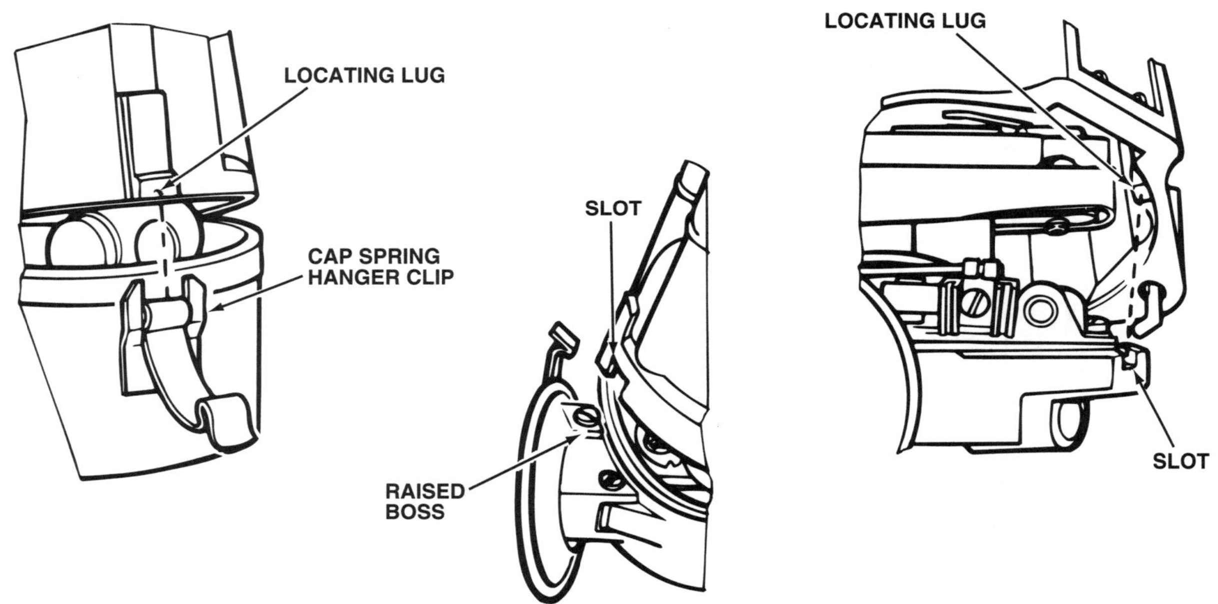

Figure 9-38. Most caps have a locating lug and install on the distributor in only one way.

Spark Plug Removal

Spark plug access is limited on many late-model engines due to a maze of air conditioning and emission control plumbing and engine-driven accessory mountings. Engine accessories may have to be loosened from their mountings and moved to get to the plugs. Air-conditioning compressors, air pumps, and power steering pumps are frequent candidates for relocation during spark plug service. When moving these accessories, be careful not to damage or strain any hoses and wiring attached to them. The spark plugs on some engines are most easily reached from underneath the vehicle. To remove the spark plugs:

1. Disconnect cables at the plug by grasping the boot and twisting gently while pulling. Do not pull on the cable. Insulated spark plug pliers provide a better grip and are recommended when working near hot manifolds, figure 9-39.

Copyright 2000 by Chek-Chart Publications

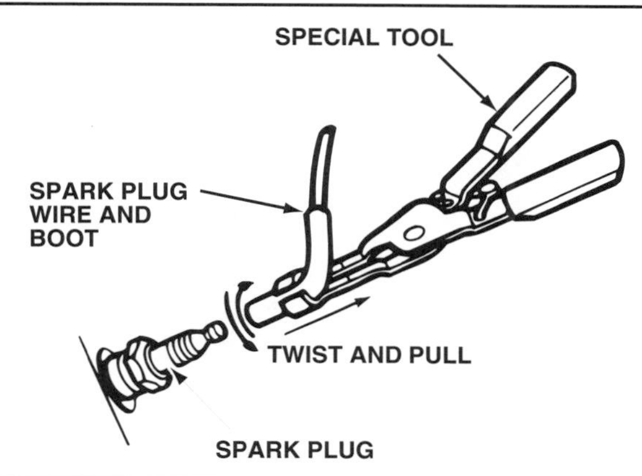

Figure 9-39. Twist and pull the boot with a cable pliers to separate it from the spark plug.

Figure 9-40. Normal used spark plug.

2. Loosen each plug one or two turns with a spark plug socket, then clear dirt away from around the plugs with compressed air.
3. Remove the plugs and keep them in cylinder number order for inspection.
4. When removing plugs with a gasket, be sure the old gasket comes out with the plug.

Spark Plug Diagnosis

Examining the firing ends of the spark plugs reveals a good deal about general engine conditions and plug operation. The insulator nose of a used plug should have a light brown-to-grayish color, and there should be very little electrode wear, figure 9-40. These conditions indicate the correct plug heat range and a healthy engine. Some common spark plug conditions that indicate problems follow.

Oil fouling

Dark, wet deposits on the plug tip are caused by excessive oil entering the combustion chamber, figure

Figure 9-41. An oil-fouled spark plug.

Figure 9-42. A carbon-fouled spark plug.

9-41. Piston ring, cylinder wall, and valve guide wear are likely causes in a high-mileage engine. Also, a defective PCV valve can draw oil vapor from the crankcase into the intake and oil-foul the plugs.

Carbon fouling

Soft, black, sooty deposits on the plug end indicate carbon fouling, figure 9-42. Carbon results from a plug that is operating too cold. Check for spark plugs with an incorrect heat range, an overly rich air-fuel mixture, weak ignition, inoperative manifold heat control valve, retarded timing, low compression, faulty plug wires or distributor cap. Carbon fouling may also result from overloading due to excessive stop-and-go driving.

Ash fouling

Certain oil or fuel additives that burn during normal combustion can create ash deposits, figure 9-43. Ash deposits are light brownish-white accumulations that form on and around the electrode. Normally, ash deposits are nonconductive, but large amounts may cause misfiring.

Copyright 2000 by Chek-Chart Publications

Figure 9-43. An ash-fouled spark plug.

Figure 9-44. A splash-fouled spark plug.

Figure 9-45. A spark plug with the gap bridged.

Figure 9-46. Insulator glazing on a spark plug.

Splash fouling
Small dark patches visible on the insulator indicate splash fouling, figure 9-44. Deposits breaking loose from pistons and valves and splashing against the hot plug insulator cause splash fouling. The condition often occurs after engine servicing that restores engine power and higher combustion temperatures. Splash-fouled plugs are generally cleaned and reinstalled.

Gap bridging
Gap bridging is usually due to conditions similar to those described for splash fouling, figure 9-45. The difference is that deposits form a bridge across the electrodes and cause a short that prevents firing. This condition is common in engines with poor oil control.

Insulator glazing
Shiny, yellow, or tan deposits are a sign of insulator glazing, figure 9-46. Frequent hard acceleration with a resulting rise in plug temperature causes glazing. The high temperature melts normal plug deposits and fuses them into a conductive coating that causes misfiring. Severe glazing cannot be removed and the plugs must be replaced.

Overheating
Spark plug overheating is indicated by a clean, white insulator tip, excessive electrode wear, or both, figure 9-47. The insulator may also be blistered. Incorrect spark plug heat range, incorrect tightening torque, overadvanced timing, a defective cooling system, or a lean air-fuel mixture may be the cause of overheating.

Detonation
Detonation causes increased heat and pressure in the combustion chamber that exerts extreme loads on engine parts. Fractured or broken spark plug insulators are a sign of detonation, figure 9-48. Overadvanced timing, a lean fuel-air mixture, low gasoline octane, and engine lugging are contributing factors. An EGR valve that fails to open is also a cause of detonation.

Copyright 2000 by Chek-Chart Publications

Figure 9-47. Overheating causes excessive spark plug electrode wear.

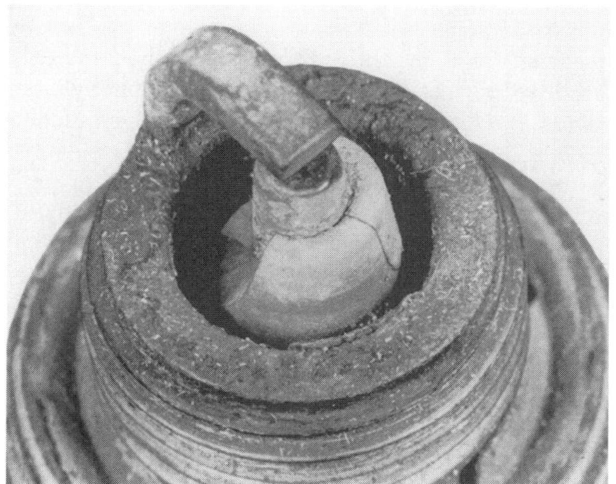

Figure 9-48. A detonation-damaged spark plug.

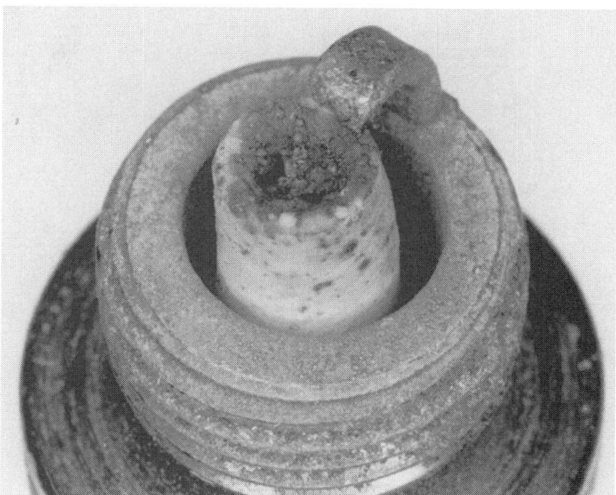

Figure 9-49. A preignition damaged spark plug.

Figure 9-50. An excessively worn spark plug.

Preignition

Preignition, which is the air-fuel charge igniting before the plug fires, causes severe damage to the spark plug electrodes, figure 9-49. Combustion chamber hot spots or deposits that hold enough heat to prematurely ignite the air-fuel charge are common causes of preignition. Other sources of preignition include crossfiring between plug cables, a plug heat range much too hot for the engine, and loose spark plugs.

Even if the color of the insulator and deposits is normal, rounded and worn electrodes indicate that a plug should be replaced, figure 9-50. These plugs are simply worn out. The voltage required to arc across the gap has increased and continues to do so with additional use. Misfiring under load is a clue to worn-out plugs. Such plugs also contribute to poor gas mileage, loss of power, and increased emissions.

Another problem that may be seen on a spark plug is carbon tracking down the insulator. Tracks appear as dark gray lines running the length of the insulator. This problem has become more common as newer spark plug designs tend to have shorter, and smooth-sided, insulators.

Spark Plug Installation

Spark plugs, both new and used, must be correctly gapped before they are installed. Although a wide variety of gapping tools is available, a round wire feeler gauge is the most efficient for used plugs, figure 9-51. Adjust the gap by carefully bending the ground electrode, figure 9-52.

- Do not assume that new plugs are correctly gapped.
- Do not make gap adjustments by tapping the electrode on a workbench or other solid object. This causes internal plug damage.

Cleaning the threaded plug holes in the cylinder head with a thread chaser ensures easy spark plug

Copyright 2000 by Chek-Chart Publications

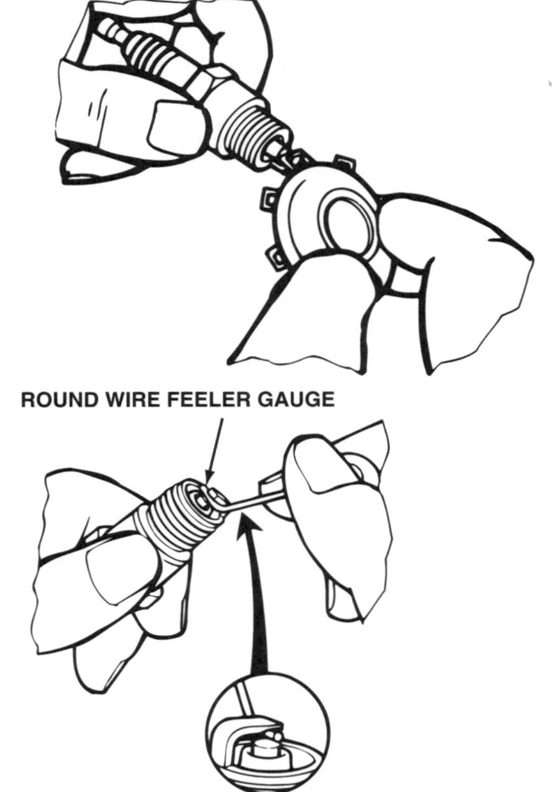

Figure 9-51. Checking spark plug gap with a feeler gauge.

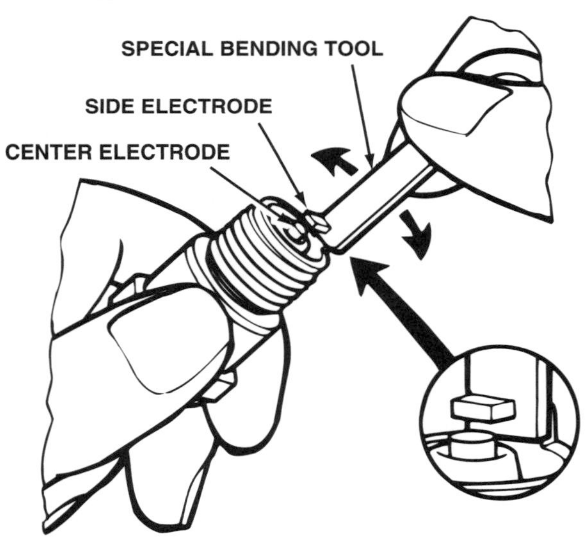

Figure 9-52. Adjust spark plug gap by carefully bending the side electrode.

PLUG TYPE	CAST-IRON HEAD		ALUMINUM HEAD	
	Foot-Pounds	Newton-Meters	Foot-Pounds	Newton-Meters
14-MM Gasketed	25-30	34-40	13-22	18-30
14-MM Tapered Seat	7-15	9-20	7-15	9-20
18-MM Tapered Seat	15-20	20-27	15-20	20-27

Figure 9-53. Always tighten spark plugs to the specified torque value.

installation. With aluminum heads, use the tool carefully to avoid damaging the threads.

Some manufacturers recommend using an antiseize compound or thread lubricant on the plug threads. Use thread lubricant only when specified by the manufacturer. Antiseize compound is commonly used when installing plugs in aluminum cylinder heads. Be sure to use the specific compound recommended by the manufacturer, as not all are compatible with aluminum. Whenever thread lubricant or antiseize is used, reduce the tightening torque slightly.

Once the plug gap has been properly set, install plugs as follows:

1. Wipe any dirt and grease from the cylinder head plug seats.
2. Check that any gaskets used on the plugs are in good condition and installed.
3. Fit the plugs in the engine and run them in by hand.
4. Tighten the plugs to specification with a torque wrench, figure 9-53.

Copyright 2000 by Chek-Chart Publications

10 Distributor Service

This chapter contains general procedures to remove, disassemble, test, repair, and install the distributor of a modern electronic ignition system. Procedures are similar for all makes and models, and these instructions apply to most distributor repair services. Always check the vehicle service manual for exact procedures and specifications. Overhaul procedures for five common domestic distributor models are presented as photographic sequences at the end of this chapter.

A modern distributor is an engine-driven switch assembly. The assembly typically contains two switches; a primary switch that provides an engine speed or position signal to the ignition control module (ICM), and a secondary switch that routes secondary voltage to the spark plugs. The ICM is part of the assembly on some distributors. Some distributor services, such as replacing the cap and rotor, are generally performed without removing the distributor from the engine. On some models, it is possible to replace the pickup coil, Hall-effect switch, or ICM with the distributor installed in the engine. However, it is often easier to remove the distributor and service it on the bench.

With the exception of V8-powered General Motors light trucks, the only domestically produced vehicles in current production that use a distributor are those with import engines, such as the 3.0L Mitsubishi V6 in Chrysler minivans, the Chevrolet Metro built by Suzuki, and the Nissan-powered Mercury Villager. Distributors are also used on some late-model vehicles from BMW, Honda, Nissan, Mercedes-Benz, Mitsubishi, Saab, Toyota, and Volvo. Although designs vary considerably, all distributors are serviced in a similar fashion.

Some late-model distributors, such as those used by BMW and Mercedes-Benz, are simply a secondary switch driven off the camshaft. The rotor bolts to a flange at the end of the camshaft and the cap bolts onto the camshaft cover. An O-ring seals the cap to the cover. Opening and closing the primary coil circuit is controlled by the PCM. The PCM receives speed and position inputs from sensors mounted elsewhere on the engine. A periodic inspection of the cap, rotor, and O-ring, which are replaced on an as-needed basis, is the only distributor service required.

Copyright 2000 by Chek-Chart Publications

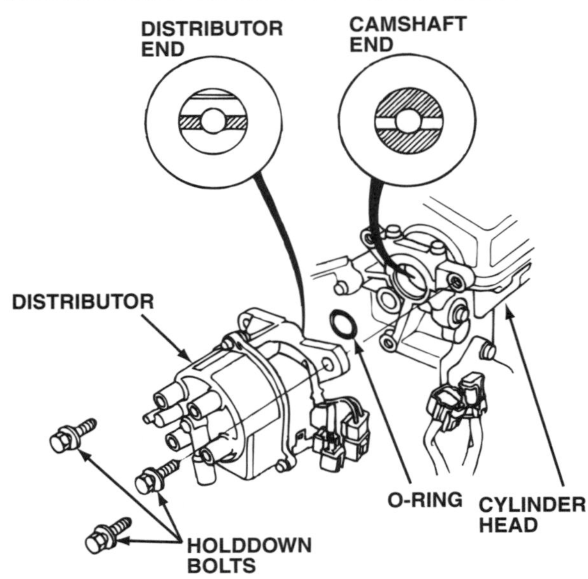

Figure 10-1. Three bolts attach this Honda camshaft-driven distributor to the cylinder head.

DISTRIBUTOR REMOVAL AND INSPECTION

The principles of distributor removal are the same for all systems, although the exact details will vary somewhat according to manufacturer and engine. Many distributors require loosening or relocating other engine accessories, such as the air cleaner or air intake ducts, in order to remove them. It may be helpful to tag all electrical leads and vacuum lines that are disconnected during distributor removal. Also, be sure to observe all electrical safety precautions and shop safety regulations during distributor removal and installation. It is always advisable to disconnect the negative battery cable to prevent accidental arcing when servicing the distributor. If not, make sure the ignition is switched off.

Removal

The distributors used on some late-model engines are driven directly off the end of the camshaft. An offset drive dog attached to the distributor shaft engages a machined slot in the camshaft, figure 10-1. Cylinder positioning has no effect on distributor removal or installation because the drive connects to the camshaft in only one position. These distributors usually have two or three slotted ears that fit over studs in the cylinder head and are retained by nuts. Remove the distributor simply by removing the nuts and lifting the assembly from the engine.

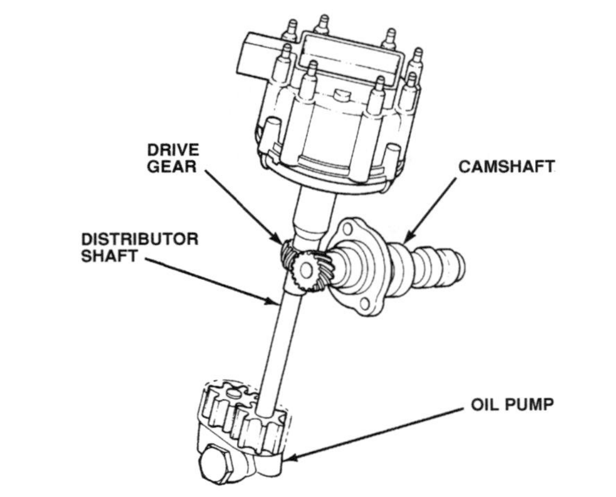

Figure 10-2. Distributor and oil pump drive are taken off the same camshaft gear on many designs.

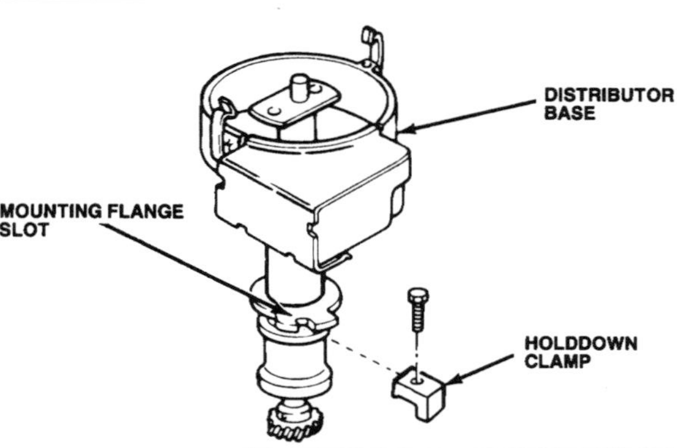

Figure 10-3. Many distributors are attached to the engine with a holddown clamp and bolt.

Most distributors install into a machined bore in the engine block and are gear-driven. A helical, or bevel, gear on the distributor gear engages a spiral gear on the camshaft or auxiliary shaft in the engine, figure 10-2. Many distributors are held in the engine with a holddown clamp and a bolt, figure 10-3. The clamp rides over a mounting flange on the distributor base. A machined slot on the distributor housing fits over a threaded stud on the engine block on other designs. A nut secures the distributor assembly to the engine. With either type, once the mounting fasteners are removed, the distributor should lift off the engine fairly easily. Be sure to mark the position of the distributor on the engine before loosening the holddown fasteners, figure 10-4. To remove a typical distributor:

Copyright 2000 by Chek-Chart Publications

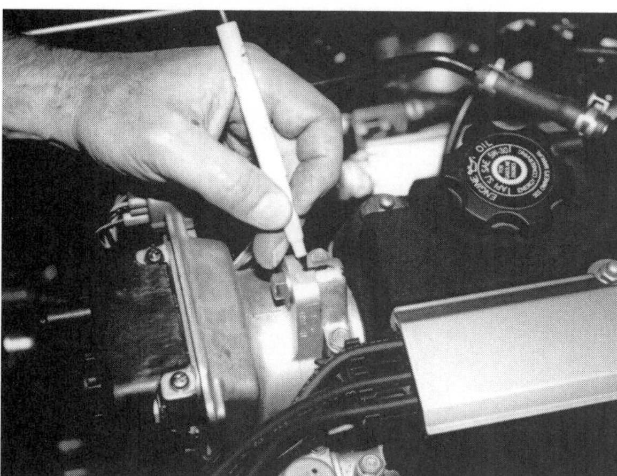

Figure 10-4. Mark the distributor position on the engine before loosening fasteners.

1. Disconnect and remove the distributor cap. On most engines, the ignition cables do not need to be disconnected from the cap; simply position the cap and wires out of the way.
2. Using a wrench on the crankshaft pulley bolt, rotate the engine by hand so that the number one cylinder is up to top dead center on the compression stroke, or the distributor rotor points straight ahead or up.
3. Mark a reference point on the distributor housing in line with the position of the rotor tip. Also mark reference points on the distributor housing and engine so the distributor can be installed in the same position, figure 10-5.
4. Disconnect the primary circuit wiring to the distributor. Disconnect any vacuum lines attached to the distributor as well.
5. Loosen and remove the distributor holddown fastener along with the holddown bracket, if used. Offset "distributor" wrenches make loosening difficult-to-reach fasteners easy, figure 10-6.
6. Twist the distributor housing gently to loosen it from the engine, then remove the distributor by pulling it up and out of the engine block bore, figure 10-7. Do not use force to remove the distributor; it should come out easily. If the distributor is stuck in the bore, it is likely the result of a dry and hardened O-ring seal. Apply a little penetrating oil to loosen it.
7. The shaft of a gear driven distributor rotates slightly as the assembly is removed and the gears disengage. Note how far the rotor moves off the reference mark as the distributor is removed. Install the distributor with the rotor in this position.

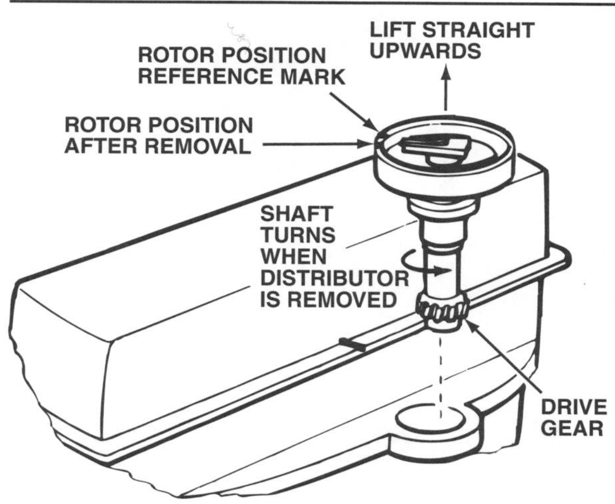

Figure 10-5. Make rotor and engine position reference marks on the distributor housing for easy assembly.

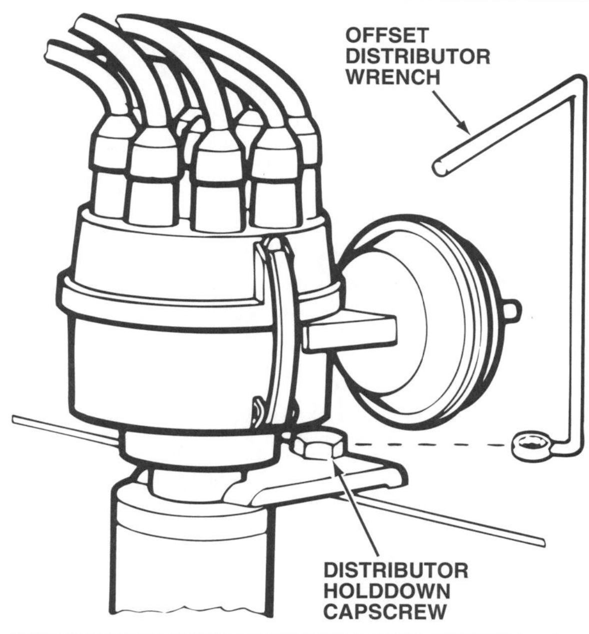

Figure 10-6. An offset wrench is needed to loosen holddown fastener on some distributors.

8. After removing the distributor, cover the engine block bore with a shop rag to keep dirt and contaminants out of the crankcase.

Many distributors have an O-ring seal that installs on the housing. Whenever the distributor is removed, inspect the O-ring and replace it as needed. Carefully remove O-rings to prevent scratching the housing,

Copyright 2000 by Chek-Chart Publications

Figure 10-7. With a slight twist to break the seal, most distributors slip easily from the bore.

figure 10-8. A metal sealing ring installs between the bottom of the distributor housing and the engine on some models. If a metal sealing ring is used, be sure to install it when fitting the distributor. Some older distributors use a gasket between the housing and the engine block.

Some engines, such as older small-block Ford V8s, use an intermediate shaft between the oil pump and the distributor. This shaft should remain in the engine when the distributor is removed. However, sludge buildup inside the engine may cause the shaft to stick in the distributor drive gear and disengage the oil pump as the distributor is removed. If the shaft comes all the way out with the distributor, there is no problem because it is easily reinstalled. But, a shaft that comes part way out and then drops off into the engine while the distributor is being removed causes a serious problem. The shaft generally falls into the front of the oil pan or timing cover, which must be removed to retrieve it.

To avoid dislodging an intermediate shaft, slowly and carefully lift the distributor just enough to reach under the housing to the bottom of the drive gear. If the intermediate shaft is coming out with the distributor, grasp it and remove it along with the distributor. Do not attempt to push the shaft back in place because it has already pulled free of the oil pump. To install an intermediate shaft, hold it firmly with a special gripping tool or long-nosed snapring pliers and lower it into the engine. Rotate the shaft to engage the drive dog with the oil pump, then release the gripping tool.

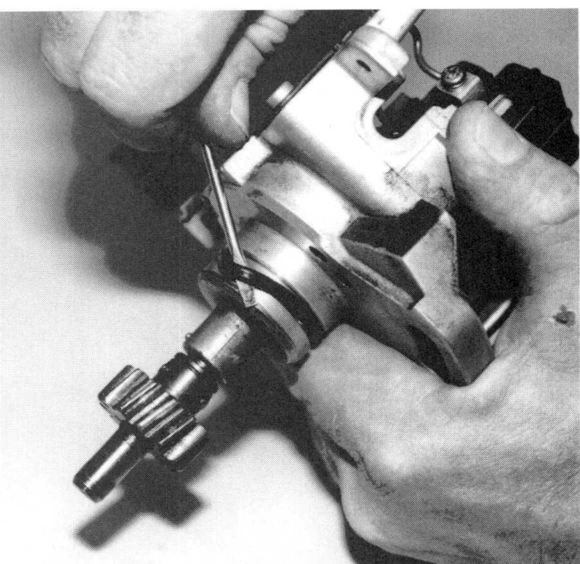

Figure 10-8. Use a screwdriver or pick to remove an O-ring.

Make sure the shaft is completely seated before installing the distributor.

Some other distributor installations have unique features that require special handling and procedures as well. Always check the service manual for the vehicle being repaired for information and specifications.

Inspection

Once the distributor is removed, use solvent and a brush to clean all oil, grease, dirt, and rust from the distributor shaft and housing. Take care to keep solvent away from the bushings, electronic components, and vacuum advance unit, if used. Dry the distributor with low-pressure compressed air and perform a preliminary inspection. Look for:

- Binding or excessive shaft movement, check end play and side play
- Worn or chipped drive gear teeth, or dog lugs, figure 10-9
- Loose or damaged electrical leads and terminal connections
- Loose or damaged component mountings
- Signs of inadequate lubrication.

If the distributor is to be serviced, install it in a bench vise with protective, or soft, jaws. If protective jaws are not available, wrap the distributor housing with shop rags to protect it. Avoid overtightening the vise, as the aluminum distributor housing is easily distorted and damaged.

Copyright 2000 by Chek-Chart Publications

Figure 10-9. Inspect the drive gear or dog for signs of wear and damage.

If shaft end play and side play feel excessive, check for wear using a dial indicator. Attach the dial indicator base to the distributor housing or the vise. The housing is preferable as it eliminates false readings from the housing moving in the vise. Position the indicator plunger on the top end of the shaft, slightly preload the plunger, and zero the dial face. Then, push up on the base of the shaft and take an indicator reading. This is the end play; compare results to specifications. Too much end play is often the result of a worn thrust washer, which usually installs under the drive gear.

To measure side play, move the indicator plunger to the side of the shaft, preload the plunger, and zero the dial face. Next, firmly grasp the distributor housing and rock the shaft back and forth. Side play is displayed on the dial indicator; compare readings to specifications. Excessive side play is the result of worn bushings or bearings, or a bent shaft. To check for a bent shaft, leave the dial indicator in position and watch the dial face while rotating the shaft through one complete revolution. If the dial indicator shows excessive runout, the shaft is bent and must be replaced.

Check the movement of the advance mechanism on older-model distributors that use mechanical weights or a vacuum diaphragm to advance the spark timing. To check mechanical systems, simply hold the shaft and twist the advance mechanism. The weights should move freely without binding and fully extend to stops, then return smoothly under spring force when released. If not, expect to find damaged bearings or bushings, or built-up dirt and corrosion between parts on disassembly. Use a hand vacuum pump to check a vacuum advance unit. Apply vacuum while watching the movement of the breaker plate. Again, watch for smooth and full movement during application and release.

Continuity of electronic devices installed in the distributor, such as a pickup coil, Hall-effect switch, optical sensor, or ignition control module, is checked with an ohmmeter before disassembly. Test points and specifications vary by model. Refer to the appropriate service manual for exact procedures.

Once the distributor has been inspected, it is possible to determine what repairs are needed to return it to service. With late-model distributors, it is often more economically feasible to replace the entire unit, rather than overhaul it. In fact, individual components are not always available to rebuild a distributor. Always consider the options and follow the course of repair that best suits the needs of the customer.

DISTRIBUTOR DISASSEMBLY AND ASSEMBLY

Distributor designs vary not only by manufacturer and engine, but often by model and year as well. Therefore, it is important to have accurate service instructions and specifications available. The procedures presented here are general and apply to most distributor overhauls. Photographic sequences that detail the overhaul of several popular domestic distributors are included following the general guidelines. Whenever a distributor is to be overhauled, read through the entire procedure in the service manual before beginning the teardown. Also be sure to have any required special tools and anticipated replacement parts available before disassembly.

Disassembly

Follow the service manual procedures and disassemble the distributor into component pieces, figure 10-10. This usually involves removing the drive gear, which is attached to the shaft with a retainer pin or snapring. Before removing the drive gear, mark it and the shaft to ensure they are in the same position on assembly. When driving out the retainer pin, make sure the distributor shaft is firmly supported to prevent damage, figure 10-11. The drive gear is an integral part of the shaft on some models. Other components, such as base plates, electronic devices, and advance mechanisms attach to the shaft or housing with small bolts, snaprings, circlips, springs, or other fasteners. Keep track of where the fasteners install, as fitting

Copyright 2000 by Chek-Chart Publications

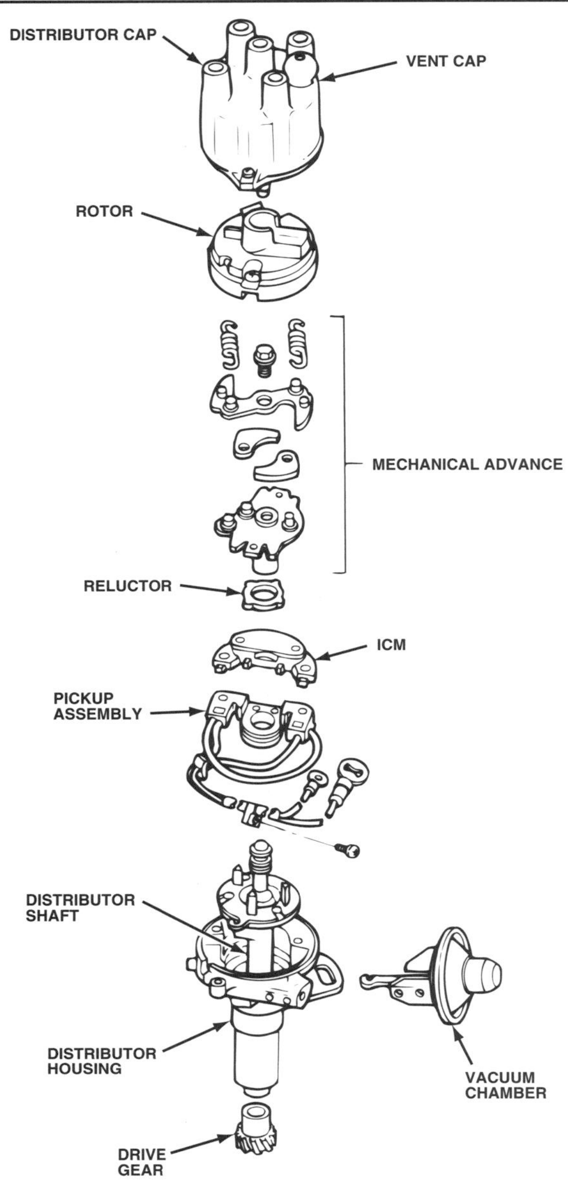

Figure 10-10. An exploded view diagram is a handy reference when overhauling a distributor.

them in the wrong location on assembly may interfere with shaft rotation or advance movement.

Most distributor shafts are supported by bushings that press-fit into the housing. However, some models use bearings rather than bushings. If the bushings or bearings require replacement, the best way to remove them is with a bushing puller. A brass drift and a hammer may be used to drive the bushings or bearings out of the housing on some models. When using a drift, take care to avoid scratching or nicking the housing bore. Also, work slowly from side to side when driving out a bushing to avoid cocking it in the bore.

Figure 10-11. Support the distributor shaft to drive out a gear retainer pin.

Once the distributor is disassembled, clean the inside of the distributor and all the moving parts, except vacuum units, with solvent and a small brush. Dry the clean parts with low-pressure compressed air. Make sure that all dirt and solvent residue are removed, especially from electrical connections. Wipe dirt off with a clean, lint-free cloth or swab with electrical contact cleaner. Carefully inspect all components for signs of damage or wear and replace parts as needed.

Assembly

Refer to the service manual instructions to correctly assemble the distributor. Always replace any O-rings or gaskets that seal the housing to the engine. Lightly lubricate all moving parts during assembly. Keep in mind, proper lubrication is essential, but too much lubrication causes problems. Distributor rotation sprays excess lubricant around the inside of the distributor where it collects dirt and causes short circuits.

Use the correct-size bearing or bushing driver to install new bearings or bushings into the distributor housing. Make sure the bearings or bushings install straight in the bore and are fully seated. With bushings, it may be necessary to ream the inside diameter to provide adequate shaft clearance once they are installed. Be sure to thoroughly clean bushing chips and shavings from the assembly after reaming.

Copyright 2000 by Chek-Chart Publications

Many solid-state distributors require that a silicone lubricant or heat sink compound be applied to specific locations within the distributor. Typical points are on the ignition module base, primary connections, rotor contact tip, and distributor connections. The silicone lubricant prevents corrosion and moisture that might interfere with voltage signals. A thin film of heat sink compound is generally applied to the mounting base of the module to help dissipate heat. Avoid applying excess lubricant or heat sink compound.

Once the distributor is assembled, check shaft rotation, end play, and side play. Also check the movement of any advance mechanisms used as previously described. Perform a few quick ohmmeter checks to verify the continuity of replacement electronic parts.

DISTRIBUTOR INSTALLATION

After the distributor has been serviced, follow these general directions to install it on the engine:

1. Make sure the negative battery cable is disconnected or the ignition is switched off to prevent accidental arcing.
2. Check that the number one cylinder of the engine is at top dead center of the compression stroke and in firing position.
3. Rotate the distributor shaft to align the rotor with the reference mark on the housing, figure 10-12. Turn an additional amount, as noted during removal, to compensate for gear engagement.
4. Align the distributor housing mark with the reference point on the engine.
5. If an O-ring or gasket is used, make sure it is in position. Lightly lubricate O-rings with motor oil to ease installation.
6. Insert the distributor into the engine, turn the rotor slightly as needed to engage the drive gears, and push lightly to seat the distributor.
7. Make sure the distributor is fully seated in the engine and engaged with the camshaft and oil pump drive.

Figure 10-12. Turn the shaft to align the rotor with the mark made earlier on the distributor.

8. Check that the rotor and reference mark are aligned. If out of position, note the amount. Then raise the distributor up, reposition the rotor the same amount, and lower it back into place.
9. When installing a distributor that attaches directly to the camshaft end, align the tangs on the distributor shaft with the slots in the end of the camshaft. Seat the distributor against the cylinder head and install the fasteners.
10. Fit the distributor holddown clamp, fasteners, and any other items used to hold the distributor in the engine. Draw the mounting fasteners up snugly, but do not fully tighten them.
11. Connect the distributor primary wiring connectors. Also attach the vacuum lines to the advance unit, if used.
12. Install the distributor cap and any other items removed during disassembly. Then, connect the negative battery cable.

After installing the distributor, start and run the engine. Check base ignition timing as described in Chapter Eleven of this *Shop Manual.* Adjust timing as needed, where applicable, then fully tighten the distributor holddown fastener.

Copyright 2000 by Chek-Chart Publications

DISTRIBUTOR OVERHAUL PROCEDURES

The following pages contain photographic procedures to disassemble, overhaul, and reassemble several common domestic solid-state distributors. Included are the:

- Delco-Remy 8-cylinder HEI model
- Delco-Remy 4-cylinder HEI-EST model
- Motorcraft Universal TFI-I model
- Chrysler 4-cylinder Hall-effect model
- Chrysler 6-cylinder optical distributor.

Chapter Thirteen of the accompanying *Classroom Manual* has additional information and illustrations of these distributors. Refer to the *Classroom Manual* as needed when overhauling a distributor. Using techniques previously explained in this chapter, inspect and test distributor components at appropriate times during the overhaul procedure.

Keep in mind, all of the distributors discussed here were used for a number of years on an assortment of models. As a result, there may be some slight variations between the examples shown and the actual distributor being serviced. Remember, these photographic sequences are for instructional purposes only and are not to be substituted for the factory service manual procedures.

Copyright 2000 by Chek-Chart Publications

DELCO-REMY 8-CYLINDER HEI DISTRIBUTOR OVERHAUL PROCEDURE

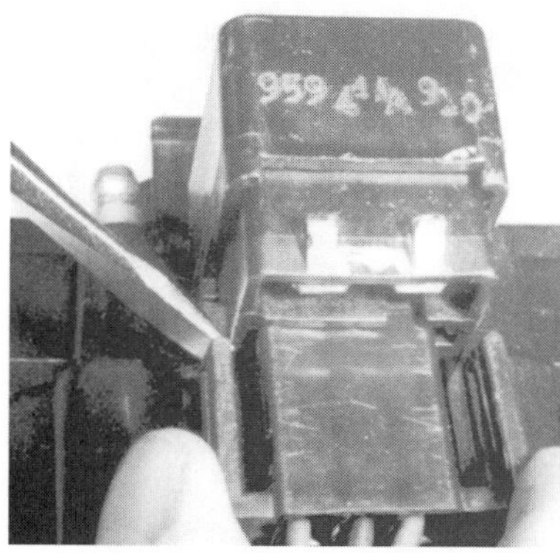

1. Carefully pry the module connector from the cap terminal with screwdriver. Release the four latches and remove the cap and coil from distributor.

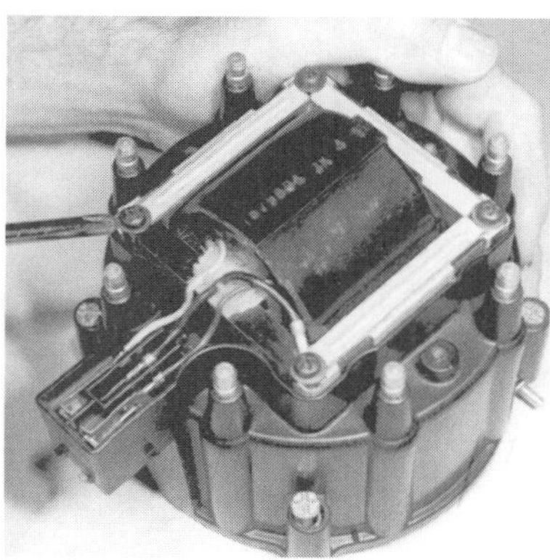

2. Remove the three screws from coil cover, then remove the four coil mounting screws. Note the position of the ground leads, then lift off the coil.

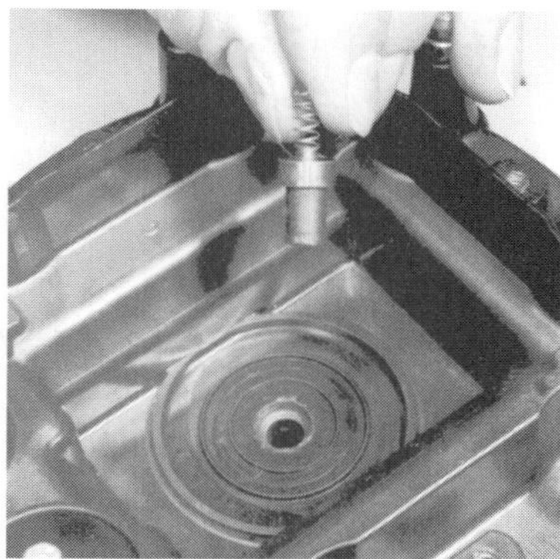

3. Remove the rubber seal, carbon button, and spring. If the seal is brittle, replace it. The button and spring are the secondary coil lead; replace them if worn or broken.

4. Remove the two attachment screws and lift off the rotor. Note the location of the pickup coil leads, tag them if needed, then disconnect them from the module.

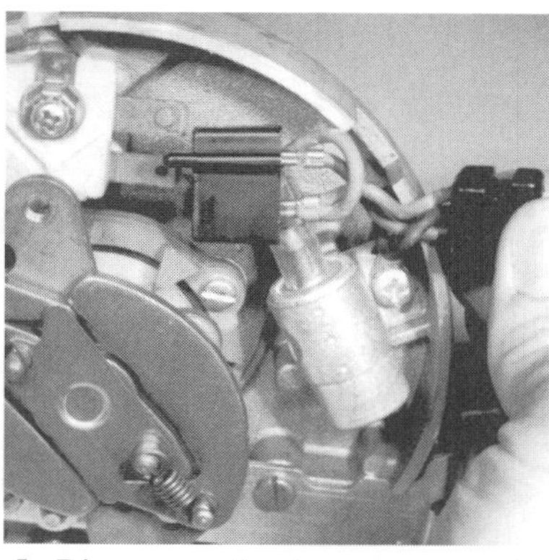

5. Disconnect the harness connector from the terminals on the opposite end of the module and slip the primary lead grommet from distributor housing.

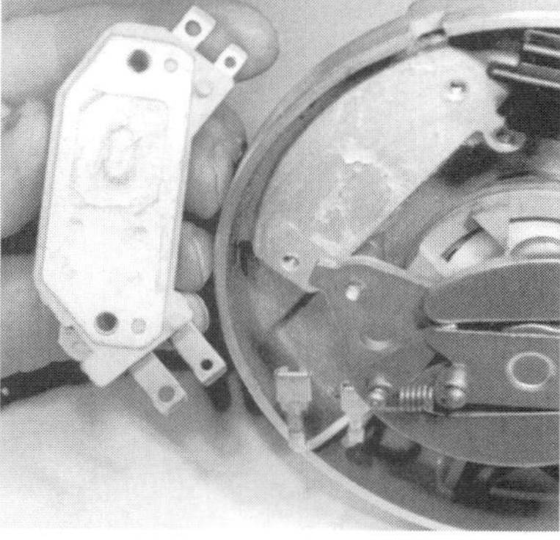

6. Remove the two mounting screws and lift the module off the distributor. Wipe the silicone grease from the module and mounting base. Apply fresh grease on assembly.

7. Remove the screw securing the RFI capacitor and lift capacitor and primary lead harness from the distributor housing.

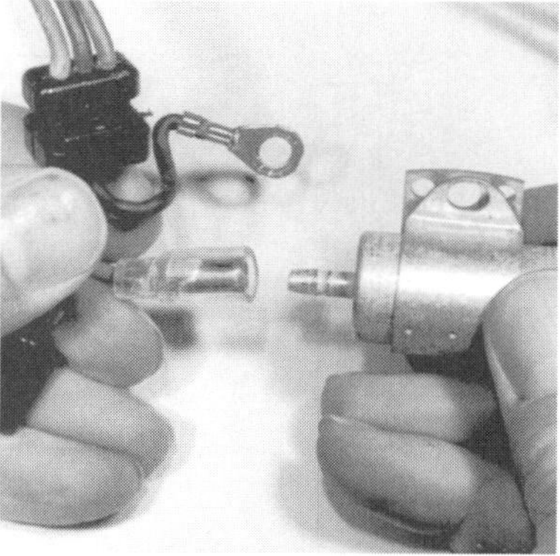

8. Disconnect the capacitor from the primary lead. Inspect and test the capacitor and primary lead for wear, continuity, and short circuits. Replace worn or damaged parts.

9. Make position marks on the advance springs, pins and weights for ease of assembly. Then, remove the two springs, weight retainer, and weights.

Copyright 2000 by Chek-Chart Publications

DELCO-REMY 8-CYLINDER HEI DISTRIBUTOR OVERHAUL PROCEDURE

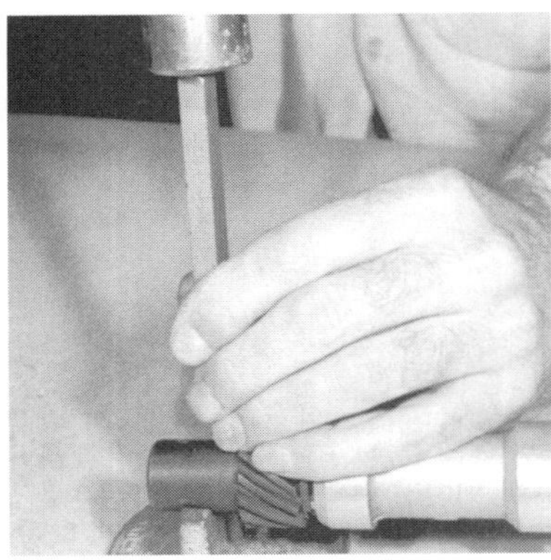

10. The shaft must be removed to remove pickup coil and pole piece. Support the gear as shown and drive out the roll pin to separate the gear and shaft.

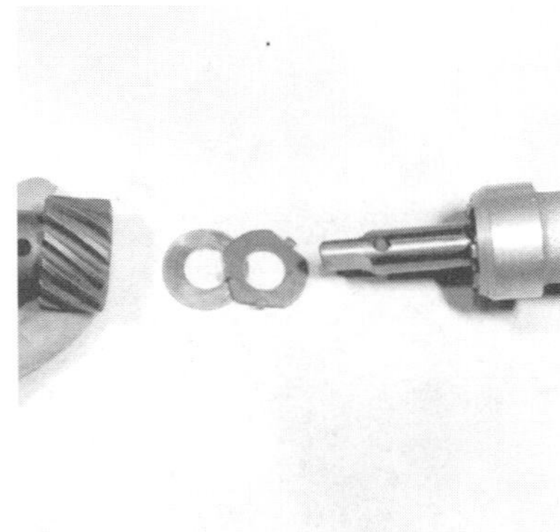

11. Remove the drive gear, shim, and tabbed washer. Note positions for assembly. The dimple toward bottom of gear must align with the rotor tip when assembled.

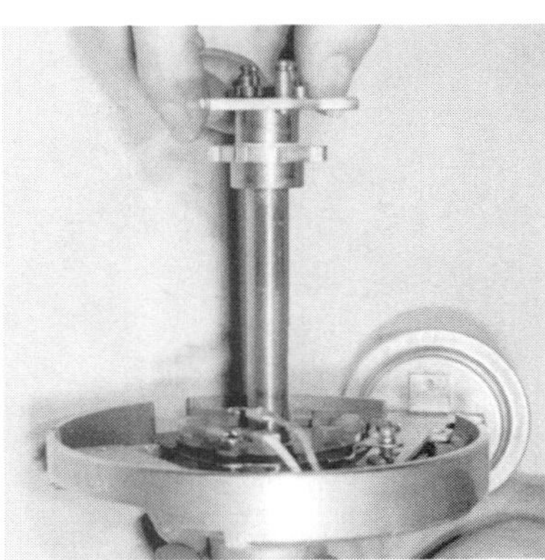

12. Carefully remove the shaft, trigger wheel, and weight base from the distributor to avoid damaging the bushings. Separate the trigger wheel from the shaft.

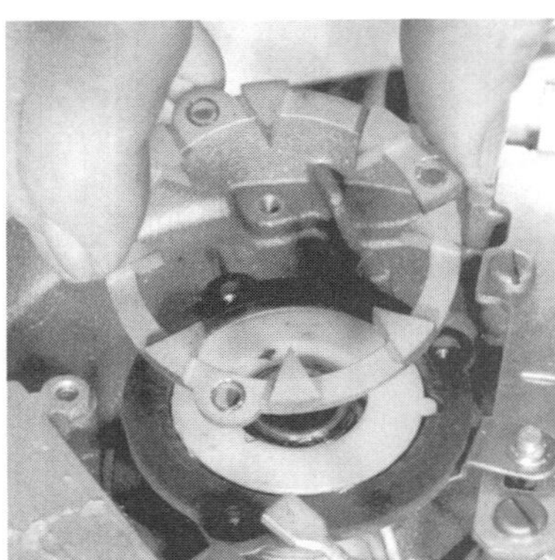

13. Remove the three screws attaching the pole piece to the pickup coil. Remove the pole piece along with the rubber gasket installed beneath it.

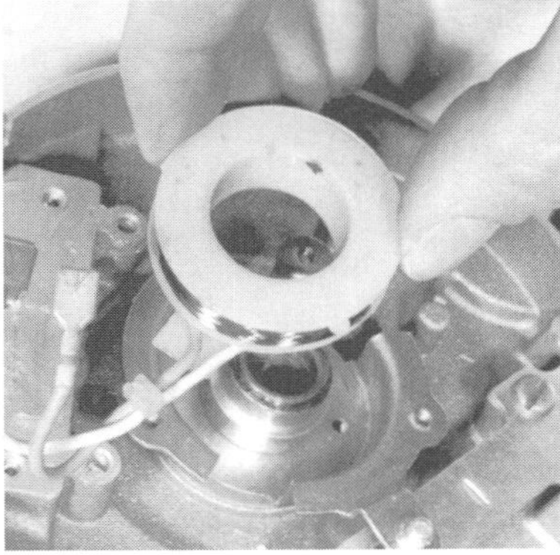

14. Slip the pickup coil from the retainer and lift it off the distributor. During operation, the retainer is rotated by vacuum to advance timing.

15. The pickup coil retainer is fastened to the bushing at the top of housing with a waved washer. Carefully pry the washer from its slot.

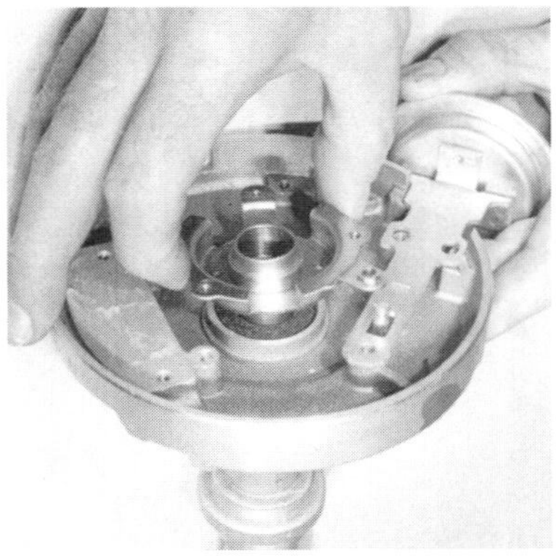

16. Separate the vacuum advance link and lift off the pickup coil retainer along with the felt washer beneath it. Remove the two mounting screws and the vacuum unit.

17. To assemble, lubricate or replace felt washer beneath pickup coil retainer and apply a thin coat of silicone grease to module mounting base.

18. Fit the vacuum unit and assemble the pickup coil into the housing. Tighten the vacuum unit screws and make sure the wave washer seats in the bushing to hold the pickup coil retainer.

Copyright 2000 by Chek-Chart Publications

DELCO-REMY 8-CYLINDER HEI DISTRIBUTOR OVERHAUL PROCEDURE

19. The trigger wheel assembles onto the distributor shaft. Make sure parts are clean and lubricate the bushings with fresh motor oil. Avoid using too much oil.

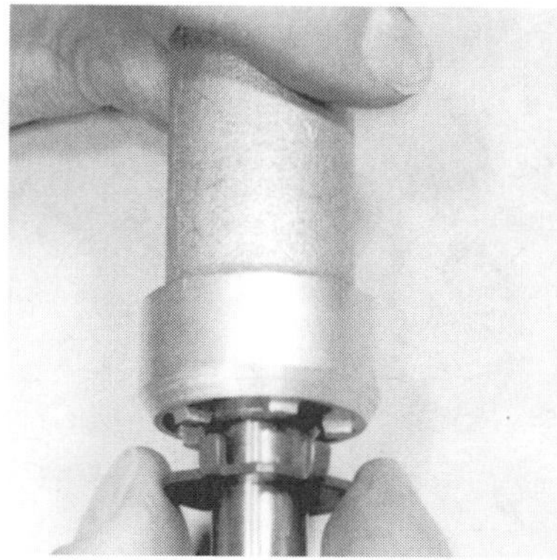

20. Carefully insert the distributor shaft and trigger wheel assembly into the housing to avoid hitting the bushings. Assemble the washer, shim, and gear onto the shaft.

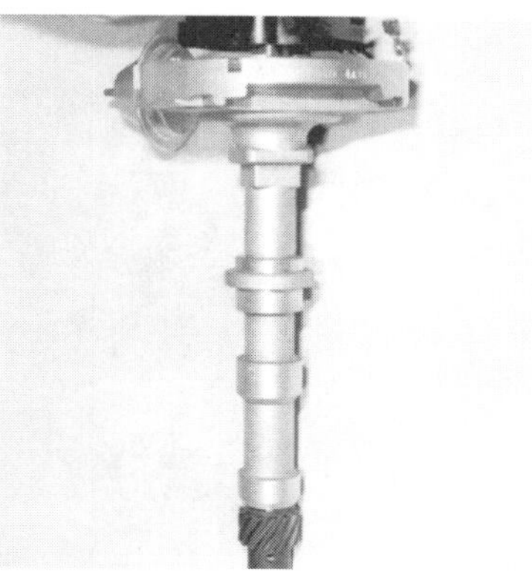

21. The drive gear is correctly installed if the dimple on the gear aligns with the rotor tip. If so, drive the roll pin through gear and shaft to secure it.

22. Assemble the advance weights in their original positions onto the shaft base plate. Fit the retainer over the pins and shaft, then install the springs in their original positions.

23. Connect the primary harness to the capacitor and fit the harness grommet into the housing slot. Install the capacitor in the distributor and tighten the screw.

24. Apply heat sink compound to the module, then attach it on the mounting base with two screws. Remember, these are ground connections and they must be clean and tight.

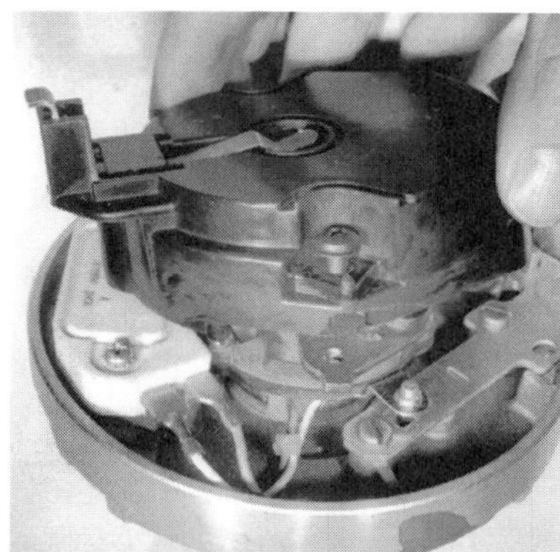

25. Attach the primary connector and pickup coil leads to the module, then check shaft rotation and advance movement. Fit the rotor and tighten two screws.

26. Fit the carbon button and spring into the cap and install the rubber seal. Then, fit the coil into the cap.

27. Install the coil mounting screws and the coil cover. Place the cap on the distributor and secure it with the hold-down latches.

Copyright 2000 by Chek-Chart Publications

DELCO-REMY 4-CYLINDER HEI-EST DISTRIBUTOR OVERHAUL PROCEDURE

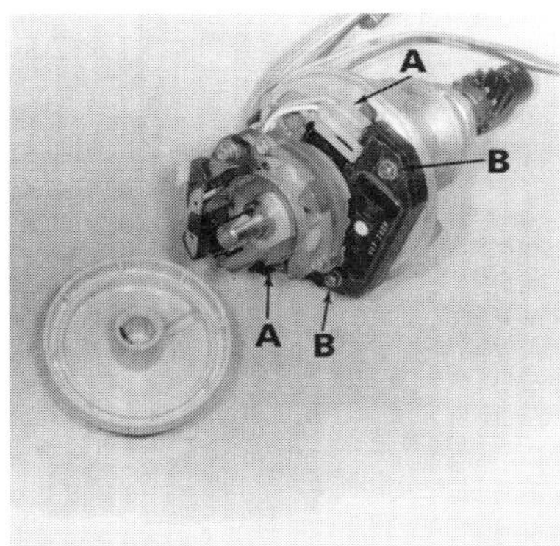

1. Pull the rotor straight off the shaft. Unclip and disconnect the leads on both sides of the HEI-EST module (A), then remove the module screws (B).

2. Lift the HEI-EST module from the distributor base. Clean the base of any silicone lubricant left by the module.

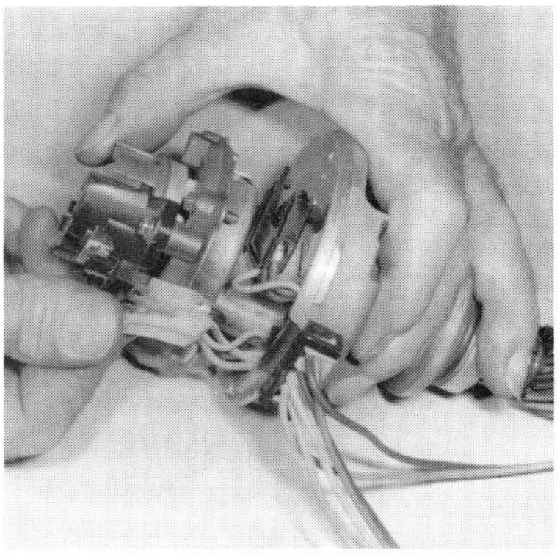

3. This Hall-effect switch provides the EST signal. Carefully unclip and remove the electrical connector from the Hall-effect switch.

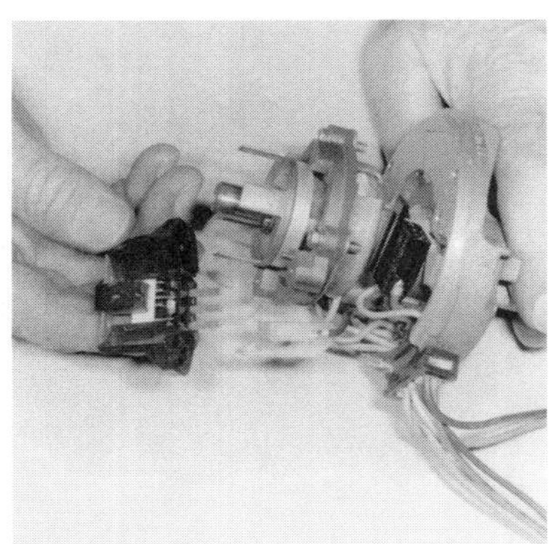

4. Remove the two screws holding the Hall-effect switch to the pickup coil assembly and lift the Hall-effect switch from the distributor.

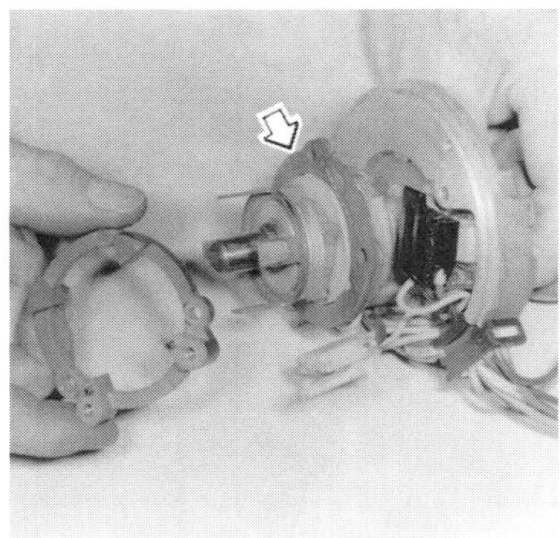

5. Remove the three screws holding the pole piece and magnet assembly. Remove the pole piece first, then remove the magnet (arrow).

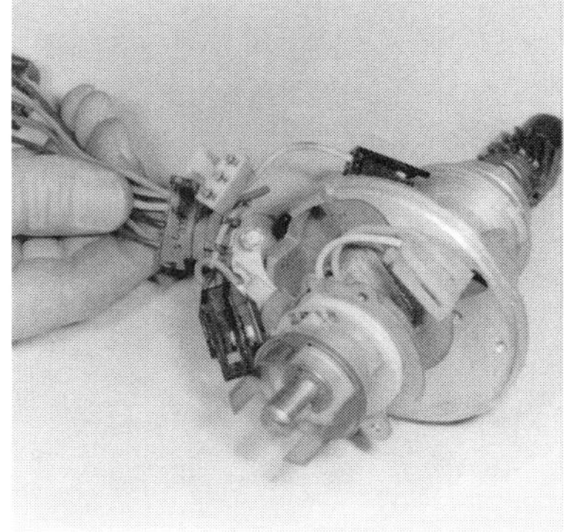

6. Remove the screw holding the wiring harness to the distributor housing and lift off the wiring harness.

Copyright 2000 by Chek-Chart Publications

DELCO-REMY 4-CYLINDER HEI-EST DISTRIBUTOR OVERHAUL PROCEDURE

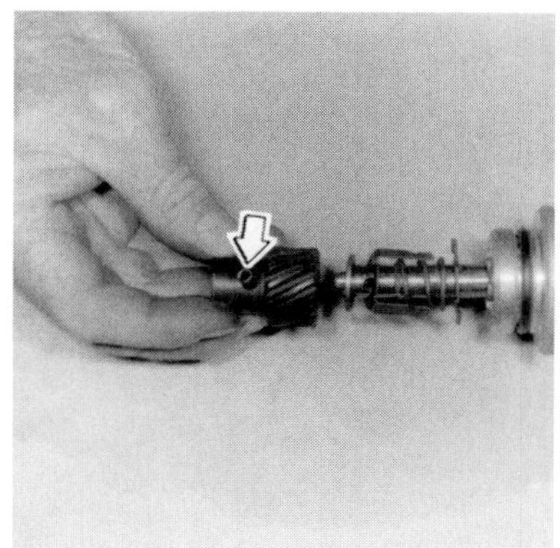

7. Drive out the roll pin (arrow) with a suitable punch to free the drive gear. Remove the drive gear, small washer, spring assembly, and large washer.

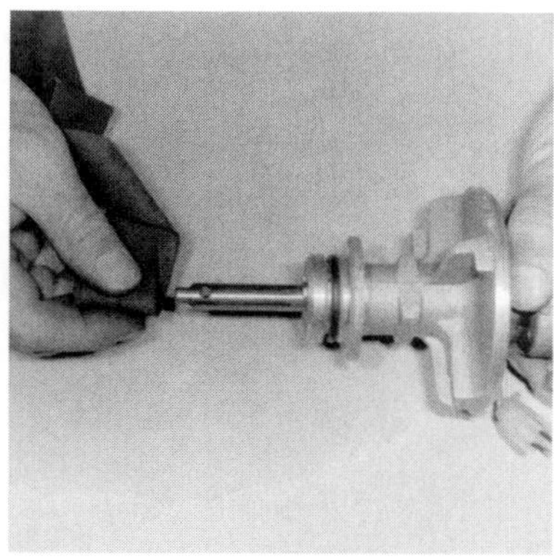

8. Deburr the distributor shaft with crocus cloth to prevent damage to the housing bushings when the shaft is removed.

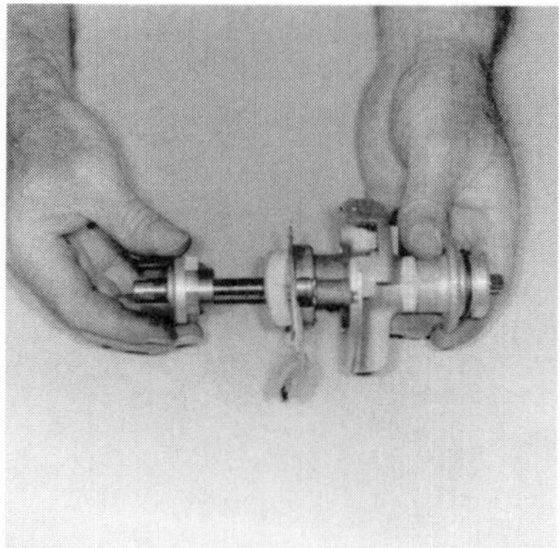

9. Carefully withdraw the shaft along with the attached shutter blade and trigger wheel from the distributor housing.

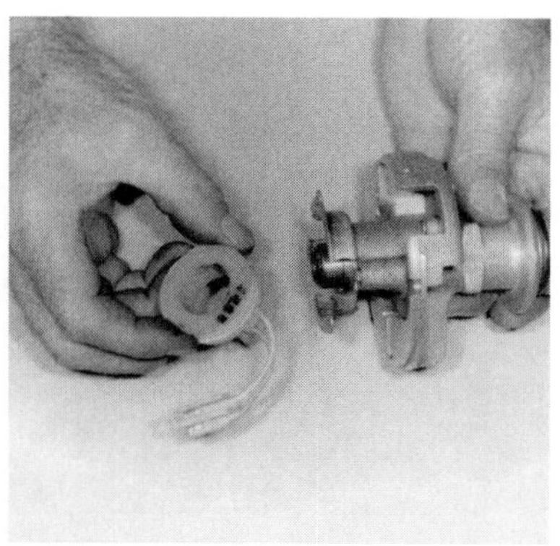

10. Remove the magnetic pulse pickup coil from the cup on the distributor base.

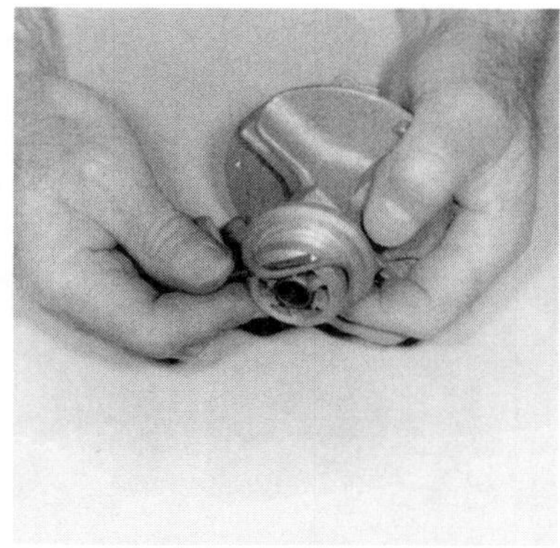

11. Use a small screwdriver as shown to remove the O-ring on the housing base. Install a new O-ring.

12. Assemble the distributor in reverse order. Be sure to apply a thin coat of silicone lubricant to the module base before installing it on the distributor base.

Copyright 2000 by Chek-Chart Publications

MOTORCRAFT UNIVERSAL TFI-I DISTRIBUTOR OVERHAUL PROCEDURE

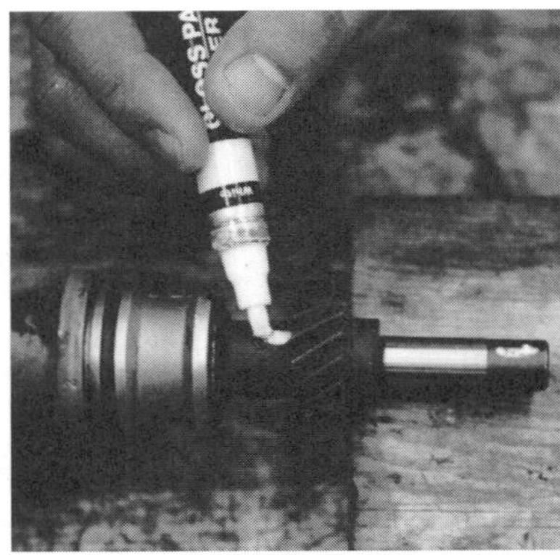

1. Remove and set aside the cap and rotor. Then, make reference marks on the distributor shaft and drive gear for correct positioning on assembly.

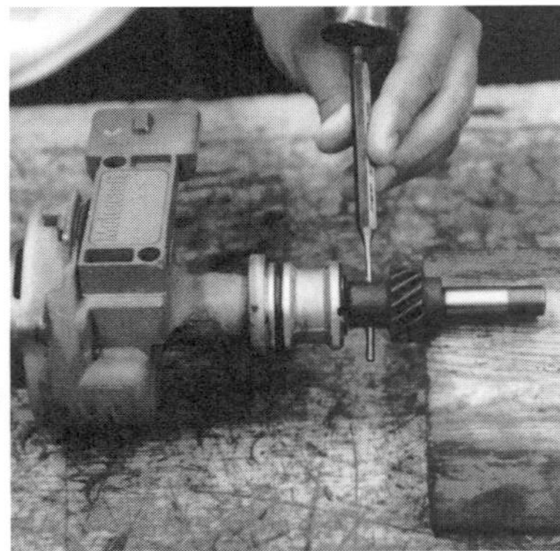

2. Support the distributor shaft and gear and use a pin punch and hammer to drive the roll pin completely out.

3. A special gear puller is available to remove the gear from the shaft. Remove the gear with a suitable puller.

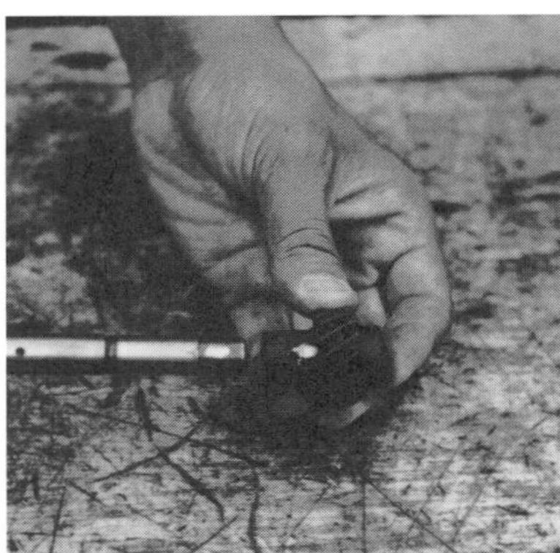

4. Once the gear is removed, clean any built-up varnish and debris from the end of shaft to prevent scoring the bushings when the shaft is removed.

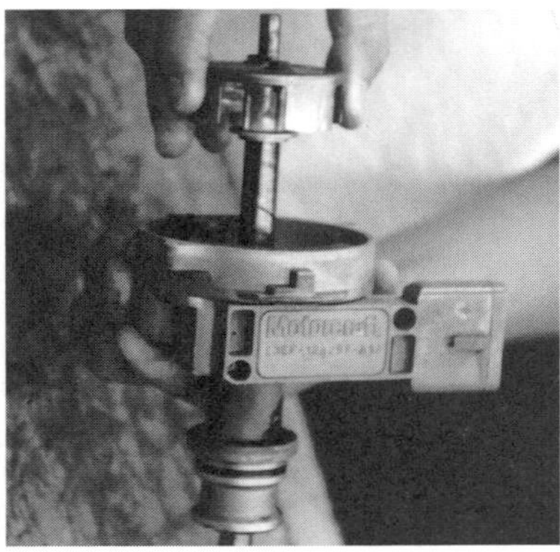

5. Carefully withdraw the distributor shaft from the distributor housing. Penetrating oil and a few light hammer taps may be needed to free the shaft.

6. Remove the two bolts holding the module in place. Then, slide the module down to disconnect the terminals and remove it from the housing.

7. Remove the two bolts that attach the magnet portion of the stator assembly to the distributor housing.

8. Remove the single bolt that attaches the stator bracket to the distributor housing.

9. Carefully pry up the stator bracket to free it from the pin on the pickup assembly, then slide the bracket out of the housing.

Copyright 2000 by Chek-Chart Publications

MOTORCRAFT UNIVERSAL TFI-I DISTRIBUTOR OVERHAUL PROCEDURE

10. Lift the stator assembly, which includes the pickup and the magnet, out of the distributor housing.

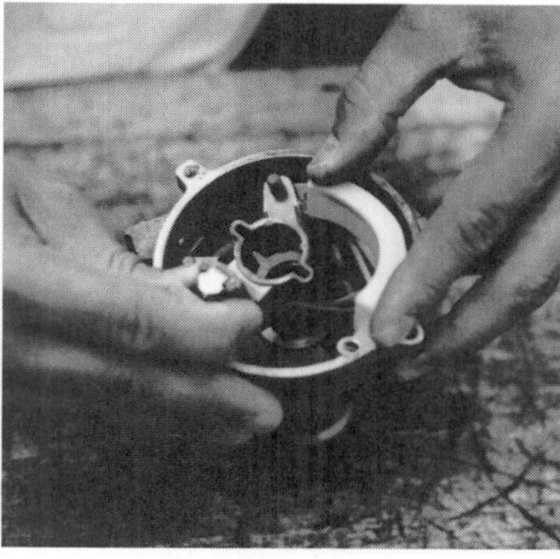

11. Fit the new stator assembly into the housing so that the magnet bolt holes align and the pickup pin is correctly positioned.

12. Fit the bracket into the housing and onto the pin. Then, install and tighten the bracket screw and the two magnet screws.

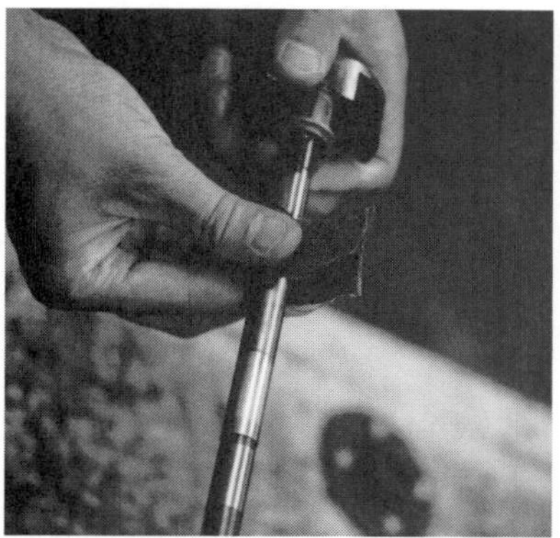

13. Polish the load-bearing area of the distributor shaft with crocus cloth to remove any nicks, burrs, or scratches. Then, slip the shaft into the housing.

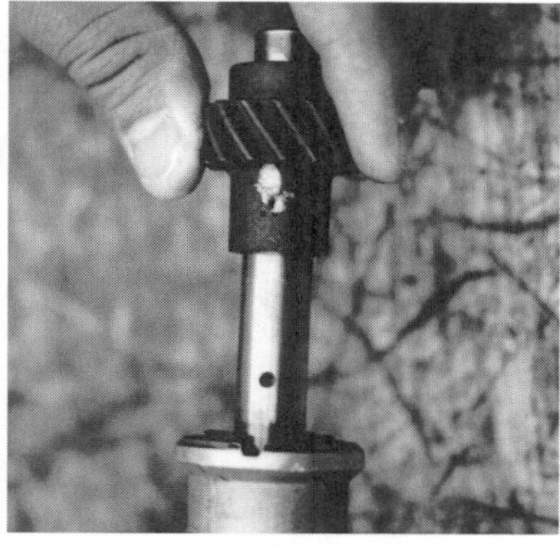

14. Carefully position the drive gear so the reference marks and the pin bores are aligned. Use a press to seat the gear on the shaft.

15. Press the gear on slowly and carefully until the bore on the gear aligns with that of the shaft. When correctly aligned, the pin should start by hand.

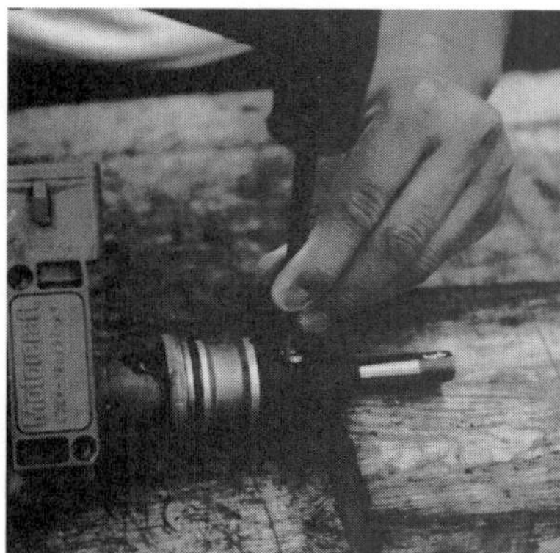

16. Install the roll pin using a punch and hammer. Drive the pin in until it is flush with the gear.

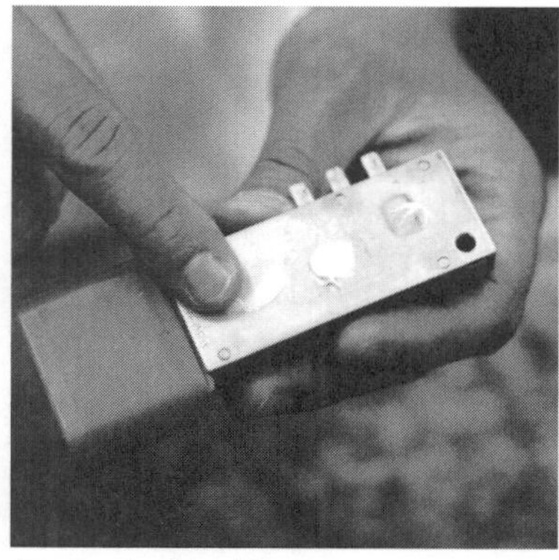

17. Apply the silicone grease supplied with the new part on the back of the module in an even coat.

18. Fit the new module into the connector terminals and onto the housing. Install the two module screws and the cap and rotor to complete the overhaul.

Copyright 2000 by Chek-Chart Publications

CHRYSLER 4-CYLINDER HALL-EFFECT DISTRIBUTOR OVERHAUL PROCEDURE

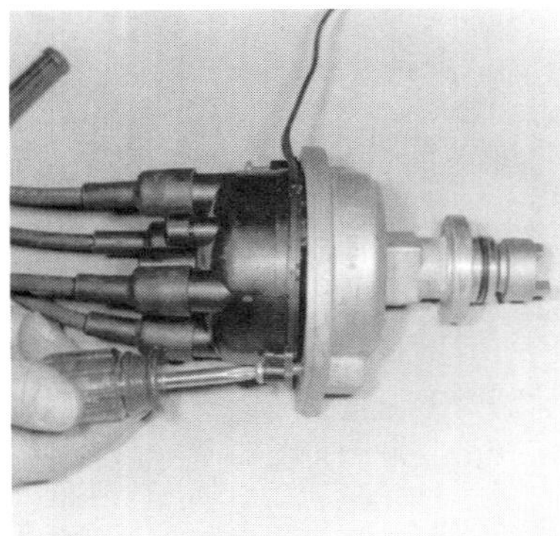

1. Loosen the two screws holding the distributor cap to the base. Lift the cap straight off to prevent rotor damage.

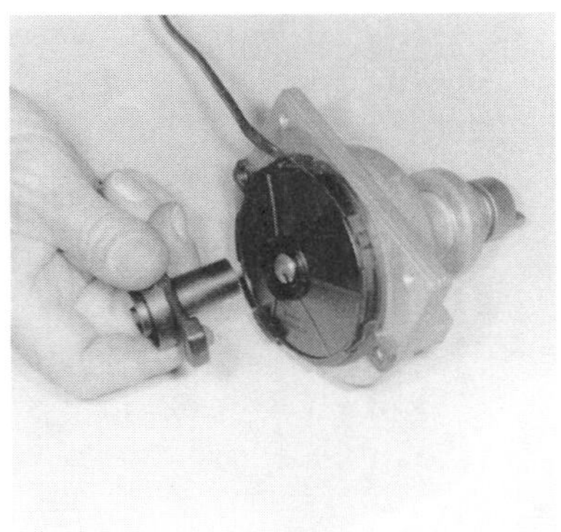

2. The rotor has an internal tab that fits into a slot in the shaft; pull the rotor straight off the distributor shaft.

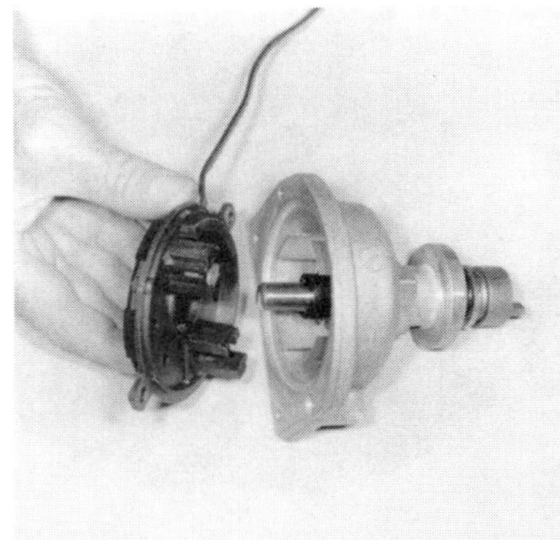

3. Lift off the Hall-effect pickup assembly. This unit is held in place by the distributor cap screws and is loose when the cap is removed.

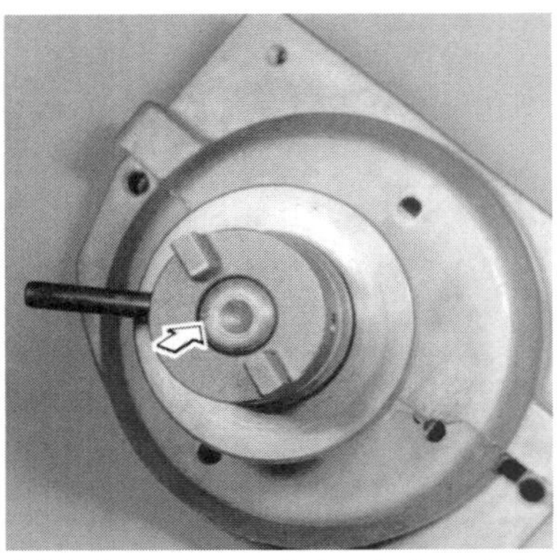

4. Mark the base of the shaft and the drive dog (arrow) to provide an alignment reference for assembly.

5. Support the drive end of the distributor, Then, carefully drive the roll pin out of the drive and shaft with a punch and hammer.

6. Remove the drive dog from the shaft, deburr the end of the shaft with crocus cloth, then carefully pull the shaft from the housing.

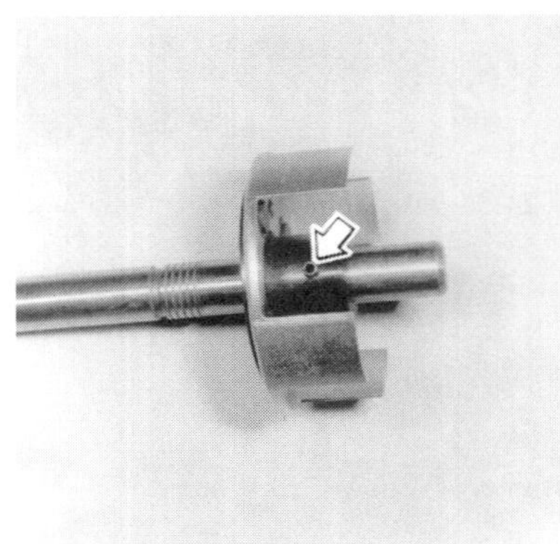

7. A small roll pin (arrow) fastens the shutter blade to the distributor shaft. Remove and install with a small punch and hammer as needed.

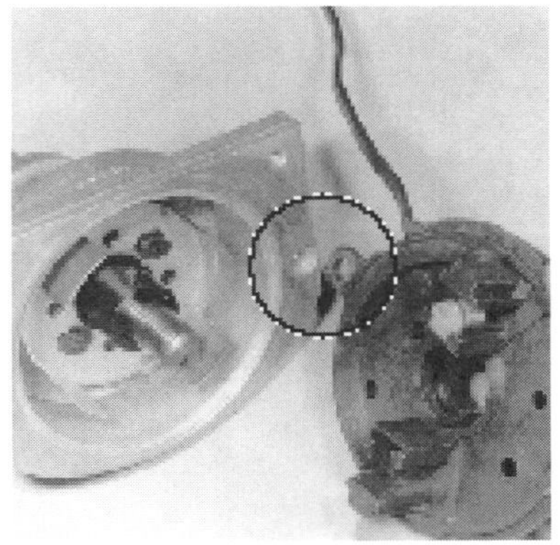

8. A tab on the Hall-effect pickup fits a recess in the housing to align the assembly. Make sure the pickup is fully seated.

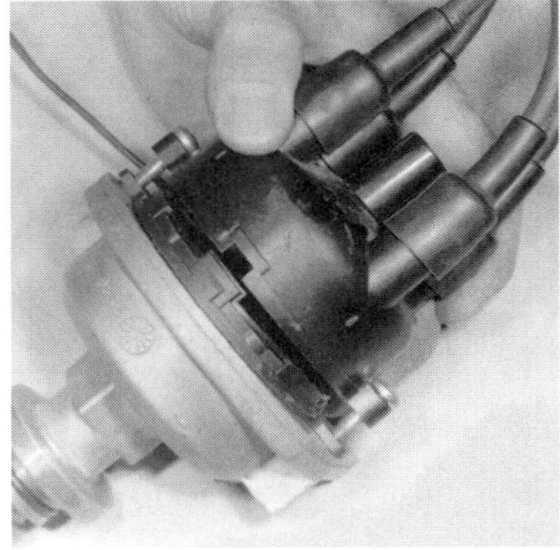

9. Fit the cap onto the Hall-effect pickup and distributor assembly. Make sure everything is aligned, then tighten the two screws to complete the assembly.

Copyright 2000 by Chek-Chart Publications

CHRYSLER 6-CYLINDER OPTICAL DISTRIBUTOR OVERHAUL PROCEDURE

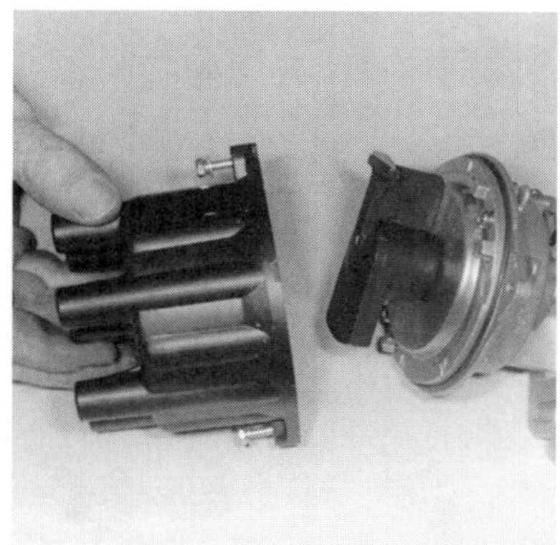

1. Loosen the two screws holding the distributor cap to the housing and remove the cap.

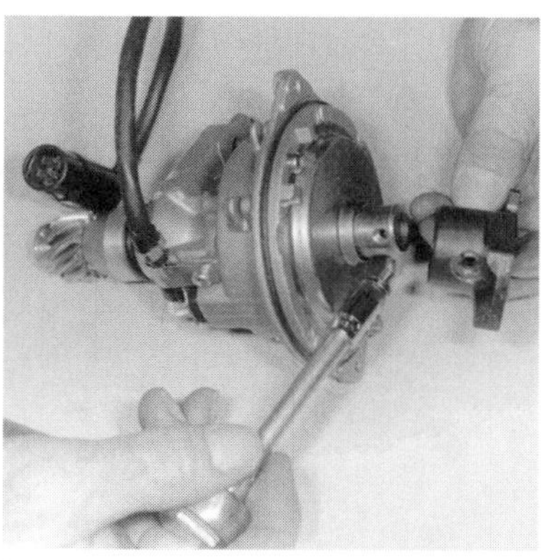

2. A screw underneath the rotor holds the rotor to the distributor shaft. Remove the screw and slip the rotor off the shaft.

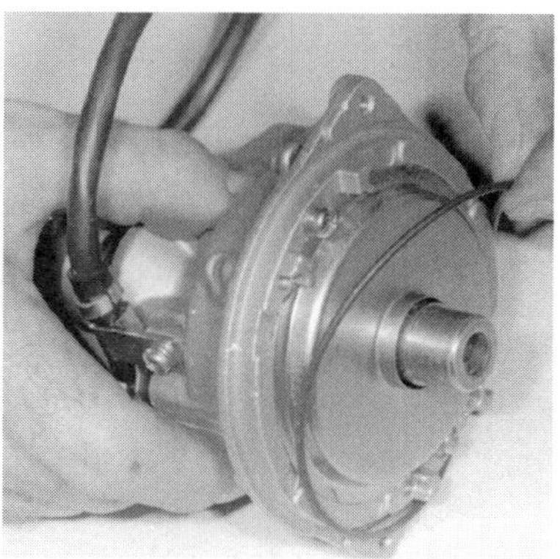

3. Carefully remove the O-ring that seals the cap to the distributor housing. Reuse the O-ring if it is not damaged or deteriorated.

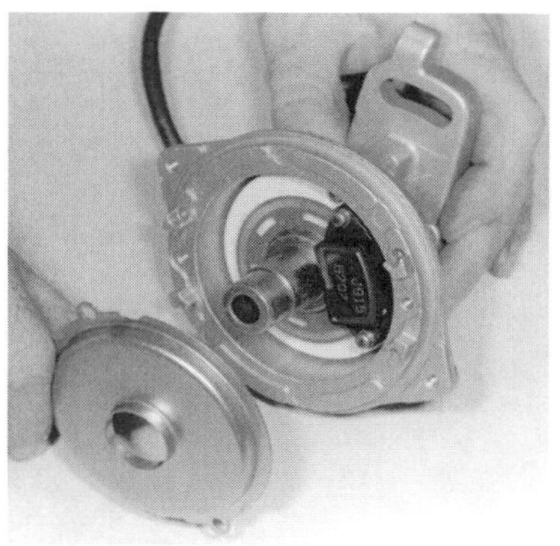

4. Remove the dust cap from the housing. This cap reduces electromagnetic interference (EMI) to prevent contamination of the sensor signal.

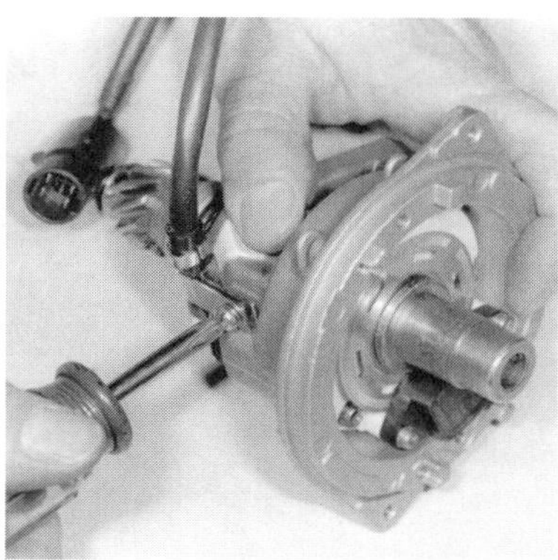

5. A screw attaches the wiring harness to the housing. Remove the screw, then disconnect the harness from the optical sensor.

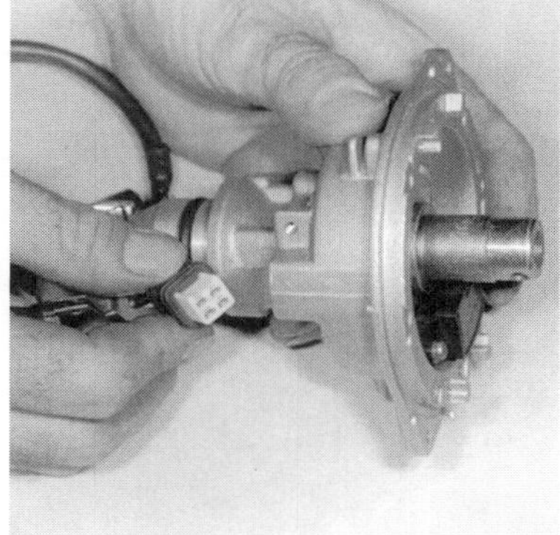

6. Gently work the wiring harness connector plug and weatherproof seal free and remove it from the base of the distributor.

7. Note that the screws holding the optical module are sealed with epoxy (A); do not try to remove them. Remove the screw in the center of the distributor shaft (B).

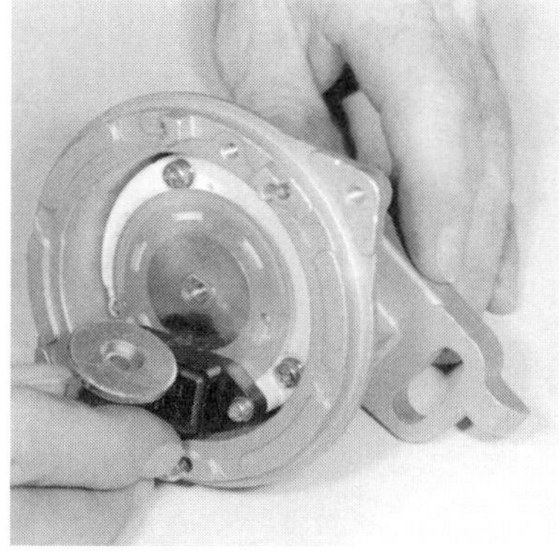

8. Once the screw is removed, slip the upper bushing of the end of the shaft to expose the disc and spacer assembly.

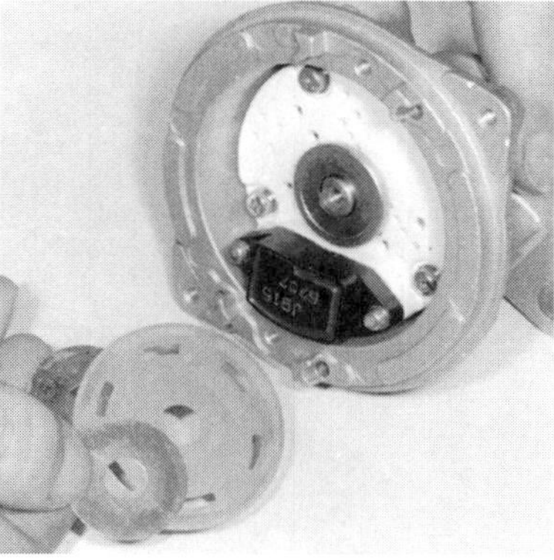

9. Note the position of the disc and spacer for assembly alignment. Then, carefully remove the disc and spacer assembly from the housing.

Copyright 2000 by Chek-Chart Publications

CHRYSLER 6-CYLINDER OPTICAL DISTRIBUTOR OVERHAUL PROCEDURE

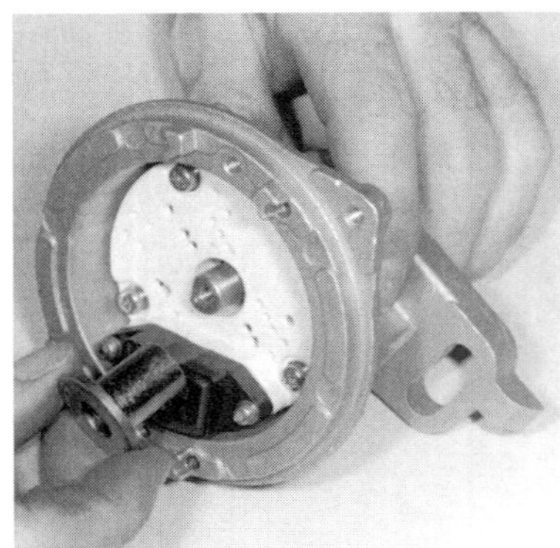

10. Pull the lower bushing out of the housing. Machined flats on the shaft and bushing align the assembly and prevent bushing rotation.

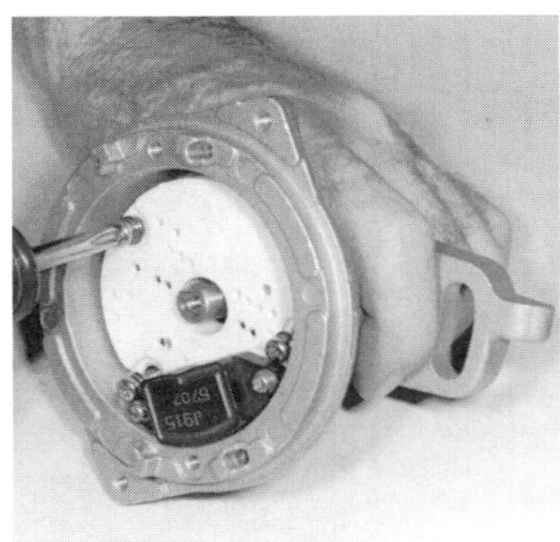

11. Three screws attach the base of the optical module assembly to the distributor housing. Remove to replace the module assembly if needed.

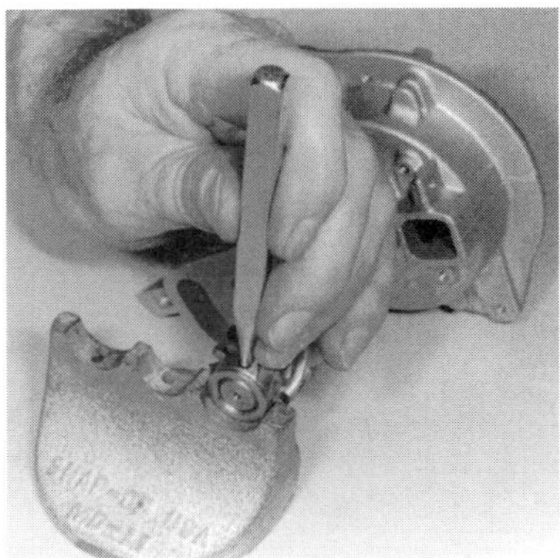

12. Support the distributor housing and drive the roll pin from the gear and shaft with a punch and hammer if shaft removal is required.

13. Slide the drive gear from the end of the shaft. There is no need to deburr the end of the shaft before removing it because the housing contains no bushings.

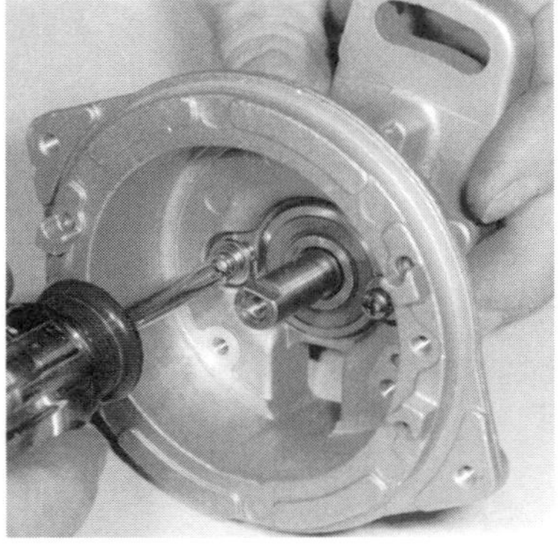

14. Remove the two screws that hold the shaft and bearing assembly in the housing, then slip the shaft and bearing out of the housing.

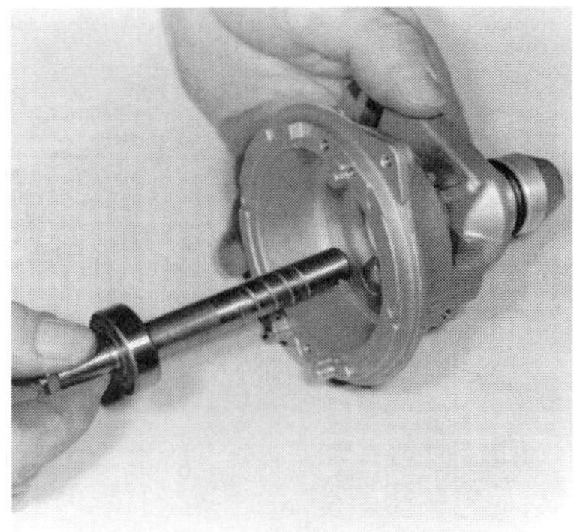

15. Replace the O-ring on the drive gear end of the housing, then assemble the distributor in reverse order.

Copyright 2000 by Chek-Chart Publications

11 Ignition Timing

Ignition timing determines the exact position of the piston in the cylinder at which the spark plug fires to ignite the fuel charge. Ignition occurs several crankshaft degrees before the piston reaches top dead center (TDC) on most engines. This is the base timing of the engine. As engine speed increases, ignition occurs sooner and the timing advances. Although ignition timing is not adjustable on many late-model engines, base timing and timing advance should be checked to verify control system operation.

Manufacturers provide base timing specifications in the service manual as well as on a Vehicle Emission Control Information (VECI) label or decal located in the engine compartment. This is generally the specification that should be followed, even if it differs from printed specifications in a manual. Timing advance specifications are available in some service manuals. Base timing should not vary from specifications, but may due to distributor wear, timing belt or chain stretch, loose or incorrectly mounted sensors, or electronic control system problems. Incorrect ignition timing causes engine performance, driveability, and emissions problems.

There are two methods of timing an engine:

- Static timing
- Dynamic timing.

Static timing is done with the engine not running and physically establishes the base timing of the engine. Dynamic timing is performed on a running engine to check base timing and timing advance.

STATIC TIMING

Static timing is a mechanical procedure for timing the engine during assembly and distributor installation. How to static time an engine was briefly explained in the distributor installation procedure in Chapter Ten of this *Shop Manual*. Check static timing when installing a distributor or servicing the timing belt or chain. Once the engine is running, check the dynamic timing. To static time an engine:

1. Rotate the engine until the first cylinder of the firing order is at TDC on the compression stroke. Both valves on number one cylinder must be closed and the crankshaft timing mark should align with the indicator on the engine.
2. The distributor rotor should be aligned with the number one terminal in the distributor cap. If not, remove the distributor and reposition it to get correct rotor alignment.

Copyright 2000 by Chek-Chart Publications

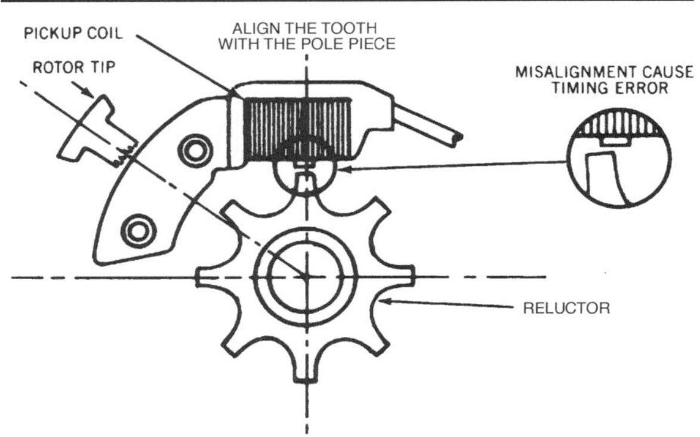

Figure 11-1. Align the pickup coil pole piece with a reluctor tooth to static time an engine.

3. Leave the holddown bolt loose and remove the rotor if necessary to get a clear view of the switching unit. With a magnetic pickup coil sensor, rotate the distributor housing in the direction of rotor rotation to align the reluctor tooth with the pole piece of the pickup coil, figure 11-1. With a Hall-effect or optical sensor, align the shutter wheel window with the switch or the light-emitting diode (LED).
4. Check that the rotor points to the number one terminal in the distributor cap, then tighten the holddown bolt.
5. Check the dynamic timing, and adjust as required.

DYNAMIC TIMING

Dynamic timing checks and adjustments are performed on a running engine. Traditionally, this is done using a stroboscopic timing light. Voltage from the number one spark plug cable triggers the timing light through an inductive clamp. The light is pointed at an indicator, degree markings, or some other reference point on the engine, which is aligned with a similar mark on the crankshaft pulley or flywheel, figure 11- 2. However, on many late-model vehicles with distributorless ignition systems (DIS) it is impossible to connect the inductive clamp to secondary ignition.

If timing is based on a crankshaft position (CKP) sensor reading directly off the crankshaft, timing is not adjustable. The position of the crankshaft in the engine block never changes, so there is no need of adjustment. On DIS systems where crankshaft position is determined by a CKP sensor reading off the camshaft, timing is adjustable and a pickup wire is

Figure 11-2. Using a timing light to check timing on a running engine.

provided. These allow for correcting ignition timing to compensate for timing chain or belt wear.

Base timing and timing advance information is displayed on the serial data stream on many electronic control systems. Access the data stream, as explained in Chapter Twelve of this *Shop Manual*, to check timing. It is possible to check timing advance with a scan tool on most nonadjustable or powertrain control module (PCM) controlled ignition systems. However, specifications are generally not available, so it is impossible to determine if timing is correct using the data stream.

Some engines have a receptacle to accept the probe of a magnetic timing meter, figure 11-3. This is a magnetic pickup coil that works exactly the same as the devices used as crankshaft position (CKP), camshaft position (CMP), engine speed (rpm), and other sensors. Timing is read on the tool, which may be built into an engine analyzer.

Always check the vehicle service manual for specific instructions when dynamic timing an engine. On most engines, timing generally is set in relation to the number one cylinder. However there are exceptions, such as the Lexus 4.0L V8 engine. On this engine, which was used on 1990-96 LS400 and SC400 models, timing is checked using the number six cylinder.

If the ignition timing is electronically controlled, the system is generally disabled in order to perform a dynamic timing check. This prevents false readings due to the control system making timing adjustments to compensate for operating conditions. Electronic timing control is bypassed using a scan tool on most

Copyright 2000 by Chek-Chart Publications

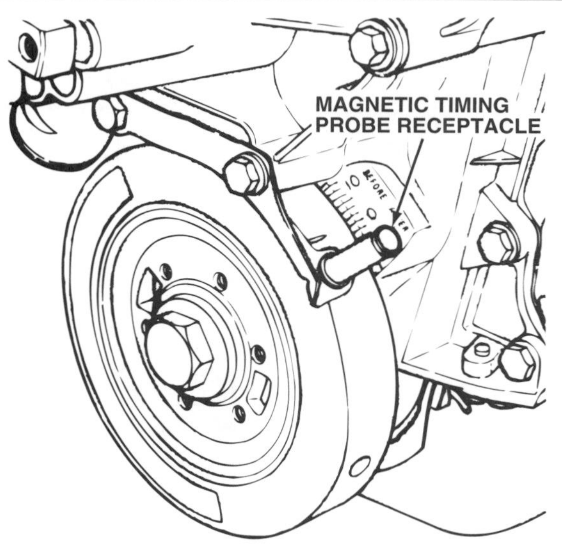

Figure 11-3. A magnetic timing probe inserts into a receptacle at the crankshaft pulley.

late-model systems, but may also be done with a jumper on some models.

Using a Timing Light

Most automotive timing lights are powered by direct current and connect to the vehicle battery, but some operate on alternating current and plug into a wall outlet. The inductive clamp, connected to the spark plug cable, flashes the strobe lamp on each time the spark plug fires. The light may be attached to an engine analyzer console, or it can be a separate piece of equipment.

A simple timing light does nothing more than flash every time the spark plug fires. This is useful for checking and adjusting initial timing and to determine if advance is occurring. However, to precisely check timing advance, an adjustable timing light is needed.

An adjustable timing light has additional circuitry that allows setting the light to flash at a specific time after, rather than at the exact moment, the spark plug fires. For example, consider an adjustable timing light hooked up to an engine that has an initial timing of TDC. If the adjustable timing light is set to zero, it flashes when the spark plug fires. Therefore, the timing marks are aligned at TDC. If the adjustable timing light is set at 5-degrees, the light flashes five degrees of engine rotation later and the timing marks align at 5-degrees after TDC, figure 11-4. The actual timing of the engine has not changed; the time at which the light

Figure 11-4. An adjustable timing light is used to check timing advance.

flashes has changed. This feature allows precise checking of timing advance and timing control systems.

Using a Magnetic Timing Meter

The magnetic timing probe is a pickup coil that is inserted into a receptacle on the engine. A notch, tab, or magnetic particle in the crankshaft, flywheel, or vibration damper generates a pulse signal every time it passes the end of the probe. On many engines, the notch, tab, or particle that creates the signal is offset from the actual number one cylinder TDC position by a specified number of degrees. Most magnetic timing meters require setting the offset specifications on the meter before checking the timing. These specifications may be found in the meter instructions or in the vehicle service manual.

Typically, a magnetic probe is used when the timing marks are almost impossible to see with a timing light. To check timing, connect the meter to the engine by inserting the probe into the receptacle. Adjust the crankshaft offset on the meter, if required. Then, start and run the engine, verify idle speed is within specifications, and read timing on the meter. Use of a magnetic timing meter is not recommended by some manufacturers, such as Ford.

Initial Timing Test and Adjustment

Procedures for checking and adjusting dynamic timing vary considerably by manufacturer, engine, and year. The underhood VECI label provides timing specifications and test conditions when timing is adjustable, and as a check specification on some

Copyright 2000 by Chek-Chart Publications

models with nonadjustable timing, figure 11-5. In general, if a timing specification is on the label, it is possible to perform a dynamic timing check. Whether the check is performed with a scan tool, timing light, or magnetic probe varies by engine; check the service manual for the vehicle being tested.

The engine should be in good running condition and at normal operating temperature when timing is checked. The following general rules for dynamic timing with a stroboscopic light apply to most models. Magnetic probe procedures are similar, and scan tool use is discussed in Chapter Twelve of this *Shop Manual.*

Timing is generally set with the engine running at a normal slow idle speed, sometimes called "curb" idle. However, some manufacturers, such as Honda and Oldsmobile, specify that timing be checked and adjusted at a higher speed on certain engines.

Often, the air cleaner must be removed to access the distributor. If so, be sure to plug any vacuum lines that are disconnected from the air cleaner.

When a vacuum advance unit is used, timing is usually set with the distributor vacuum lines disconnected and plugged. However, some manufacturers specify that the vacuum advance lines remain connected. On dual-diaphragm distributors, the manifold vacuum line that provides spark retard usually must be disconnected and plugged, while the one that provides advance remains connected. Again, this information should be on the VECI label. Note the position of vacuum lines before disconnecting them to make sure they reinstall correctly.

Locate the timing marks on the engine and crankshaft pulley, balancer, or flywheel. The timing marks on many late-model engines are difficult to find or see, and often hidden behind a maze of belts and engine accessories. If it is possible to access the timing marks, wipe the marks clean and clearly mark them with chalk or paint. If the marks cannot be reached to clean them by hand, spray the area with a chemical cleaner or degreasing agent to make them easier to see. Timing marks on some engines, particularly in vans, must be viewed from the bottom of the engine. A rubber plug must be removed from the transmission bellhousing to view the flywheel timing marks on some import engines.

On engines with electronic timing control, the system is disabled to check basic timing. This puts the ignition control module (ICM) into a bypass or "default" timing mode in which it does not control timing. This may be done using a scan tool, by disconnecting a specified connector, or installing a jumper wire. Some specific examples are included later in this chapter. On some engines with electronic timing control, it is not possible to check or set basic timing. When a distributor is removed from such an engine, it is static-timed upon installation and the electronics take over from there.

Figure 11-5. Timing specifications are found on the VECI label in the engine compartment.

To adjust the initial timing using a timing light:

1. Connect the timing light and a tachometer to the engine.
2. Disable the electronic timing control to prevent unwanted advance. If a vacuum advance unit is used, disconnect and plug the vacuum lines as required.
3. Slightly loosen the distributor holddown bolt.
4. Start and run the engine. Adjust idle speed to specifications to prevent unwanted advance.
5. Aim the timing light toward the timing marks on the engine. Carefully sight the timing marks at a right angle, figure 11-6. Be aware, looking at the marks from an incorrect position may result in an initial timing error of as much as several degrees.
6. If timing is incorrect, rotate the distributor housing until the proper marks are aligned.
7. When the timing is set to specifications, carefully tighten the distributor holddown bolt. Then, recheck the timing.

Copyright 2000 by Chek-Chart Publications

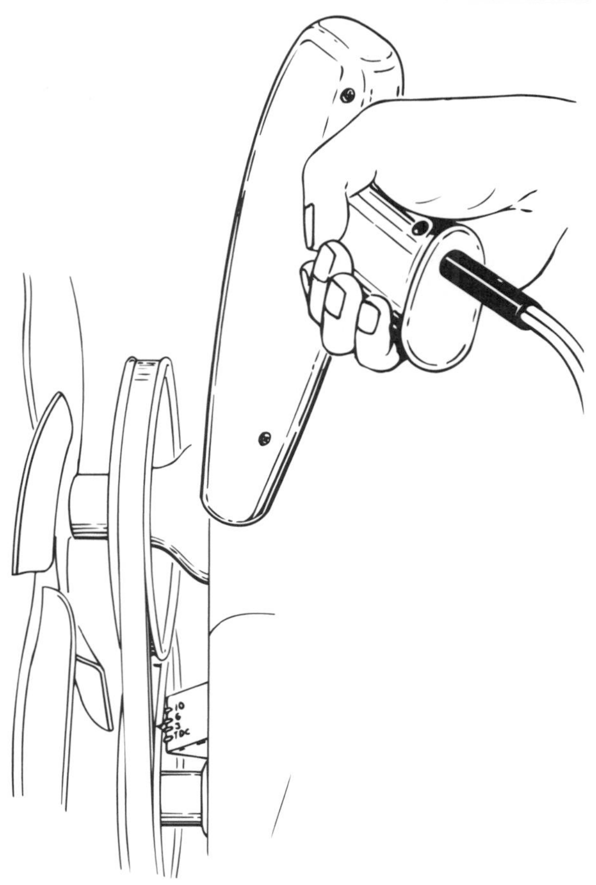

Figure 11-6. Look straight down at the marks to get an accurate reading with the timing light.

Centrifugal and vacuum advance tests

Spark advance is tested on older distributors that have centrifugal and vacuum advance units. The initial timing and idle speed must be adjusted before checking spark advance. A stroboscopic timing light, preferably with an adjustable advance meter, along with a tachometer are used to check advance. Three advance checks are made with a timing light:

- Total advance
- Centrifugal advance
- Vacuum advance.

All three checks are performed with the engine running at normal operating temperature, idle and initial timing set to specifications. To check total advance:

1. Increase engine speed to the specified rpm for checking total advance, then block the linkage to maintain the setting.
2. Adjust the timing light advance meter to bring the timing marks back into proper alignment.
3. Read the degrees of total advance on the timing light meter and compare to specifications.

If the total advance reading is within specifications, both the centrifugal and vacuum mechanisms are functioning properly. For readings not within specifications, test the individual advance devices to determine which is at fault. Check centrifugal advance as follows:

1. With the engine running at idle, disconnect and plug the distributor vacuum lines.
2. Increase and hold engine speed at the specified test speed.
3. Note the timing mark alignment and adjust the advance meter control to align the marks at the initial timing setting.

The degrees of advance recorded on the timing light meter is the centrifugal advance only. If the reading is not within specifications, the centrifugal advance mechanism must be repaired or replaced. To check the vacuum advance:

1. With the engine at specified test speed, unplug and reconnect the vacuum line to the advance unit.
2. Note the timing marks and adjust the advance meter until the marks are aligned at the initial timing setting.
3. Subtract the centrifugal advance reading of the previous test from the new reading. The result is the amount of vacuum advance.

If the reading is within specifications, the vacuum advance unit is working correctly. Replace or adjust the vacuum advance unit if the reading is not within specifications.

Distributor advance specifications may be given at several different test speeds. If so, perform the tests at all given speeds to ensure precise control of ignition timing through the range.

If the distributor being tested has a dual-diaphragm retard/advance vacuum unit, check the vacuum retard as follows:

1. Disconnect and plug both vacuum hoses at the distributor, then start and run the engine at idle.
2. While watching the timing marks, connect the manifold vacuum hose to the inner vacuum chamber.

Copyright 2000 by Chek-Chart Publications

3. Timing should immediately retard from the initial setting. Check the amount of retard with the timing light advance meter and compare it to specifications.

Many late-model distributors use a dual-diaphragm vacuum unit to provide two stages of advance, rather than advance and retard. These are checked in similar fashion. Disconnect and plug both hoses, then apply vacuum to the diaphragms one at a time and take timing readings. Make sure the hoses are connected properly, as reversing them may cause a driveability problem.

A hand-operated vacuum pump is used to test the precise vacuum advance curve of a distributor, figure 11-7. Initial timing and idle speed must be within specifications. To test, the vacuum line to the advance unit is disconnected and plugged, and the pump hose is connected to the advance unit. First, record the centrifugal advance setting at idle and at all other engine speeds specified for testing the vacuum advance unit. Then, with the engine at the test speed, operate the pump to apply 15 to 20 in-Hg of vacuum, and adjust the timing light to determine degrees of advance. Record the total advance at each test point. Subtract this reading from the centrifugal advance recorded earlier. The difference is the amount of vacuum advance. If the reading does not meet the specifications at all test points, replace the vacuum unit.

ELECTRONIC IGNITION TIMING

Ignition timing has been integrated into the electronic engine control system as a powertrain control module (PCM) function on most late-model engines. In many systems, the distributor contains no advance mechanisms: Spark advance is a computer function. Basic timing specifications are still provided, although timing may or may not be adjustable, depending upon the system. If basic timing is out of specifications, it may be the result of a control system or a mechanical problem.

The first step in checking ignition timing of an engine with electronic timing control is the same as it is with any ignition: Obtain the correct specifications. These can be found on VECI labels, in factory service manuals and service bulletins, or in independent publications such as the Chek-Chart *Car Care Guide*. The second step that applies to electronic timing control is to bypass the PCM to remove it from the control loop when setting base timing. The remainder of this chapter discusses specific procedures for checking electronic timing control on a number of popular models.

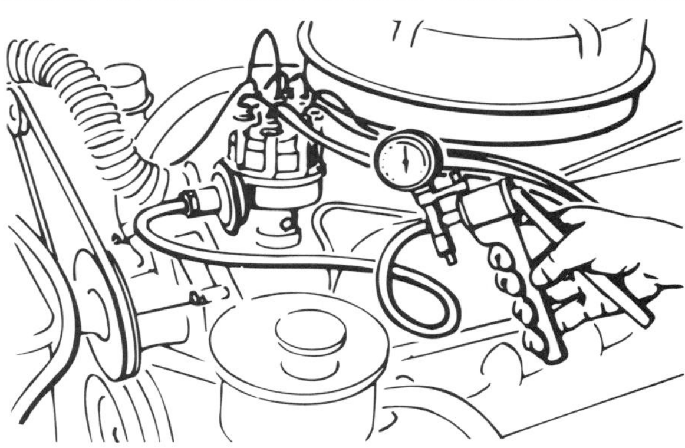

Figure 11-7. Checking vacuum advance with a hand pump.

Chrysler

Ignition timing is under complete PCM control on all late-model Chrysler vehicles and the only way to check it is by monitoring the serial data on a scan tool. However, timing may be checked with either a timing light or magnetic probe on most 1992 and older models, and adjusted on some. Timing is checked with the engine running at normal operating temperature and the idle speed set to specifications.

Disconnecting the engine coolant temperature (ECT) sensor disables electronic timing control on most models, figure 11-8. The ignition timing adjustment terminal is grounded with a jump wire on 4-cylinder 2.2L and 2.5L and V6 3.0L models with electronic spark timing (EST) control systems, figure 11-9.

While these methods are the most common ones used on domestic Chrysler systems, there are variations specified for particular models. In addition, methods for checking and adjusting the timing on import systems sold by Chrysler vary as well. Therefore, it is important to locate and use the exact procedure specified by the manufacturer for the specific year and model of the vehicle being serviced.

Ford

A diagnostic self-test of the electronic control system must be performed first, before ignition timing is checked on Ford vehicles. A diagnostic connector is provided in the engine compartment to access the

Copyright 2000 by Chek-Chart Publications

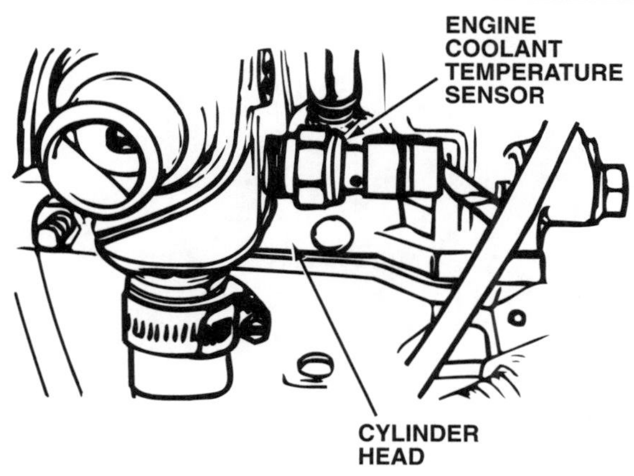

Figure 11-8. Disconnecting the ECT sensor disables timing control on most Chrysler models.

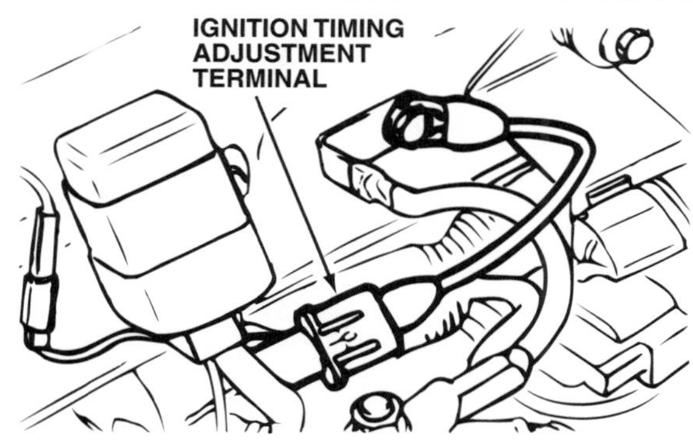

Figure 11-9. Ground the timing adjustment terminal on vehicles with electronic spark timing systems and a distributor.

self-test program on vehicles with an EEC-IV system, while EEC-V systems have an OBD II data link connector (DLC) in the passenger compartment. The EEC-IV system has a computed timing program built into the PCM self-test routines. This program is to be used to check timing with the following procedure:

1. Start the engine and run it at 2,000 rpm for two minutes, then shut it off.
2. If using a scan tool, select the timing check mode, figure 11-10. If not using a scan tool, connect a jumper wire between the ground terminal of the diagnostic connector and the separate self-test input (STI) pigtail connector, figure 11-11.
3. Start the engine and let it complete the engine-running self-test.

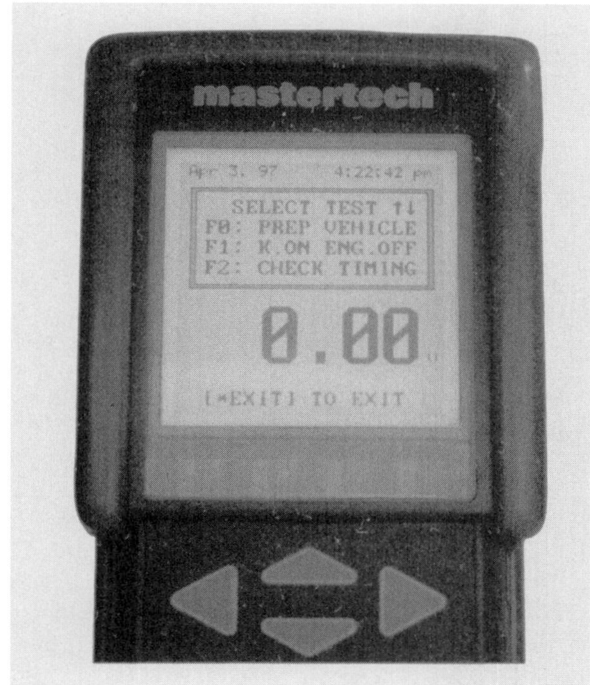

Figure 11-10. Select check timing on a scan tool to disable electronic control.

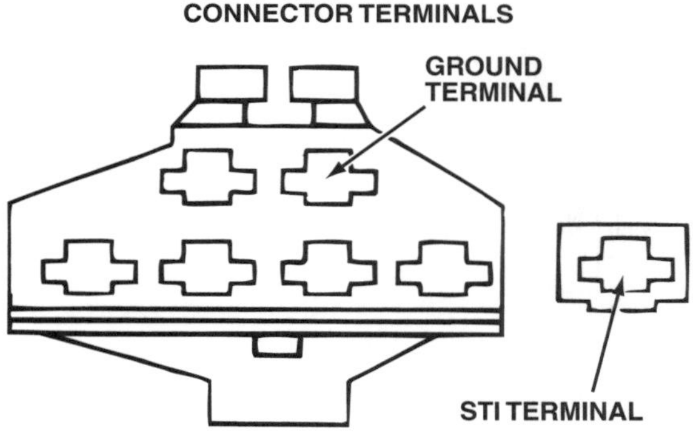

Figure 11-11. Connect the STI terminal to ground to disable spark control.

4. Once the program is completed, about one minute, engine speed increases to approximately 2,000 rpm. At this time, use the timing light to read the spark advance according to the timing mark alignment.

Under normal circumstances, timing should be advanced 20 degrees from base timing. Subtract 20 degrees from the reading taken to determine base timing. Since Ford uses a base timing of 10 degrees

Copyright 2000 by Chek-Chart Publications

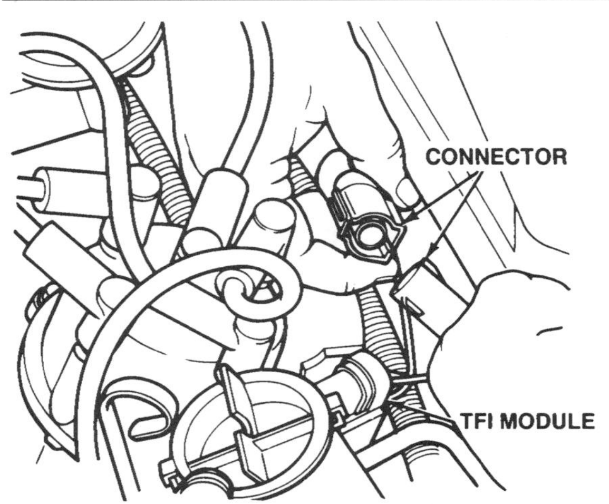

Figure 11-12. Disconnect the inline connector to check timing on EEC-IV systems TFI ignition.

BTDC on electronically controlled engines, readings taken with a timing light should be 30 degrees if base timing is correctly set.

Ignition timing is checked on EEC-IV systems with TFI ignitions by disconnecting an inline base timing connector located in the yellow wire with light green dots, figure 11-12. The connector is found in the primary harness near the distributor-mounted TFI module. Disconnecting the connector interrupts the spark out (SPOUT) circuit between the TFI module and the PCM. A shorting bar is installed in the base timing connector on some models. Remove the shorting bar to open the SPOUT circuit, figure 11-13. This locks the ignition into its base timing with no electronic control. Use a timing light to check timing mark alignment at the specified engine speed.

As with Chrysler, import models sold by Ford and some domestic models with import engines require unique procedures for checking and adjusting timing. The self-test internal (STI) terminal must be connected to the ground terminal on the underhood data link connector (DLC) with a jumper wire to check and adjust timing on most Mazda control systems used by Ford, figure 11-14. However, the Mazda 4-cylinder 2.0L engine has a Ford EEC-V control system on some Probe models. On these, the shorting bar is removed from the SPOUT connector to disable electric timing control and check timing. Disconnect the engine coolant temperature (ECT) sensor to check timing on the Nissan-built Mercury Villager.

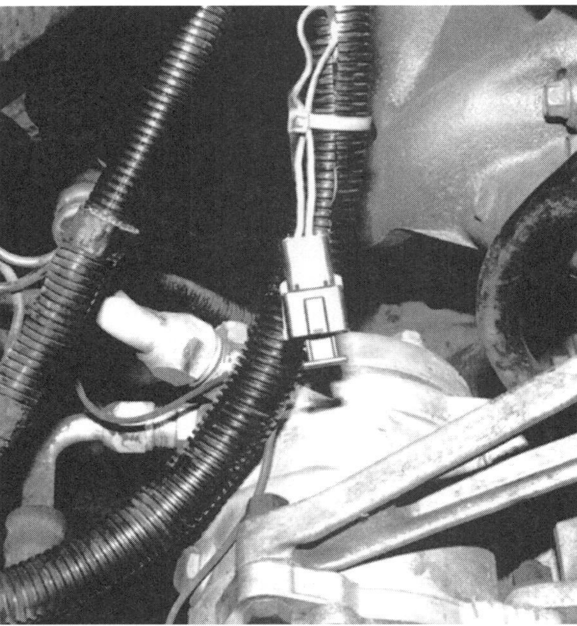

Figure 11-13. Ford inline base timing, or SPOUT, connector with a shorting bar.

On older Ford ignition systems with dual-mode modules, the module must be disconnected from the vacuum switch or barometric pressure switch, figure 11-15. On some systems, a jumper wire must be installed across the black and yellow terminals; on others, no jumper wire is necessary. Once the connector is unplugged, timing is checked with the timing light. Always follow the Ford procedures exactly for the vehicle being serviced to prevent damaging the system or setting timing incorrectly.

General Motors

Ignition timing advance is checked on a scan tool for most General Motors vehicles with electronic engine controls. On many late-model vehicles, especially those with DIS, using a scan tool is the only way to check timing. However, timing may also be checked, and adjusted in some instances, using a timing light or magnetic probe. Refer to the VECI label in the engine compartment to determine which method to use for the vehicle being serviced. If there is no VECI label, check the service manual for procedures and specifications.

To check timing, electronic timing control must be disabled. There are several ways to do this, and which method to use depends upon the model, engine, and

Copyright 2000 by Chek-Chart Publications

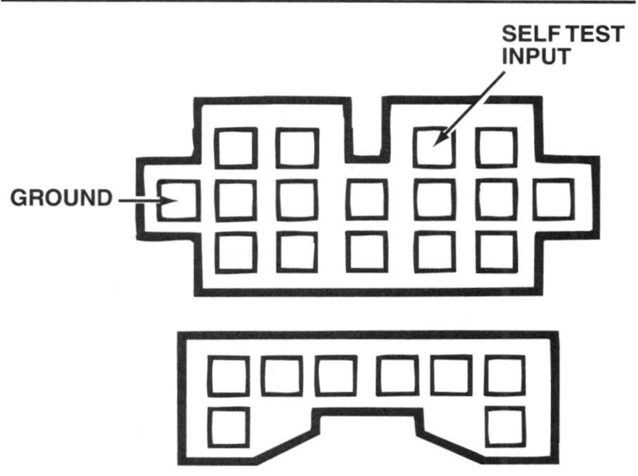

Figure 11-14. The 17-pin Mazda electronic control system test connector is used on some Ford models.

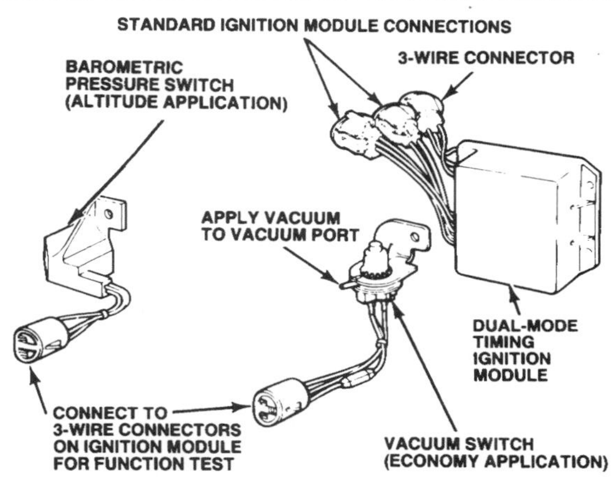

Figure 11-15 Dual-mode ignition modules on older Ford systems must be disconnected from the vacuum switch or barometric pressure switch.

year. In general, the 4-pin connector to the HEI distributor is disconnected to put the system into the bypass timing mode on engines with carburetors, figure 11-16. Four different methods are used to check timing on fuel-injected engines with an HEI distributor. It may be necessary to:

- Install a jumper wire across terminals "A" and "B" of the 12-pin assembly line data link (ALDL) connector, figure 11-17.
- Open a special set-timing connector in the distributor wiring harness.
- Ground a test connector in the engine compartment.
- Disconnect the engine control feed switch wire.

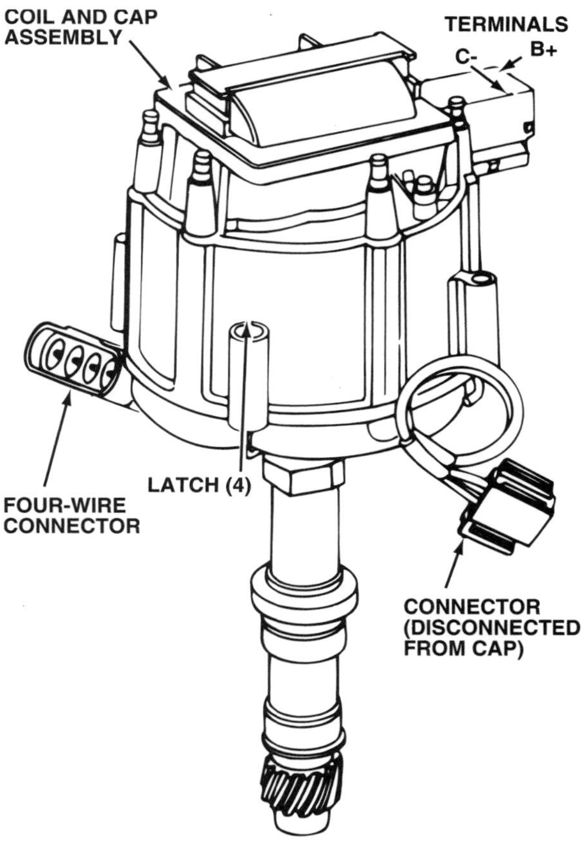

Figure 11-16. On an engine with a carburetor, disconnect the 4-pin connector at the HEI distributor.

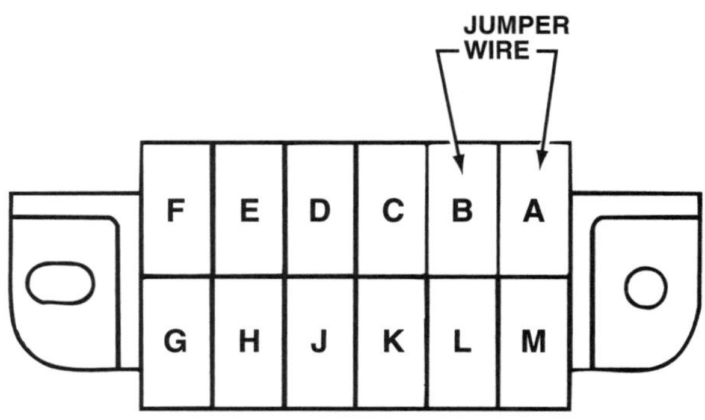

Figure 11-17. Install a jumper wire between terminals "A" and "B" of the ALDL to check timing.

Again, the correct procedure to use should be on the VECI label. Using the correct procedure is extremely important on these engines, because using the wrong method puts the system into a fixed timing mode that is *not* base timing.

Copyright 2000 by Chek-Chart Publications

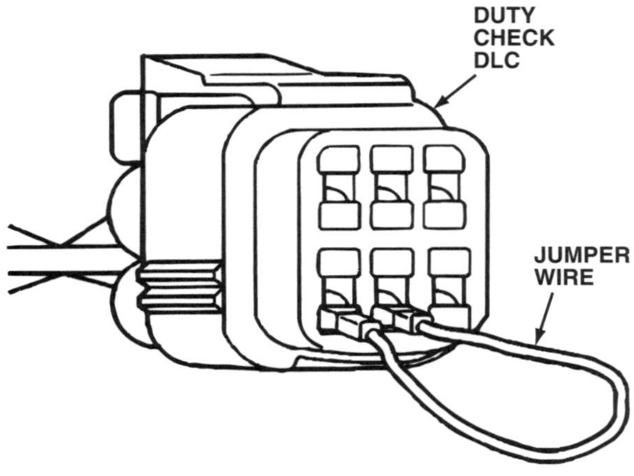

Figure 11-18. Geo Metro duty check DLC with a jumper installed to check timing.

As with the other domestic manufacturers, special procedures are used to check and adjust timing on import vehicles sold by General Motors. For example, the 3-cylinder 1.0L engine of the Geo Metro is placed in diagnostic mode by installing a jumper wire between terminals "4" and "5" of the 6-pin duty check DLC, figure 11-18. The connector is located in the passenger compartment behind the glove box and next to the PCM. Timing checks and adjustments are made on the Toyota-built Geo Prizm with a jumper wire installed either between terminals "TE1" and "E1" or "T" and "E1" of the 17-pin underhood connector, figure 11-19. Toyota engines also require the throttle switch to be closed during a timing check. Refer to the VECI label or service manual to determine which terminals to use.

Honda

Ignition timing is adjustable on most Honda and Acura models. Typically, timing is checked with a timing light and adjusted by turning the distributor. The vacuum hoses are disconnected and plugged to check timing on some older models with vacuum advance, but left connected to the advance unit on others. Refer to the VECI label or service manual for the vehicle being serviced for exact procedures.

For Honda models with electronic spark timing, the PCM is placed in diagnostic mode to prevent

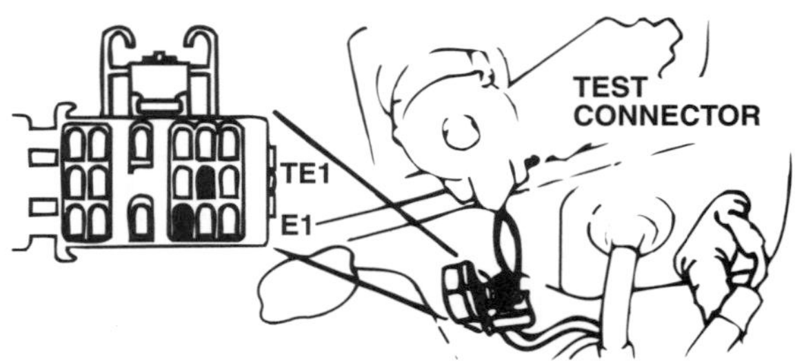

Figure 11-19. The Toyota 17-pin connector used on the Geo Prizm.

unwanted advance during a timing check by installing a jumper wire in the 2-pin service check connector, figure 11-20. The service check connector is located in the passenger compartment, generally under the dash on the right-hand side on 1990 and later models, and in the engine compartment near the ignition coil on 1988-89 models. The exact location and color of the connector vary between models, as does the timing setting. However, information for locating the connector and adjusting timing is included on the VECI label.

Mazda

Electronic spark advance is disabled to check and adjust ignition timing by grounding the diagnostic test terminal on most Mazda systems. On vehicles with a 17-pin diagnostic connector in the engine compartment, install a jumper wire between terminal "10" and the ground terminal, figure 11-21. Some older models have a 6-pin diagnostic connector along with a single-pin ground test connector located in the engine compartment, figure 11-22. On these systems, the single pin connector is grounded to disable electronic spark control. The ground test connector has a green plastic shell; be sure to ground the correct circuit.

Certain models, such as the 1993-95 626 and MX6 with a 2.0L engine and automatic transmission, use a Ford EEC-IV control system. Disconnect the SPOUT shorting bar from the connector near the distributor to check timing on these models. Ford engines and control systems are used on several Mazda truck models as well, and timing is checked using Ford procedures. Always refer to the VECI label or service manual for specific instructions on the vehicle being serviced.

Copyright 2000 by Chek-Chart Publications

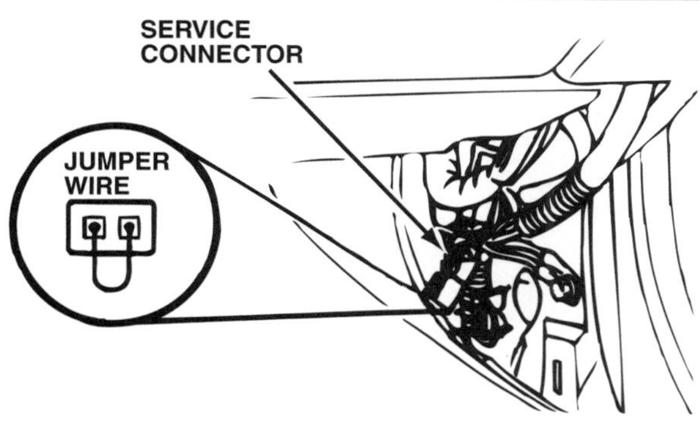

Figure 11-20. Jumper the two terminals of the service check connector to check timing on a Honda.

Figure 11-21. Install a jumper wire as shown to check timing on a Mazda with a 17-pin diagnostic connector.

Nissan

A scan tool is required to perform ignition timing checks and adjustments on late-model Nissan and Infiniti vehicles. Disable the ignition timing feedback control by selecting the ignition timing adjustment function on the scan tool, then check base timing with a timing light. Timing is adjustable on some, but not all models. Timing is typically adjusted by loosening and rotating either the crankshaft position (CKP) sensor or the camshaft position (CMP) sensor.

Timing may be checked and adjusted on older models without using a scan tool. Typically, the throttle position (TP) sensor is disconnected to disable feedback control when timing adjustments are made. Check the VECI label or service manual for specific requirements of the vehicle being serviced.

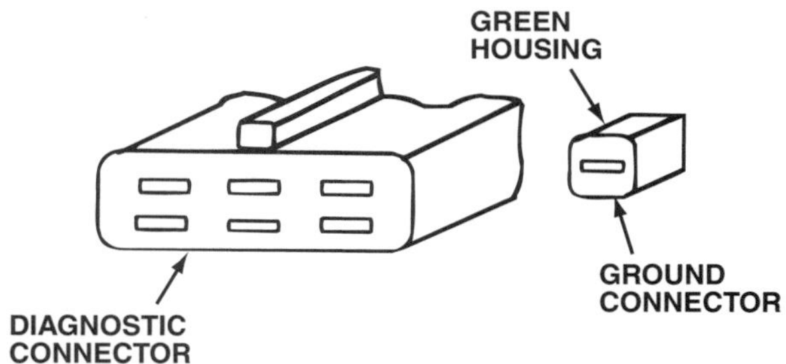

Figure 11-22. Ground the green single pin connector on a Mazda with a 6-pin diagnostic connector.

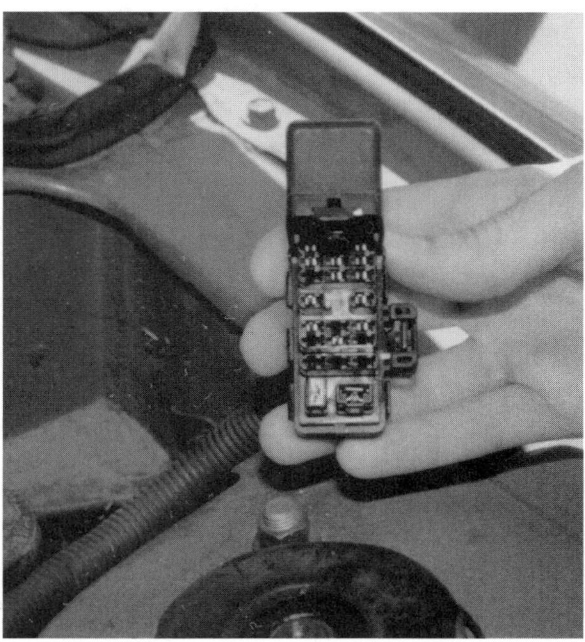

Figure 11-23. The 17-pin Toyota check connector is in the engine compartment.

Toyota

The 17-pin diagnostic connector used on the Geo Prizm is found on all Toyota models. Timing checks and adjustments are made with a jumper wire installed either between terminals "TE1" and "E1" or "T" and "E1" of the connector. The location of the test connector varies by model and year. Some are located in the engine compartment under a well-marked, rectangular-shaped protective cover, figure 11-23. Often mounted on the strut tower, Toyota calls this the check

Copyright 2000 by Chek-Chart Publications

connector in older model service manuals and data link connector one (DLC1) in late-model manuals. Other models have the test connector under the dash on the outside of the steering wheel. These Toyota diagnostic communications link (TDCL) connectors are inside a D-shaped plastic shell with a cover, figure 11-24. Be aware, some vehicles have both a check connector and a TDLC, but only one of them is connected to the system. Be sure to use the right connector. Also, Toyota EFI systems do not go into base timing mode unless the PCM is receiving a closed throttle signal from the TP sensor. Check the TP sensor circuit if timing does not change with the jumper wire correctly installed. Refer to the VECI label or appropriate service manual for specific instructions and specifications

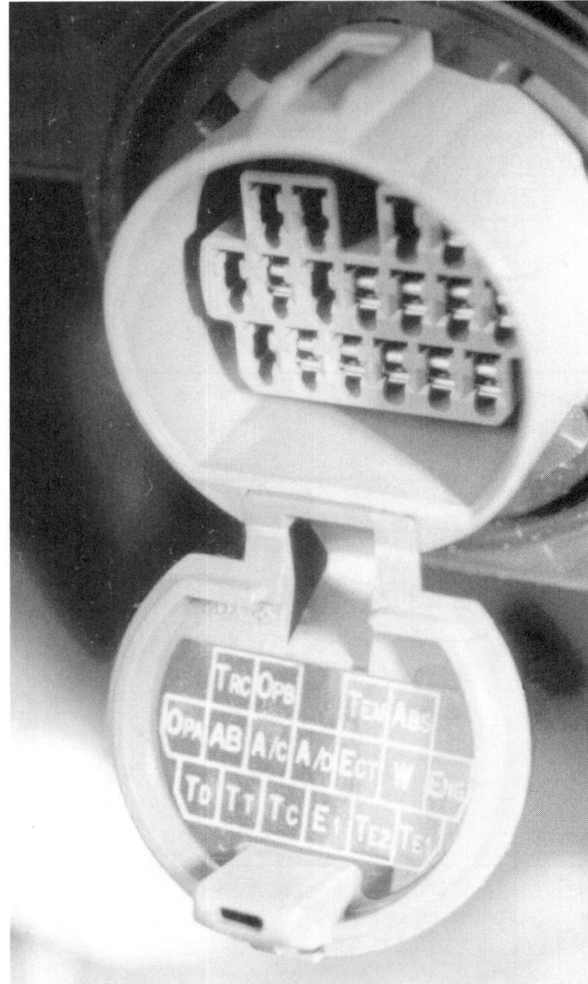

Figure 11-24. The Toyota TDLC connector is in the passenger compartment.

Copyright 2000 by Chek-Chart Publications

12 Electronic Engine Control Systems

Modern automotive engine management systems use a complex network of electronic components to keep the engine operating at peak efficiency with minimal emissions, while at the same time delivering an acceptable level of performance and driveability. Electronic control systems also regulate the operation of the antilock brakes (ABS), traction control, automatic transmission operation, climate control systems, audio systems, and other accessories and options on many vehicles. These auxiliary electronic systems may have a separate control module, or be incorporated in the powertrain control module (PCM). Regardless, multiple systems often share some sensor signals and always rely on feedback information from other control modules. Precise, rapid electronic communications between the system components is the key to maintaining this delicate balance.

Although there is a vast assortment of control systems, all manufacturers use the same basic types of circuit devices to monitor and operate the system. The design and construction of the device may vary greatly, but the internal operations are the same, as is the effect the device has on current, resistance, and voltage on the circuit.

Troubleshooting electronic engine control systems requires a familiarity with automotive electrical and electronic systems and the use of computer control systems on late-model vehicles. This chapter begins with a short review of these computer operation principles to illustrate that there are more similarities than differences among control systems.

Diagnosing performance, driveability, and emissions problems caused by an electronic control system failure is beyond the scope of this *Shop Manual*. Instead, this chapter focuses on specific circuit tests and repairs that are performed when diagnostic procedures indicate an electronic system malfunction.

The components of an electronic control system are extremely delicate and easily damaged by improper handling or testing. Be aware, your body is a conductor that is capable of producing a static electrical charge that may damage components designed to operate on a low voltage signal. The best way to avoid damage is to wear a ground strap when working with electronic components. As an alternative, make sure you are touching a ground before picking up any electronic components. Also, use only equipment designed for electronic testing. Avoid using analog test meters, which are typically designed for high current, for troubleshooting electronic systems and components.

Copyright 2000 by Chek-Chart Publications

COMPUTER CONTROL PRINCIPLES

The operation of any computer system is divided into four basic functions: input, processing, storage, and output, figure 12-1. A computer operates by converting input voltage signals to other voltage signals that represent combinations of numbers. The numbers are coded information about quantities measured by sensors. These include temperature, speed, distance, position, pressure, and other factors of engine and vehicle operation. The computer processes the voltage signals by computing the numbers they represent, comparing results to values programmed in memory, then delivering output commands to actuators that control engine and vehicle operation. Additionally, a computer stores processed information and its own operating instructions in the form of other numerical information. There are four basic functions of any computer system:

1. **Input**—Input information provided as voltage signals from system sensors is received by the computer, or PCM.
2. **Processing**—The PCM processes, or computes, the input voltage signals into combinations of binary numbers (1 and 0). It then compares the processed information to instructions and other data in its program to make logical decisions and send output commands to the system actuator devices.
3. **Storage**—Every computer has an electronic memory to store its operating instructions, or program. Some computer systems also require that some input signals be stored for later reference. Many systems can "remember" previous operating conditions and adapt their output commands to "learned" characteristics of vehicle operation. All systems have some kind of information storage capability, or memory.
4. **Output**—After receiving and processing input information, the computer sends output commands to actuator devices to control engine operation. Typical output devices are solenoids and relays. The computer may also send output information to display devices such as an electronic instrument panel.

The output commands of an engine control system regulate most, or all, of the following operations:

- Fuel metering
- Ignition timing advance
- Idle speed
- Electric fuel pump power
- Exhaust gas recirculation (EGR)
- Secondary air injection (AIR)

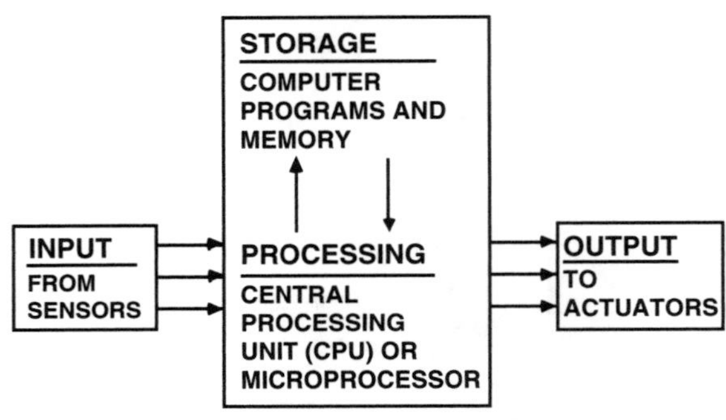

Figure 12-1. Any computer performs four functions: input, processing, storage, and output.

- Evaporative emissions vapor (EVAP) canister purging
- Intake mixture preheating, or early fuel evaporation (EFE)
- Automatic transmission torque converter clutch (TCC) lockup, also transmission shifting on some models
- Air-conditioning (AC) compressor clutch engagement
- Electric cooling fan operation.

How the system controls these operations is based on a combination of the input signals the PCM receives from the sensors and programs stored in memory. Generally, output actuator commands are not based on the input of a single or dedicated sensor. Rather, the signals from several sensors are processed to determine the correct output to a certain actuator. In addition, the input signal from a single sensor is generally used to determine the output of a number of actuators. This is especially true of vehicles that have more than one onboard computer, or control module. Multiple modules are generally linked by a communications bus, which allows them to share input sensor signals and other information as well.

Circuit layout varies considerably by manufacturer, model, and year. Accurate wiring diagrams, test procedures and sequences, and specifications for the vehicle being serviced are essential for troubleshooting and repairing electronic control systems. Most electronic control system repairs also require a scan tool and a digital multimeter (DMM), or a graphing multimeter (GMM) or a lab scope, figure 12-2.

ONBOARD DIAGNOSTIC SYSTEMS

Modern engine control systems are required to have an onboard diagnostic program that monitors operating signals and records a diagnostic trouble code (DTC) in the event of a communicated failure. In addition, certain PCM input and output signals must

Copyright 2000 by Chek-Chart Publications

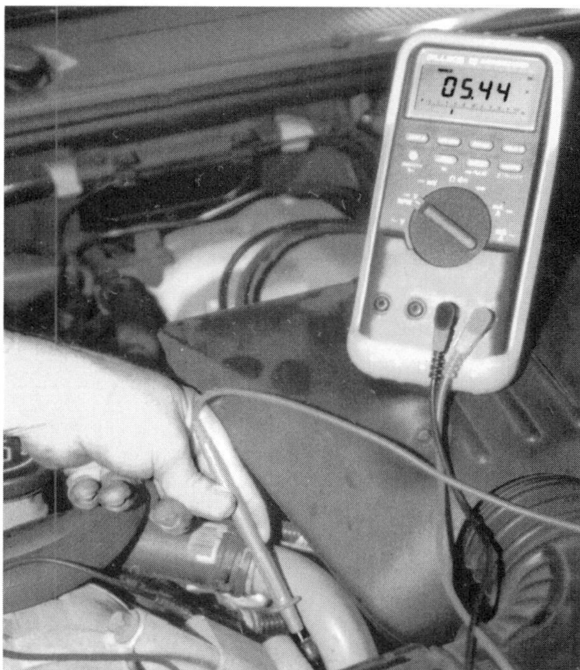

Figure 12-2. Always use digital meters designed for electronic testing when working on the control system.

be available as data parameters on the serial data stream and viewable on a scan tool. All control systems introduced since 1994 must comply with onboard diagnostic two (OBD II) standards. These systems offer scan tool access through a 16-pin data link connector (DLC) located in the passenger compartment, figure 12-3. Many older systems permit scan tool access as well, but the design and location of the diagnostic connector and the data available vary considerably between manufacturers and systems.

All late-model vehicles are required to have a malfunction indicator lamp (MIL) on the instrument panel that lights to indicate major system problems. The lamp may be labeled ENGINE, CHECK ENGINE, SERVICE ENGINE SOON, or some other term that indicates a system problem. Any MIL should illuminate when the ignition key is turned on without starting the engine, figure 12-4. This is a basic bulb check similar to the bulb check for alternator or brake system warning lamps.

If the MIL does not light with the key on, the PCM probably will not go into the diagnostic mode. The problem may be as simple as a burned-out bulb, it may be a faulty circuit, or could be an internal PCM failure. Begin by checking the bulb. Then test the lamp circuit for voltage drop on the power and ground circuits.

If the MIL lights steadily with the engine running, it indicates that a system problem exists and a DTC

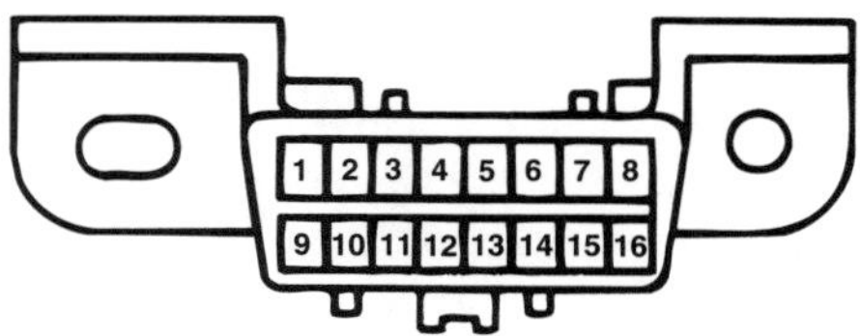

PIN NO.	ASSIGNMENTS
1.	MANUFACTURER'S DISCRETION
2.	BUS + LINE, SAE J1850
3.	MANUFACTURER'S DISCRETION
4.	CHASSIS GROUND
5.	SIGNAL GROUND
6.	MANUFACTURER'S DISCRETION
7.	K LINE, ISO 9141
8.	MANUFACTURER'S DISCRETION
9.	MANUFACTURER'S DISCRETION
10.	BUS – LINE, SAE J1850
11.	MANUFACTURER'S DISCRETION
12.	MANUFACTURER'S DISCRETION
13.	MANUFACTURER'S DISCRETION
14.	MANUFACTURER'S DISCRETION
15.	L LINE, ISO 9141
16.	VEHICLE BATTERY POSITIVE

Figure 12-3. Standard OBD II diagnostic connector and pin assignments.

Figure 12-4. The MIL should light as a bulb check when the key is switched on.

has been recorded. Not all system faults light the MIL. With some faults, the MIL may flash briefly when the code is recorded, then go out. Other problems record a DTC in memory without lighting the MIL at all. Code-setting conditions vary by manufacturer, year, and model. Accurate service information for the vehicle being tested is required for troubleshooting.

Typically, an onboard diagnostic system offers two types of information:

- DTC records
- Serial data parameters.

Diagnostic Trouble Codes

When the PCM recognizes a signal or condition that is absent or out of range, a DTC is stored in memory. A DTC indicates that a problem exists in a particular circuit or subsystem, but does not pinpoint the exact cause of the problem. Control system diagnosis always begins with checking for codes because a DTC

Copyright 2000 by Chek-Chart Publications

indicates a starting point for troubleshooting. In general, trouble codes fall into one of two categories: those that indicate a fault that exists at the time of testing, and those that indicate a fault that occurred in the past but is no longer present. Although manufacturers use different terminology to describe the types of codes, common usage refers to codes for faults present during testing as hard codes, and codes for faults not present during testing as soft codes.

To retrieve DTC records from memory, the powertrain control module (PCM) must be placed in diagnostic mode. This is done with the scan tool on late-model vehicles. Perform voltage checks at the test connector if the MIL does not light with the key on or if the PCM does not enter diagnostic mode. Most diagnostic, or data link, connectors (DLC) have a ground terminal that is used for one or more test modes. On an OBD II 16-pin connector, the chassis ground is at pin 4, and the signal ground is at pin 5. Other test connectors do not have standard pin assignments; refer to the appropriate service manual for specifications.

Use a DMM to check for continuity at the ground terminal. High resistance or an open ground circuit not only disables diagnostic mode, it also causes problems on other control circuits as well. Voltage drop on an electronic ground circuit should never exceed 0.1 volt, figure 12-5. Other terminals on the diagnostic connector may have specific levels of voltage applied to them at different times. Some may have battery, or system, voltage present under certain conditions. Others may have 5-volts, 7-volts, or a variable voltage applied for specific test conditions. Check the service manual for the vehicle being serviced.

When DTC records are in memory, manufacturers prescribe detailed instructions for isolating the source of the problem. It is important to follow the recommend troubleshooting sequence exactly to prevent false results. Remember, a DTC does not identify the exact source of a failure, it simply isolates the offending circuit. Perform tests described later in this chapter to check the devices and wiring of the suspect circuit and locate the problem. After repairs are made, clear PCM memory, drive the vehicle, and check for codes once again.

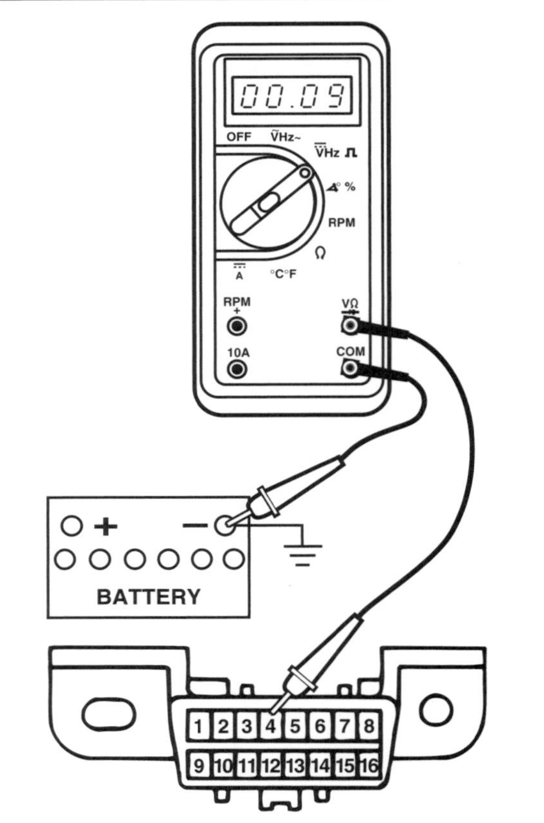

Figure 12-5. Voltage drop should be less than 0.1 volt on the DLC ground.

Figure 12-6. Input and output signals from the PCM are monitored on a scan tool.

Serial Data Parameters

By connecting a scan tool to the data link connector (DLC), a technician is able to monitor a selection of the input sensor signals being fed to the PCM, as well as selected output commands that the PCM is generating and transmitting to the actuators, figure 12-6. Each monitored signal is known as a diagnostic data parameter, or simply parameter. Parameters are transmitted in series, one after the other, until all have been displayed, then the process repeats. When parameters are transmitted in series, the available data is referred to as serial data. The list of parameters, from beginning to end before repeating itself, is known as a data frame. The entire PCM transmission is called the data stream.

Copyright 2000 by Chek-Chart Publications

DATA FRAME TRANSMISSION

```
      RPM__900 02(mV)___267 INTEGRATR_127
OPEN/CLSD LOOP_CLSD  EXHAUST OXYGEN_LEAN
TPS(V)_________0.64  BLOCK LEARN_____128
THROTTLE(%)_______0  BLM CELL__________8
IDLE AIR CONTRL_128  BASE PW (mS)____0.5
DESIRED IDLE____625  02 CROSSCOUNTS___80
MAF(gm/Sec)_______7  AIRFLOW(gm/Sec)__97
A/F LEARNED______NO  SPARK ADV(°)_____90
KNOCK____________NO  KNOCK RETARD(°)__45
PROM ID________2181  TIME__________2:20
COOLANT(°F)_____197  MAT(°F)__________97
MAP(kPa)_________40  MAP(V)_________1.60
BARO(kPa)________10  BARO(V)________0.70
02 READY________YES  CAT CONV(°F)____720
EGR DUTY CYCLE___50  EGR FDBACK(V)__1.00
BATTERY(V)_____13.8  FUEL PUMP(V)___13.7
CRANKING RPM____603  START CLNT(°F)___67
HI PS PRESSURE___NO  IDLE AIR CONTRL_228
FAN REQUEST______NO  COOLING FAN_____OFF
VEH SPEED(MPH)____0  P/N SWITCH____P-N--
TCC COMMAND______P1  TCC GROUNDED____YES
3RD GEAR_________P2  4TH GEAR_________P1
OVERDRIVE_______YES  A/C REQUEST_____YES
```

Figure 12-7. Typical data frame of a late-model General Motors vehicle.

The length of the data frame, or number of available parameters, varies by manufacturer, model year, engine, fuel system, type of ignition, emission control equipment, and the selected data list on the scan tool. The data frame on a late-model fuel-injected engine may contain more than 60 parameters, figure 12-7. A short list of certain parameters must be available to any scan tool on OBD II systems. A more complete list of parameters is available from most systems, but the factory scan tool may needed to access the complete data list.

Serial data is used to determine how well the electronic control system is performing by comparing how certain parameter values change in response to changes in operating conditions. A tremendous amount of information is available on the latest data streams. As a rule, diagnosis begins by switching the ignition on without starting the engine and reviewing the data stream. With the ignition on and engine off, any open or short circuits are readily apparent as zero or full voltage. Shorts and opens cause sensor readings to go to their maximum or minimum limits when the ignition is switched on, and these are easier to spot when all of the parameter values are constant. Keep in mind, the PCM may substitute a default value for the faulty circuit once the engine starts, and this is the value the scan tool displays when the engine is running.

Serial data displayed on the scan tool reflects what the PCM thinks is occurring and not necessarily the actual circuit conditions. Even though many circuit devices, such as pickup coils, input an analog signal, the PCM is a digital processor and the serial data is a digital record. The PCM converts, or digitizes, these input signals for processing and the digital equivalent of the analog signal is what appears on the serial data stream.

Data stream availability

All vehicles produced since 1996 and certain 1994-95 models are legally required to transmit a serial data stream by OBD II regulations. Scan tool connection is at the 16-pin DLC located in the passenger compartment. Data stream information is also available from most domestic models produced since the early 1980s. Many Japanese electronic control systems from the late 1980s on communicate with a scan tool as well. However, the factory scan tool is often required to access the data. The following Asian manufacturers allow scan tool access on some models:

- Acura
- Daihatsu
- Honda
- Hyundai
- Isuzu
- Lexus
- Mazda
- Mitsubishi
- Nissan
- Subaru
- Toyota.

With the exception of OBD II–compliant models, the electronic control systems of European vehicles cannot be accessed with an aftermarket scan tool. Serial data is often available on older models, but a special factory tester is needed to access the system.

When a data stream is available, use the information to locate faulty circuits during diagnosis, and to verify that the system is working normally after repairs. Use the procedures detailed later in this chapter to locate the source of the failure when data stream analysis indicates a circuit problem.

Special Tests

In addition to allowing access to DTC records and serial data, an OBD system supports bidirectional PCM communication. That is, the PCM accepts commands from a scan tool to perform specific tests. These may be referred to as special, functional, or actuator tests in the service manual. Special test capability is a PCM function, and the number of tests available varies

Copyright 2000 by Chek-Chart Publications

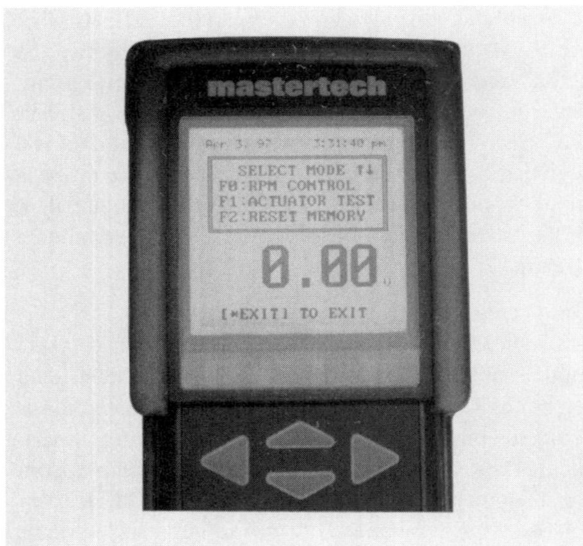

Figure 12-8. The PCM determines which special tests are available with a scan tool.

considerably by make, year, model, and equipment, figure 12-8. Special tests may include: setting ignition timing, checking EGR system function, and operating various valves, switches, and actuators used on the system.

CIRCUIT TESTS

There are two basic types of circuit on any electronic control system: input circuits and output circuits, figure 12-9. Input circuits carry instructions to the PCM, usually as a low-voltage signal from a sensor. However, some input circuits carry system, or battery, voltage. An input sensor typically transmits information to the PCM by adding a resistive load to the circuit. The amount of resistance applied by the sensor determines the voltage available on the signal circuit.

Output circuits carry commands from the PCM to the system actuators. Actuators, which are often solenoids, use the electrical energy provided by the output circuit to perform a mechanical task. This is generally done by some type of inductive coil, so the actuator device may draw a considerable amount of current. Output devices often receive power from the ignition switch or some other source rather than the PCM. The output circuit from the PCM to the actuator provides a ground path. This prevents excess heat generated by high current passing through the actuator from damaging the PCM. Be aware, when an actuator fails, too much current may travel through the ground circuit and destroy the PCM. Always check the output circuits before replacing a PCM to prevent premature failure of the new unit.

Input Sensors

An assortment of sensing devices is used throughout a modern vehicle to electronically transmit operating information to the PCM. Sensor signals describe a physical condition, such as state, temperature, position, or operating status, of the system or component they monitor. Although electronic control systems vary greatly between manufacturers and models, all of them use five basic input sensors:

- Speed sensor
- Oxygen sensor
- Position sensor
- Pressure sensor
- Temperature sensor.

The crankshaft position (CKP) signal is the primary input and the foundation upon which all other PCM functions are based. Manufacturers refer to this input as the distributor, tach, engine speed, rpm, or reference signal, depending upon the system. The purpose of this signal is to let the PCM know the engine is turning over and how fast it is turning. If there is no signal, the PCM generally does not energize the ignition system and often disables the fuel pump as well. An erratic CKP signal results in intermittent operation of the ignition system and the fuel injectors. Designs vary and the CKP sensor may be a Hall-effect switch, magneto resistive sensor, magnetic pickup, or an optical sensor.

Different electronic control systems assign different priorities to the other sensors once the engine is running. Often, a system operates without any noticeable driveability problems when only a few of the high-priority sensors are functioning. Begin troubleshooting by checking the signal of these high-priority sensors. Typically, the list includes the throttle position (TP), manifold absolute pressure (MAP) or mass airflow (MAF), and engine coolant temperature (ECT) sensors. These components, as well as other sensing devices in the system, fit one of the five categories mentioned above. Regardless of how a sensor is used, you need to know the following to analyze its performance:

- The type of signal it transmits
- How it provides information to the PCM
- What its specific application is
- How it connects to the circuitry.

The type of signal may be analog or digital, direct current (dc) or alternating current (ac). Information may be provided to the PCM as a variable voltage, a digital step signal, or a pulse train. The specific application is what the unit is sensing. A wiring diagram shows how the unit connects to the circuitry and also identifies the type of sensing device used, figure 12-10.

Copyright 2000 by Chek-Chart Publications

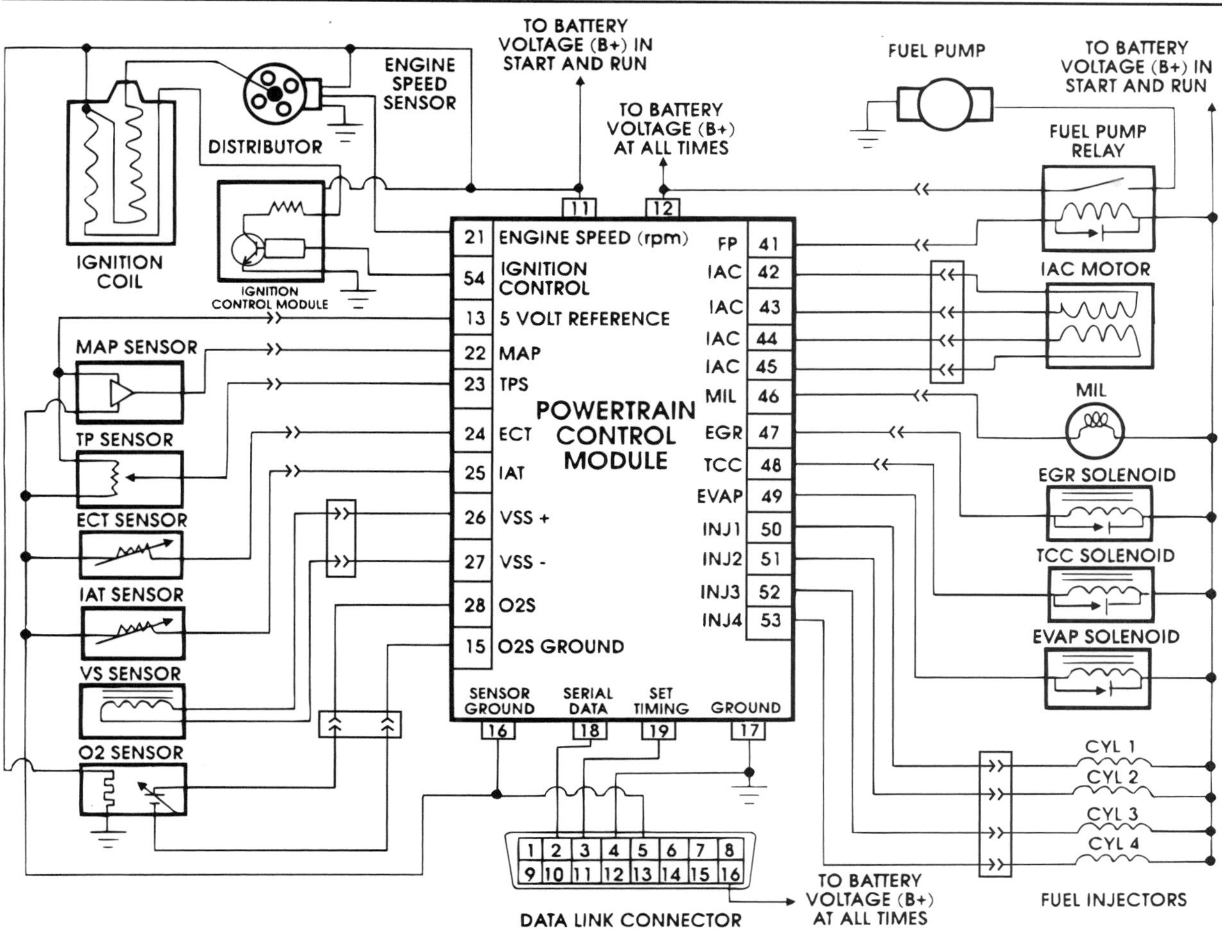

Figure 12-9. This simplified engine control system schematic shows the input and output circuits.

Speed sensors

A number of speed sensors are used on a modern vehicle to electronically determine the velocity of rotating parts. Speed sensors may be used to monitor the crankshaft, camshaft, distributor shaft, transmission components, driveshaft, axle shafts, or wheels to determine how fast they are rotating. There are four basic designs for automotive speed sensors:

- Magnetic pickup
- Hall-effect switch
- Magneto-resistive sensor
- Optical sensor.

A magnetic pickup is an analog device that produces an ac voltage, while Hall-effect switches, magneto-resistive sensors, and optical sensors are digital and produce a dc signal. For all types, the PCM uses the frequency of the signal to determine the speed of the sensed component, figure 12-11.

Magnetic pickup

As explained in Chapter Eight of this *Shop Manual*, a magnetic pickup generates an ac voltage signal whose frequency and amplitude change in proportion to the speed of the rotating component. A magnetic coil uses a two-wire circuit, a positive lead and a negative lead, to connect it to the PCM. Although the pickup coil generates its own signal, a low bias voltage is often applied to the sensor by the PCM.

It is possible to check the signal from a pickup coil with a DMM set to the ac volt or frequency scale. The resistance of the pickup coil winding may also be checked with a DMM using the ohm scale. However, checking pickup coils with a GMM or lab scope is much more accurate for detecting any glitches in the signal.

When testing with a lab scope, look for uniformity in the cycles, figure 12-12. Too much runout on the rotating part causes the trigger wheel to wobble, so the buildup and collapse of the magnetic field are uneven. This causes intermittent shifts in frequency and

Copyright 2000 by Chek-Chart Publications

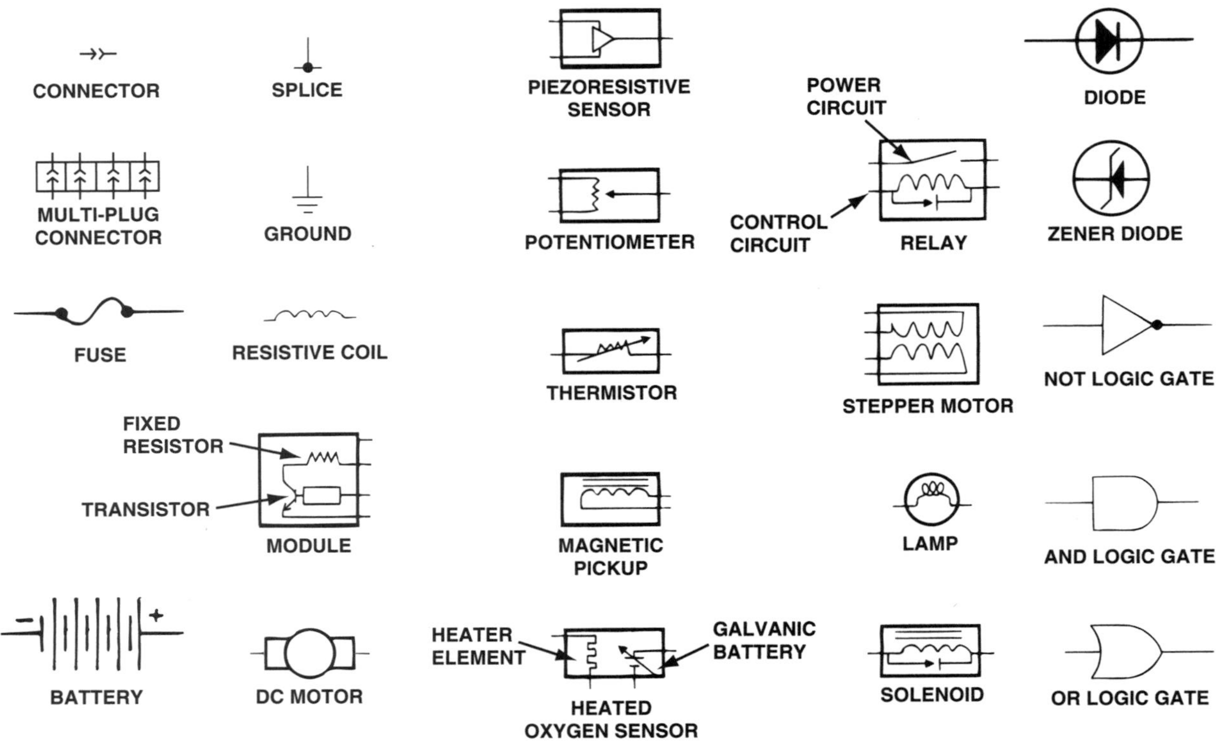

Figure 12-10. Symbols on a wiring diagram show the type of circuit devices used.

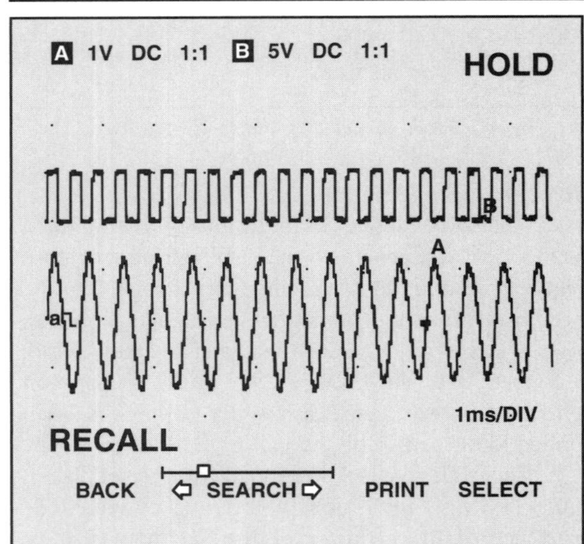

Figure 12-11. Whether digital (top) or analog (bottom), the PCM reads the frequency of a speed sensor signal.

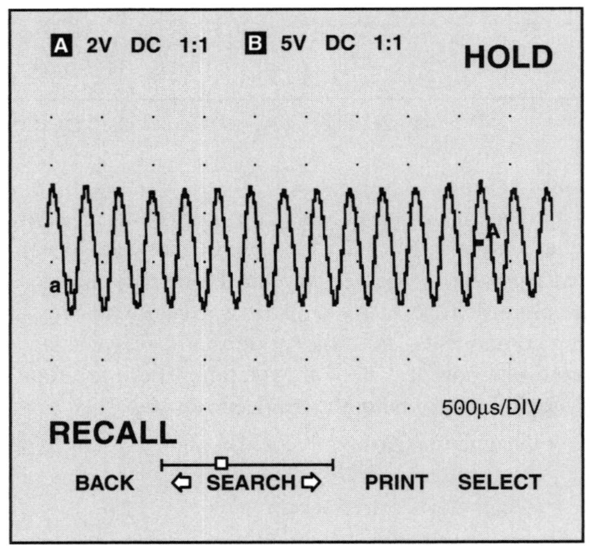

Figure 12-12. Look for even cycling and consistent amplitude on a magnetic pickup coil waveform.

produces an unstable pattern, figure 12-13. A damaged trigger wheel, such as one with a missing, bent, or broken tooth, causes a repetitive disruption to the pattern each time it passes by the pickup coil, figure 12-14.

To process a magnetic pickup coil signal, the PCM watches for voltage to switch from positive to negative and negative to positive. This should occur either at the 0-volt baseline or at the PCM applied bias voltage. If not, check voltage drop on the PCM and

Copyright 2000 by Chek-Chart Publications

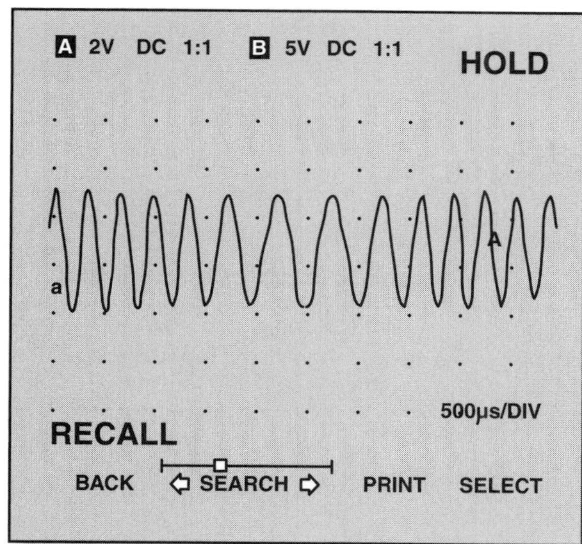

Figure 12-13. Excess shaft runout causes an erratic shift in frequency.

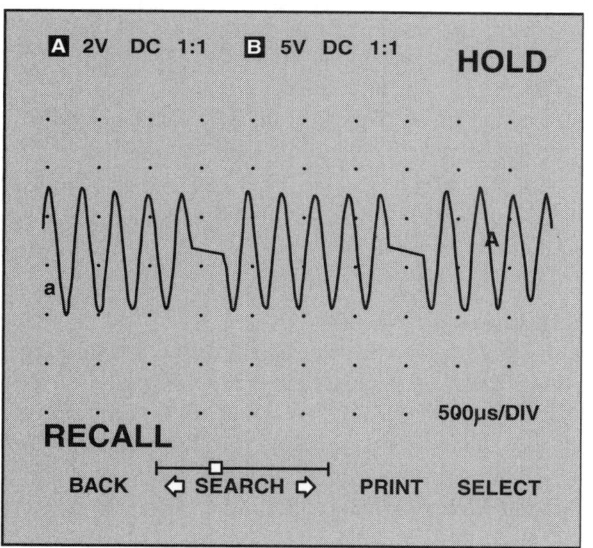

Figure 12-14. A damaged or missing ring tooth causes a regular dropout of the signal.

chassis ground circuits. The shape of the trace peak varies for different sensor designs; some are even spikes while others have a gradual vertical rise to peak voltage and a sharp drop on the falling slope, figure 12-15. Typically, the signal of a magnetic pickup must reach a minimum amplitude, difference between negative and positive peak voltages, before the PCM recognizes and begins processing it.

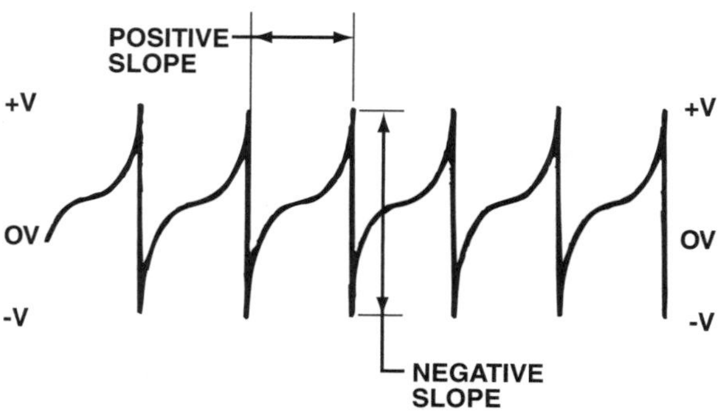

Figure 12-15. Some pickup coils are polarized and the signal rises gradually and drops off vertically.

Hall-effect switch

Exposing a Hall-element to a magnetic field energizes a transistor in the microchip assembly and removing the field switches the transistor off. Therefore, the transistor produces a digital signal, either on or off, based on the strength of the magnetic field. So, if the magnet or the element is rotating, or a rotating shutter wheel is passing between them, the frequency of the transistor signal reflects rotational speed. Most manufacturers use Hall-effect switches as input sensors on a variety of electronic control system applications. This type of sensor is popular because it produces a reliable and stable signal. Although quite a few design variations exist, all Hall-effect switches operate on the same principle and produce a similar signal.

A Hall-effect sensor usually has three wires: power, signal, and ground. Power is provided by the ignition switch or PCM as an input voltage to the element, which must be charged to produce a signal. Input voltage to the element varies by system, but is usually either five or twelve volts. The ground wire completes both the power circuit and the signal circuit and must be free of voltage drops for the unit to operate. The signal wire connects the transistor to the PCM. The PCM provides an input voltage on the signal circuit as well, which switches on and off ground as the transistor changes state. Be aware, signal voltage is not always the same as power voltage. Therefore, accurate specifications for the unit being tested are required.

Manufacturers generally provide connector pin charts along with a circuit diagram in the service manual for troubleshooting Hall-effect sensors, figure 12-16. Specifications are usually provided for input power voltage, which is easily checked with a DMM. Make sure there is less than a 0.1 volt drop on the ground circuit. Signal voltage specifications are not always available, even though the sensor may operate at 5, 7, 9, or some other peak voltage. Remember,

Copyright 2000 by Chek-Chart Publications

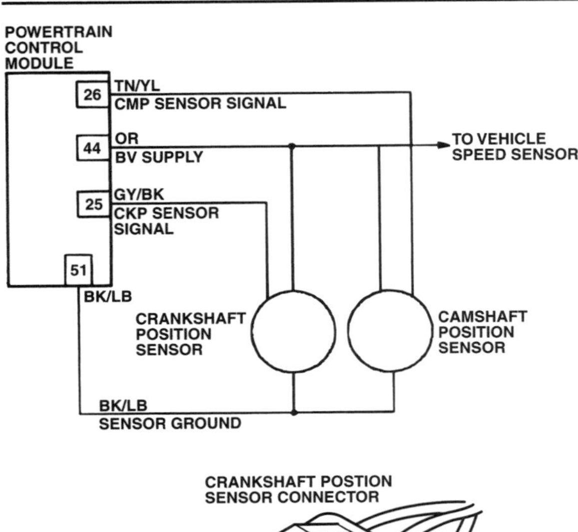

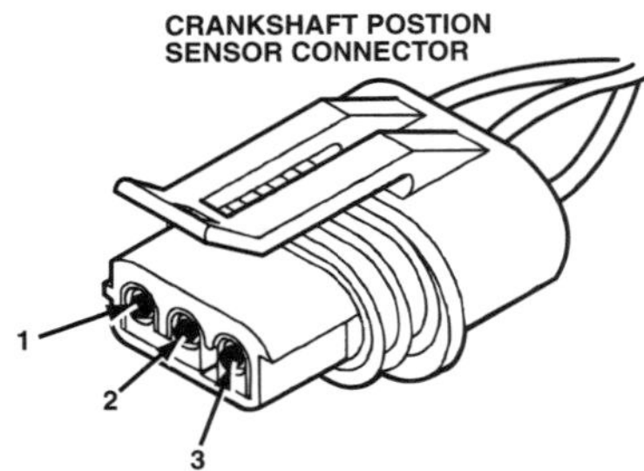

CAV	COLOR	FUNCTION
1	GY/BK	CKP SENSOR SIGNAL
2	BK/LB	SENSOR GROUND
3	OR	8-VOLT SUPPLY

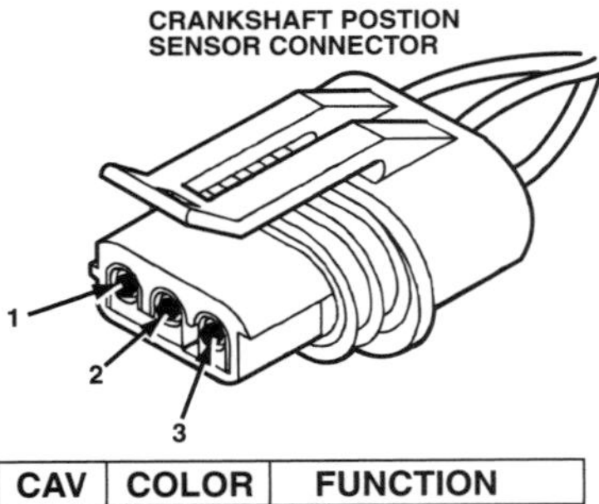

CAV	COLOR	FUNCTION
1	TN/YL	CMP SENSOR SIGNAL
2	BK/LB	SENSOR GROUND
3	OR	8-VOLT SUPPLY

Figure 12-16. A circuit diagram and connector pin identification chart are used to troubleshoot a Hall-effect sensor.

when processing a repetitive digital signal, the PCM looks for switching at the midpoint of the voltage range, not at the top or bottom, figure 12-17. The most accurate way to test a Hall switch is to monitor the signal with a GMM or lab scope.

Hall-effect switches produce a digital pulse train and should have cycles that are consistent in width and amplitude. Some sensor designs produce a signature cycle that determines the position as well as the

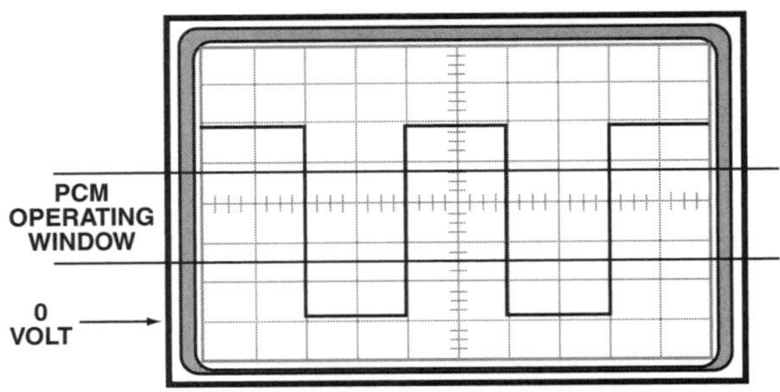

Figure 12-17. The PCM processes the switching at the midpoint of the voltage range on a repetitive signal.

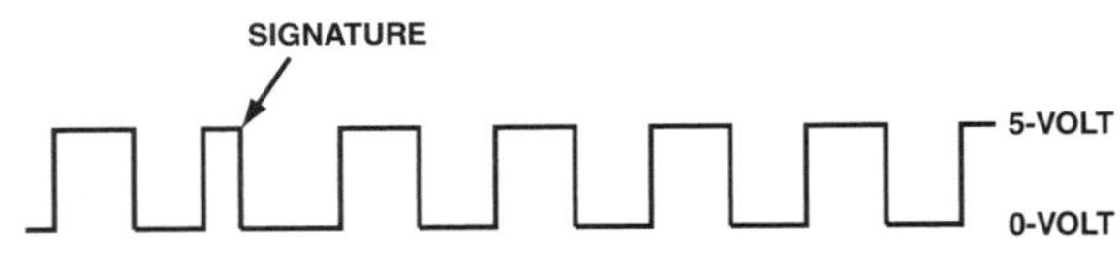

Figure 12-18. Hall sensor signals may have a signature signal to identify the position of the rotating part.

speed of the rotating part, figure 12-18. This is done by changing the shape or position of one of the shutter wheel windows. Other Hall-effect switch patterns may have a slight rounding or a notch at the top corners of the trace, which is considered normal. Make sure the signal is switching completely to ground. Check for voltage drop on the power and ground circuits. If circuit resistance is within specification and the signal does not drop to 0 volt when switching, replace the sensor.

Magneto-resistive sensor

A magneto-resistive sensor is similar to a Hall-effect switch but uses a magnetic pickup in place of the Hall-element, figure 12-19. General Motors uses a magneto-resistive device as a CKP or camshaft (CMP) sensor on a number of applications. However, General Motors usually calls the CMP a Hall-effect sensor in the service manual because both types of sensor perform the same function and generate a similar signal. The only difference is in the internal construction of the switching device used to produce the signal. On a magneto-resistive sensor, internal circuitry converts the analog output voltage of the pickup coil signal into a digital signal.

Magneto-resistive sensors use a three wire circuit: power, signal, and ground, figure 12-20. The PCM does not apply a bias voltage to the signal circuit; the sensor generates the full on and off cycle of the signal. Other than that, test and waveform analysis is the same as for a Hall-effect sensor.

Copyright 2000 by Chek-Chart Publications

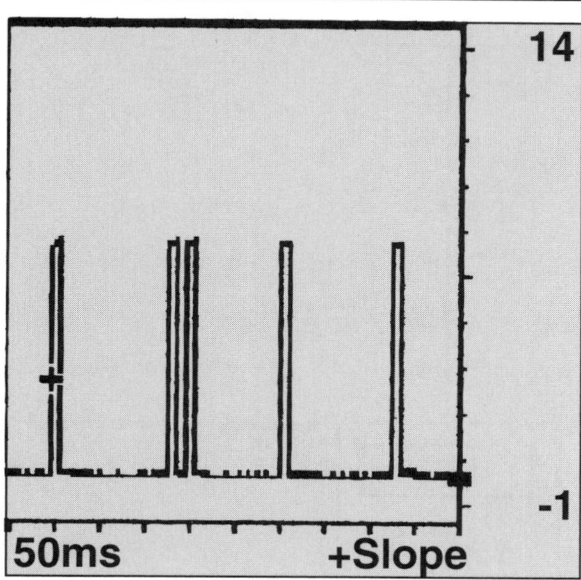

Figure 12-19. A magneto-resistive sensor converts the ac voltage generated by a pickup coil to a digital signal.

Optical sensor

An optical sensor also uses a three-wire circuit, power, ground, and signal. Two optical sensors are incorporated into a combination assembly that provides both a high and low data rate signal on some applications, figure 12-21. Refer to the appropriate service manual for specifications, connector location, and circuit identification.

The PCM applies voltage to the power circuit to energize the phototransistor on a typical optical sensor. However, power may be supplied through the ignition switch or some other source on some applications. Check the service manual for voltage specifications. The PCM also applies a low-voltage, usually 5 volts, to the signal circuit. This bias voltage energizes the light-emitting diode (LED). The ground circuit is common to both the input and signal circuit, and must have less than a 0.1-volt drop for the device to operate correctly.

As a rotating shutter wheel or blade passes between the phototransistor and LED, the signal circuit switches on and off to ground. This produces a digital pulse train, which the PCM processes to determine speed, position, or both, figure 12-22. A lab scope or GMM is the best tool for evaluating the operation of an optical sensor. Waveform structure and analysis is similar to a Hall-effect sensor.

Oxygen sensors

An oxygen sensor (O2S) is an analog voltage-generating device that produces a voltage signal based on the oxygen content of the exhaust gas, figure 12-23. An O2S provides feedback information to the PCM on how well the electronic control system is responding to changing demands for fuel. Therefore, waveform generated by an O2S is a good indicator of how well an engine is running.

The O2S produces a signal whose frequency, amplitude, voltage levels, and peak-to-peak voltages provide combustion efficiency information to the PCM. The PCM uses O2S input to regulate fuel-injector pulse width and maintain acceptable driveability, sufficient power, and peak efficiency. An OBD II system uses two sensors, an upstream O2S before the catalytic converter and downstream O2S after it. The PCM gauges converter efficiency by comparing the two signals.

Although there are several O2S types, most are galvanic batteries made of zirconium dioxide. Commonly referred to as a zirconia sensor, this type of O2S generates a maximum output voltage of approximately one volt. This produces a signal that ranges from about 0.1 to 0.9 volt (100 to 900 mV). The amount of oxygen in the exhaust, compared to the amount of oxygen in the outside air, determines how much voltage the O2S generates. Be aware, a zirconia oxygen sensor must warm to at least 300°C (572°F), before it generates a valid signal.

An O2S may have one, two, three, or four wires linking it to the PCM. Single-wire circuits deliver a signal only, and the ground path is completed through the sensor housing, figure 12-24. With these, a loose mounting or dirt and corrosion on the sensor threads create resistance on the ground circuit. With a two-wire O2S, one wire carries the signal and the other grounds the sensor through the PCM, figure 12-25. A heated oxygen sensor (HO2S) has either three or four wires. A three-wire circuit consists of an O2S signal, heater positive, and heater ground. The O2S signal grounds through the sensor housing. With a four-wire circuit, the O2S signal grounds through the PCM on the fourth lead, figure 12-26.

The PCM looks for the O2S sensor voltage signal to change direction near the 0.45-volt (450 mV) midpoint of the operating range. Ideally, the signal is evenly split and stays above and below the midpoint equal amounts of time. This indicates an oxygen content that is equivalent to the ideal, or stoichiometric, air-fuel ratio of 14.7 to 1, figure 12-27.

A zirconia O2S generates a low-voltage signal when exhaust oxygen content is high, and a high-voltage signal when the exhaust oxygen content is low. Incomplete combustion or too much fuel causes high exhaust oxygen content, while not enough fuel to meet the demands of the engine produces a low

Copyright 2000 by Chek-Chart Publications

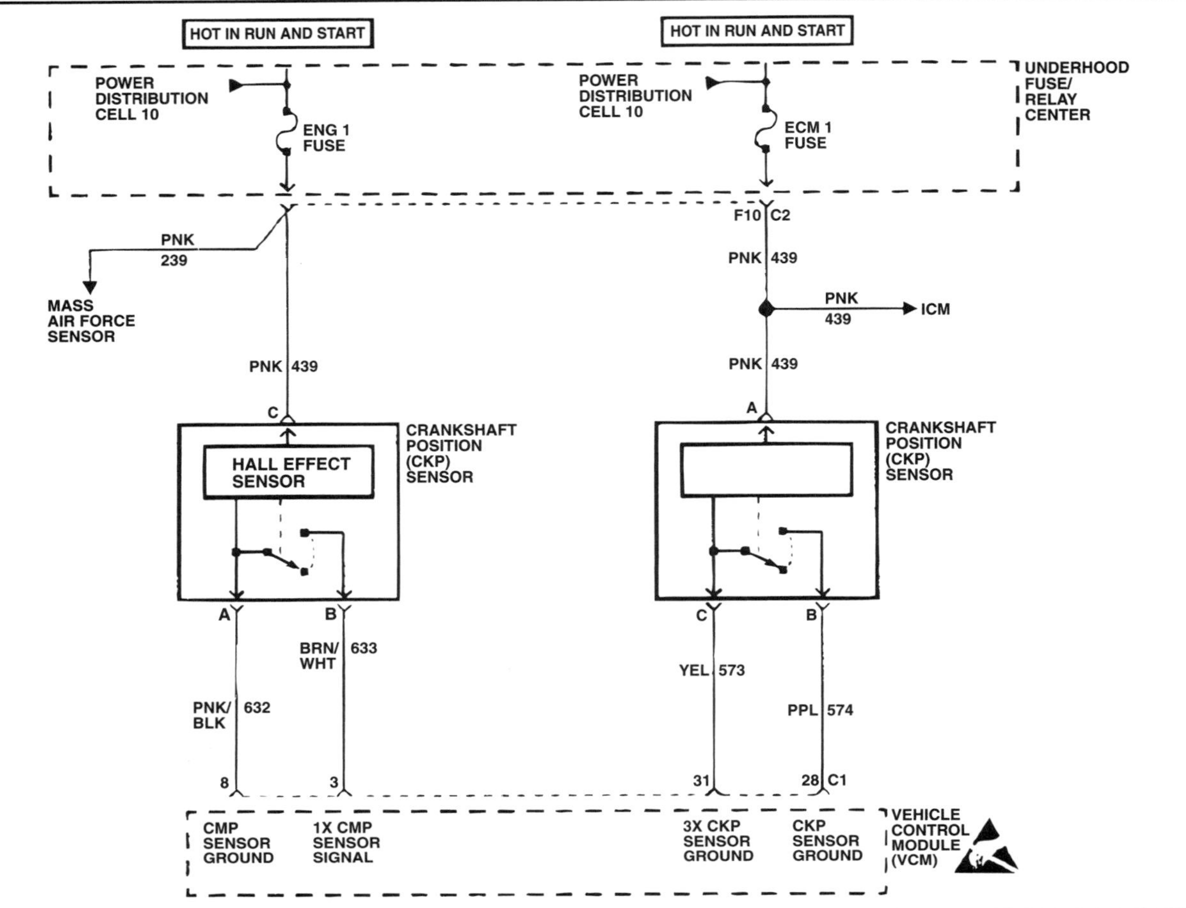

Figure 12-20. Although not identified, a magneto-resistive sensor is used as a CKP on this General Motors system.

exhaust oxygen content. An O2S signal that remains below 450 mV longer than it stays above it indicates a lean condition, figure 12-28. A waveform that spends more time above 450 mV indicates a rich running condition. The farther from the voltage midpoint the switch occurs, the more severe the mixture deviation. Exhaust gas oxygen content fluctuates in pulses that correspond to the opening of each exhaust valve.

An O2S produces a low-voltage, low-current analog signal, that is very susceptible to induced voltage interference. Since signal voltage is rapidly changing, it is difficult to get an accurate reading on a DMM. Most control systems provide O2S information on the data stream, but this in not always a reliable diagnostic aid. The best way to evaluate O2S operation is to monitor circuit activity with a GMM or lab scope.

When viewing an O2S trace on a lab scope, look for even amplitude with rounded peaks; the rising slope tends to be slightly steeper than the trailing slope. Frequency of the signal increases with engine speed. The midpoint of the wave moves up on the screen when the mixture is rich, and down when lean. Some noise on the trace is normal and is exaggerated if scope leads are too close to secondary ignition leads. A short or clipped peak can indicate a cylinder firing, EGR flow, or other problem that affects combustion.

Due to their location, an oxygen sensor is prone to contamination from combustion deposits. Because the sensor samples outside air as well, they are also susceptible to contamination from road dirt and debris. Chemicals released as some silicone gasket sealers age tend to collect on the O2S as an exhaust byproduct as well. Contaminated sensors cannot get a good measure of oxygen content. As a result, signal switching is slow to respond to changes in exhaust condition. Replace the O2S if switching is slow; these "lazy" sensors cannot be repaired by cleaning.

A heated oxygen sensor (HO2S) has a resistive coil that warms the sensor assembly, figure 12-29. The amount of voltage applied to the heater coil and when it is applied vary by system. Check the service manual for test procedures and specifications. Typically, the heater is on at startup and remains on until the sensor is transmitting a reliable feedback signal to the PCM.

Copyright 2000 by Chek-Chart Publications

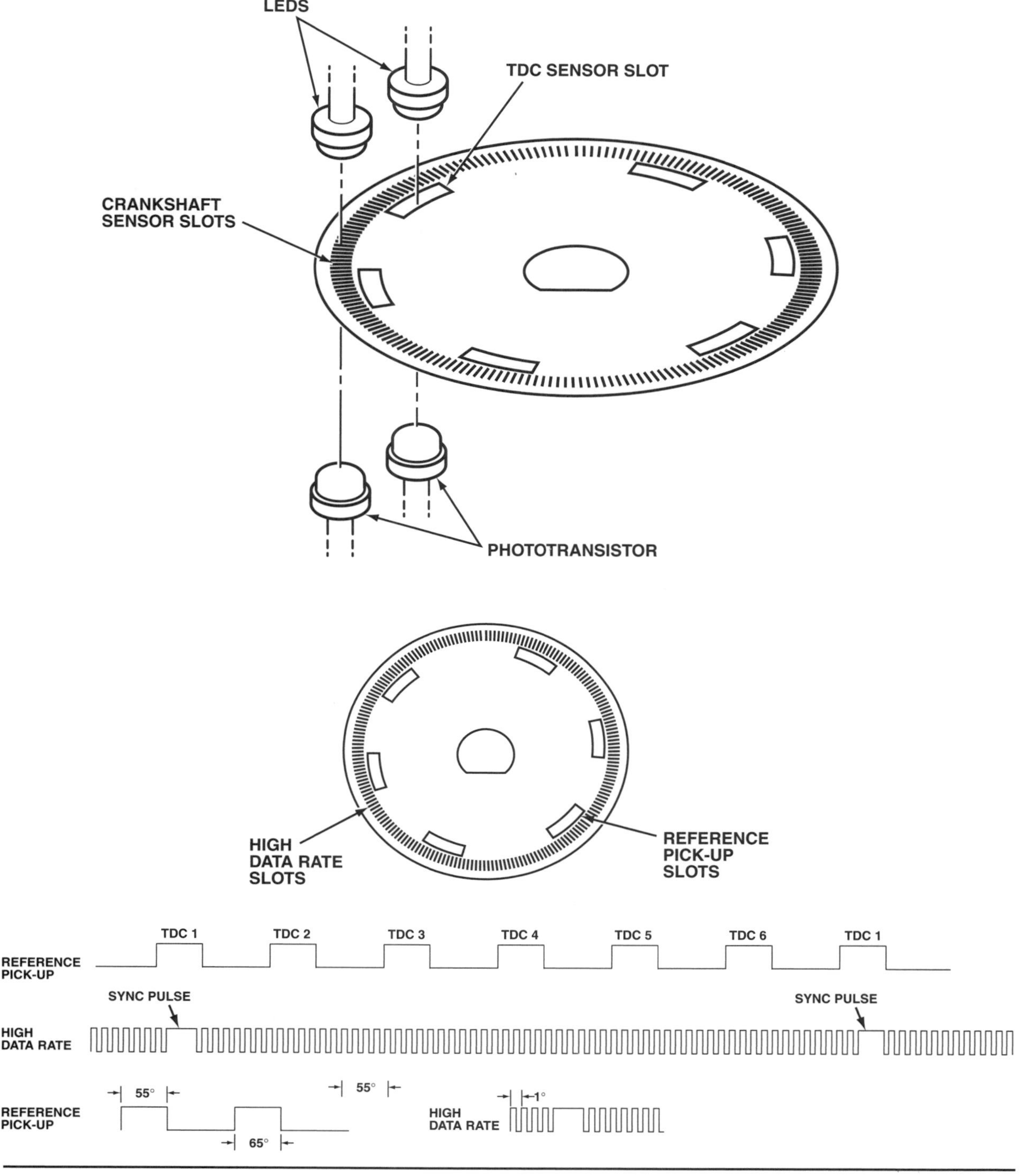

Figure 12-21. Two optical sensors in this combination assembly provide a high data signal and a reference pick-up signal.

Remember, temperature must be at least 300°C (572°F) for the sensor to generate a good signal. On some systems, the heating coil switches back on if exhaust temperature drops, such as under extended idling conditions.

Almost all of the oxygen sensors used on OBD II systems are the heated type, as are many earlier sensors. The PCM controls the ground circuit of the heater coil on most of the OBD-II systems. The heater may be a simple digital, on/off, device, or the PCM

Copyright 2000 by Chek-Chart Publications

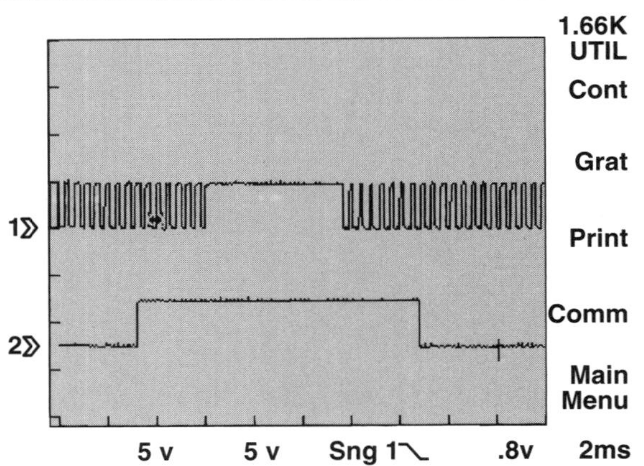

Figure 12-22. An optical sensor produces a variable-frequency, digital square wave.

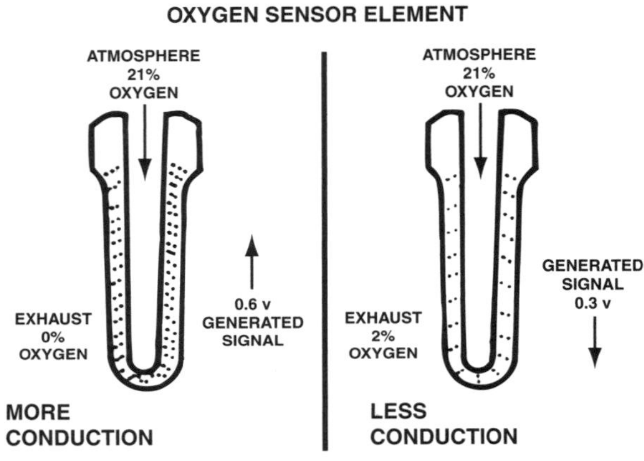

Figure 12-23. An O2S generates a voltage signal that varies in proportion to the amount of oxygen in the exhaust.

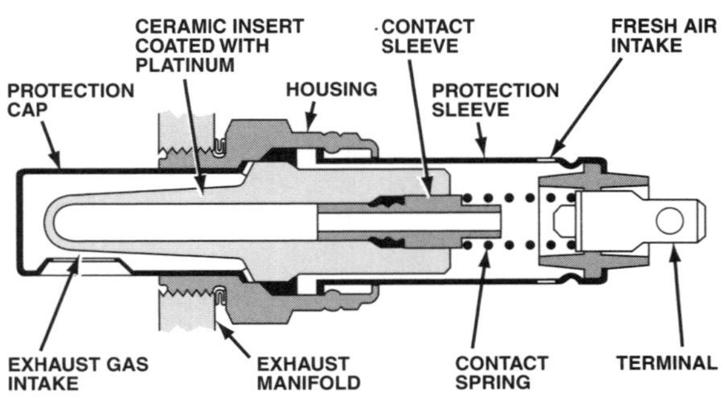

Figure 12-24. Early oxygen sensors had a single-wire circuit and grounded through the housing.

may apply a PWM signal that varies with operating conditions. If the heater circuit grounds through the O2S housing or shares a common ground with O2S itself, power is applied to the heating coil only when the engine is running.

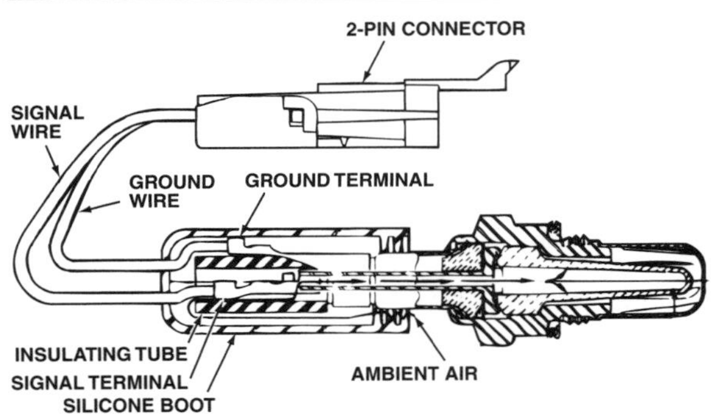

Figure 12-25. A two-wire O2S is grounded through the PCM.

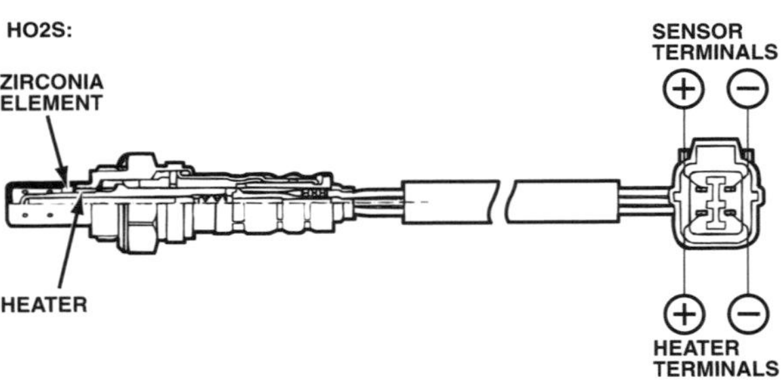

Figure 12-26. Most heated oxygen sensors have a four-wire circuit.

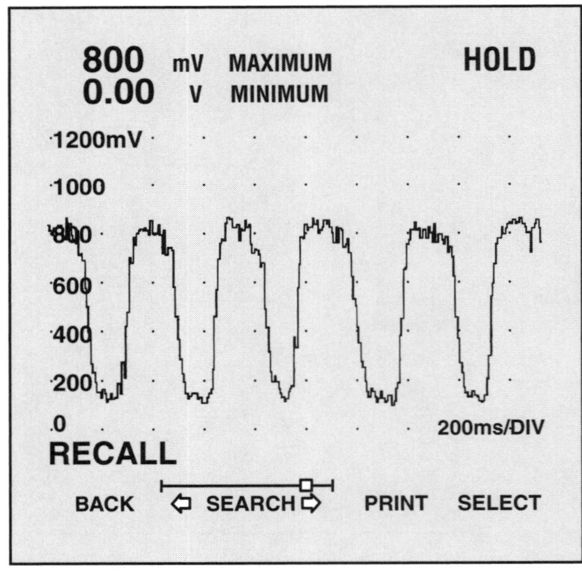

Figure 12-27. The O2S signal cycles smoothly and evenly on a good-running engine.

The downstream, or post-catalytic converter, operates the same as its upstream counterpart, but switches at a much slower rate. In fact, a scope trace may

Copyright 2000 by Chek-Chart Publications

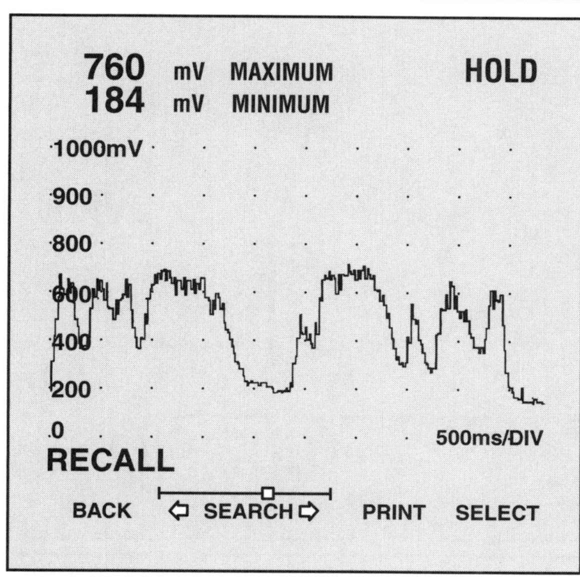

Figure 12-28. A lean condition caused by combustion or fuel mixture problems causes low O2S voltage and erratic switching.

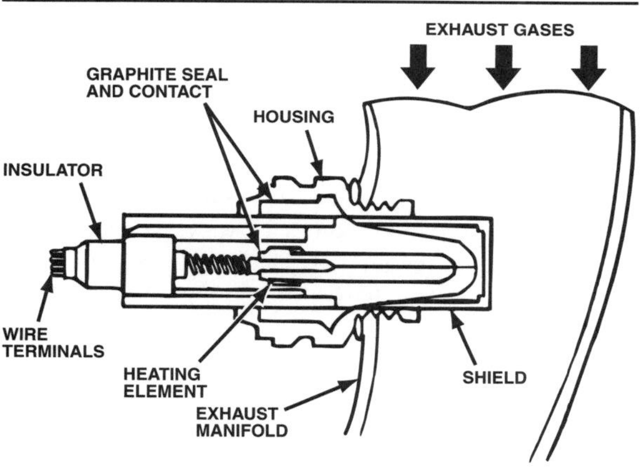

Figure 12-29. The heater circuit of a H2OS contains a resistive coil that warms the sensor.

appear almost linear as the exhaust content of the "cleaned" exhaust is fairly stable. As the catalyst deteriorates or is overloaded, the oxygen content of the treated exhaust changes. This causes the O2S sensor signal to begin switching. The PCM considers too much activity on the downstream sensor an indication of reduced converter efficiency. A DTC records under some conditions.

Circuit resistance is a concern with an O2S because it generates such a low signal voltage. Any resistance on the signal or ground circuit disrupts the voltage waveform produced by the sensor. Wiring must be in good condition, correctly routed away from the hot exhaust, and securely connected.

Position sensors

On an automotive control system, position information is generally provided to the PCM by a potentiometer sensor. A potentiometer is a variable resistor that delivers an analog voltage signal based on the motion or position of the monitored component. Most automotive systems use a potentiometer as a throttle position (TP) sensor, to provide a driver demand signal based on accelerator pedal position. Systems may also use a potentiometer to measure EGR valve opening, canister purge valve condition, and vane airflow sensor position, and provide an input signal to the PCM. Any potentiometer circuit requires three wires:

- Reference voltage
- Signal
- Ground.

All potentiometers work in a similar fashion to convert mechanical movement into a variable voltage signal. The analog signal supplies input information to the PCM as to the position of the mechanical linkage. The PCM applies a reference voltage, usually 5 volts, to one end of a variable resistor. A terminal at the opposite end of the resistor connects to a ground path through the PCM. The third terminal, which attaches to a movable wiper that sweeps across the resistor, sends the variable signal voltage back to the PCM, figure 12-30. Internal PCM circuits digitize the analog potentiometer signal for processing. When viewing a data stream, this digitized signal is displayed.

Signal voltage is high or low, depending on whether the movable wiper is near the supply end or the ground end of the resistor. Most automotive potentiometer sensors transmit a low signal voltage when the mechanical device they monitor is at rest. For example, when the throttle or EGR valve is closed, the potentiometer signal voltage is at its lowest, which is slightly above zero. As the linkage moves to its fully open position, signal voltage rises to its highest, which is slightly below reference voltage.

It is possible to check potentiometer operation by connecting a DMM to the signal and ground wires, figure 12-31. Set the meter to min/max, then move the linkage slowly to operate the device through its full range of travel. Watch for voltage to rise and fall smoothly and verify that minimum and maximum voltage is within range. Typically, normal operating range for a 5-volt potentiometer is about 0.2 to 4.9 volts. Signal voltage that is too high in the closed position indicates either a ground circuit problem or an incorrectly adjusted sensor. A signal that does not reach maximum voltage is often the result of a voltage drop on the reference circuit.

Copyright 2000 by Chek-Chart Publications

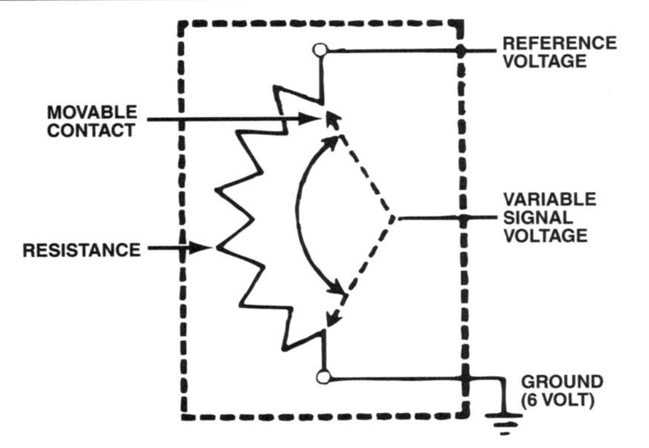

Figure 12-30. Signal voltage changes as the wiper moves across the variable resistor of a potentiometer.

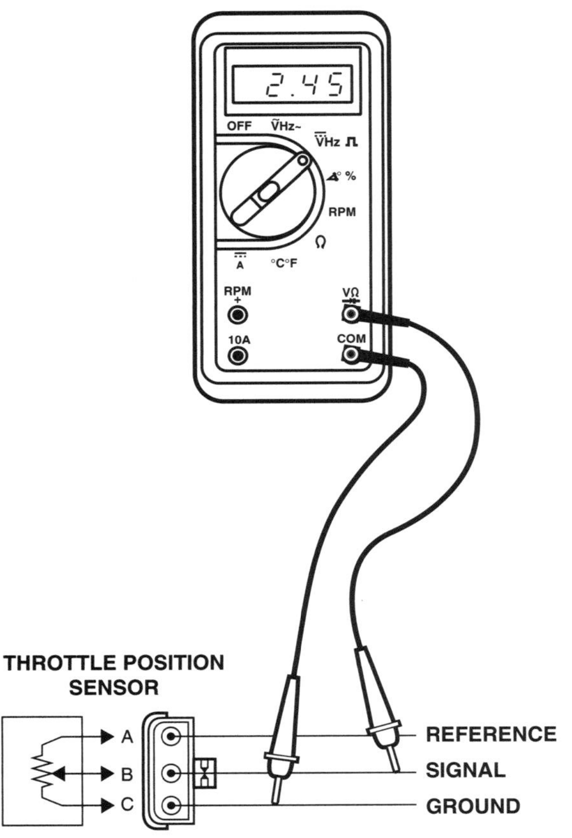

Figure 12-31. Meter connections for checking a potentiometer-type sensor with a DMM.

A common potentiometer failure is signal dropout, where the signal is lost as the wiper moves through a worn area on the resistor contact. Although difficult to isolate with a DMM, signal dropout is easily spotted when performing a sweep test with a GMM or lab scope, figure 12-32. A regular, reoccurring dropout indicates wear, while an irregular dropout indicates problems on the power, or reference voltage, side of the circuit. This can be caused by a circuit or PCM failure; troubleshoot the circuit by voltage drop testing to find the source of the problem.

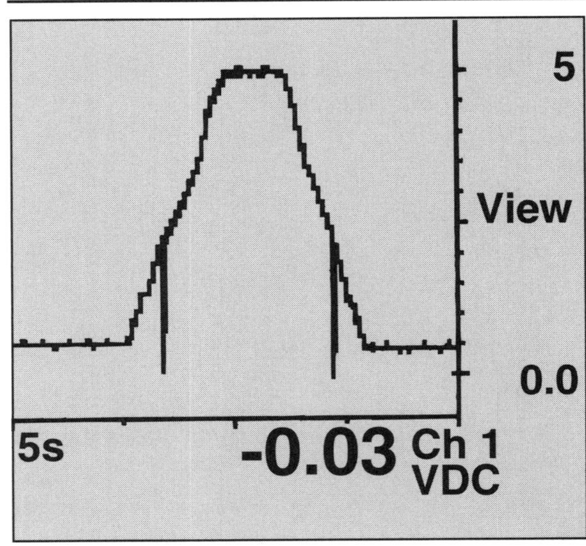

Figure 12-32. A sweep test of a potentiometer shows a worn section of the resistor contacts causing the signal to dropout.

Pressure sensors

Automotive control systems use a pressure sensor to measure manifold absolute pressure (MAP). The PCM uses information from a MAP sensor to determine the load on the engine. These sensors generally use either a piezoresistive crystal or a capacitive-ceramic device to generate an input signal to the PCM.

When pressure is applied to a piezoresistive crystal, the resistance of the crystal changes. A piezoresistive sensor uses the voltage drop caused by this resistance change to provide an analog input signal to the PCM. The PCM digitizes the signal for processing. A capacitive-ceramic pressure sensor uses intake manifold vacuum to vary the distance between two plates and open or close a circuit. These devices transmit a digital signal to the PCM. The frequency of the signal varies in response to changes in manifold vacuum.

The PCM applies a reference voltage, usually 5 volts, to a piezoresistive crystal. Resistance created by the pressure applied to the crystal determines how much of the reference voltage drops before returning to the PCM on the ground circuit. On a MAP sensor, one side of the piezoresistive crystal is inside a sealed reference chamber, and the other side is in a chamber connected to intake manifold vacuum. Some MAP sensors are a piezoresistive strain gauge design. On

Copyright 2000 by Chek-Chart Publications

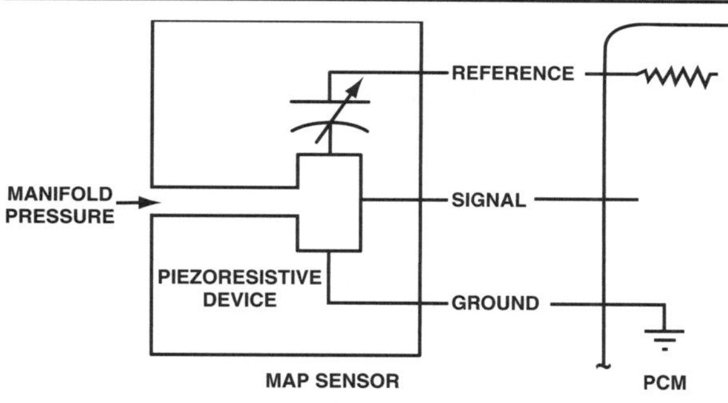

Figure 12-33. A piezoresistive MAP sensor has a three-wire circuit, reference, signal, and ground.

these sensors, a bridge network of four resistors mounts on a flexible silicon wafer. Manifold pressure acts on one side of the wafer, and the other is in a sealed chamber. As the wafer flexes, the resistance of the four resistors changes, which regulates how much reference voltage goes to ground and how much returns to the PCM as signal voltage.

Piezoresistive sensors require a three-wire circuit: reference, signal, and ground, figure 12-33. Typically, signal voltage is low, about 0.5 volt, when manifold vacuum is high, such as at idle. Signal voltage increases as manifold vacuum decreases. With no manifold vacuum, that is key on and engine off, the signal should be about 4.75 volts on domestic vehicles tested at sea level. Some Japanese manufacturers, such as Honda and Toyota, use a MAP sensor that operates on a lower voltage. On these, two to three volts on the signal circuit with the key on and engine off may be normal. Always check the specifications.

Some MAP sensors work under the same principle but produce a variable frequency instead of an analog voltage. With this type of sensor, frequency is high with low manifold vacuum and low at high vacuum, figure 12-34.

Analyzing a pressure sensor waveform is the best way to determine how the unit is operating. Keep in mind, a poorly grounded scope lead disrupts the trace. Never fail a sensor based on the first trace pattern. Disconnect and reattach the probes to rule out a scope connection problem.

Accurate specifications are needed to verify that a pressure sensor is properly calibrated. The frequency of a pressure sensor signal varies with atmospheric pressure, so it changes with altitude. A unit that is out of calibration may produce a waveform that looks good but is operating at the wrong frequency. Look for a smooth linear voltage change on the waveform as manifold vacuum increases or decreases. Use a hand vacuum pump to manipulate the sensor and perform a sweep test.

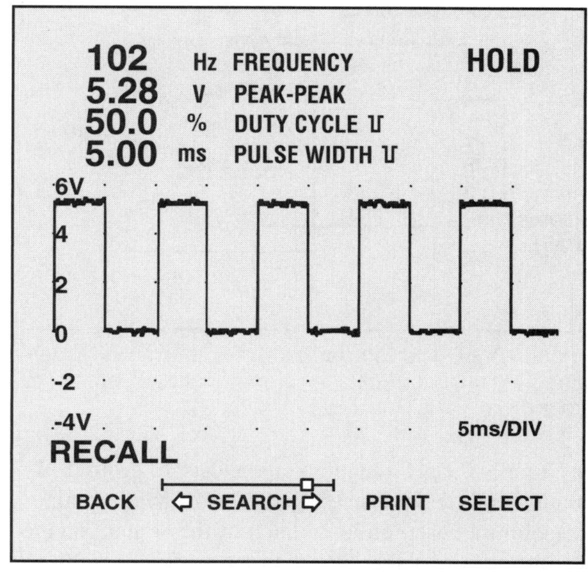

Figure 12-34. A digital MAP sensor transmits a variable-frequency square wave.

A capacitive-ceramic MAP sensor generates a square wave pattern with a variable frequency. Check for square corners where the signal comes off of ground and a vertical rise. High ground circuit resistance keeps the signal from pulling to zero. Voltage drop on the reference circuit causes a low positive peak voltage. Remember, on a digital pulse train, the PCM looks at the midpoint of the signal range to count frequency.

Temperature sensors

Temperature measurement is critical for an engine control system because most operating parameters adjust to compensate for changes in engine operating temperature. Most control systems use a negative temperature coefficient (NTC) thermistor as an engine coolant temperature (ECT) sensor. An NTC thermistor is a variable resistor, which transmits an analog voltage signal that decreases as temperature increases. There are positive temperature coefficient (PTC) thermistors as well, but these are rarely used in automotive applications. In addition to engine coolant, thermistor type sensors may be used to measure intake air temperature (IAT), ambient temperature, oil temperature, AC discharge temperature, or some other temperature on a modern automotive control system. Regardless of the application, all thermistors operate the same. However, resistance and temperature specifications vary considerably.

The PCM applies a reference voltage, usually 5 volts, through a pullup resistor, to the thermistor on the signal circuit, figure 12-35. As the thermistor heats

Copyright 2000 by Chek-Chart Publications

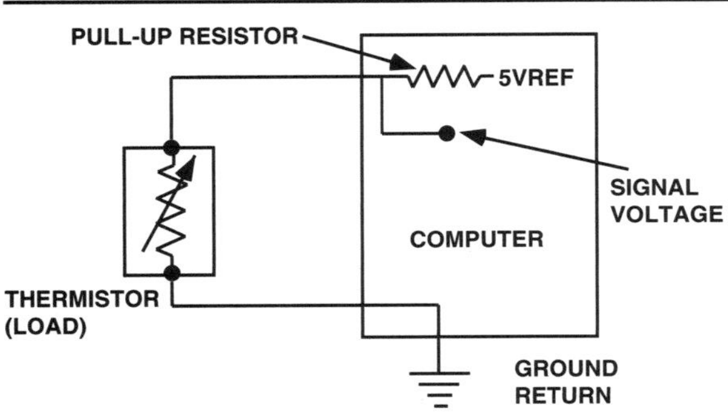

Figure 12-35. The temperature of a thermistor determines how much of the signal voltage drops to ground.

up, it pulls the reference voltage closer to ground. By monitoring the reference signal, the PCM determines temperature based on how much of the signal voltage is dropped across the thermistor. Some sensors contain an internal shunt circuit to increase their operating range. The shunt circuit activates as signal voltage drops to near ground; this reduces resistance and the signal goes high once again. A thermistor sensor requires a two-wire circuit: reference and ground. The PCM signal is the voltage drop on the reference circuit.

Most thermistor failures are due to an open or short circuit, which is detectable with a DMM. However, voltage dropout and drift are also common problems with this type of sensor. Expect signal voltage to change slowly because it responds to changing temperature. The best way to isolate signal dropout and drift is to make a timed data recording using a GMM or digital storage oscilloscope (DSO).

Manufacturers generally provide resistance and voltage drop specifications across a range of temperatures in the service manual, figure 12-36. Remember, specifications vary greatly by application and many vehicles have several thermistor sensors. Be sure to locate the correct specifications for the exact sensor being tested.

Output Actuators

The actuators are the output devices that respond to electronic commands from the PCM to control vehicle operation. These devices convert electrical energy into mechanical motion. Actuators usually contain some type of induction coil and operate at current levels that are much higher than input sensor circuits, which only carry information. The most common actuators are the ignition coils and fuel injectors. Other engine control system actuators include relays, solenoids, and force motors.

On most automotive actuators, the PCM regulates the device by controlling the ground circuit. System voltage is applied to the actuator coil to power the device through the ignition switch or a relay. The PCM opens and closes the ground circuit to control the buildup and collapse of the magnetic field in the coil.

Almost all system voltage is dropped across an actuator, which reduces the current applied to the output driver transistors in the PCM. To regulate this voltage drop, the coil windings of an actuator must meet a minimum resistance specification. If coil resistance is too low, higher voltage and current on the ground circuit may overheat and destroy the transistors in the PCM driver circuit.

Relays

The simplest actuation device is the relay, and relays are used on all automotive electrical systems. A relay is an electromagnetic switch that opens or closes depending upon whether a low-current control circuit is complete or open. When closed, the relay switch completes a high-current output circuit, which applies power to an electric device. Operation of the relay control circuit may be under PCM control, or it may be connected directly to the ignition switch, light switch, or some other source. Typically, relays are used in electronic engine control systems to operate the fuel pump, lamp drivers, and system power.

Modern vehicles typically use an assortment of relays, and the relays often install at a central location in a power distribution center, figure 12-37. However, relays may be found on an inner fender, the engine compartment bulkhead, under the dash, behind a kick panel, and other locations as well. In any case, there are only two basic relay designs: normally open and normally closed. The output circuit closes when the control circuit is complete on a normally open relay, and the output circuit opens when the control circuit is complete on a normally closed relay. In addition, the control circuit may be switched on either the power or ground side, and both types are sometimes used on the same vehicle.

The automatic shutdown (ASD) relay, used extensively on Chrysler control systems, is a good example of a relay used as a PCM output actuator, figure 12-38. On the ASD relay, the PCM completes the ground side of the circuit to direct current through the magnetic coil. Induced magnetism in the relay coil pulls the output circuit contacts closed, allowing current through the relay to power the alternator, ignition coils, fuel injectors, and oxygen sensor heaters.

To test a relay, refer to a wiring diagram to determine circuit layout and have accurate specifications

Copyright 2000 by Chek-Chart Publications

Temperature F	(C)	Sensor Voltage
248	(120)	0.25
212	(100)	0.46
176	(80)	0.84
150	(66)	1.34
140	(60)	1.55
104	(40)	2.27
86	(30)	2.60
68	(20)	2.93
32	(0)	3.59
-4	(-20)	4.24
-40	(-40)	4.90

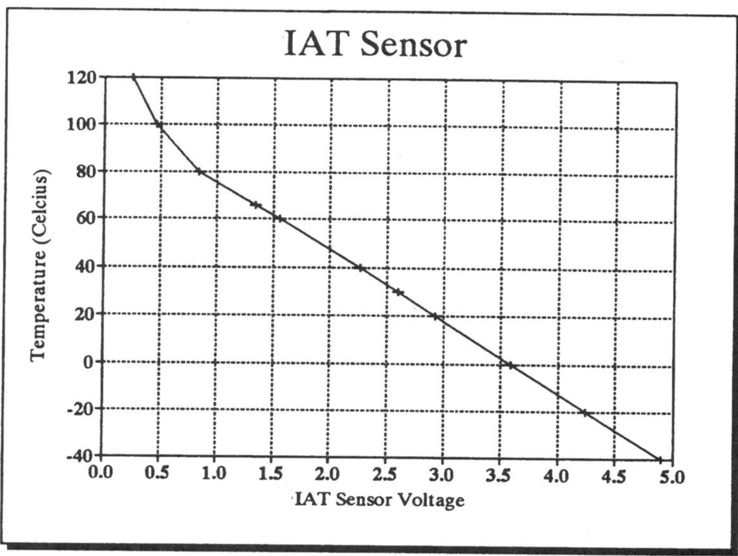

Figure 12-36. Manufactures may provide voltage drop specifications for thermistor sensors.

Figure 12-37. A number of relays are often located in a power distribution center in the engine compartment.

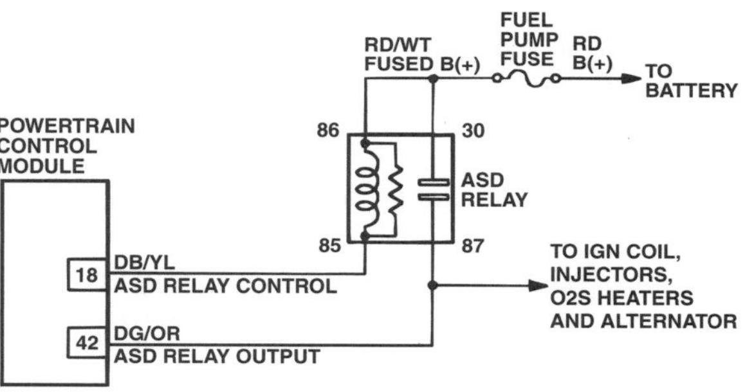

Figure 12-38. The PCM grounds the control circuit of a Chrysler ASD relay to power the alternator, ignition coils, fuel injectors, and oxygen sensor heaters.

for the relay in question. Two common relay failures are defective coil windings and insufficient contact between the points. Winding failures cause an open or short on the control circuit, and poor contact creates high output circuit resistance. Relay operation is quickly checked with a DMM.

Verify that voltage is available to the relay at both the control and output circuits, pins 86 and 30 on the Chrysler ASD relay. Often, the relay must be removed from the control panel to check available voltage on late-model vehicles. Manufacturers generally provide coil resistance specifications for checking relays with an ohmmeter. An alternative is to use jumper wires to check relay operation. Connect both relay circuits to battery voltage with jumper wires, then use another jumper wire to ground the output terminal of the control circuit. The output contacts should close, or open, depending upon the natural state of the relay. With the contacts closed, battery voltage should be available on the output terminal. If not, replace the relay.

If the relay terminals are accessible with the unit installed in the vehicle, check relay operation and circuit continuity by voltage drop testing. There should be virtually no voltage drop across the output circuit when it is complete, and all the voltage should drop on the control circuit when the coil is energized. If there is too much voltage drop and the relay is operating correctly, work down the circuit taking voltage drop readings at each connection to locate the source. Make repairs as needed and retest.

Copyright 2000 by Chek-Chart Publications

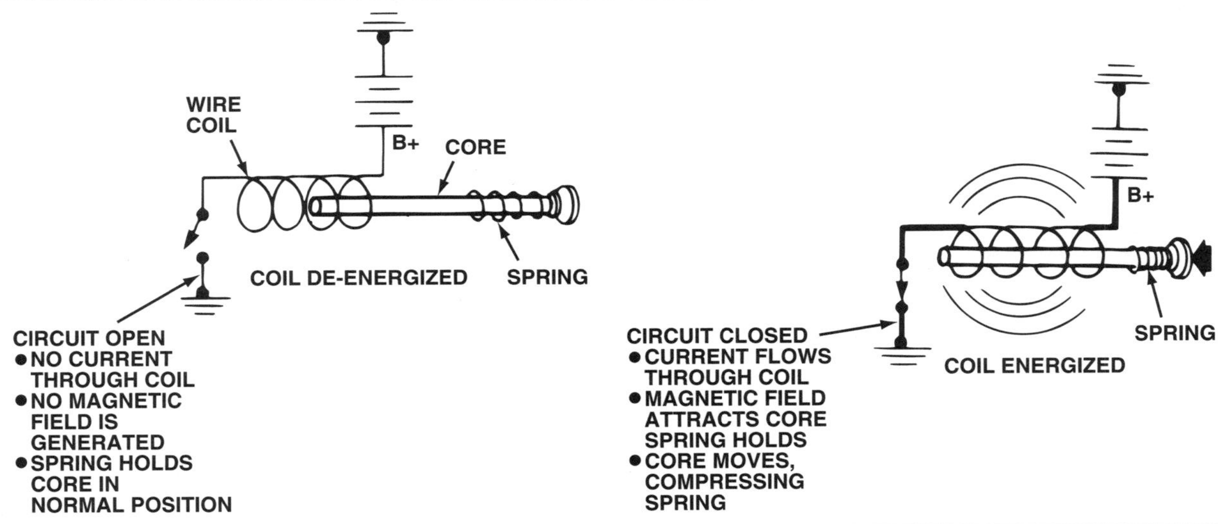

Figure 12-39. An electromagnetic field moves an iron core to open and close a solenoid.

Solenoids

A solenoid is an electromechanical device that uses magnetism to move an iron core. The core provides mechanical motion to some other system part. A solenoid thus changes electrical voltage and current into mechanical movement, figure 12-39. Solenoids are used to perform a number of mechanical tasks on modern vehicles. Solenoid design and use vary considerably and range from the large, high-current starter solenoid to the delicate, low-current fuel injector.

With the exception of the starter solenoid, most solenoids are electronically controlled. Two types of solenoids are used in automotive control systems:

- On/off
- Pulse-width modulated.

All solenoids are digital devices and have only two positions: on and off. However, the PCM is capable of varying the movement of the core in some solenoid applications. This is done by regulating the amount of time the induction coil circuit is complete in relation to the amount of time that it is open. This type of solenoid control, which is known as pulse-width modulation (PWM), adjusts the strength of the magnetic field to move the core a specific amount.

It is possible to check solenoid operation with a DMM, but using a GMM or lab scope reveals how well the device is controlling the circuit. This is especially important when dealing with PWM solenoids. Accurate service specifications are also necessary for troubleshooting a specific solenoid. The following general procedures apply to most solenoid applications. Although electronic fuel injectors are pulse-width-modulated solenoids, they are discussed in a separate section because of the uniqueness and complexity of their operation.

On/off solenoid

Like a relay, an on/off solenoid is a digital device. However, a solenoid does not control current on another circuit. Instead, it regulates the flow of air or fluid, or moves a valve or mechanical linkage. Solenoids use a two-wire circuit: power and ground. On a typical automotive application, voltage is applied to one solenoid terminal, and the PCM switches the other circuit to ground. Most solenoids are energized for varying lengths of time as determined by PCM programming, switch inputs from the driver, or input sensor signals.

On a solenoid that switches to ground, full voltage should be available to the solenoid when it is switched off. This is because the circuit is open and the solenoid not operating. A solenoid may operate on either system voltage or a lower PCM-regulated voltage. A quick check of available voltage is made with a DMM. When the solenoid energizes, or switches on, the circuit completes and voltage readings should drop to near zero. If voltage is available and the solenoid does not operate, check the resistance of the solenoid coil with an ohmmeter, figure 12-40. Manufacturers provide resistance specifications for most solenoids.

A more accurate way to check a solenoid is to measure the amperage draw through the driver circuit. For this test, the circuit must have voltage available and be under load so that current is applied to the solenoid. To test with a DMM, set the meter to the amperage

Copyright 2000 by Chek-Chart Publications

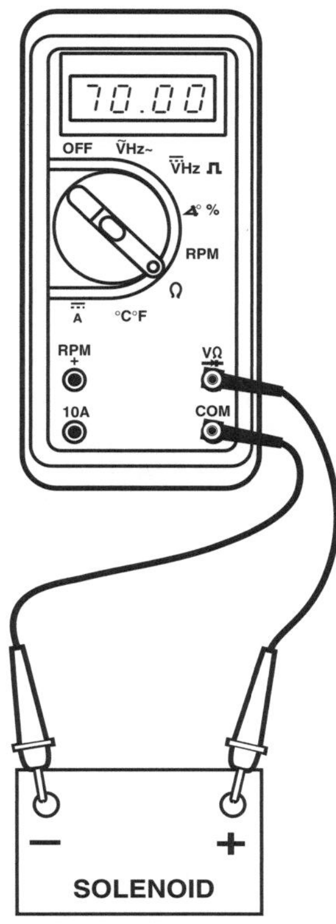

Figure 12-40. Measuring solenoid winding resistance with an ohmmeter.

scale and connect it in series between the solenoid negative terminal and ground, or the actual driver circuit if it can be energized, figure 12-41. Leave the circuit energized for 1 to 2 minutes to check the draw. Compare results to specifications.

It is also possible to check on/off solenoid operation using a GMM or lab scope. To display a solenoid trace, connect the scope probes between the load and the driver as close to the solenoid as possible. Make sure the meter lead is connected to a good chassis ground. Remember, like relays, solenoids may be switched to either ground or power, and the switch determines how the trace appears on screen. When viewing a trace, look for a good, clean transition as the solenoid energizes. The slope should be a vertical line between system voltage and ground. A signal that is not at system voltage indicates a voltage drop on the power circuit. Resistance on the ground circuit prevents the trace from pulling completely to zero when the solenoid is energized.

Be aware, when a solenoid opens, the coil collapses and voltage must be dissipated. This creates a spike, or inductive kick, and ringing on the scope trace of some solenoids. The spike may go either up or down, depending upon how the solenoid switches, figure 12-42.

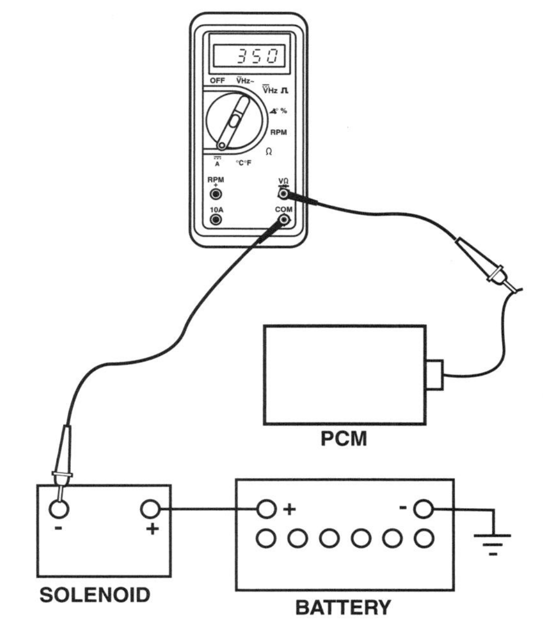

Figure 12-41. Meter connections for measuring current draw through a solenoid driver circuit.

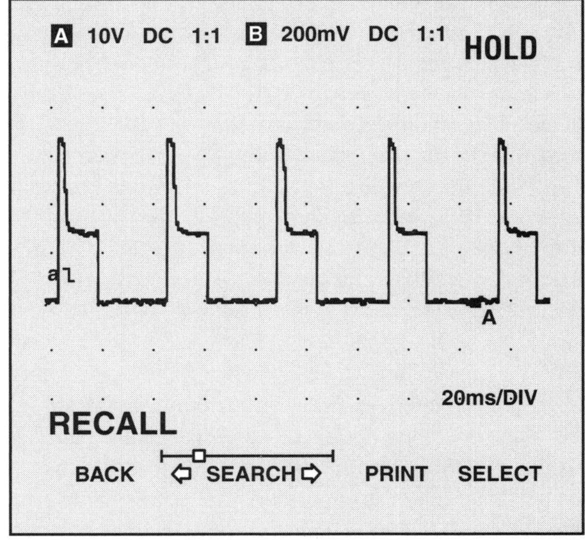

Figure 12-42. An inductive kick, or voltage spike, as the coil opens is normal on some solenoids.

Pulse-width modulation

Solenoids used in electronic applications often operate on a digital pulse train signal. That is, a continuous series of switching cycles from off to on to off. Cycling the solenoid maintains a fairly stable magnetic field to hold the core in the desired position and reduces the amount of heat buildup in the coil windings.

Copyright 2000 by Chek-Chart Publications

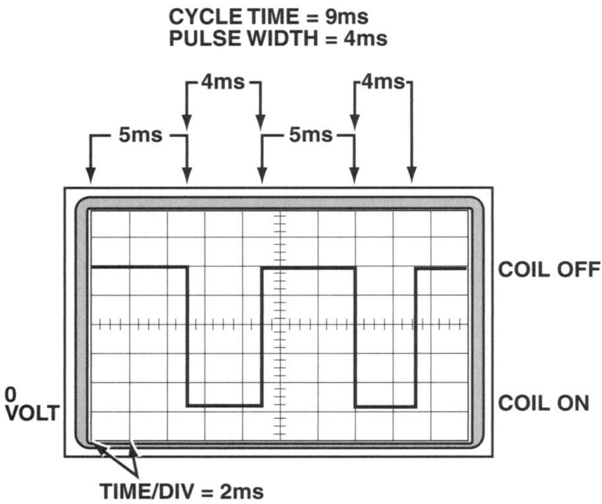

Figure 12-43. Pulse width is the amount of time the solenoid is on during each cycle.

This type of solenoid pulses on and off rapidly at a specific number of cycles per second, or hertz (Hz). The operating cycle of a pulsed solenoid is the sequence from off to on and back off again. Actuator solenoids may operate at any fixed number of cycles per second, or fixed frequency: 10 Hz, 20 Hz, 60 Hz, and so on.

The percentage of time that the solenoid is energized, or the "on" part of each cycle, is called duty cycle. When voltage and a ground are available, current travels through the windings to produce work. When the duty cycle is varied, it changes the amount of work, or position of the solenoid. This varying of duty cycle is called pulse-width modulation (PWM). The pulse width is the amount of time a solenoid is energized, or on, during one cycle and is usually measured in milliseconds (ms), figure 12-43. By using PWM, a solenoid valve may be held completely closed, completely open, or anywhere in between.

When checking duty cycle, the meter must be measuring the "on" time of the signal. If the solenoid is controlled on the ground side, the meter should be measuring the low, or negative, voltage. If the solenoid is controlled on the power side, the meter should be measuring the high, or positive, voltage.

Fuel injector solenoids use pulse-width modulation to control "on" time. This is done because of the direct relation between pulse width and the amount of fuel injected into the cylinders.

Voltage readings on a PWM solenoid taken with a DMM may be misleading because of the way the meter samples the signal and the rapid speed at which the pulses occur. For example, a DMM set to the voltage scale and connected to a 5-volt PWM solenoid

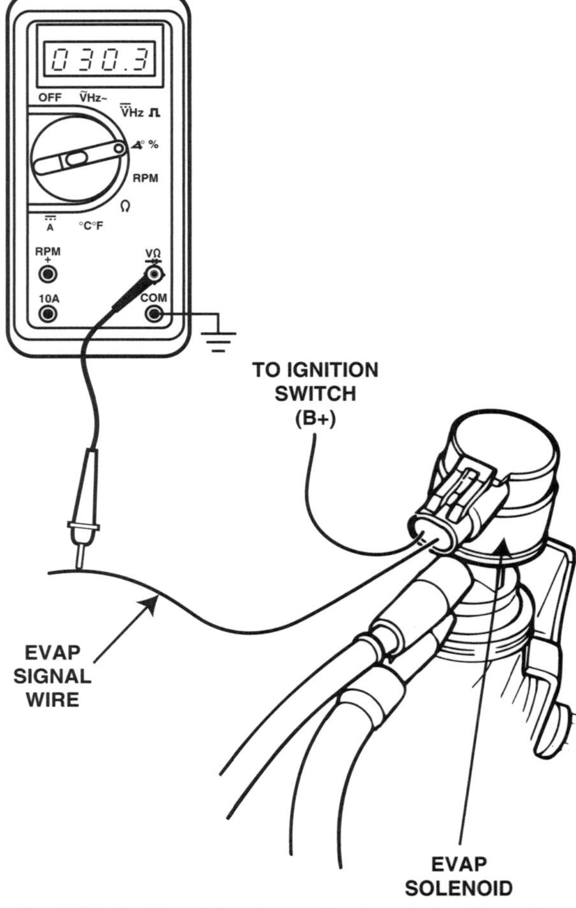

Figure 12-44. With a PWM signal, the DMM registers solenoid on-time as a percentage of the cycle.

operating at a 50-percent cycle—that is, on half the time and off half the time—would read 2.5 volts. Most DMMs designed for automotive use generally have a % or duty cycle setting. In this mode, the meter displays the signal as a percentage rather than voltage. With the above example, the meter would read 50. If the solenoid is on, voltage low, for 3ms of a 10ms cycle, the meter would read 1.5 volts on the voltage scale. With % or duty cycle selected, the meter displays 30% if triggering is on the positive slope and 70% if triggering on the negative slope, figure 12-44.

Viewing the signal waveform on a GMM or lab scope is the most accurate way to determine how well a PWM solenoid is operating. When viewing a trace, look for a good, clean transition as the solenoid energizes. The slope should be a vertical line between system voltage and ground. Remember, the collapsing coil creates an inductive kick and a spike with ringing when the unit switches on some solenoids. Resistance on the ground circuit causes the signal to stay above the zero-volt baseline when the coil is energized. For

Copyright 2000 by Chek-Chart Publications

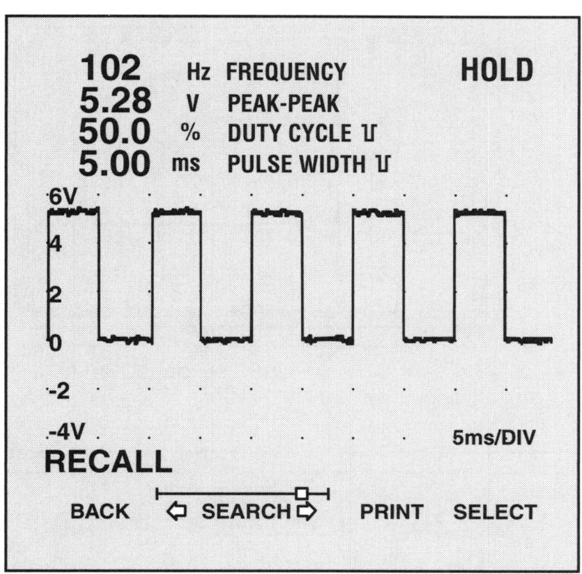

Figure 12-45. Automotive scopes often display pulse width and other signal readings along with the waveform.

best results, connect the meter leads to the ground side of the solenoid; this is the circuit the PCM is controlling.

On a traditional lab scope, precise scope triggering is needed to align the trace on the screen in order to check the duty cycle of the signal. Measure a complete cycle on the screen grid in ms, then measure how long the signal is at zero volt during the cycle. Pulse width and on-time percentage are often displayed on screen along with the signal trace on a GMM or DSO designed for automotive use, figure 12-45.

Fuel injectors

An electronic fuel injector is one of the more complex solenoid designs found on an automotive control system. A fuel injector is a type of PWM solenoid, but also operates at a variable frequency. The frequency of the injector signal, or the number of times it cycles per second, changes in proportion to engine speed. This ensures that fuel is delivered to the cylinder at the correct time regardless of how fast the crankshaft is turning. The PCM adjusts injector pulse width in relation to the amount of fuel needed by the engine at the time. Fuel need is based on engine load and operating conditions as determined by the system sensors. When engine load is high, the PCM increases the injector pulse width, which keeps the solenoid on longer during each cycle to deliver more fuel. Under light engine loads, such as at cruise or idle, the PCM shortens the pulse width to reduce fuel delivery. In general, the frequency of the signal determines when the injector opens, and how long it stays on is determined by the pulse width of the signal.

Most fuel injectors use a two-wire circuit; one wire supplies power and the other provides a ground path through the PCM. The PCM switches the ground circuit to energize the solenoid windings on some injectors and switches the power circuit to operate others. Ground switched injectors are more common and are the focus of the following discussion. There are four basic types of electronic fuel injector:

- Non-resistor—high resistance
- Series resistor—low resistance
- Peak and hold—low resistance
- PWM current controlled—low resistance.

The best way to understand how a fuel injector operates is to examine the waveform of the signal on a scope screen. Connect the meter probe to the ground side of the injector whenever possible. The ground circuit reflects current after the induction coil and provides a clearer picture of how well the solenoid is operating.

The waveform of a fuel injector signal varies depending upon the type and layout of the driver circuit. Some injector circuits contain a type of current-limiting device to protect the injector coils from overheating, prevent PCM damage, and reduce overall electrical consumption. All injector designs have common characteristics as well. Injector waveforms occur quickly and have a relatively high inductive kick. When the PCM opens the ground circuit, the magnetic field of the coil collapses, which generates an inductive kick with a spike that usually exceeds 40 volts. A typical fuel injector cycle, or event, lasts about 2 to 5ms at idle speed, and frequency increases in proportion to engine speed.

On a sequential injection system, each injector has a separate driver, so the screen display is shaped entirely by the injector being probed. With paired injectors, one driver fires two injectors simultaneously, and the waveform is shaped by activity in the windings of both units. Ganged, or banked, injectors switch all of the injectors in one bank of a V-type engine on at the same time, so the waveform is a composite of three or four injectors. On paired or banked injectors, it is impossible to display a trace for a single injector. Any of the four types of injector may be driven sequentially, paired, or banked. Therefore, it is important to check the service manual to determine how the circuits are laid out on the system being tested.

Non-resistor and series resistor

The waveforms of non-resistor and series resistor injectors are similar, and the following discussion applies to both. The main difference is that a series

Copyright 2000 by Chek-Chart Publications

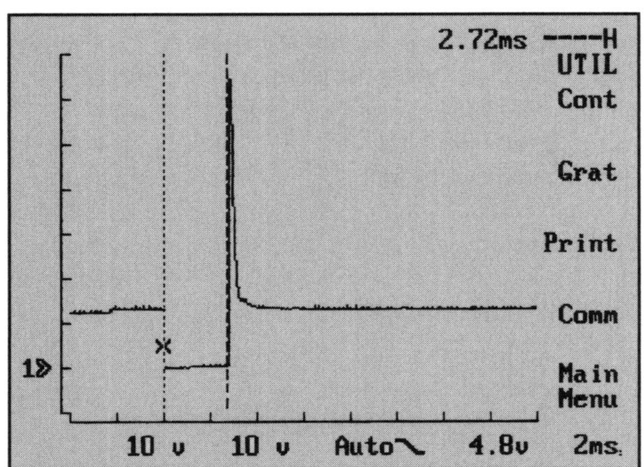

Figure 12-46. Waveform of a typical series resistor fuel injector.

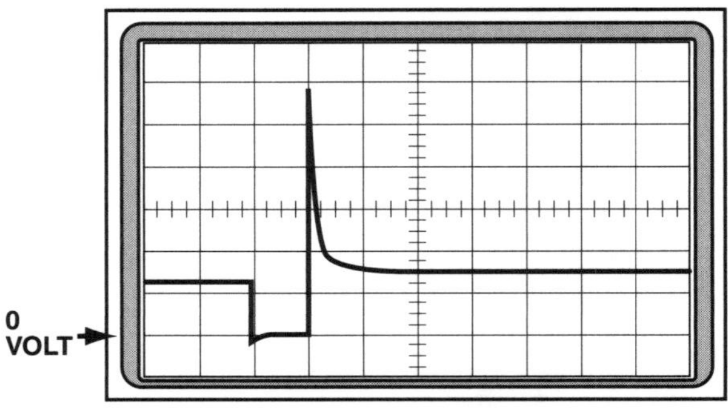

Figure 12-47. A slight voltage rise during on-time is normal for some injectors.

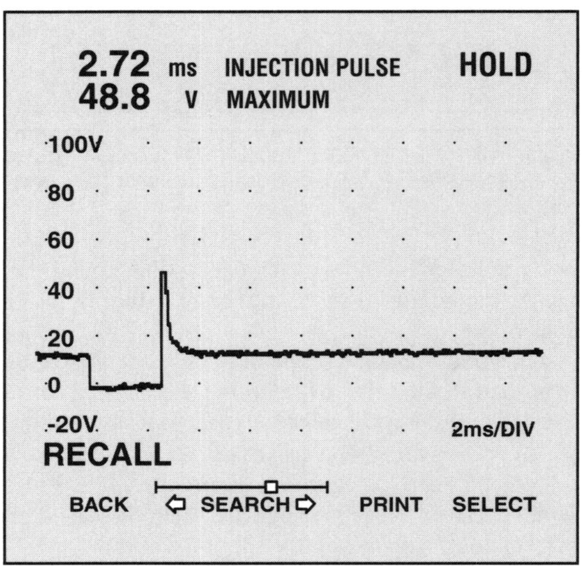

Figure 12-48. A zener diode limits peak voltage, so the waveform flattens out before it drops off.

resistor system has an external resistor on the power supply circuit to limit current. Both use the same type of driver circuit, which produces a fairly simple and easy-to-follow waveform, figure 12-46.

With the ground circuit open, injector turned off, the waveform holds steady at system voltage. When the PCM completes the ground circuit, the solenoid coil energizes to open the injector. This causes the trace to immediately drop to, or very close to, zero volts. A slow, or lazy, drop in voltage indicates a PCM driver failure. A signal that does not pull to ground is the result of high resistance in the ground circuit.

Voltage remains near zero as long as the injector solenoid is switched on. On some systems, resistance in the PCM driver circuit causes a slight rise in voltage during injector on-time. This is considered normal as long as the voltage climb remains gradual, figure 12-47. Excessive voltage rise during on-time indicates low resistance in the injector windings or high system voltage.

When the PCM opens the ground circuit, the fuel injector switches off and energy must be dissipated from the inductive coil. An injector coil carries a relatively high current, so dissipating coil voltage produces an inductive kick with a high peak voltage. The solenoid off signal must result in a sharp transition on the waveform as it climbs quickly to peak voltage. A slow, or lazy, response generally indicates a weak transistor. Some injectors use a zener diode to clip the spike and limit the amount of voltage on the circuit. This type of circuit produces a waveform with a flat top on the spike, figure 12-48. Once the injector spike peaks, it falls slightly slower than it rose, before it stabilizes at source voltage. Ringing, as the waveform drops from peak to source voltage, is normal on some circuits.

When comparing injector waveforms, look for fairly even spikes within the specified peak voltage range. With a zener diode, all peak voltages should be precisely even. A faulty voltage regulator allowing the alternator to overcharge the battery or a problem in the transistor circuit causes high peak voltage spikes. On the other hand, low system voltage, poor wiring connections at the injector, or low resistance in the injector coil, which eventually results in a short circuit, causes low peak voltage spikes.

Peak and hold

The PCM driver of a peak and hold injector has a built-in current-limiting circuit that allows the PCM to regulate current through the injector coil. A transistor switches the control circuit on and off and current through the circuit is limited by a built-in resistor.

Copyright 2000 by Chek-Chart Publications

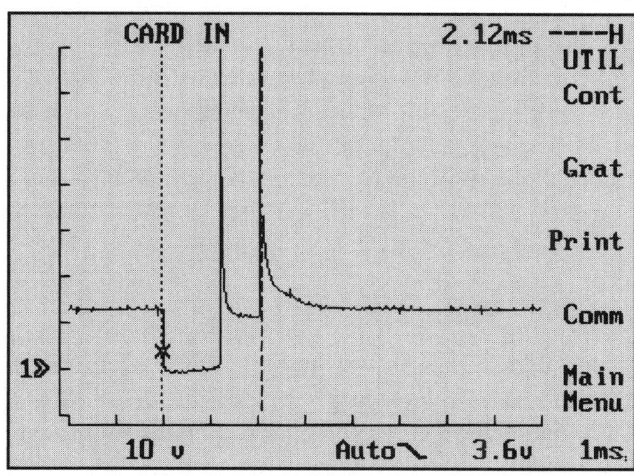

Figure 12-49. Waveform of a typical peak and hold fuel injector.

This type of injector circuit produces a waveform with two inductive spikes; the first marks the start of current limiting, and the second occurs as the injector switches off to complete the solenoid cycle, figure 12-49. This type of circuitry makes use of the principle that it takes much less current to hold an injector open than it does to initially open it. Less current reduces the likelihood of component failures due to heat damage.

The driver opens a peak and hold injector very quickly by allowing maximum current through the circuit. Once current reaches a predetermined level, the driver reduces current to about one-fourth of the initial opening level. This allows just enough current through the circuit to hold the injector open. That is, the current switches back on to energize the coil before spring force acting on the core overcomes the residual magnetism of the electromagnetic field. How long the control circuit remains on to hold the injector open determines the pulse width of the signal.

The waveform of a peak and hold injector begins with a sudden drop from system voltage to ground, then continues as a near-horizontal line with a slight ramp. When the PCM driver reduces current to begin the hold portion of the cycle, an inductive kick is produced because the injector coil field partially collapses. Peak voltage on this spike is limited by a zener diode on some systems.

Following the initial spike, the waveform drops, may ring, and holds at slightly below system voltage. The fuel injector remains open during this time. A signal that drops too far below system voltage indicates a short in the transistor circuit. The second inductive kick occurs when the transistor opens to end current limiting and switch the injector off. Typically, peak voltage of this second inductive kick is slightly lower than that of the first spike. However, both may be clipped evenly by the zener diode. Voltage descends to source voltage following this second peak and a slight ringing on the waveform is considered normal.

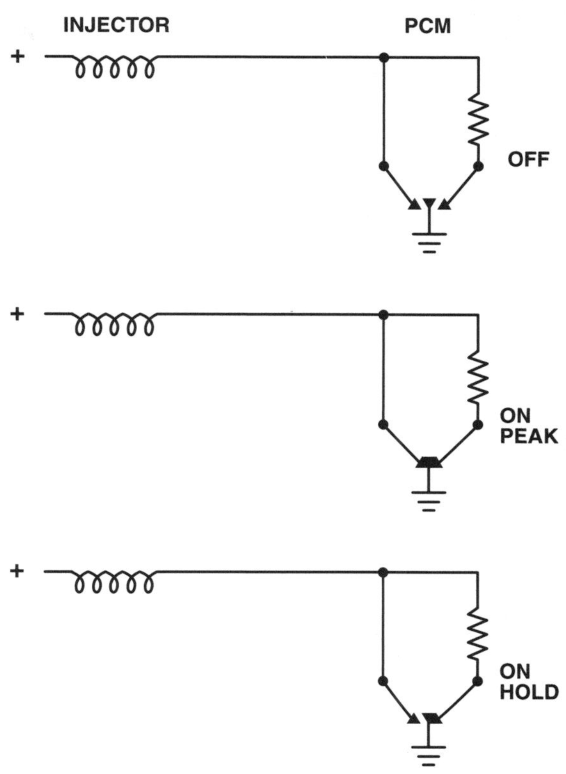

Figure 12-50. Internal PCM circuitry for a peak and hold fuel injector.

With a peak and hold injector, the PCM provides two ground paths: One path goes directly to ground and the other grounds through a resistor. Both ground circuits are open when the injector is off. To switch the injector on, the PCM momentarily completes both ground circuits, then opens the direct path to begin the "hold" portion of the cycle, figure 12-50. Now the only ground path is through the resistor, which allows just enough current through to hold the injector open.

The best way to evaluate this type of injector is to look at how long it takes to reach maximum current before the driver goes into control mode. If peak current builds too quickly, either the source voltage is too high, or there is low resistance in the circuit. A shorted injector coil winding is a common source of low resistance. Low system voltage and high circuit resistance have the opposite effect and cause a delayed peak current buildup. Poor wiring connections and defective coil windings are common causes of high circuit resistance.

Copyright 2000 by Chek-Chart Publications

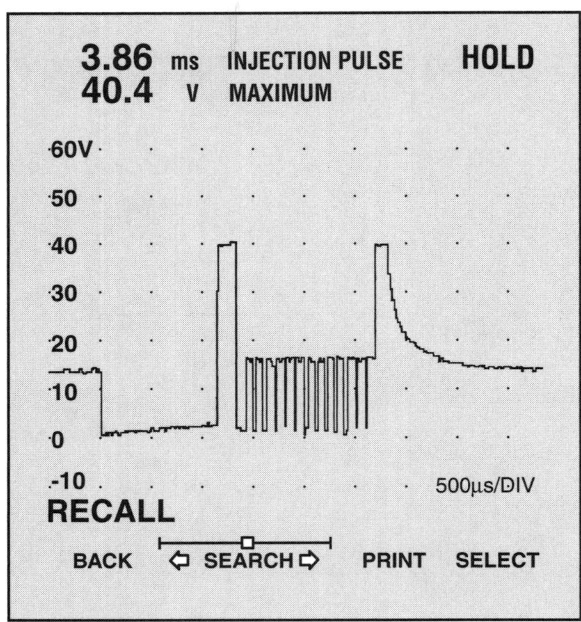

Figure 12-51. The signal cycles during injector on-time with a PWM current-controlled driver.

On a peak and hold injector, total injector on-time is from the drop to ground until the transistor opens to produce the second inductive kick. Remember, the PCM determines pulse width by varying the length of time the internal resistor circuit is open.

PWM current controlled

Although all electronic fuel injectors are PWM solenoids, this design uses a secondary modulation of the signal to control current during on-time. With PWM current control, maximum current through the circuit opens the injector quickly. Once the injector opens, the driver cycles the signal at a predetermined frequency to hold the injector open. As with a peak and hold injector, this PWM signal keeps the injector open using less current. The waveform of this type of driver circuit has two inductive kicks separated by a series of square wave pulses, figure 12-51.

The trace of a PWM current-controlled injector begins with an abrupt drop to zero, or ground, from system voltage. Either a flat or a slightly rising line follows until the current transistor switches on and the injector coil collapses. Coil collapse produces the first inductive kick, whose peak voltage may be clipped by a zener diode.

To hold the injector open, the PCM switches the transistor at a predetermined pulse width, which reduces circuit current. This modulated signal cycles extremely fast. Unless the scope is set fast enough to display the detail of the signal, the pulse train appears as ringing on the waveform. Even a good pattern with a correctly adjusted scope may appear slightly distorted due to the high rate of switching. Make sure the signal switches low enough; the transistor must pull the signal close to ground. The injector closes as the transistor stops switching and stays open. This produces the second inductive kick as the signal makes a rapid rise to peak voltage, which is followed by a more gradual drop to source voltage.

Stepper Motors

These actuators are a reversible direct-current motor that moves in increments, or steps, between off and fully energized. A stepper motor operates by moving its armature small distances in one direction or the other. A pintle valve, which does not rotate, is threaded onto the end of the armature shaft. As the armature rotates, the pintle valve moves along the threads. Which way the pintle moves depends upon the direction of armature rotation. These motors usually contain either two or four coils, but may have six or more. When two coils are used, the PCM controls the polarity of each coil, as well as the sequence of energizing them, figure 12-52. Sequencing of the coils is done in pairs when more than two coils are used.

A stepper motor moves in response to a digital signal from the PCM to a coil. To energize the coil, the PCM polarizes it. That is, one side of the coil is positive and the other side is negative. To move the coil, the PCM reverses the polarity of the coil. This polarity change attracts the armature to a different position. By changing polarity of the coils in the proper sequence, the PCM makes the armature move in small increments, or steps. Hence the name, stepper motor. The coils remain energized to hold the armature in position.

These devices commonly operate idle air control valves. To see the operation on a lab scope or GMM, connect the leads to both ends of a coil. Adjust the screen to display both positive and negative 14 volts. With the motor operating, the signal switches back and forth as the coil polarity changes, figure 12-52. The most switching activity occurs on initial startup, or when a load is placed on the engine.

In addition to idle control, stepper motors are used to operate throttle linkages, evaporative system vapor control valves, and door movement in heating and air-conditioning systems.

A force motor is used in some electronic automatic transmissions to control fluid pressure. These devices are similar to a stepper motor, but a force motor is amperage- and voltage-controlled, rather than just voltage-controlled. The PCM applies a PWM signal on the power side of the coil and regulates amperage on the ground side by varying resistance.

Copyright 2000 by Chek-Chart Publications

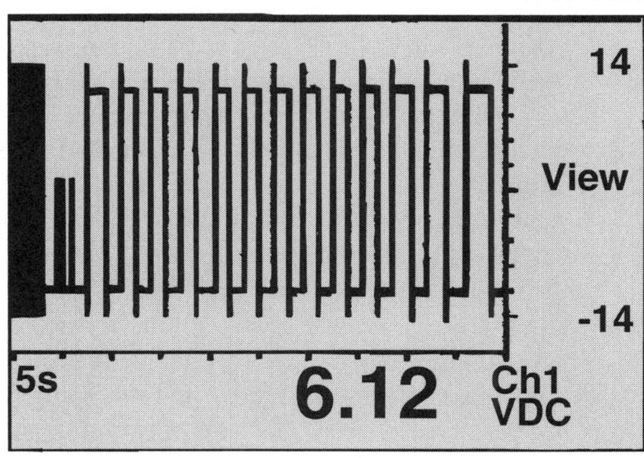

Figure 12-52. The polarity of the coil windings determines the direction the armature turns.

A force motor typically operates on voltage regulated by the PCM, and cycles at a relatively high frequency. When analyzing a force motor waveform, look for even frequency and amplitude with clean, sharp transitions, figure 12-53.

Some import models use a force motor to control idle speed.

CONTROL MODULE REPLACEMENT

Vehicle computers do fail, but not with great frequency or regularity. Too often the PCM, or some other control module, is replaced simply because the source of an electronic failure was incorrectly identified. Many control unit failures are the result of damage caused by too much current through a defective actuator. If the faulty circuit device is not replaced, the new control unit is doomed to failure. Always double-check test results when following the service manual procedure sequence recommends replacing the control module. A ground strap should be worn to prevent static electrical discharges from damaging circuitry when handling any electronic control module.

Manufacturers often use the same basic processor on a number of different vehicle applications. However, the operating instructions that are programmed into the computer are unique for each model and powertrain combination. The computer stores this information in the programmed read-only memory (PROM) of the processor. This PROM is what the processor refers to for determining what is normal or expected when making electronic decisions based on sensor inputs.

The PCM must have "flash programming" capability to comply with OBD II regulations. That is, it must be possible to download program instruction updates to the PROM using a scan tool. However, this technology is available only through the dealer service

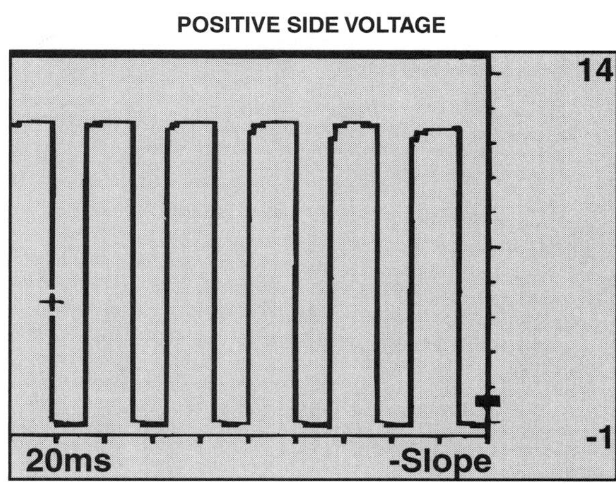

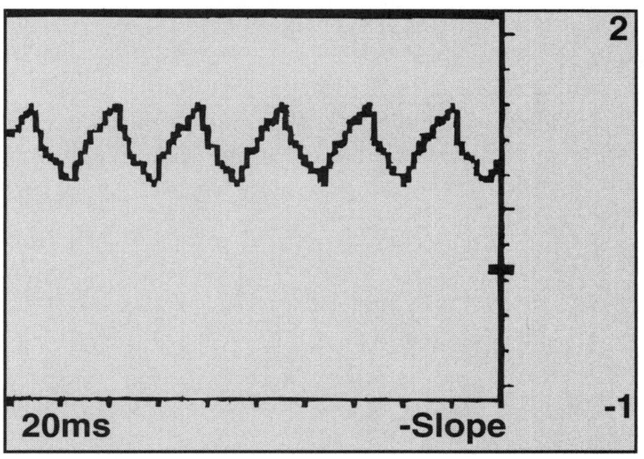

Figure 12-53. A force motor produces a rapidly cycling square wave on the positive side and an analog signal on the ground side.

department at the present time. On older designs, either the entire control module or a separate PROM chip that installs in the module is replaced to update the program instructions.

From time to time, manufacturers release revised computer operating instructions to correct specific vehicle problems. Be sure to obtain the correct part when replacing a PROM assembly. Because the PROM is designed for a given vehicle, the replacement PROM to be installed must always carry the same part number as the unit it replaces. Before deciding to replace a PCM or PROM, always check technical service bulletins (TSBs) for specific information on problems that were corrected with programming updates. With General Motors systems, a scan tool displays a PROM ID number as a data stream parameter to verify that the correct PROM is installed. Use of the incorrect PROM results in false codes and

Copyright 2000 by Chek-Chart Publications

driveability problems at the very least, and possible system damage at the other extreme.

To avoid costly, unnecessary parts replacement, check these items before ordering a PCM or PROM:

1. Battery voltage supply to the PCM and system ground continuity—Make sure the battery is fully charged and provides at least 10 volts during cranking, and that the charging system is maintaining correct battery voltage. Electronic control systems usually receive battery voltage through a fuse, fusible link, or both. Check for battery voltage available at the specified terminal of the main PCM connector. Most systems are grounded remotely through a wire in the harness. Voltage drop across the ground connection must be less than 0.1 volt to ensure good continuity.
2. Operation of a system power relay—Power to the PCM is often supplied through a system relay. If so, check the relay operation.
3. Sensor reference voltage and ground circuits—Many sensors share a common reference voltage supplied by the PCM and share a common ground as well. Incorrect or erratic reference voltage or a poor ground connection affects operation of several sensors simultaneously. The symptoms may appear as if the PCM has a major internal problem. However, a simple wiring connection repair may correct the problem.
4. Resistance and current draw of all PCM-controlled solenoids, relays, and force motors—Every output device controlled by the PCM has a minimum resistance specification. The actuator resistance limits current through the PCM output control circuit. If the actuator is shorted, current may exceed the safe maximum and damage the PCM. In most cases, current through a controlled output device should not exceed 0.75 ampere (750 milliamperes). Before replacing a PCM, check all output circuits for shorts or low resistance that could cause internal damage to the computer.

As a general rule, the PCM or PROM should be at the bottom of the list of things to replace. Again, they occasionally do fail, but a sensor or actuator problem, faulty wiring, or a mechanical fault is a more likely cause of the problem.

Copyright 2000 by Chek-Chart Publications

PART FIVE

Chassis Electrical System Service

Chapter Thirteen
Lighting System Service

Chapter Fourteen
Horn, Wiper and Washer, Cooling Fan, and Instrument Service

Chapter Fifteen
Electrical Accessory Service

Copyright 2000 by Chek-Chart Publications

13 Lighting System Service

Part Five, the final part, of this *Shop Manual* covers chassis electrical systems. This includes all the electrical systems and devices that are not necessarily required to operate the vehicle. This chapter details services performed on the vehicle lighting system; Chapter Fourteen addresses horn, windshield wiper and washer, cooling fan, and instrument systems; and Chapter Fifteen discusses other accessory items, such as power windows, seats, mirrors, and door locks. Electronic control systems, such as antilock brakes and traction control, that are traditionally considered part of the chassis, are not discussed in this section of the *Shop Manual*. Most of these systems, which are either integrated into, or linked to the PCM, are serviced in similar fashion as electronic engine control systems, which are detailed in Chapter Twelve of this *Shop Manual*.

Modern vehicles are required to have a passive restraint system to protect the driver and passengers in the event of a collision. Most manufacturers meet the requirement with a supplemental restraint system (SRS) that includes air bags, automatic tensioning belts and harnesses, or a combination of both. Any SRS must be disabled before working on the electrical system to prevent accidental deployment of the air bags. Disabling and servicing the SRS system is discussed in Chapter Fifteen of this *Shop Manual*. Refer to this chapter and disable the SRS before any chassis electrical repairs are made, especially when working under the dash or near any of the SRS sensors.

The lighting system circuits on a late-model vehicle may be complex, and often there are a number of variations to accommodate different options on the same model vehicle. Accurate specifications, wiring diagrams, and electrical schematics are critical to effectively troubleshoot lighting system problems. The following paragraphs provide general procedures for diagnosing and troubleshooting vehicle lighting problems.

LIGHTING SYSTEM DIAGNOSIS

Lighting circuit diagnosis requires the use of standard test meters and instruments to identify the three basic electrical failures:

- Short circuits
- Open circuits
- High-resistance circuits.

Refer to Chapters One and Two of this *Shop Manual* as needed for standard test procedures and meter use.

Copyright 2000 by Chek-Chart Publications

Electrical Schematics

Manufacturers provide electrical wiring diagrams that depict the entire automobile wiring system. An electrical schematic is a portion of the complete wiring diagram that details the operation of an individual circuit. All electrical information about a complete automotive circuit, including switches, connectors, loads, and other devices, is detailed in the schematic, figure 13-1. Understanding an electrical schematic is further simplified by circuit numbering, color-coded wires, and representation of components or loads by symbols. The information provided by an electrical schematic makes it easy to trace a circuit during troubleshooting.

There are several symptoms common to all electrical systems. Use the following as a general troubleshooting guideline.

With brighter than normal lights, check for:

- Incorrect bulb wattage, which causes the filament to burn brighter
- Excessive charging voltage produced by a faulty voltage regulator or a shorted alternator field circuit.

With lights that are dimmer than normal, check for:

- Low charging voltage
- Slipping drive belts
- Weak or dead battery
- High resistance in the lamp feed circuit
- High resistance in circuit ground connections.

If the charging system is not operating properly, the lights remain dim regardless of engine speed. A slipping drive belt may cause lights to decrease in brightness as engine speed increases. Lights that flare or flicker often result from the same problems as dimly lit lamps.

With lights that operate intermittently or not at all, check for:

- Defective bulb
- Blown fuse or circuit breaker
- Defective switch or other faulty component
- Loose terminal connections
- Loose ground connections.

When a bulb does not light, first check for voltage available to the bulb. If no voltage is available, check the fuse or other circuit protection devices used. If a circuit problem is indicated, check the circuit diagram, then work from the bulb toward the switch to isolate the voltage drop.

Replacing bulbs is probably the most common lighting system service performed. Other system services include headlamp aiming and circuit troubleshooting and repairs. The following paragraphs provide instructions for headlamp replacement and aiming, and for replacing other types of bulbs.

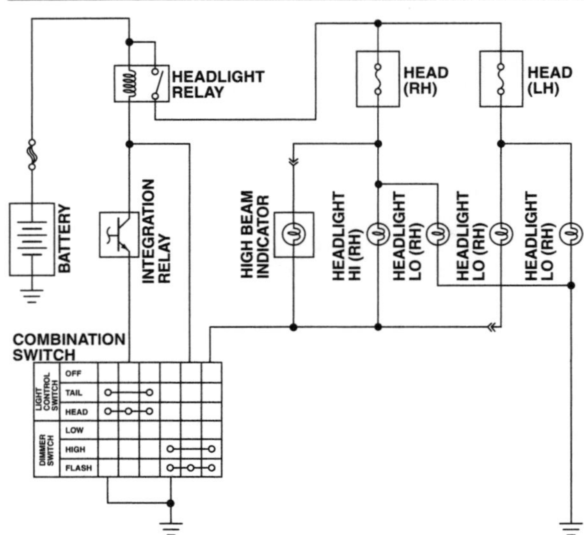

Figure 13-1. Wiring schematic for a typical headlight circuit.

HEADLIGHT SERVICE

Headlight service may involve replacing sealed beam headlamps, replacing halogen headlamp bulbs, and aiming the headlamp assembly.

Headlamp Designs

There are various types of headlights used on late-model vehicles. These may be either a sealed beam headlamp or a composite headlight with a halogen bulb inside an aerodynamic plastic lens, figure 13-2. Both conventional and halogen sealed-beam headlamps are available. There are five types of standard sealed-beam headlamps, figure 13-3:

- Type 1—Single, high-beam filament in a circular housing
- Type 1A—Single, high-beam filament in a rectangular housing
- Type 2—Double high- and low-beam filaments in a circular housing
- Type 2A—Double high- and low-beam filaments in a rectangular housing
- Type 2B—High-beam and low-beam filaments in a rectangular housing in metric dimensions.

Halogen sealed-beam headlights are like conventional headlights, except for the halogen bulb. There are the same five types of halogen sealed-beam as conventional ones, plus a high- and low-beam Type 2E. Composite headlights also may contain individual

Copyright 2000 by Chek-Chart Publications

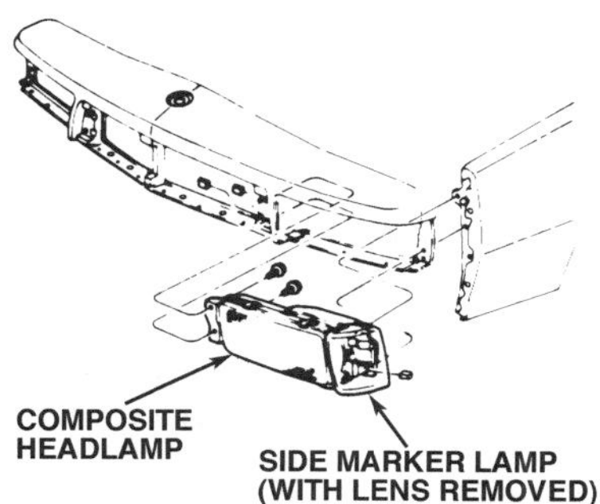

Figure 13-2. A replaceable halogen bulb fits into an aerodynamic lens assembly on a composite headlight.

halogen bulbs, one for low-beam and one for high-beam illumination, in a single lens assembly.

Headlight Replacement

Since conventional and halogen sealed-beam headlight designs are all about the same, the procedures for removal and replacement are similar for all vehicles. Replaceable halogen bulbs in composite headlights require a different replacement procedure.

Sealed-beam headlamp replacement

To replace a typical sealed-beam headlamp:

1. Make sure the headlight switch is off. If the vehicle has concealed headlights, activate the system to expose the bulbs, then switch the ignition and headlamps off.
2. Gain access to the mounting screws by removing any bezel, grille, or panel that covers the headlight retaining ring.
3. Loosen the retaining ring mounting screws and remove the retaining ring. Do not loosen the aiming bolts by mistake. For round lamps, rotate the ring slightly until the large ends of the screw slots align with the screw heads, then remove the ring, figure 13-4. For rectangular lamps, simply remove the retaining screws and lift off the retainer, figure 13-5.
4. With the retaining ring off, pull the headlamp from its housing, and unplug the connector from the back of the lamp, figure 13-6.
5. Check the connector for corrosion or damage, and clean or replace it as needed. Headlamp pigtail connectors that splice into the wiring are readily available to replace a damaged unit.
6. Attach the pigtail connector to the prongs on the new headlamp. Some manufacturers recommend using silicone grease on the bulb prongs to help prevent corrosion. If so, apply grease to the prongs, then wipe off any excess grease after making the connection.

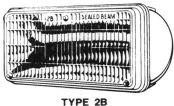

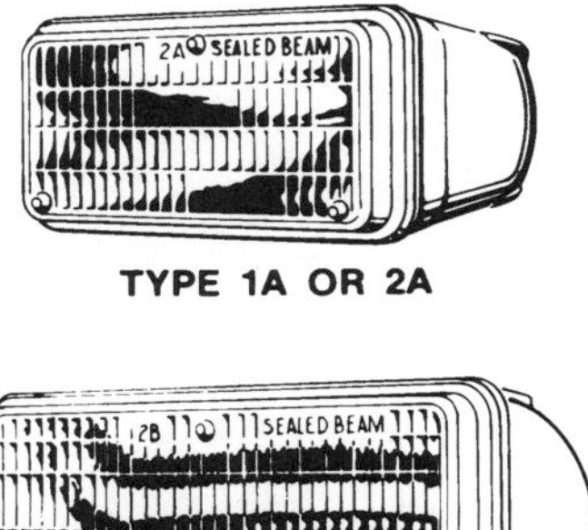

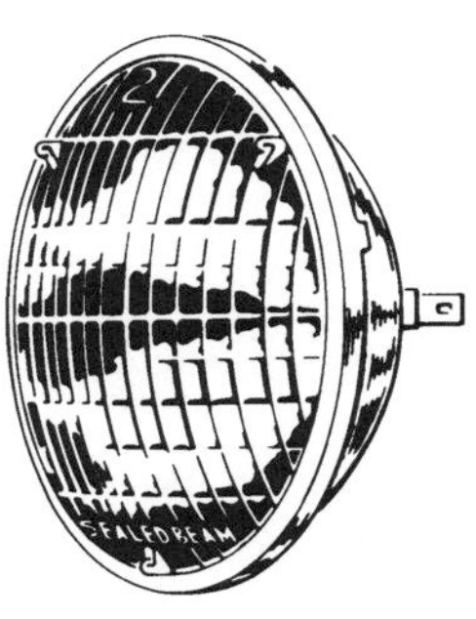

Figure 13-3. Sealed-beam headlights, both conventional and halogen, conform to design standards.

7. Align locating tabs on the lamp with the notches on the mounting while fitting the headlamp into the housing, then install the retaining ring.
8. Check headlight operation and aim; adjust if needed. Complete the installation by fitting any trim previously removed to gain access.

Composite headlamp bulb replacement

Always take care to avoid touching the glass envelope surrounding the filament of a halogen bulb when working with composite headlamps. Contact with skin leaves residual oils on the glass surface that retain heat, which causes hot spots to develop on the bulb.

Copyright 2000 by Chek-Chart Publications

Figure 13-4. On round lamps, loosen the mounting screws, then turn and lift off the retaining ring.

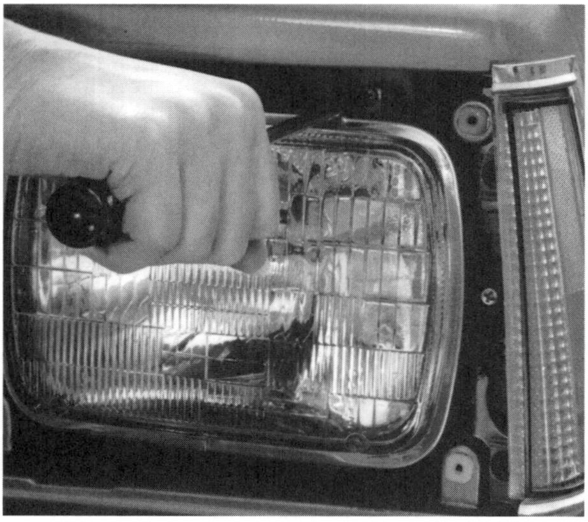

Figure 13-5. On rectangular lamps, remove the mounting screws and lift off the retainer.

These hot spots lead to premature failure of the new bulb. Most newer halogen bulb designs incorporate an insulated plastic base, which makes them easy to install without touching the glass. With older bulb designs that install into a separate socket, use a clean shop rag or paper towel to hold the bulb to avoid touching the glass during installation.

To replace the halogen bulb in a typical composite headlight assembly:

1. Make sure the headlight switch is turned off.
2. The bulb is accessed through the engine compartment. Remove or move aside any trim panels or other parts necessary to reach the headlamp electrical connector. Then, unplug the electrical connector from the bulb holder.
3. Rotate the plastic retaining ring on the bulb assembly to align the tabs and notches on the bulb holder, then slide the ring off.
4. Remove the bulb from the reflector socket by carefully pulling it straight out of the lens assembly, figure 13-7. Do not rotate the bulb during removal.
5. Hold the new bulb assembly by the plastic base and remove any protective covering from the bulb. Carefully align the bulb and socket locating tabs and insert the bulb holder into the reflector socket until it seats.
6. Slide the retaining ring over the bulb holder and rotate it to lock the assembly in place.
7. Attach the harness connector to the bulb and install any items removed previously to gain access.
8. Switch the headlamps on to check new-bulb operation.

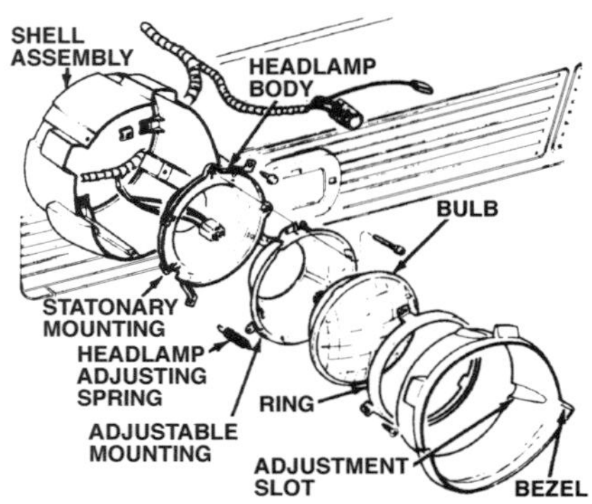

Figure 13-6. Exploded view of a typical sealed-beam headlight assembly.

Headlamp Aiming

There are three methods of aiming headlights:

- Aiming screen
- Mechanical aimer
- Photoelectric aimer.

Generally, aiming screens are the least accurate of the three methods, and are rarely used in automotive shops today. Regardless of which method is used, prepare the vehicle as follows before aiming the lamps:

- Remove any mud or ice from under the fenders.
- Inflate the tires to their specified operating pressures.
- Clean lamp lenses and replace any burned-out units.

Copyright 2000 by Chek-Chart Publications

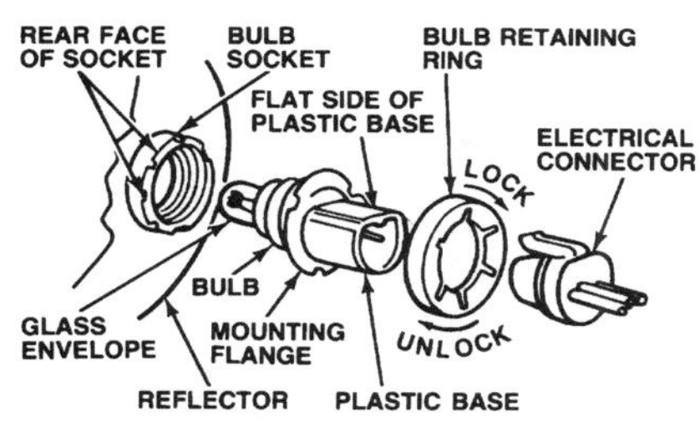

Figure 13-7. Exploded view of a typical halogen bulb of a composite headlight assembly.

- Check the service manual for any specific instructions or preconditions for the vehicle being serviced. For example, the manufacturer may specify a full tank of fuel and a driver and passenger in the front seat. If so, load the vehicle as directed.
- Cover any headlamp photocell controls to prevent their operation.

Headlights that are aimed slightly wrong greatly reduce the area illuminated by the lamps, as well as how far ahead the driver can see, figure 13-8. For this reason, headlamp aiming limits have been established by government regulations.

Aiming screens

An aiming screen is a fixed screen with guidelines on it. The headlight beams are projected on the screen and adjusted according to the guidelines on the screen. Guidelines provide horizontal and vertical centerlines, which establish a reference for positioning the focal point of the headlamp beam on the screen. The screen must be mounted perpendicular to the floor, even if the floor slopes. The screen also must be adjustable, so it can be aligned parallel to the rear axle of the vehicle.

The aiming screen must be 25 feet in front of the headlights and positioned according to the level of the floor. Darken the room and switch on the headlights to check the aiming of the low beams. Adjust as needed, then switch on the high beam headlights to verify that aiming is correct.

Although the headlight aiming limits may vary slightly from area to area, the following limits are generally accepted:

- High-beam—The center of the lamp high-intensity zone should be horizontally within 4 inches (100 mm) to the right or 4 inches (100 mm) to the left of the lamp center. The center of the lamp high-intensity zone should be vertically within 4 inches (100 mm) above or 4 inches (100 mm) below the horizontal centerline, figure 13-9.

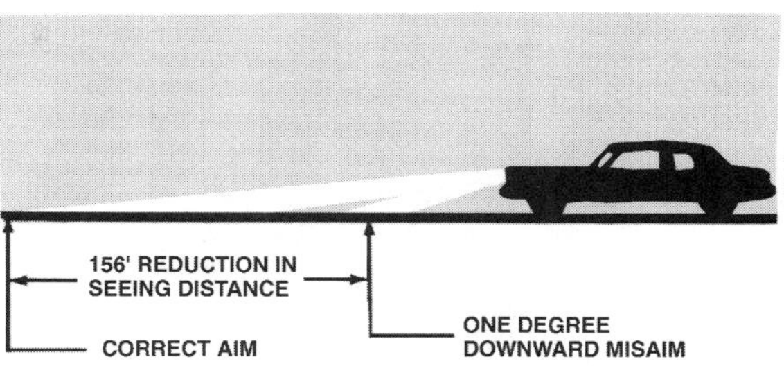

Figure 13-8. Headlights aimed one degree too low reduce visibility by more than 150 feet (45 meters).

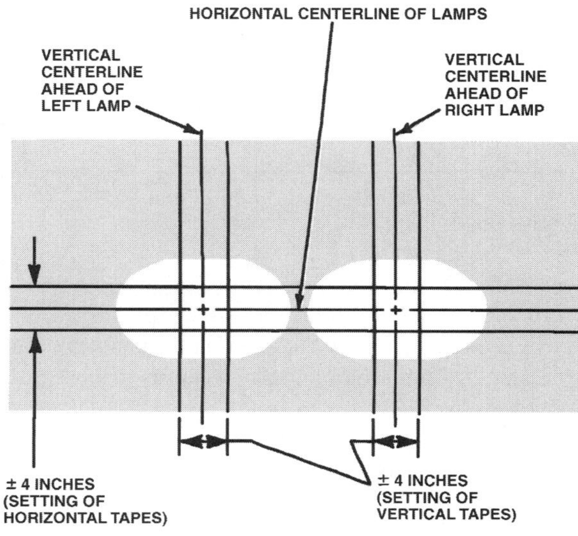

Figure 13-9. The focal point of correctly aimed high-beam headlights is centered on the screen gridlines.

- Low-beam—The left edge of the lamp high-intensity zone should be horizontally within 4 inches (100 mm) to the right or 4 inches (100 mm) to the left of the lamp center. The top edges of the lamp high-intensity zone should be vertically within 4 inches (100 mm) above or 4 inches (100 mm) below the horizontal centerline, figure 13-10.

Remember that these are maximum-allowable inspection limits. When adjusting lamp aim, be sure to center the high-intensity zones exactly, both horizontally and vertically.

Mechanical aiming

Mechanical aimers are a pair of portable devices that attach to the headlights with a suction cup, figure 13-11. The aimers rest on the three aiming pads that protrude from the face of the headlight lens. An assortment of adapters attach to the end of the unit,

Copyright 2000 by Chek-Chart Publications

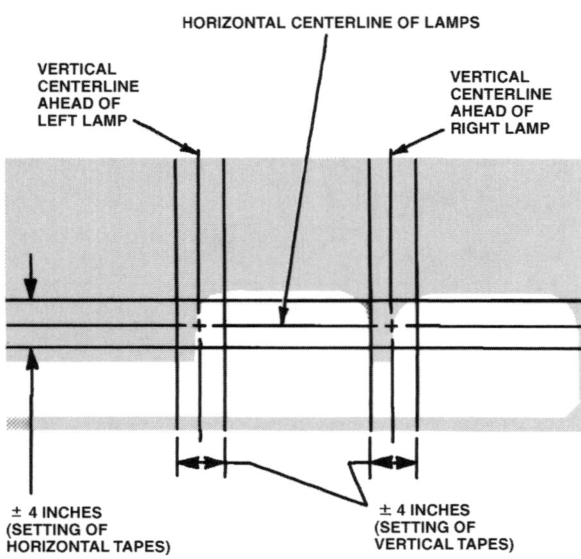

Figure 13-10. Aim low-beam headlights so the edges of the beam align with the screen gridlines.

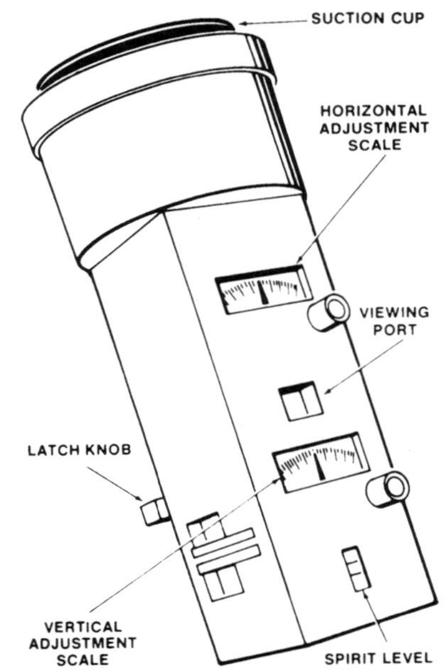

Figure 13-11. Mechanical aimers attach to the headlight with a suction cup.

which allows the aimers to be used on either round or rectangular sealed-beams, as well as on some composite headlamps. Mechanical aimers cannot be used on lamps without aiming pads or lamps that are covered by a fairing or a trim panel.

Mechanical aiming adjusts the headlights based on the position of the aiming pads, not where the light beam shines. Mechanical aiming is actually performed with the headlights switched off. To check or adjust headlamp aim with mechanical aimers:

1. Calibrate the aimers according to the equipment instructions.
2. Install the aimers on the lamp lenses using the proper adapters. This may require removing headlamp bezels or trim pieces.
3. Check the bubble spirit level for vertical level and split image for horizontal level on each aimer, figure 13-12. If necessary, turn the headlamp adjusting screws until the bubble is centered or the split image is aligned.
4. After adjusting lamp aim, bounce the vehicle to settle the aiming screws. Recheck the bubble spirit level. Remember that adjusting the vertical aim may throw off the horizontal aim, and vice versa. Double-check both before reinstalling the bezels or trim pieces.
5. If any lamp is out of adjustment, readjust all of the lamps.

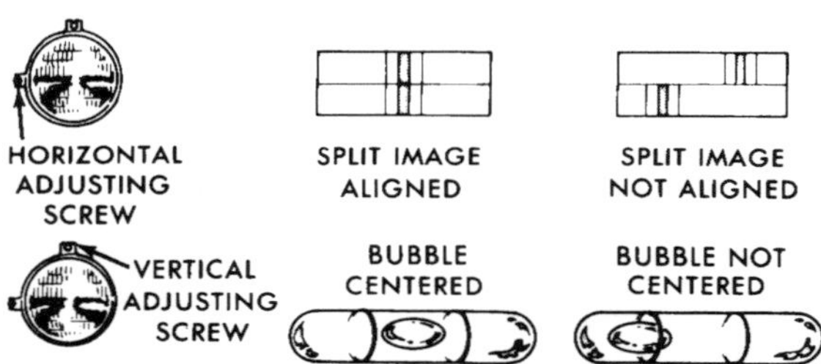

Figure 13-12. Mechanical units use either a bubble spirit level or a split image to determine headlight aim.

Any time an adjustment is made, the final turn of the adjusting screw should tighten it. This preloads the threads to help prevent the screw from loosening due to vibration. Once adjustment is determined, back it out slightly and tighten to the set position.

Photoelectric aiming

Photoelectric, or optical, aiming equipment is mounted on a frame that rides on tracks permanently installed in the shop floor. The optical aiming head is adjusted to the level of the headlamps on the test vehicle. Once the equipment is in place, the headlights are adjusted so that the hot spot of the beam projects against a target in the aimer, figure 13-13. Optical aiming is done with the headlights switched on, and the unit measures the intensity of the light beam as well as lamp aim.

Copyright 2000 by Chek-Chart Publications

Figure 13-13. A photoelectric aimer checks headlight aim as well as lamp intensity.

Headlight and Dimmer Switch Service

In addition to the lamps themselves, headlight service includes checking, testing, and replacing switches, relays, wiring, and other circuit devices that carry current through the system.

Headlight and dimmer switch testing

On most domestic headlamp circuits, the headlamp switch receives battery power at all times. The dimmer switch is in series with the low beam headlamp circuit, and the high beam headlamp circuit when switched, figure 13-14. Power is applied to the lamps through the switch, and the bulbs are grounded by a separate circuit. A different method is used on many import headlight and dimmer switch circuits. With these, the headlight switch applies power to the lamps, but the dimmer switch is installed on the ground side of the circuit. On newer vehicles, the dimmer switch is part of a column-mounted multifunction switch that also controls the headlights and turn signals, while older vehicles use a foot-operated dimmer switch mounted in the floorboard.

There are two basic locations of headlamp switches: dash mounted and steering column mounted. Dash mounted units are generally push-pull designs that often contain a rheostat for adjusting instrument lighting brightness as well. Regardless of design or location, most vehicles use a three-position main headlight switch, figure 13-15:

- First position—off, no current
- Second position—directs current to the parking lights, tail lamps, and other circuits
- Third position—directs current to both the second position circuits and to the headlight circuit.

There are a number of variations, but all headlight switches are easily checked in a similar manner. To test a headlight switch:

1. Check for battery voltage available at the headlight switch source terminal. If power is not available, check the power circuit by voltage drop testing.
2. If power is available to the switch, turn the headlight switch to the second position and check for power at the output terminal.
3. Next, move the switch to the third position and check for power at the output terminal.
4. If there is no power at the output terminal in either or both positions, the switch is defective. Replace the headlight switch.

Dimmer switch operation is also quickly checked with a voltmeter. To test the dimmer switch:

1. With the headlights turned on, check for power at the dimmer switch terminals.
2. If either the high or low beams are operational, there is power to the switch.
3. If there is power through the switch to one terminal but not the other, the dimmer switch is defective. Replace the dimmer switch.

Headlight switch replacement

There are three basic types of headlight switch:

- Lever-operated, steering column-mounted
- Push-pull, dashboard-mounted
- Rocker-type, dashboard-mounted.

Before replacing a headlamp switch, disconnect the negative battery cable. This prevents accidental short circuits during removal and installation. Remember, the switch has constant battery power, whether the ignition switch is on or off.

Dash-mounted units

Rocker-type switches are generally either snap-in units or retained by one or more screws that are concealed behind a clip-on bezel. Replace a snap-in rocker switch by prying the unit from the instrument panel with a small screwdriver. Be careful to avoid breaking any plastic locking tabs. Also, carefully pry off the bezel to access and remove retaining screws, if used. Lift the switch out and unplug the harness connector. Connect the new switch to the harness, then install it into the dash panel.

With most push-pull switches, a release button on the switch housing must be depressed to release and remove the knob before the switch is removed from the dash. Press the release button, then pull the knob

Copyright 2000 by Chek-Chart Publications

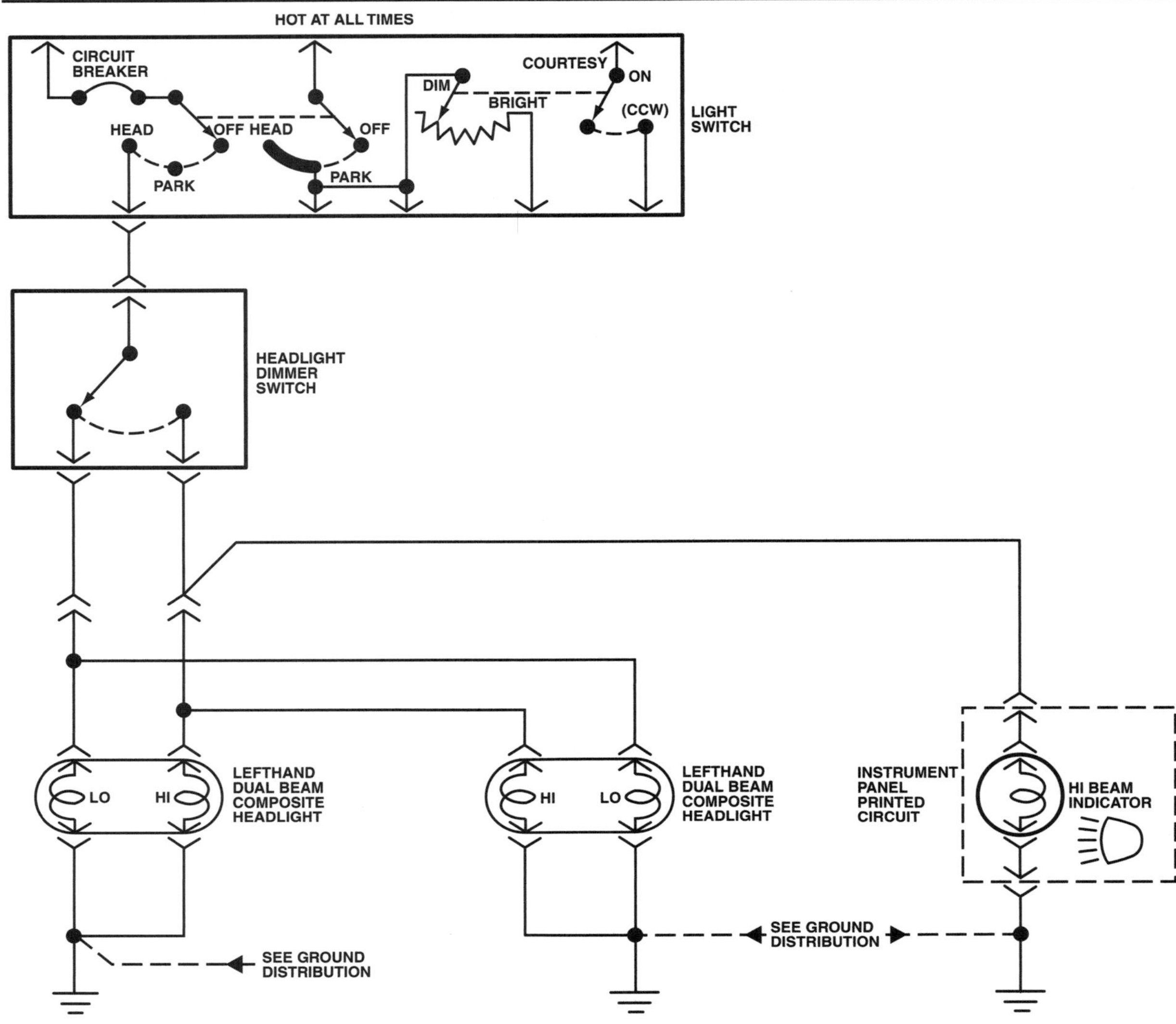

Figure 13-14. Circuit diagram of a typical domestic headlight and dimmer switch.

from the switch assembly. The knob is attached to the shaft on some designs. Remove the mounting nut that holds the switch to the instrument panel, slip the switch clear of the dash panel, and unplug the harness connector. Connect the harness to the new switch and fit the assembly into the dash panel. Then, install the mounting nut, knob, and shaft.

Column-mounted units

To replace a headlight switch mounted on the steering column, remove column shrouds as needed to gain access to the switch. Some designs require steering wheel removal and air bag assembly removal as well. Be sure to properly disable the SRS to avoid accidental deployment.

Once the switch is exposed, unplug the harness connector from the switch and remove the fasteners holding the switch to the column. Lift the switch up, disengage it from the actuator rod, and remove it from the steering column. Install and check the operation of the new switch.

Dimmer switch replacement

The dimmer switch on most late-model vehicles is incorporated into a single multifunction switch assembly that installs on the steering column. In addition to the dimmer switch, these switches may include the turn signal, horn, cruise control, windshield wiper, and interior light switches, figure 13-16. Replacing a multifunction switch requires partial disassembly of the steering column, and disabling the SRS where applicable. Procedures are similar to replacing a column-mounted headlight switch.

Copyright 2000 by Chek-Chart Publications

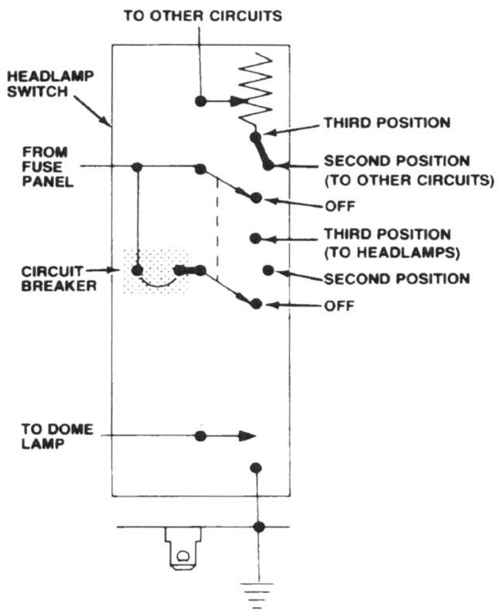

Figure 13-15. Most headlight switches are a three-position design: off, parking lights, and headlights.

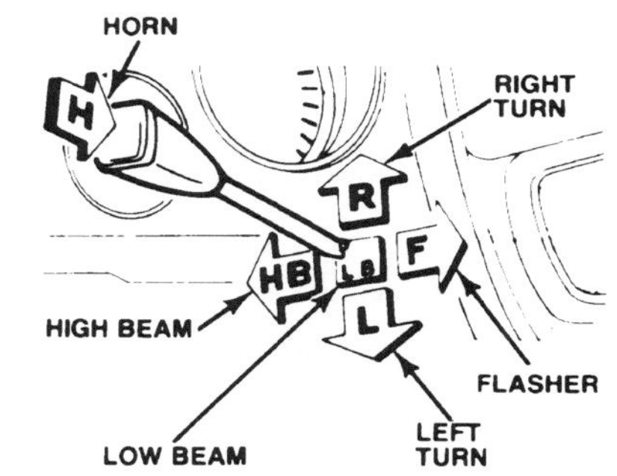

Figure 13-16. This multifunction switch contains the headlight, dimmer, turn signal, emergency flasher, and horn switches.

Retractable or Concealed Headlights

Some retractable or concealed headlights attach to the vehicle body and have a moving cover; others attach to the cover assembly and move along with it. Either an electric or vacuum motor opens or raises the headlight doors.

Electric systems have a motor-gearbox assembly mounted behind the grille, figure 13-17. On most designs, two torsion rods extend outward from the gearbox and attach to the headlight door. A double contact relay controls motor direction on a typical system. One set of contacts connects to the door-closing circuit and is closed when the relay is at rest. The second contact set connects to the door-opening circuit and these contacts close when the relay is energized. The relay control circuit connects to the headlight circuit, which directs current to open and close the doors. Additional limiting contacts, which may be in either the relay or the motor, open to stop current and prevent damage when the doors reach the end of their travel. If motor-driven doors operate slowly, check for:

- Rusted hinge points on the doors
- Binding motor bearings
- High resistance in the door circuits
- Collision damage.

Some vehicles use vacuum to operate the headlight doors, figure 13-18. A reservoir and a check valve maintain a vacuum supply while the engine is turned off or under load. On a typical system, a vacuum control manifold connected to the headlight switch directs vacuum to the motors to hold the doors in a closed position. With the headlights switched on, there is no

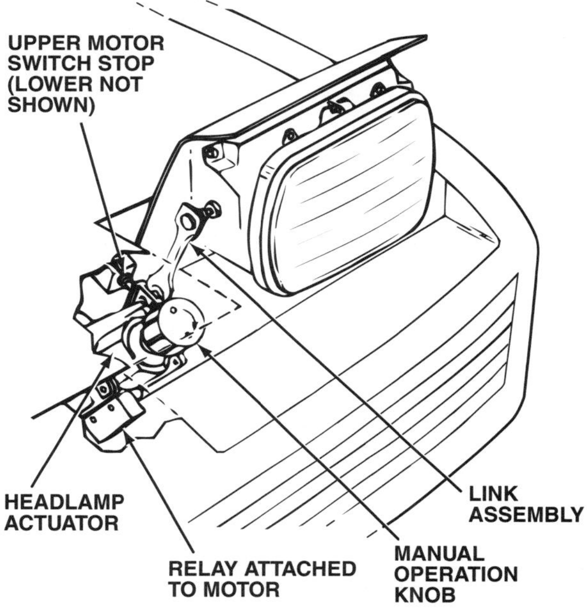

Figure 13-17. An electric motor opens and closes the headlight and door assembly on this General Motors design.

vacuum available to the door motors and spring force holds the doors open. When the headlight switch is turned off, vacuum is directed to the motors to close the doors. Air bleeds into the opposing actuator chamber through the vacuum switch. In case of a vacuum failure, the doors go to the open position. If vacuum-operated doors operate slowly or not at all, check for:

- Plugged or restricted hoses
- Faulty vacuum manifold at the headlight switch
- Vacuum leaks in the hoses or diaphragms.
- Collision damage.

Copyright 2000 by Chek-Chart Publications

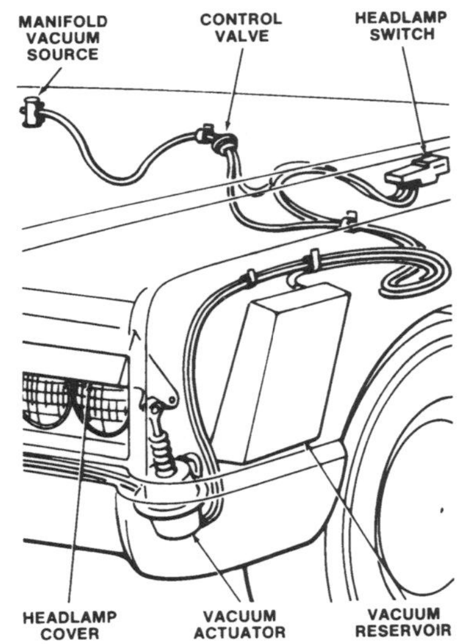

Figure 13-18. Vacuum motors operate the headlight doors on this older Ford design.

SMALL BULB REPLACEMENT

Automotive bulbs and sockets come in an assortment of shapes, sizes, and wattage, but all types conform to design standards established by either the Society of Automotive Engineers (SAE) or the International Standards Organization (ISO), figure 13-19. This reduces the possibility of installing the wrong bulb. Small bulbs may be either a single or double filament design. Double filament bulbs are used to accommodate two circuits, such as parking and directional, or stop and taillights that use the same bulb.

Small bulbs used in exterior lighting systems are usually clear and mount behind colored lenses. However, some applications that install behind a clear lens require a red or amber bulb, which is indicated by an R or NA in the standards. Bulbs have either a brass or glass wedge base, and are generally replaced from the rear of the lamp assembly.

Bulbs with a brass base fit into a matching socket that contains a single contact or double contacts to route current through the filament and complete the circuit, figure 13-20. Double-contact bulbs have an indexed base and fit into the socket only one way. Bulbs with a brass base are generally used for exterior lighting, such as tail lamps, turn signals, side markers, and backup lamps. Remove a brass-base bulb by pushing slightly to depress the tension spring while rotating the bulb to align the index pins with the slots in the socket. Then, pull the bulb straight out of the socket. Fit, push, and turn to install the new bulb.

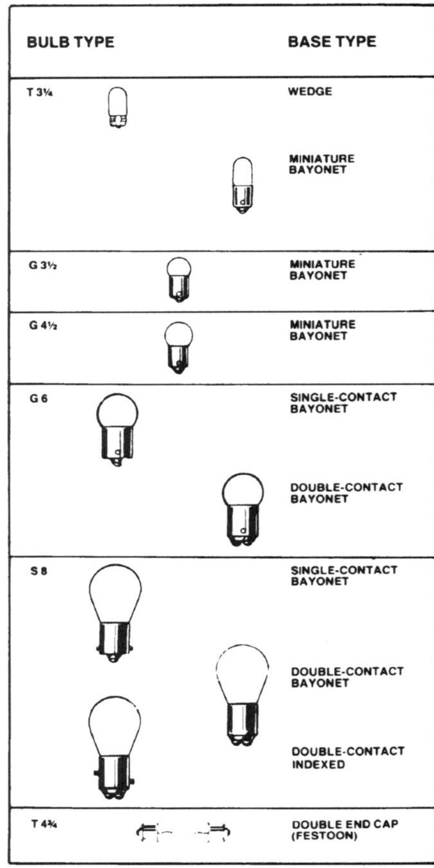

BULB TYPE	BASE TYPE
T 3¼	WEDGE
	MINIATURE BAYONET
G 3½	MINIATURE BAYONET
G 4½	MINIATURE BAYONET
G 6	SINGLE-CONTACT BAYONET
	DOUBLE-CONTACT BAYONET
S 8	SINGLE-CONTACT BAYONET
	DOUBLE-CONTACT BAYONET
	DOUBLE-CONTACT INDEXED
T 4¾	DOUBLE END CAP (FESTOON)

Figure 13-19. Automotive bulbs conform to established design standards.

Wedge-base bulbs are used in the instrument cluster and other interior lighting applications, such as dome, map, and courtesy lamps. The base and optical part of the bulb are a one-piece, formed-glass shell with four filament wires extending through the base and crimped around it to form the external contacts. Pull a wedge-base, or non-indexed, bulb straight out from the socket to remove it. Simply push in the replacement.

Most small bulbs used in exterior lighting systems are removed and replaced from the rear of the lamp assembly. The lens does not have to be removed. Rotate the socket base to align the index tabs with the slots on the lamp housing, then pull the socket and bulb out of the rear of the lamp housing, figure 13-21. Sockets are indexed in a number of different ways, figure 13-22. Be sure to remove a socket correctly to avoid damaging it.

Copyright 2000 by Chek-Chart Publications

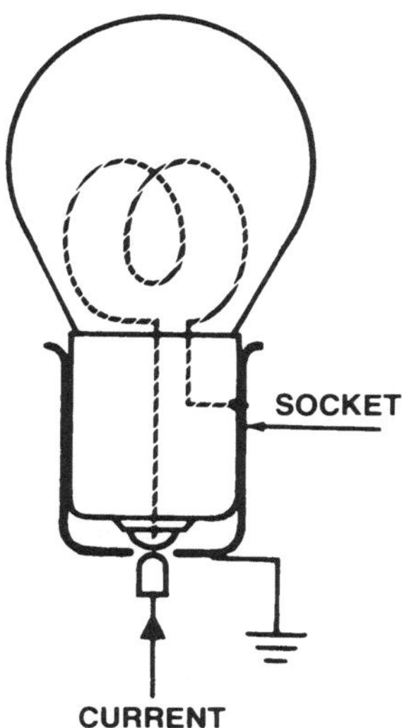

Figure 13-20. The filament of a brass-base bulb completes the circuit to ground to light the lamp.

If it is impossible to remove the socket from the rear of the lamp assembly, the lamp lens is removed to replace the bulb. Typically, screws fit through lamp lenses from the outside of the vehicle and are secured with nuts from the inside. Trim parts may need to be removed to access the fasteners. When reinstalling the lens, correctly position any gaskets and washers removed during disassembly.

If a bulb socket is corroded or rusted, it must be replaced. In most cases, replacement sockets are available. These are often installed by cutting the old socket from the wiring harness and splicing the new one into place.

Parking, Side Marker, and Taillight Service

The parking, side marker, and taillights operate when the headlight switch is in the park or headlight position on most vehicles. Typically, the parking and taillights are on a separate circuit, but share a common switch with the headlights. Side marker lights connect in parallel to the parking lights. Taillight circuits generally share a fuse with another circuit, or have a circuit breaker instead of a fuse. The license plate lamp is on the same circuit as the taillights. Circuit diagrams for the parking, side marker, and taillights are often part of a diagram that includes all of the exterior lighting circuits, figure 13-23.

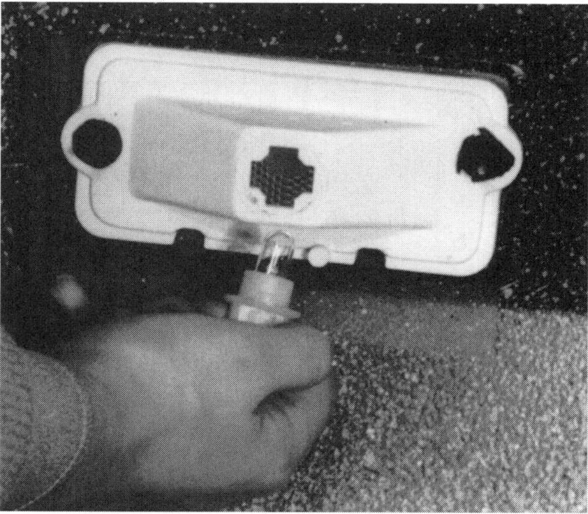

Figure 13-21. The socket and bulb are removed from the rear of the lamp assembly on most exterior lights.

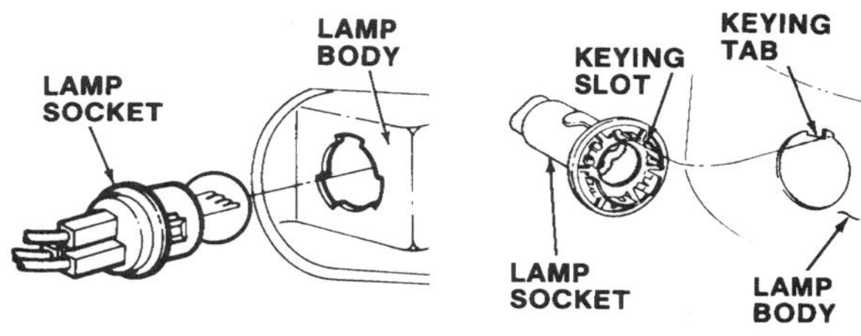

Figure 13-22. A number of methods are used to index the bulb and socket to the lamp assembly.

Parking and taillight service

The same general troubleshooting procedures apply for both parking lights and taillights. To diagnose problems in either circuit:

1. Make certain the correct bulb type is used in each socket.
2. If neither the taillights nor the license plate lamp operates, check the power supply and fuse. If the circuit is good at the fuse, check for power between the switch and the last common connector before the lights. Any open in the circuit, such as a loose connection or a faulty headlight switch, delivers power to the fuse but not to the connector.
3. If only one bulb fails to light, check for a burned-out bulb, a bad ground, or poor connection in the bulb socket.

Copyright 2000 by Chek-Chart Publications

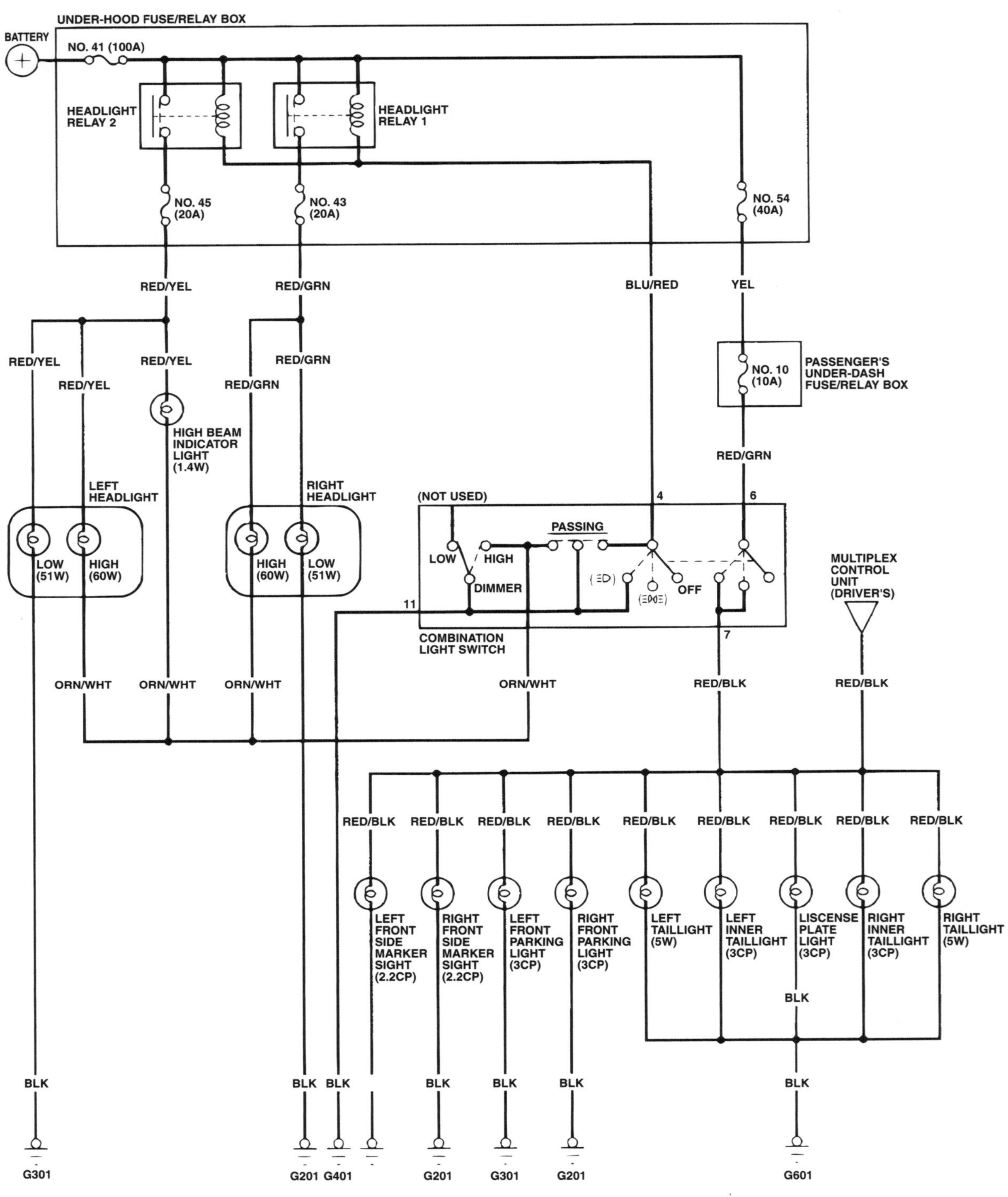

Figure 13-23. Exterior lighting circuit diagram of a Honda Accord.

Copyright 2000 by Chek-Chart Publications

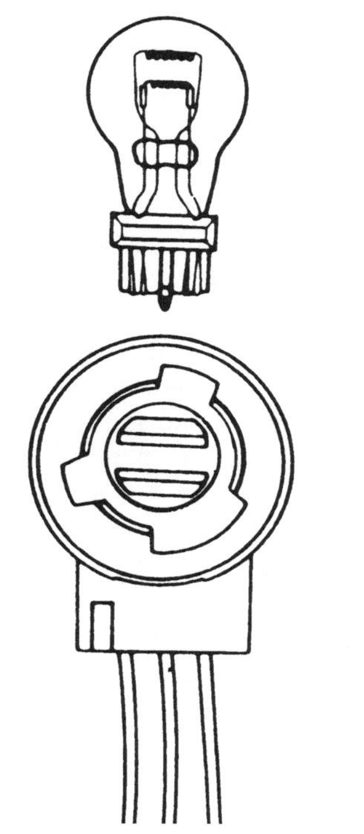

Figure 13-24. Side marker lamps often use a wedge-type bulb.

Side marker light service

Side marker lamps generally use a wedge-type bulb that mounts in an insulated socket, figure 13-24. Some bulbs are independently grounded and others ground through the turn signal filaments. Side marker lamps that ground through the turn signal filaments illuminate whenever the parking lights are switched on. However, the side marker goes out each time the turn signal flashes because the ground side of the side marker circuit is carrying current to the turn signal lamp.

The result is parking and side marker lights that are on at the same time, and side markers that flash alternately with the turn signals. With the parking lights off, the turn signal and side marker lights flash together. This makes troubleshooting the circuit a little confusing. For example, a burned-out turn signal filament also prevents the front side marker from operating. However, a burned-out parking light filament has no effect on the side marker. Use a circuit diagram to determine how current is routed, figure 13-25.

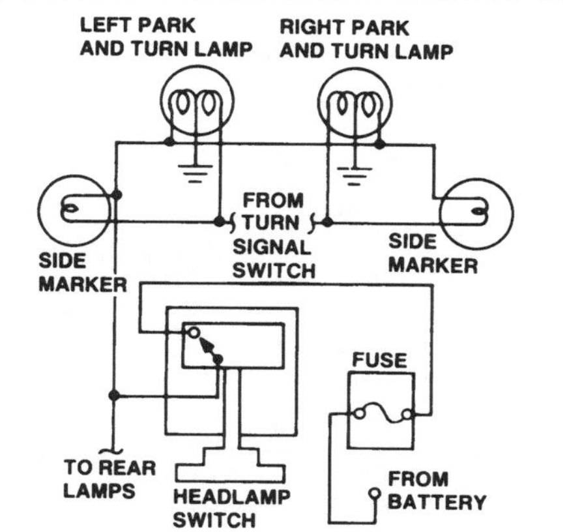

Figure 13-25. A circuit diagram is needed to determine power distribution to side marker lamps.

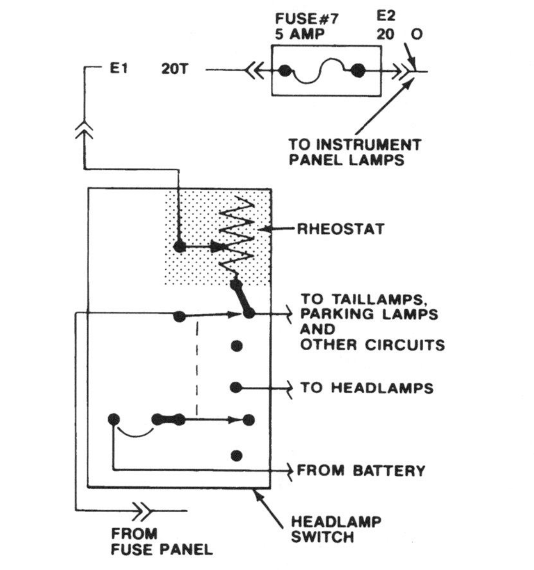

Figure 13-26. Circuitry of a headlight switch with a built-in rheostat for adjusting instrument light brightness.

Dash Light Service

Three categories of bulbs are used in instrument panel displays: indicator, warning, and illumination lamps. Dash panel illumination lamps are on a series-parallel circuit where all the bulbs connect in parallel with each other and in series with a variable resistor, or rheostat. All instrument panel circuits are grounded through a dedicated ground circuit. An open in the instrument panel ground circuit affects all of the electrical components that mount in the instrument cluster.

Copyright 2000 by Chek-Chart Publications

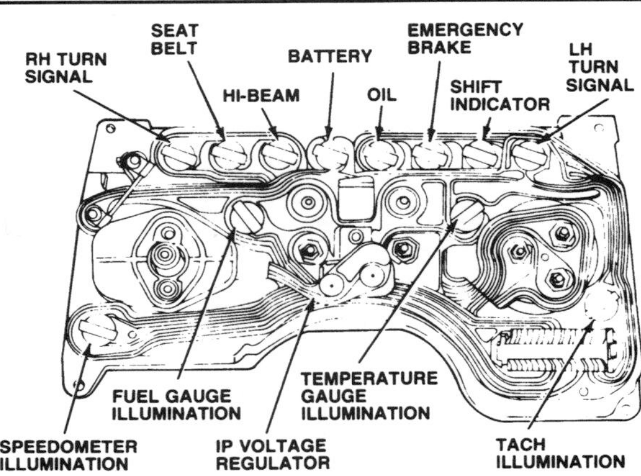

Figure 13-27. Modern instrument clusters use a printed circuit board to deliver current to the components.

Switch and rheostat service

Current to the dash lights is controlled by contacts within the main headlight switch. They receive current when the parking and taillights are lit. A rheostat allows the driver to control the brightness of the dash lights. The rheostat may be integrated into the headlight switch or a separate unit that mounts in the dash. Intermittent operation of only the instrument lights may be caused by wear or oxidation buildup on the rheostat coils. Troubleshooting these circuits is similar to that of other lighting circuits, figure 13-26.

Printed circuit boards

Printed circuit (PC) boards replaced conventional wiring behind the instrument panel many years ago. A PC board simplifies connections, conserves space and weight, and is inexpensive to manufacture compared to conventional wiring. To manufacture a PC board, a conductor plate, which is cut from a sheet of thin copper film, is laminated onto an insulator board along with the connectors and components that attach to the instrument cluster, figure 13-27. The drawback of a PC board is that the thin copper conductors cannot tolerate any overloading and a short circuit quickly destroys them. Inspect a PC board by visually following each of the circuit conductors and testing when needed with a voltmeter. Hairline cracks are difficult to see, but a voltmeter locates them quickly.

Courtesy Light Service

Dome and courtesy interior lights usually have battery voltage available to each bulb at all times. Switches installed on the ground side of the circuit regulate current through the bulb, figure 13-28. Switches may be located in the door jambs, headlight switch, or on the lamp assembly itself. The insulated, or power, side of the circuit is protected by a fuse, which blows if the circuit shorts to ground. A short to ground on the ground, or switch, side of the circuit causes the lights to stay on, but does not blow the fuse.

Check for a defective fuse if none of the dome or courtesy lights operate. If any of the lights operate, the fuse is good, so check for voltage available to the individual lights that do not operate.

Battery voltage should be available to the dome light socket at all times. If voltage is available at the socket, trigger each of the switches by opening doors as well as turning on the dome light at the headlight switch to check for ground. A dome light that does not turn off indicates a faulty door switch, a short to ground, or possibly a defective headlight switch.

Stop, Turn Signal, Hazard, and Backup Lights

Stoplight and turn signal circuits are generally combined because they connect at the turn signal switch on most vehicles. However, on some vehicles two separate circuits are used. These circuits receive voltage from two sources:

- The stoplight switch connects to the turn signal switch, so only the stoplights receive voltage when the brake pedal is depressed and the turn signal is off.
- Voltage may also be delivered from the turn signal flasher to the turn signal switch; the flasher connects to the accessory terminal on the ignition switch.

Stoplight and turn signal service

On some vehicles, the rear directional and stoplights share bulb filaments and the circuit is complete to the right and left lamps when the stoplights are on. Moving the directional switch to the right turn or left

Copyright 2000 by Chek-Chart Publications

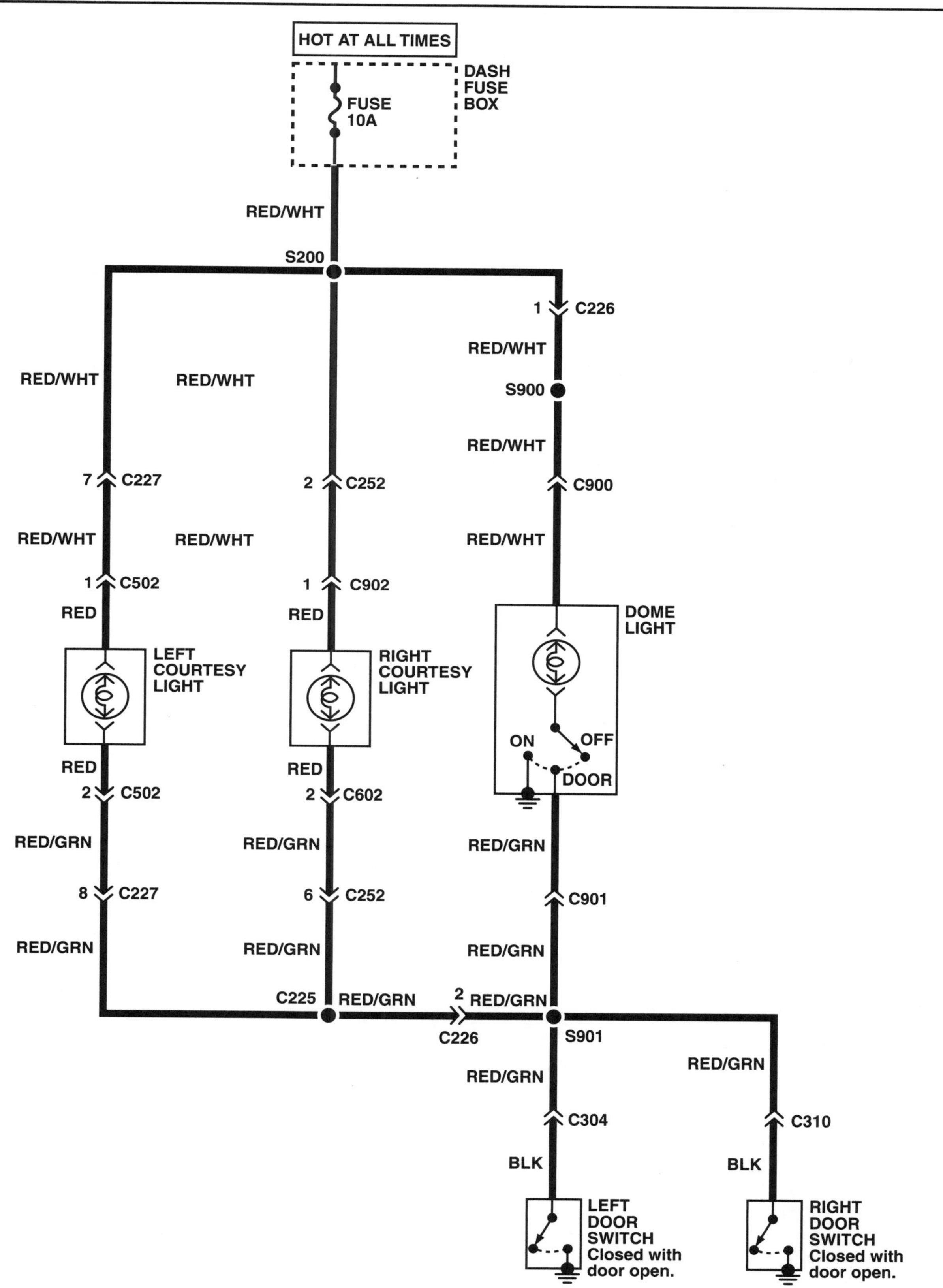

Figure 13-28. This Isuzu Amigo diagram is typical of a basic interior lighting circuit.

Copyright 2000 by Chek-Chart Publications

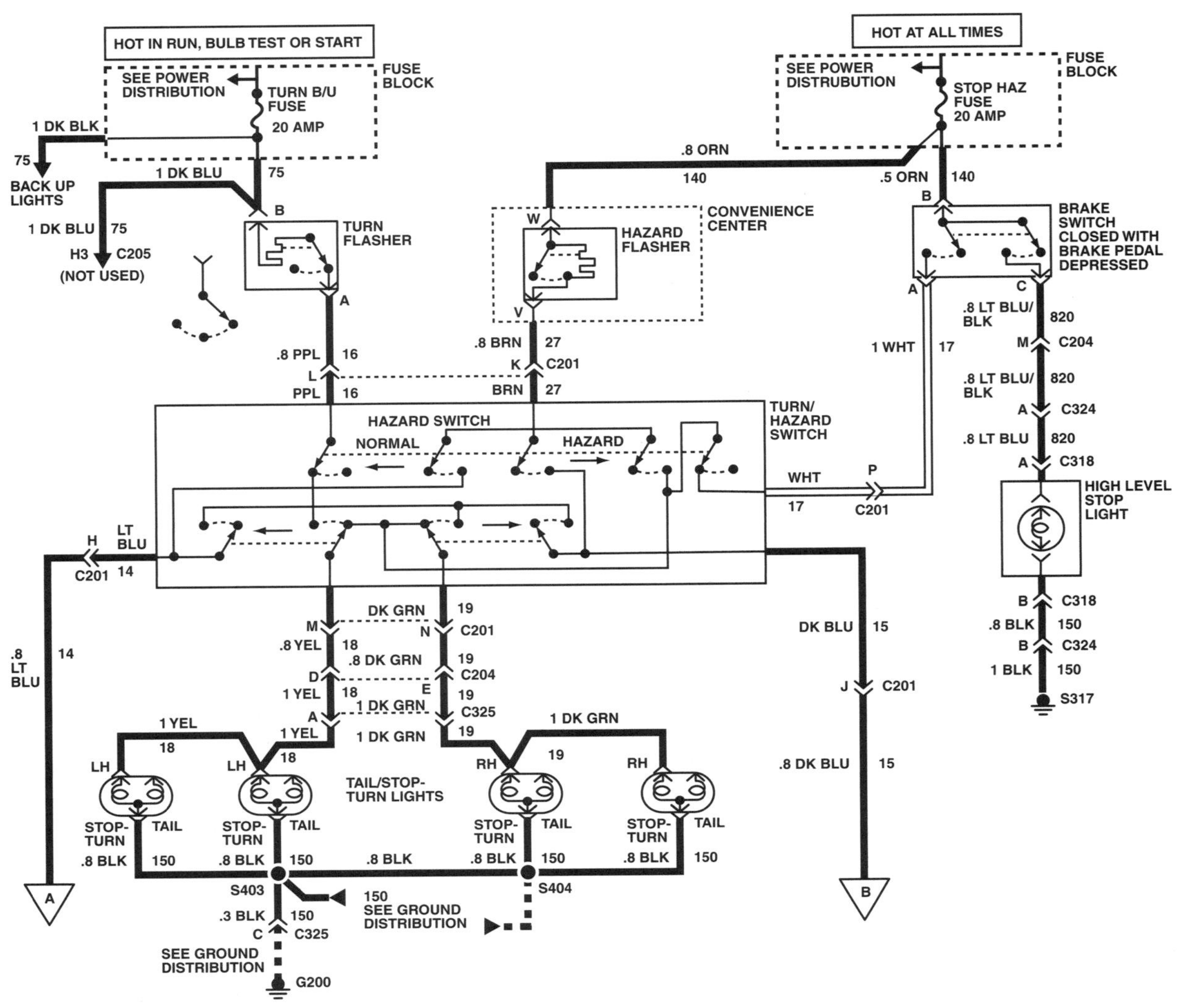

Figure 13-29. Most rear-lighting circuit designs are similar to the General Motors one shown here.

turn position removes the corresponding rear lamp from the stoplight circuit and connects it to the directional circuit. On other vehicles, the turn signals and parking lights share bulb filaments. Therefore, it is important to refer to the correct wiring diagram when troubleshooting circuit problems, figure 13-29.

Since the bulbs on each side are wired in parallel, each bulb operates independently of the other bulb on the same side. When one bulb is not operating, current is reduced. The flasher is calibrated to operate with a specified amount of current. Inoperative bulbs cause the flasher to stay on or cycle slowly.

A traditional flasher uses a bimetallic strip to open and close contacts and interrupt current through a directional switch. With the switch turned on, resistance in the strip generates heat that causes the strip to bend. This bending opens a contact set, which opens the circuit and switches off the lamp. As the strip cools, the contacts close, the circuit is complete, and the lamp illuminates again.

A switch on the brake pedal linkage actuates the stoplights when the pedal is depressed slightly. Some switches are adjustable; others are not and must be replaced if not working properly. Turn signals are controlled by a steering column mounted switch. Turn signal switch replacement is similar to that of the multifunction headlight switch discussed earlier in this chapter.

Copyright 2000 by Chek-Chart Publications

Stoplight and turn signal diagnosis

To diagnose problems in the stoplight and turn signal circuit, use the following procedure:

1. If all signal lights and indicator lights are inoperative, check for:
   - Blown fuse
   - Faulty flasher
   - Faulty switch or connector.
2. If one signal light or indicator light stays on, check for:
   - Inoperative bulb.
3. If the signal lights flash too fast, check for:
   - High voltage in circuit
   - Faulty or wrong type of flasher
   - Wrong type of bulbs.
4. If the signal lights flash too slow, check for:
   - Low voltage or high resistance in circuit
   - Faulty or wrong type of flasher
   - Wrong type of bulbs.
5. If no flashing on either side with lamps on, check for:
   - Faulty or wrong type of flasher.
6. If both stoplights are inoperative, check for:
   - Burned-out bulbs
   - Blown fuse
   - Defective or improperly adjusted stoplight switch
   - Defective turn signal switch.
7. If one stoplight is inoperative, check for:
   - Burned-out bulb, poor ground, or an open in the circuit.
8. If taillight and stoplight both work individually, but light does not operate when both are on, check for:
   - Proper ground.

Hazard light service

A separate switch attached to the directional switch enables right and left directional lights to be operated at the same time as the hazard warning lights. When the hazard light switch is on, the turn signal flasher is disconnected from the circuit and replaced with a hazard flasher. Unlike the directional lights, the hazard lights operate with the ignition switch off.

Hazard light diagnosis

If the hazard light flashing rate is too fast or too slow, turn off the hazard lights and turn on one turn signal. If the rate is normal, the problem is the flasher in the hazard warning circuit. If the flashing rate is either too fast or too slow, follow the troubleshooting procedure for turn signals. A stoplight switch or flasher failure causes the hazard lamps to illuminate but not flash.

If none of the hazard lights operate and the turn signals function normally, check for a blown fuse, faulty flasher, or open in the power circuit to the switch. A faulty hazard warning switch or an open or shorted bulb circuit prevents either one front or both rear hazard lights from operating, but the turn signals work correctly. In this case, turn the hazard switch on and check for voltage available on both sides of the switch. Power to, but not through, the switch indicates a faulty switch. If there is voltage on all the switch output leads, check for open or short circuits in the wiring to the bulbs. Locate opens and shorts by voltage drop testing the circuit.

Backup light service

Backup lights receive voltage from the accessory terminal of the ignition switch. A backup light switch that connects to the shift linkage or the transmission shift rail controls the ground circuit. The backup lights switch on when the transmission is in Reverse. The transmission range, or neutral safety, switch is combined in an assembly with the backup light switch on some vehicles, figure 13-30.

If the backup lights do not operate with the ignition switch on and transmission in reverse, check for a blown fuse, defective or improperly adjusted switch, or faulty bulb.

Copyright 2000 by Chek-Chart Publications

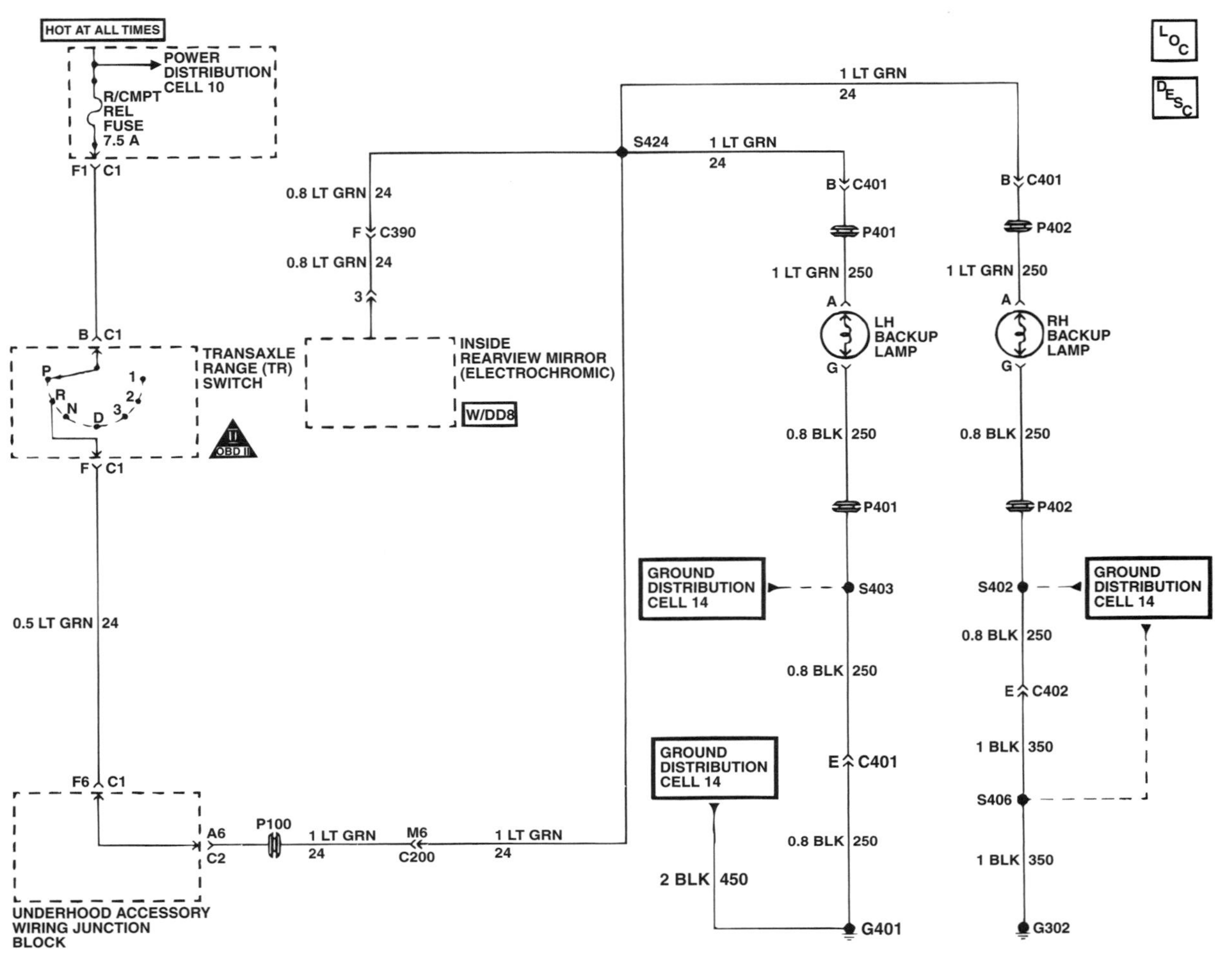

Figure 13-30. The transaxle range selector switch provides power to the backup lamps on the Oldsmobile Intrigue.

Copyright 2000 by Chek-Chart Publications

14

Horn, Wiper and Washer, Cooling Fan, and Instrument Service

These common accessory circuits generally do not require service. However, components such as switches or motors occasionally need to be replaced due to wear or damage. With any electrical service or repair, accurate specifications and circuit diagrams for the system being worked on are required to ensure a successful repair. This chapter provides general troubleshooting and repair procedures that apply to servicing most vehicles.

HORN SYSTEM

A vehicle horn is an actuator that converts an electrical signal to sound. The horn circuit includes an armature and contacts that are attached to a diaphragm. When energized, the armature causes the diaphragm to vibrate at an audible frequency. The sound created by the diaphragm is magnified as it travels through a trumpet attached to the diaphragm chamber. Systems typically use one or two horns, but some have up to four. Those with multiple horns use both high- and low-pitch units to achieve a harmonious tone. Only a high-pitched unit is used in single-horn applications. The horn assembly is marked with an "H" or "L" for pitch identification.

A fused circuit supplies battery voltage to a high-current horn circuit and the relay control circuit on a typical late-model horn system. The horn switch usually completes the ground side of the relay control circuit, figure 14-1. Some older systems do not use a relay and current is supplied directly to the horn through a switch in the steering column.

Horn System Diagnosis

There are three types of horn failure:

- No horn operation
- Intermittent operation
- Constant operation.

If a horn does not operate at all, check for:

- Burned fuse or fusible link
- Open circuit
- Defective horn
- Faulty relay
- Defective horn switch.

If a horn operates intermittently, check for:

- Loose contact at the switch
- Loose, frayed, or broken wires
- Defective relay.

A horn that sounds continuously and cannot be shut off is caused by horn switch contacts that are stuck closed, or a short to ground on the control circuit. This may be the result of a defective horn switch or a faulty

Copyright 2000 by Chek-Chart Publications

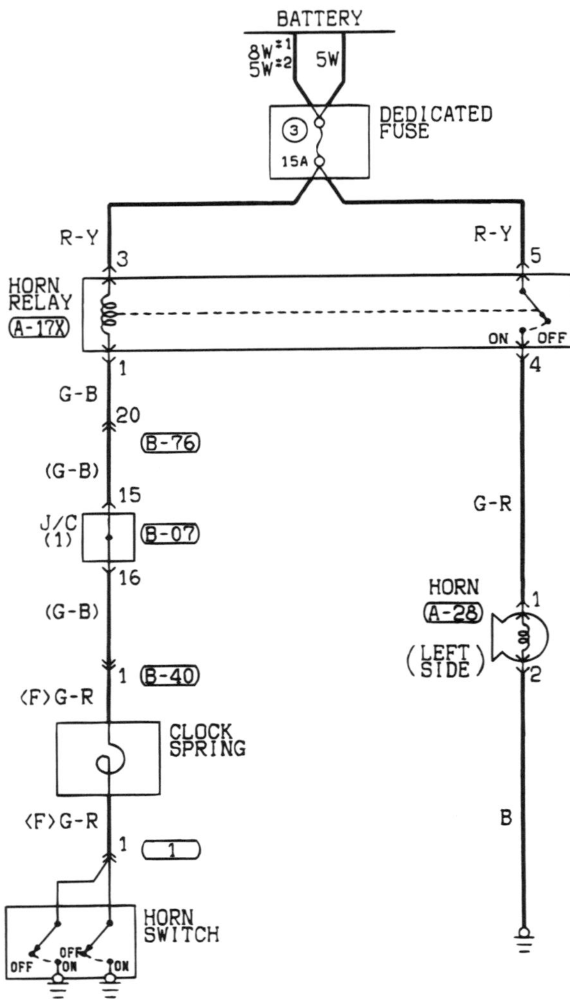

Figure 14-1. A typical horn circuit includes the horns, a relay, and the switch.

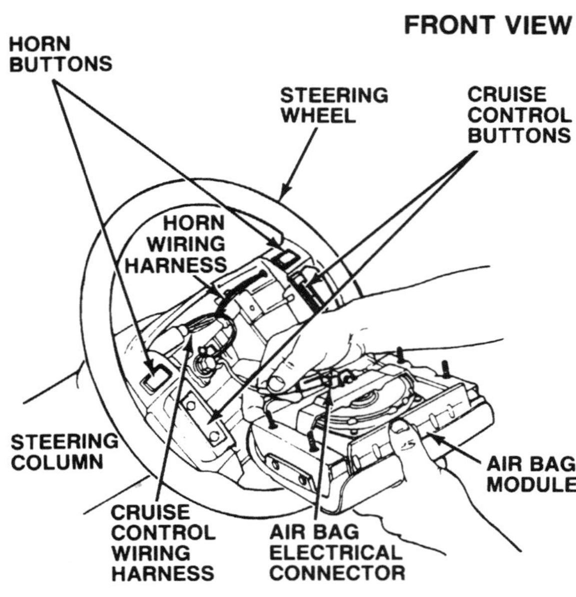

Figure 14-2. Typical steering wheel-mounted horn switch assembly.

relay. Stuck relay contacts keep the circuit complete so the horn sounds constantly. Disconnect the horn and check continuity through the horn switch and relay to locate the source of the problem.

Horn Service

When a horn malfunctions, circuit tests are made to determine if the horn, relay, switch, or wiring is the source of the failure. Typically, a digital multimeter (DMM) is used to perform voltage drop and continuity checks to isolate the failure.

Switch and relay

A momentary contact switch is used to sound the horn. The horn switch is mounted to the steering wheel in the center of the steering column on some models, figure 14-2. The horn switch is part of a multifunction switch installed on the steering column on other models, figure 14-3. These may require pulling on the stalk or depressing a button on the end of the stalk to sound the horn.

Once a switch has been disconnected from the circuit, it is easily checked with an ohmmeter. There should be continuity through the circuit only when the horn switch is depressed. Horn switch replacement may include removing the steering wheel to gain access to connections and mountings.

On most late-model vehicles, the horn relay is located in a centralized power distribution center along with other relays, circuit breakers, and fuses. The horn relay bolts onto an inner fender or the bulkhead in the engine compartment of older vehicles. Check the relay to determine if the coil is being energized and if current passes through the power circuit when the horn switch is depressed. Use a voltmeter to test input, output, and control voltage.

Circuit testing

Make sure the fuse or fusible link is good before attempting to troubleshoot the circuit. Also, check that the ground connections for the horn are clean and tight. Most horns ground to the chassis through the mounting bolts. High ground circuit resistance due to corrosion, road dirt, or loose fasteners may cause no, or intermittent, horn operation.

On a system with a relay, test the power output circuit and the control circuit. Check for voltage available at the horn, voltage available at the relay, and

Copyright 2000 by Chek-Chart Publications

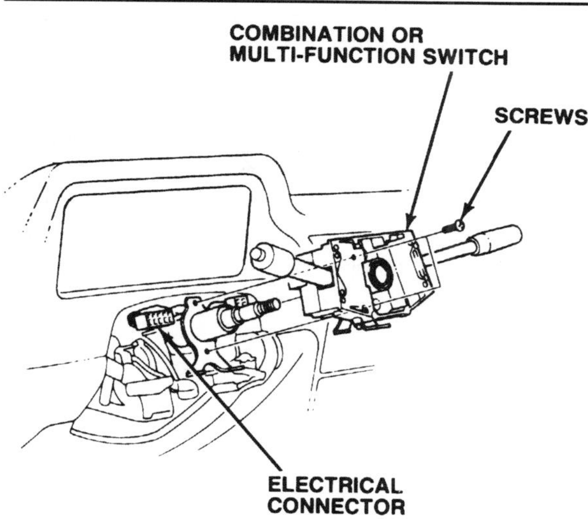

Figure 14-3. The horn switch is part of a combination switch on this design.

continuity through the switch. When no relay is used, there are two wires leading to the horn switch and a connection to the steering wheel is made with a double contact slipring. Test points on this system are similar to those of a system with a relay, but there is no control circuit.

Horn replacement

Horns are generally mounted on the radiator core support by bolts and nuts or sheet metal screws. It may be necessary to remove the grille or other parts to access the horn mounting screws. To replace a horn, simply remove the fasteners and lift the old horn from its mounting bracket, figure 14-4. Clean the attachment area on the mounting bracket and chassis before installing the new horn. Some models use a corrosion-resistant mounting screw to ensure a ground connection. If so, be sure to use it.

Adjusting horn pitch

The tone, or pitch, of an electromagnetic horn is adjustable on some models. This adjustment is used to clear up the quality of the sound. However, adjustment does not change the horn frequency.

An adjusting screw that extends through the horn housing changes the diaphragm travel to control the pitch, figure 14-5. If the horn does not work or simply clicks when the switch is depressed, loosen the adjusting screw about one-half turn and try again. If there is no improvement, the horn is defective and must be replaced. If the horn sounds, adjust the tone.

In two-horn systems, disconnect the wire from one horn while adjusting the other. Never turn the horn adjustment screw or nut while the horn is sounding. This damages the horn. Horns are usually adjusted by

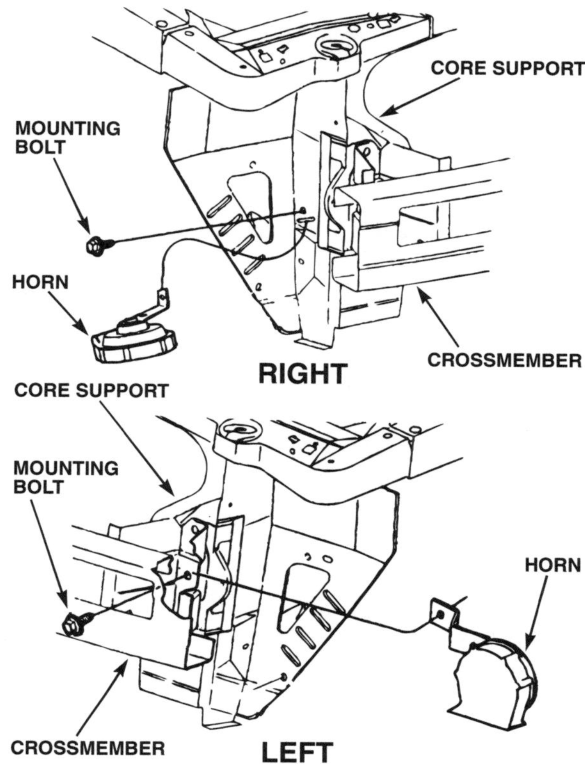

Figure 14-4. Horns typically attach to the radiator core support with a bracket.

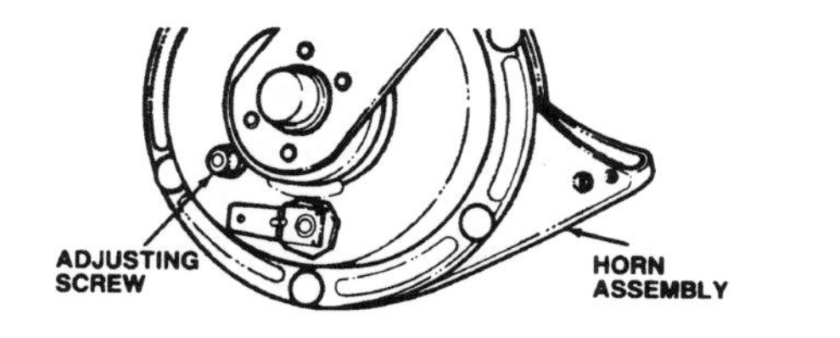

Figure 14-5. An adjusting screw is provided for setting horn pitch on some models.

sound, but may also be set using an ammeter. Connect the ammeter into the horn circuit, depress the horn switch, and note the meter reading. Most horns draw between 4.5 and 5.5 amperes. If readings are out of specifications, turn the adjusting screw slightly, about one-tenth of a turn, and check current draw again

On most horns, turning the screw or nut counterclockwise increases current; turning it clockwise decreases current. Continue making small adjustments until current draw is within specifications. If the current draw cannot be adjusted to within these limits, replace the horn.

Using a remote starter switch to energize the horn makes adjustment easier. Connect the remote starter switch between the power circuit connector of the

Copyright 2000 by Chek-Chart Publications

relay and the horn. Depress the remote starter switch to sound the horn, or get a current draw reading if using an ammeter.

WINDSHIELD WIPER AND WASHER SYSTEM

Windshield wiper systems and circuits vary greatly between manufacturers as well as between models. Most modern vehicles combine the windshield wiper and windshield washer functions into a single system. Many newer vehicles also have a rear window wiper and washer system that works independent of the windshield system. In spite of the design differences, all windshield and rear window wiper and washer systems operate in a similar fashion. Therefore, the same basic electrical tests and troubleshooting procedures apply to any system. Accurate test specifications and circuit diagrams are required for diagnosing the system, figure 14-6. A typical combination wiper and washer system consists of:

- Wiper motor
- Gearbox
- Wiper arms and linkage
- Washer pump
- Hoses and jets
- Fluid reservoir
- Combination switch.

The motor and gearbox assembly connects to the wiper switch on the instrument panel or steering column, figure 14-7. Some systems use either a one- or two-speed wiper motor, while others have a variable-speed motor. A depressed, concealed, or parking mode, which parks the wiper arm outside its normal cleaning arc when not in use, is a feature on some models.

The gearbox has an additional linkage arm to provide depressed parking. This link extends to move the wipers into the park position when the motor turns in reverse of operating direction. With depressed park, the motor assembly includes an internal park switch. The park switch completes a circuit to reverse armature polarity in the motor when the windshield wiper switch is turned off. The park circuit opens once the wiper arms are in the park position. Instead of a depressed park feature, some systems simply extend the cleaning arc below the level of the hood line.

Windshield Wiper Diagnosis

Windshield wiper failure may be the result of an electrical fault or a mechanical problem, such as binding linkage. Generally, if the wipers operate at one speed setting but not another, the problem is electrical. There is one exception: If the wipers on a depressed or a positive park system do not depress or return properly, the problem may be either mechanical or electrical.

To distinguish between an electrical and mechanical problem, access the motor assembly and disconnect the wiper arm linkage from the motor and gearbox. Then, switch the motor on to each speed. If the motor operates at all speeds, the problem is mechanical. If the motor still does not operate, the problem is electrical.

If the wiper motor does not run at all, check for a:

- Tripped circuit breaker
- Grounded or inoperative switch
- Defective motor
- Circuit wiring fault.

If the motor operates but the wipers do not, check for:

- Stripped gears in gearbox
- Loose or separated motor-to-gearbox connection
- Loose linkage to motor connection.

If the motor does not shut off, check for:

- Defective parking switch inside the motor
- Defective wiper switch
- Poor ground connection at the wiper switch.

Windshield Wiper Testing

When the wiper motor does not operate with the linkage disconnected, a few simple voltmeter tests quickly isolate the circuit fault. Refer to the circuit diagram or a connector pin chart for the vehicle being serviced to determine where to take voltage readings, figure 14-8. To test the wiper system:

1. Switch the ignition on and set the wiper switch to a speed at which the motor does not operate.
2. Check for battery voltage available at the appropriate wiper motor terminal for the selected speed. If voltage is available to the motor, an internal motor problem is indicated. Replace the motor. No voltage available indicates a switch or circuit failure; continue testing.
3. Check that battery voltage is available at the motor side of the wiper switch. If battery voltage is available, the circuit is open between the switch and motor. Locate the open by voltage drop testing. Repair the wiring, and retest. No voltage available indicates either a faulty switch or a power supply problem.
4. Check for battery voltage available at the power input side of the wiper switch. If voltage is available, the switch is defective. Replace the switch. No voltage available to the switch indicates a circuit problem between the battery and switch. Locate the fault by voltage drop testing. Repair the wiring as needed, and retest.

Copyright 2000 by Chek-Chart Publications

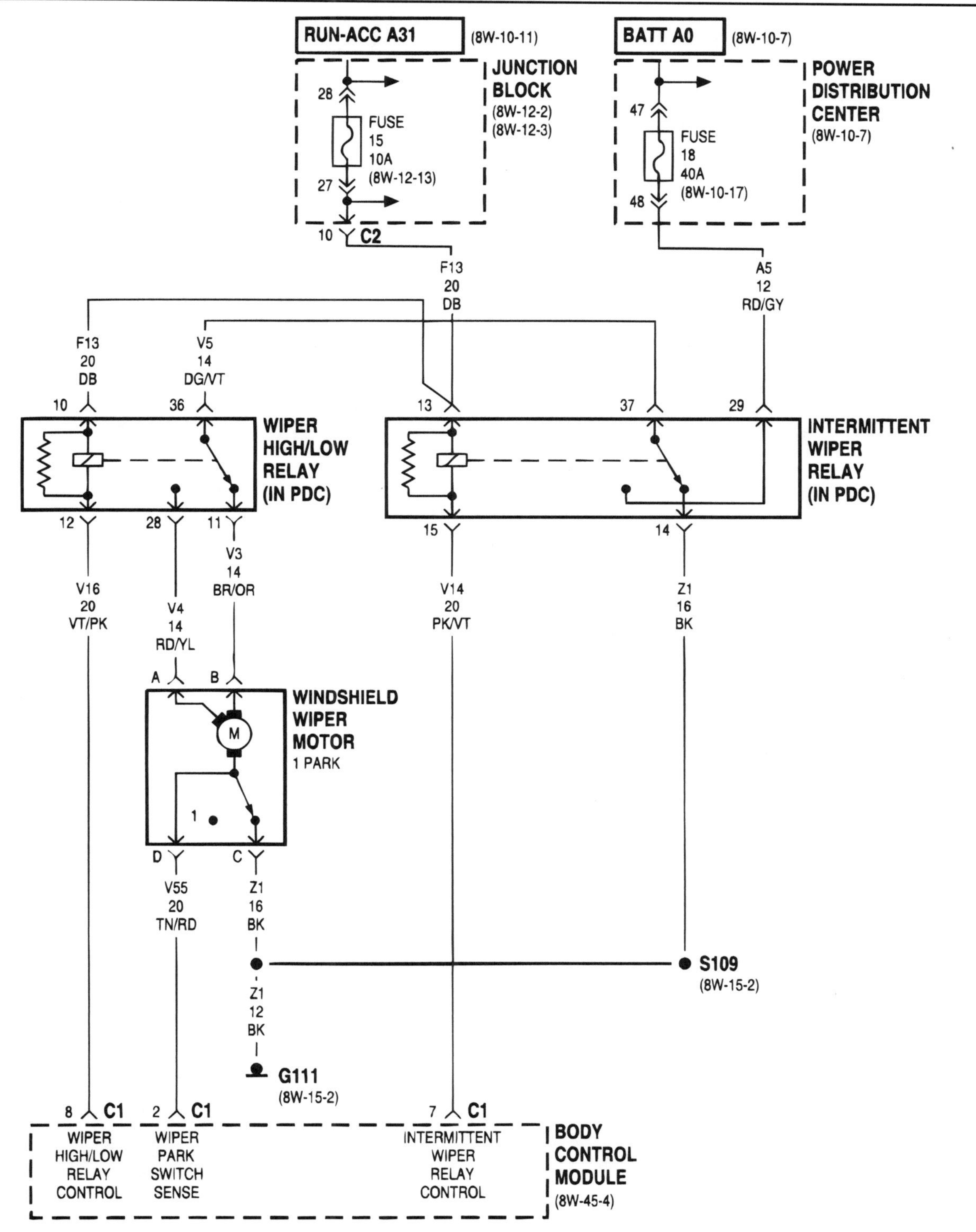

Figure 14-6. A circuit diagram is necessary to troubleshoot a windshield wiper problem.

Windshield Wiper Service

Wiper motors are replaced if defective. The motor usually mounts in the cowl or at some point on the bulkhead below the windshield. Bulkhead-mounted units are accessible from under the hood, while the cowl panel is removed to service a motor mounted in

Copyright 2000 by Chek-Chart Publications

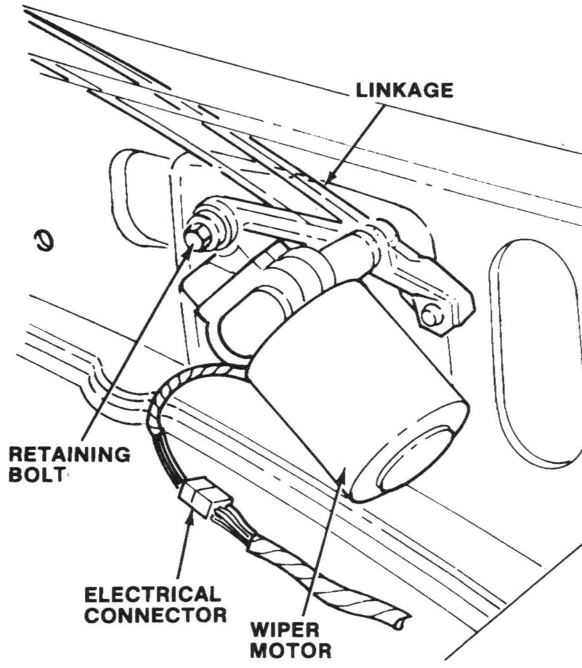

Figure 14-7. The motor and linkage bolt to the body and connect to the switch with a wiring harness.

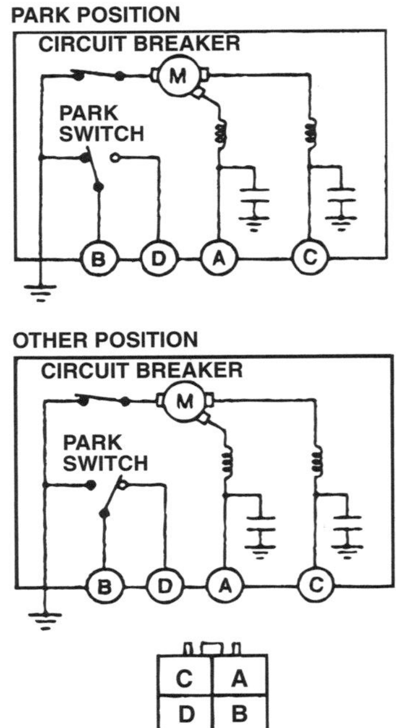

Terminal	Operation speed
C	Low
A	High

Figure 14-8. Mazda Millenia wiper motor connector pin chart and test specifications.

the cowl, figure 14-9. After gaining access to the motor, removal is simply a matter of disconnecting the linkage, unplugging the electrical connectors, and unbolting the motor. Move the wiper linkage through its full travel by hand to check for any binding before installing the new motor.

Rear window wiper motors are generally located inside the rear door panel of station wagons, or the rear hatch panel on vehicles with a hatchback or liftgate, figure 14-10. After removing the trim panel covering the motor, replacement is essentially the same as replacing the front wiper motor.

Wiper control switches install either on the steering column or on the instrument panel. Instrument panel switches are either snap-in units or are retained by one or more screws covered by a snap-in bezel, figure 14-11. Steering column wiper switches, which are operated by controls on the end of a switch stalk, require partial disassembly of the steering column for replacement, figure 14-12. The steering wheel must be removed to replace the wiper switch on some models.

Pulse-Wipe Systems

Windshield wipers may also incorporate a delay, or intermittent operation, feature commonly called pulse wipe. The length of the delay, or the frequency of the intermittent operation, is adjustable on some systems. Pulse-wipe systems may rely on simple electrical

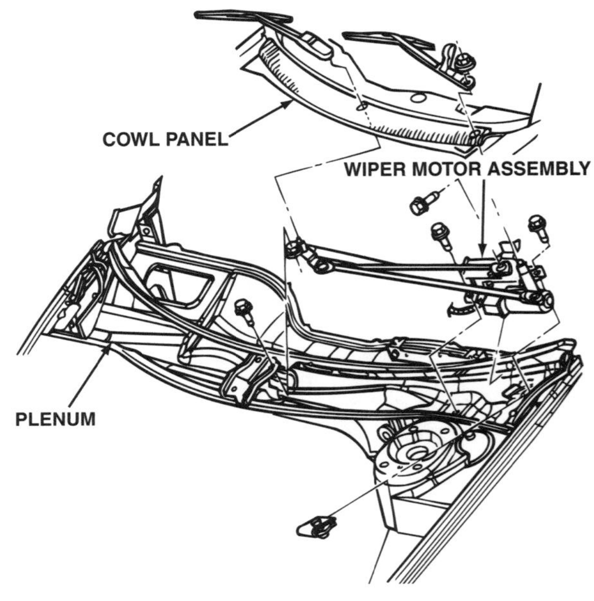

Figure 14-9. The wiper motor and linkage mount under the cowl panel on many vehicles.

Copyright 2000 by Chek-Chart Publications

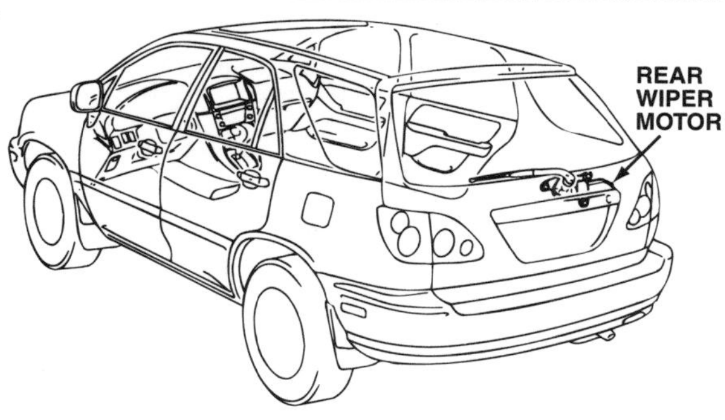

Figure 14-10. A single rear-window wiper mounts directly to the motor on most applications.

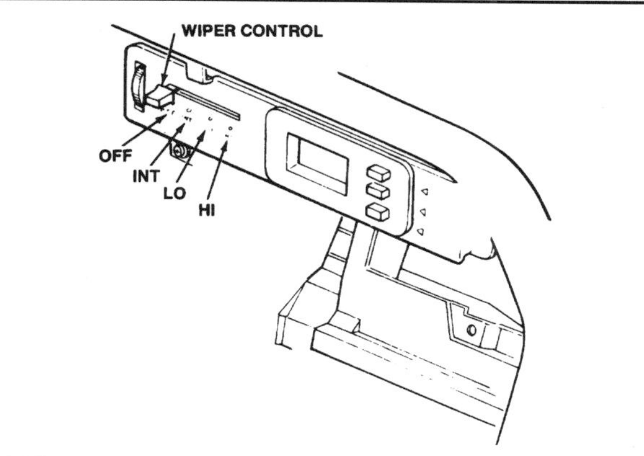

Figure 14-11. Instrument panel-mounted windshield wiper control switch assembly.

controls, such as a variable resistance switch, or be controlled electronically through a control module. Mercedes-Benz uses an electronic pulse system that actually senses water on the windshield and automatically switches on the wipers. The speed or pulse of the wiper motor is determined by how much water is on the glass, figure 14-13.

With any electronic control system, it is important to follow the diagnosis and test procedures recommended by the manufacturer for that specific vehicle. Refer to Chapter Twelve of this *Shop Manual* for additional electronic control system service information.

A typical pulse, or interval, wiper system uses either a governor or a solid-state module that contains either a variable resistor or rheostat and capacitor. The module connects into the electrical circuitry between the wiper switch and wiper motor. The variable resistor or rheostat controls the length of the interval between wiper pulses. A solid-state pulse-wipe timer regulates the control circuit of the pulse relay to direct current to the motor at the prescribed interval, figure 14-14. The following troubleshooting procedure applies to most models.

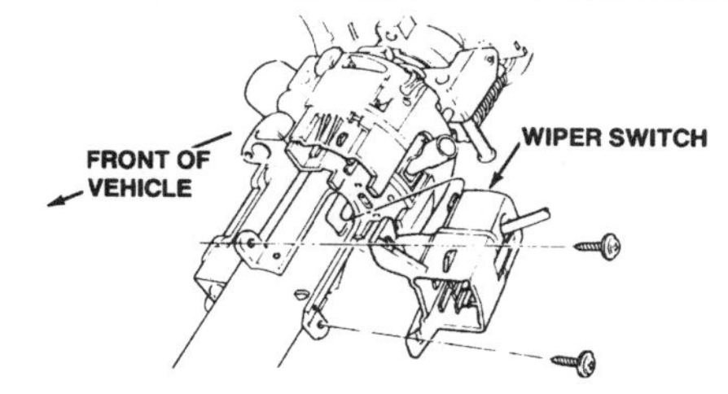

Figure 14-12. The wiper switch attaches to the steering column on many late-model vehicles.

If the wipers do not run at all, check the wiper fuse, fusible link, or circuit breaker and verify that voltage is available to the switch. Refer to a wiring diagram of the switch to determine how current is routed through it to the motor in the different positions. Next, disconnect the switch and use jumper wires to apply power directly to the motor on the different speed circuits. If the motor now runs, the problem is in the switch or module. Check for continuity in the circuit for each speed through the control to ground if the wiper motor runs at some, but not all, speeds.

Windshield Washer Diagnosis

Most vehicles use a positive-displacement or centrifugal-type washer pump located in the washer reservoir. However, some older models use a pulse-type pump attached to the body of the wiper motor. A momentary-contact switch, which is usually part of a steering column-mounted combination switch assembly, energizes the washer pump.

Inoperative windshield washers may be caused by a:

- Blown fuse
- Empty reservoir
- Clogged nozzle
- Broken, pinched, or clogged hose
- Loose or broken wire
- Blocked reservoir screen
- Leaking reservoir.

To quick-check any washer system, make sure the reservoir has sufficient fluid, then disconnect the pump hose and operate the washer switch, figure 14-15. If fluid squirts from the pump, the delivery system is at fault, not the motor, switch, or circuitry. If no fluid squirts from the pump, the problem is most likely a circuit failure, defective pump, or faulty switch. However, a clogged reservoir screen may be preventing fluid from entering the pump.

Windshield Washer Service

When a fluid delivery problem is indicated, check for blocked, pinched, broken, or disconnected hoses,

Copyright 2000 by Chek-Chart Publications

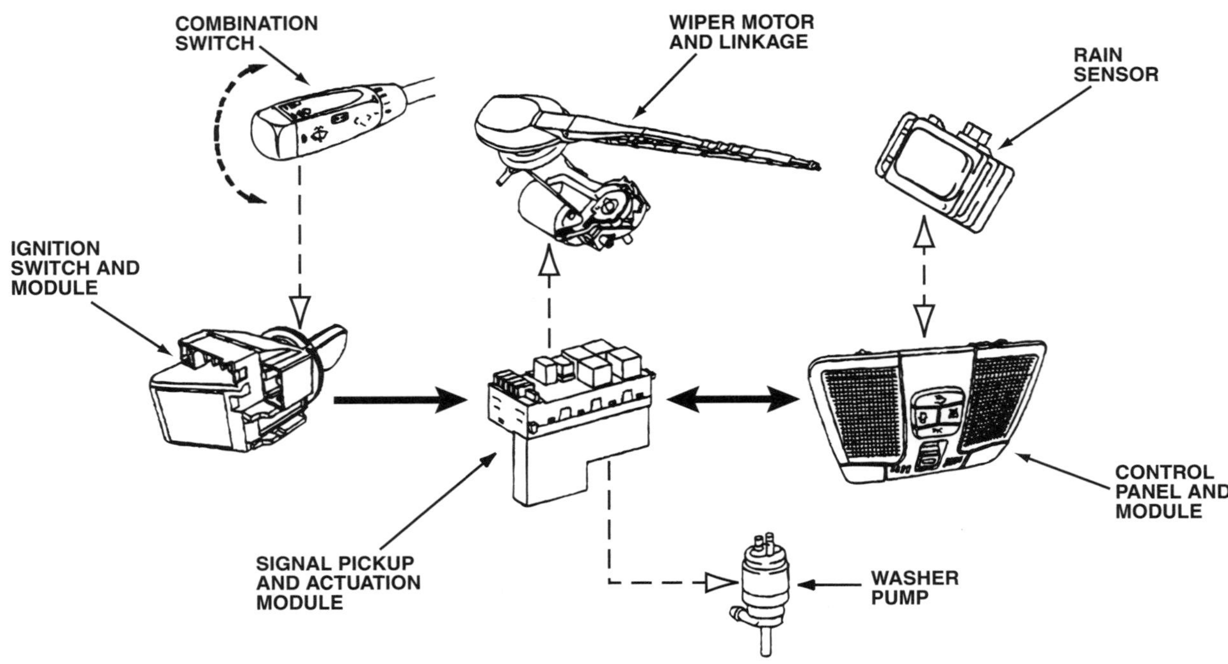

Figure 14-13. This Mercedes-Benz system adjusts wiper speed based on the amount of water on the windshield.

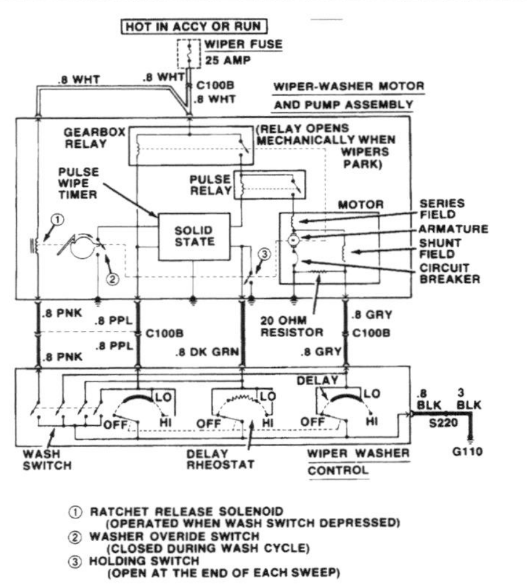

Figure 14-14. Circuit diagram of a rheostat-controlled, electronically timed, interval wiper.

clogged nozzles, or a blocked washer pump outlet. If the pump motor does not operate, check for battery voltage available at the pump while operating the washer switch. If voltage is available and the pump does not run, check for continuity on the pump ground circuit. If there is no voltage drop on the ground circuit, replace the pump motor.

If battery voltage is not available at the motor, check for power through the washer switch. If voltage

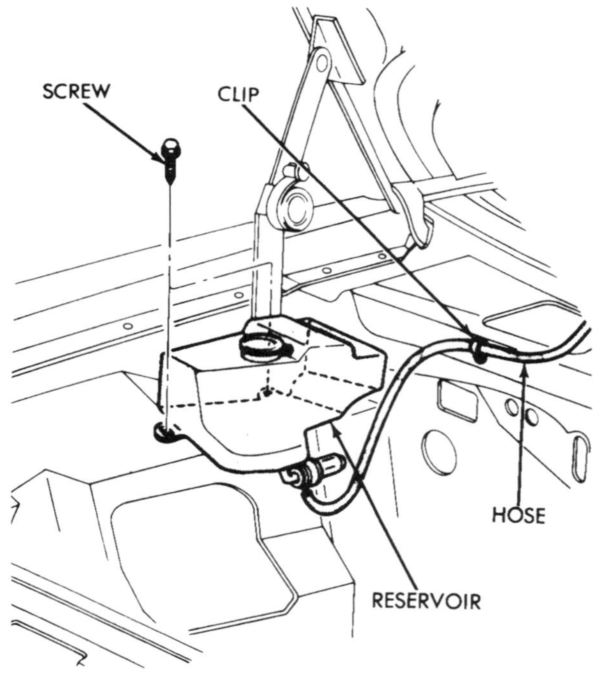

Figure 14-15. Disconnect the hose at pump and operate the switch to check a washer pump.

is available at and through the switch, there is a problem in the wiring between the switch and pump. Perform voltage drop tests to locate the fault. Repair

Copyright 2000 by Chek-Chart Publications

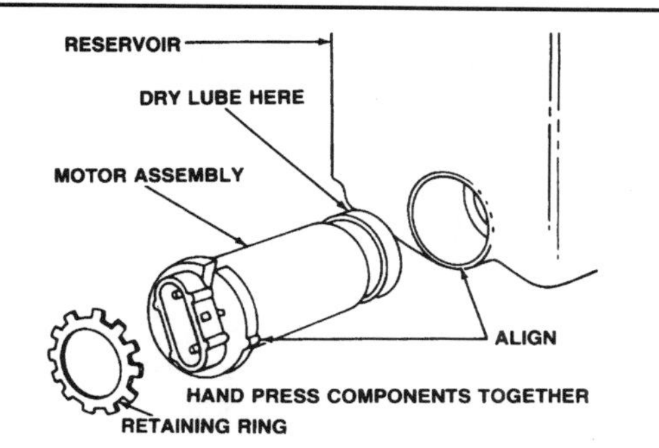

Figure 14-16 Washer pumps usually install into the reservoir and are held in place with a retaining ring.

the wiring as needed and retest. If voltage is available to but not through the switch, replace the switch. Locate and correct the open or short circuit between the switch and the battery if battery voltage is not available to the switch.

Washer motors are not repairable and are simply replaced if defective. Centrifugal or positive-displacement pumps are located on or inside the washer reservoir tank or cover and secured with a retaining ring or nut, figure 14-16. Washer pump switches are installed either on the steering column or on the instrument panel.

ELECTRIC COOLING FAN SYSTEM

Electric cooling fans, which are designed to operate only when necessary, are switched on and off by a temperature-sensitive switch. Commonly called the fan switch, the unit installs in the radiator on some models, figure 14-17. On other models, the switch installs on the engine, generally in the cylinder head. Several methods are used to supply current to the fan motor:

- A coolant temperature switch, usually mounted in the engine, that energizes the control circuit of a relay. The relay provides power to the fan motor.
- A coolant temperature switch that contains an internal contact set. The contacts inside the switch close to complete either the power or ground side of the fan motor circuit. This type of switch may be mounted in either the engine or radiator.
- An air-conditioning (AC), or high discharge pressure, switch that energizes the control circuit of a relay to turn on the fan motor. These switches, which may be actuated either by high-side pressure or the AC power circuit, are used in addition to the coolant temperature switch.
- Electronically controlled relays that operate on an output signal from a control module to energize the fan motor. These systems switch the fan motor on and off based on the signal of the engine coolant temperature (ECT) sensor.

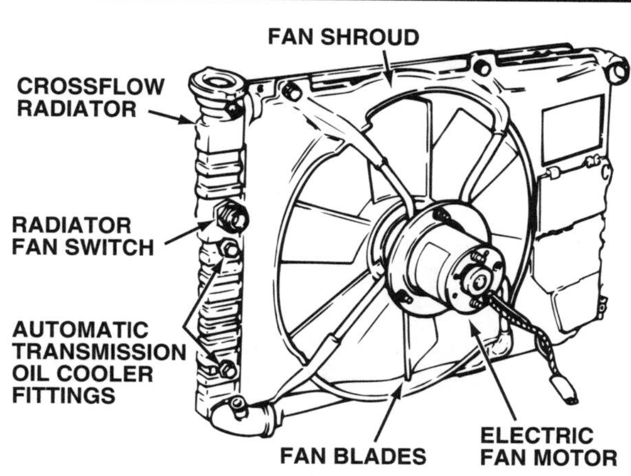

Figure 14-17. A radiator-mounted switch controls the motor on this cooling fan.

Typical electric cooling fans switch on when engine coolant temperature reaches from about 212° to 225°F (100° to 107°C). Some systems may have either a two-speed fan or two separate fans to provide a high rate of air flow under extreme conditions. These systems control fan use as needed based on temperature and other factors. On models with air conditioning, the fan is also used to increase condenser air flow and reduce AC system high-side pressure when needed, figure 14-18. A pressure switch installed somewhere in the high-pressure side of the system provides a control signal to the relay to energize the fan motor.

An electronically controlled fan motor is switched on to maintain normal operating temperature whenever the engine coolant begins to overheat, or when there is no input signal from the ECT sensor. Electronic control systems generally store a diagnostic trouble code (DTC) if there is no ECT signal.

Any diagnosis of the cooling fan begins with an examination of a circuit diagram. This diagram provides the most accurate and timely understanding of how a particular system should operate.

Circuit Testing

As explained in the *Classroom Manual*, there are a considerable number of electric fan circuit variations. However, there are a few features common to all cooling fan systems. There are two types of cooling fan failure: a fan motor that does not run and a motor that runs continuously.

The most basic electric cooling fan circuit is found on older vehicles without AC or electronic controls. These systems typically provide a path to ground for

Copyright 2000 by Chek-Chart Publications

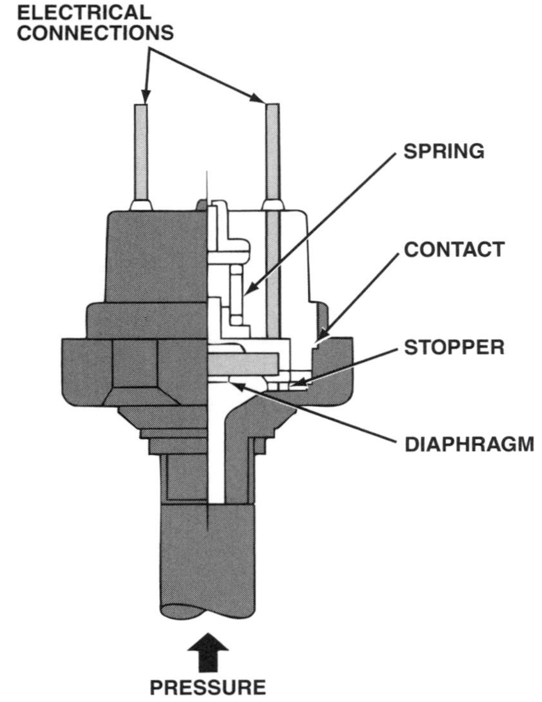

Figure 14-18. This switch energizes the fan relay when AC pressure exceeds the switch setting.

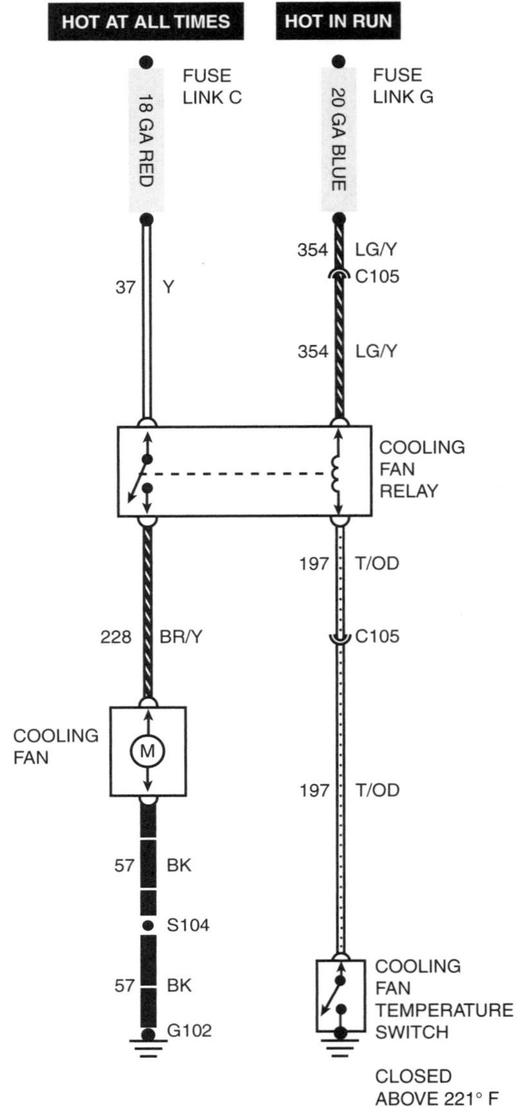

Figure 14-19. Circuit diagram of a Ford single-speed cooling fan system.

the fan relay control circuit through the temperature switch when engine coolant reaches a specified temperature. Once energized, the relay applies voltage to the fan motor, figure 14-19.

The first step in troubleshooting a fan motor that does not run is to verify that battery voltage is available to the relay. If no voltage is available, check the circuit fuse and fusible links. Perform voltage drop tests on the power circuit as needed to locate the open. If voltage is available to the relay, check the fan motor.

To check the fan motor, disconnect it from the wiring harness and use jumper wires to connect the motor terminals to ground and battery voltage. Always use a fused jumper wire to connect the power circuit. Also, make the jumper wire ground connection away from the battery to prevent arcing and a possible explosion. A motor that does not run when connected directly to the battery is defective; replace the motor. A motor that runs with the jumper wires installed indicates a circuit failure. Check the switch, relay, and wiring.

Stuck contacts in either the temperature switch or the relay cause the fan motor to run continuously. To check, simply disconnect the electrical connector at the temperature switch. If the fan stops running, the temperature switch contacts are stuck closed. Replace the switch. If the fan continues running with the switch disconnected, the relay is likely at fault. However, a short to ground in the wiring produces the same result. Check the relay and replace it if needed. If the relay is working and the motor continues to run, there is a short to ground somewhere in the circuit. Locate the short by voltage drop testing and repair as needed.

A common variation of the basic system uses two relays to power the fan motor, figure 14-20. One is the temperature-controlled, cooling fan relay just described and the other relay is controlled by the AC system. The AC relay runs the fan whenever the compressor is turned on, regardless of engine coolant temperature. If the AC is turned off while the vehicle is being driven, control of the cooling fan returns to the

Copyright 2000 by Chek-Chart Publications

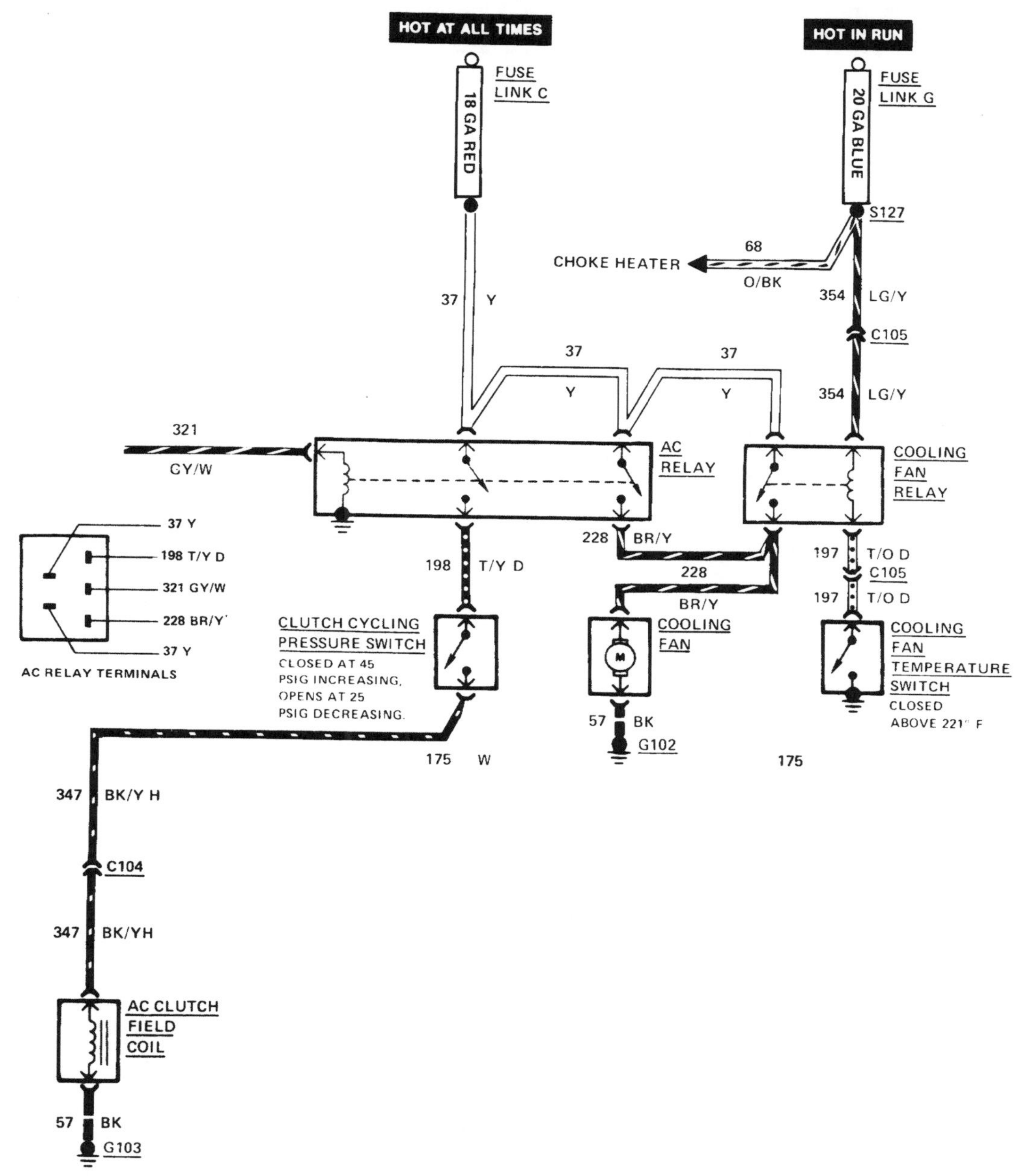

Figure 14-20. Circuit diagram of a Ford dual-relay cooling fan system.

basic fan circuit, through the cooling fan relay. With this type of system, check the cooling fan and AC relays separately by disabling one while testing the other.

Most late-model cooling fan systems are electronically controlled by the powertrain control module (PCM). Therefore, it is important to work carefully to avoid accidental circuit damage. A number of vehicles use a system with two fan motors, each of which may be controlled by several relays, figure 14-21. In the system shown, current travels through the right hand fan motor to the series parallel relay when the low speed relay is energized. When the series parallel relay is deenergized, current is routed through the left hand motor, which places both motors in series to reduce speed. Energizing the series parallel relay energizes the high-speed relay as well. Under these conditions, the series parallel relay routes current from the right-hand motor directly to ground and the high-speed relay provides power to the left-hand

Copyright 2000 by Chek-Chart Publications

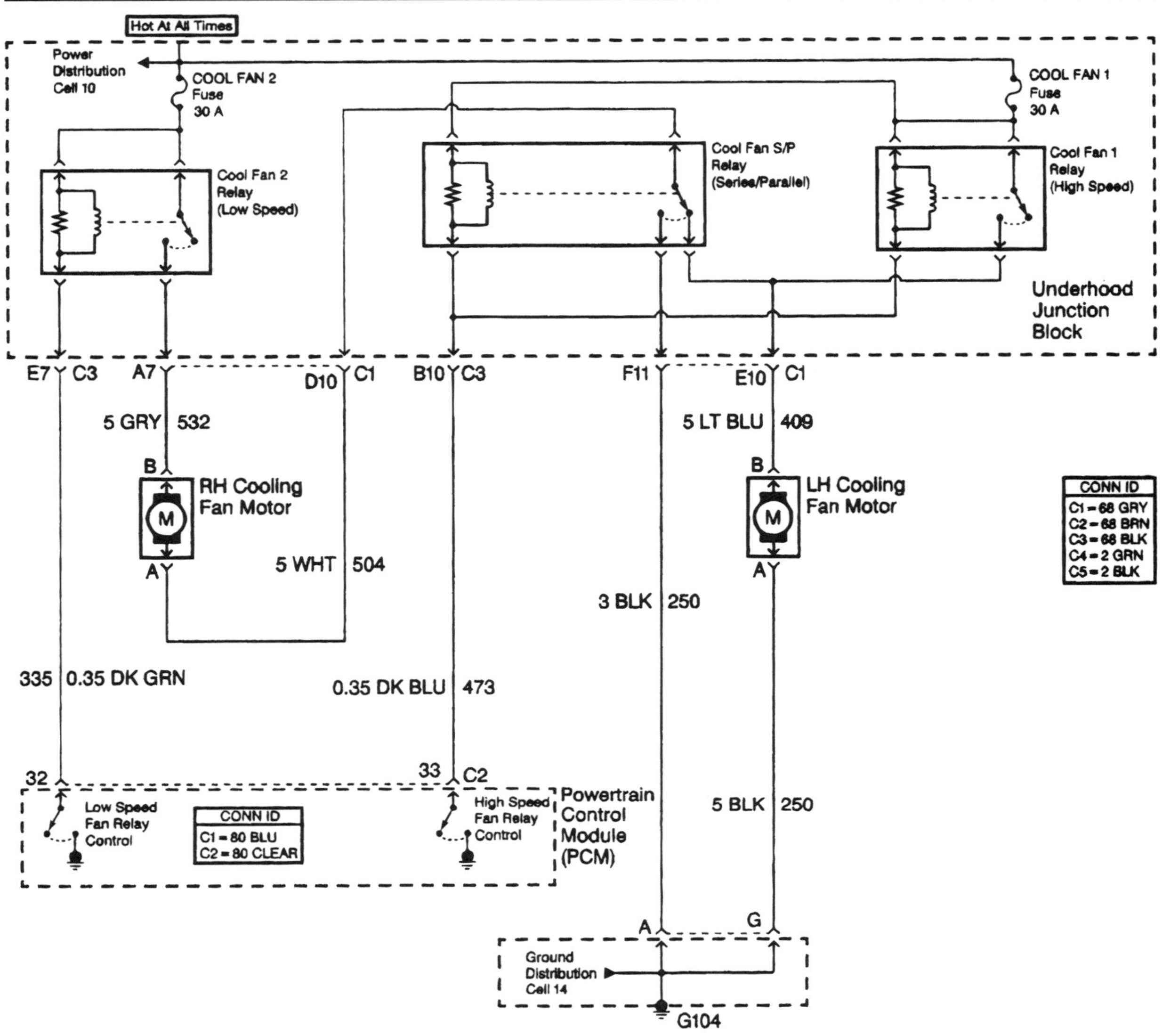

Figure 14-21. Circuit diagram of a two-fan system with multiple relays.

motor. Now, both motors are energized in parallel and speed increases.

The circuitry on a newer system may appear complex, but they are simply a combination of basic relay and motor circuits. Access the onboard diagnostic system to see if the failure set a diagnostic trouble code (DTC). Repair the source of any DTC failure before testing the cooling fan circuits. Never attempt to troubleshoot a circuit without an accurate diagram. Starting at the motor, perform voltage drop checks to locate circuit faults.

Temperature Switch Tests

A simple DMM check determines if a cooling fan temperature switch is operational without removing it from the engine. However, the test does not reveal if the switch is operating within or outside specifications.

With the engine at normal operating temperature, but not running, use the DMM to check continuity between the cooling fan temperature switch body and the cylinder head. Any resistance here creates a poor ground path for the signal circuit. Corrosion and dirt buildup around the switch mounting are common sources of high ground circuit resistance. Slightly

Copyright 2000 by Chek-Chart Publications

loosening and tightening the switch may restore continuity. If so, remove the switch, clean the contact surfaces, and reinstall it.

If there is continuity between the switch body and engine, disconnect the temperature switch harness and install a jumper wire between the switch lead and a good engine ground. Turn the ignition switch to the RUN position. If the fan motor runs with the connector grounded but not when the connector is reinstalled, replace the temperature switch. Be sure the coolant temperature is hot enough to close the switch before replacing it.

An alternative way to test a cooling fan temperature switch is to capture the signal on a graphing multimeter as the engine warms up and the fan cycles on. Signal voltage pulls to ground as the switch closes to complete the circuit, which energizes the relay sending power to the fan, figure 14-22. A common fan switch failure is due to coolant sediment buildup on the switch. The deposits form a layer of insulation that dissipates coolant heat before it reaches the sensor, which delays switching and causes overheating problems.

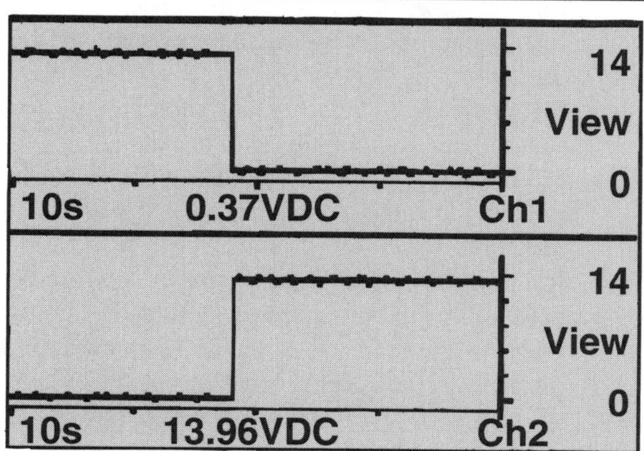

Figure 14-22. When the fan switch signal goes to ground (CH1), the relay power circuit goes to system voltage (CH2).

Relay Tests

A cooling fan relay is a normally open relay. Many systems use a double contact relay but use only the normally open set of contacts. Check the circuit diagram to determine which type of relay is being tested. As explained earlier in this *Shop Manual*, relay operation is checked with either an ohmmeter or a voltmeter.

Using an ohmmeter, there should be continuity across the control circuit. There should be no continuity across the power circuit when the relay is not energized and continuity when energized.

Using a voltmeter, there should be about 12 volts on both sides of the control circuit when not energized. When the relay energizes, voltage should drop to zero on the temperature-switch side of the circuit. The power circuit should have battery voltage available to the power source or the fan at all times and across the relay when energized.

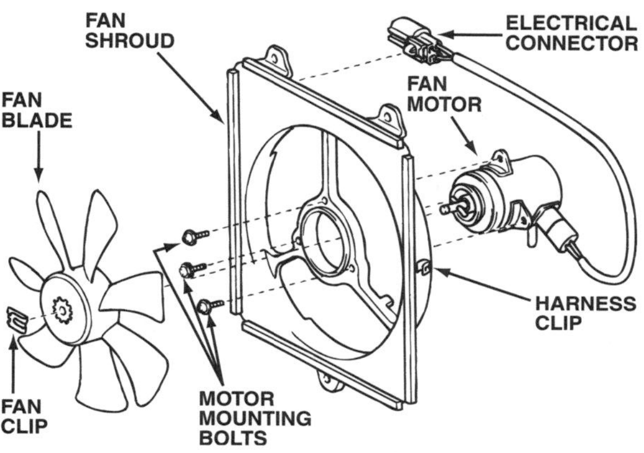

Figure 14-23. Typical cooling fan motor installation.

Fan Motor Replacement

If a fan motor does not run when it is disconnected from the wiring harness and connected directly to battery voltage and ground with jumper wires, the motor is likely defective and must be replaced. However, the fan may be bound against the shroud or radiator as a result of collision damage or shroud distortion. If the fan spins free by hand, replace the motor. Cooling fan motors are usually attached to a fan shroud that bolts up to the radiator or the radiator core support, figure 14-23. The fan and shroud are removed from the vehicle as an assembly and the motor is replaced on the bench. To replace a typical fan motor:

1. Separate the fan motor connector from the wiring harness. Also, remove any clips that route the wiring along the shroud.
2. Support the assembly while removing the screws or bolts holding the shroud to the radiator or support. Once the fasteners are removed, carefully lift the shroud and motor assembly from the vehicle.
3. Next, remove the fan blade from the motor shaft. Some fans are held to the shaft with a retaining clip that pries off, while others use nuts that are removed with a wrench.
4. Remove the fasteners that attach the fan motor to the fan shroud support. Then, separate the motor from the support.

Copyright 2000 by Chek-Chart Publications

5. Fit the new motor into the shroud support, install the mounting fasteners, and tighten securely.
6. Place the fan blade on the motor shaft and secure with the retaining clip or nuts.
7. Fit the shroud and motor assembly onto the radiator, install the fasteners, and tighten them securely.
8. Rotate the motor by hand to make sure the fan blades clear the radiator and shroud.
9. Connect the fan motor to the wiring harness and install any routing clips used.

GAUGES, WARNING DEVICES, AND DRIVER INFORMATION SYSTEMS

Gauges, which indicate various vehicle conditions such as coolant temperature, oil pressure, fuel level, and battery voltage, may be either analog or digital devices. Gauge and instrument operations on most late-model vehicles are electronically controlled by an onboard computer and are often linked to the engine management system. Diagnostic trouble code (DTC) information is available on some systems to assist in troubleshooting. Gauges and instrumentation are unique for each model of vehicle, so service manual specifications and procedures are needed for correct diagnosis and repair. The information presented here consists of general procedures that apply to most models.

Analog Gauges

Before testing any gauge or instrument that appears to be defective, make sure that the condition it monitors is normal. For example, if an engine coolant temperature gauge or warning lamp indicates the engine is overheating, test the cooling system before assuming that the gauge or lamp is inaccurate.

Analog gauges operate on one of three principles:

- Mechanical
- Thermal
- Electromagnetic.

Mechanical gauges are directly operated by what they measure using fluid pressure, fluid temperature, or cables. Thermal gauges use current passing through a bimetallic strip to heat one side of the strip faster than the other. This causes the strip to bend, which moves the needle on the gauge. Electromagnetic gauges use the interaction of magnetic fields to move the gauge needle.

Thermal or electromagnetic gauges use a signal modified by a sending unit. A sending unit is a transducer that changes a mechanical, hydraulic, or temperature signal into an electrical signal. Several designs are in use to generate signals based on pressure, level, or temperature.

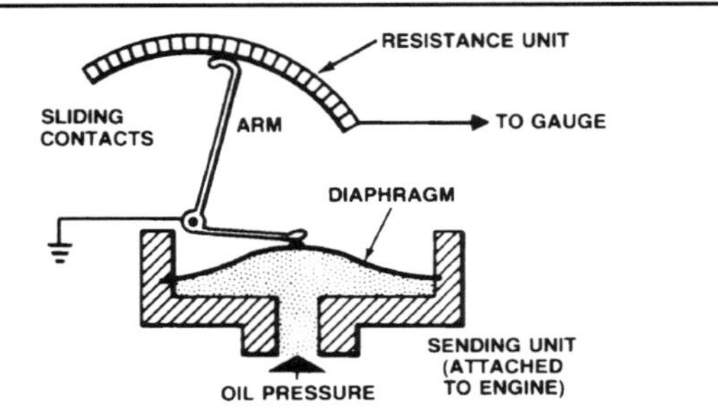

Figure 14-24. Pressure sending units are a transducer that uses the position of the diaphragm to vary resistance.

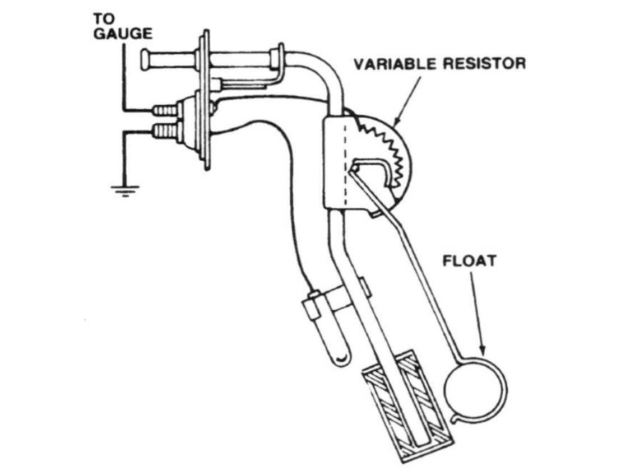

Figure 14-25. Level sending units are potentiometers that vary resistance according to the position of the arm.

Pressure sending units use a diaphragm to operate a sliding contact against a resistor, thus changing the movement of the diaphragm into an electrical signal, figure 14-24. Level sending units use a float in a reservoir to move a sliding contact along a variable resistor, so a change in fluid level produces a change in gauge circuit resistance, figure 14-25. Thermal sending units use a heat-sensing element, or thermistor, whose electrical resistance varies along with temperature, figure 14-26.

Intermittent or nonoperation of an analog gauge is often caused by an electrical problem in the gauge circuit. High or low gauge readings may be the result of a defective sending unit, instrument voltage regulator (IVR), or faulty circuitry. Check the circuit diagram to determine what devices are used in the circuit being tested.

Copyright 2000 by Chek-Chart Publications

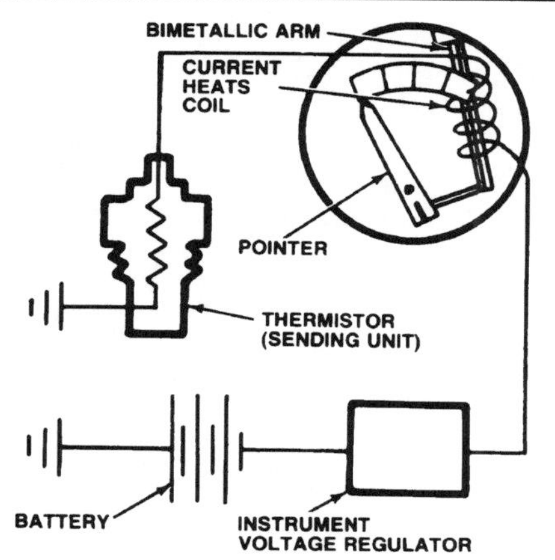

Figure 14-26. A thermistor, whose resistance varies by temperature, is used as a temperature sending unit.

Circuit Voltage Limiters

Most gauges require a continuous, controlled amount of voltage to operate. This may be either battery voltage or a lower regulated voltage, which is usually about 5 to 6 volts. Regulated voltage is provided by an IVR, of which there are several types.

An older type of IVR consists of a set of contacts and a bimetallic strip with a heating coil wrapped around it, figure 14-27. The bimetallic strip bends as the coil heats and bends back as it cools, which opens and closes the contact points. The points act like a self-setting circuit breaker to keep gauge voltage at a specific average level.

A solid-state device that delivers a constant, consistent voltage to the gauges is used on newer models. The voltage limiter may be a separate unit on the printed circuit (PC) board, or an integral part of one of the dash units.

Testing an IVR

If the IVR is not working properly, the gauges it controls give inaccurate readings. Be aware, gauges may be damaged by excessive voltage if the IVR fails. An IVR fault causes all regulated gauges to read inaccurate. Typical symptoms include:

- Gauges fail all at once.
- Gauges give inaccurate, either all high or all low, readings.
- Readings vibrate by more than the width of the needle.

Use a voltmeter or test lamp to determine if the IVR unit is functioning. Be careful not to ground or short any of the regulator terminals when testing it. Doing so causes IVR and instrument panel wiring harness damage.

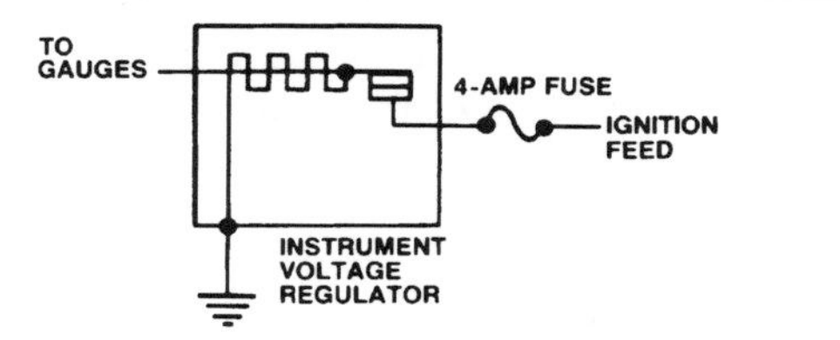

Figure 14-27. An instrument voltage regulator (IVR) provides a constant voltage to the gauges.

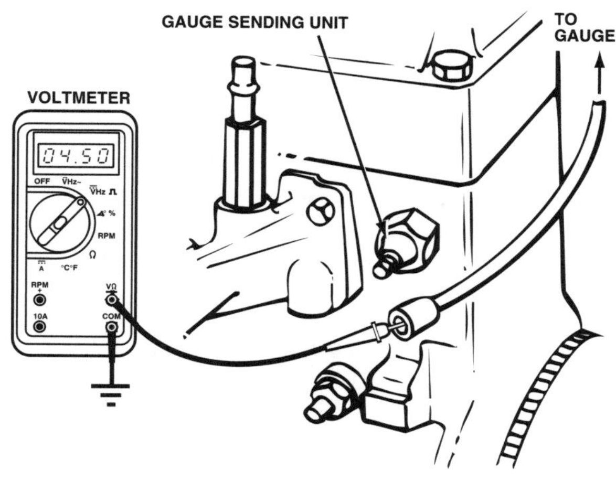

Figure 14-28. Using a sending-unit circuit to check IVR operation.

The IVR is often difficult to reach for testing. On most vehicles, the instrument cluster must be removed from the dash because the IVR mounts on the back side of the cluster. However, it is possible to use a gauge sending unit in the engine compartment to make a quick test of IVR operation. To test:

1. Check the circuit fuse and replace it, if necessary.
2. Disconnect one of the gauge sending units from the wiring harness.
3. Connect the positive voltmeter lead to the sending unit wire and attach the negative lead meter lead to ground, figure 14-28.
4. Switch the ignition on while watching the voltmeter.

Voltage should either hold steady at the regulated voltage or pulse between zero and a positive voltage at about the same rate as the turn signal flashers. An analog voltmeter displays this pulsing, but a digital meter displays the average of the high and low voltages. However, the min/max feature captures and plays

Copyright 2000 by Chek-Chart Publications

back the high and low voltages. A scope or graphing multimeter (GMM) also displays the cycling of the voltage signal. If the meter reading is higher or lower than specified regulated voltage, or does not pulse, replace the IVR.

Replacing an IVR

Instrument voltage regulators are generally either separate units that are held to the back of the instrument cluster panel by screws or nuts, or plugged into a printed circuit (PC) board. Remove the instrument cluster to gain access to the IVR. On some designs, the IVR is built into one of the gauges. The entire gauge must be replaced if the IVR is defective on this type of system. The pulsing relay of an IVR may also be a source of electromagnetic interference (EMI) that affects gauge operation. Some manufacturers eliminate the IVR from their clusters by using air core gauges, which are electronically controlled using pulse-width modulation.

Gauge and Sending Unit Service

With the exception of ammeters and voltmeters, all electrical gauges use a variable-resistance sending unit to control current through the gauge itself.

Analog gauge design is simple, and with the low-voltage and light-current load carried by most gauges, they easily last the life of the vehicle. When a gauge appears to work improperly, the cause is most likely a problem in the wiring, a malfunctioning IVR, or a defective sending unit, rather than the gauge itself. If a single gauge fails or shows an inaccurate reading, the problem is most likely in the circuit branch or sending unit for that particular gauge. When all of the gauges fail or show inaccurate readings, the problem is most likely in the IVR or their shared circuitry.

Gauge testing

Most gauges may be tested with a variable resistance gauge tester. The tester connects into the circuit in place of the sending unit and is set to duplicate the resistance of the sending unit. A gauge tester is basically an adjustable resistor that supplies a substitute signal for the sending unit. With the gauge tester set for the correct amount of resistance and the sending unit wiring harness disconnected, connect one test lead to the sending unit wiring harness and the other test lead to the circuit ground. The gauge should register the correct setting.

As with any electrical circuit, the first place to check is the fuse and main power supply. If the fuse is

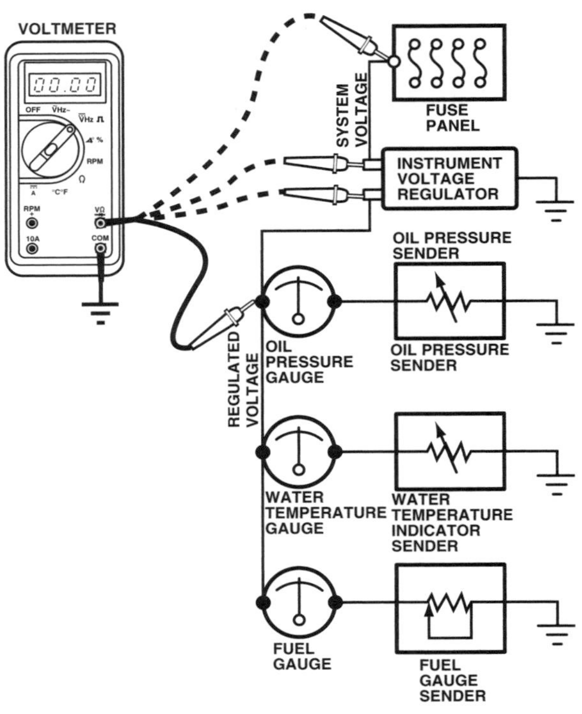

Figure 14-29. Locate circuit problems by voltage drop testing from power to the gauge.

good, work down the circuit from the power source to the gauge performing voltage drop checks, figure 14-29. Switch the ignition on and disconnect the sending unit. Full battery voltage should be available at the IVR input terminal. If battery voltage is available on the output terminal of the IVR, the IVR is either defective or not properly grounded. Readings at the IVR output terminal and at the gauge should pulse to an average of about 4.5 volts on a thermostatic system or equal battery voltage on an electromagnetic gauge system. This same signal voltage should be available at the sending unit. Avoid grounding the sending unit lead, as this causes gauge damage.

Printed circuit board testing

Troubleshooting a printed circuit (PC) board is quick and easy. However, the printed circuit, which is composed of copper foil bonded to a mylar film mounted on a thin composition board, is easily damaged by improper handling. Any PC defect requires replacement of the entire board.

Never use a probe when testing PC board circuits, as this pierces and damages the circuit or copper conductors. Use a self-powered test lamp or an ohmmeter for this procedure:

Copyright 2000 by Chek-Chart Publications

1. Remove the instrument cluster and visually inspect the printed circuit carefully.
2. Using a circuit diagram, connect the test lamp or ohmmeter lead to the proper pin plug terminal for the circuit being tested. Trace the circuit between each uncoated position leading to the gauge, indicator, or bulb in that circuit.
3. Check each uncoated position on the other side of the gauge, indicator, or bulb circuit.
4. Connect one test lead to the pin of the circuit being tested. Touch all remaining pin terminals one at a time with the other test leads to check for continuity between circuits.

Ammeter and voltmeter testing

Since ammeters and voltmeters measure the performance of the electrical system, they do not require a sending unit to control current through them. Therefore, test procedures are slightly different for these types of gauges.

Ammeter

An ammeter connects in series or parallel between the alternator and the battery. If connected in series, a conductor bar is mounted between the two ammeter connectors. Parallel circuits use two points in the wiring, one close to the battery and the other closer to the alternator. Current passing through the conductor bar, or shunt circuit, creates a voltage drop. The direction and amount of the voltage drop are used to determine total current into or out of the battery.

A loose connection at the ammeter terminal increases resistance and results in intermittent meter operation. Continued operation produces excess heat that damages the wiring and gauge.

To test an ammeter, turn the ignition switch, headlights, and other accessories on; the gauge should show a discharge. Use a voltmeter or 12-volt test light to check for battery voltage available on both sides of the gauge, figure 14-30.

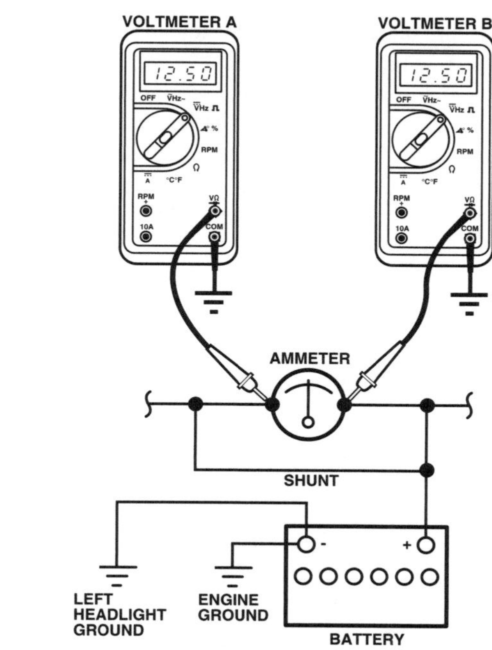

Figure 14-30. Checking voltage drop across an ammeter gauge.

Voltmeter

A voltmeter indicates the system, or battery, voltage using an electromagnet and a return spring. Return spring force attempts to keep the needle in the zero position. The field strength of an electromagnet, which varies according to system voltage, opposes return spring force to move the needle up and down the scale. The balance of return spring force and field strength is calibrated into volts and displayed on the

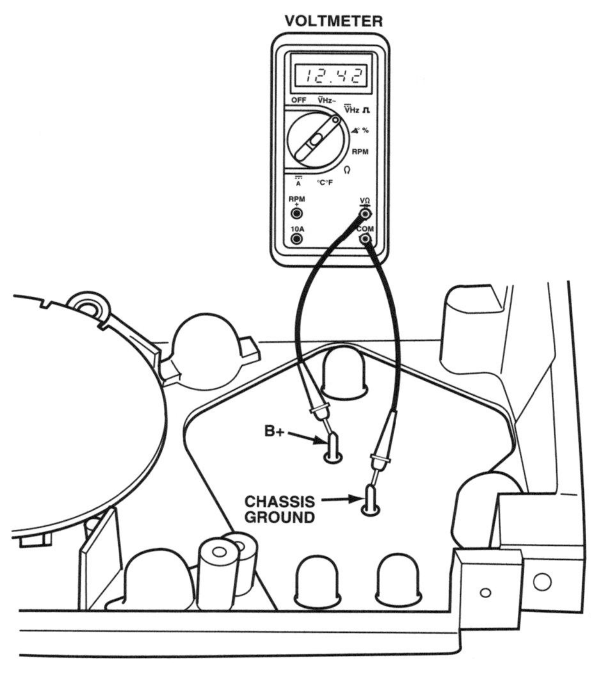

Figure 14-31. Checking continuity of a voltmeter gauge.

Copyright 2000 by Chek-Chart Publications

gauge face. The voltmeter gauge, which connects in parallel to the battery, receives system voltage through the ignition switch.

To test the voltmeter, remove the instrument cluster and disconnect or remove the gauge. Switch the ignition on and check for battery voltage at the gauge connections, figure 14-31. On a combination gauge, there are several connection pins; refer to the service manual instructions.

Warning Lamps

Warning lamps are controlled by one or more switches. The exception to this is a charging system warning lamp, which is controlled by the alternator producing voltage equal to battery voltage. The remaining warning lamps are either grounding units controlled by insulated switches, or insulated units controlled by grounding switches. Seatbelt warning systems often include a timed circuit breaker so that the lamp works for a brief period of time and then shuts off.

As with gauges, it is important to verify that the system the warning lamp is monitoring is operating correctly before looking for circuit faults. Locate a circuit diagram for the particular unit being serviced to determine circuit layout and test points.

Some vehicles use warning lamps in the instrument cluster instead of gauges; others use a combination of lamps and gauges. A charging system warning lamp is directly controlled by charging voltage, while a sending unit is used to operate all other warning lamps. Warning lamp sending units are simple on/off digital switches, rather than the variable resistors used for gauges, figure 14-32.

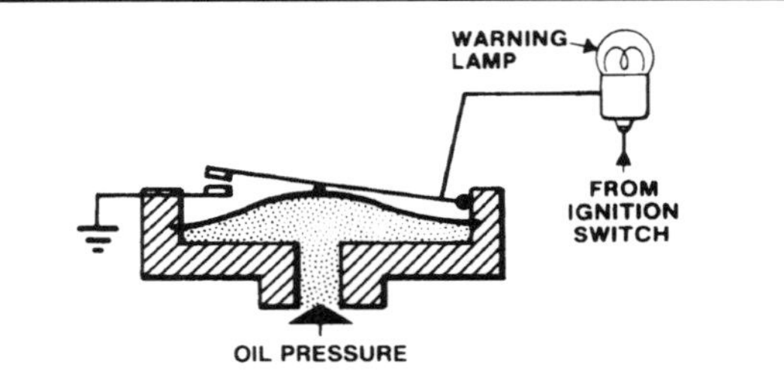

Figure 14-32. Internal contact points open and complete the circuit on a warning-lamp sending unit.

Warning lamp circuits operated with a sending unit are checked using the same procedures as for interior lighting circuits, which are detailed in Chapter Thirteen of this *Shop Manual*. Before troubleshooting any warning lamp circuit, check the battery and charging systems for proper operation. Also check the system being monitored. When a circuit failure is indicated, conduct voltage drop tests to locate and repair the fault.

Electronic Digital Instrument Clusters

Electronic digital instrument clusters differ considerably in their design and in the type of devices used on the display. However, any electronic instrument cluster serves the same purpose and performs the same functions as an analog instrument cluster. Digital instruments are electronically controlled by an onboard computer, which may be the PCM, the body control module (BCM), or a dedicated instrument control module. Sending units, similar to those used for analog gauges, provide the input signals. Once the computer processes these input signals, it sends output signals to the instrument cluster to control the display panel.

Regardless of its level of sophistication, an electronic instrument panel combines conventional sending units, such as a coolant temperature switch or the variable resistor of a fuel tank float, with the solid-state equivalent of analog gauges. The display device may be a light-emitting diode (LED), a liquid crystal display (LCD), a vacuum fluorescent display (VFD), cathode ray tube (CRT), or fiber-optic panel. The control module outputs voltage signals, which are based on sensor readings, to operate the instrument display according its design.

Always make sure that the engine condition monitored by any electronic instrument that appears to be defective is truly normal. Test the engine condition before assuming that the instrument is wrong.

Because of the wide array of instrument cluster designs, it is extremely important to have accurate service information. Never attempt to diagnose a problem without accurate diagrams, specifications, and procedures for the particular model being tested. Most late-model systems have a self-diagnostic program; refer to the service manual to access and test the system. Always disable the supplemental restraint system (SRS) and disconnect the negative battery cable to prevent damage when removing or installing a digital instrument cluster.

Gauge testing

The displays in an electronic cluster are part of an electronic system that often contains a self-diagnostic program or test sequence. If a gauge display is faulty

Copyright 2000 by Chek-Chart Publications

and the control module successfully completes a self-diagnostic test, the source of the failure is outside the cluster. Check for problems in the wiring, connections, sensors, and sending units.

An inoperative gauge is quickly checked. Simply disconnect the sending unit, switch the ignition on, and ground the gauge circuit with a jumper wire. Usually, if the gauge shows a maximum reading, the sending unit is defective. There are exceptions, such as General Motors fuel gauges, which read empty with the sending unit grounded. When all of the gauges display maximum readings with the engine running, check for loose or damaged connections or a short to ground at the gauge module.

When all of the gauges work intermittently or drop to zero after the engine starts, check dedicated ground connections for the gauge module. Poor ground connections on a digital instrument cluster cause the displays to fade or disappear entirely.

Display replacement

In almost all cases, an electronic instrument cluster is serviced as an assembly by replacing it. Removal and installation procedures are the same as with a conventional cluster. If one instrument is defective, the entire cluster must be replaced. Trip computers and other electronic display devices are also serviced by replacement.

A considerable amount of disassembly is required to replace the cluster on most vehicles. Most of this involves removing trim panels that are easily bent, scratched, or broken if handled incorrectly. Follow the service manual procedure for the specific model being repaired. Special tools are required for some models.

If an electronic cluster uses an odometer memory chip, the chip must be removed from the defective cluster and installed in the new one, figure 14-33. State laws vary regarding the installation of new odometer memory chips to replace a defective one. Some require that the original mileage be posted on a door jamb label; others require the chip to be programmed to display the mileage of the previous chip. In areas where the law requires the display of original mileage in the odometer, refer to the procedure from the manufacturer to set the mileage when installing a new chip.

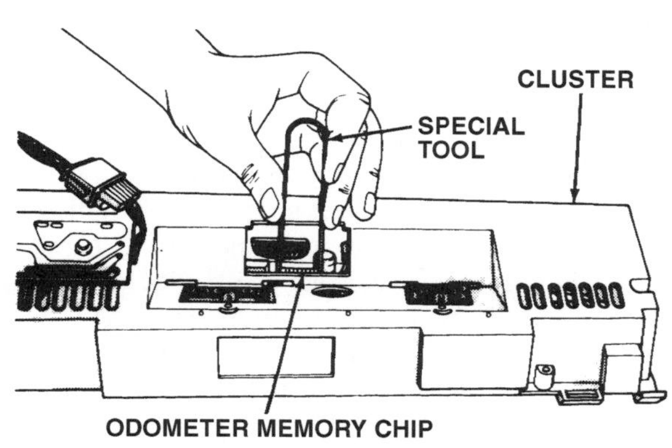

Figure 14-33. Remove and install an odometer memory chip with a special tool to avoid damaging the chip.

Driver Information Centers

Many late-model vehicles are equipped with electronic instrumentation that provides a wide variety of information to the driver. These units range from simple trip computers to more complicated electronic message centers that check the level of each fluid, the operation of each lamp, the opening of doors, hood, and trunk, as well as tire inflation on some models. The module that operates these indicators receives power from the ignition-run circuit.

These electronic devices vary in levels of complexity, but like electronic digital clusters, they rely on input from outside sensors and circuits. Most contain a self-diagnostic program that, if successfully completed, indicates a failure in the wiring, connectors, sensors, or sending units. For this reason, diagnosing problems in such units requires the service manual diagnostic charts, specifications, and circuit diagrams. In all cases, a problem found to be in the unit is corrected by replacement.

Audible Warning Devices

Audible warning devices, such as buzzers and chimes, are used in many areas to alert the driver if the:

- Seat belts are not fastened
- Key is in switch with door open
- Door is not closed
- Vehicle speed is excessive
- Headlights are on with the door open.

Copyright 2000 by Chek-Chart Publications

Like the vehicle horn, these devices typically use a set of contact points and a vibrating diaphragm to make noise, figure 14-34. A time delay switch connected to the seat belt latch turns the buzzer off after a few seconds on some models.

When an audible warning device fails to operate, check the circuit fuse first. If the fuse is okay, disconnect the warning device from the wiring harness. Using jumper wires, connect the device to battery voltage and ground to see if it operates. If the buzzer operates, check the circuit switches. Warning devices generally are controlled by switches connected to the ground side of the circuit. Use voltage drop checks to locate and repair circuit failures.

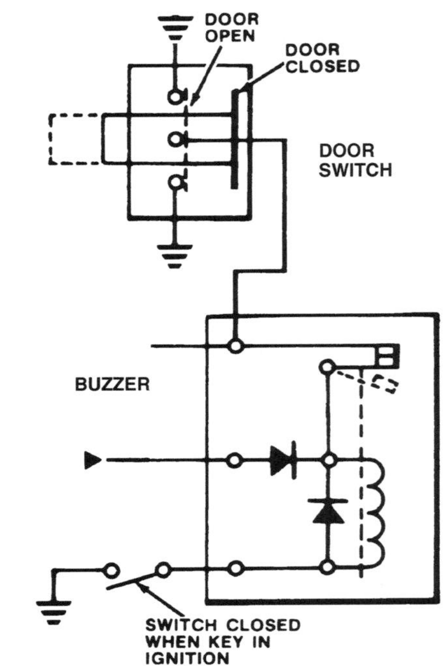

Figure 14-34. Circuit diagram of a typical door-ajar warning buzzer.

Copyright 2000 by Chek-Chart Publications

15 Electrical Accessory Service

Electric and electronic accessories designed for driver convenience and comfort are found on virtually all late-model vehicles. Items such as power windows and door locks, which were once available only as options on luxury models, are now common even on base-model vehicles. The list of accessories supplied as standard or optional equipment is long, and continues to grow. Electrical accessories lists may include:

- Airbag or supplemental restraint system (SRS)
- Air-conditioning (AC) system
- Anti-theft system
- Audio system
- Cigarette lighter or power receptacle
- Clock
- Cruise control
- Heated rear view mirror
- Heated seats
- Heated windshield
- Keyless entry system
- Power door locks
- Power seats
- Power sunroof or convertible top
- Power windows
- Rear window defroster.

These common accessory circuits seldom require service. However, component failures due to wear and damage do occur. Often, the source of an electrical failure is a mechanical problem, such as binding linkage that creates resistance and generates excessive heat. Typical electrical accessory repairs include replacing fuses, switches, relays, motors, and linkage assemblies, as well as repairing damaged wiring and connections.

Regardless of the number of accessories available, troubleshooting is similar for most of them. With the exception of the airbag, AC, and cruise control, which are complete systems, most accessories fall into one of three categories: motor, solenoid, or resistor. All have some type of switch to activate them, and many use a relay to control current. Keeping this in mind, circuit failures are easy to isolate when troubleshooting with accurate wiring and circuit diagrams.

This chapter briefly discusses common electrical and electronic accessory diagnosis, testing, and service. General procedures, which apply to most models, are presented here. Many modern accessories are electronically monitored by the body control module (BCM) or another onboard computer. These systems usually have a self-diagnostic function and are checked or tested using a scan tool. See Chapter Twelve of this *Shop Manual* for electronic control system service information.

Copyright 2000 by Chek-Chart Publications

New vehicles have at least one airbag built into the steering wheel to protect the driver, and many have a passenger-side airbag as well. Additional side airbags may be installed in the seats, doors, or body as part of the complete SRS. All airbags are pyrotechnic devices, which means they use the expanding gas of an explosion to inflate them. Accidental deployment may cause severe injuries and damage to the vehicle. Always follow the service manual procedure to disarm the SRS before working on accessory components, especially in the passenger compartment.

AIRBAG SYSTEMS

An airbag system consists of two basic subsystems: the airbag module and the electronic control system. The airbag module contains the airbag and the ignitor that inflates it. The electrical system includes the crash sensors and control module, along with the relays, wiring, and circuit protection devices, figure 15-1. Typically, a dedicated airbag control module, which is mounted near the center of the chassis, operates the SRS. However, this module is part of the communications network that includes the powertrain control module (PCM), body control module (BCM), and other onboard computers, figure 15-2. An airbag system always includes a capacitor, which stores enough voltage to trigger the detonators in the event the battery is immediately taken out of the circuit on impact. The capacitor is typically built into the airbag module. Be aware, not allowing enough time for the capacitor to discharge before making repairs is the cause of many accidental airbag deployments.

All airbag systems require that special precautions be observed when testing or servicing. To prevent deployment:

- Always disconnect the negative battery cable and tape the terminal to prevent arcing.
- Always wait the time specified by the manufacturer after disconnecting the battery for the system capacitor to discharge.
- Never use self-powered test equipment unless specified by the service manual test procedure.
- Never probe airbag connectors.
- Always wear safety glasses when servicing an airbag system.

The crash sensors of an SRS react to impacts according to the direction and force of the impact. Also called a deceleration, inertia, or G-force sensor, a crash sensor is capable of discriminating between impacts that require airbag inflation and those that do not. When struck with enough force in the proper direction, the roller inside the crash sensor unseats and closes a contact set to complete a circuit, figure 15-3. This transmits an input signal to the electronic control module (ECM). The ECM responds immediately by delivering an output signal to deploy the airbag. The entire event is over in a matter of seconds, but a considerable amount of interior damage, in addition to that of the collision that triggered the sensor, is left behind.

Airbag Testing and Service

Airbag system components and their location in the vehicle vary according to system design, but the basic principles of testing are the same as for other electrical circuits. Use an accurate diagram to determine how the circuit is designed and the correct sequence of tests to be followed.

Some airbag systems require the use of special testers. The built-in safety circuits of such testers prevent accidental deployment of the airbag. If such a tester is not available, follow the recommended alternative test procedures specified by the manufacturer exactly. Access the self-diagnostic system and check for diagnostic trouble code (DTC) records. The factory scan tool is needed to access the data stream on some systems.

An SRS has a diagnostic module that detects system electrical faults, disables the system, and notifies the driver through a system readiness indicator, or airbag warning lamp in the instrument cluster. Depending on circuit design, a system fault may cause the warning lamp to fail to illuminate, remain lit continuously, or flash. Some systems use a tone generator that produces an audible warning when a system fault occurs if the warning lamp is inoperative.

The warning lamp should illuminate with the ignition key on and engine off as a bulb check. If not, the diagnostic module is likely disabling the system. Some warning lamp circuits have a timer that extinguishes the lamp after a few seconds. The SRS generally does not require service unless there is a failed component. However, a steering wheel–mounted airbag module is routinely removed and replaced in order to service switches and other column mounted devices.

Airbag Module Replacement

Carefully follow the procedures provided by the vehicle manufacturer for the specific model being serviced to disable and remove the airbag module. Failure to do so may result in serious injury and extensive damage to the vehicle. Replacing a discharged airbag is costly. The following procedure reviews the basic steps for removing an airbag module. Do not substitute these general instructions for the specific procedure recommended by the manufacturer:

Copyright 2000 by Chek-Chart Publications

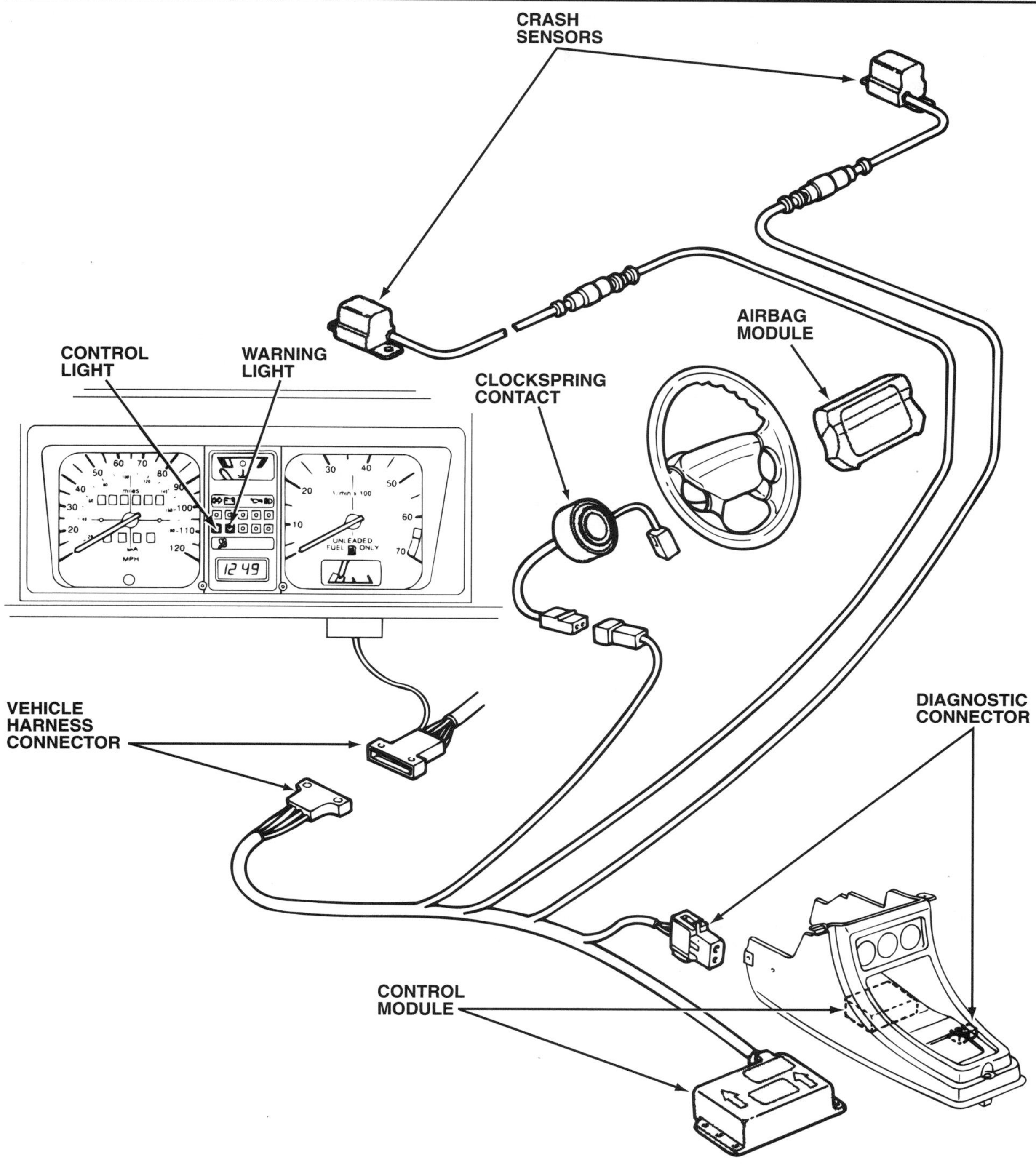

Figure 15-1. Components of a simple airbag system.

1. Turn the steering wheel until the front wheels are positioned straightahead. Some components on the steering column are removed only when the front wheels are straight.
2. Switch the ignition off, and disconnect the negative battery cable, which cuts power to the airbag module.
3. Once the battery is disconnected, wait as long as recommended by the manufacturer before continuing. When in doubt, wait at least 10 minutes, to make sure the capacitor is completely discharged.
4. Loosen and remove the nuts or screws that hold the airbag module in place. On some vehicles,

Copyright 2000 by Chek-Chart Publications

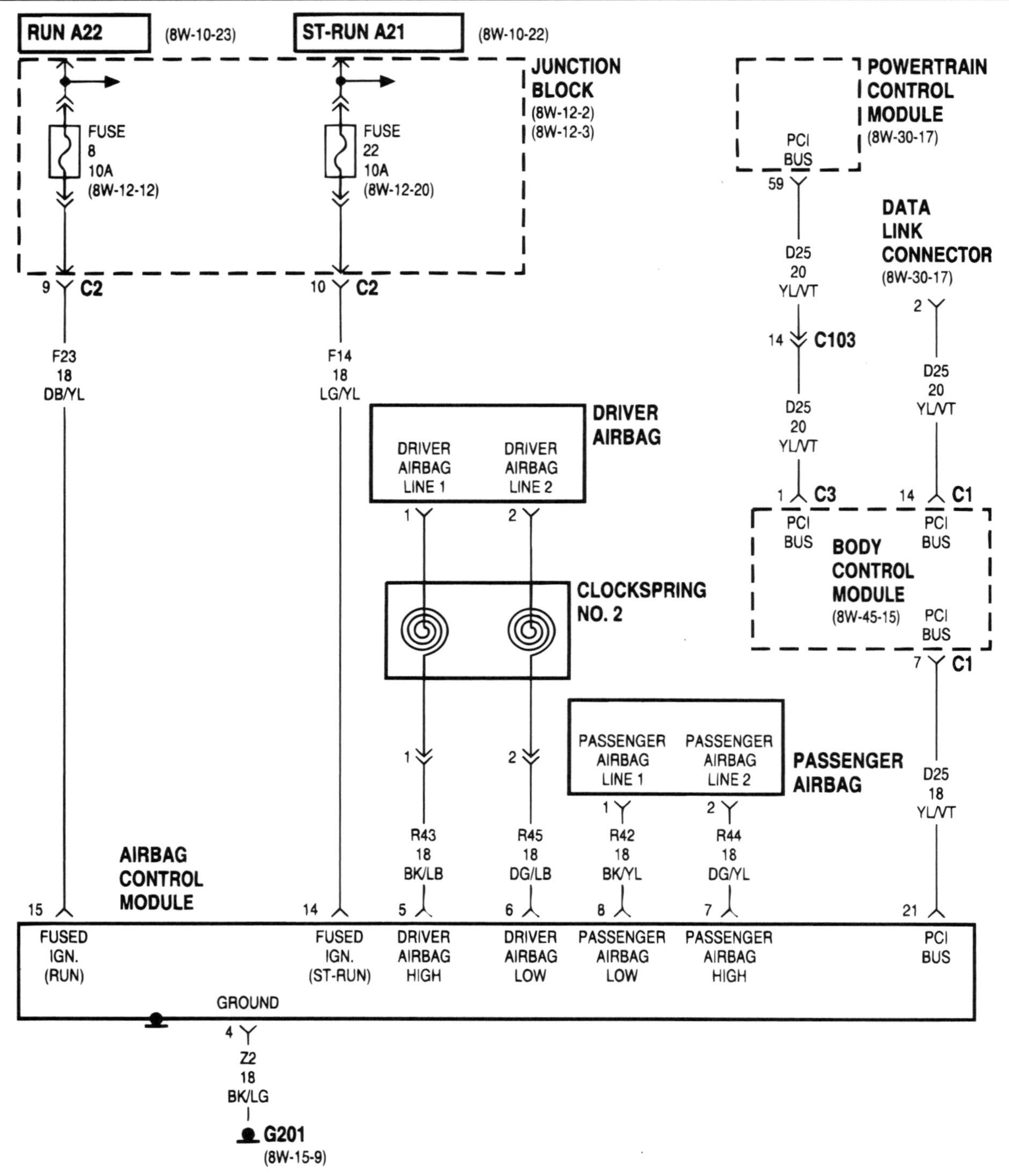

Figure 15-2. The airbag control module is linked to the PCM and BCM on this Chrysler system.

these fasteners are located on the back of the steering wheel, figure 15-4. On others, they are located on each side of the steering wheel. The fasteners may be concealed with plastic finishing covers that must be pried off with a small screwdriver to access them, figure 15-5. Use a socket wrench, Torx bit, or screwdriver as required to remove the fasteners. Discard the old fasteners and replace them with new ones during assembly.

Copyright 2000 by Chek-Chart Publications

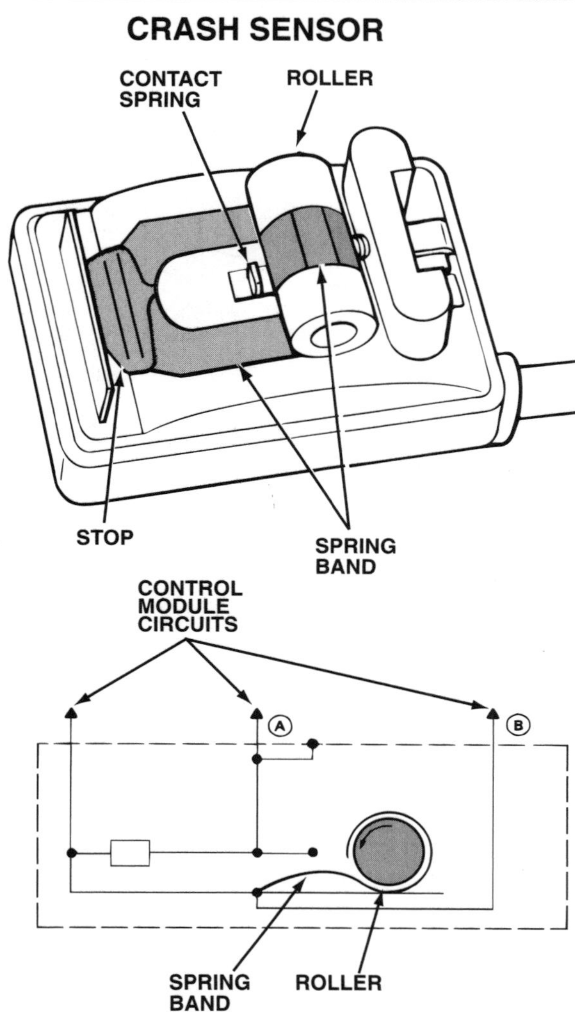

Figure 15-3. The roller of this Volkswagen crash sensor unseats on impact to complete a circuit.

5. Carefully lift the airbag module from the steering wheel and disconnect the electrical connector. Connector location varies: Some are below the steering wheel behind a plastic trim cover, while others are at the top of the column under the module, figure 15-6.
6. Store the module, pad side up, in a safe place where it will not be disturbed or damaged while the vehicle is being serviced. Do not attempt to disassemble the airbag module. If the airbag is defective, replace the entire assembly.

When installing the airbag module, make sure the clockspring is correctly positioned to ensure module-to-steering column continuity. Always route the wiring exactly as it was before removal. Also, make sure the module seats completely into the steering wheel. Secure the assembly using new fasteners.

ANTI-THEFT SYSTEMS

Anti-theft devices flash lights or sound an alarm if the vehicle is broken into or vandalized. In addition to the alarm, some systems prevent the engine from starting by disabling the starter, ignition, or fuel system once the anti-theft device is activated. Others permit the engine to start, but then disable it after several seconds. Switches in the door jambs, trunk, and hood provide an input signal to the control module should an undesirable entry occur on a typical system, figure 15-7. Some anti-theft systems are more complex and also have electronic sensors that trigger the alarm if there is a change in battery current draw, a violent vehicle motion, or if glass is broken. These sensors also provide an input signal to the control module, which may be a separate anti-theft unit or incorporated into the PCM or BCM.

Anti-Theft System Diagnosis

Most factory-installed anti-theft systems are integrated with several other circuits to form a complex, multiple-circuit system. Therefore, it is essential to have accurate diagrams, specifications, and test procedures for the specific model being serviced. The easiest way to reduce circuit complexity is to use the wiring diagram to break the entire system into its subcircuits, then check only those related to the problem. If any step indicates that a subcircuit is not complete, check the power source, ground, the components, and the wiring in that subcircuit.

Modern anti-theft systems, especially those supplied as original equipment, are electronically regulated and have a self-diagnostic program. This self-diagnostic program is generally accessed and activated using a scan tool. Diagnostic and test procedures are similar as for any of the other electronic control systems used on the vehicle. Refer to Chapter Twelve of this *Shop Manual* for additional information on electronic control systems.

Anti-Theft System Testing and Service

Before performing any diagnostic checks, make sure that all of the following electrical devices are operational:

- Parking and low-beam headlights
- Dome and courtesy lights
- Horn
- Wipers
- Clock
- Electric door locks.

Copyright 2000 by Chek-Chart Publications

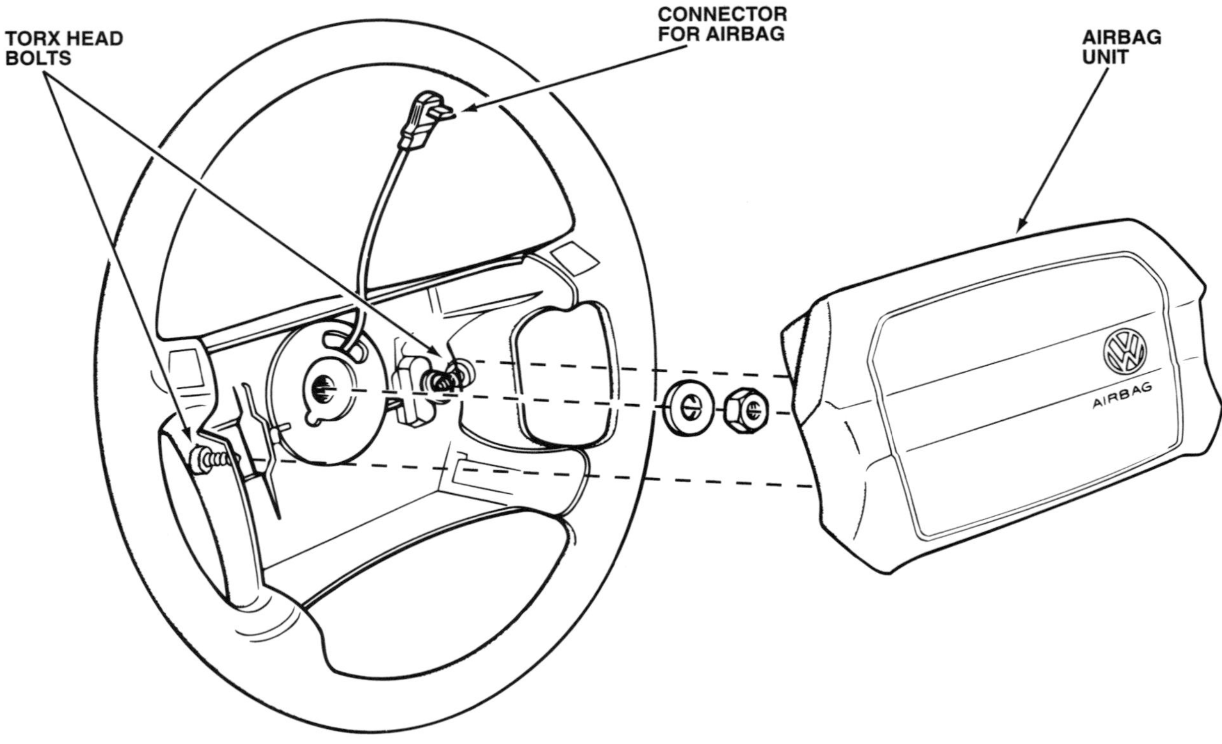

Figure 15-4. This Volkswagen airbag module is attached by bolts on the back side of the steering wheel.

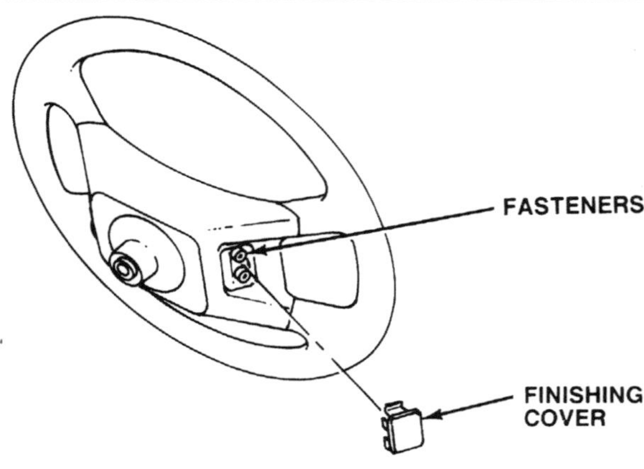

Figure 15-5. Airbag module fasteners are often concealed behind a plastic finishing cover.

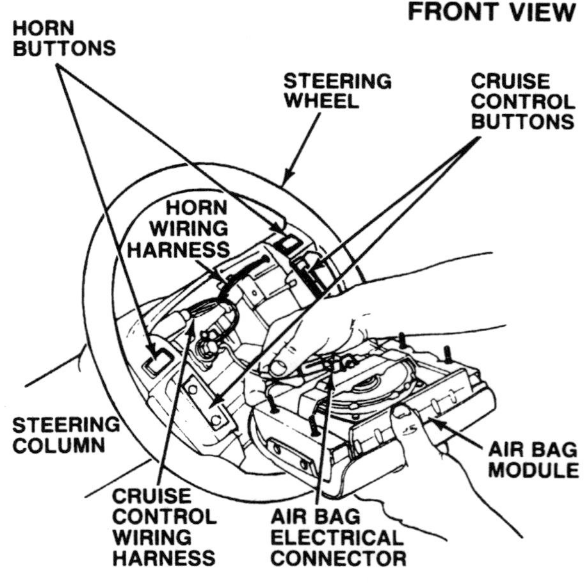

Figure 15-6. Lift the airbag module from the steering wheel and separate the electrical connector.

Circuit information from these devices often provides basic inputs to the control module. If a problem is detected in any of these circuits, such as a missing signal or a signal that is out of range, the control module disables the anti-theft system and may record a DTC.

If all of the above-mentioned devices are operational, check all the circuits leading to the anti-theft control module. Make sure all switches are in their normal, or off, positions. Door jamb switches complete the ground circuit when a door is opened, figure 15-8. Frequently, corrosion that builds up on the switch contacts prevents the switch from operating properly. Conduct voltage drop tests to isolate faulty

Copyright 2000 by Chek-Chart Publications

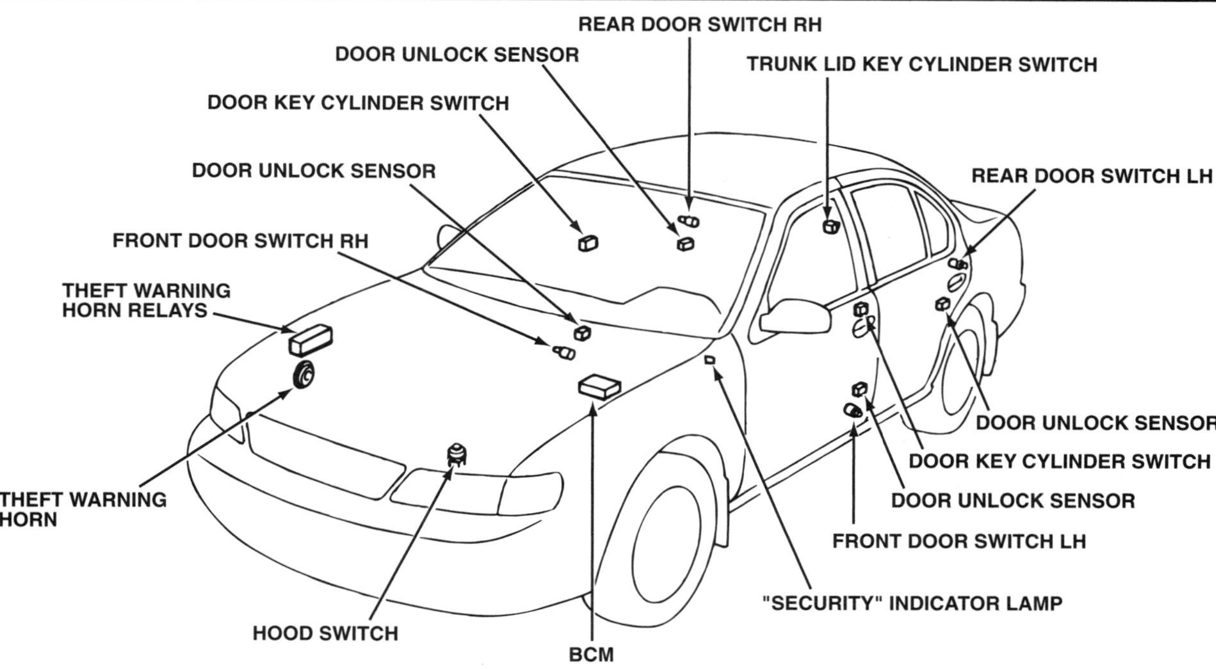

Figure 15-7. Component locator for a Nissan Maxima anti-theft system.

components and circuit problems. Repair as needed and retest to confirm that the system is operational. Follow procedures from the manufacturer to clear DTC records, then run the self-diagnostic program to verify repairs.

AIR-CONDITIONING (AC) AND HEATING SYSTEMS

The primary job of all air-conditioning (AC) and heater systems is to control the temperature inside the passenger compartment. How this is done varies considerably by make and model, but there are a number of components common to all systems.

When troubleshooting any temperature-control system, the first step is to make sure that the problem is really in the electrical system. Make the following preliminary checks before attempting to diagnose electrical problems:

- Coolant level
- System operating pressure
- Drive belt tension
- Vacuum line routing and connections
- Radiator airflow
- Electric cooling fan operation
- Interior sensor air intake suction, if used.

The blower motor circuit is common to all heater and AC systems, and all cycling clutch and orifice tube AC systems have a compressor clutch control circuit.

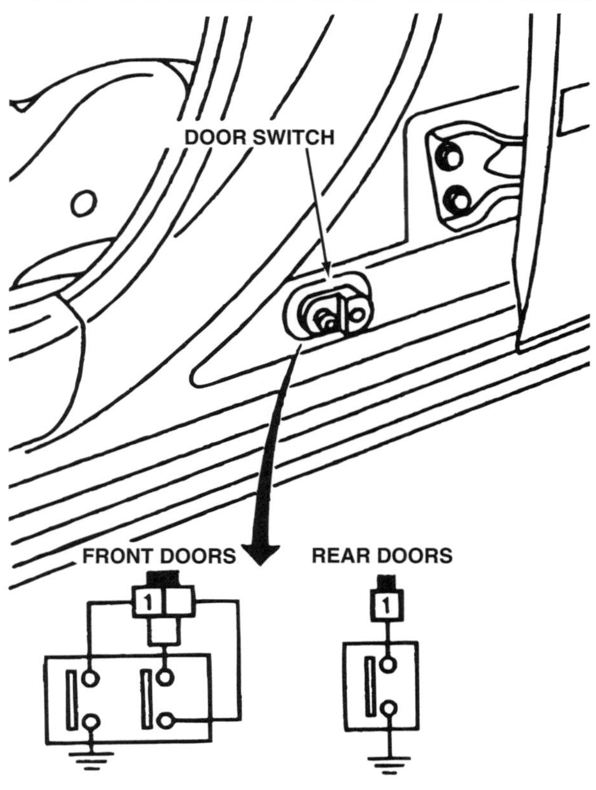

Figure 15-8. Door switches complete the ground circuit with the door open, and are a common source of high resistance.

Copyright 2000 by Chek-Chart Publications

If the vehicle has a temperature-control system, various other sensors, switches, and relays may be included in the control circuitry. Modern temperature-control systems are electronically controlled, either by a dedicated microprocessor, the BCM, or the PCM. These temperature-control systems have self-diagnostic capability, which is usually accessed using a scan tool.

Blower Motor Circuit

The blower motor circuit includes the heater-AC function control assembly on the instrument panel, the blower switch, the resistor block, and the blower motor, figure 15-9. Setting the function control to the heat or defrost mode directs current to the blower motor when the ignition switch is on.

Some blower control circuits regulate the ground side to control blower speeds, while others use positive-side switching, figure 15-10. Although the basic operation of the blower motor is identical, how power is routed to the motor differs on the two designs. Power for a circuit that switches to ground comes from the fuse panel, through the function selector switch, to the blower motor, then to the blower speed switch. The blower motor switch completes the circuit to ground through the resistor. The opposite occurs in positive-side switching, as power reaches the switch first, and is then routed to the motor.

All blower control circuits use a resistor block. The resistor block has one less resistor than the number of blower switch positions. That is, a motor with four speeds uses three resistors, while one with three speeds has only two resistors. The resistors create a voltage drop before the motor, which reduces the speed of the motor. When the blower switch is set to its lowest speed, all of the resistors are in the circuit. When the switch is set to its highest speed, voltage is routed around the resistor block and applied directly to the motor. In addition, some systems use a thermal limiter on the resistor block as a protective device. The thermal limiter is a fuse that opens at a specific temperature, which indicates excessive current, to protect the circuit.

Blower motors are tested in similar fashion as explained for windshield wiper motors in Chapter Fourteen of this *Shop Manual*. Gain access to the motor and rotate it by hand to eliminate the possibility of seizure or a binding fan. Use a connector pin chart and a jumper wire to connect the motor directly to ground. Use a fused jumper wire to apply battery voltage to the motor. If the motor runs with the jumper wires installed, the problem is in the control circuit before the motor. If the motor does not run, it has an internal problem; replace it.

Compressor Clutch Control

The amount of cooling that occurs in any air-conditioning system depends upon the flow of refrigerant through the evaporator core. An AC compressor has an electromagnetic clutch in the drive pulley assembly. When the clutch engages, it locks the compressor shaft to the pulley and pumps refrigerant through the system.

Compressor clutch control circuits vary on different systems but all operate on similar principles. That is, the clutch engages when the AC controls are switched on, the ambient temperature is above the calibrated value of the temperature control switch, AC system pressure is within normal operating range. Circuit and component failures are easily located by voltage drop testing, provided an accurate wiring diagram and test specifications are available, figure 15-11.

If the clutch is not engaging and refrigerant pressure is satisfactory, that is, the low-pressure switch is closed, check the clutch as follows:

1. Start the engine and set the AC control switch for maximum cooling.
2. Check for battery voltage available to the compressor clutch terminal.
3. If battery voltage is not available, there is an open in the circuit between the control assembly and the clutch. Locate the open by voltage drop testing. Repair as needed and retest.
4. To check for clutch engagement, switch the engine off and disconnect the clutch circuit. Attach one end of a fused jumper wire to the clutch terminal and momentarily connect the other end of the jumper wire to battery voltage. The clutch should engage.
5. If the clutch does not engage, disconnect the jumper wire and check the resistance of the clutch coil with an ohmmeter, figure 15-12. Compare results to specifications and replace the clutch if needed.

Other AC and heater circuit devices, such as switches, relays, and sensors, are checked using standard electrical tests explained previously in this *Shop Manual*. With an electronically controlled system, be sure to follow procedures recommended by the manufacturer to access the self-diagnostic program. Keep in mind, the refrigeration system must be fully charged and operational in order to troubleshoot electrical problems in an AC system.

Copyright 2000 by Chek-Chart Publications

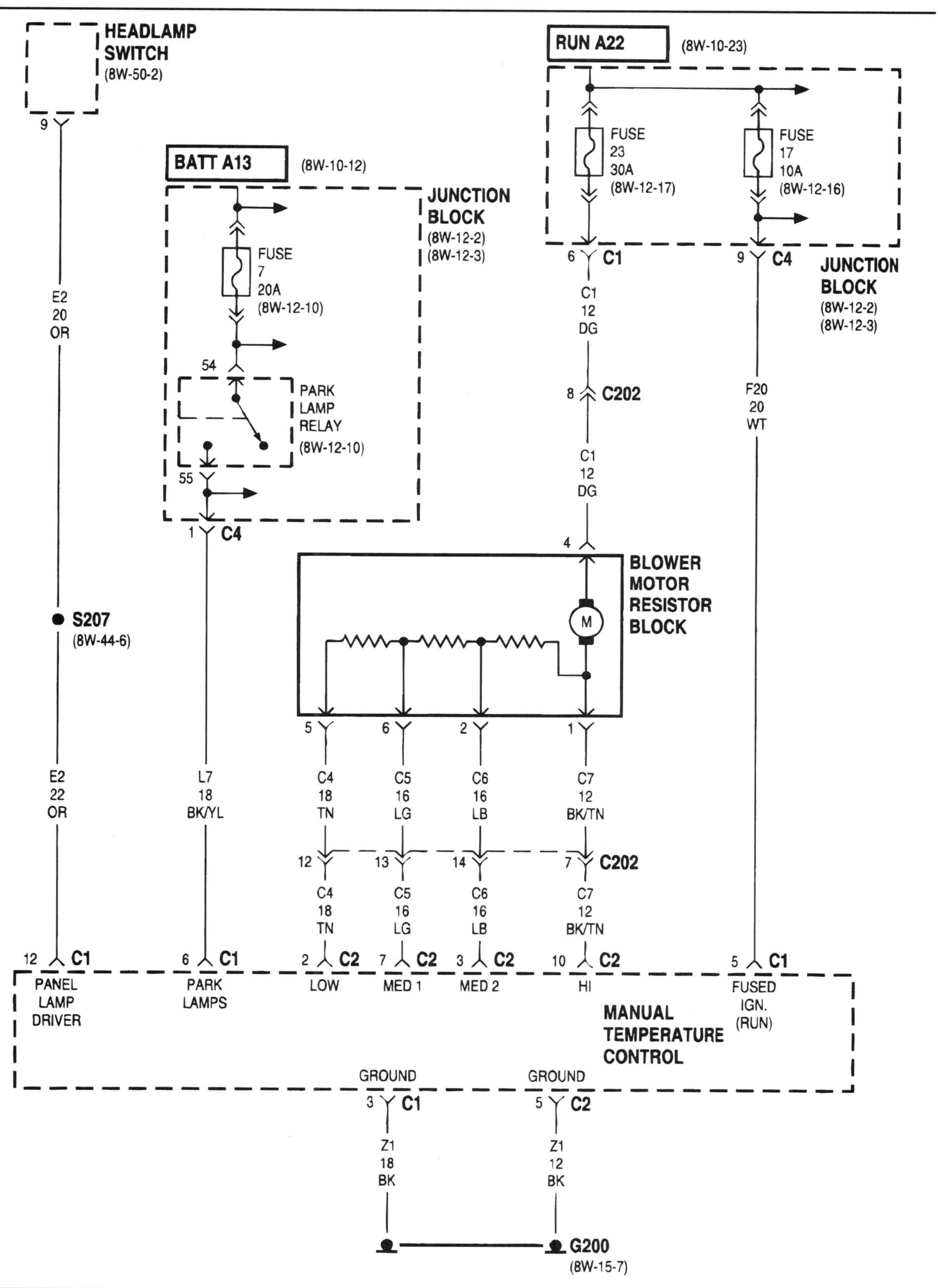

Figure 15-9. This Chrysler manual control switch routes current through the resistor block to the motor.

Copyright 2000 by Chek-Chart Publications

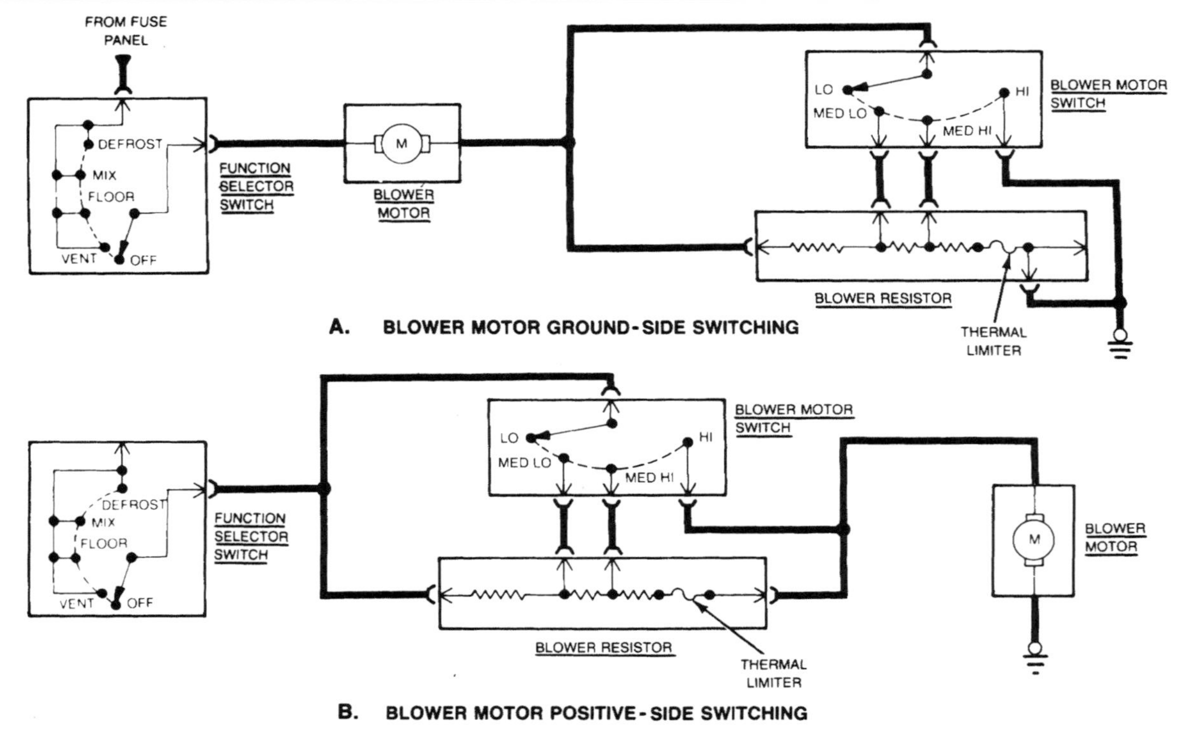

Figure 15-10. A blower motor may be controlled on either the ground (A) or power (B) side of the circuit.

AUDIO SYSTEMS

Modern original equipment (OE) audio systems are extremely sophisticated and often include an electronic tuner, compact disc player, amplifier, and a number of speakers. Aftermarket audio systems, which are as complex as OE systems, are common. With any audio system service, it is essential to know exactly what components are used and how all of the circuits are arranged, figure 15-13. With wiring diagrams and specifications from the manufacturer, standard electrical and electronic tests are used to troubleshoot any audio system.

Always determine the exact nature of the problem before removing audio components for service. Knowing whether the condition is constant or intermittent, occurs with the engine on or off, or only occurs when the vehicle is either parked or moving, helps pinpoint the problem.

Radio Diagnosis

The most common causes of poor, intermittent, or no radio reception are:

- Vehicle in a poor reception area
- Antenna trim improperly adjusted
- Defective antenna.

Most modern sound systems use a separate ground circuit for the speakers, while some older systems use the vehicle chassis as ground. Any loose connector affects the operation of part or all of the system. Intermittent operation and crackling speakers may be caused by poor connections.

Servicing Radio Components

As always, the first step is to check for available voltage. Battery voltage must be available to the power terminal on the radio tuner. Many radio tuners have a low-amperage fuse on the power circuit to prevent damage from overloading. The fuse is either inline between the ignition switch and the tuner, or in a fuse holder mounted on the back of the radio chassis. Internal circuit problems are indicated if voltage is available but the radio does not operate. Remove the radio for service.

Speakers are quickly checked using a common "AA" (1.5-volt) battery. Simply disconnect both speaker leads at the connector and momentarily connect the battery across the speaker terminals. The speaker should make a popping noise as the battery is connected and disconnected. If so, the problem is in circuitry, not the speaker. A speaker that makes no sound is defective and must be replaced.

Copyright 2000 by Chek-Chart Publications

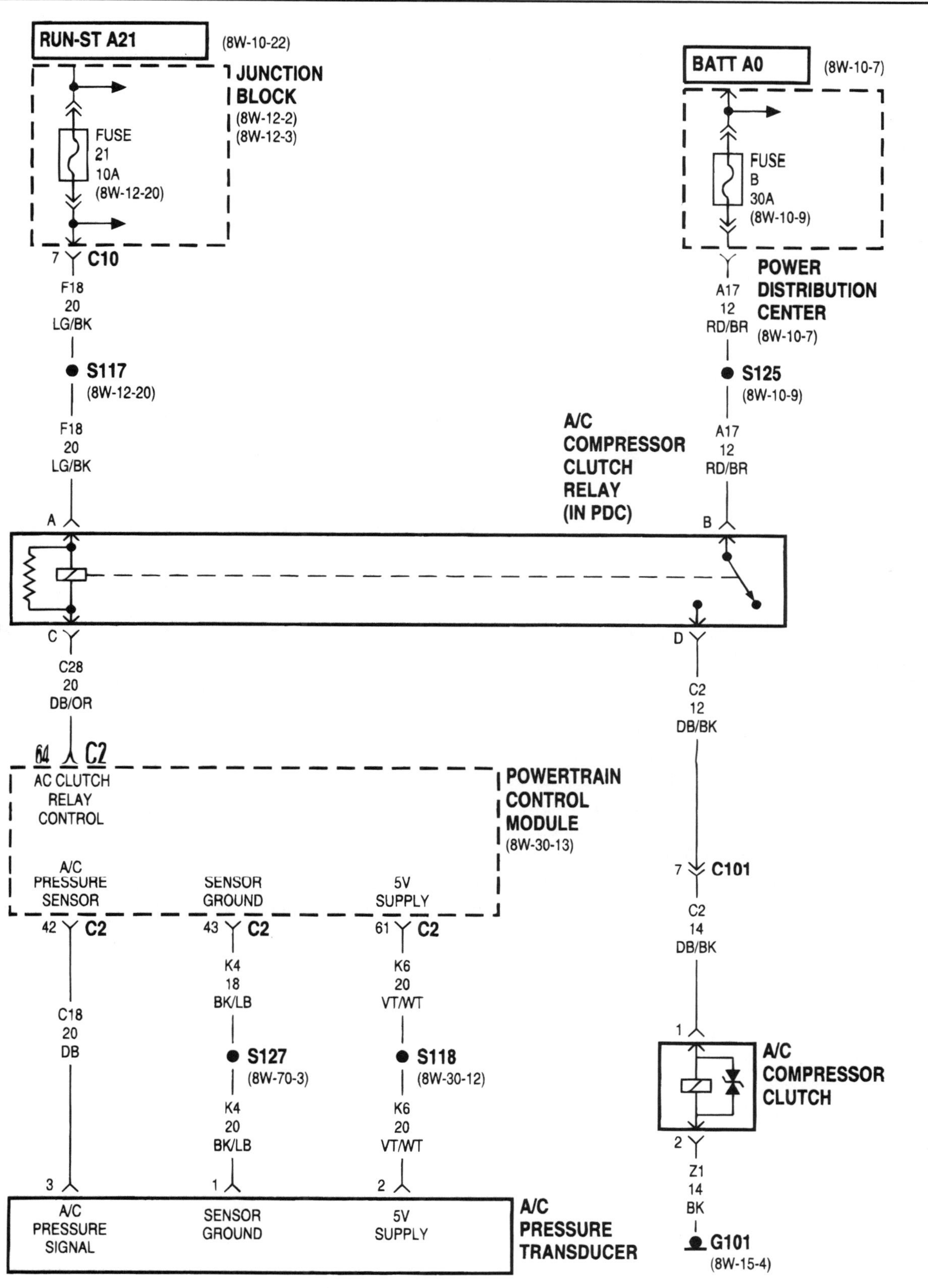

Figure 15-11. This Chrysler AC compressor clutch circuit is typical of an electronically controlled system.

Copyright 2000 by Chek-Chart Publications

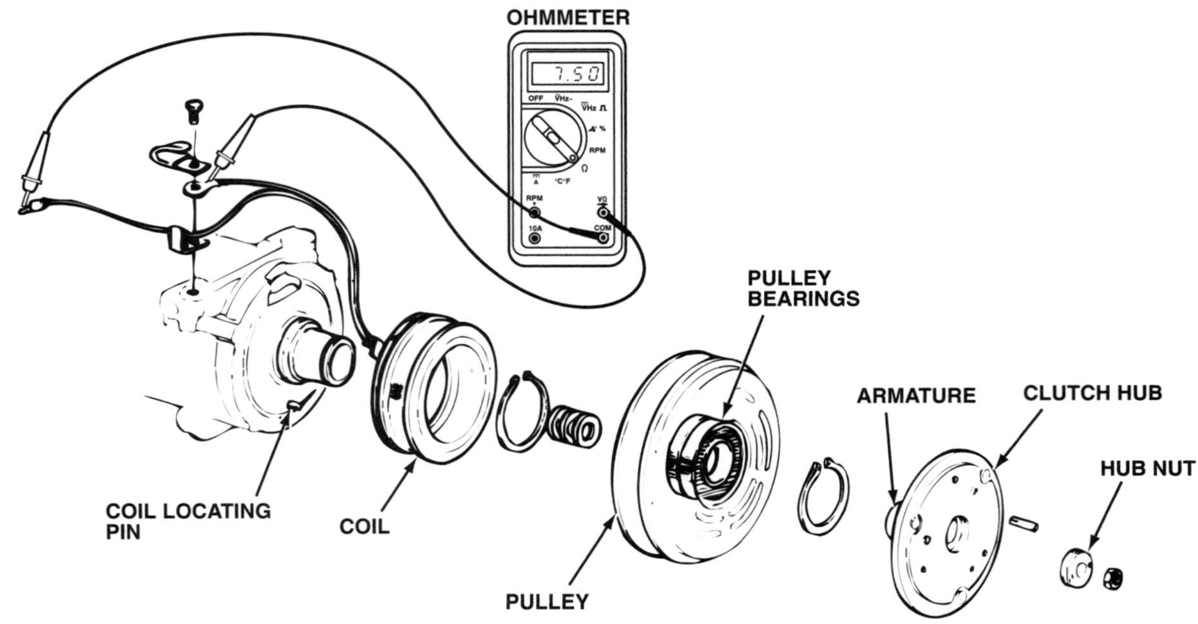

Figure 15-12. Checking AC compressor clutch coil resistance with an ohmmeter.

Antenna service

An antenna may be a fixed mast, a manually adjustable mast, a motor-driven mast, or a grid on the rear window. All antennas carry a signal and the shield around the circuit that carries the signal must be grounded. Power antennas use an electric motor to automatically rise when the radio is turned on and automatically lower when the radio is switched off.

The antenna lead is a coaxial cable that carries the signal through the center conductor. The outer conductor of the cable acts as a shield to protect the radio signal from interference. For the cable to be effective as a shield, it must be securely grounded at the body connection. A poor ground causes excess ignition noise in AM reception, or erratic sound. To check antenna ground with a fixed antenna:

1. Tune the radio for a weak AM station or signal.
2. Unscrew and remove the antenna mast.
3. Connect a short jumper wire between the mast mounting stud and the cable lead.

If the radio station is not received, the antenna ground is good. If the radio station is still received, the ground is poor or open.

To check antenna ground with a power antenna:

1. Fully lower the antenna and separate the motor connector.
2. Connect an alligator clip near the top of the antenna.
3. Tune the radio for a weak AM station or signal.
4. Remove the alligator clip and connect a short jumper between the mounting bracket and the top of the mast.

If the radio station is not received, the antenna ground is good. If the radio station is still received, the ground is poor or open.

Power antennas use a reversible direct current (dc) motor to raise and lower the mast, figure 15-14. Power is usually routed to the motor through the power control switch of the tuner. Reversing the polarity of the voltage applied to the armature reverses the direction of motor rotation.

To troubleshoot a power antenna problem, locate a pin identification chart for the motor. Check for voltage available to the armature and for continuity on the ground circuit. If the circuitry is sound and voltage is available, the failure is likely an internal motor problem. Check the current draw of the motor if specifications are available. Antenna motors are not generally a serviceable item, and are simply replaced if defective.

Noise-suppression components

Two kinds of electrical interference, radiated and conducted, may affect radio reception. Radiated noise, or radiofrequency interference (RFI), results from an accessory that gives off a signal that is picked up along with the desired radio signal by the antenna. Interference from radiated noise is controlled by a

Copyright 2000 by Chek-Chart Publications

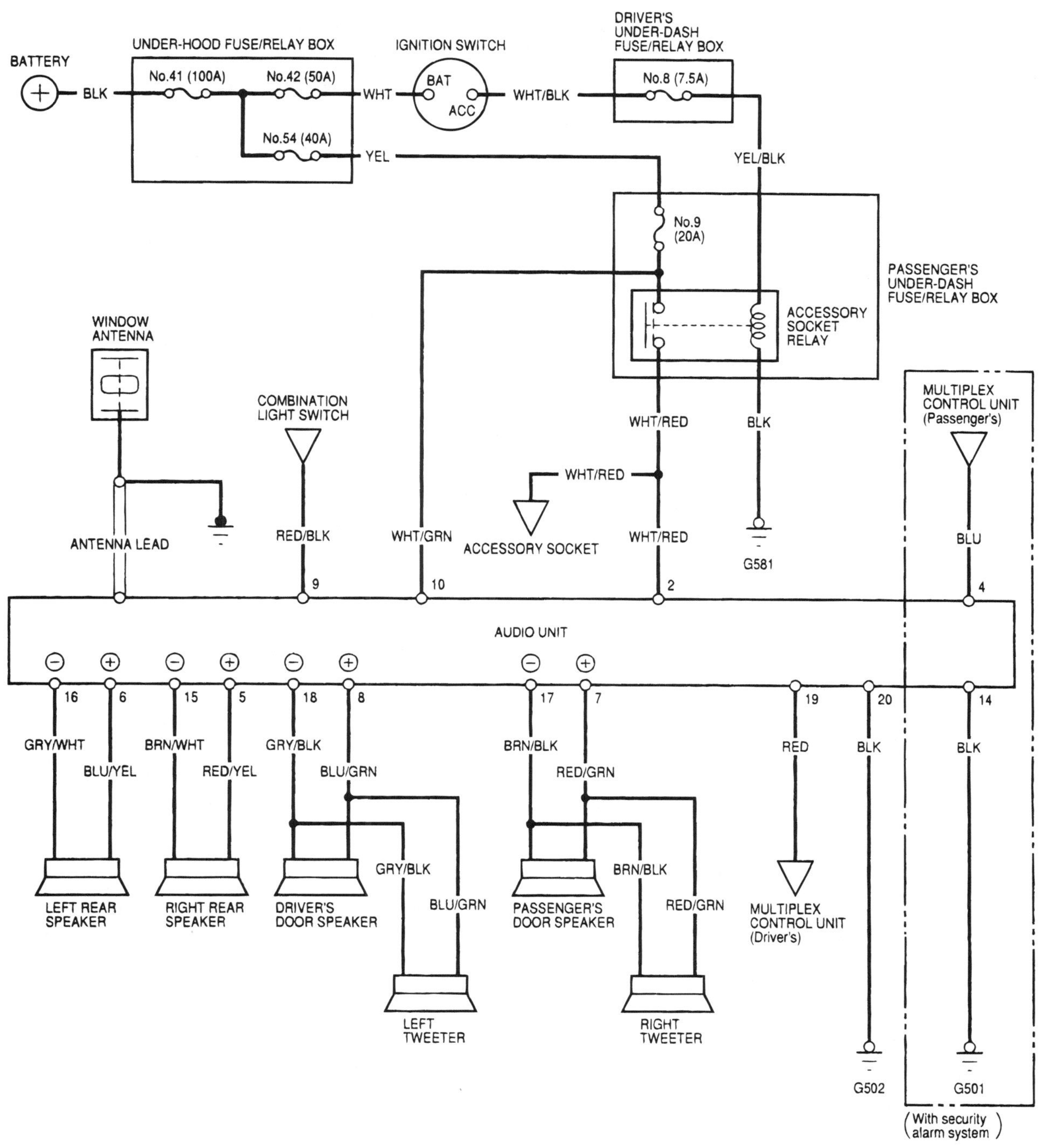

Figure 15-13. Circuit diagrams are essential for troubleshooting a modern audio system.

capacitor that installs on the back of the tuner, figure 15-15. Common sources of radiated interference include:

- Defective ignition components
- Heater blower, wiper, fan, or AC system motors
- Electronic components
- Electric fuel pumps
- An overhead compass
- Loose ground strap or loose antenna mount.

Radiated interference from operating devices such as turn signals or the cigarette lighter may cause a popping noise on weak or distant AM signals.

Copyright 2000 by Chek-Chart Publications

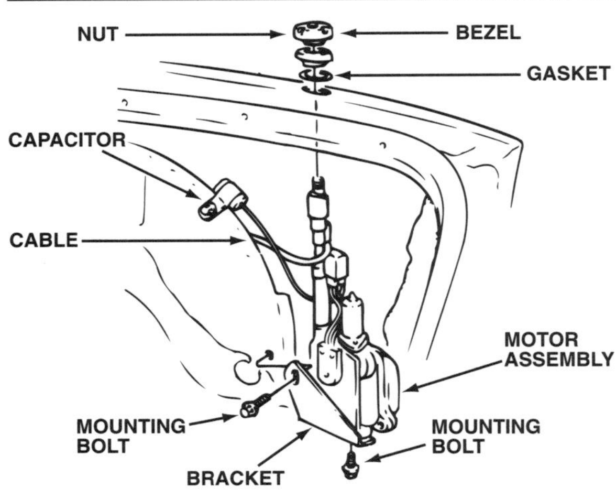

Figure 15-14. A power antenna uses an electric motor to raise and lower the mast.

Conducted interference is audible at very low volume and results from problems on the insulated, or power, circuit. An inline filter, or radio choke, that installs in the input circuit from the ignition switch is used to control this type of interference. These filters prevent unwanted and random signals on the insulated circuit from reaching the radio. Typical sources of conducted interference include:

- The alternator
- Control modules
- Trim, interior, or courtesy lights.

Radio static also may originate from an outside source, such as high-tension power lines or power tools being used nearby. To determine the cause of excessive radio noise, disconnect the antenna cable at the back of the radio. If the noise ceases, replace the antenna. If the noise continues, the problem is located in the radio wiring.

Trimming the antenna

Each time the antenna or radio is repaired or replaced, the antenna must be trimmed to balance reception. Trim is adjusted with an adjustment screw located either near the antenna lead connector on the tuner or accessed through the instrument panel trim. Tune the radio to a station as close as possible to 1400 kHz on the AM dial. Then, use a nonmagnetic screwdriver and adjust trim by slowly turning the screw both directions until the radio plays the loudest.

CIGARETTE LIGHTER OR POWER RECEPTACLE

A cigarette lighter is standard equipment on most older models, but available only as an option on many newer vehicles. However, many late-model vehicles have a power port in place of the lighter to accommodate cell phones, laptop computers, and other electronic equipment. Both of these devices are similar, except the power port does not have a heating element. Lighters and power ports often receive power through a subcircuit of the interior or courtesy light circuit, which connects to constant battery voltage through the main fuse block.

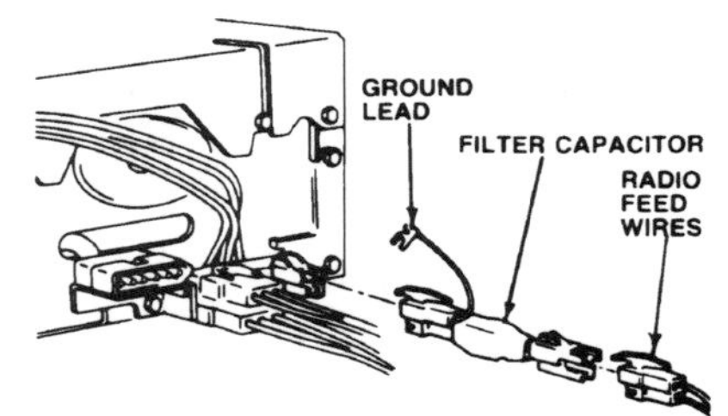

Figure 15-15. This filter capacitor on the back of the tuner reduces radiated interference.

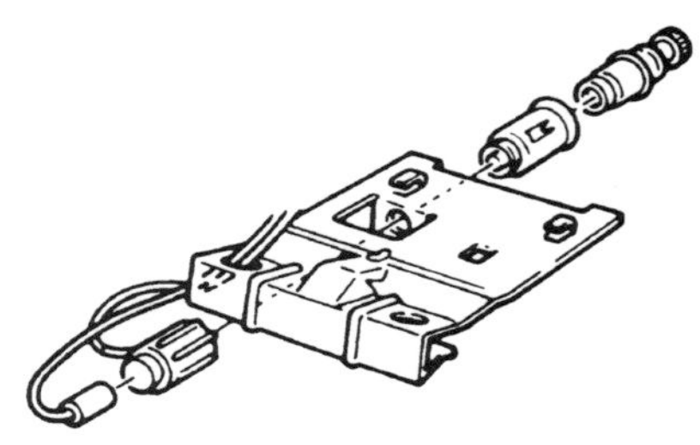

Figure 15-16. A typical cigarette lighter consists of an element and a socket.

A cigarette lighter consists of an element and a socket, figure 15-16. The element is a high-resistance heating coil attached to the knob. The socket installs in the ashtray or instrument panel and is held in position with a sleeve that threads onto the socket from the rear. On a lighter, a heat-sensitive bimetallic clip holds the heating element in once it is pressed into the socket. Current travels from the socket through the clip to heat the element. When the element is heated, the clip releases the element, allowing it to return to a ready position. The most common causes of lighter malfunctions are:

- Carbon accumulation in the socket that shorts the circuit
- Burned-out or corroded element that opens the circuit
- Defective socket.

To check the lighter, visually inspect the components for damage. Then, check for voltage available at the

Copyright 2000 by Chek-Chart Publications

socket, and continuity on the ground circuit. If voltage is available and there is no unwanted ground resistance, replace the lighter element. Check the socket of a power port in similar fashion.

CLOCK

An automotive clock connects to constant battery voltage at the main fuse block. A fuse is installed on the rear of the clock on some models. The clock may be a self-contained unit, or a function of the radio. Digital clocks usually combine other functions, such as a timer and calendar.

An open circuit or poor ground causes a loss of the display on a digital clock. A clock that burns fuses or does not operate correctly is serviced by replacing the unit. Replacement generally requires dismantling the instrument panel or removing the radio.

CRUISE CONTROL SYSTEMS

Cruise, or automatic speed-control maintains a constant vehicle speed over a variety of driving conditions. Older versions, which are electromechanical systems, use a transducer connected to the throttle by mechanical linkage to modulate vacuum, based on an electrical signal. Newer electronic versions precisely control vehicle speed using the ECM, figure 15-17. This may be either a dedicated cruise control module or incorporated into the BCM.

Cruise Control Diagnosis

All cruise control systems use information, such as the speed of the transmission output shaft or the speedometer cable, to determine if the vehicle is moving at the selected speed. If not, a servo connected to the throttle linkage mechanically increases or decreases throttle opening to maintain the set speed. Perform a thorough visual inspection of all system components. Diagnose cruise control problems based on symptoms, figure 15-18.

Cruise Control Testing and Service

Stoplight switches used on vehicles with cruise control have two circuits: a stoplight circuit and a cruise control circuit. The two circuits work opposite of each other. The stoplight circuit completes to direct current to the brake lamps when the brake pedal is depressed, while the cruise control circuit opens to stop current to the control module when the pedal is depressed.

An incorrectly adjusted servo throttle cable allows vehicle speed to drop several miles per hour below the set speed. Vehicle speed is determined by a speed sensor located on the servo assembly, the transmission, differential, or other driveline component. Servo-mounted speed sensors are usually driven by the speedometer cable. Electronic systems generally use an amplifier to signal the control module that operates the servo.

Any defective component prevents the system from operating. Always check for battery voltage through the fuse. Inspect and repair any poor circuit connections, broken or damaged wires, and vacuum leaks. Further electrical cruise control service consists of checking for ground and insulated circuit continuity by voltage drop testing. Accurate wiring and circuit diagrams are essential for troubleshooting cruise control circuitry.

HEATED SIDE VIEW MIRROR SYSTEMS

An electrically heated side view mirror is generally incorporated into the rear window defroster circuitry and is activated by the same switch, figure 15-19. The circuit typically includes the switch, a relay with a timer circuit, the mirror and rear window heater grids, and the wiring that connects them. With the control switch on, the timer-relay contacts close to provide current to both the rear defroster grid and the heated mirror element. A separate fuse, installed between the relay and heating element, is often used to protect the mirror circuit.

The heating function of the mirror is often combined with other power mirror functions, such as adjustment and memory settings, and regulated through an electronic control module (ECM). Follow procedures from the manufacturer to troubleshoot and repair the electronic control system.

Heated Side View Mirror Testing and Service

If neither the defroster grid nor the heated mirror works, troubleshoot the rear defroster system first. If the grid works but the heated mirror does not, use a circuit diagram and a DMM to isolate the problem. Check for battery voltage available to the switch. If voltage is available, perform voltage drops along the power circuit between the switch and mirror. Also check for high resistance or an open ground circuit. Repair any circuit faults and retest. If no problem is found in the circuitry and the relay is operating correctly, the heating element is defective. Replace the mirror.

Copyright 2000 by Chek-Chart Publications

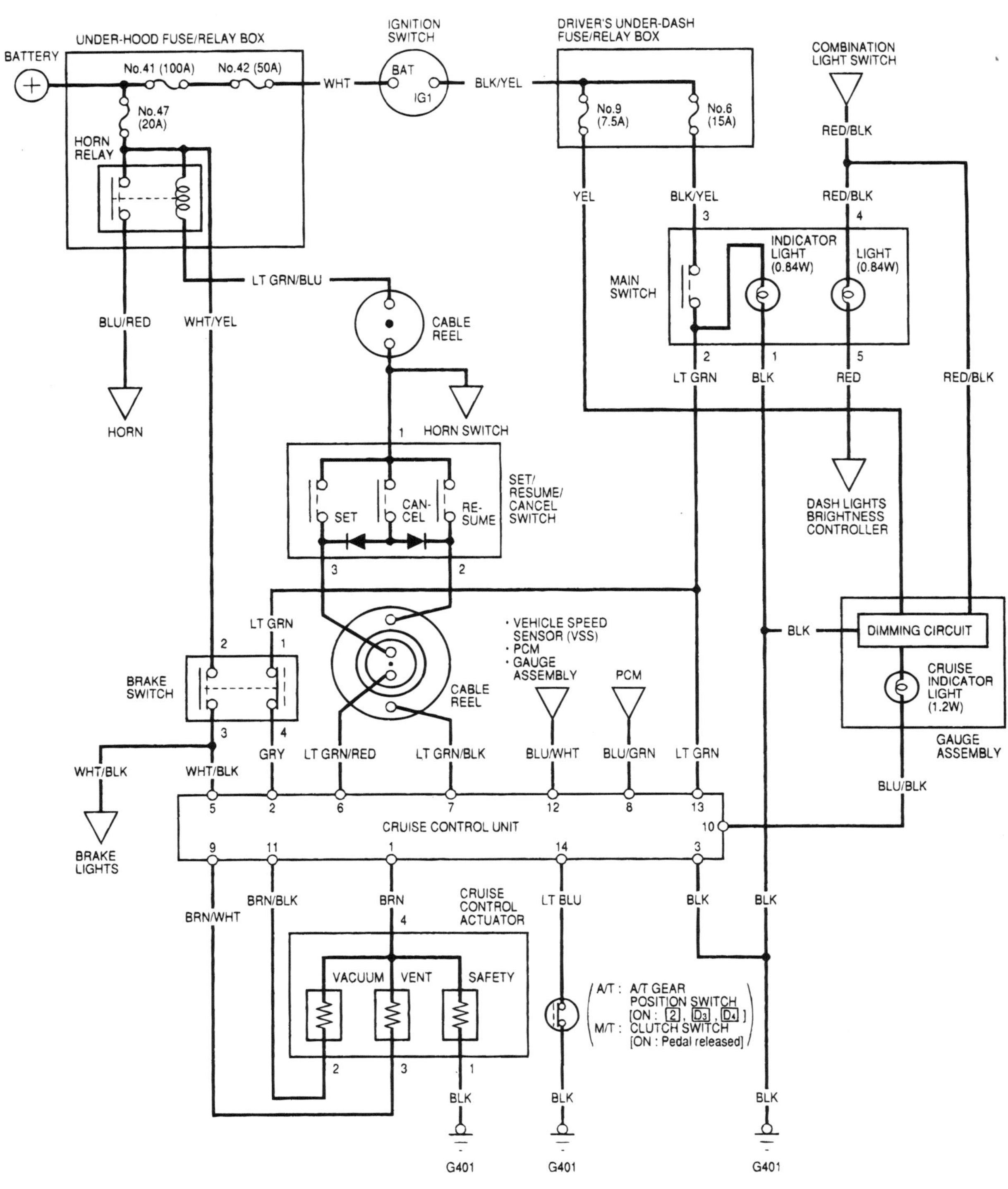

Figure 15-17. Circuit diagram of a Honda electronic cruise control system.

Copyright 2000 by Chek-Chart Publications

ELECTRONIC SPEED CONTROL TROUBLESHOOTING	
PROBLEM	**CHECK**
Speed control operates, but does not accelerate or coast down properly	1. Control switch 2. Control switch circuit 3. Servo assembly
Speed changes up or down constantly	1. Throttle linkage adjustment 2. Servo assembly 3. Speedometer cable and sensor 4. Amplifier or reserve
Does not disengage when brakes are applied	1. Brake switch and circuit 2. Vacuum dump valve 3. Servo assembly 4. Amplifier or reserve
Does not disengage when clutch pedal is depressed	1. Clutch switch 2. Clutch switch circuit
Speed does not set in system	1. Throttle linkage adjustment 2. Control switch and circuit 3. Vacuum dump valve 4. Clutch or brake switch 5. Servo assembly 6. Speed sensor
Speed wanders up or down after it is set	1. Actuator cable adjustment 2. Vacuum dump valve 3. Servo assembly
System operates but does not resume properly	1. Control switch and circuit 2. Servo assembly 3. Amplifier or reserve
Speed will resume below 20 mph	Control module
Speed engages without operating set button	Control switch and circuit

Figure 15-18. Cruise control problems are initially diagnosed by symptom.

HEATED SEATS

Heated seat circuitry is similar to that of a heated side view mirror. The heater is activated by a switch on the dashboard, which connects to either the control circuit of a timed relay or a thermostatic switch that opens the circuit once a preset temperature is reached, figure 15-20. As with mirrors, the heating function is often combined with other power seat functions and regulated through an electronic control module (ECM).

Follow procedures from the manufacturer to troubleshoot and repair the electronic control system. When circuit problems are indicated, conduct voltage drop tests to locate the source of the failure.

HEATED WINDSHIELD

Components of an optional heated windshield are quite similar to those of a heated mirror or rear window defroster. However, a heated windshield receives power directly from the alternator rather than through the ignition switch. Therefore, it is essential to check the charging system thoroughly before troubleshooting a heated windshield problem.

Heated windshields are designed primarily for use when the vehicle is parked with the engine warming up on a cold morning. It is possible to activate a heated windshield at any temperature for testing. However, some electronic control systems prevent activation above a preset temperature and the system must be placed in diagnostic mode to test the system. When testing these systems, follow the service manual procedures from the manufacturer. Also, closely monitor the windshield surface temperature and turn the system off if the windshield gets too warm. As a general rule, the heater should never be allowed to operate for more that two minutes at a time. Overheating the windshield may cause permanent optical damage to the glass.

Copyright 2000 by Chek-Chart Publications

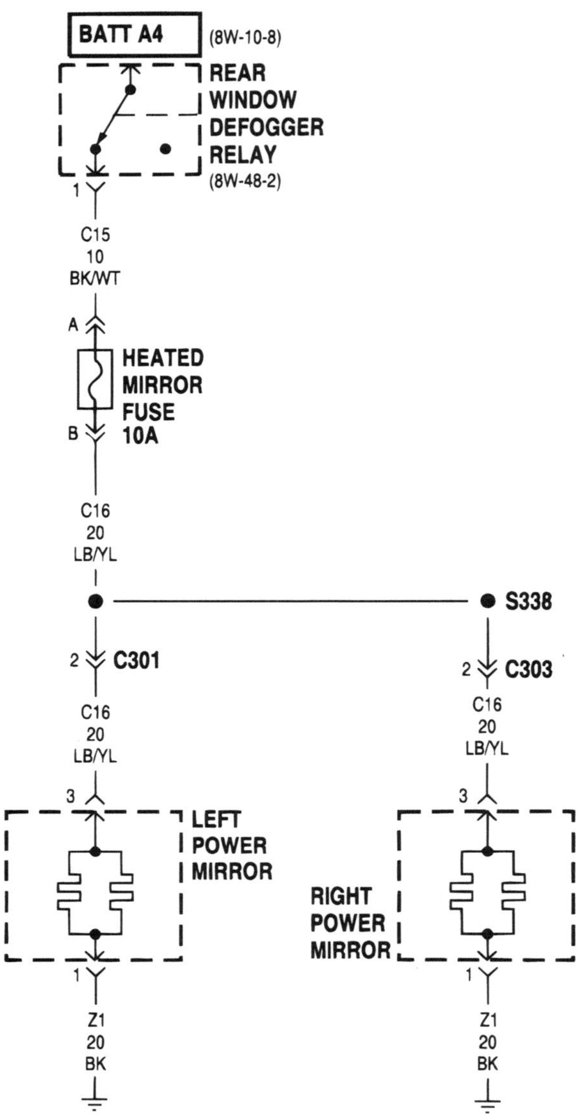

Figure 15-19. Heated side view mirror circuits are combined with the rear window defrost system on this Chrysler design.

Refer to a wiring diagram and perform voltage drop tests to isolate problems in the windshield heating circuit. Verify that the timed relay is operating as designed and switches off once the glass is warm. If testing indicates a problem in the heating element, the windshield must be replaced.

KEYLESS ENTRY SYSTEM

The major function of a keyless entry system is to open the vehicle doors without a key. This is usually done with a wireless transmitter built into the key or key fob. However, a keypad located on the outside of the door is used to unlock some older Ford systems. The transmitter or keypad broadcasts a signal that is received by an ECM, which is generally mounted in the trunk or under the instrument panel, figure 15-21. The ECM responds to the input by transmitting output signals to the locking actuator motors located in the doors.

A small battery powers the transmitter built into the key, and a weak battery is a common cause of the locks not operating. Replace the battery if the transmitter does not operate the locks, but the power locks work normally when using the interior switches. Intermittent operation of a keyless entry system is often caused by a loose wire or connector. If the system is inoperative, check for:

- Mechanical binding in the door locks
- Low battery voltage
- Blown fuse
- Open circuit to control module
- Defective module
- Defective keypad actuator
- Defective transmitter.

Basic keyless entry systems use a relatively simple circuit. However, many systems are wired into corresponding accessories, such as an automatic door lock or anti-theft system, which makes diagnosis appear more complex. Service manual procedures, circuit diagrams, and specifications are required for effective troubleshooting. Use the circuit diagram to isolate suspect subcircuits and devices. Perform voltage drop tests to locate the source of the failure.

POWER LOCK AND LATCH SYSTEMS

Electric latches controlled by either solenoids or electric motors are used on doors, rear decks, tailgates, and fuel filler doors. A master control switch allows the driver to lock or unlock all the doors while seated. Some systems provide switches on each door to operate each lock separately. However, these individual switches may be overridden by the master control switch. In addition, the door locks may also be controlled by a keyless entry system as previously described.

On a typical power door lock system, each door lock is connected to a reversible dc electric motor or double-acting solenoid through a relay. Two relays, one for locking and the other for unlocking the door, are used on some models. Reversing the polarity of the armature or solenoid coil circuits changes the direction in which motor or solenoid moves. The

Copyright 2000 by Chek-Chart Publications

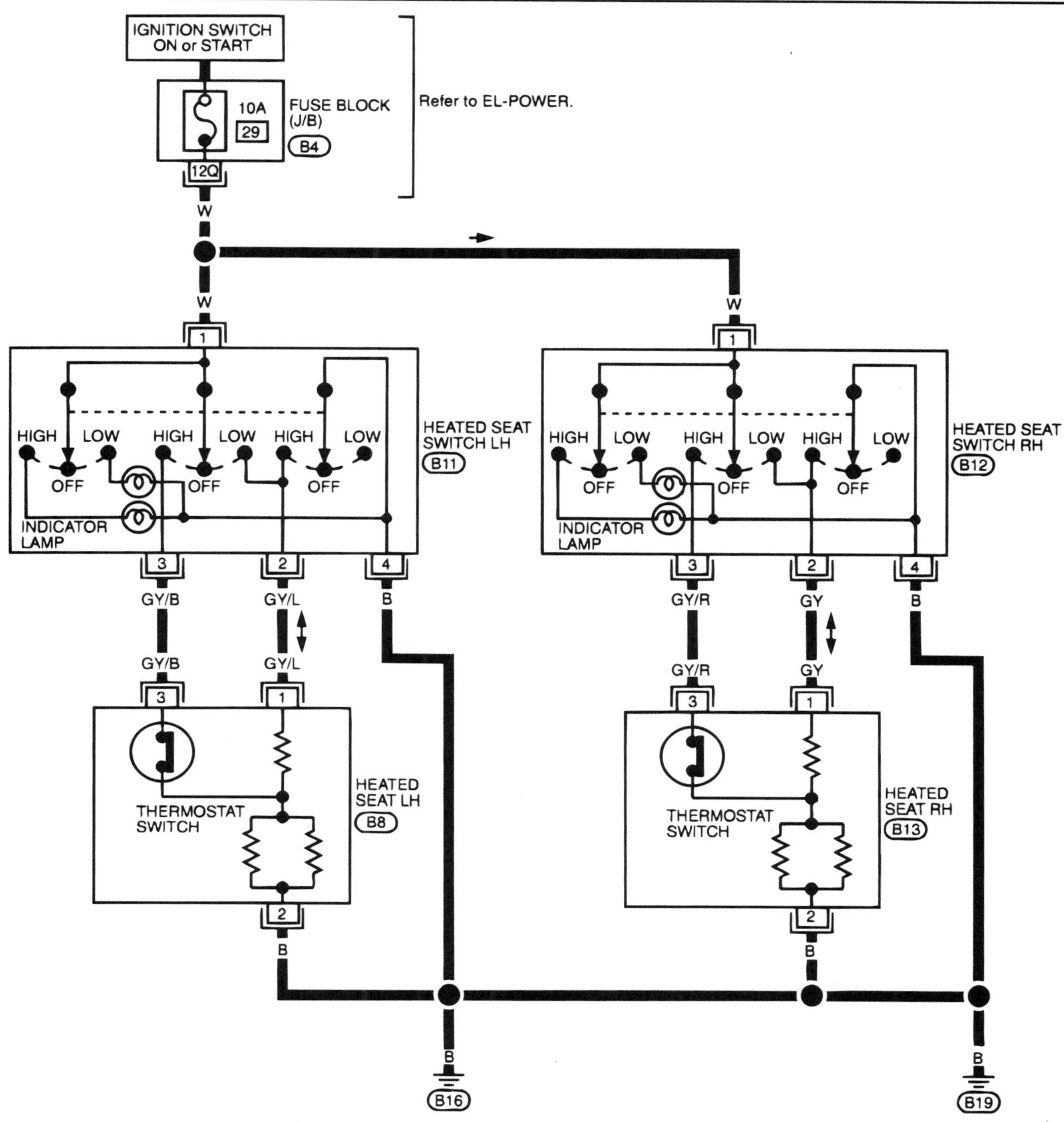

Figure 15-20. The thermostat switch opens once the seat heating grid reaches a preset temperature on this Nissan system.

solenoid or armature connects to a mechanical linkage that locks and unlocks the door.

The power door locks on models with an automatic transmission may be connected to the gear selector lever as well. On these systems, all of the doors automatically lock when the gear selector is placed into drive position. Moving the gear selector to park automatically unlocks all doors. Doors may also be unlocked either manually or with the control switches while the transmission is in drive.

In addition to power door locks, many vehicles have a power rear deck, or trunk latch, and a remotely activated fuel filler door. Although these may operate similarly to the power door locks, each is a separate system. An electric trunk latch is usually powered by the ignition-run circuit and the release

Copyright 2000 by Chek-Chart Publications

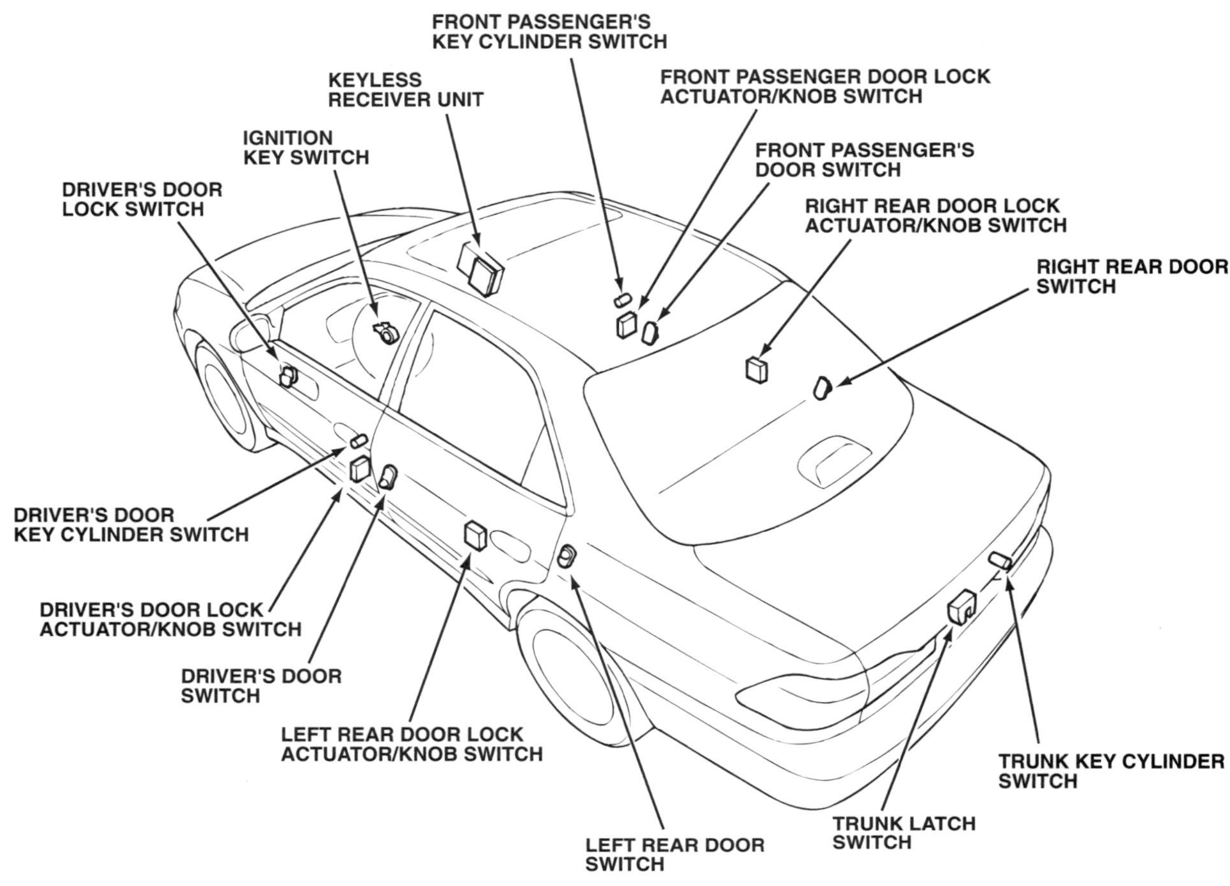

Figure 15-21. Component locator of a Honda keyless entry system.

switch is often concealed in the glove compartment or center console. The button activates a solenoid attached to the latch. The circuit consists of a solenoid, switch, wiring, and fuse.

Remote fuel filler doors are often cable controlled, but some use an electric solenoid to release the latch. A simple circuit composed of a switch, solenoid, fuse, and wiring controls an electric fuel filler door.

Electric Lock Testing and Service

Similar standard electrical tests and troubleshooting procedures are used to locate problems in any latch and lock system. Refer to wiring and circuit diagrams to locate system components. Check for voltage available at the solenoid, relay, and switch and isolate circuit problems, figure 15-22.

An inoperative power door lock system may be caused by a number of problems, including:

- Tripped circuit breaker, or blown fuse or fusible link
- Open circuit
- Defective switch
- Defective relay
- Defective motor or solenoid
- Loose connections
- Mechanical latch linkage problems.

If the fuse, fusible link, or circuit breaker is blown, check for short circuits and excessive current draw in the motors or solenoids. Mechanical problems, such as binding linkage, are often the cause of a blown fuse because the circuit draws too much current in an attempt to overcome the mechanical resistance.

Copyright 2000 by Chek-Chart Publications

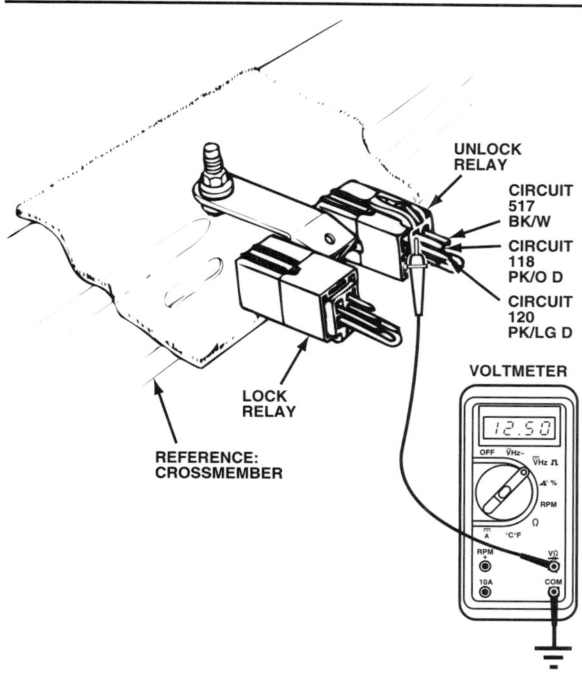

Figure 15-22. Checking the operation of a power door lock relay.

Linkage problems are usually the result of lack of lubrication, but may also be the result of badly worn connection points, especially on older vehicles.

Study the diagram to determine how current is routed through the system and approach troubleshooting logically to locate the source of the problem. In general, if none of the locks operate, the cause is likely in the main power supply circuit or the master control switch. If only one latch fails to operate, the fault is probably in the circuit or motor for that particular door.

Component replacement

Master control switches install either on the armrest of the left-front door or in the center console, while individual door switches install in the door panel of the door they service. Most switches press fit into the door panel or console and are retained by a plastic clip molded onto the switch body. These switches are easily removed for testing and replacement by gently prying them out with a small screwdriver. To install, simply push the switch in until the clip snaps into place.

Motors, solenoids, and relays mount inside the door frame on a bracket attached to the door with screws, pop rivets, or clips. Door panel trim must be removed to access these components for testing and replacement. Some motor and solenoid assemblies have slotted brackets to permit adjustment. Adjust the motor or solenoid to move the lock mechanism to its locked position when its plunger is fully extended.

POWER SEAT SYSTEMS

There are several movement designs for electrically adjustable seats:

- Forward and backward
- Forward, backward, up, and down
- Forward, backward, up and down, and tilt forward and backward.
- Reclining seat back.

These are commonly referred to as 2-way, 4-way, and 6-way respectively because of the planes in which they move. Additional movements, such as an adjustable headrest, are available on some models. Modern automotive seats may also include heating grids and an adjustable lumbar, or back, support. Seat movement is accomplished using reversible dc motors. An inflatable air bladder that assembles into the seat back is generally used to provide lumbar support adjustment. These have inflatable back supports that are powered by a small electric pump mounted in the seat frame.

Typically, the different seat functions, movement, heating, and inflation, operate independently of each other. However, many modern seating systems are electronically controlled and a single ECM regulates all functions. In addition, the wiring for all the devices is combined into a single harness. The electronic control systems on some models have a memory seat feature, which allows the driver to program different seat positions into a control module for later recall.

Power seat circuit and drive mechanism designs vary considerably by manufacturer and model. One method of providing 6-way power seat movement uses three reversible motor armatures assembled into a single housing, figure 15-23. Other designs use three separate motors. One motor moves the seat horizontally forward and backward, one moves the seat vertically up and down, and the other motor tilts the seat back forward and backward. Many newer models have 8-way power seats that use four motors, two of which adjust seat height, figure 15-24. This design places one height-adjusting motor at the front of the seat and another at the rear. Using two height-adjusting motors allows the driver to adjust the pitch, or tilt of the seat.

Regardless of the number used or how they assemble to the seat, permanent-magnet motors are used and movement is reversed by reversing the polarity of the armature current. Power to the armature is regulated through a switch on the ground circuit that opens and closes the control circuit of a relay. An internal circuit breaker is often used to protect the motor. Vertical gear drives and horizontal rack-and-pinion or worm drives provide the seat movement.

Copyright 2000 by Chek-Chart Publications

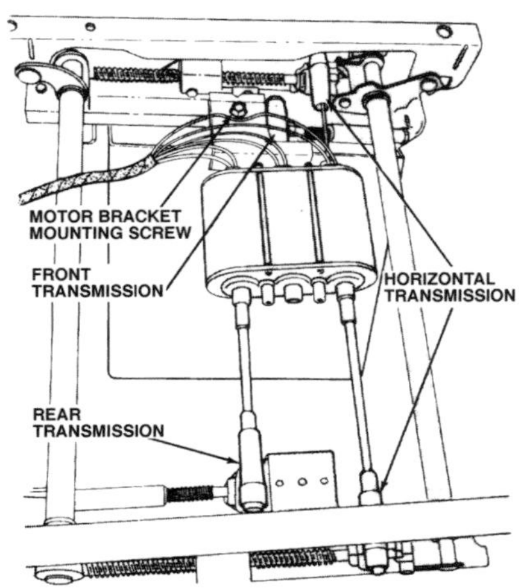

Figure 15-23. This power seat motor assembly houses three armatures to provide 6-way adjustment.

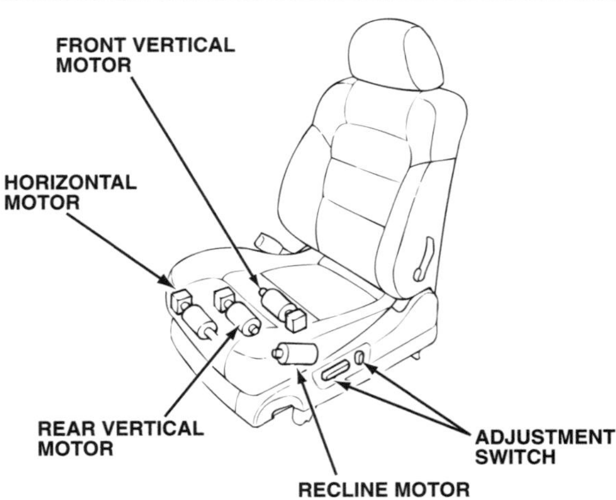

Figure 15-24. Four motors are used to provide 8-way power seat adjustment.

Due to the complexity of modern power seat designs, it is virtually impossible to troubleshoot electrical problems without accurate wiring and circuit diagrams. Most systems with electronic controls have a self-diagnostic function that is accessed using a scan tool.

Power Seat Testing and Service

Troubleshooting power seats is essentially the same as that used for other motor-driven accessories. Check for battery voltage available at the circuit breaker and the input connector of the switch. If voltage is available to the switch, remove the switch for continuity testing. Consult the service manual circuit diagram to test for correct continuity for all switch positions. If the switch is operational, the seat must be removed from the vehicle to check the motor assembly and wiring harness. Be sure to disable the SRS before removing the seat to avoid accidental deployment of the airbag.

With a memory seat system, determine if a discharged or recently disconnected battery is the cause a preset memory loss. In some systems, all the power seat functions are directed through the control module and will not work if the module is not installed or is not functional. As a first step in troubleshooting this type of system, check voltage and ground to the control module.

Component replacement

The design of most switches installed in a console or armrest allows them to be pried out and pressed back in place. However, the armrest is removed to access the mounting screws or clips on some models. If installed on the side of the seat frame, they are held in place by screws. Power seat motors are located underneath the seat on the track assembly. The seat assembly must be removed for testing and service.

POWER SUNROOF AND CONVERTIBLE TOP

Electric sunroof panels are opened and closed by a motor moving cables through a tube. The motor generally has a clutch that allows slippage when the motor stalls at the end of the cable travel or the panel is obstructed. The control switch may be located on the instrument panel, in the center console, or on a panel on the headliner. Overload protection is provided by a circuit breaker, which is often located in the fuse block and may also serve the power window circuit.

Power convertible tops may be operated by two double-acting hydraulic cylinders, which are driven by an electric pump motor, or by two or more reversible dc motors attached to a linkage assembly. Two relays, one for raising and one for lowering the top, direct current through the motors. The relay control circuits connect to a switch mounted on the instrument panel. A typical convertible-top system uses three circuit protection devices: a 20-amp fuse, a fusible link, and a 25-amp circuit breaker. This is important to know when troubleshooting this type of circuit.

Sunroof Diagnosis

A sunroof that does not operate properly is often the result of binding or improper adjustment. Always eliminate the possibility of a mechanical failure

Copyright 2000 by Chek-Chart Publications

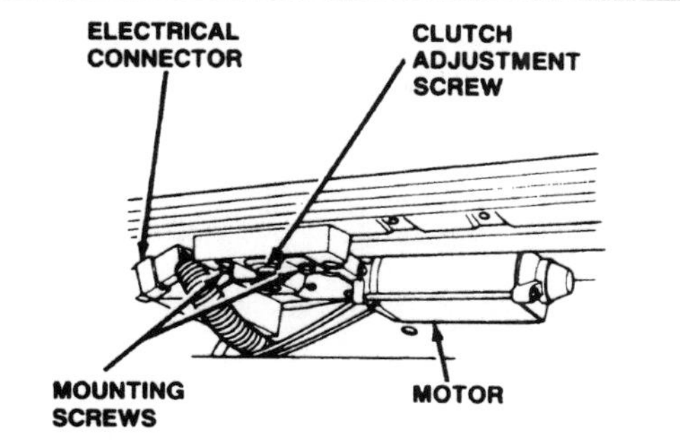

Figure 15-25. Clutch slippage is adjusted by turning the clutch adjustment screw on this sunroof motor.

before attempting to locate an electrical fault. Some sunroof systems have a clutch adjustment screw that controls the amount of slippage, figure 15-25. If the clutch is slipping, tighten the screw and operate system again. If the clutch slips after adjustment or the motor stalls before opening or closing the sunroof, replace the motor.

Convertible Top Diagnosis

If the convertible top system is inoperative, check for:

- Low battery voltage
- Defective circuit breaker
- Mechanical binding in linkage
- Loose or corroded ground connections
- Lack of hydraulic fluid
- Hydraulic system leakage
- Restrictions in hydraulic system
- Defective cylinder or pump.

Testing and Service

These electrical circuits are relatively simple to troubleshoot because they are single circuits that are not integrated with other accessory circuits, figure 15-26. However, they may share a circuit breaker with the power windows. Switches, relays, and wiring are checked as in other electrical circuits.

Sunroofs generally are mounted to the roof as a module, with the motor and drive gear assembly attached to the module, and may require headliner removal to service the components.

Convertible-top motor and pump units generally mount on the floor behind the rear seat, and are accessed by removing the rear seat back and cushion. Hydraulic cylinders are usually located inside each rear quarter panel behind interior trim panels, as are the motors on a motor-driven top, figure 15-27.

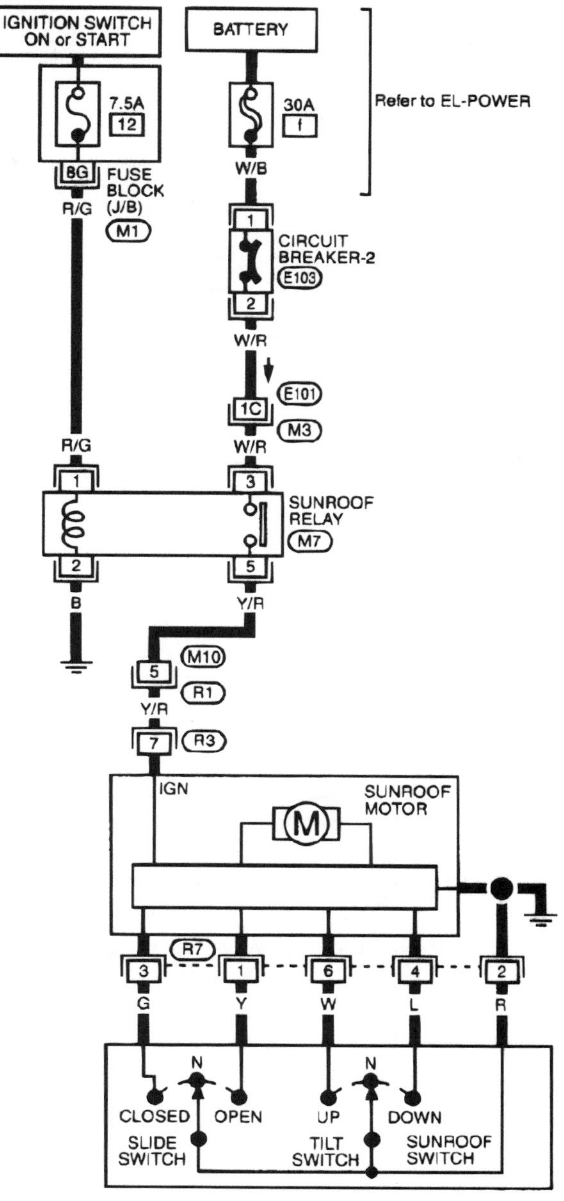

Figure 15-26. This Nissan power sunroof diagram shows the simplicity of the circuitry.

POWER WINDOW SYSTEMS

Vehicle doors and tailgates with power windows contain motors and a regulator assembly to raise and lower the window glass, figure 15-28. The power window system consists of the motors and regulators, relays, individual control switches at each door, a master switch assembly, and connecting wiring. The circuit is powered from the accessory terminal of the ignition switch and is generally protected by a circuit

Copyright 2000 by Chek-Chart Publications

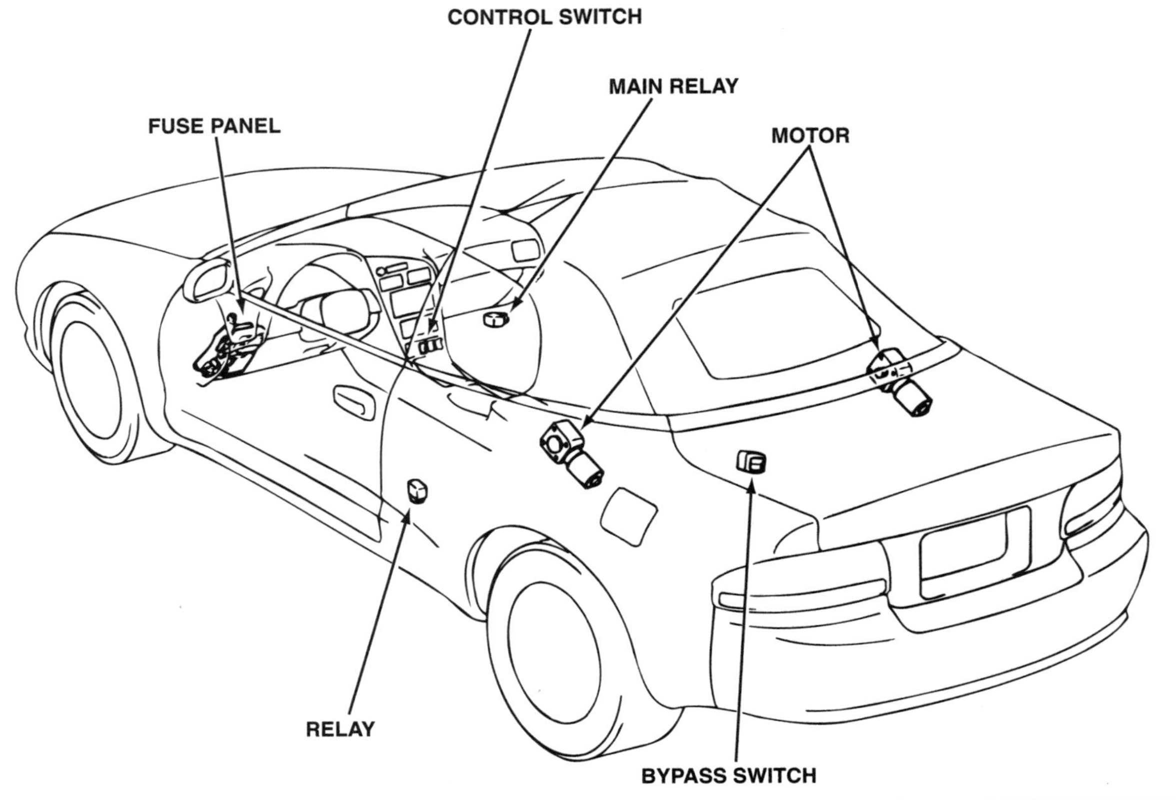

Figure 15-27. Two dc motors drive the convertible top-linkage on a Toyota Celica.

breaker located in the main fuse block. The power window circuit has both sides of the motor connected to ground when not in use. When the window is operated, one side of the window is disconnected from ground and connected to power while the other side remains grounded. Reversing the polarity reverses the motor, and thus the direction of window travel. Power window regulators may be a scissors-type or flex-drive design.

Power Window Diagnosis

If power window operation is slow or intermittent, check for:

- Incorrectly adjusted or aligned regulator
- Motor or regulator gears dry of lubricant
- Motor bushings dry of lubricant
- Defective circuit breaker
- Loose wiring connections
- Window channels dry.

If a power window is inoperative, check for:

- Defective motor
- Defective switch
- Open wiring circuit.

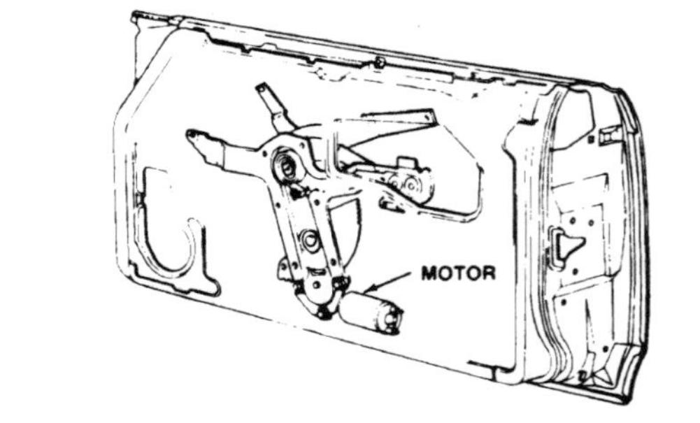

Figure 15-28. An electric motor and a regulator assembly raise and lower the glass on a power window.

Power Window Testing and Service

Common causes of slow power window operation are low battery voltage and high circuit resistance. Make sure the battery is in good condition and fully charged. Also, check for voltage available to and through the switch and continuity on the ground circuit. Once these conditions are met, test power window motor operation as follows:

Copyright 2000 by Chek-Chart Publications

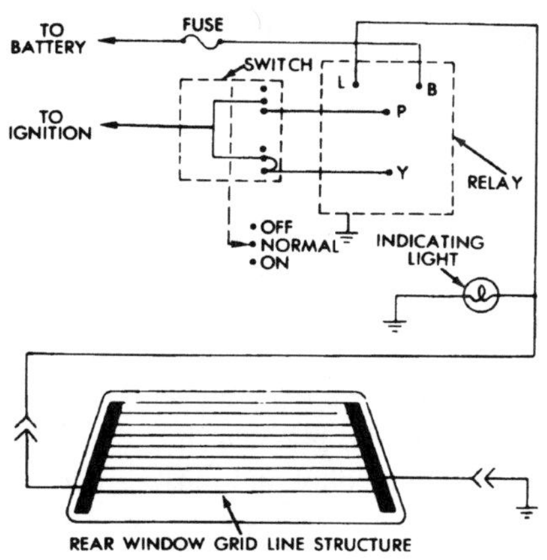

Figure 15-29. A switch and relay control current through the heating grid of a rear window defroster.

1. Remove the appropriate door trim panel.
2. Disconnect the electrical connections at the motor terminals. Connect one of the motor terminals to a chassis ground with a jumper wire and use a fused jumper wire to momentarily connect the other motor terminal to battery voltage. Refer to a connector pin chart to determine which side of the motor to apply power to based on the position of the window.
3. The motor should operate normally when connected directly to battery voltage. If so, reverse the jumper wire connections at the connector to check for movement in the opposite direction.

If the motor operates at normal speed when connected to battery voltage, the problem is most likely high resistance in the switch, relay, or circuit. Isolate the source of the failure by voltage drop testing. If the motor does not operate with voltage applied, it has an internal problem. Replace the motor.

Component replacement

Since power window motors mount inside the door frame, the door panel trim must be removed to replace the motor or regulator. Power window circuit relay locations vary and may be mounted on a bracket under the instrument panel, inside the door frame, or behind a kick panel.

REAR WINDOW DEFROSTER SYSTEMS

A heated rear window defroster, like all other electric automotive heaters, uses a high-resistance circuit to produce heat. A grid of electrically conductive lines

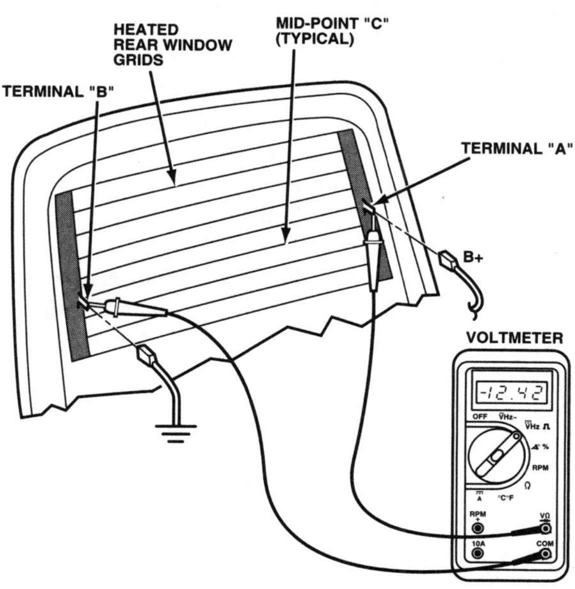

Figure 15-30. Checking for voltage available at the grid of a rear window defroster.

bonded to the glass surface warms the glass as resistance impedes current. Current through the grid is controlled by a relay and switch, figure 15-29. The switch and relay may be separate units or be combined into a single assembly. A timer relay automatically switches off the heating element on some models. A warning lamp, either an LED or bulb, in the switch or on the instrument panel, illuminates when the grid is on. Most late-model systems use a solid-state timer module to switch the grid current off after a specified length of time. The grid in these systems is typically protected by either a fusible link or circuit breaker, while the relay control circuit is fused.

Rear Window Defroster Testing and Service

To check the operation of a rear window defroster grid, switch the ignition on without starting the engine. Then, switch the defroster on while watching the vehicle ammeter or voltmeter. The meter needle should deflect as the switch is turned on. If the vehicle uses an indicator lamp instead of an ammeter or voltmeter, a temperature difference should be felt on the window surface within 2 to 4 minutes.

If the window is not heating, check for battery voltage available at the grid, figure 15-30. Low voltage to the grid may be caused by a loose or corroded connection at the grid feed wire, a weak fusible link, or a

Copyright 2000 by Chek-Chart Publications

defective circuit breaker. Check for excessive ground side resistance by voltage drop testing.

If battery voltage is available at the grid, an open ground circuit may be the cause of the problem. Isolate the failure by voltage drop testing. Keep in mind, a break, or open circuit, on one grid wire causes only that one wire to malfunction. All of the wires would have to be broken to render the entire grid inoperative.

To check for an open circuit in the grid, connect the negative lead of a voltmeter to a chassis ground and switch the defroster system on. Next, take available voltage readings at the midpoint of each grid line. Take care not to scratch or nick the grid lines with the probe. Readings should be approximately 6 volts if the circuit is complete. No voltage available indicates the grid circuit is open between the test point and the insulated, or positive side of the grid. If the reading equals battery voltage, the ground side of the grid circuit is open.

Excess grid resistance results in a grid that operates, but does not produce enough heat. To check, disconnect both grid terminals, measure grid resistance with an ohmmeter, and compare the reading to specifications.

Grid lines may be repaired with a special epoxy conductor. Clean the glass in the area of the broken grid circuit with alcohol and mask it before applying the epoxy.

Copyright 2000 by Chek-Chart Publications

ASE Technician Certification Sample Test

This sample test is similar in format to the series of tests given by the National Institute for Automotive Service Excellence (ASE). Each of the ASE exams covers a specific area of automotive repair and service. The tests are given every fall and spring throughout the United States.

To earn certification in a particular field, a technician must successfully complete one of these tests and have at least two years of "hands on" experience, or a combination of work experience and formal automotive technical training. A person who successfully completes all of the tests is a certified ASE Master Automobile Technician.

The questions in this sample test follow the format of the ASE exams. If you plan to apply for certification later in your career, learning to take this kind of test helps you prepare. The answers for this sample test are on page 337 of this *Shop Manual*.

For test registration forms or additional information on the automobile technician certification program, write to:

National Institute for
AUTOMOTIVE SERVICE EXCELLENCE
13505 Dulles Technology Drive, Suite 2
Herndon, VA 20171-3421

1. Which of the following methods should NOT be used to repair electrical wires?
   a. Splicing with insulated solderless connectors
   b. Twisting the wires together, soldering with acid core solder, and insulating with heat-shrink tubing
   c. Twisting the wires together, soldering with resin core solder, and taping
   d. Splicing with noninsulated connectors and insulating with heat-shrink tubing
2. When checking diode resistance by reversing the leads of an analog ohmmeter, a good diode produces:
   a. Two low readings
   b. Two high readings
   c. One high and one low reading
   d. One high and one infinite reading
3. High resistance in a circuit may cause all of the following conditions EXCEPT:
   a. Defroster grid not hot enough
   b. Motors run slowly
   c. Inoperative horn
   d. Blown fuse
4. Technician A says General Motors recommends using petroleum jelly when repairing aluminum wiring to seal the spliced area after a repair is made.
   Technician B says the aluminum wire is a solid conductor and must always be replaced with a section of the same gauge and length.
   Who is right?
   a. A only
   b. B only
   c. Both A and B
   d. Neither A nor B
5. An infinite reading on an autoranging digital ohmmeter indicates:
   a. The instrument is set on the incorrect range
   b. The instrument should be zeroed
   c. A shorted circuit
   d. An open circuit
6. A higher than normal ammeter reading when performing a current draw test on most circuits indicates:
   a. An open circuit
   b. Excessive circuit resistance
   c. A short circuit
   d. Infinite resistance
7. Technician A says the battery must be able to provide at least 10 volts while cranking the engine.
   Technician B says a voltage drop of more than 0.2 volt across the battery ground cable can result in low cranking voltage.
   Who is right?
   a. A only
   b. B only
   c. Both A and B
   d. Neither A nor B
8. Technician A says the PCM allows an engine with direct ignition to start once it receives an input signal for crankshaft speed.
   Technician B says the PCM must receive both crankshaft speed and position, or "synch," signals before it allows the engine to start.
   Who is right?
   a. A only
   b. B only
   c. Both A and B
   d. Neither A nor B
9. The starter control circuit includes all of the following EXCEPT:
   a. The ignition switch
   b. The starter motor
   c. The starter relay or solenoid winding
   d. The starting safety switch

Copyright 2000 by Chek-Chart Publications

10. Technician A says high resistance in an electronic control circuit causes problems because these systems use low-voltage components.
    Technician B says low resistance in an electronic actuator may cause PCM failure because low resistance allows too much current to pass through the PCM.
    Who is right?
    a. A only
    b. B only
    c. Both A and B
    d. Neither A nor B

11. Technician A says the loss caused by resistance in an operating circuit is called voltage drop.
    Technician B says there should not be any voltage drop across a harness connector.
    Who is right?
    a. A only
    b. B only
    c. Both A and B
    d. Neither A nor B

12. Technician A says the engine should be running and all of the accessories should be turned off to test the ground circuit of an alternator.
    Technician B says the best way to test the ground circuit of an alternator is to use a carbon pile battery tester to load the circuit.
    Who is right?
    a. A only
    b. B only
    c. Both A and B
    d. Neither A nor B

13. The temperature-corrected figure for a hydrometer reading of 1.240 taken at an electrolyte temperature of 30°F (-1°C) would be:
    a. 1.256
    b. 1.260
    c. 1.224
    d. 1.220

14. An electronic input device that provides a signal voltage based on the position of a moveable wiper on a variable resistor is called a:
    a. Thermistor
    b. Motion detector
    c. Potentiometer
    d. Piezoelectric generator

15. Technician A says to replace the shift fork if the starter motor pinion clearance is out of specifications.
    Technician B says too much starter motor pinion clearance indicates a worn starter drive or an incorrectly mounted starter motor.
    Who is right?
    a. A only
    b. B only
    c. Both A and B
    d. Neither A nor B

16. Technician A says a high firing and short spark line on a secondary oscilloscope trace is the result of low resistance from a short circuit.
    Technician B says a damaged plug wire, worn distributor cap, or excessive plug gap results in a high firing and short spark line on a secondary oscilloscope trace.
    Who is right?
    a. A only
    b. B only
    c. Both A and B
    d. Neither A nor B

17. What is the state-of charge of a battery with a specific gravity reading of 1.200 at 80°F (25°C)?
    a. Completely discharged
    b. About 50 percent charged
    c. About 75 percent charged
    d. Fully charged

18. There is an uneven ripple in the waveform when checking the charging system on an oscilloscope. The most likely cause of the ripple would be:
    a. High diode resistance
    b. A shorted stator winding
    c. A shorted diode
    d. An open field winding

19. Technician A says the charging system circuit wiring is good as long as voltage drop on either the positive circuit or the negative circuit is less than 0.5 volt.
    Technician B says the total voltage drop of the charging system, both the positive and the negative, circuit should not exceed 1.0 volt.
    Who is right?
    a. A only
    b. B only
    c. Both A and B
    d. Neither A nor B

20. Technician A says with the starter cranking, a voltmeter reading of 3.5 volts with the meter connected to the starter relay battery terminal and the relay switch terminals indicates high resistance in the relay control circuit.
    Technician B says this could indicate high resistance in the connections at the battery terminal lead to the ignition switch.
    Who is right?
    a. A only
    b. B only
    c. Both A and B
    d. Neither A nor B

21. When testing an airbag system, do all of the following EXCEPT:
    a. Wear safety glasses
    b. Probe airbag connectors to check voltage
    c. Disconnect the negative battery cable
    d. Allow system capacitor to discharge prior to testing

22. Technician A says when diagnosing the ignition system, an excessively high secondary voltage discharge may be caused by high primary circuit resistance.
    Technician B says in an ignition system, a loss of secondary voltage causes a greater loss of primary voltage.
    Who is right?
    a. A only
    b. B only
    c. Both A and B
    d. Neither A nor B

23. Technician A says a pulse-width modulated (PWM) solenoid can be checked with a good DMM designed for automotive use.
    Technician B says the only way to check a PWM solenoid is with an oscilloscope.
    Who is right?
    a. A only
    b. B only
    c. Both A and B
    d. Neither A nor B

24. Technician A says a problem of a dim stop light lamp may be caused by corrosion in the lamp socket.
    Technician B says a short in the lamp socket could be the cause of dim stoplight bulbs.
    Who is right?
    a. A only
    b. B only
    c. Both A and B
    d. Neither A nor B

Copyright 2000 by Chek-Chart Publications

25. The most accurate way to check a PCM-controlled solenoid is to:
    a. Measure the voltage drop to ground
    b. Measure the current draw through the driver circuit
    c. Measure voltage on the power circuit
    d. Measure solenoid resistance with an ohmmeter

26. The purpose of using shielded cables on certain automotive circuits is to:
    a. Protect the signals against electromagnetic interference (EMI) and radio frequency interference (RFI)
    b. Protect the conductor against heat
    c. Protect the high-current conductor from shorts
    d. Protect the signals from jumping between conductors

27. Technician A says when a Weather-Pack® connector fails, cut the old connector off and splice a new connector into place.
    Technician B says when a Weather-Pack® connector fails, it is repaired by replacing the seals and insulating with grease.
    Who is right?
    a. A only
    b. B only
    c. Both A and B
    d. Neither A nor B

28. Technician A says as long as the voltage drop on an electronic input sensor circuit is 0.5 volt or less, it should not affect sensor operation.
    Technician B says most electronic input sensors have a separate ground connection to the computer to eliminate ground problems.
    Who is right?
    a. A only
    b. B only
    c. Both A and B
    d. Neither A nor B

29. All of the following can cause an excessive voltage drop in a circuit EXCEPT:
    a. Corrosion on a power feed connection
    b. A loose plug-type connector
    c. An overtightened ground connection
    d. Incorrect assembly of a ground connection

30. Technician A says a charging system oscilloscope trace that regularly drops out or spikes down is most likely caused by a shorted diode.
    Technician B says a shorted stator winding or high diode resistance cause an alternator scope trace to drop out or spike down.
    Who is right?
    a. A only
    b. B only
    c. Both A and B
    d. Neither A nor B

31. Which is the LEAST likely to happen in a circuit with a high-resistance problem?
    a. Lamps are dim
    b. Motors run slowly
    c. Battery overcharges
    d. Horn does not work

32. Technician A says there should be a 12-volt voltage drop across a motor in a 12-volt circuit.
    Technician B says there should be no voltage drop on a switch in a 12-volt circuit.
    Who is right?
    a. A only
    b. B only
    c. Both A and B
    d. Neither A nor B

33. Technician A says a short to ground in a component that is not turned off by the ignition could be the cause of a battery that goes dead while the vehicle sits overnight.
    Technician B says a short to ground in the alternator could drain the battery and cause it to go dead overnight.
    Who is right?
    a. A only
    b. B only
    c. Both A and B
    d. Neither A nor B

34. Technician A says a loose headlight ground connection could be the cause of one headlight being brighter in warm weather than in cold weather.
    Technician B says the cause of one headlight being brighter in warm weather than in cold weather is most likely a short to ground.
    Who is right?
    a. A only
    b. B only
    c. Both A and B
    d. Neither A nor B

35. Technician A says if the measurement changes when the wires are wiggled while checking voltage drop on a connection, the connector may have a loose contact.
    Technician B says heat may cause a good connector to go bad or a faulty connector to work.
    Who is right?
    a. A only
    b. B only
    c. Both A and B
    d. Neither A nor B

36. Technician A says a diode offers little or no resistance in one direction and very high resistance in the other.
    Technician B says a diode makes a good one way electrical check valve.
    Who is right?
    a. A only
    b. B only
    c. Both A and B
    d. Neither A nor B

37. A dome light that operates correctly off one door switch but not the other may be caused by all of the following EXCEPT:
    a. Faulty switch
    b. Faulty bulb
    c. Open connector
    d. Broken wire

38. Technician A says when diagnosing a stoplight circuit problem a component locator should be checked to see if the bulbs are also used by the directional circuit.
    Technician B says a circuit schematic should be checked when diagnosing a stop light circuit problem to see if there are parallel current paths to the bulbs.
    Who is right?
    a. A only
    b. B only
    c. Both A and B
    d. Neither A nor B

39. If lights are dim, the probable cause is:
    a. High ground circuit resistance
    b. Low voltage regulator output
    c. Faulty light switch
    d. Loose terminal connections

40. A fast turn signal flashing rate may be caused by all of the following EXCEPT:
    a. Loose terminal connections
    b. The wrong type of flasher
    c. The wrong type of bulbs
    d. High circuit voltage

Copyright 2000 by Chek-Chart Publications

41. Which of the following statements about halogen sealed-beam headlights is NOT true?
    a. Replace them in the same way as conventional sealed-beam headlights
    b. Install them inside an aerodynamic plastic lens assembly
    c. Size standards are the same as conventional sealed-beam headlights
    d. Three aiming points are used to adjust the beam

42. A battery can be fast-charged for up to 1 hour if the corrected specific gravity reading is:
    a. 1.150 or less
    b. 1.150 to 1.175
    c. 1.175 to 1.200
    d. 1.200 to 1.250

43. Technician A says a power window fuse that blows every time the down position of the switch is pressed is likely caused by a short to ground between the switch and the window motor. Technician B says a previous wiring repair using wire that is too small in diameter could be causing the power window fuse to blow.
    Who is right?
    a. A only
    b. B only
    c. Both A and B
    d. Neither A nor B

44. All of the following statements about analog gauges are true EXCEPT:
    a. They may be mechanical, thermal, or electromagnetic
    b. They use the same sending units as digital gauges
    c. The reading is displayed with a needle
    d. They require a controlled amount of voltage

45. A horn that sounds continuously and cannot be shut off, is most likely caused by:
    a. Horn switch contacts stuck closed
    b. Horn switch contacts stuck open
    c. Battery voltage too high
    d. The alternator is overcharging

46. Which of the following is a likely cause of a windshield wiper arm NOT moving while the motor is running?
    a. Blown circuit breaker
    b. Defective motor or switch
    c. Binding linkage or gears
    d. Wiring problems

47. When the needles on all the regulated-voltage gauges vibrate by more than the width of the needle, the most likely cause would be a defective:
    a. Battery
    b. Gauge package
    c. Instrument voltage regulator
    d. Instrument cluster wiring connection

48. A variable-resistance sending unit is used on all electrical gauges EXCEPT:
    a. Ammeters and voltmeters
    b. Fuel gauges
    c. Temperature gauges
    d. Oil pressure gauges

49. Which warning lamp does NOT use an on/off switch as a sending unit?
    a. Coolant temperature
    b. Oil pressure
    c. Charging system
    d. Check engine

50. The most likely problem of a rear defroster grid that operates but does not generate enough heat would be:
    a. Low circuit voltage
    b. Circuit current too high
    c. High circuit resistance
    d. Low alternator output

Copyright 2000 by Chek-Chart Publications

Answers to ASE Sample Test Questions

1-B 2-C 3-D 4-C 5-D 6-C
7-C 8-B 9-B 10-C 11-C 12-B
13-D 14-C 15-B 16-B 17-B
18-A 19-D 20-C 21-B 22-D
23-A 24-C 25-B 26-A 27-D
28-C 29-C 30-D 31-C 32-C
33-C 34-A 35-C 36-C 37-B
38-B 39-A 40-A 41-B 42-A
43-A 44-B 45-A 46-C 47-C
48-A 49-C 50-C

Copyright 2000 by Chek-Chart Publications

Index

Copyright 2000 by Chek-Chart Publications

Copyright 2000 by Chek-Chart Publications

Copyright 2000 by Chek-Chart Publications

Copyright 2000 by Chek-Chart Publications

Copyright 2000 by Chek-Chart Publications

Copyright 2000 by Chek-Chart Publications

NOTES

NOTES

NOTES

NOTES

NOTES

NOTES

NOTES

NOTES

NOTES

NOTES